Wildflowers & Plant Communities
OF THE SOUTHERN APPALACHIAN MOUNTAINS & PIEDMONT

Wildflowers & Plant Communities

OF THE SOUTHERN APPALACHIAN MOUNTAINS
& PIEDMONT

A Naturalist's Guide to the Carolinas, Virginia, Tennessee, & Georgia

Timothy P. Spira

THE UNIVERSITY OF NORTH CAROLINA PRESS   CHAPEL HILL

NEW HANOVER COUNTY
PUBLIC LIBRARY
201 CHESTNUT STREET
WILMINGTON, NC 28401

A SOUTHERN GATEWAYS GUIDE

© 2011 THE UNIVERSITY OF NORTH CAROLINA PRESS

Photographs: © 2011 Timothy P. Spira
All rights reserved.
Designed and set by Kimberly Bryant with Rebecca Evans in Arnhem and TheSans types.

Manufactured in China

The paper in this book meets the guidelines for permanence and durability of the Committee on Production Guidelines for Book Longevity of the Council on Library Resources. The University of North Carolina Press has been a member of the Green Press Initiative since 2003.

cloth   15 14 13 12 11   5 4 3 2 1
paper   15 14 13 12 11   5 4 3 2 1

Library of Congress Cataloging-in-Publication Data
Spira, Timothy P.
Wildflowers and plant communities of the southern Appalachian Mountains and Piedmont : a naturalist's guide to the Carolinas, Virginia, Tennessee, and Georgia / Timothy P. Spira. — 1st ed.
    p. cm.
Includes bibliographical references and indexes.
ISBN 978-0-8078-3440-4 (cloth : alk. paper) —
ISBN 978-0-8078-7172-0 (pbk : alk. paper)
1. Wild flowers — Appalachian Region, Southern — Identification. 2. Wild flowers — Piedmont (U.S. : Region) — Identification. 3. Plant communities — Appalachian Region, Southern. 4. Plant communities — Piedmont (U.S. : Region) I. Title. II. Title: Naturalist's guide to the Carolinas, Virginia, Tennessee, and Georgia.
QK122.3.S65 2011
582.130975 — dc22   2010037828

For those who

PROMOTE AND PROTECT

native plants and natural habitats

Contents

Region Covered ix / Acknowledgments xi

Part I. Introduction 1
1 HOW TO USE THIS FIELD GUIDE 5
2 THE MOUNTAINS 8
3 THE PIEDMONT 15
4 UNDERSTANDING NATURAL COMMUNITIES 19

Part II. Photo Key 29
1 THE MOUNTAINS 31
  Spruce-Fir Forest 31
  Grassy Bald 34
  Heath Bald 36
  High-Elevation Rock Outcrop 39
  High-Elevation Red Oak Forest 42
  Northern Hardwood Forest 46
  Rich Cove Forest 50
  Acidic Cove Forest 54
  Spray Cliff 57
  Rocky Streamside 59
  Mountain Bog 62
  Chestnut Oak Forest 66
  Pine-Oak-Heath 69
  Forest Edge 72

2 THE PIEDMONT 77
  River Bluff Forest 77
  Alluvial Forest 80
  Basic Mesic Forest 84
  Oak-Hickory Forest 88
  Xeric Hardpan Forest 92
  Granite Outcrop 95
  Roadside and Field 99

Part III. Plant Community Profiles 103

1 THE MOUNTAINS 105
High-Elevation Communities 105
- Spruce-Fir Forest 105
- Grassy Bald 110
- Heath Bald 115
- High-Elevation Rock Outcrop 119
- High-Elevation Red Oak Forest 124
- Northern Hardwood Forest 129

Low-Elevation Moist to Wet Communities 135
- Rich Cove Forest 135
- Acidic Cove Forest 141
- Spray Cliff 147
- Rocky Streamside 151
- Mountain Bog 156

Low-Elevation Dry Communities 163
- Chestnut Oak Forest 163
- Pine-Oak-Heath 168

Forest Edge 173

2 THE PIEDMONT 179
Moist to Wet Communities 179
- River Bluff Forest 179
- Alluvial Forest 184
- Basic Mesic Forest 190

Dry Communities 195
- Oak-Hickory Forest 195
- Xeric Hardpan Forest 200
- Granite Outcrop 205

Roadside and Field 211

Part IV. Species Profiles 217

1 TREES 219
2 SHRUBS AND WOODY VINES 269
3 HERBACEOUS PLANTS 325

Glossary of Botanical Terms 471 / Selected Natural Areas 476 /
Suggested Reading 495 / Websites 498 / Index of Scientific Plant Names 499 /
Index of Common Plant Names 509

Illustrations of basic plant structures appear at the back of the book, after the indexes.

The Region Covered

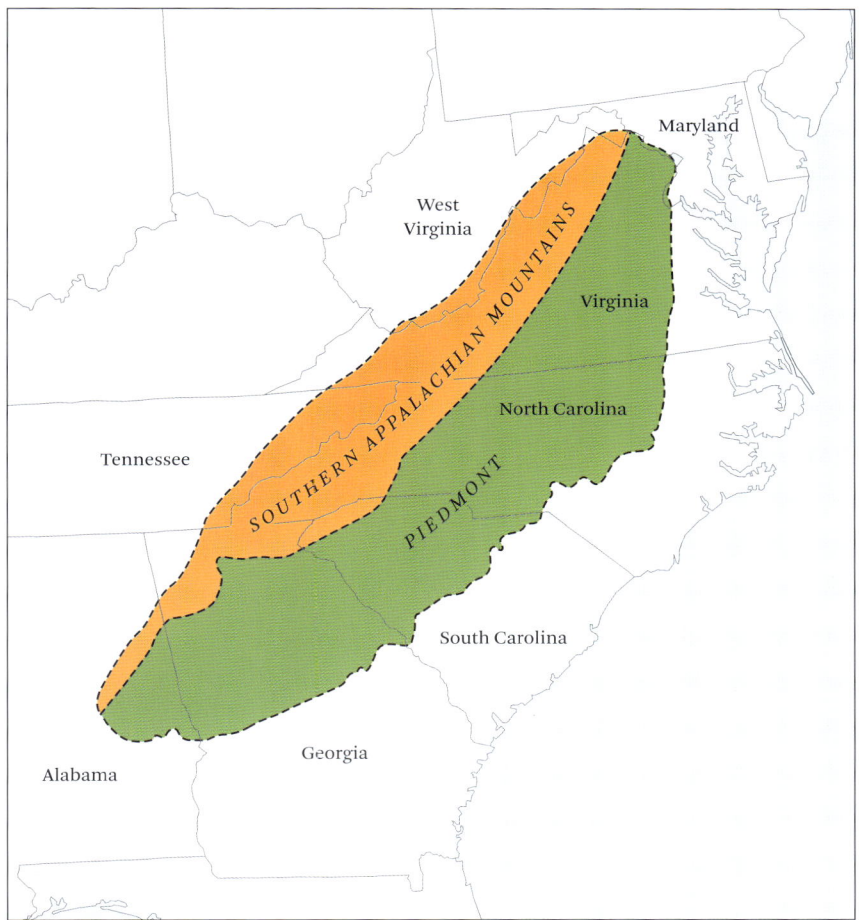

Map 1. The southern Appalachian mountain and piedmont regions of the southeastern United States

The 21 major plant communities described in this book are best represented in the southern Appalachian mountains and the adjoining piedmont. Readers outside these regions may also find this book of interest, as many of the 340 plant species described here are widely distributed throughout the Southeast.

Acknowledgments

I thank my spouse, Lisa Wagner, for her support and understanding—not only did she tolerate my long hours, she also carefully read the entire manuscript and provided invaluable advice (not to mention good companionship). Patrick McMillan shared his knowledge, helped with plant identification, and reviewed the manuscript. Douglas Rayner, Peter White, and Robert Wyatt also provided helpful comments on various versions of the manuscript. I gratefully acknowledge the contributions of Jim Allison, Cyndi Banks, Jennifer Bausman, Henry Chambers, Keith Clay, Dixie Damrel, Tim Lee, Richard Porcher, Johnny Townsend, and Ronald and Blanche Wagner. Special thanks to the staff at the University of North Carolina Press, especially senior editor Elaine Maisner, who provided encouragement and guidance from the start.

I am indebted to Clemson University, and especially to Hap Wheeler, Department Chair of Biological Sciences, for allowing me to spend so much time on this project. Teaching courses in field botany, plant ecology, and the natural history of wildflowers had me out in the woods and sparked my interest in writing this book. A work like this reflects the contributions of numerous scientists—their discoveries are woven throughout these pages.

I would like to acknowledge Great Smoky Mountains National Park, the Blue Ridge Parkway, the Botanical Gardens at Asheville, and the Highlands Botanical Garden, as they were especially fertile sites for capturing the photographs that appear in this book.

Exploring the southern Appalachian mountains and the adjoining piedmont has been a joyful experience. As a token of my appreciation, all royalties from the sale of this book will go toward promoting and conserving native plants and natural habitats.

Wildflowers & Plant Communities
OF THE SOUTHERN APPALACHIAN MOUNTAINS & PIEDMONT

PART I

Introduction

One of the joys of being a naturalist is that there is always something new to discover and interpret. While many find identifying wildflowers satisfying, identification is the beginning rather than the end of the journey. If you're interested in learning more about plants, including less familiar information about their ecology and natural history, you'll find this book to be a valuable reference as well as a worthwhile companion on field trips and wildflower walks.

The key idea at the center of the book is the organization of plants into 21 major communities. Often, you'll see wildflower books organized by flower color or family affinity, but the natural community emphasis used here is an exciting, fresh approach that is connected to our growing understanding of the environment and how all parts of the natural world are mutually dependent.

Whether you're just learning about wildflowers or are already familiar with many of our native plants, this book will help you identify major natural communities and their representative species. The term "wildflower" is used in a broad sense to include both woody and nonwoody flowering plants because both are conspicuous components of most communities. Using this book, you'll get a sense of the landscape being a mosaic of different communities that harbor particular groups of plants. By recognizing the distinctive vegetation associated with particular habitats, you can begin to read the landscape.

This book is intended to benefit a wide audience of nature lovers including wildflower enthusiasts, naturalists, hikers, birders, gardeners, and students. Organized into 4 major sections, Part I lays the groundwork by describing the region covered and introducing you to the fundamental properties of natural communities. Next is a photo key consisting of 760 thumbnail photos of plants arranged by community type. This user-friendly feature enables you to rapidly preview plants that you're likely to encounter within a particular community.

Part III profiles 21 major plant communities, including spruce-fir forest, grassy bald, rich cove forest, mountain bog, oak-hickory forest, and granite outcrop. The discussion of each community includes a description of its distinctive features, vegetation, seasonal aspects, distribution, dynamics, and conservation. I have also included a list of characteristic species, most of which are illustrated in the photo key.

Part IV comprises detailed descriptions of 340 species, including 65 trees, 75 shrubs and woody vines, and 200 herbaceous plants (along with accompanying photos). Most plants were chosen because they're prominent species, but examples of rare and unusual plants are also included. I've provided more information on the ecology and natural history of individual species than is typically found in wildflower books and have included information on interesting interactions between plants and animals. Among the sections at the back of the book are a glossary of botanical terms, a list of sources for obtaining additional information, and descriptions of exceptional natural areas to visit. Line drawings of basic plant structures are also included.

The region covered represents one of the most biologically diverse areas of North America. In addition to having the highest mountains of eastern North America, the southern Appalachians harbor some of the most extensive broad-leaved temperate forests in the world, as well as the largest remaining stands of old-growth forest in the eastern United States. No other mountain region in North America has more species of plants. In some areas, the climate is so moist that the vegetation has been designated a temperate rainforest, the only such area east of the Pacific Northwest. Spectacular spring wildflowers, the grandeur of old-growth forests, and brilliant fall colors take your breath away, encouraging you to return again and again.

The piedmont (which literally means "foot of the mountain") is a vast area of gently rolling hills dissected by numerous streams and rivers. Extending from the Blue Ridge Mountains to the west and the coastal plain to the east, the piedmont is best represented in the region covered in this book. Once largely cultivated, much of the piedmont has reverted to pine and hardwood forests interspersed with fields in various stages of succession. Granite outcrops, river bluff forest, alluvial forest, basic mesic forest, and remnant prairies are just a few of the interesting communities represented.

Exploring plants "in the wild" elicits a sense of adventure, surprise, and delight. With so much to discover, let's get started!

1 : How to Use This Field Guide

Wildflower Identification Tips

1. If you know the common name or scientific name of a species, refer to the index to find the page number where the species is described and illustrated by a photograph.
2. To identify an unfamiliar plant, turn to the photo key (Part II). This pictorial guide presents thumbnail photos of representative species arranged by plant community, including the corresponding page number for the species description. Choose the community that most closely fits the plant's surroundings. If you don't see the plant in the selected community, choose the next best community that resembles the plant's surroundings. When you find what looks like a good match, turn to the page on which the species is described (Part IV) to either confirm or reject your identification (and to read about the species).
3. If you don't find the species, try thumbing through other similar communities in the photo key. While this isn't the quickest way to identify plants, it will help familiarize you with plants in the various communities, which will help in future searches. Again, keep in mind that not every species is included in this book.

Species Profiles (Part IV)

PLANTS INCLUDED

Because it's impossible to include all species in a field guide such as this, I've chosen prominent plants as well as a sprinkling of rare and unusual species. The 340 species described are grouped by habit: trees, shrubs and woody vines, and herbaceous plants. Trees are usually over 15 ft. tall and generally have a single main stem, whereas shrubs are smaller woody plants, usually with multiple stems arising from (or close to) the ground. Vines have elongate stems adapted for climbing and may or may not have woody tissue. Herbaceous plants (herbs) lack aboveground woody tissue. In addition to flowering plants, I have included a small number of ferns, mosses, and lichens among the herbaceous plants. Nonnative species (those introduced by humans) are indicated by an asterisk in this section as well as in the photo key.

Abbreviations

Scientific names: "sp." (species); "spp." (more than one species in a genus); "var." (variety).

Months of the year (mainly for flowering and fruiting times): Jan., Feb., Mar., Apr., May, June, July, Aug., Sept., Oct., Nov., and Dec.

English units are used because they remain the most widely understood: "in." (inches) and "ft." (feet).

Format for Species Profiles

1. *Scientific name.* A plant's scientific name is the most reliable name because, no matter how widely distributed, each species has only one valid scientific name. Scientific names consist of two parts: the genus name (capitalized) and a specific epithet (lowercased). *Quercus alba* Linnaeus is an example of a full scientific name. The generic name is *Quercus*, the specific epithet is *alba*, and Linnaeus refers to the botanical authority (the person who first described the plant). Note that scientific names are italicized and that generic names are sometimes abbreviated, as in *Q. alba*, where *Q.* stands for *Quercus*. An asterisk placed before the species name indicates that it's an introduced rather than a native species in the region covered in this book. New information based on molecular studies has resulted in many taxonomic changes over the last decade, including those at the family, genus, and species levels.

    The scientific names used in this field guide generally conform to the terminology found in Alan Weakley's *Flora of the Carolinas, Virginia, Georgia, Northern Florida, and Surrounding Areas* (2008; available at www.herbarium.unc.edu/flora.htm). Family names, flowering and fruiting times, habitats, and ranges also follow Weakley's *Flora*.

2. *Common name(s).* One or 2 common names are listed for each species. While common names are widely used by wildflower enthusiasts, you should be aware of their pitfalls. For example, common names may vary from region to region, and the same common name can refer to more than one species.

3. *Family name.* The scientific family name (which ends in "-aceae") and the common family name (listed in parentheses) are included. As mentioned above, recent studies have resulted in many taxonomic revisions, including family relationships, resulting in some species being placed in new or different families.

4. *Description.* The plant descriptions provided here are abbreviated versions of those found in more formal taxonomic treatments. These abbreviated descriptions can be used (along with accompanying photographs) as a guide to help identify individual plants. I have tried to minimize the use of specialized botanical terms, but some terms may still be unfamiliar. If clarification is needed, please refer to the glossary (for a list of botanical terms) or the illustrations of basic plant structures at the very back of the book. Flowering and fruiting times are given, but note that considerable variation can occur between years (as well as over elevational and latitudinal gradients), due to differences in overall weather conditions.

5. *Habitat/range.* For each species, the ecological setting (habitat), frequency, and range are described. Keep in mind that the terms used to indicate frequency ("locally abundant," "common," "uncommon," "occasional," and "rare") are highly subjective and difficult to apply as the abundance of species can vary regionally.

6. *Taxonomy.* This section includes information on topics such as the number of species in a genus, the characteristics that distinguish similar species, and the derivation of names.

7. *Ecology.* Detailed information on the ecology and natural history of representative species is presented, much of which isn't available in other wildflower books.

8. *Wildlife.* Plants and animals interact in myriad ways, sometimes cooperatively, other times antagonistically. Plants, for example, are grazed, browsed, and sometimes eaten whole by herbivores, while their flowers are pollinated and their fruits and seeds are dispersed by various kinds of animals. These and other interactions are discussed in this section.
9. *Uses.* Various ways that people use plants are briefly described. Before tasting a plant listed as edible, make sure that you have properly identified it because some plants are toxic. Note that plants thought to be of little use to humans are often valuable components of the communities they inhabit.
10. *Synonym.* If a particular species has recently been given a different scientific name, the previously used scientific name (called a synonym) is listed.

2 : The Mountains

The plant communities presented in this book pertain most closely to the eastern portion of the southern Appalachians, including southwestern Virginia, western North Carolina, northwestern South Carolina, eastern Tennessee, and northern Georgia. However, many of the species profiled are widely distributed in the mountains (and beyond), including in the three physiographic provinces described below. Elevations vary from about 1,000 ft. at the base of the Blue Ridge Mountains to numerous peaks greater than 6,000 ft.

Physiographic Provinces

Three parallel geographic regions, known as physiographic provinces, based on characteristic landforms, geology, and soils, make up the southern Appalachian mountains. From east to west, they are the Blue Ridge, Valley and Ridge, and Cumberland Plateau. These provinces are part of the Appalachian mountain region that extends more than 2,000 miles from northern Georgia and Alabama to the Gaspé Peninsula in Quebec, Canada. Differences in climate and overall habitat conditions in each province greatly influence plant distribution patterns and contribute to the rich diversity of communities represented in the mountain region.

BLUE RIDGE PROVINCE

The Blue Ridge province represents a nearly unbroken chain of mountains that runs from Virginia to Georgia. The 2 main mountain ranges, the Blue Ridge and Unaka Mountains, run in a northeast to southwest direction and are interconnected by numerous cross-ranges, including the Black Mountains, the Balsam Ranges, and the Nantahala Mountains. The width of the Blue Ridge province ranges from about 20 miles in northern Virginia to about 70 miles in southwestern North Carolina. Steep slopes, broad ridges, intermountain basins, and large, rounded peaks are common landforms. The Blue Ridge province has the largest number of high mountains in eastern North America, including 43 peaks topping 6,000 ft. in western North Carolina. Here, Mount Mitchell, the tallest mountain east of the Rocky Mountains, rises to an elevation of 6,684 ft. Only a small portion of northeastern Georgia and northwestern South Carolina is part of the Blue Ridge province.

The steep eastern slope of the Blue Ridge Mountains, known as the Blue Ridge Escarpment, drops 2,000 to 3,000 ft. in as little as 3 miles. This rugged region of narrow ridges, deep gorges, major rivers, and plunging waterfalls provides some of the most spectacular scenery in the southern Appalachians. The variable topography and steep elevational gradients of the escarpment region provide habitats that differ in moisture availability, soils, and climate over very short distances, resulting in a rich mosaic of plant species and communities.

The plant communities described in this book are best represented within the Blue Ridge province.

VALLEY AND RIDGE PROVINCE

This province is characterized by multiple rows of long, narrow ridges separated by fertile valleys punctuated by streams and rivers. The undulating landscape is a manifestation of the underlying geology—valleys occur where more easily erodible rock such as limestone and shale occur; ridges are associated with areas of more durable rock (such as sandstone and quartzite) that have resisted erosion over the ages. The parent rock material also influences the type of soil formed. For example, the sandstone and quartzite rock on ridges gives rise to relatively thin acidic soils, whereas the limestone and shale in valleys form thicker, more fertile soils that harbor a more diverse flora.

CUMBERLAND PLATEAU PROVINCE

Much of this province consists of closely spaced mountains interspersed with steep-sided valleys where rivers have cut through the more gentle topography of the plateau. Unlike mountains in the Valley and Ridge province, the mountains here are broad with mostly flat tops, with an average elevation of about 2,000 ft. Underlain with sandstone, the Cumberland Plateau has mostly dry, acidic soils. In contrast, the valleys dissecting the plateaus have mostly calcium-rich limestone that weathers to form less acidic, more nutrient-rich soils. The different substrates and variable topography are major factors contributing to the diverse vegetation of this province.

Geologic History

One of the world's oldest mountain ranges, the Appalachians have a long and complex geologic history. From about 500 to 250 million years ago, 3 separate mountain-building periods occurred in which the eastern North American continental plate successively collided with and broke apart from the European and African continents, causing older rock to be pushed above younger rock, gradually forming what are now called the Appalachian Mountains. Over the past 200 million years, the Appalachians have been gradually eroding due to wind and water; deep glaciers also shaped the northern Appalachians. Perhaps once as tall as any modern mountain chain, the Appalachians today are only a remnant of what was once a much taller mountain range. Unlike the sharp mountain peaks of much younger mountains (such as the Rockies), the peaks of the southern Appalachians experienced hundreds of millions of years of weathering, forming the rounded peaks that characterize the southern Appalachians today.

Past Climate Change

Climate plays a central role in determining the distribution of plants and therefore the type of vegetation found in a particular place. As the climate changes, so does the vegetation. Let's consider the interplay of past climate and vegetation change in the southeastern United States during the Pleistocene Epoch or "Ice Age" which began about 2 million years ago and lasted until about 10,000 years ago. During the Wisconsin glaciation, the last of 4 major glacial periods, massive sheets of ice covered the Northern Hemisphere, reaching its maximum southern extent about 18,000 years ago south of the Great Lakes region in central Illinois. Even though glaciers didn't reach the Southeast, they brought about a cold, dry climate that resulted in vegetation radically different from that of today.

Studies reconstructing past vegetation from fossil pollen found in lake beds indicate that at the peak of the Wisconsin glaciation much of the southeastern landscape was a mix of boreal forest interspersed with prairie or sagebrush, with open woodlands forming park-like savannas. Boreal forest dominated by jack pine and spruce occurred as far south as present-day Atlanta. Deciduous forest dominated by oaks occurred south of the boreal forest. Large grazing animals such as bison, elk, caribou, woolly mammoths, and many other species ranged throughout much of the region, lending support to the existence of extensive areas of open, prairie-like vegetation.

Climatic change during the ice ages drastically altered habitats and effectively reshuffled ecological communities. Long periods of low temperatures, punctuated by warmer temperatures and the ebb and flow of glaciers, resulted in species expanding and contracting their ranges. Plant species migrated at different rates depending on their mode of dispersal, habitat requirements, and chance events. As a result, plants rearranged themselves into new species assemblages (communities) as they moved across the landscape.

In the Southeast, cold-weather species such as spruce and jack pine expanded their range during cold periods and then retreated when temperatures warmed. Warm-weather species such as oak and hickory retreated south during glacial advances and then spread northward when temperatures rose. About 18,000 years ago, a warming trend began that resulted in a major rearrangement of communities. By 12,500 years ago, oak-hickory forest had replaced boreal forest over much of the southeastern landscape.

Following the Pleistocene, an interglacial period known as the Holocene epoch began (and continues to this day). About 9,500 years ago, a pronounced warming trend began and reached maximum temperatures between about 7,500–5,000 years before the present, in what is referred to as the hypsithermal period. The hot, dry climate during this period dramatically affected the distribution and composition of communities. Cool-temperate and boreal species such as spruce and fir shifted to higher elevations, while deciduous forests dominated by oaks characterized the forested landscape over much of the Southeast. Frequent fires resulted in more open forests (woodlands) interspersed with prairies. As the climate became cooler and moister about 5,000 years ago, the vegetation began to stabilize and communities began to resemble present-day vegetation.

Climate

The mountain region's highly variable topography, including a wide range of elevations, produces many different climate regimes. In fact, some have described the range of climates represented from the lower slopes of the Blue Ridge escarpment at about 1,000 ft. to the top of Mount Mitchell at 6,684 ft. as being similar to the climates a traveler from Georgia to Canada would encounter. With increasing elevation, the climate becomes cooler and wetter, with more frequent clouds, fog, and mist. At the highest elevations, snow may fall from late October to early May. Elevation also influences the length of the frost-free season, decreasing from 200 days at lower elevations to around 100 days at higher elevations.

Rainfall is generally abundant but highly variable. Asheville, North Carolina, for example, receives less than half the rainfall of Mount Mitchell, which is less than 30 miles away. At the lower extreme, areas on the leeward sides of mountains (such as Asheville and the Shenandoah Valley, Virginia) average about 40 in. of annual rain due to the rain-shadow effect. Conversely, moist air masses moving northward from the Gulf of Mexico cool and subsequently release unusually heavy amounts of rainfall as they encounter the upper slopes of higher mountains. Here, as well as on steep south-facing slopes along the Blue Ridge Escarpment, average annual rainfall amounts approach 90 in., the highest amount in North America outside the Pacific Northwest. The climate in these areas is so wet that the vegetation has been designated a temperate rainforest.

Precipitation amounts are fairly uniform throughout the year, with a slight drop in autumn (September–November). Frequent summer thunderstorms originating from moist, warm air from the Gulf of Mexico are an important source of moisture, as are late-summer and fall hurricanes (originating in the Atlantic Ocean, Caribbean, or Gulf) in some years. Winter-season cyclonic storms, which originate west of the Mississippi River or along the Gulf coast and generally move northeasterly, are another primary source of moisture for the region.

Exceptional Biodiversity

The southern Appalachians have an extraordinarily rich flora. With upwards of 2,500 species of flowering plants, 130 species of trees, and more than 400 species of mosses, the region comprises some of the most species-rich, temperate deciduous forests in the world. About 1,500 species of vascular plants occur in Great Smoky Mountains National Park alone, more than in any other national park. The southern Appalachians support more tree species than any other area of comparable size in North America and include the largest and oldest representatives of a number of species. A highly variable topography, coupled with a wide diversity of soils, climates, and geology, has fostered the enormous diversity of species that we see today, particularly in the southern part of the Appalachians, where glaciers never scoured the land.

Vegetation

The region supports a large number of vegetation types between the cool, high mountain peaks and the hot, humid lower slopes. The mountains are mostly a forested landscape, with evergreen coniferous forest on the highest slopes and broad-leaved deciduous forest below. Spruce-fir forest is restricted to elevations above 5,000 ft. where the growing season is short and cool and the winters are long and cold. Dominated by needle-leaved evergreen species, spruce-fir forest is more similar to the boreal forests of Maine and eastern Canada than to other vegetation types in the South.

High-elevation red oak and northern hardwood forests commonly occur below spruce-fir forest. On ridgetops exposed to high winds, the stunted canopy trees display gnarled trunks and branches. American chestnut (*Castanea dentata*) was once a dominant canopy species in high-elevation red oak forest. Today, this community is dominated by a single species, northern red oak (*Quercus rubra*). Northern hardwood forest occurs on moist slopes dominated by a mixture of deciduous species, including American beech (*Fagus grandifolia*), yellow birch (*Betula alleghaniensis*), and yellow buckeye (*Aesculus flava*). A dense carpet of wildflowers often decorates the forest floor, particularly in spring before the canopy trees have leafed out.

The southern Appalachians lack a true timberline and the associated alpine tundra that is found at more northerly latitudes. Scattered across the high mountain landscape are several mostly treeless communities, including open, meadow-like areas known as grassy balds. The dense herbaceous vegetation that characterizes grassy balds has a rich diversity of wildflowers, including a number of rare species. Heath balds, in contrast, form dense shrublands that have relatively few species. The mostly treeless, high-elevation rock outcrop community is dominated by low-growing species that form dense "mats" of vegetation where shallow soils have accumulated. Multicolored lichens and pin cushion-like mosses grow on bare rocks, while shrubs and stunted trees are restricted to scattered pockets of deep soil.

Cove forests occur on moist valley flats, sheltered slopes, and other protected areas. Underlain by base-rich rocks with elevated soil pH, rich cove forests have spectacular spring wildflower displays and greater species diversity than any other community in the southern Appalachians. Acidic cove forests occupy similar sites, but because of relatively infertile soils derived from acidic rocks, have much lower species diversity. Chestnut oak forests and pine-oak-heath are fire-prone communities found on upper slopes and ridgetops at mid-elevations.

Wetland communities include rocky streamsides and mountain bogs. Lower areas along rocky streamsides are often sparsely vegetated because of frequent flooding, whereas on more elevated (and stable) sites, plants are more abundant and diverse. Despite their small size and rarity, mountain bogs have a rich diversity of wildflowers. The vegetation associated with the spectacular waterfalls in the steep gorges of the Blue Ridge Escarpment consists of an unusual assemblage of algae, bryophytes (mosses and liverworts), ferns, and flowering plants that is known as the spray cliff community.

Natural and Human-Caused Disturbance

Fire, wind, ice, and heavy precipitation are the main causes of natural disturbance in the mountain region. Relatively dry forests such as pine-oak-heath and chestnut oak forest are particularly vulnerable to fire. More mesic forests, such as cove forests and northern hardwood forests are usually too moist to burn. High winds are common at high elevations, sometimes exceeding 100 mph. Forests on ridgetops and other exposed areas often have stunted, twisted trees with numerous downed branches strewn across the forest floor. Occasional tornadoes and localized "microbursts" of intense winds knock down trees, sometimes over large areas. Ice accumulating on stems and leaves causes branches to snap and damages the crowns of trees. The heavy rains and high winds associated with tropical storms and hurricanes topple trees and cause debris avalanches on steep mountain slopes. Widespread evidence of past floods, landslides, and mudflows includes the many stream channels filled with rock, soil, and woody debris.

Native Americans used fire for a variety of reasons, including in the mountains (see "Impact of Native Americans," in the introduction to the piedmont). Looking for available land, European settlers moved from the piedmont up to the mountains in the seventeenth and eighteenth centuries, where they farmed and raised livestock. Fire was frequently used to clear the forest for farming and to open the woods for grazing by free-ranging livestock.

Large-scale commercial logging from 1850 to 1930 had an enormous impact on the forests of eastern North America. Prior to the railroads, trees were harvested to supply the timber and fuel needs of nearby villages, with very limited export to other areas. The building of railroads linking population centers to more remote forested areas set the stage for extensive logging of southeastern forests. From 1880 to 1930, railroads opened up the southern Appalachians to commercial logging. Hardwood forests at lower elevations and coniferous forests at higher elevations were rapidly exploited. Forestry practices resulted in the accumulation of enormous amounts of highly flammable logging slash that eventually burned, creating very hot, damaging fires.

Conservation Concerns

While not pristine wilderness, the southern Appalachians have recovered remarkably well from widespread deforestation early in the twentieth century. Today, some of the most extensive contiguous forest in eastern North America occurs in the region. This reflects the poor suitability of much of the landscape for agricultural use and large-scale urban development; in addition, federal and state governments manage substantial amounts of forested land. With 3 national parks (Great Smoky Mountains National Park, the Blue Ridge Parkway, and Shenandoah National Park) and 6 national forests (Pisgah, Nantahala, Cherokee, Jefferson, Sumter, and Chattahoochee), the southern Appalachians have the greatest concentration of public land in the eastern United States. These areas, along with other protected sites in the region, provide critical habitat for an enormously rich diversity of plants and animals.

Humans continue to alter the southern Appalachians in numerous ways, including forest management activities such as logging and fire suppression. Another concern is suburban encroachment into previously intact forest from retirement and second-home developments. These semi-domesticated forest fragments require access roads and forest-fire protection, often to the detriment of natural forest function. The elimination of large predators (and other factors) has led to historically high deer populations in some areas. Overbrowsing by deer has severely diminished the shrub layer and the abundance and diversity of wildflowers on the forest floor.

Air pollution is another issue. The Blue Ridge derives its name from the soft blue haze in the mountains, caused by substances naturally emitted from the vegetation. The Great Smoky Mountains were named for a similar reason. Today, the burning of fossil fuels releases air pollutants into the atmosphere that can damage plants directly by damaging their tissues or indirectly by altering soil chemistry. For example, acid rain can result in the release of aluminum ions from soil minerals, resulting in toxic levels of aluminum that impair plant growth and contribute to forest decline.

Increasing temperatures associated with climate change, coupled with dramatic changes in rainfall patterns and the frequency and intensity of storms, could have dramatic effects on vegetation. For example, the distribution patterns of individual plant and animal species could shift (e.g., increase in elevation, latitude, or both), thereby changing the composition and distribution of communities. The biggest difference between past and present climate change is that current changes are occurring at a much faster rate, making it more difficult for species to migrate or adapt to changing conditions. Habitat fragmentation is also an issue, as forests and other natural habitats are often smaller and more patchily distributed across the landscape, making it more difficult for species to migrate.

The introduction of exotic species, including vectors of disease, have had a devastating impact on southern Appalachian forests. The American chestnut was lost as a dominant canopy tree in the early twentieth century, and spruce-fir forests have been decimated by the balsam woolly adelgid since the 1950s. The hemlock woolly adelgid is currently eliminating both Canada and Carolina hemlock over much of their ranges. Millions of acres of forested land in the Southeast are currently occupied by nonnative plants. Kudzu and Japanese honeysuckle each cover about 7 million acres. Almost 400 species of exotic (nonnative) plants have been identified in Great Smoky Mountains National Park. Although most are thought to be ecologically benign, about 35 species pose a serious threat due to their potential to displace native species and alter natural areas.

A century after the southern Appalachians were devastated by widespread deforestation, much of the region is again forested and recovering its biodiversity. While the threats outlined above are cause for concern, the region's biota has proven to be remarkably resilient. Current trends suggest that with strong human commitment and sound sustainable stewardship, humans and nature can continue to coexist in the region into the next century and beyond.

Additional conservation issues are discussed in the plant community descriptions (Part III).

3 : The Piedmont

Millions of years of erosion have lowered and smoothed the former mountains of the piedmont, creating an undulating landscape of gently rolling hills and valleys dissected by rivers and streams. Bounded by the Blue Ridge Mountains to the west and the coastal plain to the east, the piedmont province stretches from New Jersey to central Alabama. Relatively narrow in the north, the piedmont is best developed in Virginia, the Carolinas, and Georgia where its maximum width varies from 100 to nearly 200 miles (map 1). Elevations range from about 1,000 to 1,500 ft. at the base of the Blue Ridge escarpment to roughly 200–300 ft. at the fall line, where the piedmont ends and the coastal plain begins. Scattered in the western (inner) piedmont are a number of more or less isolated, rounded mountain peaks and ridges composed of granite and other resistant rock, Stone Mountain in Georgia, Pilot Mountain in North Carolina, and Paris Mountain in South Carolina among them.

The term "fall line" was first used by early boatmen traveling inland along rivers and streams. They encountered rapids, and in some cases, falls where the flatlands of the coastal plain adjoin the gentle rolling hills of the piedmont. The rapids and falls reflect the stream channels becoming steeper where the relatively hard rock of the piedmont encounters the softer, more erodible strata of the coastal plain. These areas were among the first places populated, because the falls and rapids generally marked the limit of upstream travel for boats coming inland, and the falls provided power for mills. Prominent fall-line towns include Richmond, Virginia, Raleigh, North Carolina, Columbia, South Carolina, and Augusta, Georgia.

Climate and Soils

Hot summers, mild winters, high humidity, and annual rainfall amounts of 40–50 in. are similar to those in the coastal plain. The growing season is relatively long (180–240 days), and because rainfall is fairly evenly distributed throughout the year, there are no pronounced wet or dry seasons. While piedmont soils are generally acidic and low in nutrients, scattered outcrops of mafic rocks such as amphibolite, diabase, or gabbro give rise to more basic soils that are rich in both nutrients and plant species.

Impact of Native Americans

Ancient peoples, or Paleo-Indians, arrived in North America from Asia more than 12,000 years ago. These early Americans often traveled considerable distances in search of prey and used fire to drive game as well as to open the forest to improve visibility and travel. Thick forests and dense brush offered Native Americans very little to eat. By using fire, Native Americans promoted more open forests with grasses, forbs, and shrubs that provided good forage for game as well as food for themselves. Trees such as oaks and hickories produced many more acorns and nuts in more open forests, as did berry-producing plants such as blueberries and huckleberries. While some fires resulted from lightning, most were human caused. Once ignited, fires often spread widely because little or no effort was made by Native Americans to extinguish them, and because a relatively dry climate provided favorable conditions for fire. Fires burned out when they encountered natural firebreaks (e.g., rivers), precipitation, or a reduction in combustible fuel.

The frequent use of fire by Native Americans had a widespread and long-lasting impact on southeastern vegetation. Unlike the dense, closed-canopy forests typical of many areas today, the frequently burned landscapes of prehistoric forests were a diverse mosaic of prairies, savannas, and woodlands with widely spaced trees in park-like savannas. Frequent fires favored the widespread dominance of fire-tolerant species such as oak, hickory, and pine, and their dominance in the pollen record for thousands of years indicates a fire-disturbed vegetation. The American chestnut oak–dominated forests of the southern Appalachians, the oak-hickory-pine forests of the piedmont, and the longleaf pine savannas of the coastal plain all represent ecosystems that were maintained by thousands of years of fires. Because fires reduced the density and size of woody plants in the understory, frequent low-intensity fires increased the diversity and abundance of herbaceous plants on the forest floor.

At the time of Columbus, it's estimated that nearly 2 million Native Americans lived in the Southeast. These early Americans were both numerous enough and sufficiently skilled at manipulating the environment through their use of fire to have significantly altered the vegetation. Had aboriginal people not been part of the North American landscape for thousands of years, the vegetation first observed by Europeans 500 years ago would have been very different.

Disease, coupled with displacement by European settlers, reduced Native American populations by up to 95 percent within 2 centuries of the arrival of Columbus in 1492. With far fewer Native Americans, the frequency of fires decreased and the appearance of the landscape began to change as prairies became savannas and woodlands became dense forests.

Impact of Widespread Agriculture

Widespread forest-clearing and farming by European settlers in the piedmont began in the eighteenth century and continued through the nineteenth and early twentieth centuries. A shifting agricultural system prevailed whereby tracts were cut over and farmed until the soil became depleted of nutrients or eroded. Farmers then moved to a new area and repeated the process. As a result, there were often waves of occupants over time on any given tract of land. Land that escaped being cleared and farmed was almost always on less productive or hard to cultivate topography such as steep slopes, rocky outcrops, and permanently wet areas.

It was only after land decreased in availability that more permanent residency ensued. By the early twentieth century, widespread clearing and nearly continuous farming of row crops (such as cotton and tobacco) on sloping surfaces led to severe erosion throughout much of the piedmont. With the loss of most of its once fertile topsoil, productivity in piedmont farms decreased and many abandoned farms reverted to forest.

Signs of past farming are scattered across the piedmont landscape. Many forested areas retain a washboard corrugation on the soil surface, indicating old row crops. Other signs of farming include old terraces, drainage ditches, and large piles of rocks that were removed from fields to facilitate plowing. Old plow furrows, remnants of house foundations, chimneys or cisterns, and remnant populations of cultivated plants often indicate home sites on old farms. Signs of past livestock grazing include old fencing material nailed onto trees as well as old traps or pens used to capture and hold roaming stock.

Fire Suppression

A serious effort to prevent fires on public lands began in the early 1930s. The highly effective "Smokey the Bear" campaign, begun in the 1940s, convinced 2–3 generations of Americans that forest fires were harmful. Unfortunately, foresters and other land-use managers failed to understand that many of the forest systems they were trying to protect depend on fires for their long-term persistence. Fires weren't completely eliminated, but the frequency of wildland fires decreased dramatically over the twentieth century, significantly altering the vegetation in many areas.

Today, public land managers are generally aware of the benefit of fire to many vegetation types in the Southeast. For example, wildland fires promote a greater diversity of communities, thereby enhancing the biodiversity of plants and animals. Also, more than 50 percent of the rare plants in the Southeast are fire-dependent species. As a result, land managers have begun to more actively use prescribed burns as a management tool.

Vegetation

Apart from urban areas, the piedmont landscape is largely a patchwork of secondary forest, fields in various stages of succession, pastures, and small farms. Early successional forests typically have a large component of pines and shade-intolerant hardwoods such as shortleaf pine (*Pinus echinata*) and loblolly pine (*P. taeda*) along with tulip tree (*Liriodendron tulipifera*) and sweetgum (*Liquidambar styraciflua*). More mature forests vary in composition, depending on soil type, moisture level, topography, and disturbance history.

One of the more widespread piedmont communities is oak-hickory forest. Dominated by a variety of hardwood species and scattered with pines, it occupies habitats ranging from dry south-facing slopes and ridges to fairly moist lower slopes and flats. River bluff forest dominated by American beech (*Fagus grandifolia*) is restricted to steep, north-facing river bluffs and sheltered ravines on moist acidic soils. Mountain species such as catawba rhododendron (*Rhododendron catawbiense*) and Canada hemlock (*Tsuga canadensis*) occur here due to the relatively cool, moist microclimate.

The narrow floodplain forests on the margins of many rivers and streams that cross the piedmont are called alluvial forest because of the nutrient-rich alluvium that is deposited when rivers and streams overflow their banks. Flood-tolerant trees such as sycamore (*Platanus occidentalis*), river birch (*Betula nigra*), and winged elm (*Ulmus alata*) are dominant. Here too, a rich diversity of wildflowers carpets the forest floor.

Several interesting and unusual communities occur in the piedmont region, including basic mesic forest, xeric hardpan forest, and granite outcrops. The moist, nearly neutral (basic) soils that characterize basic mesic forest produce colorful wildflower displays, particularly in early spring before the canopy trees leaf out. Xeric hardpan forest is a relatively rare community restricted to shallow soils underlain by a clay hardpan or shallow rock layer. Resident plants must cope with a soil that fluctuates between being a gummy paste in wet periods and a hard brick-like substrate when dry. Stunted trees, ephemeral pools with unusual wetland plants, and species-rich, prairie-like habitats highlight this community.

The granite outcrop community consists of a diverse mosaic of lichen- and moss-covered rocks and herb- and shrub-dominated patches with spectacular spring wildflower displays. High solar radiation and the absorption of heat by the rock surfaces commonly produce summer temperatures in excess of 120°F on ground surfaces. The mostly low-growing vegetation consists of a highly specialized group of plants that cope with the desert-like environment in a variety of fascinating ways.

Conservation Concerns

The rapid rate of residential and commercial development in the piedmont is adversely affecting natural communities and the species they harbor. Rapid expansion of large metropolitan areas such as Richmond, Virginia, Charlotte and Greensboro, North Carolina, Atlanta, Georgia, and Greenville-Spartanburg, South Carolina, has resulted in widespread habitat loss. Communities such as oak-hickory forest that once formed large uninterrupted tracts now form scattered patches of forest interspersed by roads, fields, housing developments, and other human activities.

The process whereby a large, continuous area of habitat is reduced in size and divided into fragments is called habitat fragmentation. These "islands" of natural habitat are often isolated from each other by highly degraded landscapes creating barriers for normal dispersal and colonization. For example, if the movement of mammals between forest patches is impeded, then plants whose fleshy fruits or barbed seeds are dispersed by mammals are likely to be adversely affected. Habitats that are broken up or fragmented are also more vulnerable to colonization by invasive species, and because smaller habitat patches generally have fewer species than larger patches, fragmented habitats show reduced species diversity.

Fire suppression is another serious problem as highways, subdivisions, and commercial developments increasingly surround fire-dependent habitats. Concerns about smoke management, air quality, damage to structures, and budget constraints make it difficult to implement prescribed burns. The lack of fire has resulted in a decline in the extent and quality of piedmont habitats such as oak-hickory forests, oak woodlands and savannas, prairies, and canebrakes.

With continued human population growth and urban sprawl, problems associated with habitat loss and fragmentation are likely to worsen. On the positive side, state and federal agencies, along with private conservation groups such as the Nature Conservancy, are working to purchase and manage natural areas that represent both typical piedmont landscapes as well as unusual habitats that harbor less common communities and species.

4 : Understanding Natural Communities

An ecological community is an assemblage of plants, animals, and other organisms living together at the same place and time. Species aren't isolated entities but interact with each other in intricate ways. Co-occurring plants compete with each other for light, water, nutrients, and space. Animals interact with plants by pollinating their flowers, dispersing their seeds, and grazing on their tissues. For many nature enthusiasts, the enjoyment of native plants isn't just a celebration of their natural beauty, or the satisfaction that comes with learning their names, but also stems from an understanding of the complex interrelationships among species in their natural environments.

Communities provide the context within which species interact with each other and their physical environment. The structure and composition of natural communities varies, largely due to changes in the physical environment. Regional landscapes often have a mosaic of communities present, reflecting differences in moisture availability, soil type, topography, and other factors. Because adjoining communities often grade into one another, it can be difficult to tell where one community ends and another begins.

Plants play a dominant role in community classification because they're highly visible and form the base of the food chain. This section describes some of the key characteristics of natural communities, including the factors that determine their distribution across the landscape.

Community Characteristics

VERTICAL STRATIFICATION

For the most part, the mountain and piedmont regions are forested. Unlike pine plantations, natural forest communities typically have several layers. The canopy forms the top layer, followed by the subcanopy, shrub layer, herbaceous layer, and forest floor. These layers are more developed in older, more mature forests than in younger, more recently disturbed forests. The canopy generally consists of mature trees that reach heights greater than 100 ft. in some forest types. In a closed forest, the crowns of the canopy trees overlap, forming a nearly continuous ceiling. Most of a forest's photosynthesis occurs in the canopy, where light levels are highest and leaves are most concentrated. The understory includes smaller individuals of canopy species, such as American beech (*Fagus grandifolia*), as well as smaller trees that never reach the canopy, such as flowering dogwood (*Cornus florida*). In some areas, shrubs form dense thickets. In other areas, the shrub layer is sparse or totally absent. The herbaceous layer includes plants with soft rather than woody stems (often called herbs), very low-growing shrubs, and the seedlings of woody plants. The herbaceous layer varies from dense to sparse, depending on environmental factors such as the amount of light, soil pH, and soil moisture. The herbaceous layer is most conspicuous early in the growing season when the spring wildflowers are in bloom. The forest floor consists of leaves, twigs, and other kinds of organic matter that are broken down by decomposers into carbon dioxide, nitrogen, calcium, and other substances that are returned to the soil and air where they can be taken up and reused by plants.

DOMINANT AND INDICATOR SPECIES

The most abundant or conspicuous species are community dominants. Chestnut oak forest, spruce-fir forest, and oak-hickory forest are examples of communities whose names reflect the dominant species. In contrast, communities such as cove forest, northern hardwood forest, and alluvial forest lack clear dominants. The term "indicator species" refers to species that are more or less unique to a particular community, or due to their abundance, impart a distinct identity to the community. Fraser fir (*Abies fraseri*), for example, is considered to be an indicator species of spruce-fir forest as it's both abundant and largely restricted to this community type.

SPECIES RICHNESS

Species richness varies considerably among different community types. For example, a rich cove forest may have 25 tree species per acre while a spruce-fir forest may have fewer than 10 tree species per acre. Whether or not a species is present within a particular habitat or community depends on several factors. First, seeds have to reach the area. This is largely due to chance, although some species produce more seeds and disperse them over a wider area than other species. Second, species must survive conditions in the area. The tolerance range of a species includes both biotic factors such as potential competitors and pathogens, as well as abiotic factors such as climate, soil type, and light levels. Finally, past disturbance (as discussed below) plays an important role in determining the composition of species in a particular area.

ECOTONES

Natural communities aren't always easy to identify and name. This is particularly true in areas where adjoining communities grade into one another. The transition zone from one community to another is called an ecotone. The gradation may be fairly abrupt (a narrow ecotone) if there is a sudden change in soil type, moisture regime, or disturbance history. More commonly, there is a gradual change from one community type to another (a broad ecotone). Ecotones typically have relatively high species richness since they contain a mixture of species from adjoining communities.

GAPS

A gap is an opening in the vegetation caused by a disturbance. Gaps may be small or large depending on the scale of the disturbance (e.g., the death of a single canopy tree versus an entire hurricane-impacted forest). Because light levels increase dramatically in gaps, species that require high light levels are able to become established in gaps, but not in the deeply shaded forest understory. Consequently, gaps play an important role in maintaining species diversity in forests. Forests typically consist of a mosaic of gaps of varying sizes and ages with new gaps forming and others filling in. Thus, even mature forests are dynamic rather than stable environments with young, mid- and more mature stages of regrowth represented in gaps of varying sizes.

SUCCESSION

Succession is the replacement of one community by another over time. The process begins either by the exposure of a previously unvegetated substrate (e.g., a river sandbar) or by some form of disturbance (e.g., fire, logging, windthrow). Succession is always occurring within communities: it occurs after a single tree falls in the forest, as well as after a fire sweeps through an area. Thus, succession occurs at spatial scales ranging from very small to very large. The communities that occur sequentially in a given area (seral stages) are influenced by interacting factors including climate, soil, frequency and intensity of disturbance, and the pool of species available for colonization. Plants colonize disturbed areas by dormant seeds already present in the soil or new seeds dispersed by wind, water, and birds. Previously established plants may also resprout following disturbance and spread vegetatively by rhizomes or stolons.

Species diversity increases during early succession as new species arrive, but diversity may decline in later seral stages as dominant species eliminate less competitive ones. While some plant species are limited to one or two seral stages, others are able to occupy a wider spectrum of communities. As plant communities change, the animal life each supports also changes. Species diversity of both plants and animals is generally highest in areas that have a variety of seral stages represented. A diversity of seral stages within an area often reflects environmental variability (e.g., differences in topography, soil, and moisture availability), as well as different disturbance histories across the landscape. In areas heavily disturbed by humans, many early successional habitats are represented (e.g., fields, shrublands, and young forests), whereas later successional habitats (e.g., mature forests) are uncommon. Ecologists used to think succession had a stable end-stage called a climax community. Today, ecologists have largely abandoned this idea as most communities are in a state of flux due to species introductions, climate change, and other kinds of disturbance. The dynamic nature of communities is illustrated by the changes in distribution and composition of vegetation in the southeastern United States over the last 20,000 years, as discussed earlier.

FOREST AGE

By looking for certain characteristics, it's often possible to make an educated guess about the maturity of a particular forest. Key characteristics associated with most older forests include a well-defined canopy and understory, relatively large and loosely spaced canopy trees, scattered, dead standing trees with a deeply shaded forest floor and a thick layer of decomposing leaves. In contrast, young or immature forests typically have a high density of small-diameter trees (trees that look crowded and spindly). The understory, if present, is often poorly defined, and the forest floor has a relatively thin layer of decomposing leaves. The species present in the canopy are also a good indicator of forest age. For example, large American beech (*Fagus grandifolia*), yellow buckeye (*Aesculus flava*), or Canada hemlock (*Tsuga canadensis*) are good indicators of a mature forest, whereas pin cherry (*Prunus pensylvanica*), black locust (*Robinia pseudoacacia*), and sweetgum (*Liquidambar styraciflua*) are associated with younger forests.

PREDICTING FOREST CHANGE

To some extent, one can predict forest change by comparing the species composition of trees in the canopy to the tree species that are growing as seedlings/saplings on the forest floor. If the canopy trees and tree seedlings/saplings on the forest floor are similar, this indicates that the current forest is self-perpetuating. In contrast, if the young trees (saplings) are different from the canopy trees, this indicates that the composition of the forest will change over time. For example, because pines are generally shade intolerant, they are often unable to regenerate under their own canopies. As a result, saplings of shade-tolerant hardwoods such as oaks, hickories, and beech, rather than pines, typically occur in the understory of dense pine forests. In the absence of fire or other major disturbance, such forests will gradually undergo succession from pine to hardwood-dominant forest as hardwoods eventually replace adult pines. Because the lifespan of trees can be quite long, a change in forest composition or type can take many years.

Determinants of Community Type

CLIMATE

Climate plays an important role in determining the composition and distribution of communities across the landscape. Temperature, precipitation, sunlight, wind, and the length of the growing season influence plant growth and development, with species' responding differently according to genetic composition and adaptability. While average values are important, so are extremes. Temperature, moisture, and sunlight vary greatly across the landscape, creating a range of localized climates. Because plants are sedentary, the climate immediately surrounding individual plants (the microclimate) is more important than the overall climate of the area. Microclimates are strongly influenced by topography (the shape of the land) as well as by surrounding plants, which intercept sunlight, provide windbreaks, humidify air (through evaporative water loss from leaves), and buffer temperature. The air temperature in a patch of vegetation can vary dramatically from the soil surface to the top of the canopy. Elevation also influences climate. As elevation increases from the piedmont to the mountains, temperatures become cooler, precipitation increases, and the growing season shortens. The same pattern occurs with increasing latitude.

TOPOGRAPHY

Features of local topography include changes in elevation, steepness of slope, and slope direction. On sites with little slope, the influence of topography is slight. On steep slopes, changes in temperature, moisture, and other factors influence the distribution of plants and natural communities. Soil, water, and dissolved nutrients are pulled downhill on steep slopes, creating a gradient in soil development, moisture, and nutrient levels. On cliffs and other very steep slopes, there is little or no soil development and the vegetation is often stunted and sparse. Conversely, at the base of slopes where nutrients and moisture slowly accumulate over time, dense forests of tall trees can form. In hilly areas, the direction of slope influences microclimate and therefore community distribution. South-facing slopes, for example, typically receive more sunlight and are warmer and drier than north-facing slopes. In the mountains, communities such as northern hardwood forest and cove forest typically occur on cool, moist, north-facing slopes, whereas chestnut oak forest and pine-oak-heath generally occur on warmer, drier, south-facing slopes. In the piedmont region, river bluff forest and basic mesic forest commonly occur on north-facing slopes.

GEOLOGY AND SOILS

A variety of rocks occur in our region, including granite, limestone, schists, gneiss, and amphibolite. Each has its own characteristic chemistry, texture, and rate of erosion, which in turn affect plant- and community-distribution patterns. Rocks such as limestone, dolomite, and marble have high concentrations of calcium carbonate and weather fairly rapidly, contributing calcium, magnesium, and other important plant nutrients to soils. Calcium is an essential plant nutrient and acts as a buffer to maintain pH levels close to neutral. At a near-neutral pH, most nutrients are readily available for plant use. Non-carbonate rocks such as granite and gneiss don't break down easily, produce acidic soils, and generally don't provide important nutrients for plants.

Like sunlight, soil is vital to plants, as it provides water, nutrients, and the physical support necessary for growth and survival. Soil is a mixture of mineral particles (derived from rocks), organic matter (both living and dead), and spaces (pores) between soil particles that are filled with air and water. Soil properties such as texture, acidity, nutrient availability, and water-holding capacity are important factors determining the distribution of communities. The relative proportion of 3 main soil particles—sand (the largest), silt (intermediate), and clay (the smallest)—determine soil texture. With their relatively large grains, sandy soils are well aerated (oxygen is readily available to plant roots) but have poor water-holding capacity. As a result, sandy soils are often dry. Clay soils, in contrast, consist of tiny, closely packed soil particles that retain moisture but are sometimes poorly aerated. Sandy soils are most common in the coastal plain, while clay soils are common in the piedmont and mountain regions.

Soils range from being extremely acidic to slightly alkaline. Most soils in our region are acidic and the vegetation consists largely of acid-tolerant species. While acidic soils predominate, scattered islands of higher pH soils (> 6.0) are scattered throughout the region. Sites with more basic (circumneutral) soils generally have increased species diversity and density, particularly in the herbaceous layer. Species-rich communities associated with circumneutral soils include rich cove forests (in the mountains) and basic mesic forests (in the piedmont). While some species (e.g., heath shrubs) are restricted to acidic soils and others (e.g., white basswood, *Tilia americana*) to basic soils, most mountain and piedmont plants tolerate a fairly broad range of soil acidity.

Soil moisture also has a strong influence on vegetation. Mesic communities have well-drained, moderately moist soils. Such communities generally have relatively high species diversity and often appear rather lush. Examples include northern hardwood forest, cove forest, river bluff forest, and basic mesic forest. Xeric communities occur on sandy, rocky, or otherwise poor soils that are frequently dry. Examples include heath balds, rock outcrops, chestnut oak forest, and xeric hardpan forest. Hydric communities such as alluvial forests and mountain bogs are associated with low-lying areas where the soil is often water-saturated.

PAST DISTURBANCE

Changes in vegetation at a landscape level are often the result of different disturbance histories. Important causes of disturbance include fire, windthrow, logging, and insect and disease outbreaks. Disturbances differ in extent, severity, and frequency. A windstorm, for example, might blow down several trees, while several thousand might be blown down by a hurricane. The "severity" of a disturbance refers to the amount of change it causes. A forest fire, for example, can be a low-intensity ground fire that burns the herbaceous layer along with low-growing shrubs and trees, while a crown fire spreads from the crown of one tree to another, eventually destroying most of the canopy trees and other vegetation within an area. The "frequency" of disturbance refers to how often, on average, a particular type of disturbance occurs in a particular place. Small disturbances of low intensity are much more common than large, severe disturbances.

Without natural disturbance, species diversity would drop dramatically as many species are restricted to recently disturbed habitats. With too much disturbance, later successional communities and the species associated with them would likely be lost. The near absence of old-growth forest in the piedmont region, for example, is indicative of a heavily disturbed landscape.

Fire

Occasional fires are part of a natural process that benefits many forests and other community types. Both natural (caused by lightning) and human-induced fires (particularly ones set by precolonial Native Americans) have had an important influence on the vegetation of the southeastern United States. Plant species cope with fire in various ways. The trees most likely to survive a burn are the largest individuals with the thickest bark, as bark provides insulation from the heat of fire. Small and medium-sized trees are easily killed by fire, as are thin-barked species such as birch, maple, hemlock, and beech. As they grow, some trees shed their lower branches and thereby make it more difficult for fire to reach the canopy. Following topkill by fire, many trees, shrubs, and herbaceous plants have the ability to resprout from dormant buds on roots and rhizomes. Other species regenerate primarily by seed, taking advantage of the increased light, reduced competition, and enhanced soil nutrients that follow a fire.

Widespread suppression of wildfires began in the 1930s. Lightning fires were quickly extinguished and human-induced fires were strongly discouraged. The lack of fire altered the vegetation in many areas, and the increased amount of woody debris on the forest floor increased the risk of much larger, uncontrollable fires. Due to a better understanding of the role of fire as a natural process, many federal and state agencies (as well as private land managers) now let naturally occurring wildfires burn themselves out, except where human lives or property are threatened. Land managers also use prescribed burns to reduce the risk of catastrophic crown fires and to maintain fire-dependent communities such as pine-oak-heath.

Windthrow

Minor windstorms frequently cause single trees to fall, creating small gaps in forests. In communities where fires are infrequent due to moist conditions (e.g., in northern hardwood forest, cove forest, and river bluff forest), single tree blowdowns are the dominant form of disturbance. Trees most vulnerable to windthrow include dead or diseased trees, tall trees with shallow roots, and large trees on slopes. On steep slopes, a single large windthrown tree can take several others with it, creating gaps an acre or more in size. Once a tree-fall gap occurs, neighboring trees become more susceptible to being blown down. Extremely powerful storms such as tornadoes and hurricanes occur much less frequently than minor windstorms, affecting large tracts of forest, both uprooting trees and snapping them like matchsticks at mid-trunk level. Gaps of varying size created by windthrow are an important component of forest dynamics as they contribute to a continuously changing and diverse array of species.

Ice and Snow Loading

Periodic ice storms cause freezing rain to accumulate in layers of ice on exposed surfaces, causing scattered branches to break, sometimes damaging numerous trees, which creates gaps similar to those caused by windthrow. Snow can also build up and break off tree limbs. Pines are particularly susceptible to ice damage while the conical shapes of spruce and fir help them shed heavy snow loads.

Insects and Disease

In forests where evidence of fire is lacking, numerous dead or dying trees are usually a sign of forest pathogens: insects and diseases that kill trees. Southern pine beetles, for example, kill large numbers of pines, particularly those that are old, drought-stressed, or growing in dense pine plantations. Introduced insects such as the balsam woolly adelgid and the hemlock woolly adelgid have devastated populations of Fraser fir (*Abies fraseri*), Canada hemlock (*Tsuga canadensis*), and Carolina hemlock (*T. caroliniana*) in recent years. Gypsy moth outbreaks are also a concern as caterpillars can defoliate large tracts of forest, sometimes killing numerous trees. Trees that die following defoliation usually do so because their roots are starved of carbohydrates.

Plants are subject to diseases caused by fungi, bacteria, and viruses. Plant diseases can have a sudden onset, dramatically affecting populations, or can be chronic, persisting in populations for years. The most devastating example of a plant disease in eastern North America is the chestnut blight. This fungus, accidentally introduced from Asia early in the twentieth century, eliminated the American chestnut (*Castanea dentata*) as a dominant canopy tree in eastern deciduous forests. The indirect effect of the chestnut blight altered the ecology of the communities in which the American chestnut had been abundant. Other significant diseases include dogwood anthracnose, Dutch elm disease, beech bark disease, and white pine blister rust, each of which is caused by a fungal pathogen whose spread is facilitated by insects. Forest pathogens (both insects and disease) will undoubtedly continue to have a profound effect on our forests.

Humans

Humans are the most pervasive cause of disturbance to natural communities. While people have altered the southeastern landscape for over 12,000 years, the extent and frequency of human-caused disturbance has increased dramatically over the last 200 years. The conversion of forest to farmland or pasture, commercial logging, urban sprawl, the introduction of nonnative species, and global climate change are among the many ways humans have changed the landscape. Many of these topics are discussed elsewhere in this book.

Conservation Benefits

Some communities are common, others rare. A community can be rare because it occurs in a specialized habitat that is rare. For example, the unusual soil conditions associated with the xeric hardpan forest community limit its occurrence to a small number of widely scattered sites in the piedmont. In other cases, a community is rare because human activities have seriously altered or destroyed most of the physical environment in which the community occurs. Communities particularly vulnerable to human disturbance include those that occur on soils that are highly productive for agriculture, landscapes that are highly desirable for development, and areas where natural fire regimes have been altered by fire suppression. Some of the rarest communities occur in habitats that are both rare and subject to human disturbance, such as mountain bogs.

Here, I briefly consider some of the benefits of maintaining natural communities. For example, intact communities play a critical role in reducing floods, protecting watersheds, and reducing soil erosion. Leaves on trees, shrubs, and herbs, as well as dead, decomposing leaves on the forest floor, intercept rain and thereby reduce runoff. Plant roots and soil organisms also penetrate and aerate the soil, increasing the soil's capacity to absorb water and reduce flooding. Dams and reservoirs in the mountain and piedmont regions provide drinking water to nearby communities. Maintaining the vegetation within the watershed (e.g., by restricting logging) helps ensure a steady supply of high-quality water. Intact communities also protect the local soil, thereby maintaining productivity. If vegetation is removed, rates of soil erosion and landslides increase dramatically. Soils that take decades to form can quickly wash away.

Natural communities also help buffer and moderate local, regional, and global climates. At the local level, even a small patch of forest provides shade and transpires water, reducing temperatures in hot weather. At the regional level, water lost by plants through transpiration recycles rainwater back into the atmosphere, which can return as rain. One of the potential consequences of large-scale deforestation is a reduction in regional rainfall amounts. At the global level, plant growth is tied into the carbon cycle: removing the vegetation from an area results in reduced CO_2 uptake by plants, which in turn contributes to the rise in the atmospheric CO_2 levels driving global climate change. Maintaining large areas of continuous forest, such as those in the southern Appalachians, provides an important carbon sink that helps reduce climate change.

The southern Appalachians are a haven for outdoor recreation, attracting hikers, wildflower enthusiasts, bird-watchers, fishermen, kayakers, campers, picnickers, and people who simply want to enjoy the scenery. Great Smoky Mountains National Park (which has more than twice the annual visitors of any other U.S. National Park), Shenandoah National Park, the Blue Ridge Parkway, and the region's national forests attract millions of visitors each year. From an economic perspective, attracting nature-oriented tourists and the revenue they bring in is another reason to preserve forests, grassy balds, and other natural communities.

Finally, many conservation-oriented groups want to protect and conserve viable populations of all native species. This is a huge task, complicated by the fact that we don't know very much about the biology of many species, especially less conspicuous groups such as fungi, mosses, lichens, and invertebrates. The simplest and best way to conserve large numbers of species is to take a community-based approach. For example, we don't know (or understand) the habitat requirements of all the species that live in a rich cove forest, but if we protect multiple high-quality examples of rich cove forests, then we're likely to protect many of the species associated with this community. Because of the benefits of this kind of preservation, a number of organizations and agencies now emphasize protecting entire communities rather than single species.

PART II

This pictorial guide will enable you to rapidly preview plants that you're likely to encounter within each of the 21 plant communities described in Part III. If you're about to explore a rich cove forest, for example, you can quickly refer to the 50 thumbnail photos included for this community, to get an idea of what plants you might find. Within each community, plants are arranged alphabetically by trees, shrubs and woody vines, and herbaceous plants. The scientific and common names are listed beneath each of the 760 photos included here. An asterisk in front of a scientific name indicates that the species is introduced, rather than native. If you'd like to learn more about a particular species, turn to the page(s) indicated for a description of the plant.

Photo Key

1 : The Mountains

Spruce-Fir Forest

Abies fraseri
Fraser fir, p. 219

Acer pensylvanicum
Striped maple, p. 221

Acer spicatum
Mountain maple, pp. 223–24

Amelanchier laevis
Smooth serviceberry, pp. 225–26

Betula alleghaniensis
Yellow birch, pp. 226–27

Picea rubens
Red spruce, p. 248

Prunus pensylvanica
Fire cherry, p. 254

Sorbus americana
Mountain ash, pp. 262–63

Ilex montana
Mountain holly, pp. 288–89

PHOTO KEY / THE MOUNTAINS / SPRUCE-FIR FOREST

Menziesia pilosa
Minniebush, pp. 295–96

Rhododendron catawbiense
Catawba rhododendron, pp. 301–2

Rhododendron vaseyi
Pinkshell azalea, pp. 304–5

Ribes rotundifolium
Appalachian gooseberry, p. 308

Rubus allegheniensis
Allegheny blackberry, p. 310

Sambucus racemosa
Red elderberry, p. 313

Viburnum lantanoides
Witch hobble, p. 321

Ageratina altissima
White snakeroot, pp. 328–29

Athyrium asplenioides
Southern lady fern, p. 340

Carex pensylvanica
Pennsylvania sedge, pp. 343–44

Chelone lyonii
Pink turtlehead, pp. 348–49

Clintonia borealis
Bluebead lily, pp. 352–353

Dryopteris campyloptera
Mountain wood fern, p. 366

Eurybia chlorolepis
Mountain wood aster, pp. 371–72

Maianthemum canadense
Canada mayflower, pp. 400–401

Oclemena acuminata
Whorled aster, p. 409

Oxalis montana
Mountain wood sorrel, p. 414

Solidago glomerata
Skunk goldenrod, pp. 443–44

Trillium undulatum
Painted trillium, pp. 459–60

Veratrum viride
False hellebore, pp. 463–64

PHOTO KEY / THE MOUNTAINS / SPRUCE-FIR FOREST

Grassy Bald

Abies fraseri
Fraser fir, p. 219

Amelanchier laevis
Smooth serviceberry, pp. 225–26

Crataegus macrosperma
Bigfruit hawthorn, p. 236

Prunus pensylvanica
Fire cherry, p. 254

Kalmia latifolia
Mountain laurel, pp. 291–92

Rhododendron calendulaceum
Flame azalea, p. 301

Rhododendron catawbiense
Catawba rhododendron, pp. 301–2

Rubus allegheniensis
Allegheny blackberry, p. 310

Vaccinium corymbosum
Highbush blueberry, p. 317

PHOTO KEY / THE MOUNTAINS / GRASSY BALD

Achillea millefolium
Yarrow, p. 325

Angelica triquinata
Mountain angelica, pp. 333–34

Avenella flexuosa
Wavy hairgrass, pp. 341–42

Carex pensylvanica
Pennsylvania sedge, pp. 343–44

Danthonia compressa
Mountain oat grass, pp. 359–60

Dennstaedtia punctilobula
Hayscented fern, p. 360

Fragaria virginiana
Wild strawberry, pp. 373–74

Houstonia serpyllifolia
Appalachian bluet, pp. 387–88

Lilium grayi
Gray's lily, pp. 396–97

Lysimachia quadrifolia
Whorled loosestrife, pp. 399–400

Minuartia groenlandica
Mountain sandwort, p. 405

*Phleum pratense
Timothy grass, pp. 421–22

35

Pteridium aquilinum
Bracken fern, p. 432

Rudbeckia laciniata
Cutleaf coneflower, pp. 433–34

Schizachyrium scoparium
Little bluestem, pp. 436–37

Sibbaldiopsis tridentata
Three-tooth cinquefoil, pp. 438–39

Solidago glomerata
Skunk goldenrod, pp. 443–44

Heath Bald

Prunus pensylvanica
Fire cherry, p. 254

Aronia melanocarpa
Black chokeberry, p. 272

Clethra acuminata
Mountain sweet pepperbush, pp. 278–79

PHOTO KEY / THE MOUNTAINS / HEATH BALD

Diervilla sessilifolia
Southern bush honeysuckle, p. 282

Kalmia buxifolia
Sand myrtle, pp. 290–91

Kalmia latifolia
Mountain laurel, pp. 291–92

Menziesia pilosa
Minniebush, pp. 295–96

Rhododendron calendulaceum
Flame azalea, p. 301

Rhododendron catawbiense
Catawba rhododendron, pp. 301–2

Rhododendron maximum
Rosebay, pp. 302–3

Rhododendron vaseyi
Pinkshell azalea, pp. 304–5

Rubus allegheniensis
Allegheny blackberry, p. 310

Smilax rotundifolia
Common greenbrier, pp. 314–15

Vaccinium corymbosum
Highbush blueberry, p. 317

Viburnum cassinoides
Wild raisin, pp. 320–21

Cuscuta rostrata
Appalachian dodder, pp. 356–57

Epigaea repens
Trailing arbutus, pp. 368–69

Galax urceolata
Galax, pp. 374–75

Gaultheria procumbens
Wintergreen, pp. 376–77

Geum radiatum
Spreading avens, p. 379

Pteridium aquilinum
Bracken fern, p. 432

Trillium undulatum
Painted trillium, pp. 459–60

High-Elevation Rock Outcrop

Abies fraseri
Fraser fir, p. 219

Amelanchier laevis
Smooth serviceberry, pp. 225–26

Betula alleghaniensis
Yellow birch, pp. 226–27

Picea rubens
Red spruce, p. 248

Pinus pungens
Table mountain pine, pp. 249–50

Quercus rubra
Northern red oak, pp. 259–60

Sorbus americana
Mountain ash, pp. 262–63

Tsuga caroliniana
Carolina hemlock, pp. 265–66

Aronia melanocarpa
Black chokeberry, p. 272

Diervilla sessilifolia
Southern bush honeysuckle, p. 282

Hudsonia montana
Mountain golden heather, pp. 286–87

Hypericum buckleyi
Granite dome St. John's wort, pp. 287–88

Kalmia buxifolia
Sand myrtle, pp. 290–91

Kalmia latifolia
Mountain laurel, pp. 291–92

Menziesia pilosa
Minniebush, pp. 295–96

Rhododendron catawbiense
Catawba rhododendron, pp. 301–2

Rhododendron vaseyi
Pinkshell azalea, pp. 304–5

Vaccinium corymbosum
Highbush blueberry, p. 317

Asplenium montanum
Mountain spleenwort, p. 339

Avenella flexuosa
Wavy hairgrass, pp. 341–42

Danthonia compressa
Mountain oat grass, pp. 359–60

Gaultheria procumbens
Wintergreen, pp. 376–77

Geum radiatum
Spreading avens, p. 379

Grimmia laevigata
Dry rock moss, p. 381

Heuchera villosa
Rock alumroot, pp. 385–86

Liatris helleri
Heller's blazing star, p. 396

Micranthes petiolaris
Cliff saxifrage, p. 403

Minuartia groenlandica
Mountain sandwort, p. 405

Oclemena acuminata
Whorled aster, p. 409

Packera millefolium
Blue ridge ragwort, pp. 415–16

Schizachyrium scoparium
Little bluestem, pp. 436–37

Selaginella tortipila
Twisted hair spikemoss, p. 437

Sibbaldiopsis tridentata
Three-tooth cinquefoil, pp. 438–39

Solidago glomerata
Skunk goldenrod, pp. 443–44

Umbilicaria mammulata
Smooth rock tripe, pp. 461–62

Xerophyllum asphodeloides
Turkeybeard, p. 468

High-Elevation Red Oak Forest

Acer pensylvanicum
Striped maple, p. 221

Acer rubrum
Red maple, p. 222

Betula alleghaniensis
Yellow birch, pp. 226–27

Castanea dentata
American chestnut, pp. 231–32

Crataegus macrosperma
Bigfruit hawthorn, p. 236

Quercus montana
Chestnut oak, pp. 258–59

Quercus rubra
Northern red oak, pp. 259–60

Robinia pseudoacacia
Black locust, pp. 260–61

Cornus alternifolia
Alternate leaf dogwood, p. 279

Corylus cornuta
Beaked hazelnut, pp. 280–81

Gaylussacia ursina
Bear huckleberry, p. 284

Hamamelis virginiana
Witch hazel, pp. 285–86

Ilex montana
Mountain holly, pp. 288–89

Kalmia latifolia
Mountain laurel, pp. 291–92

Rhododendron calendulaceum
Flame azalea, p. 301

Rhododendron catawbiense
Catawba rhododendron, pp. 301–2

Rhododendron maximum
Rosebay, pp. 302–3

Rubus allegheniensis
Allegheny blackberry, p. 310

43

Viburnum lantanoides
Witch hobble, p. 321

Ageratina altissima
White snakeroot, pp. 328–29

Athyrium asplenioides
Southern lady fern, p. 340

Carex pensylvanica
Pennsylvania sedge, pp. 343–44

Clematis viorna
Leather flower, p. 352

Clintonia umbellulata
Speckled wood lily, pp. 353–54

Conopholis americana
Squawroot, p. 355

Dennstaedtia punctilobula
Hayscented fern, p. 360

Dioscorea villosa
Wild yam, pp. 363–64

Dryopteris campyloptera
Mountain wood fern, p. 366

Eurybia macrophylla
Bigleaf aster, p. 372

Galax urceolata
Galax, pp. 374–75

Laportea canadensis
Wood nettle, p. 395

Lysimachia quadrifolia
Whorled loosestrife, pp. 399–400

Maianthemum canadense
Canada mayflower, pp. 400–401

Oclemena acuminata
Whorled aster, p. 409

Osmunda claytoniana
Interrupted fern, pp. 413–14

Pedicularis canadensis
Lousewort, p. 419

Smilax herbacea
Carrion flower, pp. 440–41

Solidago curtisii
Curtis's goldenrod, p. 443

Thelypteris noveboracensis
New York fern, pp. 451–52

Trillium erectum
Wake robin, p. 457

PHOTO KEY / THE MOUNTAINS / HIGH-ELEVATION RED OAK FOREST

Northern Hardwood Forest

Acer pensylvanicum
Striped maple, p. 221

Acer saccharum
Sugar maple, pp. 222–23

Acer spicatum
Mountain maple, pp. 223–24

Aesculus flava
Yellow buckeye, pp. 224–25

Amelanchier laevis
Smooth serviceberry, pp. 225–26

Betula alleghaniensis
Yellow birch, pp. 226–27

Fagus grandifolia
American beech, pp. 237–38

Fraxinus americana
White ash, pp. 238–39

Magnolia acuminata
Cucumber tree, pp. 243–44

Picea rubens
Red spruce, p. 248

Tilia americana
White basswood, pp. 263–64

Aristolochia macrophylla
Pipevine, pp. 271–72

*Celastrus orbiculatus
Oriental bittersweet, p. 277

Cornus alternifolia
Alternate leaf dogwood, p. 279

Hydrangea arborescens
Wild hydrangea, p. 287

Rhododendron catawbiense
Catawba rhododendron, pp. 301–2

Ribes rotundifolium
Appalachian gooseberry, p. 308

Rubus allegheniensis
Allegheny blackberry, p. 310

Rubus odoratus
Flowering raspberry, p. 311

Sambucus racemosa
Red elderberry, p. 313

Viburnum lantanoides
Witch hobble, p. 321

Actaea racemosa
Black cohosh, pp. 326–27

Ageratina altissima
White snakeroot, pp. 328–29

Arisaema triphyllum
Jack-in-the-pulpit, p. 335

Aruncus dioicus
Goat's beard, p. 336

Carex pensylvanica
Pennsylvania sedge, pp. 343–44

Caulophyllum thalictroides
Blue cohosh, pp. 345–46

Claytonia caroliniana
Carolina spring beauty, pp. 350–51

Dennstaedtia punctilobula
Hayscented fern, p. 360

Diphylleia cymosa
Umbrella leaf, pp. 364–65

Epifagus virginiana
Beechdrops, pp. 367–68

Erythronium umbilicatum
Dimpled trout lily, pp. 370–71

Impatiens pallida
Yellow jewelweed, pp. 391–92

Laportea canadensis
Wood nettle, p. 395

Maianthemum racemosum
False Solomon's seal, p. 401

Monarda didyma
Crimson bee balm, pp. 406–7

Phacelia fimbriata
Fringed phacelia, pp. 419–20

Rudbeckia laciniata
Cutleaf coneflower, pp. 433–34

Solidago curtisii
Curtis's goldenrod, p. 443

Stellaria pubera
Giant chickweed, p. 447

Trillium erectum
Wake robin, p. 457

Uvularia grandiflora
Large-flowered bellwort, p. 462

Viola canadensis
Canada violet, pp. 465–66

PHOTO KEY / THE MOUNTAINS / NORTHERN HARDWOOD FOREST

49

Rich Cove Forest

Acer pensylvanicum
Striped maple, p. 221

Acer saccharum
Sugar maple, pp. 222–23

Aesculus flava
Yellow buckeye, pp. 224–25

Betula lenta
Sweet birch, p. 227

Carpinus caroliniana
Ironwood, pp. 228–29

Cladrastis kentukea
Yellowwood, pp. 234–35

Cornus florida
Flowering dogwood, pp. 235–36

Fagus grandifolia
American beech, pp. 237–38

Fraxinus americana
White ash, pp. 238–39

Halesia tetraptera
Carolina silverbell, p. 239

Liriodendron tulipifera
Tulip tree, pp. 242–43

Magnolia acuminata
Cucumber tree, pp. 243–44

Magnolia fraseri
Fraser magnolia, pp. 244–45

Ostrya virginiana
Hop hornbeam, pp. 246–47

Prunus serotina
Black cherry, pp. 254–55

Tilia americana
White basswood, pp. 263–64

Aristolochia macrophylla
Pipevine, pp. 271–72

Asimina triloba
Pawpaw, p. 274

Calycanthus floridus
Sweet shrub, pp. 275–76

Hydrangea arborescens
Wild hydrangea, p. 287

Lindera benzoin
Spicebush, pp. 293–94

PHOTO KEY / THE MOUNTAINS / RICH COVE FOREST

Actaea pachypoda
Doll's eyes, pp. 325–26

Actaea racemosa
Black cohosh, pp. 326–27

Adiantum pedatum
Maidenhair fern, p. 327

Allium tricoccum
Ramps, pp. 329–30

Anemone quinquefolia
Wood anemone, p. 333

Arisaema triphyllum
Jack-in-the-pulpit, p. 335

Asarum canadense
Wild ginger, pp. 336–37

Caulophyllum thalictroides
Blue cohosh, pp. 345–46

Claytonia caroliniana
Carolina spring beauty, pp. 350–51

Clintonia umbellulata
Speckled wood lily, pp. 353–54

Cypripedium parviflorum
Yellow lady's slipper, pp. 358–59

Dicentra cucullaria
Dutchman's britches, pp. 362–63

Galearis spectabilis
Showy orchis, p. 375

Geranium maculatum
Wild geranium, p. 378

Hepatica acutiloba
Acute-lobed hepatica, pp. 384–85

Hydrastis canadensis
Goldenseal, pp. 388–89

Impatiens capensis
Orange jewelweed, pp. 390–91

Laportea canadensis
Wood nettle, p. 395

Maianthemum racemosum
False Solomon's seal, p. 401

*Microstegium vimineum
Japanese stiltgrass, pp. 403–4

Panax quinquefolius
American ginseng, p. 417

Podophyllum peltatum
Mayapple, p. 426

Polygonatum biflorum
Solomon's seal, pp. 428–29

Sanguinaria canadensis
Bloodroot, p. 435

PHOTO KEY / THE MOUNTAINS / RICH COVE FOREST

53

Thalictrum thalictroides
Meadowrue, p. 451

Tiarella cordifolia
Foamflower, pp. 452–53

Trillium grandiflorum
Large-flowered trillium, pp. 457–58

Trillium vaseyi
Vasey's trillium, pp. 460–61

Viola canadensis
Canada violet, pp. 465–66

Acidic Cove Forest

Acer rubrum
Red maple, p. 222

Betula alleghaniensis
Yellow birch, pp. 226–27

Betula lenta
Sweet birch, p. 227

Fagus grandifolia
American beech, pp. 237–38

Halesia tetraptera
Carolina silverbell, p. 239

Ilex opaca
American holly, pp. 239–40

Liriodendron tulipifera
Tulip tree, pp. 242–43

Magnolia acuminata
Cucumber tree, pp. 243–44

Magnolia fraseri
Fraser magnolia, pp. 244–45

Pinus strobus
Eastern white pine, p. 251

Quercus rubra
Northern red oak, pp. 259–60

Tsuga canadensis
Canada hemlock, pp. 264–65

Decumaria barbara
Climbing hydrangea, p. 281

Euonymus americanus
Strawberry bush, pp. 283–84

Kalmia latifolia
Mountain laurel, pp. 291–92

PHOTO KEY / THE MOUNTAINS / ACIDIC COVE FOREST

Leucothoe fontanesiana
Mountain doghobble, p. 292

*Ligustrum sinense
Chinese privet, pp. 292–93

Rhododendron catawbiense
Catawba rhododendron, pp. 301–2

Rhododendron maximum
Rosebay, pp. 302–3

Viburnum acerifolium
Mapleleaf viburnum, pp. 319–20

Arisaema triphyllum
Jack-in-the-pulpit, p. 335

Cymophyllus fraserianus
Fraser's sedge, p. 357

Epigaea repens
Trailing arbutus, pp. 368–69

Erigeron pulchellus
Robin's plantain, p. 369

Galax urceolata
Galax, pp. 374–75

Hexastylis shuttleworthii
Large flower heartleaf, p. 387

Medeola virginiana
Indian cucumber root, pp. 402–3

Mitchella repens
Partridge berry, p. 406

Polystichum acrostichoides
Christmas fern, p. 429

Shortia galacifolia
Oconee bells, p. 438

Thelypteris noveboracensis
New York fern, pp. 451–52

Viola hastata
Halberdleaf yellow violet, pp. 466–67

Spray Cliff

Kalmia latifolia
Mountain laurel, pp. 291–92

Rhododendron maximum
Rosebay, pp. 302–3

Xanthorhiza simplicissima
Yellowroot, pp. 322–23

PHOTO KEY / THE MOUNTAINS / SPRAY CLIFF

Adiantum pedatum
Maidenhair fern, p. 327

Asplenium montanum
Mountain spleenwort, p. 339

Asplenium rhizophyllum
Walking fern, pp. 339–40

Cymophyllus fraserianus
Fraser's sedge, p. 357

Galax urceolata
Galax, pp. 374–75

Heuchera parviflora
Cave alumroot, p. 385

Houstonia serpyllifolia
Appalachian bluet, pp. 387–88

Impatiens capensis
Orange jewelweed, pp. 390–91

Marchantia species
Liverwort, p. 402

Micranthes petiolaris
Cliff saxifrage, p. 403

Oenothera fruticosa
Sundrops, pp. 410–11

Oxalis montana
Mountain wood sorrel, p. 414

Podostemum ceratophyllum
Riverweed, p. 427

Sphagnum species
Sphagnum, p. 445

Thalictrum clavatum
Mountain meadowrue, p. 450

Rocky Streamside

Betula nigra
River birch, p. 228

Platanus occidentalis
Sycamore, p. 253

Alnus serrulata
Tag alder, pp. 269–70

Arundinaria gigantea
Giant cane, pp. 273–74

Calycanthus floridus
Sweet shrub, pp. 275–76

Cephalanthus occidentalis
Buttonbush, p. 278

Clethra acuminata
Mountain sweet pepperbush, pp. 278–79

Cornus amomum
Silky dogwood, p. 280

Itea virginica
Virginia willow, pp. 289–90

Kalmia latifolia
Mountain laurel, pp. 291–92

Leucothoe fontanesiana
Mountain doghobble, p. 292

Rhododendron arborescens
Sweet azalea, p. 300

Rhododendron maximum
Rosebay, pp. 302–3

Rhododendron periclymenoides
Wild azalea, p. 304

Rhododendron viscosum
Swamp azalea, p. 305

Salix nigra
Black willow, pp. 311–12

Sambucus canadensis
Common elderberry, pp. 312–13

Xanthorhiza simplicissima
Yellowroot, pp. 322–23

Campanulastrum americanum
Tall bellflower, p. 343

Carex torta
Twisted sedge, pp. 344–45

Chelone glabra
White turtlehead, pp. 347–48

Eutrochium fistulosum
Joe Pye weed, p. 373

Houstonia serpyllifolia
Appalachian bluet, pp. 387–88

Impatiens capensis
Orange jewelweed, pp. 390–91

Impatiens pallida
Yellow jewelweed, pp. 391–92

Justicia americana
American water willow, pp. 393–94

Lobelia cardinalis
Cardinal flower, p. 399

*Microstegium vimineum
Japanese stiltgrass, pp. 403–4

Osmunda cinnamomea
Cinnamon fern, pp. 412–13

Podostemum ceratophyllum
Riverweed, p. 427

PHOTO KEY / THE MOUNTAINS / ROCKY STREAMSIDE

61

Rudbeckia laciniata
Cutleaf coneflower, pp. 433–34

Schizachyrium scoparium
Little bluestem, pp. 436–37

Sorghastrum nutans
Indiangrass, p. 444

Vernonia noveboracensis
New York ironweed, p. 465

Mountain Bog

Acer rubrum
Red maple, p. 222

Betula alleghaniensis
Yellow birch, pp. 226–27

Nyssa sylvatica
Black gum, pp. 245–46

Picea rubens
Red spruce, p. 248

Pinus rigida
Pitch pine, p. 250

Pinus strobus
Eastern white pine, p. 251

Tsuga canadensis
Canada hemlock, pp. 264–65

Alnus serrulata
Tag alder, pp. 269–70

Aronia melanocarpa
Black chokeberry, p. 272

Ilex verticillata
Winterberry, p. 289

Kalmia latifolia
Mountain laurel, pp. 291–92

Leucothoe fontanesiana
Mountain doghobble, p. 292

Menziesia pilosa
Minniebush, pp. 295–96

Rhododendron maximum
Rosebay, pp. 302–3

Rhododendron viscosum
Swamp azalea, p. 305

Salix nigra
Black willow, pp. 311–12

Vaccinium corymbosum
Highbush blueberry, p. 317

Vaccinium macrocarpon
Cranberry, pp. 317–18

Viburnum cassinoides
Wild raisin, pp. 320–21

Xanthorhiza simplicissima
Yellowroot, pp. 322–23

Drosera rotundifolia
Roundleaf sundew, pp. 365–66

Eutrochium fistulosum
Joe Pye weed, p. 373

Gaultheria procumbens
Wintergreen, pp. 376–77

Gentiana saponaria
Soapwort gentian, pp. 377–78

Helonias bullata
Swamp pink, pp. 383–84

Lilium grayi
Gray's lily, pp. 396–97

Onoclea sensibilis
Sensitive fern, p. 411

Osmunda cinnamomea
Cinnamon fern, pp. 412–13

Osmunda claytoniana
Interrupted fern, pp. 413–14

Parnassia asarifolia
Kidneyleaf grass of parnassus, pp. 417–18

*Phleum pratense
Timothy grass, pp. 421–22

Platanthera ciliaris
Yellow-fringed orchid, p. 424

Platanthera integrilabia
Monkey face orchid, p. 425

Sagittaria latifolia
Arrowhead, p. 434

Sarracenia purpurea
Purple pitcher plant, pp. 435–36

Sphagnum species
Sphagnum, p. 445

Spiranthes cernua
Nodding ladies' tresses, pp. 446–47

Symplocarpus foetidus
Skunk cabbage, p. 448

Veratrum viride
False hellebore, pp. 463–64

PHOTO KEY / THE MOUNTAINS / MOUNTAIN BOG

65

Chestnut Oak Forest

Acer rubrum
Red maple, p. 222

Carya glabra
Pignut hickory, pp. 229–30

Carya tomentosa
Mockernut hickory, p. 231

Castanea dentata
American chestnut, pp. 231–32

Liriodendron tulipifera
Tulip tree, pp. 242–43

Nyssa sylvatica
Black gum, pp. 245–46

Oxydendrum arboreum
Sourwood, p. 247

Pinus strobus
Eastern white pine, p. 251

Quercus alba
White oak, pp. 255–56

Quercus coccinea
Scarlet oak, p. 256

Quercus montana
Chestnut oak, pp. 258–59

Quercus rubra
Northern red oak, pp. 259–60

Sassafras albidum
Sassafras, pp. 261–62

Arundinaria appalachiana
Hill cane, pp. 272–73

Clethra acuminata
Mountain sweet pepperbush, pp. 278–79

Corylus cornuta
Beaked hazelnut, pp. 280–81

Gaylussacia ursina
Bear huckleberry, p. 284

Kalmia latifolia
Mountain laurel, pp. 291–92

Pyrularia pubera
Buffalo nut, pp. 299–300

Rhododendron calendulaceum
Flame azalea, p. 301

Rhododendron maximum
Rosebay, pp. 302–3

PHOTO KEY / THE MOUNTAINS / CHESTNUT OAK FOREST

Rhododendron minus
Gorge rhododendron, p. 303

Smilax rotundifolia
Common greenbrier, pp. 314–15

Vaccinium pallidum
Lowbush blueberry, p. 318

Vaccinium stamineum
Deerberry, p. 319

Amianthium muscitoxicum
Fly poison, p. 331

Aureolaria laevigata
Appalachian oak leach, p. 341

Chimaphila maculata
Pipsissewa, p. 349

Dennstaedtia punctilobula
Hayscented fern, p. 360

Epigaea repens
Trailing arbutus, pp. 368–69

Galax urceolata
Galax, pp. 374–75

Gaultheria procumbens
Wintergreen, pp. 376–77

Goodyera pubescens
Rattlesnake orchid, pp. 379–80

Iris verna
Dwarf iris, p. 393

Maianthemum racemosum
False Solomon's seal, p. 401

Medeola virginiana
Indian cucumber root, pp. 402–3

Monotropa hypopithys
Pinesap, pp. 407–8

Pedicularis canadensis
Lousewort, p. 419

Polygonatum biflorum
Solomon's seal, pp. 428–29

Pine-Oak-Heath

Acer rubrum
Red maple, p. 222

Castanea dentata
American chestnut, pp. 231–32

Nyssa sylvatica
Black gum, pp. 245–46

PHOTO KEY / THE MOUNTAINS / PINE-OAK-HEATH

Oxydendrum arboreum
Sourwood, p. 247

Pinus pungens
Table mountain pine, pp. 249–50

Pinus rigida
Pitch pine, p. 250

Pinus virginiana
Virginia pine, pp. 252–53

Quercus coccinea
Scarlet oak, p. 256

Quercus montana
Chestnut oak, pp. 258–59

Sassafras albidum
Sassafras, pp. 261–62

Symplocos tinctoria
Horse sugar, p. 263

Tsuga caroliniana
Carolina hemlock, pp. 265–66

Gcylussacia ursina
Bear huckleberry, p. 284

Kalmia latifolia
Mountain laurel, pp. 291–92

Rhododendron catawbiense
Catawba rhododendron, pp. 301–2

Rhododendron maximum
Rosebay, pp. 302–3

Smilax glauca
Whiteleaf greenbrier, p. 314

Smilax rotundifolia
Common greenbrier, pp. 314–15

Vaccinium pallidum
Lowbush blueberry, p. 318

Vaccinium stamineum
Deerberry, p. 319

Aureolaria laevigata
Appalachian oak leach, p. 341

Chimaphila maculata
Pipsissewa, p. 349

Coreopsis major
Whorled coreopsis, pp. 355–56

Cypripedium acaule
Pink lady's slipper, pp. 357–58

Epigaea repens
Trailing arbutus, pp. 368–69

Galax urceolata
Galax, pp. 374–75

Gaultheria procumbens
Wintergreen, pp. 376–77

Lilium michauxii
Carolina lily, pp. 397–98

Pityopsis graminifolia
Grassleaf golden aster, pp. 423–24

Polygala paucifolia
Fringed polygala, pp. 427–28

Pteridium aquilinum
Bracken fern, p. 432

Tephrosia virginiana
Goat's rue, pp. 449–50

Xerophyllum asphodeloides
Turkeybeard, p. 468

Forest Edge

Acer rubrum
Red maple, p. 222

Liquidambar styraciflua
Sweetgum, p. 242

Liriodendron tulipifera
Tulip tree, pp. 242–43

Nyssa sylvatica
Black gum, pp. 245–46

Oxydendrum arboreum
Sourwood, p. 247

Pinus taeda
Loblolly pine, pp. 251–52

Pinus virginiana
Virginia pine, pp. 252–53

Robinia pseudoacacia
Black locust, pp. 260–61

Sassafras albidum
Sassafras, pp. 261–62

Aralia spinosa
Devil's walkingstick, pp. 270–71

Aristolochia macrophylla
Pipevine, pp. 271–72

Arundinaria appalachiana
Hill cane, pp. 272–73

*Celastrus orbiculatus
Oriental bittersweet, p. 277

Hydrangea arborescens
Wild hydrangea, p. 287

Kalmia latifolia
Mountain laurel, pp. 291–92

PHOTO KEY / THE MOUNTAINS / FOREST EDGE

73

Ligustrum sinense
Chinese privet, pp. 292–93

Lonicera japonica
Japanese honeysuckle, pp. 294–95

Parthenocissus quinquefolia
Virginia creeper, pp. 296–97

Phoradendron serotinum
American mistletoe, pp. 297–98

Pueraria montana
Kudzu, pp. 298–99

Rubus odoratus
Flowering raspberry, p. 311

Sambucus canadensis
Common elderberry, pp. 312–13

Smilax rotundifolia
Common greenbrier, pp. 314–15

Toxicodendron radicans
Poison ivy, pp. 315–16

Achillea millefolium
Yarrow, p. 325

Ageratina altissima
White snakeroot, pp. 328–29

Aruncus dioicus
Goat's beard, p. 336

Asclepias syriaca
Common milkweed, pp. 337–38

Coreopsis major
Whorled coreopsis, pp. 355–56

Erigeron pulchellus
Robin's plantain, p. 369

Eurybia chlorolepis
Mountain wood aster, pp. 371–72

Eutrochium fistulosum
Joe Pye weed, p. 373

Fragaria virginiana
Wild strawberry, pp. 373–74

Helianthus strumosus
Roughleaf sunflower, pp. 382–83

Lilium superbum
Turk's cap lily, p. 398

Maianthemum racemosum
False Solomon's seal, p. 401

Oenothera fruticosa
Sundrops, pp. 410–11

Phlox carolina
Carolina phlox, p. 422

Platanthera ciliaris
Yellow-fringed orchid, p. 424

Prunella vulgaris
Heal all, pp. 431–32

Rudbeckia hirta
Black-eyed Susan, pp. 432–33

Rudbeckia laciniata
Cutleaf coneflower, pp. 433–34

Silene virginica
Fire pink, p. 439

2 : The Piedmont

River Bluff Forest

Acer floridanum
Southern sugar maple, pp. 219–20

Acer rubrum
Red maple, p. 222

Cornus florida
Flowering dogwood, pp. 235–36

Fagus grandifolia
American beech, pp. 237–38

Halesia tetraptera
Carolina silverbell, p. 239

Ilex opaca
American holly, pp. 239–40

Liriodendron tulipifera
Tulip tree, pp. 242–43

Ostrya virginiana
Hop hornbeam, pp. 246–47

Oxydendrum arboreum
Sourwood, p. 247

Quercus rubra
Northern red oak, pp. 259–60

Symplocos tinctoria
Horse sugar, p. 263

Tsuga canadensis
Canada hemlock, pp. 264–65

Euonymus americanus
Strawberry bush, pp. 283–84

Kalmia latifolia
Mountain laurel, pp. 291–92

Lonicera sempervirens
Coral honeysuckle, p. 295

Rhododendron minus
Gorge rhododendron, p. 303

Rhododendron periclymenoides
Wild azalea, p. 304

Vaccinium stamineum
Deerberry, p. 319

Botrypus virginianus
Rattlesnake fern, p. 342

Chamaelirium luteum
Fairywand, pp. 346–47

Chimaphila maculata
Pipsissewa, p. 349

Desmodium nudiflorum
Beggar's ticks, p. 361

Epifagus virginiana
Beechdrops, pp. 367–68

Erythronium umbilicatum
Dimpled trout lily, pp. 370–71

Geranium maculatum
Wild geranium, p. 378

Hepatica acutiloba
Acute-lobed hepatica, pp. 384–85

Hexastylis arifolia
Little brown jugs, pp. 386–87

Oxalis violacea
Violet wood sorrel, pp. 414–15

Panax quinquefolius
American ginseng, p. 417

Podophyllum peltatum
Mayapple, p. 426

Polystichum acrostichoides
Christmas fern, p. 429

Sanguinaria canadensis
Bloodroot, p. 435

Stellaria pubera
Giant chickweed, p. 447

Tiarella cordifolia
Foamflower, pp. 452–53

Trillium catesbaei
Catesby's trillium, p. 455

Trillium reliquum
Relict trillium, p. 459

Uvularia perfoliata
Perfoliate bellwort, pp. 462–63

Viola hastata
Halberdleaf yellow violet, pp. 466–67

Alluvial Forest

Acer negundo
Box elder, pp. 220–221

Acer rubrum
Red maple, p. 222

Betula nigra
River birch, p. 228

Carpinus caroliniana
Ironwood, pp. 228–29

Carya ovata
Shagbark hickory, p. 230

Celtis laevigata
Hackberry, pp. 232–33

Ilex opaca
American holly, pp. 239–40

Juglans nigra
Black walnut, pp. 240–41

Liquidambar styraciflua
Sweetgum, p. 242

Liriodendron tulipifera
Tulip tree, pp. 242–43

Morus rubra
Red mulberry, p. 245

Platanus occidentalis
Sycamore, p. 253

Ulmus alata
Winged elm, p. 266

Aesculus sylvatica
Painted buckeye, p. 269

Alnus serrulata
Tag alder, pp. 269–70

Arundinaria gigantea
Giant cane, pp. 273–74

Asimina triloba
Pawpaw, p. 274

Bignonia capreolata
Crossvine, p. 275

Cornus amomum
Silky dogwood, p. 280

Euonymus americanus
Strawberry bush, pp. 283–84

Itea virginica
Virginia willow, pp. 289–90

Leucothoe fontanesiana
Mountain doghobble, p. 292

*Ligustrum sinense
Chinese privet, pp. 292–93

Lindera benzoin
Spicebush, pp. 293–94

*Lonicera japonica
Japanese honeysuckle, pp. 294–95

Parthenocissus quinquefolia
Virginia creeper, pp. 296–97

Salix nigra
Black willow, pp. 311–12

Sambucus canadensis
Common elderberry, pp. 312–13

Toxicodendron radicans
Poison ivy, pp. 315–16

Viburnum acerifolium
Mapleleaf viburnum, pp. 319–20

Xanthorhiza simplicissima
Yellowroot, pp. 322–23

Arisaema triphyllum
Jack-in-the-pulpit, p. 335

Chasmanthium latifolium
River oats, p. 347

Claytonia virginica
Spring beauty, pp. 351–52

Erythronium umbilicatum
Dimpled trout lily, pp. 370–71

Galium aparine
Catchweed bedstraw, p. 376

*Microstegium vimineum
Japanese stiltgrass, pp. 403–4

Osmunda cinnamomea
Cinnamon fern, pp. 412–13

Pleopeltis polypodioides
Resurrection fern, pp. 425–26

PHOTO KEY / THE PIEDMONT / ALLUVIAL FOREST

83

Polystichum acrostichoides
Christmas fern, p. 429

Stellaria pubera
Giant chickweed, p. 447

Vernonia noveboracensis
New York ironweed, p. 465

Zephyranthes atamasca
Atamasco lily, pp. 469–70

Basic Mesic Forest

Acer floridanum
Southern sugar maple, pp. 219–20

Acer rubrum
Red maple, p. 222

Carpinus caroliniana
Ironwood, pp. 228–29

Celtis laevigata
Hackberry, pp. 232–33

Cercis canadensis
Eastern redbud, pp. 233–34

Cornus florida
Flowering dogwood, pp. 235–36

Fagus grandifolia
American beech, pp. 237–38

Juglans nigra
Black walnut, pp. 240–41

Liriodendron tulipifera
Tulip tree, pp. 242–43

Magnolia acuminata
Cucumber tree, pp. 243–44

Ostrya virginiana
Hop hornbeam, pp. 246–47

Quercus rubra
Northern red oak, pp. 259–60

Ulmus rubra
Slippery elm, pp. 266–67

Aesculus sylvatica
Painted buckeye, p. 269

Asimina triloba
Pawpaw, p. 274

PHOTO KEY / THE PIEDMONT / BASIC MESIC FOREST

85

Calycanthus floridus
Sweet shrub, pp. 275–76

Hydrangea arborescens
Wild hydrangea, p. 287

Lindera benzoin
Spicebush, pp. 293–94

*Lonicera japonica
Japanese honeysuckle, pp. 294–95

Ptelea trifoliata
Hoptree, p. 298

Ribes echinellum
Miccosukee gooseberry, pp. 307–8

Actaea pachypoda
Doll's eyes, pp. 325–26

Actaea racemosa
Black cohosh, pp. 326–27

Adiantum pedatum
Maidenhair fern, p. 327

Asarum canadense
Wild ginger, pp. 336–37

Asplenium rhizophyllum
Walking fern, pp. 339–40

Claytonia virginica
Spring beauty, pp. 351–52

Cypripedium parviflorum
Yellow lady's slipper, pp. 358–59

Dicentra cucullaria
Dutchman's britches, pp. 362–63

Erythronium umbilicatum
Dimpled trout lily, pp. 370–71

Hepatica acutiloba
Acute-lobed hepatica, pp. 384–85

Panax quinquefolius
American ginseng, p. 417

Podophyllum peltatum
Mayapple, p. 426

Polystichum acrostichoides
Christmas fern, p. 429

Primula meadia
Shooting star, pp. 430–31

Sanguinaria canadensis
Bloodroot, p. 435

Tiarella cordifolia
Foamflower, pp. 452–53

Trillium cuneatum
Sweet Betsy, pp. 455–56

Trillium discolor
Pale yellow trillium, pp. 456–57

PHOTO KEY / THE PIEDMONT / BASIC MESIC FOREST

Trillium reliquum
Relict trillium, p. 459

Oak-Hickory Forest

Acer rubrum
Red maple, p. 222

Carya glabra
Pignut hickory, pp. 229–30

Carya ovata
Shagbark hickory, p. 230

Carya tomentosa
Mockernut hickory, p. 231

Cercis canadensis
Eastern redbud, pp. 233–34

Cornus florida
Flowering dogwood, pp. 235–36

Liquidambar styraciflua
Sweetgum, p. 242

Liriodendron tulipifera
Tulip tree, pp. 242–43

Nyssa sylvatica
Black gum, pp. 245–46

Oxydendrum arboreum
Sourwood, p. 247

Pinus echinata
Shortleaf pine, pp. 248–49

Pinus strobus
Eastern white pine, p. 251

Pinus virginiana
Virginia pine, pp. 252–53

Quercus alba
White oak, pp. 255–56

Quercus falcata
Southern red oak, p. 257

Quercus stellata
Post oak, p. 260

Sassafras albidum
Sassafras, pp. 261–62

Arundinaria appalachiana
Hill cane, pp. 272–73

PHOTO KEY / THE PIEDMONT / OAK-HICKORY FOREST

89

Gelsemium sempervirens
Carolina jessamine, p. 285

*Lonicera japonica
Japanese honeysuckle, pp. 294–95

Phoradendron serotinum
American mistletoe, pp. 297–98

*Pueraria montana
Kudzu, pp. 298–99

Smilax glauca
Whiteleaf greenbrier, p. 314

Toxicodendron radicans
Poison ivy, pp. 315–16

Vaccinium arboreum
Sparkleberry, p. 316

Vaccinium stamineum
Deerberry, p. 319

Vitis rotundifolia
Muscadine, p. 322

Amphicarpaea bracteata
Hog peanut, pp. 331–32

Aureolaria laevigata
Appalachian oak leach, p. 341

Chimaphila maculata
Pipsissewa, p. 349

Conopholis americana
Squawroot, p. 355

Cypripedium acaule
Pink lady's slipper, pp. 357–58

Desmodium nudiflorum
Beggar's ticks, p. 361

Diphasiastrum digitatum
Running cedar, p. 364

Echinacea laevigata
Smooth coneflower, p. 367

Goodyera pubescens
Rattlesnake orchid, pp. 379–80

Hexastylis arifolia
Little brown jugs, pp. 386–87

Monotropa uniflora
Indian pipe, pp. 408–9

Pityopsis graminifolia
Grassleaf golden aster, pp. 423–24

Spigelia marilandica
Indian pink, pp. 445–46

Tipularia discolor
Cranefly orchid, p. 453

Trillium catesbaei
Catesby's trillium, p. 455

PHOTO KEY / THE PIEDMONT / OAK-HICKORY FOREST

Xeric Hardpan Forest

Carya glabra
Pignut hickory, pp. 229–30

Cercis canadensis
Eastern redbud, pp. 233–34

Chionanthus virginicus
Fringetree, p. 234

Diospyros virginiana
Persimmon, p. 237

Fraxinus americana
White ash, pp. 238–39

Juniperus virginiana
Eastern red cedar, pp. 241–42

Liquidambar styraciflua
Sweetgum, p. 242

Pinus echinata
Shortleaf pine, pp. 248–49

Pinus virginiana
Virginia pine, pp. 252–53

Quercus alba
White oak, pp. 255–56

Quercus marilandica
Blackjack oak, pp. 257–58

Quercus stellata
Post oak, p. 260

Ulmus alata
Winged elm, p. 266

Elaeagnus umbellata
Autumn olive, pp. 282–83

Lonicera japonica
Japanese honeysuckle, pp. 294–95

Rosa carolina
Carolina rose, pp. 308–9

Vaccinium arboreum
Sparkleberry, p. 316

Vaccinium pallidum
Lowbush blueberry, p. 318

Vaccinium stamineum
Deerberry, p. 319

Agalinis purpurea
Purple gerardia, p. 328

Andropogon virginicus
Broomsedge, pp. 332–33

Asclepias tuberosa
Butterfly weed, p. 338

Clematis viorna
Leather flower, p. 352

Commelina erecta
Erect dayflower, p. 354

Coreopsis major
Whorled coreopsis, pp. 355–56

Echinacea laevigata
Smooth coneflower, p. 367

Eryngium yuccifolium
Rattlesnake master, p. 370

Helianthus schweinitzii
Schweinitz's sunflower, p. 382

Helianthus strumosus
Roughleaf sunflower, pp. 382–83

*Microstegium vimineum
Japanese stiltgrass, pp. 403–4

Oenothera fruticosa
Sundrops, pp. 410–11

Polygonatum biflorum
Solomon's seal, pp. 428–29

Rudbeckia hirta
Black-eyed Susan, pp. 432–33

Schizachyrium scoparium
Little bluestem, pp. 436–37

Silphium terebinthinaceum
Prairie dock, p. 440

Sorghastrum nutans
Indiangrass, p. 444

Tephrosia virginiana
Goat's rue, pp. 449–50

Granite Outcrop

Chionanthus virginicus
Fringetree, p. 234

Diospyros virginiana
Persimmon, p. 237

Juniperus virginiana
Eastern red cedar, pp. 241–42

PHOTO KEY / THE PIEDMONT / GRANITE OUTCROP

Pinus echinata
Shortleaf pine, pp. 248–49

Pinus taeda
Loblolly pine, pp. 251–52

Pinus virginiana
Virginia pine, pp. 252–53

Ulmus alata
Winged elm, p. 266

Aesculus sylvatica
Painted buckeye, p. 269

Bignonia capreolata
Crossvine, p. 275

Gelsemium sempervirens
Carolina jessamine, p. 285

*Ligustrum sinense
Chinese privet, pp. 292–93

Ptelea trifoliata
Hoptree, p. 298

Rhododendron minus
Gorge rhododendron, p. 303

Rhus copallinum
Winged sumac, p. 306

Vaccinium arboreum
Sparkleberry, p. 316

96

Andropogon virginicus
Broomsedge, pp. 332–33

Aquilegia canadensis
Eastern columbine, pp. 334–35

Castilleja coccinea
Indian paintbrush, p. 345

Cladina rangiferina
Gray reindeer lichen, p. 350

Commelina erecta
Erect dayflower, p. 354

Diamorpha smallii
Elf orpine, pp. 361–62

Erythronium umbilicatum
Dimpled trout lily, pp. 370–71

Gratiola amphiantha
Pool sprite, pp. 380–81

Grimmia laevigata
Dry rock moss, p. 381

Hypericum gentianoides
Pineweed, p. 389

Minuartia glabra
Appalachian sandwort, pp. 404–5

Oenothera fruticosa
Sundrops, pp. 410–11

Opuntia humifusa
Eastern prickly pear, p. 412

Packera millefolium
Blue ridge ragwort, pp. 415–16

Packera tomentosa
Woolly ragwort, pp. 416–17

Phemeranthus teretifolius
Appalachian rock pink, pp. 420–21

Portulaca smallii
Small's portulaca, p. 430

Schizachyrium scoparium
Little bluestem, pp. 436–37

Tradescantia hirsuticaulis
Hairy spiderwort, pp. 453–54

Yucca filamentosa
Beargrass, pp. 468–69

Roadside and Field

Albizia julibrissin
Mimosa, p. 225

Diospyros virginiana
Persimmon, p. 237

Juniperus virginiana
Eastern red cedar, pp. 241–42

Liquidambar styraciflua
Sweetgum, p. 242

Liriodendron tulipifera
Tulip tree, pp. 242–43

Pinus taeda
Loblolly pine, pp. 251–52

Pinus virginiana
Virginia pine, pp. 252–53

Prunus serotina
Black cherry, pp. 254–55

Campsis radicans
Trumpet vine, pp. 276–77

Elaeagnus umbellata
Autumn olive, pp. 282–83

Ligustrum sinense
Chinese privet, pp. 292–93

Lonicera japonica
Japanese honeysuckle, pp. 294–95

Parthenocissus quinquefolia
Virginia creeper, pp. 296–97

Pueraria montana
Kudzu, pp. 298–99

Rhus copallinum
Winged sumac, p. 306

Rhus glabra
Smooth sumac, pp. 306–7

Rosa multiflora
Multiflora rose, pp. 309–10

Smilax rotundifolia
Common greenbrier, pp. 314–15

Toxicodendron radicans
Poison ivy, pp. 315–16

Vitis rotundifolia
Muscadine, p. 322

Achillea millefolium
Yarrow, p. 325

Ambrosia artemisiifolia
Common ragweed, pp. 330–31

Andropogon virginicus
Broomsedge, pp. 332–33

Asclepias tuberosa
Butterfly weed, p. 338

Coreopsis major
Whorled coreopsis, pp. 355–56

Fragaria virginiana
Wild strawberry, pp. 373–74

Galium aparine
Catchweed bedstraw, p. 376

*Hypericum perforatum
Common St. John's wort, p. 390

Ipomoea pandurata
Bigroot morning glory, pp. 392–93

*Lamium amplexicaule
Henbit, pp. 394–95

Oenothera biennis
Common evening primrose, pp. 409–10

Passiflora incarnata
Maypops, pp. 418–19

Phytolacca americana
Pokeweed, pp. 422–23

PHOTO KEY / THE PIEDMONT / ROADSIDE AND FIELD

101

Pteridium aquilinum
Bracken fern, p. 432

Rudbeckia hirta
Black-eyed Susan, pp. 432–33

Solanum carolinense
Horse nettle, pp. 441–42

Solidago altissima
Tall goldenrod, p. 442

*Taraxacum officinale
Common dandelion, pp. 448–49

*Trifolium repens
White clover, pp. 454–55

*Verbascum thapsus
Woolly mullein, p. 464

Viola sororia
Common blue violet, p. 467

PART III

Plant Community Profiles

1 : The Mountains

High-Elevation Communities

SPRUCE-FIR FOREST

Distinguishing Features

Spruce-fir forest can be distinguished from all other mountain communities in that red spruce or Fraser fir—or a mix of the two—dominates the canopy.

Introduction

Spruce-fir forest occurs along the Appalachian Mountains from Canada south to North Carolina and Tennessee. A band of similar forest (called boreal forest) circles the northern hemisphere at high latitudes, stretching from Alaska and Canada to Scandinavia, Russia, and China. Needle-leaved evergreen conifers are the dominant species in spruce-fir forest and many of the same species (or their close relatives) occur in true boreal forest. In the northeastern United States (e.g., Maine), spruce-fir forest extends from the mountains to the ocean's edge, but is restricted to high-elevation peaks in the southern Appalachians, where the growing season is short and cool and winters are long and cold. Severe conditions at high elevations are a serious challenge for plants as freezing temperatures, sleet, and snow can occur in any season. Wind-driven ice particles can damage plant tissues, and very low temperatures can cause ice crystals to form within plants, tearing apart cell membranes and dehydrating cells. High winds and ice storms can break and topple trees, creating small gaps that facilitate the establishment and growth of shade-intolerant species such as yellow birch (*Betula alleghaniensis*) and fire cherry (*Prunus pensylvanica*). In contrast, spruce and fir tolerate shade, forming large "sapling banks" that persist in a suppressed condition under a closed canopy until released by a light gap. High rainfall, low temperatures, fog drip, and shading by canopy trees help keep the thick organic soil moist and the vegetation lush. A nonnative insect (the balsam woolly adelgid) and air pollution currently threaten this community.

Vegetation

The two dominants, red spruce (*Picea rubens*) and Fraser fir (*Abies fraseri*), are evergreen conifers with needle-like leaves whose conical shape enables them to shed heavy snow loads much as a steeply pitched roof does. Fraser fir has upright cones and leaves that are flat and narrow with white stripes on their undersides, whereas red spruce has pendant cones and leaves that are prickly, slightly curved, and lacking stripes. Red spruce is most abundant at lower elevations and more sheltered sites, while Fraser fir is dominant on exposed sites at higher elevations (> 6,000 ft.), where it often forms nearly pure stands. Less common are deciduous trees such as yellow birch, mountain maple (*Acer spicatum*), mountain ash (*Sorbus americana*), and fire cherry.

Shrubs are sparse to common, depending on the degree of disturbance. In open areas, blackberries (*Rubus*) form dense thickets that suppress herbaceous plants and can slow tree regeneration. Other shrubs such as red elderberry (*Sambucus racemosa*), witch hobble (*Viburnum lantanoides*), and Appalachian gooseberry (*Ribes rotundifolium*) also increase with disturbance. In more intact forest, shrubs are less common and the ground layer can be dense with mosses, ferns, and flowering plants. In shaded forests with moist soils, mosses grow on just about everything: soil, rocks, tree trunks, and fallen logs. Lichens also do well, covering the trunks of trees and absorbing moisture directly from the air. More than 200 species of bryophytes (mosses and liverworts) and 225 species of lichens have been identified in spruce-fir forests. Ferns are also common, especially mountain wood fern (*Dryopteris campyloptera*) and the southern lady fern (*Athyrium asplenioides*).

Seasonal Aspects

In spring, fire cherry, mountain ash, witch hobble, red elderberry, and blackberries produce clusters of whitish flowers that develop into brightly colored fleshy fruits in summer and fall. Other spring-flowering plants include painted trillium (*Trillium undulatum*), bluebead lily (*Clintonia borealis*), and mountain wood sorrel (*Oxalis montana*). Painted trillium has a single upright flower with 3 white petals, each of which has a distinct red, inverted, v-shaped mark near the base. The pink-veined white flowers and clover-like leaves of mountain wood sorrel form prostrate mats on cool, moist soils, whereas bluebead lily's nodding, greenish yellow flowers rise well above several large basal leaves. In summer, false hellebore (*Veratrum viride*) produces yellowish green flowers on stout, leafy stems. The short terminal spikes of pink turtlehead (*Chelone lyonii*) attract bumblebees that squeeze into the closed flowers to gather nectar. In late summer and early fall, look for the daisy-like flowers of mountain wood aster (*Eurybia chorolepis*) and whorled aster (*Oclemena acuminata*), whose yellow disk (central) flowers turn red or purplish as they age. Evergreens such as Fraser fir, red spruce, and Catawba rhododendron (*Rhododendron catawbiense*) stand out in winter in an otherwise mostly leafless forest.

Distribution

Southern Appalachian spruce-fir forest is restricted to the high mountains of southwest Virginia, western North Carolina, and eastern Tennessee, at elevations above 4,500 ft. The mountains of other southeastern states aren't high enough to support this community type. Nearly half of the spruce-fir forest in the region occurs in Great Smoky Mountains National Park.

> *Balsam woolly adelgid devastates Fraser fir.* Accidentally introduced from Europe in the 1950s, this aphid-like insect has eliminated more than 90 percent of adult Fraser fir trees in the southern Appalachians. The white, threadlike protective covering of this microscopic insect gives it the appearance of dots of "wool" on the trunk, branches, and twigs of Fraser fir. Heavy infestations of the adelgid reflect its high reproductive rate and wide dispersal (mostly by wind, but also by humans, animals, and nursery stock). Most vulnerable to adelgids are older, larger firs with furrowed bark and numerous crevices. Smooth bark with few crevices makes young fir trees less susceptible. Adelgids inject salivary compounds into the bark, which result in abnormal xylem (conducting) cells that impair the flow of water and nutrients in the tree. Within a few years of attack, the needles turn red and fall off the tree, due to severe water stress. The bleached skeletons of standing dead trunks are a conspicuous part of many present-day spruce-fir forests. Other trunks are strewn across the ground, overgrown with brambles or dense patches of young spruce and fir. Dense stands of Fraser fir saplings have appeared since the dieback of adult trees, but whether or not they can survive long enough to reproduce before they are killed by adelgids is a critical question in the future status of this species. If the younger trees don't reach cone-bearing age, if the production of viable seed is low, or if adelgid populations don't decline, Fraser fir could eventually be lost from the forest.

Dynamics

From 1880–1930, large-scale logging and associated fires eliminated huge areas of southern Appalachian spruce-fir forest. With the canopy removed, the moist, spongy, organic soil dried out and was able to carry fire. Fires sparked by railroad operations and homesteaders burning slash piles (to clear the ground for pastures) killed the "sapling banks" of spruce and fir and consumed most of the soil's organic matter. Because spruce and fir are generally unable to recolonize sites that have been cleared and burned, large areas haven't returned to spruce-fir forest.

A tiny, introduced insect, the Balsam woolly adelgid, has also had a devastating impact on Fraser fir populations over the past half-century, killing more than 1.5 million trees on Mount Mitchell, North Carolina, alone. Widespread mortality of Fraser fir opened up previously dense spruce-fir forests, which in some areas has created a tangle of standing dead and fallen trees, young spruce and/or fir trees, dense shrubs, and relatively few herbaceous plants. While not susceptible to the adelgid, higher winds associated with a more open forest have toppled trees and snapped the trunks of red spruce.

Conservation Aspects

Spruce-fir forest is a unique mountain community. The vegetation is distinct, the climate is especially harsh, and the forest harbors a number of rare and unusual species. During the height of the last ice age, some 18,000 years ago, temperatures were much colder and spruce-fir forest covered a much larger area of the Southeast. As the climate became warmer, these forests "retreated" up the southern Appalachian Mountains, where today they are restricted to a few scattered high-elevation peaks. These high mountain refugia provide critical habitat for a number of rare plants that can't tolerate warmer, drier climates, including Fraser fir, pinkshell azalea (*Rhododendron vaseyi*), and Rugel's ragwort (*Rugelia nudicaulis*). Spruce-fir forest also provides important habitat for rare animals such as high-elevation salamanders, the northern flying squirrel, and the spruce-fir moss spider.

Spruce-fir forest is currently one of the Southeast's rarest and most threatened communities. Large-scale logging and associated fires eliminated about 50 percent of the total area of southern Appalachian spruce-fir forest by the early twentieth century. Today, most spruce-fir forest is publicly owned, and because timber harvesting is prohibited, logging is no longer an immediate threat. The balsam woolly adelgid continues to affect spruce-fir forest by killing adult Fraser firs, thereby opening up the canopy and altering the character of the forest. While widespread dieback hasn't occurred in red spruce, declining growth rates and unhealthy trees, perhaps due to air pollution, are major concerns.

High levels of ozone, nitrogen oxides, and other chemicals from factories, power plants, and automobiles are frequently carried into high-elevation communities by clouds, fog, rain, and snow. Acid rain is causing soil acidification, which adversely affects some plants and may have substantial long-term impacts on forests. Many of these same air pollutants are also responsible for obscuring formerly expansive vistas.

SUGGESTED READING

Marchand, P. 1996. *Life in the Cold: An Introduction to Winter Ecology*. 3rd ed. Lebanon, N.H.: University Press of New England.
Stephenson, S. L., and H. S. Adams. 1984. The Spruce-Fir Forest on the Summit of Mount Rogers in Southwestern Virginia. *Bulletin of the Torrey Botanical Club* 111:69–75.
White, P. S., ed. 1984. The Southern Appalachian Spruce-Fir Ecosystem: Its Biology and Threats. *USDI, National Park Service, Research/Resources Management Report SER 71*.

SPRUCE-FIR FOREST: CHARACTERISTIC PLANTS

Trees

ABUNDANT SPECIES

Abies fraseri	Fraser fir	p. 219
Picea rubens	Red spruce	p. 248

OCCASIONAL TO LOCALLY ABUNDANT SPECIES

Acer pensylvanicum	Striped maple	p. 221
Acer spicatum	Mountain maple	pp. 223–24
Amelanchier laevis	Smooth serviceberry	pp. 225–26
Betula alleghaniensis	Yellow birch	pp. 226–27
Prunus pensylvanica	Fire cherry, Pin cherry	p. 254
Sorbus americana	Mountain ash	pp. 262–63

Shrubs

OCCASIONAL TO LOCALLY ABUNDANT SPECIES

Ilex montana	Mountain holly	pp. 288–89
Menziesia pilosa	Minniebush	pp. 295–96
Rhododendron catawbiense	Catawba rhododendron	pp. 301–2
Ribes rotundifolium	Appalachian gooseberry	p. 308
Rubus allegheniensis	Allegheny blackberry	p. 310
†*Rubus canadensis*	Smooth blackberry	
Sambucus racemosa	Red elderberry	p. 313
†*Vaccinium erythrocarpum*	Highbush cranberry	
Viburnum lantanoides	Witch hobble, Hobblebush	p. 321

Herbs

OCCASIONAL TO LOCALLY ABUNDANT SPECIES

Ageratina altissima	White snakeroot	pp. 328–29
Athyrium asplenioides	Southern lady fern	p. 340
Carex pensylvanica	Pennsylvania sedge	pp. 343–44
Chelone lyonii	Pink turtlehead	pp. 348–49
Clintonia borealis	Bluebead lily	pp. 352–53
Dryopteris campyloptera	Mountain wood fern	p. 366
Eurybia chlorolepis	Mountain wood aster	pp. 371–72
Maianthemum canadense	Canada mayflower	pp. 400–401
Oclemena acuminata	Whorled aster	p. 409
Oxalis montana	Mountain wood sorrel	p. 414
Solidago glomerata	Skunk goldenrod	pp. 443–44
Trillium undulatum	Painted trillium	pp. 459–60
Veratrum viride	False hellebore	pp. 463–64

Rare Plants

†*Betula cordifolia*	Mountain paper birch	
Rhododendron vaseyi	Pinkshell azalea	pp. 304–5
†*Rugelia nudicaulis*	Rugel's ragwort	

† = *plant not included in the species profiles (Part IV)*

GRASSY BALD

Distinguishing Features

Grassy balds are distinguished from other communities by their extensive areas of dense herbaceous vegetation at high elevations. Areas invaded by shrubs or small trees are generally considered to be grassy balds; however, if the herbaceous layer is largely absent, then the term "shrub bald" is used.

Introduction

Grassy balds are open, meadow-like areas with patches of shrubs and small trees that occur on high-elevation ridgetops, domes, and gentle slopes. Like most high-elevation habitats, grassy balds are exposed to strong winds, high rainfall, dense fog, and low temperatures. The dense herbaceous vegetation that characterizes this community supports an extremely diverse flora, including a number of unusual and rare species. While the origin of grassy balds is something of a mystery, it's clear that most grassy balds are currently undergoing succession from open, grassy habitats to shrub thickets and forest, a process that threatens to obscure the panoramic views and decrease the rich diversity of wildflowers that make this one of the most distinctive and cherished communities in the mountain region.

Vegetation

Like the prairies of the Midwest, this is a community dominated by grasses, including mountain oat grass (*Danthonia compressa*), wavy hairgrass (*Avenella flexuosa*), and velvet grass (*Holcus lanatus*). Rather than creating a dense sod, these mostly clump-forming grasses make up a patchwork of mounds or hummocks.

On wetter soils, sedges may dominate, including Pennsylvania sedge and brown sedge (*Carex pensylvanica* and *C. brunnescens*). Grasses can be distinguished from sedges by their stems: grasses usually have round, jointed stems with a hollow center, whereas sedges typically have triangular stems, lack joints, and have a solid center. Among the grasses and sedges are low-growing broad-leaved herbs such as three-tooth cinquefoil (*Sibbaldiopsis tridentata*), wild strawberry (*Fragaria virginiana*), and dwarf cinquefoil (*Potentilla canadensis*). Taller herbs that emerge above the grasses include mountain angelica (*Angelica triquinata*), mountain phlox (*Phlox latifolia*), and skunk goldenrod (*Solidago glomerata*). Gray's lily (*Lilium grayi*) is a well-known rare plant that appears in the community. Grassy balds have a number of weedy species introduced from Europe, including Timothy grass (*Phleum pratense*), velvet grass, sheep sorrel (*Rumex acetosella*), white clover (*Trifolium repens*), and common St. John's wort (*Hypericum perforatum*). The most common woody plants are blackberries (*Rubus* spp.) and heath shrubs, including Catawba rhododendron (*Rhododendron catawbiense*), flame azalea (*R. calendulaceum*), highbush blueberry (*Vaccinium corymbosum*), and mountain laurel (*Kalmia latifolia*). Small trees such as smooth serviceberry (*Amelanchier laevis*), fire cherry (*Prunus pensylvanica*), and bigfruit hawthorn (*Crataegus macrosperma*) are also common. Many of these shrubs and small trees produce showy flowers in late spring or early summer.

Seasonal Aspects

Wild strawberry produces white flowers that develop into sweet, edible red fruits by late spring–early summer. Like the wild strawberry, dwarf cinquefoil and three-tooth cinquefoil are low-growing plants in the rose (Rosaceae) family with open, bowl-shaped flowers and palmately compound leaves. Dwarf cinquefoil produces yellow flowers in the spring, whereas the white flowers of three-tooth cinquefoil don't appear until summer. Appalachian bluet (*Houstonia serpyllifolia*) is another low-growing plant that blooms in spring. Its tiny blue flowers (with yellow centers) sit above a mat of green leaves, attracting our attention and that of the small bees and flies that function as pollinators. Two taller plants flowering from spring through summer are yarrow (*Achillea millefolium*), with small white flowers in dense terminal clusters, and whorled loosestrife (*Lysimachia quadrifolia*), with solitary yellow flowers on long stalks. In early summer, both hummingbirds and butterflies seek nectar from the dark red bell-shaped flowers of Gray's lily. In mid- to late summer, bees and other insects visit the dense umbels of Mountain angelica's tiny, greenish yellow flowers. Flower visitors to mountain angelica often behave erratically, apparently due to an intoxicating substance in the nectar.

Two members of the sunflower (Asteraceae) family that bloom in summer and fall are cutleaf coneflower (*Rudbeckia laciniata*), a tall plant with showy, long-stalked flower heads with drooping yellow ray flowers, and skunk goldenrod, a relatively short plant with densely packed yellow flower heads at the stem tip. If you smell skunk, the latter species may be nearby. One of the more conspicuous plants of autumn is stiff gentian (*Gentianella quinquefolia*). Bumblebees enter the narrow, tubular violet-blue to lilac-colored flowers seeking nectar. Bigfruit hawthorn, allegheny blackberry (*Rubus allegheniensis*), and highbush blueberry produce fleshy fruits whose seeds are widely dispersed by animals into communities such as grassy balds.

Distribution

Grassy balds are widely scattered in the mountains at elevations above 4,500 ft. in southern Virginia, western North Carolina, and Tennessee.

> *Grazers and grassy balds.* Fossil excavations in the mountains of Virginia and Tennessee reveal that a magnificent array of large native herbivores ("megaherbivores") once roamed the southern Appalachians, including musk oxen, mastodons, ground sloths, mammoths, moose, caribou, bison, and elk. The open grasslands created by ice age climate change (as described above) would have attracted large herds of these animals, which would have grazed and browsed herbaceous plants as well as the seedlings and saplings of woody plants, thereby preventing the succession of grassy balds to woodlands. About 10,000 years ago, most of these "megaherbivores" suddenly vanished. Following the "great megafauna extinction," elk and bison likely became the dominant grazers of grassy balds until they too were extirpated by European settlers in the early nineteenth century. This last event might have led to the end of grassy balds as well, had settlers not introduced their own domestic livestock, which functioned as surrogate megaherbivores. The grazing hypothesis, as described here, implies that large herbivores were part of a disturbance regime that played a key role in the persistence of grassy balds for thousands of years. The widespread loss of grassy balds would probably not be happening today if they were intact ecosystems complete with their large native herbivores.

Dynamics

Grassy balds contain patches of open vegetation in a landscape dominated by forest. The southern Appalachians aren't high enough for a climatic treeline, so why do these open, treeless areas exist? Biologists have debated this issue for decades, yet still aren't sure how balds originated and why they've persisted over time. With regard to their origin, one school of thought emphasizes "natural" factors, the other, "anthropogenic" factors. The distribution of grassy balds is apparently not determined by physical factors such as topography, geology, or soil type, nor is there evidence that fire is a causal factor, at least not under present-day conditions. It's possible that various factors along with past climatic change produced forest openings. One plausible scenario is that severe climate conditions during the most recent ice age (which peaked about 18,000 years ago) eliminated trees from high-elevation areas of the southern Appalachians, replacing forests with open grasslands, some of which persisted for thousands of years. Alternatively, grassy balds could be the result of Native Americans using fire to open forests for hunting and the gathering of nuts and berries, a process followed by European settlers clearing woods to create pasture for summer livestock. Regardless of the origin of grassy balds, historical records indicate that from the early 1800s, settlers brought cattle, sheep, and horses up from lower elevations to grassy balds for summer grazing. As soon as grazing by domestic animals came to a halt in the

1930s due to economic changes and land protection, woody plants began to invade, steadily reducing the amount of herbaceous vegetation. By 1970, almost half of the more than 100 known grassy balds were lost due to successional change. Because natural processes don't currently maintain grassy balds or create new ones, balds are vulnerable to extinction.

Conservation Aspects

Grassy balds are a rare and threatened community with various origins and histories, ranging from being naturally occurring balds to those that are clearly the result of human activities. In the early to mid-twentieth century, approximately two-thirds of the balds in the southern Appalachians came under federal ownership as national parks and forests. The removal of grazing livestock from public lands led to invasion by woody plants, and over the last century more than half of known balds have become forested. Those that remain are significant sites for plant diversity, rare species, historic preservation, and recreational opportunities, including scenic vistas in a landscape where unobstructed views are uncommon. To protect these resources, active management is needed to prevent the succession from open balds to shrub thickets and forests. Although additional grassy balds are likely to be lost in the future, land managers are currently using techniques such as mowing, hand cutting, grazing, and prescribed fire to preserve some of the grassy balds in our national parks and forests.

SUGGESTED READING

Mark, A. F. 1958. The Ecology of Southern Appalachian Grass Balds. *Ecological Monographs* 28:293–336.

White, P. S., and R. D. Sutter. 1999. Managing Biodiversity in Historic Habitats: Case History of the Southern Appalachian Grassy Balds. In Peine, J. D., ed., *Ecosystem Management for Sustainability: Principles and Practices Illustrated by a Regional Biosphere Reserve Cooperative*, 375–95. Boca Raton, Fla.: Lewis Publishers.

Weigl, P. D., and T. W. Knowles. 1995. Megaherbivores and Southern Appalachian Grass Balds. *Growth and Change* 26:365–82.

GRASSY BALD: CHARACTERISTIC PLANTS

Trees

Abies fraseri	Fraser fir	p. 219
Amelanchier laevis	Smooth serviceberry	pp. 225–26
Crataegus macrosperma	Bigfruit hawthorn	p. 236
Prunus pensylvanica	Fire cherry, Pin cherry	p. 254

Shrubs

OCCASIONAL TO LOCALLY ABUNDANT SPECIES

Kalmia latifolia	Mountain laurel	pp. 291–92
Rhododendron calendulaceum	Flame azalea	p. 301
Rhododendron catawbiense	Catawba rhododendron	pp. 301–2
Rubus allegheniensis	Allegheny blackberry	p. 310
Vaccinium corymbosum	Highbush blueberry	p. 317

Herbs

ABUNDANT SPECIES

Angelica triquinata	Mountain angelica, Filmy angelica	pp. 333–34
Avenella flexuosa	Wavy hairgrass	pp. 341–42
Carex pensylvanica	Pennsylvania sedge	pp. 343–44
Danthonia compressa	Mountain oat grass	pp. 359–60
†*Holcus lanatus*	Velvet grass	
†*Potentilla canadensis*	Dwarf cinquefoil	
Sibbaldiopsis tridentata	Three-tooth cinquefoil	pp. 438–39

OCCASIONAL TO LOCALLY ABUNDANT SPECIES

Achillea millefolium	Yarrow	p. 325
Dennstaedtia punctilobula	Hayscented fern	p. 360
Fragaria virginiana	Wild strawberry	pp. 373–74
†*Gentianella quinquefolia*	Stiff gentian	
Houstonia serpyllifolia	Appalachian bluet	pp. 387–88
Lysimachia quadrifolia	Whorled loosestrife	pp. 399–400
Minuartia groenlandica	Mountain sandwort	p. 405
Pteridium aquilinum	Bracken fern	p. 432
Rudbeckia laciniata	Cutleaf coneflower	pp. 433–34
Schizachyrium scoparium	Little bluestem	pp. 436–37
Solidago glomerata	Skunk goldenrod	pp. 443–44

Invasive Exotic Plants

Phleum pratense	Timothy grass	pp. 421–22
†*Rumex acetosella*	Sheep sorrel	

Rare Plants

†*Gentiana austromontana*	Blue ridge gentian	
Lilium grayi	Gray's lily	pp. 396–97

† = *plant not included in the species profiles (Part IV)*

HEATH BALD

Distinguishing Features

Heath balds differ from other higher-elevation communities by the dominance of heath shrubs, with only scattered, stunted trees and a sparse herbaceous layer. Rock outcrops commonly have patches of shrubs of the same species as those found on heath balds, making the distinction between the two communities difficult to see. If the community is predominately covered by shrubs, rather than bare rock or scattered herbs, it's considered a heath bald.

Introduction

Heath balds are dense shrublands that grow at mid- to high elevations on exposed peaks, on narrow, sharp ridges, and on adjacent slopes with rocky, acidic soils. Locals refer to them simply as "balds" or "slicks," for the near absence of trees or the smooth appearance of the vegetation from a distance. Up close, the vegetation is anything but smooth, often consisting of a tangled mass of branches that makes off-trail hiking nearly impossible. A striking feature of this community is its low species diversity: a typical heath bald has just 10–20 vascular plant species, mostly shrubs belonging to a single plant family, the heath family (Ericaceae). Nearly all shrubs found in this community also occur as understory species in surrounding forests. The reason for the presence of heath balds on some ridges and slopes but not on others is often a mystery. An important piece of the puzzle is disturbance history, as heath balds frequently occur on previously forested sites where logging, fires, or windfall eliminated the trees but not the understory shrubs.

Vegetation

The vegetation ranges from dense impenetrable thickets 3–12 ft. tall to more open shrubland. Dominant shrub species vary with elevation, geographic location, and topographic features such as slope and aspect. High-elevation balds are commonly dominated by Catawba rhododendron (*Rhododendron catawbiense*), an evergreen species with showy clusters of deep pink to purple flowers that attract thousands of visitors to the mountains each spring. Other common shrubs include highbush blueberry (*Vaccinium corymbosum*), mountain sweet pepperbush (*Clethra acuminata*), and wild raison (*Viburnum cassinoides*). The rare pinkshell azalea (*Rhododendron vaseyi*) produces striking clusters of pink flowers on bare stems in late spring. On lower elevation balds, mountain laurel (*Kalmia latifolia*) and black chokeberry (*Aronia melanocarpa*) commonly occur. The herbaceous layer is generally sparse due to the dense cover of shrubs and exposed rock. Low-growing evergreens such as galax (*Galax urceolata*), wintergreen (*Gaultheria procumbens*), and trailing arbutus (*Epigaea repens*), along with deciduous species such as bracken fern (*Pteridium aquilinum*) and painted trillium (*Trillium undulatum*), occur sporadically.

Seasonal Aspects

Spring-flowering evergreen shrubs include Catawba rhododendron, mountain laurel, and sand myrtle (*Kalmia buxifolia*). Catawba rhododendron produces spectacular displays of rose-pink to purple flowers in dense clusters at the tips of leafy branches. Dense thickets of mountain laurel with crooked branches bear showy clusters of white to pinkish cup-shaped flowers. Sand myrtle is a low-growing shrub with small white or pinkish flowers in umbrella-like clusters. Deciduous shrubs that flower in spring include flame azalea (*Rhododendron calendulaceum*), pinkshell azalea, and minniebush (*Menziesia pilosa*). Clusters of bright orange, yellow, or red flowers of flame azalea light up the mountains in late spring. Nearly as striking are the pink flowers that cover the bare stems of pinkshell azalea. Less conspicuous but equally interesting are minniebush's small, urn-shaped white flowers with a reddish tinge.

In summer, look for small clusters of yellow trumpet-shaped flowers near the stem tips of southern bush honeysuckle (*Diervilla sessilifolia*), a small clump-forming deciduous shrub. Long-tongued, bee-like moths known as bumblebee hawkmoths visit the flowers for nectar on daytime foraging bouts. Mountain sweet pepperbush, a multistemmed shrub with distinctive cinnamon-like, reddish brown bark, produces elongate clusters of small white flowers in summer. Orange spaghetti-like strands wrapped around the leaves and stems of plants are the leafless stems of Appalachian dodder (*Cuscuta rostrata*), a parasitic flowering plant. Look for dense clusters of tiny white flowers on its orange stems in late summer.

Fire cherry (*Prunus pensylvanica*), wild raisin, highbush blueberry, black chokeberry, and allegheny blackberry (*Rubus allegheniensis*) produce colorful fruits in summer and fall. At ground level, one might also encounter the bright red fruits of painted trillium and wintergreen.

Distribution

In the southern Appalachians, heath balds are scattered in the higher mountains of Virginia, North Carolina, and Tennessee.

Dynamics

Heath balds form in various ways. On some sites, heath shrubs colonize open areas such as rock outcrops, landslide scars, and grassy balds. Heath balds also form on previously forested sites where high winds, intense fires, or logging have eliminated the trees but not the understory heath shrubs. Once a heath shrubland has formed, dense shade, deep leaf litter, and shallow, dry, acidic soils make it difficult for trees to establish from seed, thereby hindering succession back to forest. On sites exposed to desiccating winds and shallow nutrient-poor soils, heath balds can persist as a stable climax community.

> *When to be evergreen.* Some plants shed their leaves after two months, whereas others retain their leaves for as long as 40 years. Deciduous plants have leaves that last less than a year, while evergreens produce leaves that are retained for one year or more. Leaves of evergreens tend to be thick, tough, and waxy, whereas those of deciduous species are usually thinner with a larger surface area. Initially, it might seem advantageous to be evergreen, as a plant could photosynthesize (and therefore grow) whenever light is available. As it turns out, however, there are tradeoffs associated with being evergreen. Evergreens invest heavily in materials such as lignin and fiber that protect the leaf and contribute to its long lifespan, whereas deciduous species invest heavily in materials that facilitate high rates of photosynthesis and growth. The leaf traits of evergreens reduce water and nutrient loss and provide protection from herbivores, but they also reduce rates of photosynthesis and growth. As a result, evergreens are poor competitors on moist, fertile soils. But they commonly dominate vegetation on nutrient-poor sites, due to their ability to retain nutrients in their persistent leaves, stems, and roots. In the mountains and piedmont, widespread evergreens such as pines and heath shrubs commonly occur on nutrient-poor, acidic soils. Evergreens (e.g., those found in spruce-fir forests) are also common at higher elevations and latitudes where the growing season is short and resources too limiting to produce a new "crop" of leaves each year.

Conservation Aspects

More than half the heath balds in the southern Appalachians are located in national parks and forests. Because heath balds occur as scattered islands of shrubland, they occupy a relatively small area. For example, the more than 400 heath balds in Great Smoky Mountains National Park cover less than one percent of the total land area. Heath balds generally occur in inaccessible, well-protected sites, although the trampling of low-growing heath shrubs can be a problem along popular trails or overlooks.

SUGGESTED READING

White, P. S., S. P. Wilds, and D. A. Stratton. 2001. The Distribution of Heath Balds in the Great Smoky Mountains, North Carolina and Tennessee. *Journal of Vegetation Science* 12:453–66.

Whittaker, R. H. 1956. Vegetation of the Great Smoky Mountains. *Ecological Monographs* 26:1–80.

———. 1979. Appalachian Balds and Other North American Heathlands. In Specht, R. L., ed., *Ecosystems of the World. Series Publication 9A. Heathlands and Related Shrublands: Descriptive Studies*, 427–40. New York: Elsevier Scientific.

HEATH BALD: CHARACTERISTIC PLANTS

Trees

Prunus pensylvanica	Fire cherry, Pin cherry	p. 254

Shrubs and Woody Vines

ABUNDANT SPECIES

Kalmia latifolia	Mountain laurel	pp. 291–92
Rhododendron catawbiense	Catawba rhododendron	pp. 301–2
Rhododendron maximum	Rosebay rhododendron	pp. 302–3

OCCASIONAL TO LOCALLY ABUNDANT SPECIES

Aronia melanocarpa	Black chokeberry	p. 272
Clethra acuminata	Mountain sweet pepperbush	pp. 278–79
Diervilla sessilifolia	Southern bush honeysuckle	p. 282
[†]*Gaylussacia baccata*	Black huckleberry	
Kalmia buxifolia	Sand myrtle	pp. 290–91
Menziesia pilosa	Minniebush	pp. 295–96
[†]*Pieris floribunda*	Mountain fetterbush	
Rhododendron calendulaceum	Flame azalea	p. 301
Rubus allegheniensis	Allegheny blackberry	p. 310
[†]*Rubus canadensis*	Smooth blackberry	
Smilax rotundifolia	Common greenbrier	pp. 314–15
Vaccinium corymbosum	Highbush blueberry	p. 317
[†]*Vaccinium erythrocarpum*	Highbush cranberry	
Viburnum cassinoides	Wild raisin	pp. 320–21

Herbs

OCCASIONAL TO LOCALLY ABUNDANT SPECIES

Cuscuta rostrata	Appalachian dodder	pp. 356–57
Epigaea repens	Trailing arbutus	pp. 368–69
Galax urceolata	Galax, Skunkweed	pp. 374–75
Gaultheria procumbens	Wintergreen	pp. 376–77
Pteridium aquilinum	Bracken fern	p. 432
Trillium undulatum	Painted trillium	pp. 459–60

Rare Plants

Geum radiatum	Spreading avens	p. 379
Rhododendron vaseyi	Pinkshell azalea	pp. 304–5

[†] = *plant not included in the species profiles (Part IV)*

HIGH-ELEVATION ROCK OUTCROP

Distinguishing Features

High-elevation rock outcrops differ from surrounding communities by having extensive areas of bare or lichen-covered rock scattered with herb-dominated mats on shallow soils. Trees are stunted and largely restricted to outcrop margins and crevices where deeper soils accumulate. Patches of shrubs are often present, but large areas dominated by shrubs are considered heath balds. High-elevation rock outcrops are differentiated from low-elevation rock outcrops not only by elevation (the boundary is about 3,000 ft.) but by vegetation as well. Annual plants and weedy species, for example, are common in the hot, dry, more frequently disturbed habitats associated with granite outcrops in the piedmont, but they are rare on high-elevation outcrops.

Introduction

This community occurs on rock outcrops on exposed ridges, peaks, and upper slopes at elevations above 3,000 ft. Outcrops consist of various types of rock, including granite, gneiss, schist, and amphibolite; soils vary from bare rock with no soil, to thin soils over rock, to deeper soils in crevices and forest borders. High rainfall, low temperatures, and frequent fog characterize the climate and keep the thin soils moist, reducing the incidence of drought stress. Species composition varies depending on soil depth and moisture, elevation, exposure, and geology. Two different types of high-elevation rock outcrop occur. Granitic domes consist of smooth, exfoliating granite or similar rock material that is largely free of crevices. Rocky summits, in contrast, have irregular, fractured rocks where cracks and crevices accumulate pockets of soil, providing additional habitat for plants to grow. The vegetation consists of lichens and mosses growing on bare rock, mat-forming species on thin soils, with shrubs and stunted trees on deeper soils. While many rock outcrop species also occur in surrounding forests and balds, a number of distinctive species occur, including rare endemics and northern disjuncts.

Vegetation

A patchwork of lichen and moss-covered rocks, low-growing, mat-forming herbaceous plants, scattered shrubs, and stunted trees characterize the vegetation. Lichens growing on bare rocks include brightly colored crustose lichens, whose circular patches appear to be "painted" on rocks, several species of *Cladonia* lichens (with grayish green upright branches), and the smooth rock tripe (*Umbilicaria mammulata*), whose large, leathery, leaf-like structure curls up and appears brittle when dry but which has a slimy, rubbery feel when wet. Two common mosses are dry rock moss (*Grimmia laevigata*) and the Appalachian haircap moss (*Polytrichum appalachianum*). The pincushion mounds of *Grimmia* are vivid green when actively growing, black when dormant. Twisted hair spikemoss (*Selaginella tortipila*) keeps a low profile by forming compact mounds of tightly packed, moss-like leaves. Cliff saxifrage (*Micranthes petiolaris*) commonly occurs on both moist and dry sites.

    The most lush and species-rich sites are persistently wet due to seepage. Areas with deeper soil, such as older well-established mats, rock crevices in rocks, and outcrop margins support various shrubs and trees. Low-growing shrubs include Granite Dome St. John's wort (*Hypericum buckleyi*), mountain golden heather (*Hudsonia montana*), and sand myrtle (*Kalmia buxifolia*). Curiously, sand myrtle, turkeybeard (*Xerophyllum asphodeloides*), and pinebarrens death camas (*Stenanthium leimanthoides*) grow on high-elevation rock outcrops and near sea level in the New Jersey pine barrens. Scattered, mostly stunted trees include Fraser fir (*Abies fraseri*), red spruce (*Picea rubens*), yellow birch (*Betula alleghaniensis*), table mountain pine (*Pinus pungens*), Carolina hemlock (*Tsuga caroliniana*), and smooth serviceberry (*Amelanchier laevis*). Tree flagging results from branches being buffeted by winds and ice, causing the buds to be killed, occurring to such an extent that there is little growth on the windward side of trees.

Seasonal Aspects

Common spring-flowering shrubs include Catawba rhododendron (*Rhododendron catawbiense*), mountain laurel (*Kalmia latifolia*), and sand myrtle, all of which are evergreen shrubs in the heath family (Ericaceae). Catawba rhododendron and mountain laurel produce spectacular floral displays at the tips of shoots with thick leathery leaves, whereas sand myrtle is a relatively short shrub with clusters of small, white flowers and narrow leaves. Deciduous heath shrubs include pinkshell azalea (*Rhododendron vaseyi*), a rare species whose showy pink flowers cover leafless stems in spring, and highbush blueberry (*Vaccinium corymbosum*), a medium to large multistemmed shrub whose small white to pinkish pendulous flowers develop into sweet, edible berries in summer.

The yellow trumpet-shaped flowers of southern bush honeysuckle (*Diervilla sessilifolia*) bloom at the tips of leafy stems in summer, whereas prostrate mats of Granite Dome St. John's wort produce bright yellow flowers and red cone-shaped fruits. Its flowers lack nectar but the numerous stamens attract pollen-collecting bees that function as pollinators. Another prostrate subshrub is the rare mountain golden heather—look for its yellow flowers among needle-like evergreen leaves from late spring through summer. Herbaceous plants that flower in summer include cliff saxifrage, whose open inflorescence of small but distinctive white flowers overtops a basal rosette of semisucculent green to red leaves with coarsely toothed margins. Rock alumroot (*Heuchera villosa*) has large maple-like basal leaves and upright stalks that produce numerous small whitish flowers from early summer to fall. Mountain dandelion (*Krigia montana*) is easily recognized by its basal leaves and dandelion-like yellow flower heads.

Three rare, summer-flowering herbs are spreading avens (*Geum radiatum*), Heller's blazing star (*Liatris helleri*), and mountain sandwort (*Minuartia groenlandica*). Spreading avens has large, mostly basal leaves with conspicuous bowl-shaped yellow flowers. Heller's blazing star produces small upright stems culminating in showy clusters of lavender flower heads, and from late spring through early fall mountain sandwort forms prostrate "cushions" with numerous tiny white flowers.

Distribution

High-elevation rock outcrops occur mainly in the high peaks region of the southern Appalachians, primarily in North Carolina and Tennessee, less frequently in Virginia and Georgia.

Dynamics

Lichens and mosses are the first plants to colonize bare rock. These slow-growing plants collect small amounts of soil that allow hardy vascular plants to get established. The small mats of vegetation that gradually form go through a succession of species largely driven by the amount and rate of soil accumulation. As new species invade and previously established plants spread horizontally, the mat gets progressively larger. Once a mat has built up to a depth of several inches, seedlings of woody plants have a chance to colonize. Such seedlings have slow growth rates and high mortality. The mats themselves are often ephemeral as increasing weight causes them to slide downslope, unless their roots find anchorage in cracks or crevices. High winds can blow trees over, lifting up and destroying the mat in which they're rooted. Most outcrops remain relatively open habitats dominated by herbaceous plants, due to exfoliating rock, soil erosion, vegetation loss, and other factors.

Climate change, alpine relicts, and rare species. In today's climate, the southern Appalachians aren't high enough for an alpine zone, as the tallest peaks are covered with trees and grassy balds and outcrops aren't true alpine communities. Temperatures were apparently cold enough during the last ice age (in the Pleistocene epoch) as a treeline and a true alpine community occurred at elevations above 5,000 ft, as are indicated by pollen and macrofossil evidence. The alpine zone lasted until about 12,000 years ago, when temperatures began warming and trees were able to migrate up to the highest peaks. Remnants of an alpine flora still persist in certain small, isolated high-elevation outcrops where a combination of cooler temperatures, shallow soils, high light, and diminished competition closely resembles past alpine conditions. Among the ice age relicts are a small number of species whose distributions are centered in the alpine and arctic habitats of New England and Canada that have disjunct (isolated) populations at high elevations in the southern Appalachians, including mountain sandwort, three-tooth cinquefoil (*Sibbaldiopsis tridentata*), and deerhair bulrush (*Trichophorum cespitosum*). Conversely, a number of rare species most closely affiliated with the coastal plain, including Heller's blazing star and mountain golden heather, apparently colonized mountain outcrops during a previously hot, dry climate. Climatic change during the last ice age contributed to the large number of species endemic (restricted) to the southern Appalachians, as widespread population loss would have left some species with only a few surviving populations within a restricted geographic area. Currently, more than 40 species of rare plants occur on high-elevation rock outcrops.

Conservation Aspects

Most high-elevation rock outcrops in the southern Appalachians have some level of protection as they occur in National Parks, National Forests, state and local parks, and private reserves. Nonetheless, protected areas with public access often have problems with trampling by hikers attracted to rock outcrops by the good views the outcrops provide. Low growth forms and shallow soils make rock outcrop plants particularly vulnerable to trampling damage by unwitting nature enthusiasts and rock climbers. Other threats include habitat destruction by development activities such as ski slopes, resorts, private homes, and rock quarries. And plants restricted to cool microclimates on mountain summits are particularly vulnerable to global climate change.

SUGGESTED READING

Cogbill, C. V., P. S. White, and S. K. Wiser. 1997. Predicting Treeline Elevation in the Southern Appalachians. *Castanea* 62:137–46.

Wiser, S. K., and P. S. White. 1999. High-Elevation Outcrops and Barrens of the Southern Appalachian Mountains. In Anderson, R. C., J. S. Fralish, and J. M. Baskin, eds., *Savannas, Barrens and Rock Outcrop Communities of North America*, 119–32, New York: Cambridge University Press.

Wiser, S. K., R. K. Peet, and P. S. White. 1996. High Elevation Rock Outcrop Vegetation of the Southern Appalachian Mountains. *Journal of Vegetation Science* 7:703–22.

HIGH-ELEVATION ROCK OUTCROP: CHARACTERISTIC PLANTS

Trees

OCCASIONAL TO LOCALLY ABUNDANT SPECIES

Abies fraseri	Fraser fir	p. 219
Amelanchier laevis	Smooth serviceberry	pp. 225–26
Betula alleghaniensis	Yellow birch	pp. 226–27
Picea rubens	Red spruce	p. 248
Pinus pungens	Table mountain pine	pp. 249–50
Quercus rubra	Northern red oak	pp. 259–60
Sorbus americana	Mountain ash	pp. 262–63
Tsuga caroliniana	Carolina hemlock	pp. 265–66

Shrubs

OCCASIONAL TO LOCALLY ABUNDANT SPECIES

Aronia melanocarpa	Black chokeberry	p. 272
Diervilla sessilifolia	Southern bush honeysuckle	p. 282
Kalmia buxifolia	Sand myrtle	pp. 290–91
Kalmia latifolia	Mountain laurel	pp. 291–92
Menziesia pilosa	Minniebush	pp. 295–96
†*Pieris floribunda*	Mountain fetter-bush	
Rhododendron catawbiense	Catawba rhododendron	pp. 301–2
Vaccinium corymbosum	Highbush blueberry	p. 317

Herbs

OCCASIONAL TO LOCALLY ABUNDANT SPECIES

Asplenium montanum	Mountain spleenwort	p. 339
Avenella flexuosa	Wavy hairgrass	pp. 341–42
Danthonia compressa	Mountain oat grass	pp. 359–60
Gaultheria procumbens	Wintergreen	pp. 376–77
Grimmia laevigata	Dry rock moss	p. 381
Heuchera villosa	Rock alumroot, Crag jangle	pp. 385–86
†*Krigia montana*	Mountain dandelion	
Liatris helleri	Heller's blazing star	p. 396
Micranthes petiolaris	Cliff saxifrage	p. 403
Minuartia groenlandica	Mountain sandwort	p. 405
Oclemena acuminata	Whorled aster	p. 409
Schizachyrium scoparium	Little bluestem	pp. 436–37
Selaginella tortipila	Twisted hair spikemoss	p. 437
Solidago glomerata	Skunk goldenrod	pp. 443–44
Xerophyllum asphodeloides	Turkey beard, Beargrass	p. 468

Lichens

Umbilicaria mammulata	Smooth rock tripe	pp. 461–62

Rare Plants

Geum radiatum	Spreading avens	p. 379
Hudsonia montana	Mountain golden heather	pp. 286–87
Hypericum buckleyi	Granite dome St. John's wort	pp. 287–88
Packera millefolium	Blue Ridge ragwort	pp. 415–16
Rhododendron vaseyi	Pinkshell azalea	pp. 304–5
Sibbaldiopsis tridentata	Three-tooth cinquefoil	pp. 438–39

† = plant not included in the species profiles (Part IV)

HIGH-ELEVATION RED OAK FOREST

Distinguishing Features

High-elevation red oak forest differs from all other high-elevation forests in that northern red oak makes up 75 percent or more of the canopy.

Introduction

Northern red oak (*Quercus rubra*) grows as a canopy species in a variety of communities in the mountain and piedmont regions. While it shares dominance with other canopy species in most communities, northern red oak is the overwhelming dominant in some high mountain areas. High-elevation red oak forest occurs on dry to mesic slopes and ridgetops at elevations between 3,500 and 5,500 ft. with well-drained, rocky, acidic soils. The forest varies from being a closed canopy of large well-formed trees on middle and upper slopes to an open canopy of gnarled, stunted trees (called oak orchards) on ridges exposed to high winds and frequent ice storms.

Vegetation

In addition to northern red oak, other canopy trees include chestnut oak (*Q. montana*) and red maple (*Acer rubrum*), with small patches of red spruce (*Picea rubens*) at higher elevations. American chestnut (*Castanea dentata*) was once a canopy dominant or co-dominant before an introduced fungus (commonly known as the chestnut blight) decimated it in the early twentieth century. Today, this once magnificent species persists as root sprouts and slowly rotting trunks.

The understory has low to moderate coverage with small trees or shrubs such as bigfruit hawthorn (*Crataegus macrosperma*), smooth serviceberry (*Amelanchier laevis*), mountain holly (*Ilex montana*), and witch hazel (*Hamamelis virginiana*). Shrubs in the heath family (Ericaceae) are common, including evergreen species such as mountain laurel (*Kalmia latifolia*), rosebay (*Rhododendron maximum*), and Catawba rhododendron (*R. catawbiense*), as well as deciduous species such as flame azalea (*R. calendulaceum*) and blueberries (*Vaccinium* spp.). The herbaceous layer is often dense and fairly diverse in "oak orchards" as an open canopy increases the amount of light reaching the forest floor. Common herbs include speckled wood lily (*Clintonia umbellulata*), white snakeroot (*Ageratina altissima*), bigleaf aster (*Eurybia macrophylla*), whorled loosestrife (*Lysimachia quadrifolia*), and lousewort (*Pedicularis canadensis*). A diverse mixture of herbaceous plants grows under deciduous shrubs, with fewer herbs under the denser shade of evergreen shrubs.

Seasonal Aspects

Spring-flowering trees include black locust (*Robinia pseudoacacia*), a fast-growing tree with deeply furrowed bark, paired thorns at the base of compound leaves, and white pea-like flowers in drooping clusters. If a thorn appears to move it's likely a locust treehopper, a sap-sucking insect that likes to play hide and seek. Bigfruit hawthorn, a small thicket-forming tree also has thorns (long, sharp ones!) and white to pink flowers in dense flat-topped clusters. In late spring, the brightly colored tubular flowers of flame azalea light up the forest understory. Subtler are the succulent, tumor-like green galls on its stem tips, which typically appear from early spring through mid-late summer. Alternate leaf dogwood (*Cornus alternifolia*), a multistemmed shrub with widely spreading horizontal branches, produces small white flowers in flat-topped clusters in spring and dark blue berry-like fruits on red stalks in late summer and fall. The inconspicuous, wind-pollinated late-winter and early spring flowers of American and beaked hazelnut (*Corylus americana* and *C. cornuta*) develop into edible nuts in late summer and fall. Squirrels, blue jays, and other wildlife species very quickly harvest the tasty nuts enclosed within large leafy bracts.

Carrion flower (*Smilax herbacea*), an herbaceous climbing vine, derives its name from the carrion-like odor associated with its numerous yellow-green flower clusters (umbels). Shiny carrion flies often hang out near the flowers, perhaps looking for (but not finding) a place to lay their eggs. Another herbaceous climbing vine is wild yam (*Dioscorea villosa*). Its tiny yellow-green spring flowers develop into showy, three-winged fruits in late summer and fall. Other spring-flowering herbs include lousewort, Canada mayflower (*Maianthemum canadense*), and whorled loosestrife. Bumblebees frequently visit lousewort's yellowish to reddish brown tubular flowers in tightly packed heads. Canada mayflower forms dense mats of short-stemmed plants bearing 1–3 broadly ovate leaves. Its tiny white flowers develop into translucent red berries in late summer. Whorled loosestrife is a relatively tall plant whose solitary yellow flowers on long stalks emerge from whorled leaves in late spring and summer.

Summer-flowering species include rosebay, leather flower (*Clematis viorna*), bigleaf aster, and occasionally, the root sprouts of American chestnut. Bumblebees forage for nectar on the white to pale-pink flower clusters of rosebay as well as the striking urn-shaped red-purple flowers of leather flower, an herbaceous climbing vine. Bigleaf aster has large, heart-shaped, basal leaves with upright shoots whose pale purple ray flowers surround yellow disk flowers that become reddish with age. In open, sunny areas, the thin shoots of the American chestnut sometimes accumulate sufficient resources to produce elongate clusters of small, fragrant cream-colored flowers, but rarely are fruits with viable nuts produced.

In late summer and fall, mountain holly, bigfruit hawthorn, and wake robin (*Trillium erectum*) produce conspicuous reddish fruits, whereas alternate leaf dogwood, blackberries (*Rubus* spp.), carrion flower, and speckled wood lily produce clusters of dark blue-black fruits. The leaves of northern red oak, often filled with circular holes made by June beetles (a nocturnal buzzing insect), turn a deep scarlet color in autumn. Providing contrast are the butter-yellow autumn leaves of striped maple (*Acer pensylvanicum*) and witch hazel.

> *Red oaks and white oaks.* Oaks are divided into 2 distinct groups, red oaks and white oaks, based on characteristics associated with their leaves and acorns. The red oak group includes species such as northern red oak, scarlet oak (*Q. coccinea*), and black oak (*Q. velutina*), whereas white oak (*Q. alba*), chestnut oak, and post oak (*Q. stellata*) are members of the white oak group. Leaves of the red oak group have bristles on their leaf tips and leaf lobes; leaves of the white oak group don't. Acorns in the white oak group mature in one summer and germinate the following autumn, shortly after they drop from the trees. Acorns in the red oak group take 2 summers to mature, and because an overwintering period is required, germinate in spring, rather than autumn. Acorns in the red oak group are rich in fats and have high tannin concentrations serving as a chemical defense compound. Acorns in the white oak group are lower in lipids and have lower concentrations of tannins. The higher tannins found in the acorns of the red oak group presumably reflect their greater vulnerability to seed predators, as they remain dormant for a longer period prior to germinating. Differences in acorn chemistry also influence the behavior of seed predators/dispersers. Squirrels eat the acorns of the white oak group immediately, or they excise the seedling embryo (thereby preventing germination and loss of food energy) prior to burial. Acorns of the red oak group are generally buried undamaged in autumn and consumed in winter. Unrecovered acorns often germinate and form seedlings, but few survive to become trees.

Distribution

High-elevation red oak forest is found at higher elevations in the mountains of Virginia, North Carolina, Tennessee, and Georgia, particularly on broad ridges with southerly aspects. Where spruce-fir forest is absent, high-elevation red oak forest may extend to the highest peaks.

Dynamics

High-elevation red oak forest is susceptible to disturbance by high winds, ice storms, and fires. On exposed ridges, winds gusting at more than 100 mph bend, twist, and blow down trees. Ice and snow build up and break off branches, exposing trees to attack by insects and fungi. Lightning splits and injures trees and periodically ignites low-intensity surface fires. Periodic disturbance facilitates forest regeneration by opening up the canopy and increasing the amount of light reaching the forest floor. Because northern red oak is relatively light demanding, occasional disturbance plays a critical role in its persistence as a canopy dominant. The loss of American chestnut as a canopy dominant in the 1930s provided an unusual opportunity for northern red oak to recruit new individuals into the canopy. As a result, higher-elevation forests dominated by northern red oak currently cover a larger area than they did prior to the chestnut blight in the 1930s.

Conservation Aspects

Most high-elevation red oak forests have been logged. Logging, coupled with chestnut blight in the early twentieth century, opened up the forest, thereby providing an opportunity for shade-intolerant, opportunistic species such as black locust, tulip tree (*Liriodendron tulipifera*), and yellow birch (*Betula alleghaniensis*) to get established. Past disturbance and fire exclusion have increased the density of both heath shrubs and fast-growing understory species such as red maple, which can hinder northern red oak regeneration. An infestation of gypsy moths is an additional threat as the caterpillars have led to repeated defoliation and widespread mortality in oak-dominated forests of the central and northern Appalachians.

SUGGESTED READING

Crow, T. R. 1988. Reproductive Mode and Mechanisms for Self-Replacement of Northern Red Oak (*Quercus rubra*)—A Review. *Forest Science* 34:19–40.

DeLapp, J. 1978. Gradient Analysis and Classification of the High Elevation Red Oak Community of the Southern Appalachians. M.S. thesis, North Carolina State University, Raleigh.

Stephenson, S. L., and H. S. Adams. 1989. The High-Elevation Red Oak (*Quercus rubra*) Community Type in Western Virginia. *Castanea* 54:217–29.

HIGH-ELEVATION RED OAK FOREST: CHARACTERISTIC PLANTS

Trees

ABUNDANT SPECIES		
Quercus rubra	Northern red oak	pp. 259–60
OCCASIONAL TO LOCALLY ABUNDANT SPECIES		
Acer pensylvanicum	Striped maple	p. 221
Acer rubrum	Red maple	p. 222
Betula alleghaniensis	Yellow birch	pp. 226–27
Castanea dentata	American chestnut	pp. 231–32
Crataegus macrosperma	Bigfruit hawthorn	p. 236

| *Quercus montana* | Chestnut oak | pp. 258–59 |
| *Robinia pseudoacacia* | Black locust | pp. 260–61 |

Shrubs

OCCASIONAL TO LOCALLY ABUNDANT SPECIES

Cornus alternifolia	Alternate leaf dogwood	p. 279
Corylus cornuta	Beaked hazelnut	pp. 280–81
Gaylussacia ursina	Bear huckleberry	p. 284
Hamamelis virginiana	Witch hazel	pp. 285–86
Ilex montana	Mountain holly	pp. 288–89
Kalmia latifolia	Mountain laurel	pp. 291–92
Rhododendron calendulaceum	Flame azalea	p. 301
Rhododendron catawbiense	Catawba rhododendron	pp. 301–2
Rhododendron maximum	Rosebay	pp. 302–3
Rubus allegheniensis	Allegheny blackberry	p. 310
Viburnum lantanoides	Witch hobble, Hobblebush	p. 321

Herbs

OCCASIONAL TO LOCALLY ABUNDANT SPECIES

Ageratina altissima	White snakeroot	pp. 328–29
Athyrium asplenioides	Southern lady fern	p. 340
Carex pensylvanica	Pennsylvania sedge	pp. 343–44
Clematis viorna	Leather flower	p. 352
Clintonia umbellulata	Speckled wood lily	pp. 353–54
Conopholis americana	Squawroot, Cancer root	p. 355
Dennstaedtia punctilobula	Hayscented fern	p. 360
Dioscorea villosa	Wild yam	pp. 363–64
Dryopteris campyloptera	Mountain wood fern	p. 366
Eurybia macrophylla	Bigleaf aster	p. 372
Galax urceolata	Galax, Skunkweed	pp. 374–75
Laportea canadensis	Wood nettle	p. 395
Lysimachia quadrifolia	Whorled loosestrife	pp. 399–400
Maianthemum canadense	Canada mayflower	pp. 400–401
Oclemena acuminata	Whorled aster	p. 409
Osmunda claytoniana	Interrupted fern	pp. 413–14
Pedicularis canadensis	Lousewort, Wood betony	p. 419
Smilax herbacea	Carrion flower	pp. 440–41
Solidago curtisii	Curtis's goldenrod	p. 443
Thelypteris noveboracensis	New York fern	pp. 451–52
Trillium erectum	Wake robin	p. 457

Rare Plants

| [†]*Eutrochium purpureum* | Purple node Joe Pye weed |
| [†]*Prenanthes roanensis* | Appalachian rattlesnake root |

† = *plant not included in the species profiles (Part IV)*

NORTHERN HARDWOOD FOREST

Distinguishing Features

Northern hardwood forest can be distinguished from other high elevation forest types by the dominance of mesophytic canopy trees (American beech, yellow birch, yellow buckeye, and sugar maple) since other high mountain forest types generally have northern red oak, red spruce, or Fraser fir as canopy dominants.

Introduction

Northern hardwood forest occurs on medium- to high-elevation (generally over 4,000 ft.) slopes, coves, and flats, often on north-facing slopes. The soil is usually moist, due to high rainfall and low temperatures. The relatively large trees form a dense forest except on exposed high-elevation sites where trees are dwarfed and the forest is more open. The broad-leaved deciduous trees that dominate northern hardwood forest contrast with the needle-leaved evergreens of spruce-fir forest. Perhaps the most striking feature of northern hardwood forest is its brilliant display of autumn colors. The autumn air is clearer and cooler than in summer and at no other time of year is the rich array of trees more apparent.

Vegetation

Mesophytic (moisture-loving) trees, primarily American beech (*Fagus grandifolia*), yellow birch (*Betula alleghaniensis*), yellow buckeye (*Aesculus flava*), and sugar maple (*Acer saccharum*) dominate the canopy. Other canopy species include white basswood (*Tilia americana*), white ash (*Fraxinus americana*), and at higher elevations, red spruce (*Picea rubens*). Common understory trees include striped maple

(*Acer pensylvanicum*), mountain maple (*Acer spicatum*), and smooth serviceberry (*Amelanchier laevis*). Pipevine (*Aristolochia macrophylla*), a climbing vine with large heart-shaped leaves, is found on the edge and other well-lit areas of the forest. A sparse to fairly dense shrub layer includes witch hobble (*Viburnum lantanoides*), wild hydrangea (*Hydrangea arborescens*), and Appalachian gooseberry (*Ribes rotundifolium*). The herbaceous layer is often dense and quite diverse, particularly on sheltered sites with deep, moist soils. Common herbs include false Solomon's seal (*Maianthemum racemosum*), blue cohosh (*Caulophyllum thalictroides*), Curtis's goldenrod (*Solidago curtisii*), wake robin (*Trillium erectum*), and large-flowered bellwort (*Uvularia grandiflora*). Scattered patches of mosses and lichens are easily overlooked, except in winter, when plants in the other layers have died back and the forest floor is mostly a drab brown. Along streams and seepage areas, plant cover can be lush with characteristic species such as flowering raspberry (*Rubus odoratus*), umbrella leaf (*Diphylleia cymosa*), and crimson bee balm (*Monarda didyma*). Almost all herbaceous plants in mountain forests are long-lived perennials that store nutrients in autumn in underground rhizomes, bulbs, or roots that provide the resources needed for resprouting in spring. Fringed phacelia (*Phacelia fimbriata*) and yellow jewelweed (*Impatiens pallida*) are unusual in that they are short-lived (annual) plants that regenerate from seed each year.

BEECH GAP FOREST

A variant of northern hardwood forest called beech gap forest occurs primarily in gaps and ridgetops at elevations greater than 4,500 ft., where trees are exposed to desiccating winds, frequent low temperatures, and ice storms. The severe climatic conditions result in canopy trees that are stunted and have a distinctly gnarled appearance. Despite their small size, the canopy trees are often quite old. The canopy is dominated by American beech with lesser amounts of yellow buckeye and yellow birch. There is little or no subcanopy or shrub layer, but the herbaceous layer can be very dense. Common herbs include Pennsylvania sedge (*Carex pensylvanica*), white snakeroot (*Ageratina altissima*), black cohosh (*Actaea racemosa*), hayscented fern (*Dennstaedtia punctilobula*), and beechdrops (*Epifagus virginiana*), a flowering plant that is a root parasite on American beech. Beech gaps occur in small patches surrounded by other high-elevation forest types and by grassy or heath balds.

Seasonal Aspects

Seen from afar, the white flower clusters of smooth serviceberry resemble white clouds against a mostly leafless forest in early spring. Another early blooming species is yellow buckeye—bumblebees and hummingbirds seeking energy in the form of its sugar-rich nectar actively visit and pollinate its yellow tubular flowers. Wind-pollinated trees such as American beech, yellow birch, and sugar maple release enormous amounts of pollen from relatively inconspicuous flowers in spring. Striped maple differs from most maples in that its small, bell-shaped, nectar-producing flowers are pollinated by insects (small bees and flies), rather than by the wind.

The dense mats of the white to pink flowers of Carolina spring beauty (*Claytonia caroliniana*) produce spectacular displays in early spring. Fringed phacelia also forms colorful patches in spring—its numerous small white flowers collectively resemble a light cover of newly fallen snow. Wake robin produces maroon or white flowers on upright stalks whose fetid odor attracts flies and beetles that function as pollinators. Queen bumblebees pollinate the limp (even when fresh), nodding butter-yellow flowers of the large-flowered bellwort. Other plants to observe in spring include the white lacy flowers at the tips of the arching stems of false Solomon's seal, and umbrella leaf's white flowers on stalks above pairs of large umbrella-shaped leaves.

In spite of its common name, hummingbirds (not bees) pollinate the bright-red tubular flowers of crimson bee balm. Other summer-flowering woodland herbs include black cohosh, white snakeroot, yellow jewelweed, and wood nettle (*Laportea canadensis*). The numerous white stamens within each black cohosh flower give its long, narrow inflorescences a fuzzy white appearance. White snakeroot's white flower heads at the tips of leafy shoots also have a fuzzy look. Bumblebees frequently visit yellow jewelweed's flowers to obtain nectar from the down-curved nectar spur. Touching the narrow, elongate ripe fruits of jewelweed causes them to explode, thereby dispersing the seeds. Touching wood nettle's hairy foliage is less fun, as a stinging sensation lasts for several minutes.

Wild raspberry produces showy, deep pink to purple bowl-shaped flowers in summer that mature into fleshy red fruits. In summer and fall, pipevine swallowtail caterpillars (black with reddish spots) can be seen feeding on the large heart-shaped leaves of Dutchman's pipe, a woody climbing vine whose flowers resemble an old-fashioned smoking pipe. Red squirrels feed on the winged seeds of sugar maple, as well as on the sweet sap oozing from stem wounds. Because goldenrods typically occur in fields and roadsides, you may be surprised to discover Curtis's goldenrod in the forest understory—its yellow flower heads occur in small clusters within the upper leaf axils in late summer and fall.

Distribution

Northern hardwood forest is restricted to the southern Appalachians of western North Carolina, eastern Tennessee, southwestern Virginia, and, less frequently, northeastern Georgia. A similar forest type in the northeastern United States has significantly fewer species due to the species loss caused by Pleistocene glaciers. On more sheltered slopes, "bowls," and upper coves, the boundaries between northern hardwood forest and rich cove forest, are often blurred as they share many of the same species and as the transition between community types can be gradual.

Dynamics

High winds and ice storms create openings in the forest canopy, providing an opportunity for new trees to get established and releasing shade-suppressed saplings. The large number of broken branches on the forest floor and scattered downed trees reflect frequent wind and ice damage. Fires occur infrequently due to moist conditions; however, fires can be quite damaging during drought periods as many trees in this forest have relatively thin bark. Clusters of opportunistic species such as yellow birch, fire cherry (*Prunus pensylvanica*), and black locust (*Robinia pseudoacacia*) are good indicators of past logging or fires.

European wild boars impact vegetation. This species, like wild pigs everywhere, eats just about anything it can find, including acorns, hickory nuts, beechnuts, tubers, and bulbs. Wild boars also eat, uproot, and trample wildflowers such as spring beauty, trout lily, and trillium and damage tree roots, seedlings, and saplings. They tear up rhododendron thickets, dig up sod on grassy balds, pollute streams, and compete with native animals for berries, acorns, and nuts. Because fruit availability fluctuates markedly from year to year, this competition can have serious consequences for native wildlife. The potential impact of wild boars is exacerbated by their high reproductive output. A female boar can produce 10 young per litter, whereas a female black bear, for example, normally produces 2 cubs every other year. While large numbers of wild boars have been trapped or shot, totally eliminating them is virtually impossible. Increasing numbers of wild boars, now in the thousands in the southern Appalachians, could substantially reduce populations of black bear, squirrels, and other wildlife, as well as significantly reduce the abundance and diversity of herbaceous plants.

Conservation Aspects

Northern hardwood forest is limited to higher-elevation sites (generally over 4,000 ft.) within the relatively small geographic area of western North Carolina, eastern Tennessee, southwestern Virginia, and northeastern Georgia. This community usually occurs on public lands administered by the U.S. Forest Service (e.g., Pisgah, Nantahala, Cherokee, Jefferson, and Chattahoochee National Forests) and the National Park Service (e.g., Great Smoky Mountains National Park, Shenandoah National Park, and the Blue Ridge Parkway) and are thought to be reasonably well protected at the present time. Threats include invasive species, disease, and air pollution. For example, grazing and soil disturbance by European wild boars have reduced herbaceous plant cover in beech gap forests by up to 90 percent. Beech bark disease, a complex made up of the beech scale insect and two closely associated fungi, has caused mortality of numerous American beech trees. High-elevation plant communities are particularly vulnerable to atmospheric deposition of air pollutants such as acid rain and ground-level ozone.

SUGGESTED READING

McLeod, D. E. 1988. Vegetation Patterns, Floristics and Environmental Relationships in the Black and Craggy Mountains. Ph.D. diss., University of North Carolina, Chapel Hill.

Russell, N. 1953. The Beech Gaps of the Great Smoky Mountains. *Ecology* 34:366–74.

White, P. S., E. Buckner, J. D. Pittillo, and C. V. Cogbill. 1993. High-Elevation Forests: Spruce-Fir Forests, Northern Hardwood Forests, and Associated Communities. In Martin, W. H., S. G. Boyce, A. C. Echternacht, eds., *Biodiversity of the Southeastern United States: Upland Terrestrial Ccommunities*, 305–38. New York: Wiley and Sons.

NORTHERN HARDWOOD FOREST: CHARACTERISTIC PLANTS

Trees

ABUNDANT SPECIES
Aesculus flava	Yellow buckeye	pp. 224–25
Betula alleghaniensis	Yellow birch	pp. 226–27
Fagus grandifolia	American beech	pp. 237–38

OCCASIONAL TO LOCALLY ABUNDANT SPECIES
Acer pensylvanicum	Striped maple	p. 221
Acer saccharum	Sugar maple	pp. 222–23
Acer spicatum	Mountain maple	pp. 223–24
Amelanchier laevis	Smooth serviceberry	pp. 225–26
Fraxinus americana	White ash	pp. 238–39
Magnolia acuminata	Cucumber tree	pp. 243–44
Picea rubens	Red spruce	p. 248
Tilia americana	White basswood	pp. 263–64

Shrubs and Woody Vines

OCCASIONAL TO LOCALLY ABUNDANT SPECIES
Aristolochia macrophylla	Pipevine, Dutchman's pipe	pp. 271–72
Cornus alternifolia	Alternate leaf dogwood	p. 279
Hydrangea arborescens	Wild hydrangea	p. 287
Rhododendron catawbiense	Catawba rhododendron	pp. 301–2
Ribes rotundifolium	Appalachian gooseberry	p. 308
Rubus allegheniensis	Allegheny blackberry	p. 310
Rubus odoratus	Flowering raspberry	p. 311
Sambucus racemosa	Red elderberry	p. 313
Viburnum lantanoides	Witch hobble, Hobblebush	p. 321

Herbs

ABUNDANT SPECIES
Ageratina altissima	White snakeroot	pp. 328–29
Dennstaedtia punctilobula	Hayscented fern	p. 360
Laportea canadensis	Wood nettle	p. 395
Maianthemum racemosum	False Solomon's seal	p. 401
Viola canadensis	Canada violet	pp. 465–66

OCCASIONAL TO LOCALLY ABUNDANT SPECIES
Actaea racemosa	Black cohosh, Bugbane	pp. 326–27
Arisaema triphyllum	Jack-in-the-pulpit	p. 335
Aruncus dioicus	Goat's beard	p. 336
Carex pensylvanica	Pennsylvania sedge	pp. 343–44
Caulophyllum thalictroides	Blue cohosh	pp. 345–46
Claytonia caroliniana	Carolina spring beauty	pp. 350–51
Diphylleia cymosa	Umbrella leaf	pp. 364–65
Epifagus virginiana	Beechdrops	pp. 367–68
Erythronium umbilicatum	Dimpled trout lily	pp. 370–71
Impatiens pallida	Yellow jewelweed	pp. 391–92
Monarda didyma	Crimson bee balm	pp. 406–7
Phacelia fimbriata	Fringed phacelia	pp. 419–20
Rudbeckia laciniata	Cutleaf coneflower	pp. 433–34
Solidago curtisii	Curtis's goldenrod	p. 443

Stellaria pubera	Giant chickweed	p. 447
Trillium erectum	Wake robin, Stinking Willie	p. 457
Uvularia grandiflora	Large-flowered bellwort	p. 462

Invasive Exotic Plants

Celastrus orbiculatus	Oriental bittersweet	p. 277

Rare Plants

†*Aconitum reclinatum*	White monkshood
†*Corallorhiza maculata*	Spotted coralroot

† = *plant not included in the species profiles (Part IV)*

Low-Elevation Moist to Wet Communities

RICH COVE FOREST

Distinguishing Features

You can recognize rich cove forest by its diverse mixture of moisture-loving trees and lush, species-rich herbaceous layer. Acidic cove forest, which occurs on similar sites, but with more acidic soils, has fewer tree species, a dense heath shrub layer, and a relatively sparse herbaceous layer.

Introduction

In narrow valleys, broad ravines, and concave slopes where the soil is rich, the climate mild, and rainfall abundant, one of the most species-rich communities in eastern North America occurs. Rich cove forest occurs at low to moderate elevations where adjacent slopes and a dense canopy of tall, mostly deciduous trees moderate temperature and wind and intercept the sun so that deep shade is present much of the year. The terrain is often rugged with steep slopes, fallen logs, and scattered boulders. The deep, dark soils of this forest are generally more nutrient-rich and less acidic than surrounding areas, due to the presence of base-rich rocks (such as amphibolite, marble, and limestone) that release calcium (or magnesium) into the soil as they weather. A fertile, generally circumneutral (less acidic) soil, coupled with a favorable climate, results in conditions that favor an unusually rich diversity of plants. Within a single stride, one can encounter a dozen different species of spring wildflowers, while thousands of herbaceous plants may occupy a single two-acre patch of forest. No other community in eastern North America has so many kinds of trees coupled with such a lush and species-rich herbaceous layer.

Vegetation

A variety of trees form a dense canopy of overlapping crowns that deeply shade the forest floor, much like a dense tropical forest. Rooted in moist, fertile soils, the canopy trees grow faster, taller, and wider than in most other forests. Among the most common canopy species are tulip tree (*Liriodendron tulipifera*), American beech (*Fagus grandifolia*), white basswood (*Tilia americana*), yellow buckeye (*Aesculus flava*), and sugar maple (*Acer saccharum*). Other canopy species include white ash (*Fraxinus americana*), sweet birch (*Betula lenta*), cucumber tree (*Magnolia acuminata*), and yellowwood (*Cladrastis kentukea*). The usually open understory consists of smaller individuals of the canopy species as well as typical subcanopy trees such as Carolina silverbell (*Halesia tetraptera*), Fraser magnolia (*Magnolia fraseri*), flowering dogwood (*Cornus florida*), hop hornbeam (*Ostrya virginiana*), ironwood (*Carpinus caroliniana*), striped maple (*Acer pensylvanicum*), and pawpaw (*Asimina triloba*). A generally sparse shrub layer includes species such as sweet shrub (*Calycanthus floridus*), spicebush (*Lindera benzoin*), and wild hydrangea (*Hydrangea arborescens*). The herbaceous layer is particularly striking in that it's both species-rich and dense, often forming a continuous carpet of lush vegetation on the forest floor. Among the many conspicuous species are black cohosh (*Actaea racemosa*), blue cohosh (*Caulophyllum thalictroides*), acute-lobed hepatica (*Hepatica acutiloba*), mayapple (*Podophyllum peltatum*), Solomon's seal (*Polygonatum biflorum*), bloodroot (*Sanguinaria canadensis*), meadowrue (*Thalictrum thalictroides*), and various trilliums (*Trillium* spp.). By midsummer, wood nettle (*Laportea canadensis*) is readily apparent both visually and to the touch (due to its stinging hairs). The abundance and diversity of herbaceous plants is often greatest on lower slopes, benches, and coves where soil nutrients, organic matter, and moisture accumulate in a downslope movement to form a rich, compost-like soil.

Seasonal Aspects

Among the many trees found in rich cove forests are spring-flowering species such as yellow buckeye, tulip tree, cucumber tree, Carolina silverbell, white basswood, and yellowwood. Yellow buckeye is one of the first trees to leaf out and flower in early spring—its clusters of yellow tubular flowers are frequently visited by bumblebees, but hummingbirds also occasionally visit and pollinate the nectar-rich flowers. The greenish yellow tulip-shaped flowers of tulip tree, as well as the fragrant greenish yellow cup-shaped flowers of cucumber tree, often go unnoticed, as they blend in with the foliage up in the canopy. Carolina silverbell is a common understory tree whose nodding white bell-shaped flowers hang in conspicuous clusters from leafless branches in early spring. Yellowwood, a relatively rare small to medium-sized tree produces hanging clusters of white pea-like flowers in spring that develop into flat seedpods in summer. Day-flying bees and night-flying moths pollinate white basswood's yellowish green flowers, which hang from distinctive leaf-like bracts in late spring.

Three common spring-flowering shrubs are spicebush, pawpaw, and sweet shrub. Spicebush produces round clusters of tiny yellow flowers on leafless plants in late winter and early spring. The nodding purple flowers of pawpaw also emerge before the leaves in early spring. Sweet shrub's upright maroon flowers occur on leafy stems through much of spring, producing a spicy fragrance that attracts small beetles.

An amazing diversity of spring-flowering herbaceous plants covers the forest floor early in the growing season. Bloodroot's large white solitary flower with numerous golden anthers emerges above a single large leaf in early spring, whereas the solitary white flower of mayapple lies partially hidden beneath its paired umbrella-like leaves. Various trilliums bloom in early spring, including the large, white, funnel-shaped flowers of large-flowered trillium (*Trillium grandiflorum*), which turn pink with age. Foamflower (*Tiarella cordifolia*) produces a dense raceme of white flowers with abundant orange (rather than yellow) pollen held well above its maple-like basal leaves. Blue cohosh, a smooth upright plant with large compound leaves, produces clusters of small yellowish green to purple-green flowers that form dark blue berry-like seeds. Showy orchis (*Galearis spectabilis*) has 2 large, fleshy basal leaves and a single stout flower stalk with showy pink to lavender flowers. In late spring, the creamy white bell-shaped flowers of Solomon's seal hang below its leaves on long, arching stems. The most common violet in cove forests is probably Canada violet (*Viola canadensis*)—its upright leafy stems produce white flowers with a yellow center from spring through early summer (and sporadically in the fall). From late spring through summer, black cohosh produces tassel-like flowers on tall stalks whose fetid odor attracts carrion flies and beetles that function as pollinators. The small white flowers of ramps (*Allium tricoccum*) bloom in round clusters early in the summer, long after its large flat leaves, with a strong onion odor, have withered away.

The high diversity of plants that characterize this community provides a rich palette of leaf colors in autumn. A rich array of fleshy fruits appearing from summer through fall adds additional color and provides an important food source for numerous birds and mammals. Examples include the bright red fruits of flowering dogwood, spicebush, and jack-in-the-pulpit (*Arisaema triphyllum*); the dark blue to black fruits of Solomon's seal, speckled wood lily (*Clintonia umbellulata*), and black cherry (*Prunus serotina*); the white waxy berries of doll's eyes (*Actaea pachypoda*); and the large green to brown pod-like fruits of sweet shrub, Carolina silverbell, and yellow buckeye.

Distribution

Rich cove forest is fairly widespread in the mountains at low to middle elevations and occurs sporadically in the upper piedmont.

Dynamics

Small openings in the canopy of rich cove forest play an important role in forest regeneration and maintaining diversity, particularly in the tree and herbaceous layers. These canopy gaps are primarily due to high winds, the frailty of trees in old age, and other natural causes toppling individual trees. Though common in forests on upper slopes and ridges, fires occur infrequently in cove forests, due to moist conditions. Areas that have been logged tend to have a greater abundance of shade-intolerant trees (such as tulip tree and black locust), a higher density of shrubs, and a less abundant and diverse herbaceous layer.

> *American ginseng.* The roots of American ginseng (*Panax quinquefolius*) have been dug up and exported to Asia for nearly 300 years. In the nineteenth century, an average of 381,000 lbs. of wild ginseng roots were exported each year from the United States. By the late twentieth century, exports dropped to an average of 121,000 lbs. per year. In 2003, about 75,000 lbs. of ginseng roots were harvested from wild populations and exported to Asia. Based on an average of 330 field-collected plants per pound of ginseng roots (dry weight), it can be estimated that almost 25 million plants were harvested in 2003 alone. With wild plants becoming scarce, less than 4 percent of exported American ginseng currently comes from wild-collected roots. Demand for wild roots remains high, however, as Asians prefer wild roots over cultivated ones. This preference is reflected in ginseng prices: $250–$500 per lb. for wild roots versus less than $20 per lb. for cultivated roots. At the time of this writing, collecting wild American ginseng in National Forests of Virginia, the Carolinas, Tennessee, and Georgia was legal (in designated areas, with a permit). This could change if ginseng populations continue to decline. Within the National Park System, harvesting of all native plants is prohibited, but poaching of ginseng and other medicinal plants continues to be a serious problem.

Conservation Aspects

Rich cove forest can be thought of as a living museum of an extremely old association of plants, animals, and microbes. Sheltered from winds, temperature extremes, and major environmental changes (such as glaciation and ocean inundation), cove forests have persisted for millions of years in the southern Appalachians. This antiquity, along with moist, fertile soils and a favorable climate, has resulted in tremendous plant diversity.

Rich cove forest includes some of the best examples of old-growth deciduous forest in eastern North America. Here one encounters unusually large trees with wide trunks, some of which are more than 500 years old, an exceptional age for species in eastern North American forests. The largest tracts of old-growth cove forest occur in Great Smoky Mountains National Park, where trees such as white basswood, tulip tree, yellow buckeye, Carolina silverbell, and American beech reach or approach record heights. Some of the best spots for viewing spring wildflowers also occur in old-growth rich cove forests.

Current threats to the forest include the clearing of adjoining slopes for residential development, invasive species such as Chinese privet (*Ligustrum sinense*) and autumn olive (*Elaeagnus umbellata*), and the overharvesting of medicinal plants, including goldenseal (*Hydrastis canadensis*), black cohosh, bloodroot, and American ginseng.

ACIDIC COVE FOREST

Distinguishing Features

Acidic cove forest is similar to rich cove forest but has more acidic soils with a dense layer of heath shrubs and a much lower diversity of trees and herbaceous species.

Introduction

Acidic cove forest occurs on moist, sheltered sites such as narrow, rocky gorges, steep ravines, and lower slopes and ridges within coves. The terrain is often rugged, with steep slopes, boulders, fallen logs, and stumps. Ephemeral creeks, seeps, and springs often dot the landscape. Underlain by quartzite, granite, or other acidic bedrock, the soils have a low pH, usually less than 4.5, compared to the higher soil pH (about 6.0) associated with rich cove forest. Acid-tolerant mesophytic trees, a dense evergreen shrub layer, and a relatively small group of acid-tolerant herbaceous species characterize this community.

Vegetation

Acidic cove forest generally has a dense canopy consisting of a relatively small number of mesophytic species, including tulip tree (*Liriodendron tulipifera*), sweet birch (*Betula lenta*), yellow birch (*B. alleghaniensis*), and red maple (*Acer rubrum*). Species such as white basswood (*Tilia americana*), white ash (*Fraxinus americana*), and American beech (*Fagus grandifolia*) are much less common in acidic cove forest than in rich cove forest. Canada hemlock (*Tsuga canadensis*) is currently threatened by the hemlock woolly adelgid, an introduced insect pest. A relatively open subcanopy includes Fraser magnolia (*Magnolia fraseri*) along with smaller individuals of the canopy species. Dense heath shrub thickets make travel difficult and inhibit the growth of herbaceous plants. Common shrubs include rosebay (*Rhododendron maximum*) and mountain doghobble (*Leucothoe fontanesiana*) on more mesic sites and mountain laurel (*Kalmia latifolia*) on drier sites. The sparse and species-poor herbaceous layer includes slow-growing evergreens such as largeflower heartleaf (*Hexastylis shuttleworthii*), skunkweed (*Galax urceolata*), and partridge berry (*Mitchella repens*) as well as semi-evergreen species such as foamflower (*Tiarella cordifolia*) and Robin's plantain (*Erigeron pulchellus*). Three common ferns, Christmas fern (*Polystichum acrostichoides*), New York fern (*Thelypteris noveboracensis*), and hayscented fern (*Dennstaedtia punctilobula*) form dense mats under an open canopy. Rare plants include Oconee bells (*Shortia galacifolia*), Fraser's sedge (*Cymophyllus fraseri*), and Appalachian twayblade (*Listera smallii*).

Asian connection. A surprisingly large number of plants (as well as fungi, insects, and freshwater fish) of eastern North America have their closest relatives in eastern Asia. For example, 65 genera of seed plants occur in both eastern North America and eastern Asia and nowhere else. More genera with disjunct relatives in Asia occur in southern Appalachian cove forests than in any other forest type in eastern North America. Examples include trees such as *Liriodendron* (tulip tree) and *Halesia* (Carolina silverbell), shrubs such as *Hamamelis* (witch hazel) and *Lindera* (spicebush), vines such as *Decumaria* (climbing hydrangea) and *Parthenocissus* (Virginia creeper), and numerous herbs, including *Panax* (ginseng), *Podophyllum* (mayapple), and *Shortia* (Oconee bells). Typically, a genus is represented by closely related but different species on each continent. For example, the genus *Liriodendron* is represented by *L. tulipifera* in eastern North America and *L. chinense* in eastern Asia. In rare instances, the same species is native to both eastern North America and eastern Asia (e.g., sensitive fern, *Onoclea sensibilis*).

What accounts for the close floristic affinity between eastern Asia and eastern North America? One important piece of the puzzle is that millions of years ago, plant migration across continents was possible because land bridges once joined North America, eastern Asia, and northern Europe. In addition, a warm climate fostered the development of a north temperate flora that was once more or less continuously distributed across the northern hemisphere. As extreme climatic cooling occurred several million years ago, the forest became highly fragmented. While some genera managed to persist in Europe (such as *Hepatica*) and in western North America (such as *Cornus* and *Trillium*), the southern Appalachians and mountains at comparable latitudes in eastern Asia, with their warm, moist climates and diverse topographies, became primary refugia for many of these north temperate forest plants. Thus, most genera currently restricted to eastern North America and eastern Asia were much more widely distributed in the past than in the present.

Seasonal Aspects

Spring flowering trees include Fraser magnolia, Carolina silverbell (*Halesia tetraptera*), and horse sugar (*Symplocos tinctoria*). The pleasantly fruity odor and large creamy white flowers of Fraser magnolia attract beetles, its primary pollinator. The showy white nodding flowers of Carolina silverbell develop into four-winged pod-like fruits in summer. Horse sugar produces cream-colored to yellow flowers in dense clusters at the tips of mostly leafless stems in early spring. Sweet birch, whose name reflects the strong wintergreen odor of its leaves and twigs (when crushed or broken), produces slender, drooping male catkins near the tips of twigs that release enormous amounts of wind-dispersed pollen in early spring. Much like poison ivy, climbing hydrangea (*Decumaria barbara*), a semi-evergreen vine, climbs trees via numerous aerial rootlets arising from its stems. Look for climbing hydrangea's creamy white flowers in dense terminal clusters in late spring.

Mountain laurel, rosebay, and mountain doghobble are thicket-forming shrubs with thick evergreen leaves and showy flowers. Mountain laurel's white to pinkish bowl-shaped flowers in dense showy clusters are a spectacular sight in spring. Dense, drooping clusters of white urn-shaped flowers on the leafy stems of mountain doghobble fill the spring air with a pleasantly sweet or strongly musky odor. Rosebay's white to pale pink flowers in dense clusters brighten the forest understory in summer, as do the pink warty fruits and orange to scarlet seeds of strawberry bush (*Euonymus americanus*) in autumn.

Spring-flowering woodland herbs include Robin's plantain, halberdleaf yellow violet (*Viola hastata*), Oconee bells, Jack-in-the-pulpit (*Arisaema triphyllum*), and partridge berry. The conspicuous daisy-like flower heads of Robin's plantain, a common trailside plant, rise above a basal rosette of spoon-shaped leaves. Halberdleaf yellow violet produces one to several bright yellow flowers on slender stalks just above its arrowhead-shaped basal leaves. Oconee bells, a well-known but rare clump-forming evergreen with shiny circular leaves produces solitary white nodding flowers on short leafless stalks. Jack-in-the-pulpit's unusual "flower" consists of a large green or purple-striped spathe within which tiny male or female flowers (rarely both) occur at the base of a columnar spadix. The female flowers mature into dense clusters of bright red berries in autumn. Partridge berry produces paired white trumpet-shaped flowers in spring that develop into round red berries that persist through winter.

Distribution

Acidic cove forest is widespread at low to moderate elevations in the mountains and upper piedmont.

Dynamics

Canopy openings of varying size and frequency play an important role in forest regeneration. Shade-intolerant trees such as tulip tree, sweet birch, and yellow birch depend on openings in the forest to get established, grow, and eventually reach the canopy, whereas shade-tolerant species such as Canada hemlock and

Fraser magnolia grow slowly while persisting under a shaded canopy. Natural gaps (openings) in cove forests are usually caused by high winds toppling tall trees (windthrows). The lower parts of forests in narrow, steep gorges are also susceptible to floods. Moist conditions provide protection from most fires, benefiting thin-barked fire-sensitive species such as sweet birch, yellow birch, American beech, and Canada hemlock.

Conservation Aspects

IMPACT OF RHODODENDRON THICKETS

Rosebay (*Rhododendron maximum*) is an evergreen shrub or small tree that forms dense thickets in acidic cove forest. The almost impenetrable tangled mazes of branches and twisted trunks are called "laurel hells" by southern highlanders. Historically a riparian species, rosebay moved upslope and greatly increased its coverage following heavy logging, the chestnut blight, and fire suppression in the twentieth century. Rosebay thickets alter the environment by creating deep shade, reducing availability of water and soil nutrients, forming a thick leaf litter layer, and increasing soil acidity. Collectively, these changes inhibit the growth of herbaceous plants and other shrubs and limit tree regeneration. Because rosebay thrives on disturbance and inhibits the growth of other plants, it has become an ecologically dominant species. Without major change, rosebay thickets may persist indefinitely, since established plants are potentially long-lived (100 years or more) and self-replacing (by vegetative reproduction and by seed). As adult trees within rhododendron thickets die and aren't replaced, the forest canopy becomes patchier and less diverse. To counter this successional trend, some land managers have begun using prescribed burns to reduce the area covered by rosebay thickets.

HEMLOCK LOSS

Canada hemlock can reach heights greater than 100 ft. and live more than 400 years, yet an insect the size of a pinhead can kill a mature hemlock tree in just a few years. Accidentally introduced from Asia on nursery stock of Asian hemlocks, hemlock woolly adelgids weaken and eventually kill our native hemlocks by inserting their piercing mouthparts into the base of needles and sucking nutrients, eventually starving the tree to death. Adelgid-infested trees can be recognized by the appearance of tiny "cotton balls" at the base of needles as well as a thinning crown due to needle loss.

The hemlock woolly adelgid was first detected in eastern North America in Richmond, Virginia, in 1951. With no natural enemies and an abundant food source to exploit, its population exploded. Easily dispersed by wind, migratory birds, and mammals (including humans), it has now spread from Virginia north to Maine and south to Georgia. The rate of infestation has increased rapidly over the last decade and without adequate control threatens the survival of our two native hemlocks, Canada hemlock and Carolina hemlock (*Tsuga caroliniana*) throughout their respective ranges. Widespread reduction or elimination of hemlocks could have an ecological impact similar in magnitude to that of the loss of American chestnut as a dominant canopy tree in the 1930s.

Prior to the adelgid infestation, Canada hemlock was an important component of old-growth forests in eastern North America. The best examples occurred in Great Smoky Mountains National Park where Canada hemlock was a common species in about 8,500 acres of old-growth forest. Many of these acres were never logged and hemlock trees 300–600 years old and up to 170 ft. tall could be found. To put this in a historical perspective, a 400-year-old hemlock virtually spanned the entire period of European settlement of the region.

Hemlocks provide numerous benefits, including cover for wildlife such as grouse, wild turkeys, rabbits, and deer, as well as homes for innumerable insects and other invertebrates. Along streams, dense hemlock foliage provides deep shade that helps maintain cool stream temperatures critical to the survival of trout and other cold-water organisms. Sites disturbed by hemlock loss are vulnerable to exotic plant invasions by species such as Chinese privet (*Ligustrum sinense*), multiflora rose (*Rosa multiflora*), and Japanese stiltgrass (*Microstegium vimineum*). The opening of the canopy also provides an opportunity for rosebay thickets to expand, which can in turn inhibit tree regeneration as described above.

Adelgid-infested hemlocks on public lands can be treated with foliar applications of insecticidal soaps or by systemic insecticides near visitor centers and campgrounds, but such treatments are generally not practical or economically viable in large forest stands. A potential remedy for infested forests is the use of biocontrol methods whereby natural enemies of the hemlock woolly adelgid are introduced into infested hemlock stands. Entomologists are currently releasing predatory beetles from Asia that feed exclusively on hemlock woolly adelgids. So far, these biocontrol agents have had little success reducing hemlock mortality.

SUGGESTED READING

Koch, F. H., H. M. Cheshire, and H. A. Devine. 2006. Landscape-Scale Prediction of Hemlock Woolly Adelgid, *Adelges tsugae* (Homoptera: Adelgidae), Infestation in the Southern Appalachian Mountains. *Environmental Entomology*: 35:1313–23.

Lei, T. T., S. W. Semones, J. F. Walker, B. D. Clinton, and E. T. Nilsen. 2002. Effects of *Rhododendron maximum* Thickets on Tree Seed Dispersal, Seedling Morphology and Survivorship. *International Journal of Plant Sciences* 163:991–1000.

Turner, M. G., S. M. Pearson, P. Bolstad, and D. N. Wear. 2003. Effects of Land-Cover Change on Spatial Patterns of Forest Communities in the Southern Appalachian Mountains (USA). *Landscape Ecology* 18:449–64.

ACIDIC COVE FOREST: CHARACTERISTIC PLANTS

Trees

ABUNDANT SPECIES		
Acer rubrum	Red maple	p. 222
Betula lenta	Sweet birch, Cherry birch	p. 227
Liriodendron tulipifera	Tulip tree, Yellow poplar	pp. 242–43
Tsuga canadensis	Canada hemlock, Eastern hemlock	pp. 264–65
OCCASIONAL TO LOCALLY ABUNDANT SPECIES		
Betula alleghaniensis	Yellow birch	pp. 226–27
Fagus grandifolia	American beech	pp. 237–38

Halesia tetraptera	Carolina silverbell	p. 239
Ilex opaca	American holly	pp. 239–40
Magnolia acuminata	Cucumber magnolia	pp. 243–44
Magnolia fraseri	Fraser magnolia	pp. 244–45
Pinus strobus	Eastern white pine	p. 251
Quercus rubra	Northern red oak	pp. 259–60

Shrubs and Woody Vines

ABUNDANT SPECIES

Kalmia latifolia	Mountain laurel	pp. 291–92
Leucothoe fontanesiana	Mountain doghobble	p. 292
Rhododendron maximum	Rosebay	p. 302–3

OCCASIONAL TO LOCALLY ABUNDANT SPECIES

Decumaria barbara	Climbing hydrangea	p. 281
Euonymus americanus	Strawberry bush, Hearts-a-bustin'	pp. 283–84
Rhododendron catawbiense	Catawba rhododendron	pp. 301–2
Viburnum acerifolium	Mapleleaf viburnum	pp. 319–20

Herbs

ABUNDANT SPECIES

Galax urceolata	Galax, Skunkweed	pp. 374–75
Mitchella repens	Partridge berry	p. 406
Polystichum acrostichoides	Christmas fern	p. 429
Thelypteris noveboracensis	New York fern	pp. 451–52
Viola hastata	Halberdleaf yellow violet	pp. 466–67

OCCASIONAL TO LOCALLY ABUNDANT SPECIES

Arisaema triphyllum	Jack-in-the-pulpit	p. 335
Epigaea repens	Trailing arbutus	pp. 368–69
Erigeron pulchellus	Robin's plantain	p. 369
Hexastylis shuttleworthii	Large flower heartleaf, Wild ginger	p. 387
Medeola virginiana	Indian cucumber root	pp. 402–3

Invasive Exotic Plants

Ligustrum sinense	Chinese privet	pp. 292–93

Rare Plants

Cymophyllus fraserianus	Fraser's sedge	p. 357
†*Listera smallii*	Appalachian twayblade	
†*Lysimachia fraseri*	Fraser's loosestrife	
Shortia galacifolia	Oconee bells	p. 438

† = *plant not included in the species profiles (Part IV)*

SPRAY CLIFF

Distinguishing Features

The spray cliff community is readily identified by the presence of a waterfall.

Introduction

Fast-flowing water splashing over rocks as it cascades down a cliff enhances the appeal of this community. Spray cliffs occur on vertical to gently sloping rock faces that are constantly wet from the spray of waterfalls, sometimes supplemented by seepage water. The numerous ledges, crevices, and other protected niches near waterfalls provide an unusually equable environment as the substrate is always wet or at least moist and temperatures are moderated by spray water and shelter from the sun and wind. As such, spray cliffs are generally cooler in summer and warmer in winter than the surrounding environment. The moist microclimate, combined with relatively mild temperatures, contributes to the rich diversity of plants found here, including a number of endemics and rare disjuncts. Take care when exploring this community as steep terrain and slippery rocks create a perilous environment.

Vegetation

A unique assemblage of algae, bryophytes (mosses and liverworts), ferns, and flowering plants characterize the continuously moist vegetation. Bryophytes are particularly abundant because of their unusual ability to grow on bare rock substrates. Examples include various species of sphagnum moss along with liverworts in the genus *Marchantia* that form dense, prostrate mats. Many of the mosses and liverworts, and some ferns, are narrow endemics, restricted to this community type; others are tropical disjuncts, living far north of their main range. One of the more interesting tropical disjuncts is the Appalachian shoestring fern (*Vittaria appalachiana*)—it grows in highly sheltered habitats (such as cavities and fissures) in moist gorges and spray cliffs where its asexual spores (gemmae) germinate and establish tiny plantlets called gametophytes that never develop into sporophytes (the stage in the fern life cycle we normally think of as a fern). How did this normally tropical fern get here? One possible scenario is that in the distant past (between 65 and 35 million years ago), the climate was much warmer than in the present and tropical plants such as the shoestring fern flourished over much of the eastern United States. As the climate cooled (culminating in the ice ages), tropical species were gradually replaced by more cold-tolerant species. The sporophytes of shoestring fern couldn't tolerate the change in climate and disappeared, but the gametophytes persist to this day as relicts in highly specialized habitats where temperatures never get too cold or too hot.

Sparse soil limits the presence of vascular plants. A notable exception is riverweed (*Podostemum ceratophyllum*), a submersed aquatic vascular plant that grows on bare rock in river rapids and waterfalls where it's held in place by small disk-like holdfasts. A few stunted stems of shrubs such as rosebay (*Rhododendron maximum*) and mountain laurel (*Kalmia latifolia*) sometimes occur in rock crevices where sufficient soil has accumulated. Trees are rare, but adjoining forests often provide shade, thereby contributing to the relatively cool summer temperatures.

Seasonal Aspects

Moderate temperatures and a continuously moist substrate enable most plants to have a long growing season. In spring, the numerous small blue-violet flowers of Appalachian bluet (*Houstonia serpyllifolia*) appearing above a mat of tiny green leaves provide an attractive mosaic. The yellow center of each flower helps guide potential pollinators (small bees and flies) to the nectar within. From late spring through early summer, mountain meadowrue (*Thalictrum clavatum*) produces delicate white flowers on slender stalks that develop into curved (scimitar-shaped) fruits. Bumblebees visit the bright yellow flowers of sundrops (*Oenothera fruticosa*) from spring through summer. Cave alumroot (*Heuchera parviflora*) grows in deeply shaded cliffs and ledges where most other flowering plants can't grow. It has large round basal leaves and produces numerous tiny white flowers in branched racemes in summer. One of the most striking plants of the spray cliff community is orange jewelweed (*Impatiens capensis*), a tall annual with smooth, branching stems and orange-yellow trumpet-shaped flowers. Both bees and hummingbirds visit the nectar-rich flowers from late spring through early fall.

Distribution

Scattered in the mountains and rare in the upper piedmont, spray cliffs are best developed on the steep gorge walls of the Southern Blue Ridge Escarpment of southwestern North Carolina, northwestern South Carolina, and northeastern Georgia. Spray cliffs also occur west of the escarpment in eastern Tennessee and are loosely scattered in Virginia.

Dynamics

Periodic flooding, rock falls, and erosion can dislodge vegetation mats. The openings that result provide an opportunity for colonizing species to get established. In the absence of disturbance, species diversity decreases when dominant species exclude less competitive ones.

> *Southern Blue Ridge Escarpment.* An unusually high concentration of species, particularly mosses and liverworts, occur in the Southern Blue Ridge Escarpment near where the borders of North Carolina, South Carolina, and Georgia come together. Along the escarpment, there is an abrupt drop in elevation from the crest of the Blue Ridge at about 4,000 ft. to the piedmont nearly 3,000 ft. below. As prevailing moist air masses moving northward from the Gulf of Mexico encounter the steep face of the escarpment, the rising air cools and drops up to 100 in. of rain per year, making this the wettest spot in eastern North America. Over time, the rain-swollen Eastatoee, Toxaway, Horsepasture, Thompson, and Whitewater rivers have carved out deep, narrow gorges punctuated by high waterfalls in their steep descent from the escarpment to the piedmont. Within these 5 river gorges (collectively known as the Jocassee Gorges), and at the base of waterfalls, there is a remarkably high concentration of bryophytes, including more than 75 endemic and disjunct species. Along a 4-mile stretch of the Whitewater River gorge alone, more than 285 species of mosses have been identified. This represents nearly one-fourth of the total number of mosses known from the United States and Canada. One of the most famous plants in the Blue Ridge Escarpment is Oconee Bells (*Shortia galacifolia*), a rare endemic that was first discovered by the famous French botanist André Michaux in 1787 and later characterized by nineteenth-century Harvard botanist Asa Gray as "perhaps the most interesting plant in North America."

Conservation Aspects

Many spray cliffs occur in remote mountain areas that have escaped direct disturbance. Others have been impacted by logging or development on adjacent lands or by large numbers of visitors trampling the vegetation. High species diversity coupled with a large number of endemic, disjunct, and rare species make this an important community to preserve.

SUGGESTED READING

Anderson, L. E., and R. H. Zander. 1973. The Mosses of the Southern Blue Ridge Province and their Phytogeographic Relationships. *Journal of the Elisha Mitchell Scientific Society* 89:15–60.

Billings, W. D., and L. E. Anderson. 1966. Some Microclimatic Characteristics of Habitats of Endemic and Disjunct Bryophytes in the Southern Blue Ridge. *The Bryologist* 69:76–95.

Zartman, C. E., and J. D. Pittillo. 1998. Spray Cliff Communities of the Chattooga Basin. *Castanea* 63:217–40.

SPRAY CLIFF: CHARACTERISTIC PLANTS

Shrubs

OCCASIONAL TO LOCALLY ABUNDANT SPECIES

Kalmia latifolia	Mountain laurel	pp. 291–92
Rhododendron maximum	Rosebay	pp. 302–3
Xanthorhiza simplicissima	Yellowroot	pp. 322–23

Herbs

OCCASIONAL TO LOCALLY ABUNDANT SPECIES

Adiantum pedatum	Maidenhair fern	p. 327
Asplenium montanum	Mountain spleenwort	p. 339
Asplenium rhizophyllum	Walking fern	pp. 339–40
†*Asplenium trichomanes*	Maidenhair spleenwort	
Galax urceolata	Galax, skunkweed	pp. 374–75
Heuchera parviflora	Cave alumroot	p. 385
Houstonia serpyllifolia	Appalachian bluet	pp. 387–88
Impatiens capensis	Orange jewelweed	pp. 390–91
Marchantia species	Liverwort	p. 402
Micranthes petiolaris	Cliff saxifrage	p. 403
Oenothera fruticosa	Sundrops	pp. 410–11
Oxalis montana	Mountain wood sorrel	p. 414
Podostemum ceratophyllum	Riverweed	p. 427
†*Polypodium virginianum*	Common rockcap fern	
Sphagnum species	Sphagnum	p. 445
Thalictrum clavatum	Mountain meadowrue	p. 450

Rare Plants

†*Boykinia aconitifolia*	Brook saxifrage	
Cymophyllus fraserianus	Fraser's sedge	p. 357
†*Huperzia porophila*	Rock clubmoss	
†*Vittaria appalachiana*	Appalachian shoestring fern	

† = *plant not included in the species profiles (Part IV)*

ROCKY STREAMSIDE

Distinguishing Features

The rocky streamside community occurs along rivers and streams that are too rocky, wet, or frequently flooded for trees to reach maturity.

Introduction

Mountain and piedmont rivers have enough energy to erode the landscape, forming narrow valleys with small floodplains and fairly straight channels. After heavy rains, the rivers swell and overflow their banks and the erosive force of fast-moving water periodically washes away plants and transports and deposits large numbers of cobbles, stones, and even boulders downstream. One of our most dynamic (changeable) communities, rocky streamsides occur along large rivers and streams that are too rocky, wet, or severely flooded to harbor canopy trees. The substrate varies from rock outcrops to piled cobbles and boulders to gravel bars, with soils consisting of fine to course alluvial materials deposited among the rocks. Flooding can occur at any time of year, resulting in a shifting substrate, waterlogged soils, and total submergence of the vegetation. The vegetation is highly variable, due to differences in stream size, differing substrates, and variations in the frequency and intensity of flooding. Lower areas along river margins are generally more frequently flooded, have less stable substrates, and are sparsely vegetated. In the more stable (elevated) zones along river margins, flooding occurs less frequently and herbaceous and woody plants are more abundant and diverse.

Vegetation

The herbaceous plants found on gravelly sandbars include bluets (*Houstonia caerulea* and *H. serpyllifolia*), pink smartweed (*Polygonum pensylvanicum*), and mountain dandelion (*Krigia montana*). On high-energy stretches of rivers where cobbles and boulders accumulate, a dominant species is twisted sedge (*Carex torta*), a tenaciously rooted perennial with a densely clumped growth form that is particularly well adapted to fast-water environments. Riverweed (*Podostemum ceratophyllum*) is a highly unusual flowering plant that grows submerged in the swift current of rocky streams and rapids, strongly attached to rocks by unique holdfasts. Large slabs of bedrock along rivers are mostly bare except for cracks and fissures where pockets of soil accumulate. On slightly elevated (more stable) shorelines grow a number of species typically associated with prairie grasslands. These "scour prairies" are densely vegetated with grasses and forbs, including prairie species such as Indiangrass (*Sorghastrum nutans*), little bluestem (*Schizachyrium scoparium*), and obedient plant (*Physostegia virginiana*).

Cinnamon fern (*Osmunda cinnamomea*) and royal fern (*O. regalis*) are common ferns with upright compound leaves and separate fertile and sterile fronds. Clump-forming shrubs include tag alder (*Alnus serrulata*), black willow (*Salix nigra*), Virginia willow (*Itea virginica*), mountain doghobble (*Leucothoe fontanesiana*), and yellowroot (*Xanthorhiza simplicissima*). Rhododendrons that grow along rocky streamsides include evergreen species such as rosebay (*Rhododendron maximum*) and deciduous species such as sweet azalea (*R. arborescens*), wild azalea (*R. periclymenoides*), and swamp azalea (*R. viscosum*). Saplings of trees such as sycamore (*Platanus occidentalis*) and river birch (*Betula nigra*) sometimes occur, but rarely reach maturity, due to frequent or prolonged flooding.

Seasonal Aspects

Abundant sunlight and moisture create an environment in which plants flower from early spring through late autumn. Wild azalea produces striking clusters of pleasantly fragrant white to pinkish funnel-shaped flowers on leafless plants in early spring. Equally spectacular (and even more fragrant) are the white to pinkish tubular flowers of sweet azalea and swamp azalea from late spring to early summer. Yellow root, a low-growing shrub with highly divided leaves, produces drooping clusters of small brownish purple to yellowish green flowers. Virginia willow's long, narrow clusters of white flowers are a colorful sight in late spring. Silky dogwood (*Cornus amomum*), a tall multistemmed shrub with hairy dark red twigs, produces flat-topped clusters of small white flowers that develop into bluish fruits (with whitish blotches) in late summer and fall. Common elderberry (*Sambucus canadensis*) also has white flowers in flat-topped clusters that form shiny black to purple fruits in summer that are quickly stripped by birds. Black willow's female catkins produce enormous numbers of small seeds with tufts of white hairs that float in the wind. Its short-lived seeds lose viability within just a few days if they don't land in a favorable site for germination.

Pollinators actively visit many of the showier herbaceous plants of summer and fall. Butterflies, bees, and other insects frequently visit the flat-topped flower heads on the tall stems of Joe Pye weed (*Eutrochium fistulosum*) and New York ironweed (*Vernonia noveboracensis*). Both hummingbirds and butterflies visit the brilliant red flowers of cardinal flower (*Lobelia cardinalis*), while both bees and hummingbirds pollinate the nectar-rich flowers of jewelweed (*Impatiens capensis* and *I. pallida*). Bumblebees squeeze into the tubular flowers of white turtlehead (*Chelone glabra*) and work the blue flowers of tall bellflower (*Campanulastrum americanum*) and the pink tubular flowers of obedient plant. On moist sand near streams, butterflies frequently cluster in groups exhibiting a behavior called puddling, in which they take up water (and dissolved minerals such as sodium) through their coiled proboscises (mouth parts).

> *Rivers as dispersal corridors.* Because plants are rooted in place, their ability to migrate into new areas or to recolonize previously occupied sites depends largely on fruit and seed dispersal. Rivers and river margins can serve as corridors for dispersal by water, wind, and animals. Even small rivers may transport enormous numbers of seeds. Water-dispersed seeds often have buoyancy-enhancing traits such as corky or fibrous tissues that trap air, impermeable seed coats, or in the case of tiny seeds, high surface to volume ratios. Plants are also dislodged and transported downstream by floods. Seeds dispersed by wind are either very small (such as the dust-sized seeds of orchids) or have structures that catch the wind, thereby reducing their rate of fall. River corridor plants such as willows and sycamores have fuzzy or woolly seeds that float on a breeze and can be carried long distances, while the winged (and heavier) seeds of ash and maple flutter as they fall and are dispersed shorter distances. Other plants rely on animals to disperse their seeds along river corridors. Some seeds have hooks, barbs, or bristles that stick to the fur or feathers of a passing animal. Seeds can also be dispersed after getting stuck to an animal's muddy foot or beak. Many plants have their seeds carried internally by animals. Water birds such as mallards and teal feed on plants and pass intact seeds through their guts. Other birds feed on fleshy fruits, digest the pulp, and disperse the seeds in their droppings. Fish aren't important seed dispersers, at least not in North America. By using river corridors as flyways, birds disperse seeds both up and down streams. Seeds transported by wind are also dispersed in various directions, enabling species to colonize sites both up and downstream. How seeds of water-dispersed plants colonize upstream sites remains a mystery.

Distribution

The rocky streamside community is common in the mountains (and less so in the piedmont) along major rivers and their tributaries.

Dynamics

The frequency and intensity of flooding, causing the scouring and reworking of the substrate, has a major influence on the vegetation. In frequently disturbed sites, rocky streamside habitats tend to be sparsely vegetated, whereas moderate to dense shrub thickets often occur on less disturbed sites. The fibrous roots and rhizomes of twisted sedge trap soil particles along the margins of fast-moving, rocky streams. As this material builds up and stabilizes the substrate, other species colonize the area.

Conservation Aspects

Conservation of riverside habitats requires attention to the surrounding watershed, since countless activities far removed from the river corridor affect its biological integrity. Many streamside habitats have been dramatically altered or eliminated by the construction of power-generating and flood control dams. Other changes in hydrology and increased sedimentation resulting from logging, uncontrolled development, and other factors affect habitat quality and species composition along river margins. Rocky streamside habitats are vulnerable to invasive exotic plants, due to the frequent exposure of bare soil following flood scouring.

SUGGESTED READING

Allan, J. D. 2004. *Stream Ecology: Structure and Function of Running Waters*. New York: Springer.

Barrat-Segretain, M. H. 1996. Strategies of Reproduction, Dispersion and Competition in River Plants: A Review. *Vegetatio* 123:13–37.

Tobe, J. D., J. E. Fairey III, and L. L. Gaddy. 1992. Vascular Flora of the Chauga River Gorge, Oconee County, South Carolina. *Castanea* 57:77–109.

ROCKY STREAMSIDE: CHARACTERISTIC PLANTS

Trees

Betula nigra	River birch	p. 228
Platanus occidentalis	Sycamore	p. 253

Shrubs

ABUNDANT SPECIES

Alnus serrulata	Tag alder	pp. 269–70
Arundinaria gigantea	Giant cane	pp. 273–74
Cephalanthus occidentalis	Buttonbush	p. 278
Cornus amomum	Silky dogwood	p. 280
Itea virginica	Virginia willow	pp. 289–90
Salix nigra	Black willow	pp. 311–12
Sambucus canadensis	Common elderberry	pp. 312–13
Xanthorhiza simplicissima	Yellowroot	pp. 322–23

OCCASIONAL TO LOCALLY ABUNDANT SPECIES

Calycanthus floridus	Sweet shrub	pp. 275–76
Clethra acuminata	Mountain sweet pepperbush	pp. 278–79
Kalmia latifolia	Mountain laurel	pp. 291–92
Leucothoe fontanesiana	Mountain doghobble	p. 292

Rhododendron arborescens	Sweet azalea	p. 300
Rhododendron maximum	Rosebay	pp. 302–3
Rhododendron periclymenoides	Wild azalea, Pinxterflower	p. 304
Rhododendron viscosum	Swamp azalea, Clammy azalea	p. 305

Herbs

ABUNDANT SPECIES

Carex torta	Twisted sedge	pp. 344–45
Houstonia serpyllifolia	Appalachian bluet	pp. 387–88
Impatiens capensis	Orange jewelweed	pp. 390–91
Justicia americana	American water willow	pp. 393–94

OCCASIONAL TO LOCALLY ABUNDANT SPECIES

Campanulastrum americanum	Tall bellflower	p. 343
Chelone glabra	White turtlehead	pp. 347–48
Eutrochium fistulosum	Joe Pye weed	p. 373
Impatiens pallida	Yellow jewelweed	pp. 391–92
Krigia montana	Mountain dandelion	
Lobelia cardinalis	Cardinal flower	p. 399
Osmunda cinnamomea	Cinnamon fern	pp. 412–13
†*Osmunda regalis*	Royal fern	
†*Physostegia virginiana*	Obedient plant	
Podostemum ceratophyllum	Riverweed	p. 427
†*Polygonum pensylvanicum*	Pink smartweed	
Rudbeckia laciniata	Cutleaf coneflower	pp. 433–34
Schizachyrium scoparium	Little bluestem	pp. 436–37
Sorghastrum nutans	Indiangrass	p. 444
Vernonia noveboracensis	New York ironweed	p. 465

Invasive Exotic Plants

Microstegium vimineum	Japanese stiltgrass	pp. 403–4
†*Sorghum halepense*	Johnsongrass	

† = *plant not included in the species profiles (Part IV)*

MOUNTAIN BOG

Distinguishing Features

Mountain bogs are small, isolated wetlands with a wide range of herb-, shrub-, and tree-dominated areas and significant amounts of peat moss (sphagnum).

Introduction

Mountain bogs are isolated wetlands surrounded by terrestrial communities. Bogs are inherently rare because flat or gently sloping wet sites are scarce in the southern Appalachians. Drainage, changes in grazing or mowing, and development have further reduced the number and extent of mountain bogs. Despite their small size and rarity, bogs have high species diversity and harbor a large number of rare and endangered species, including swamp pink (*Helonias bullata*), Gray's lily (*Lilium grayi*), and monkey face orchid (*Platanthera integrilabia*).

Vegetation

Species composition varies from bog to bog, reflecting differences in elevation, topography, hydrology, underlying rock, and recent land-use history. Three distinct types of bog are described: southern Appalachian bog, the swamp forest–bog complex, and cataract bogs. Bogs are technically known as fens, though they are commonly called bogs, a term that is retained here.

SOUTHERN APPALACHIAN BOG

These bogs occur on relatively flat areas along valley bottomlands as well as on gentle slopes along the margins of mountain streams. Rainwater and a high water table keep bottomland sites moist, whereas gentle slopes receive moisture from seepage flow. Soils are generally acidic and nutrient-poor, but rich in organic matter. The vegetation consists of a mosaic of low-growing shrub thickets and herb-dominated areas with scattered trees. Common trees include red maple (*Acer rubrum*), eastern white pine (*Pinus strobus*), and pitch pine (*Pinus rigida*) along with shrubs such as winterberry (*Ilex verticillata*), wild raisin (*Viburnum cassinoides*), cranberry (*Vaccinium macrocarpon*), and swamp azalea (*Rhododendron viscosum*). The herbaceous layer is relatively sparse under shrub thickets but is dense and species-rich in more open areas. Sedges (*Carex* and *Rhynchospora* spp.) are often abundant, along with thick mats of peat moss (*Sphagnum* spp.), kidneyleaf grass of parnassus (*Parnassia asarifolia*), scattered ferns, and showy orchids. Introduced pasture species such as Timothy grass (*Phleum pratense*), velvet grass (*Holcus lanatus*), and fescue (*Festuca arundinacea*) also commonly occur in southern Appalachian bogs.

SWAMP FOREST–BOG COMPLEX

This forested wetland community is associated with small streams that have level or gently sloping areas whose soils are often water-saturated and strongly acidic. The vegetation is characterized by a broken canopy with an open to dense shrub layer and small boggy openings less than an acre in size. Sites vary in the relative amount of closed forest, shrub thickets, and boggy openings they contain. At lower elevations, red maple, tulip tree (*Liriodendron tulipifera*), and black gum (*Nyssa sylvatica*) are dominant, while on poorly drained sites at higher elevations, red spruce (*Picea rubens*) can dominate. Once common at higher elevations, Canada hemlock (*Tsuga canadensis*) is increasingly rare due to an infestation of hemlock woolly adelgid. The shallow roots of red maple and other canopy trees result in frequent tree-falls, which create openings (gaps in the canopy) that provide habitat for species that require high light levels.

Dominant shrubs include rosebay (*Rhododendron maximum*) and mountain laurel (*Kalmia latifolia*) as well as more typical wetland species such as tag alder (*Alnus serrulata*) and winterberry. Both red and black chokeberry (*Aronia arbutifolia*, *A. melanocarpa*) also occur. Boggy openings in small depressions typically have dense mats of peat moss along with herbaceous plants such as sedges, false hellebore (*Veratrum viride*), arrowhead (*Sagittaria latifolia*), and cinnamon fern (*Osmunda cinnamomea*). Rare species include swamp pink and marsh marigold (*Caltha palustris*).

In Virginia and northern North Carolina, this community is called a "skunk cabbage bog" because of abundant skunk cabbage (*Symplocarpus foetidus*), which has large cabbage-like leaves and unpleasantly pungent (to the human nose) winter-blooming flowers.

CATARACT BOG

This rare and unusual community occurs alongside streams that flow over the rock surface of granite domes. Here water slides, rather than falls, over the rock surface, providing a nearly constant source of moisture for small mats of vegetation that form along the water's edge. In this narrow linear community, conditions are ideal for bog plants because light levels are high, moisture is readily available, and the miniature pockets of soil that collect on the smooth rock substrate inhibit succession to a shrub- or tree-dominated vegetation. Be careful when exploring this community as algae growing on the wet rocks make the substrate extremely slippery.

Among the rich array of typical bog plants are insectivorous plants such as pitcher plants (e.g., *Sarracenia purpurea* and *S. jonesii*), roundleaf sundew (*Drosera rotundifolia*), and horned bladderwort (*Utricularia cornuta*). Other notable plants include orchids such as the common grass pink (*Calopogon tuberosus*). Shrubs such as tag alder, witch alder (*Fothergilla major*), and yellowroot (*Xanthorhiza simplicissima*) occur on deeper soils.

When streams dry up due to prolonged drought, margins of vegetation mats curl up. In subsequent storms, entire mats may be washed away and the process of soil accumulation and plant colonization starts anew. Steeper slopes have sparser vegetation because soil pockets are less likely to form and vegetation mats are more frequently carried downslope.

Seasonal Aspects

Spring-flowering species include swamp pink, purple pitcher plant, and swamp azalea. Striking clusters of pink flowers with conspicuous blue anthers at the tips of largely leafless stalks distinguish swamp pink, a federally listed species. The purple-streaked leaves of purple pitcher plant (*Sarracenia purpurea*) are modified into keeled, pitcher-shaped containers that attract and capture insects. Its solitary, purple, nodding flowers (on leafless stalks well above the leaves) depend on bumblebees for pollination while insects captured in the leaves provide an important source of nutrients for the plant. Swamp azalea's long, slender white to pinkish tubular flowers in dense clusters bloom from late spring through early summer. The flowers are particularly fragrant in the evening, when its primary pollinators (moths) are most active.

Other summer-blooming plants include Gray's lily, a rare species whose dark red, bell-shaped flowers are pollinated by hummingbirds (fritillary butterflies also visit the flowers for nectar but apparently aren't effective pollinators of this plant). Roundleaf sundew has small white flowers on short upright stalks that are pollinated by mosquitoes, gnats, and midges. An insectivorous plant, its small round prostrate leaves are covered by reddish sticky hairs that capture and digest insects. False hellebore, a plant highly toxic to humans (if ingested), has stout leafy stems with dense clusters of yellow-green flowers. Arrowhead derives its name from its large arrowhead-shaped basal leaves; the 3-petalled white flowers on the lower portion of the upright stalk are usually female, the upper ones male.

Three of the showier plants of late summer and fall are kidneyleaf grass of parnassus, nodding ladies' tresses (*Spiranthes cernua*), and soapwort gentian (*Gentiana saponaria*). Kidneyleaf grass of parnassus has kidney-shaped basal leaves and showy white flowers with conspicuous green veins that radiate from the center of the flower, guiding insect pollinators to the nectar. Nodding ladies' tresses is an orchid whose small, white, spirally arranged flowers on an upright stalk usually bloom through the first heavy frost. The bluish purple tubular flowers of soapwort gentian also persist well into fall—look for bumblebees pushing their way into the closed flowers to access nectar.

Winterberry produces dense clusters of bright red berries in autumn that persist on the plant well into winter. When other foods are scarce, birds and small mammals eat the fruits and disperse the seeds. Similarly, the red berries of cranberry and wintergreen (*Gaultheria procumbens*) ripen in fall but persist on the plant into winter. The large basal leaves of skunk cabbage emerge in spring and die back in fall, but its tiny flowers enclosed in a hood-like brownish purple spathe bloom in winter.

Distribution

Bogs are more common in the northern Appalachians than the southern Appalachians, largely because receding glaciers scoured out basins favorable for bog development in the north but not in the south. The swamp forest–bog complex is scattered throughout the Appalachians from Pennsylvania to Georgia, but the Southern Appalachian bog type is largely restricted to Virginia and North Carolina, mostly at mid- to high elevations. Cataract bogs are rare, known only from South Carolina; other locations are likely but have yet to be documented.

Dynamics

Factors responsible for creating and maintaining mountain bogs are poorly understood. Some mountain bogs are of relatively recent origin, but others are known to be at least 10,000–12,000 years old. Beavers, large grazers, and fires play important roles in bog dynamics.

BEAVERS

By building dams and flooding stream and river valleys, beavers create boggy habitats that are subsequently colonized by peat moss and other typical bog plants. Beavers also help keep boggy habitats open by cutting down trees and shrubs. Over time, abandoned beaver ponds typically undergo succession from being herb-dominated communities to shrubby bogs to complex mosaics of forest, shrubland, and herbaceous cover. By the early 1900s, overhunting led to the extinction of beavers in our region, which probably reduced the acreage covered by bogs. Beavers have made a comeback due to a successful reintroduction program. Their effect on mountain bogs has been somewhat mixed: new bogs have been created, but flooding has damaged some previously established bogs that supported rare species.

LARGE GRAZERS

Bison, elk, and other large grazers likely played an important role in keeping bogs and other wetland habitats open (much like the role they played in grassy balds). The grasses, sedges, and other herbaceous plants found in bogs would have attracted large grazers. By also foraging on woody plants, large grazers helped prevent bogs from undergoing succession to shrub thickets or forested landscapes. Following their extinction, domestic animals (such as cows) played a similar ecological role in many bogs.

FIRE

The role of fire in maintaining mountain bogs is unclear. Both lightning-induced fires and the burning of bogs by Native Americans likely occurred, but we don't know how frequently bogs burned. The presence of numerous species whose distributions are centered in fire-maintained coastal plain bogs suggests that fire played a role in maintaining some mountain bogs. In the Blue Ridge Escarpment region and other relatively low-elevation sites, fires probably occurred frequently enough to keep bogs open, but fires were probably less frequent and important in maintaining bogs in the cool, moist air at higher elevations.

> *Biogeography of bogs.* About one-third of the more than 600 species of vascular plants found in "boggy" wetlands of the southern Appalachians are widely distributed in eastern North America, including red maple, tag alder, and swamp rose (*Rosa palustris*). Species distributed primarily in the northeastern United States and adjacent areas in Canada make up another third of the total number of species, including many species at or near the southern limit of their range in Georgia, the Carolinas, and Tennessee. Examples include cranberry, dragon's mouth (*Arethusa bulbosa*), and cotton grass (*Eriophorum virginicum*). A third group of species is comprised mostly of coastal plain species that have disjunct populations in mountain bogs, including Carolina sheeplaurel (*Kalmia carolina*), netted chain fern (*Woodwardia areolata*), and purple pitcher plant. Very few species are restricted (endemic) to southern Appalachian "boggy" wetlands.

Conservation Aspects

Bogs in the southern Appalachians are inherently rare because flat, wet sites are scarce. Habitat degradation and destruction (e.g., drainage, logging, conversion to agriculture, and clearing for resort and residential development) have substantially reduced the number and extent of mountain wetlands. Most remaining bogs are small (less than 5 acres) and have an altered hydrology that threatens their long-term persistence. In the absence of grazing and hay mowing, shrubs and trees are invading many bogs, which, if left unchecked, could eliminate many of the herbaceous species that characterize bog vegetation. Some mountain bogs have persisted for thousands of years, so this recent change from relatively open, boggy habitat to shrub thicket or forest is cause for concern.

The ecology of mountain bogs is poorly understood. Nevertheless, it's clear that slight changes in the surrounding landscape can have major effects. For example, many bogs formerly surrounded by forest now occur adjacent to agricultural fields, pastures, or Christmas tree farms. Since forested slopes release water more slowly and constantly than unforested slopes, bogs adjacent to cultivated land are more likely to dry out. Similarly, the channeling of an adjacent stream can lower the local water table, causing substantial drying and thereby allowing woody plants to invade when an unaltered water table would have prevented their establishment. Once established, shrubs and trees take up huge amounts of water, further drying up bogs and accelerating their succession to shrub thicket or forest. Other threats include changes in water quality due to increased sediment load from soil erosion and soil chemistry altered by nearby agriculture. For example, excess nutrient input causes a decline in peat moss abundance, which subsequently promotes succession to woody plants. Collectors of commercially valuable species such as rare orchids, insectivorous plants, and bog turtles (a threatened species) also degrade bogs.

SUGGESTED READING

Moorhead, K. K., and I. M. Rossell. 1998. Southern Mountain Fens. In M. G. Messina, and W. H. Conner, eds., *Southern Forested Wetlands: Ecology and Management*, 379–403. Boca Raton, Fla.: Lewis Publishers.

Murdock, N. A. 1994. Rare and Endangered Plants and Animals of Southern Appalachian Wetlands. *Water, Air and Soil Pollution* 77:385–405.

Pittillo, J. D. 1994. Vegetation of Three High Elevation Southern Appalachian Bogs and Implications of Their Vegetational History. *Water, Air and Soil Pollution* 77:333–48.

MOUNTAIN BOG: CHARACTERISTIC PLANTS

Trees

OCCASIONAL TO LOCALLY ABUNDANT SPECIES

Acer rubrum	Red maple	p. 222
Betula alleghaniensis	Yellow birch	pp. 226–27
Nyssa sylvatica	Black gum	pp. 245–46
Picea rubens	Red spruce	p. 248
Pinus rigida	Pitch pine	p. 250
Pinus strobus	Eastern white pine	p. 251
Tsuga canadensis	Canada hemlock, Eastern hemlock	pp. 264–65

Shrubs

ABUNDANT SPECIES

Alnus serrulata	Tag alder	pp. 269–70
Ilex verticillata	Winterberry	p. 289
Kalmia latifolia	Mountain laurel	pp. 291–92
Leucothoe fontanesiana	Mountain doghobble	p. 292
Rhododendron maximum	Rosebay	pp. 302–3
†*Rosa palustris*	Swamp rose	
Vaccinium corymbosum	Highbush blueberry	p. 317

OCCASIONAL TO LOCALLY ABUNDANT SPECIES

Aronia melanocarpa	Black chokeberry	p. 272
Menziesia pilosa	Minniebush	pp. 295–96
Rhododendron viscosum	Swamp azalea, Clammy azalea	p. 305
Salix nigra	Black willow	pp. 311–12
†*Salix sericea*	Silky willow	
†*Spiraea tomentosa*	Steeplebush	
†*Toxicodendron vernix*	Poison sumac	
Vaccinium macrocarpon	Cranberry	pp. 317–18
Viburnum cassinoides	Wild raisin	pp. 320–21
Xanthorhiza simplicissima	Yellowroot	pp. 322–23

Herbs

OCCASIONAL TO LOCALLY ABUNDANT SPECIES

Drosera rotundifolia	Roundleaf sundew	pp. 365–66
Eutrochium fistulosum	Joe Pye weed	p. 373
Gaultheria procumbens	Wintergreen	pp. 376–77
Onoclea sensibilis	Sensitive fern	p. 411
Osmunda cinnamomea	Cinnamon fern	pp. 412–13
Osmunda claytoniana	Interrupted fern	pp. 413–14
Phleum pratense	Timothy grass	pp. 421–22
Platanthera ciliaris	Yellow fringed orchid	p. 424
Sagittaria latifolia	Arrowhead, Duck potato	p. 434
Sphagnum species	Sphagnum	p. 445
Spiranthes cernua	Nodding ladies' tresses	pp. 446–47
Veratrum viride	False hellebore	pp. 463–64

Rare Plants

[†]*Caltha palustris*	Marsh marigold	
Helonias bullata	Swamp pink	pp. 383–84
Lilium grayi	Gray's lily	pp. 396–97
Parnassia asarifolia	Kidneyleaf grass of parnassus	pp. 417–18
Platanthera integrilabia	Monkey face orchid	p. 425
[†]*Sarracenia jonesii*	Mountain sweet pitcher plant	
Sarracenia purpurea	Purple pitcher plant	pp. 435–36
Symplocarpus foetidus	Skunk cabbage	p. 448

[†] = *plant not included in the species profiles (Part IV)*

Low-Elevation Dry Communities

CHESTNUT OAK FOREST

Distinguishing Features

Chestnut oak forest differs from all other mountain forest types by the dominance of chestnut oak or scarlet oak.

Introduction

Forests dominated by chestnut oak (*Quercus montana*) can be found in the coastal plain, the piedmont, and the mountains, but ecologists have traditionally limited the chestnut oak forest designation to low- to mid-elevation communities of the mountains and piedmont where American chestnut was the dominant or co-dominant canopy species prior to the chestnut blight in the early twentieth century. Today, American chestnut persists primarily as a shrub from root sprouts, although fallen chestnut logs and old dead stumps can still be seen on the forest floor. Chestnut oak forest typically occurs on dry upper slopes and ridgetops at elevations up to about 4,000 ft. Steep slopes and thin rocky soils result in subxeric conditions that favor slow-growing, drought-tolerant species such as chestnut oak and scarlet oak (*Q. coccinea*). An abundance of heath shrubs is a good indicator of this community's acidic, nutrient-poor soils.

Vegetation

A dense canopy of tall, well-formed trees occurs on more favorable sites, whereas stunted trees with gnarled shapes form an open canopy on drier sites. The dominant canopy tree is generally chestnut oak, although scarlet oak is more abundant on ridges and upper slopes, due to its greater tolerance of drought. Other canopy trees include black oak (*Q. velutina*), white oak (*Q. alba*), northern red oak (*Q. rubra*), mockernut hickory (*Carya tomentosa*), and eastern white pine (*Pinus strobus*). Additional understory trees include red maple (*Acer rubrum*), sassafras (*Sassafras albidum*), and black gum (*Nyssa sylvatica*). An often dense shrub layer is dominated by tall evergreen heath shrubs such as mountain laurel (*Kalmia latifolia*), with lesser amounts of rosebay (*Rhododendron maximum*) and gorge rhododendron (*R. minus*). Low-growing deciduous heath shrubs include lowbush blueberry (*Vaccinium pallidum*), deerberry (*V. stamineum*), and bear huckleberry (*Gaylussacia ursina*). Prostrate plants with thick leathery leaves and a slightly woody base include trailing arbutus (*Epigaea repens*) and wintergreen (*Gaultheria procumbens*).

Where shrubs are less dense, the diversity and abundance of herbaceous plants usually increase. Hayscented fern (*Dennstaedtia punctilobula*) sometimes forms a dense groundcover in forest openings that reduces the diversity of woodland herbs and inhibits the establishment of woody plants, thereby slowing succession back to forest. Root parasites such as buffalo nut (*Pyrularia pubera*), Appalachian oak leach (*Aureolaria laevigata*), and pinesap (*Monotropa hypopithys*) draw nutrients and water from neighboring plants.

Seasonal Aspects

One of the earliest plants to flower is trailing arbutus, a prostrate plant whose fragrant white to pale pink flowers are often partially hidden beneath its leathery leaves. Other spring-flowering members of the heath family (Ericaceae) include evergreen species such as mountain laurel and gorge rhododendron, as well as deciduous species such as flame azalea (*Rhododendron calendulaceum*) and deerberry. The white to pinkish flowers of mountain laurel and gorge rhododendron add color to the forest understory, as do the intensely bright orange, red, or yellow flowers of flame azalea. Deerberry differs from our other blueberries in having open, bell-shaped flowers with exerted stamens and stigmas. Another deciduous shrub is buffalo nut—its alternate, conspicuously veined leaves with numerous upright spikes of small greenish flowers in spring develop into a few large pear-shaped fruits in summer and fall.

Dwarf iris (*Iris verna*) has dense clusters of upright leaves and showy lavender flowers with a yellowish orange stripe. Other spring-flowering herbaceous plants include fly poison (*Amianthium muscitoxicum*), pipsissewa (*Chimaphila maculata*), and galax (*Galax urceolata*). Fly poison produces small white flowers in dense terminal racemes above grass-like basal leaves. Pulp from its crushed bulbs was once used to attract and kill houseflies, hence its common name. Pipsissewa is a small but common evergreen herb whose nodding white to pink waxy flowers in loose clusters overtop lance-shaped leaves with whitish-green stripes along the veins. Galax commonly forms dense colonies of round shiny leaves with clusters of small white flowers on tall slender stalks from late spring to early summer. Its other name, skunkweed, reflects its sometimes skunky odor.

In summer, rosebay produces showy clusters of white to pink flowers, particularly in open, sunny areas. Its thick, leathery leaves curl up tight (looking like fat cigars) and hang down during times of drought or extreme cold. Mountain sweet pepperbush (*Clethra acuminata*), a multistemmed shrub with distinctive, cinnamon-like, reddish brown bark, produces fragrant white flowers in upright racemes. Lowbush blueberry's sweet, edible blue-black berries ripen in summer, whereas the red to black fruits of the related bear huckleberry vary from sweet to tasteless. In summer, birds quickly strip the dark blue lipid-rich fruits from sassafras (*Sassafras albidum*). Hill cane (*Arundinaria appalachiana*), a relatively low-growing (up to 5 ft. tall) native bamboo with grass-like leaves, forms large colonies via underground stems but rarely flowers and sets seed.

Autumn colors include the bright red foliage of scarlet oak, the brilliant red to orange leaves of black gum and red maple, and the distinctive golden yellow foliage of hickories. The basal rosettes of rattlesnake orchid (*Goodyera pubescens*), with bluish green leaves and a network of white veins, stand out in winter against the mostly grayish brown forest floor.

Distribution

Chestnut oak forest occurs at low to middle elevations on upper slopes and ridgetops in the mountains. It's less common in the piedmont where it generally occurs on north-facing slopes at higher elevations. On more xeric sites, chestnut oak forest intergrades to pine-oak-heath, which has a canopy that ranges from being open to closed, with more pines and a denser understory of heath shrubs. On more mesic or sheltered sites, chestnut oak forest intergrades to cove forest.

Dynamics

The devastation caused by the chestnut blight opened up the canopy, increasing the number of chestnut oak, scarlet oak, tulip tree, red maple, and eastern white pine as well as the density of mountain laurel and other heath shrubs. Dry slopes, flammable shrubs, and thick leaf litter make chestnut oak forest susceptible to periodic fires, favoring oak regeneration. Wind-thrown trees are common on ridgetops and open slopes, due to the shallowness of roots in thin soils underlain by rock.

Conservation Aspects

Chestnut oak forest is subject to common kinds of disturbance, including clear cutting, conversion to pine plantation, fire suppression, development, and invasive species.

Acorns and hickory nuts. Acorns and hickory nuts are an important food source for animals. Both types of nuts are large and extremely nutritious relative to the fruits and seeds of most eastern trees. While nut production varies tremendously from year to year, a single large oak tree can produce more than 28,000 acorns in a good year. These energy-rich food packets are consumed by a diverse array of birds, insects, and mammals, including bears, deer, squirrels, mice, jays, and wild turkeys. Most of these animals are nut predators because the seeds are immediately eaten and destroyed. In contrast, some small mammals (such as squirrels, mice, and chipmunks) and birds (such as blue jays) facilitate seed dispersal by storing nuts in the ground. For example, gray squirrels cache large numbers of acorns and hickory nuts by burying them and then using them as a primary food source in fall and winter. By pushing nuts into the soil or by tucking them under leaf litter, the seeds are placed in an environment that favors germination and seedling establishment. While gray squirrels typically find and eat most buried nuts, unrecovered nuts can germinate and give rise to new plants. Blue jays also function as both acorn predators and dispersers. Acorns are a main component of the jay's diet, especially in fall, when they consume or cache a significant portion of the acorn crop. Squirrels and other small mammals disperse nuts over a relatively small area, whereas blue jays disperse acorns over a much larger areas, thereby facilitating oak regeneration in disturbed landscapes.

SUGGESTED READING

Keever, C. 1953. Present Composition of Some Stands of the Former Oak-Chestnut Forest in the Southern Blue Ridge Mountains. *Ecology* 34:44–54.

McShea, W. J., and W. M. Healy, eds. 2002. *Oak Forest Ecosystems: Ecology and Management for Wildlife*. Baltimore: John Hopkins University Press.

Stephenson, S. L., A. N. Ash, and D. F. Stauffer. 1993. Appalachian Oak Forests. In Martin, W. H., S. G. Boyce, A. C. Echternacht, eds., *Biodiversity of the Southeastern United States: Upland Terrestrial Communities*, 255–303, New York: Wiley and Sons.

CHESTNUT OAK FOREST: CHARACTERISTIC PLANTS

Trees

ABUNDANT SPECIES

Quercus coccinea	Scarlet oak	p. 256
Quercus montana	Chestnut oak	pp. 258–59

OCCASIONAL TO LOCALLY ABUNDANT SPECIES

Acer rubrum	Red maple	p. 222
Carya glabra	Pignut hickory	pp. 229–30
Carya tomentosa	Mockernut hickory	p. 231
Castanea dentata	American chestnut	pp. 231–32
Liriodendron tulipifera	Tulip tree, Yellow poplar	pp. 242–43
Nyssa sylvatica	Black gum	pp. 245–46

Oxydendrum arboreum	Sourwood	p. 247
Pinus strobus	Eastern white pine	p. 251
Quercus alba	White oak	pp. 255–56
Quercus rubra	Northern red oak	pp. 259–60
†*Quercus velutina*	Black oak	
Sassafras albidum	Sassafras	pp. 261–62

Shrubs and Woody Vines

ABUNDANT SPECIES

Gaylussacia ursina	Bear huckleberry	p. 284
Kalmia latifolia	Mountain laurel	pp. 291–92
Rhododendron maximum	Rosebay	pp. 302–3
Vaccinium pallidum	Lowbush blueberry	p. 318

OCCASIONAL TO LOCALLY ABUNDANT SPECIES

Arundinaria appalachiana	Hill cane	pp. 272–73
Clethra acuminata	Mountain sweet pepperbush	pp. 278–79
Corylus cornuta	Beaked hazelnut	pp. 280–81
Pyrularia pubera	Buffalo nut	pp. 299–300
Rhododendron calendulaceum	Flame azalea	p. 301
Rhododendron minus	Gorge rhododendron, Punctatum	p. 303
Smilax rotundifolia	Common greenbrier	pp. 314–15
Vaccinium stamineum	Deerberry	p. 319

Herbs

OCCASIONAL TO LOCALLY ABUNDANT SPECIES

Amianthium muscitoxicum	Fly poison	p. 331
Aureolaria laevigata	Appalachian oak leach	p. 341
Chimaphila maculata	Pipsissewa, Striped wintergreen	p. 349
Dennstaedtia punctilobula	Hayscented fern	p. 360
Epigaea repens	Trailing arbutus	pp. 368–69
Galax urceolata	Galax, Skunkweed	pp. 374–75
Gaultheria procumbens	Wintergreen	pp. 376–77
Goodyera pubescens	Rattlesnake orchid	pp. 379–80
Iris verna	Dwarf iris	p. 393
Maianthemum racemosum	False Solomon's seal	p. 401
Medeola virginiana	Indian cucumber root	pp. 402–3
Monotropa hypopithys	Pinesap	pp. 407–8
Pedicularis canadensis	Lousewort, Wood betony	p. 419
Polygonatum biflorum	Solomon's seal	pp. 428–29

Rare Plants

†*Fothergilla major*	Large witch alder
†*Thermopsis mollis*	Appalachian golden banner

† = plant not included in the species profiles (Part IV)

PINE-OAK-HEATH

Distinguishing Features

Dense heath shrubs beneath a somewhat stunted canopy of pines and dry-site oaks characterize the pine-oak-heath community.

Introduction

Pine-oak-heath occurs on exposed ridges and slopes in the mountains and upper piedmont on dry, nutrient-poor, acidic soils. Stunted pines and drought-tolerant oaks and a dense layer of heath shrubs dominate the vegetation. Herbaceous plants are sparse and overall plant diversity is low. On most sites, fire suppression has increased the density of heath shrubs and allowed longer-lived, shade-tolerant oaks to gradually replace shade-intolerant pines.

Vegetation

Species composition varies with elevation, exposure, and soil depth. The two most common oaks are scarlet oak (*Quercus coccinea*) and chestnut oak (*Q. montana*). Dominant pines vary with elevation: Virginia pine (*Pinus virginiana*) and short leaf pine (*P. echinata*) at lower elevations, pitch pine (*P. rigida*) at intermediate elevations, and table mountain pine (*P. pungens*) at the highest elevations. Common subcanopy trees include black gum (*Nyssa sylvatica*), red maple (*Acer rubrum*), sourwood (*Oxydendrum arboreum*), and sassafras (*Sassafras albidum*). Dense shrub thickets are dominated by members of the heath family (Ericaceae), including bear huckleberry (*Gaylussacia ursina*), mountain laurel (*Kalmia latifolia*), lowbush blueberry (*Vaccinium pallidum*), rosebay (*Rhododendron maximum*), and catawba rhododendron (*R. catawbiense*). Vines include common greenbrier and whiteleaf greenbrier (*Smilax rotundifolia* and *S. glauca*). Where shrubs are absent or less dense, herbs such as trailing arbutus (*Epigaea repens*), pipsissewa (*Chimaphila maculata*), galax (*Galax urceolata*), wintergreen (*Gaultheria procumbens*), bracken fern (*Pteridium aquilinum*), pink lady's slipper (*Cypripedium acaule*), whorled coreopsis (*Coreopsis major*), and turkeybeard (*Xerophyllum asphodeloides*) may occur.

Seasonal Aspects

Round clusters of yellowish green sassafras flowers emerge on leafless stems in early spring, as do the elongate clusters of cream-colored to yellow flowers of horse sugar (*Symplocos tinctoria*). Another early spring bloomer is trailing arbutus—its fragrant white to pink flowers are often partially obscured by its evergreen leaves. Lowbush blueberry, deerberry (*Vaccinium stamineum*), and bear huckleberry produce small, nodding whitish flowers that are pollinated by bees. The larger white to pink bowl-shaped flowers of mountain laurel (*Kalmia latifolia*) have spring-loaded stamens that shower the dorsal surfaces of large bees with pollen, some of which is inadvertently transferred onto the stigmas of other flowers, resulting in pollination. Turkeybeard (*Xerophyllum asphodeloides*) produces showy white flowers at the tips of tall stalks in late spring, particularly in years when fires have opened the canopy, allowing additional light to reach the forest floor. One of the most striking plants of the pine-oak-heath community is the pink lady's slipper, an orchid whose flower has a magnificent pink pouch that attracts bumblebees (and delights the human eye!).

Grassleaf golden aster (*Pityopsis graminifolia*) and whorled coreopsis produce bright yellow flower heads that persist well into fall. Bumblebees seeking nectar frequently enter the trumpet-shaped yellow flowers of the Appalachian oak leach (*Aureolaria laevigata*), while butterflies lap up nectar from the nodding orange-red flowers of the Carolina lily (*Lilium michauxii*). The red to black fruits of bear huckleberry, and the colorful leaves of black gum, sourwood, red maple, and scarlet oak are among the many species that contribute threads to the rich tapestry of autumn colors.

Distribution

Pine-oak-heath is widespread in the mountains and on scattered peaks and ridges (monadnocks) in the upper piedmont at elevations from 1,000 to more than 4,000 ft.

Dynamics

Periodic fires play a key role in facilitating the regeneration and maintenance of the pine-oak-heath community. This vegetation is vulnerable to fire, as exposed ridgetops and upper slopes are exposed to lightning and high winds, conditions are often dry, and a thick leaf litter layer and dense shrubs provide abundant fuel. Extensive clearing and burning of southern Appalachian forests in the late 1800s and early 1900s favored the spread of pine-dominant forests, including the pine-oak-heath community. Beginning in the 1930s, federal and state agencies implemented a massive program of fire suppression. Stands of pine-oak-heath, which previously experienced fires about every 10–15 years, rarely burned. As a result, pine regeneration was greatly reduced and heath shrubs and subcanopy trees such as mountain laurel, black gum, sassafras, and red maple became more abundant. In the absence of fire, canopy trees such as chestnut oak and scarlet oak increase in size, overtop pines, and eventually shade them out. As the canopy pines die out and aren't replaced, succession to a hardwood forest occurs. Only on the most xeric sites, where growth and recruitment of oaks is reduced, is pine-oak-heath self-maintaining in the absence of fire.

> *Fire-adapted pines.* Because most pines are intolerant of shade and competition, they depend on periodic fires and other kinds of disturbance to persist. Two pines particularly well-adapted to fire are table mountain pine and pitch pine. Both species have thick bark that insulates their vascular tissue from low-intensity fires that can kill other species. While more intense fires often kill table mountain pine, fire-damaged pitch pine readily resprouts from dormant buds along the trunk and base of the tree. To varying degrees, both species have closed (serotinous) cones that remain closed until the heat of fire melts the resin on the woody cone scales, allowing them to crack open and release their seeds when conditions are most favorable for seedling establishment and growth.
>
> Closed cones containing viable seeds can persist on table mountain pine for 5–25 years, although some cones open in the absence of fire when high temperatures melt the resin that seals the cone scales. The degree of serotiny in pitch pine varies geographically. In regions with long histories of frequent fires (such as in the New Jersey Pine Barrens), pitch pine produces cones that remain closed on trees for many years. In contrast, where fires have historically been less frequent (such as in the southern Appalachians), individuals produce cones that typically open and release their seeds soon after maturity.

Conservation Aspects

The greatest threat to the pine-oak-heath community is fire suppression. Where possible, management plans should include fires, particularly high-intensity fires, to kill enough trees in the overstory to ensure successful pine regeneration. Using fire as a management tool helps maintain pine-dominated forests, which in turn enhances species and community diversity in the southern Appalachians.

Another factor that adversely affects pines is the southern pine beetle. Populations of this native beetle usually occur in low numbers in forests; however, when trees are stressed by drought or shading, beetle populations can explode, killing large numbers of pines (infested trees have yellow or red needles). Beetle attacks are cyclical, with major outbreaks occurring every 10 years or so, lasting for 2–3 years.

SUGGESTED READING

Harrod, J. C., M. E. Harmon, and P. S. White. 2000. Post-Fire Succession and 20th Century Reduction in Fire Frequency on Xeric Southern Appalachian Sites. *Journal of Vegetation Science* 11:465–72.

Welch, N. T., and T. A. Waldrop. 2001. Restoring Table Mountain Pine (*Pinus pungens* Lamb.) Communities with Prescribed Fire: An Overview of Current Research. *Castanea* 66:42–49.

Williams, C. E. 1998. History and Status of Table Mountain Pine–Pitch Pine Forests of the Southern Appalachian Mountains (USA). *Natural Areas Journal* 18:81–90.

PINE-OAK HEATH: CHARACTERISTIC PLANTS

Trees

ABUNDANT SPECIES

Pinus pungens	Table mountain pine	pp. 249–50
Pinus rigida	Pitch pine	p. 250
Pinus virginiana	Virginia pine	pp. 252–53
Quercus coccinea	Scarlet oak	p. 256

OCCASIONAL TO LOCALLY ABUNDANT SPECIES

Acer rubrum	Red maple	p. 222
Castanea dentata	American chestnut	pp. 231–32
†*Castanea pumila*	Chinquapin	
Nyssa sylvatica	Black gum	pp. 245–46
Oxydendrum arboreum	Sourwood	p. 247
Quercus montana	Chestnut oak	pp. 258–59
Sassafras albidum	Sassafras	pp. 261–62
Symplocos tinctoria	Horse sugar, Sweet leaf	p. 263
Tsuga caroliniana	Carolina hemlock	pp. 265–66

Shrubs and Woody Vines

ABUNDANT SPECIES

Gaylussacia ursina	Bear huckleberry	p. 284
Kalmia latifolia	Mountain laurel	pp. 291–92
Vaccinium pallidum	Lowbush blueberry	p. 318

OCCASIONAL TO LOCALLY ABUNDANT SPECIES

Rhododendron catawbiense	Catawba rhododendron	pp. 301–2
Rhododendron maximum	Rosebay	pp. 302–3
Smilax glauca	Whiteleaf greenbrier	p. 314
Smilax rotundifolia	Common greenbrier	pp. 314–15
Vaccinium stamineum	Deerberry	p. 319

Herbs

OCCASIONAL TO LOCALLY ABUNDANT SPECIES

Aureolaria laevigata	Appalachian oak leach	p. 341
Chimaphila maculata	Pipsissewa, Striped wintergreen	p. 349
Coreopsis major	Whorled coreopsis	pp. 355–56
Cypripedium acaule	Pink lady's slipper	pp. 357–58
Epigaea repens	Trailing arbutus	pp. 368–69
Galax urceolata	Galax, Skunkweed	pp. 374–75
Gaultheria procumbens	Wintergreen	pp. 376–77
Lilium michauxii	Carolina lily	pp. 397–98
Pityopsis graminifolia	Grassleaf golden aster	pp. 423–24
Polygala paucifolia	Fringed polygala, Bird-on-the-wing	pp. 427–28
Pteridium aquilinum	Bracken fern	p. 432
Tephrosia virginiana	Goat's rue	pp. 449–50
Xerophyllum asphodeloides	Turkeybeard, Beargrass	p. 468

† = *plant not included in the species profiles (Part IV)*

Forest Edge

Distinguishing Features

The forest edge community is easily recognized by its location on the margin of forests.

Introduction

A forest edge represents the interface between the outer band of a forest and very different kinds of habitat, including fields, roadsides, and rivers. Edges can occur naturally (as those on boundaries between forests and lakes do), or as a result of human activities such as agriculture, forestry, or urban development. Numerous environmental changes occur near edges, including changes involving light levels, wind speed, and the temperature of the soil relative to the forest interior. Higher light levels associated with edges often result in more abundant flower and fruit production than occurs under the forest canopy. Species richness can also be higher on the forest edge, due to a mixing of species from forests and more open habitats such as fields and roadsides. Not all plants respond to edges in the same way. Some species grow well and thrive along forest edges, whereas others are largely confined to the forest interior. Shade-intolerant species are generally favored near edges, as they tend to grow faster and outcompete shade-tolerant species in areas of abundant sunlight. Most edge species can tolerate frequent disturbance and are generalists, occupying a variety of habitats.

Vines: how (and why) they climb. Vines are plants that grow upward and outward by using other plants or objects as a means of support. Woody vines occur in almost every plant community where there are trees or shrubs to support them. Most of the nearly 60 species of woody vines found in the Southeast occur most commonly in areas where light levels are high, such as along riverbanks, forest edges, tree-fall gaps and early- to midsuccessional forests. Vines have great economic impact as weeds, particularly exotic species such as kudzu and Japanese honeysuckle, and some provide valuable forage, fruits, and seeds for wildlife. Since woody vines don't receive food from their host plants, they aren't parasitic. However, the foliage of woody vines can shade the leaves and thereby slow the growth of their host plants. Because vines use other plants for support, they don't have to expend energy on thick, woody stems. This enables vines to rapidly extend their stems into better-lit areas of the forest canopy. While "groping" for trees to climb, some vines grow as trailing plants, forming a dense groundcover in well-lit areas. Described below are three different climbing mechanisms used by vines.

1. *Root-climbers.* Vines such as English ivy (*Hedera helix*), poison ivy, and climbing hydrangea (*Decumaria barbara*) have stems with densely covered aerial roots that attach firmly to the host structure. Root climbers generally occur on tree trunks and larger branches, and not on less stable, smaller-diameter branches and twigs.
2. *Twining vines.* These are woody vines whose stems wrap around supporting structures, usually the stems of smaller trees and shrubs. Twining vines include kudzu, Japanese honeysuckle, yellow jessamine (*Gelsemium sempervirens*), and pipevine.
3. *Vines with tendrils.* Tendrils are modified parts of leaves, leaf stalks, stems, or stipules that facilitate climbing by either twining around the host structure or by adhering to it. Vines with adhesive-disk tendrils, such as Virginia creeper, are particularly effective climbers since adhesion enables them to climb large objects such as tree trunks as well as less stable, smaller-diameter branches high up in the canopy where light levels are greatest. Other tendril-climbing vines include common greenbrier (*Smilax rotundifolia*), muscadine (*Vitis rotundifolia*), and crossvine (*Bignonia capreolata*).

Vegetation

Common forest edge species include fast-growing trees such as tulip tree (*Liriodendron tulipifera*), sweet gum (*Liquidambar styraciflua*), and Virginia pine (*Pinus virginiana*). The vegetation can also include a thick growth of shrubs, with species such as wild hydrangea (*Hydrangea arborescens*), common elderberry (*Sambucus canadensis*), and devil's walkingstick (*Aralia spinosa*), along with woody vines such as pipevine (*Aristolochia macrophylla*), poison ivy (*Toxicodendron radicans*), and Virginia creeper (*Parthenocissus quinquefolia*). Exotic species such as Chinese privet (*Ligustrum sinense*), Japanese honeysuckle (*Lonicera japonica*), and kudzu (*Pueraria montana*) thrive in the abundant sunlight and periodic disturbance. Common herbaceous plants include numerous members of the sunflower family, such as black-eyed Susan (*Rudbeckia hirta*), cutleaf coneflower (*Rudbeckia laciniata*), roughleaf sunflower (*Helianthus strumosus*), Joe Pye weed (*Eutrochium fistulosum*), whorled coreopsis (*Coreopsis major*), yarrow (*Achillea millefolium*), and white snakeroot (*Ageratina altissima*). Other common herbs include Turk's cap lily (*Lilium superbum*), sundrops (*Oenothera fruticosa*), and heal all (*Prunella vulgaris*).

Seasonal Aspects

Black locust (*Robinia psuedoacacia*) produces clusters of fragrant white pea-like flowers in spring. Two soft-stemmed shrubs, common elderberry and wild hydrangea, produce dense clusters of small white flowers in spring, as does Chinese privet, an invasive species whose woody stems form dense thickets that outcompete native vegetation. Hidden among the large heart-shaped leaves of pipevine are inconspicuous brown-purple flowers that resemble an old-fashioned smoking pipe. Woodland herbs that flower in spring to early summer include the scarlet red flowers (with deeply notched petals) of fire pink (*Silene virginica*), the arching branches and large feathery inflorescences of goat's beard (*Aruncus dioicus*), and the showy lavender to pink flowers of Carolina phlox (*Phlox carolina*) on short upright stems. From late spring to fall, you may observe the blue-violet flowers of heal all (*Prunella vulgaris*), as well as the bright yellow flowers of sundrops (*Oenothera fruticosa*).

The white lace-like flower clusters of sourwood (*Oxydendrum arboreum*) stand out in woodland borders and other sunny areas in summer. Sharp prickles cover the leaves and stems of devil's walkingstick—its large showy terminal clusters of small greenish white flowers of summer mature into purple-black fruits in autumn. Sassafras (*Sassafras albidum*) has a mix of leaf shapes—unlobed, 2-lobed, and 3-lobed (mitten-shaped), which usually occur on the same plant. Spicebush swallowtail caterpillars (which resemble the head of a small snake) feed on sassafras leaves at night and often hide within a folded leaf margin during the day. During summer drought, some tulip tree leaves turn yellow and fall off prematurely. A conspicuous vine is kudzu, an invader with long stems reaching high into the forest canopy, its trifoliate leaves forming dense patches that smother other plants. Kudzu's climbing stems often produce long, drooping clusters of very fragrant, purple, pea-like flowers in summer and fall.

Summer-flowering herbaceous plants include Turk's cap lily, common milkweed (*Asclepias syriaca*), and yellow-fringed orchid (*Platanthera ciliaris*). Various swallowtail butterflies pollinate the spectacular orange to red nodding flowers of Turk's cap lily. Swallowtail butterflies, including spicebush swallowtails, also pollinate yellow-fringed orchid flowers, which are bright yellow to deep orange with a fringed lip petal and a long nectar spur. The tall stems of common milkweed produce dense umbels of purplish-green flowers that attract numerous long-tongued butterflies, bees, wasps, and other insects seeking nectar. The yellow to orange flower heads of various sunflowers (Asteraceae family) such as whorled coreopsis, roughleaf sunflower, black-eyed Susan, and cutleaf coneflower are a conspicuous part of woodland borders in late summer and fall as are Joe Pye weed's large clusters of showy pink-purplish flower heads on tall stems. Forest edges are also great places to enjoy the rich autumn colors that characterize the southern Appalachians.

Distribution

Forest edges are a frequent component of the mountain and piedmont landscape.

Dynamics

Shade-intolerant, early- to midsuccessional species typically dominate forest edges, whereas late-successional species are most prevalent in the forest interior. Increased exposure to wind along forest margins can physically damage trees, causing stunted growth and tree-falls. Wind also dries out the soil, decreases relative humidity, and increases transpirational water loss, creating a drier environment that can increase the risk and frequency of fires.

Conservation Aspects

Urban sprawl, roads, industry, and agriculture have subdivided forests into smaller more isolated fragments, which in turn have increased the abundance of forest edge habitat. Human activities such as littering, fertilizer runoff from adjacent farmlands, escaping fires, plant-poaching, and other forms of disturbance are associated with edges. Forest edges can have relatively high species diversity, consisting mostly of widely distributed species that can tolerate frequent disturbance. Few plant species are restricted to forest edges or are considered to be rare. Edges tend to have dense shrubs and vines that provide abundant food (including insects and small fruits) and thick cover for birds and mammals that are well adapted to disturbed situations. Exotic species are typically most abundant near forest edges, but wind and animals can disperse seeds into the forest interior, which can result in the movement of exotic invasives into forests.

SUGGESTED READING

Forman, R. T. T. 1995. *Land Mosaics: The Ecology of Landscapes and Regions.* Cambridge: Cambridge University Press.
Matlock, G. R. 1993. Vegetation Dynamics of the Forest Edge—Trends in Space and Successional Time. *Journal of Ecology* 82:113–23.
McDonald, R. I., and D. L. Urban. 2006. Edge Effects on Species Composition and Exotic Species Abundance in the North Carolina Piedmont. *Biological Invasions* 8:1049–60.

FOREST EDGE: CHARACTERISTIC PLANTS

Trees

ABUNDANT SPECIES

Acer rubrum	Red maple	p. 222
Liquidambar styraciflua	Sweetgum	p. 242
Liriodendron tulipifera	Tulip tree, Yellow poplar	pp. 242–43
Pinus taeda	Loblolly pine	pp. 251–52
Pinus virginiana	Virginia pine	pp. 252–53

OCCASIONAL TO LOCALLY ABUNDANT SPECIES

Nyssa sylvatica	Black gum	pp. 245–46
Oxydendrum arboreum	Sourwood	p. 247
Robinia pseudoacacia	Black locust	pp. 260–61
Sassafras albidum	Sassafras	pp. 261–62

Shrubs and Woody Vines

ABUNDANT SPECIES

Parthenocissus quinquefolia	Virginia creeper	pp. 296–97
Smilax rotundifolia	Common greenbrier	pp. 314–15
Toxicodendron radicans	Poison ivy	pp. 315–16

OCCASIONAL TO LOCALLY ABUNDANT SPECIES

Aralia spinosa	Devil's walkingstick	pp. 270–71
Aristolochia macrophylla	Pipevine, Dutchman's pipe	pp. 271–72
Arundinaria appalachiana	Hill cane	pp. 272–73
Hydrangea arborescens	Wild hydrangea	p. 287
Kalmia latifolia	Mountain laurel	pp. 291–92
Phoradendron serotinum	American mistletoe	pp. 297–98
Rubus odoratus	Flowering raspberry	p. 311
Sambucus canadensis	Common elderberry	pp. 312–13

Herbs

ABUNDANT SPECIES

Coreopsis major	Whorled coreopsis	pp. 355–56
Eutrochium fistulosum	Joe Pye weed	p. 373
Helianthus strumosus	Roughleaf sunflower	pp. 382–83
Phlox carolina	Carolina phlox	p. 422
Rudbeckia hirta	Black-eyed Susan	pp. 432–33
Rudbeckia laciniata	Cutleaf coneflower	pp. 433–34

OCCASIONAL TO LOCALLY ABUNDANT SPECIES

Achillea millefolium	Yarrow	p. 325
Ageratina altissima	White snakeroot	pp. 328–29
Aruncus dioicus	Goat's beard	p. 336
Asclepias syriaca	Common milkweed	pp. 337–38
Erigeron pulchellus	Robin's plantain	p. 369
Eurybia chlorolepis	Mountain wood aster	pp. 371–72
Fragaria virginiana	Wild strawberry	pp. 373–74
Lilium superbum	Turk's cap lily	p. 398
Maianthemum racemosum	False Solomon's seal	p. 401
Oenothera fruticosa	Sundrops	pp. 410–11
Platanthera ciliaris	Yellow-fringed orchid	p. 424
Prunella vulgaris	Heal all	pp. 431–32
Silene virginica	Fire pink	p. 439

Invasive Exotic Plants

Celastrus orbiculatus	Oriental bittersweet	p. 277
Ligustrum sinense	Chinese privet	pp. 292–93
Lonicera japonica	Japanese honeysuckle	pp. 294–95
Pueraria montana	Kudzu	pp. 298–99

† = *plant not included in the species profiles (Part IV)*

2 : The Piedmont

Moist to Wet Communities

RIVER BLUFF FOREST

Distinguishing Features

A canopy dominated by American beech and other mesophytic trees on relatively cool, moist slopes and ravines characterizes river bluff forest. Oaks other than northern red oak are generally not well represented.

Introduction

River bluff forest (or beech forest, as it's sometimes called) occurs on steep north-facing river bluffs and sheltered ravines with acidic soils. A dense tree canopy, steep slopes, and a proximity to water result in a mesic environment characterized by low light intensity and relatively cool, humid air. Steep slopes, fallen trees, and scattered boulders present a more rugged terrain than typically found in the piedmont. Some river bluff forests still harbor large old trees, having escaped human-influenced disturbance.

Vegetation

Two main characteristics define this community: an abundance of American beech (*Fagus grandifolia*) and few oaks (other than northern red oak, *Quercus rubra*). Other canopy dominants include tulip tree (*Liriodendron tulipifera*) and red maple (*Acer rubrum*). Common understory trees include flowering dogwood (*Cornus florida*), hop hornbeam (*Ostrya virginiana*), Carolina silverbell (*Halesia tetraptera*), horse sugar (*Symplocos tinctoria*), and American holly (*Ilex opaca*). Shrubs include strawberry bush (*Euonymus americanus*), gorge rhododendron (*Rhododendron minus*), and deerberry (*Vaccinium stamineum*). The herbaceous layer varies from sparse to moderate in density and diversity, depending on position on slope, the nature of the soil, and other factors. Where moisture, nutrients, and soil accumulate at the base of concave slopes, a rich carpet of wildflowers often occurs; in contrast, the herbaceous layer is usually sparse in deeply shaded areas. Among the more conspicuous woodland herbs are mayapple (*Podophyllum peltatum*), wild geranium (*Geranium maculatum*), foamflower (*Tiarella cordifolia*), and perfoliate bellwort (*Uvularia perfoliata*). A common but less conspicuous species is beechdrops (*Epifagus virginiana*), a parasitic flowering plant that frequently occurs under the canopy of American beech.

Seasonal Aspects

In early spring, look for the flowers of understory trees such as Carolina silverbell (whose white bell-shaped flowers hang in groups below its branches), flowering dogwood (whose 4 large, petal-like white bracts surround a central cluster of small, inconspicuous flowers), and horse sugar (bearing dense clusters of white to yellowish flowers with long stamens at the tips of mostly leafless stems). Two native rhododendrons—wild azalea (*Rhododendron periclymenoides*, a deciduous species) and gorge rhododendron (*R. minus*, an evergreen)—produce showy clusters of white to pink flowers in spring. Coral honeysuckle (*Lonicera sempervirens*), a native vine that is much less aggressive (weedy) than its introduced relative, Japanese honeysuckle (*L. japonica*), has red tubular flowers that attract both butterflies and hummingbirds. The nodding yellow flowers of dimpled trout lily (*Erythronium umbilicatum*) and the whitish flowers of acute-lobed hepatica (*Hepatica acutiloba*) are among the first woodland herbs to bloom in late winter and early spring. Foamflower, giant chickweed (*Stellaria pubera*), and fairywand (*Chamaelirium luteum*) produce numerous small white flowers in spring; in contrast, a single large white flower occurs at the tip of the leafless stalk of bloodroot (*Sanguinaria canadensis*). Mayapple's large, solitary white flower is partially hidden beneath 2 broad, umbrella-like leaves. Other spring flowers include the showy pink flowers of wild geranium, the nodding, pale yellow flowers of perfoliate bellwort, and the fleshy flowers of little brown jugs (*Hexastylis arifolia*) that lie hidden beneath its evergreen leaves. Rattlesnake fern (*Botrypus virginianus*) produces 2 fronds—one vegetative, the other reproductive (with bright yellow spore cases resembling tiny grapes).

In early summer, honeybees actively harvest nectar from the white flowers of sourwood (*Oxydendrum arboreum*), producing a prized honey. Less conspicuous are the tiny yellow flowers of American ginseng (*Panax quinquefolius*), a plant that is increasingly rare due to overcollecting. In late summer and fall, look for the nodding yellowish white flower heads of lion's foot (*Prenanthes serpentaria*), the warty red fruits of strawberry bush (*Euonymus americanus*), and the deep scarlet leaves of northern red oak. The reddish orange fruits of American holly and the persistent tan leaves of American beech stand out in winter, as do the evergreen fronds of Christmas fern (*Polystichum acrostichoides*).

Distribution

River bluff forest occurs throughout the piedmont region.

Dynamics

Fires occur infrequently and with low intensities, due to fairly moist conditions. Periodic, selective timber harvesting has resulted in a decrease in red oaks while noncommercial hardwoods such as American beech have increased in number. Human-influenced disturbance has increased the number of opportunistic trees such as tulip tree, sweetgum (*Liquidambar styraciflua*), and pines.

> *Mountain disjuncts.* The relatively cool, moist conditions that characterize this community provide an environment more akin to the mountains than the piedmont. It's not surprising, then, to find a number of typically mountainous species in river bluff forests, including trees such as Canada hemlock (*Tsuga canadensis*) and white pine (*Pinus strobus*), shrubs such as Catawba rhododendron (*Rhododendron catawbiense*) and mountain laurel (*Kalmia latifolia*), and herbs such as galax (*Galax urceolata*), mountain spleenwort (*Asplenium montanum*) and Catesby's trillium (*Trillium catesbaei*). Sprouts of American chestnut (*Castanea dentata*), a species generally uncommon in the piedmont, can also be found on river bluffs. Some mountain disjuncts were more widely distributed across the Southeast in the colder climates of the last ice age (over 10,000 years ago), with small populations persisting in scattered piedmont sites where relatively cool, moist conditions prevail. Other disjuncts probably reflect more recent colonization, the effect of long-distance seed dispersal by birds, wind, or rivers.

Conservation Aspects

River bluff forests are fairly common. On steep, nearly inaccessible slopes, they are less disturbed than most piedmont communities. While most sites have been logged and grazed by domestic livestock, some escaped being farmed. Small remnant patches of old-growth forest can still be found on some sites, with unusually large American beech, tulip tree, and other species, some well over 100 years old. While many river bluff forests are recovering from past disturbance (and may eventually reach old-growth status), others continue to be threatened by logging, development, and other factors.

SUGGESTED READING

Adams, H. S., S. L. Stephenson, S. Ware, and M. Schnittler. 2003. Forests of the Central and Southern Appalachians and Eastern Virginia Having Beech as a Major Component. *Castanea* 68:222–32.
Hardin, J. W., and A. W. Cooper. 1967. Mountain Disjuncts in the Eastern Piedmont of North Carolina. *The Journal of the Elisha Mitchell Scientific Society* 83:139–50.
Oosting, H. J. 1942. An Ecological Analysis of the Plant Communities of Piedmont, North Carolina. *American Midland Naturalist* 28:1–126.

RIVER BLUFF FOREST: CHARACTERISTIC PLANTS

Trees

ABUNDANT SPECIES

Acer rubrum	Red maple	p. 222
Cornus florida	Flowering dogwood	pp. 235–36
Fagus grandifolia	American beech	pp. 237–38
Liriodendron tulipifera	Tulip tree, Yellow poplar	pp. 242–43
Ostrya virginiana	Hop hornbeam	pp. 246–47
Quercus rubra	Northern red oak	pp. 259–60

OCCASIONAL TO LOCALLY ABUNDANT SPECIES

Acer floridanum	Southern sugar maple	pp. 219–20
Halesia tetraptera	Carolina silverbell	p. 239
Ilex opaca	American holly	pp. 239–40
Oxydendrum arboreum	Sourwood	p. 247
Symplocos tinctoria	Horse sugar, Sweet leaf	p. 263
Tsuga canadensis	Canada hemlock, Eastern hemlock	pp. 264–65

Shrubs and Woody Vines

OCCASIONAL TO LOCALLY ABUNDANT SPECIES

Euonymus americanus	Strawberry bush, Heart's-a-bustin'	pp. 283–84
Kalmia latifolia	Mountain laurel	pp. 291–92
Lonicera sempervirens	Coral honeysuckle	p. 295
Rhododendron minus	Gorge rhododendron, Punctatum	p. 303
Rhododendron periclymenoides	Wild azalea, Pinxterflower	p. 304
Vaccinium stamineum	Deerberry	p. 319

Herbs

ABUNDANT SPECIES

Desmodium nudiflorum	Beggar's ticks	p. 361
Erythronium umbilicatum	Dimpled trout lily	pp. 370–71
Hexastylis arifolia	Little brown jugs	pp. 386–87
Podophyllum peltatum	Mayapple	p. 426
Polystichum acrostichoides	Christmas fern	p. 429
Tiarella cordifolia	Foamflower	pp. 452–53

OCCASIONAL TO LOCALLY ABUNDANT SPECIES

Botrypus virginianus	Rattlesnake fern	p. 342
Chamaelirium luteum	Fairywand, Devil's bit	pp. 346–47

Chimaphila maculata	Pipsissewa, Striped wintergreen	p. 349
Epifagus virginiana	Beechdrops	pp. 367–68
Geranium maculatum	Wild geranium	p. 378
Hepatica acutiloba	Acute-lobed hepatica	pp. 384–85
Oxalis violacea	Violet wood sorrel	pp. 414–15
†*Prenanthes serpentaria*	Lion's foot	
Sanguinaria canadensis	Bloodroot	p. 435
Stellaria pubera	Giant chickweed	p. 447
Trillium catesbaei	Catesby's trillium	p. 455
Uvularia perfoliata	Perfoliate bellwort	pp. 462–63
Viola hastata	Halberdleaf yellow violet	pp. 466–67

Rare Plants

†*Euonymus atropurpureus*	Burning bush	
†*Magnolia macrophylla*	Bigleaf magnolia	
Panax quinquefolius	American ginseng, Sang	p. 417
Trillium reliquum	Relict trillium	p. 459

† = *plant not included in the species profiles (Part IV)*

ALLUVIAL FOREST

Distinguishing Features

Alluvial forest in the piedmont and lower mountains is easily recognized by its location in floodplains and its characteristic species, such as sycamore, river birch, and box elder.

Introduction

Alluvial forest occurs along streams and rivers that seasonally or intermittently flood their banks. Alluvial forests vary in size from broad river valleys to narrow strips of streamside vegetation. The relatively small floodplain forests of the piedmont are called alluvial forests for the nutrient rich "alluvium" that is deposited when rivers and streams overflow their banks. The brown color of the water is the result of silt and clay particles that erode from mountain and piedmont soils and are then carried downstream in the sediment. Moist, nutrient-rich soils, long growing seasons, and high summer temperatures provide favorable conditions for plant growth. Flooding benefits plants by continually replenishing soil nutrients and moisture, but long periods of standing water deplete soils of oxygen and can limit plant growth. Because plant species differ in their ability to cope with poorly aerated soils, the frequency and duration of flooding has a strong influence on the distribution and composition of plants within floodplain forests.

Vegetation

Alluvial forests in the piedmont and lower mountains have a well-developed canopy, an open to dense understory, and an herbaceous layer that is both dense and diverse. Common canopy trees include sycamore (*Platanus occidentalis*), river birch (*Betula nigra*), sweetgum (*Liquidambar styraciflua*), tulip tree (*Liriodendron tulipifera*), and green ash (*Fraxinus pennsylvanica*). Understory trees include box elder (*Acer negundo*), red maple (*Acer rubrum*), ironwood (*Carpinus caroliniana*), and American holly (*Ilex opaca*). A species-rich shrub layer includes spicebush (*Lindera benzoin*), pawpaw (*Asimina triloba*), strawberry bush (*Euonymus americanus*), silky dogwood (*Cornus amomum*), painted buckeye (*Aesculus sylvatica*) and giant cane (*Arundinaria gigantea*). Vines are common and diverse and include species such as poison ivy (*Toxicodendron radicans*), Virginia creeper (*Parthenocissus quinquefolia*), and crossvine (*Bignonia capreolata*).

A dense herbaceous layer often develops beneath a fairly open canopy. Two tall herbs are giant ragweed (*Ambrosia trifida*) and New York ironweed (*Vernonia noveboracensis*). Common ferns include Christmas fern (*Polystichum acrostichoides*), royal fern (*Osmunda regalis*), and resurrection fern (*Pleopeltis polypodioides*), a species that grows on the trunks or branches of trees, and on large rocks. Grasses and sedges are also common, including river oats (*Chasmanthium latifolium*), an ecologically important species that traps and stabilizes soils (thereby reducing erosion).

Natural levees sometimes occur near the water's edge. These slightly elevated areas form when silt and other particulates are deposited at the base of streamside vegetation. Dominant species include sycamore, river birch, and box elder. In lower parts of the floodplain, where standing water persists for longer periods, swamp forests can occur. Species diversity is relatively low in swamp forests because only species tolerant of prolonged flooding can survive. Canopy dominants include sweet gum, willow oak (*Quercus phellos*), red maple, swamp cottonwood (*Populus heterophylla*), and green ash. Vines are common in swamp forests, but the herbaceous layer is generally sparse.

Seasonal Aspects

In early spring, woody trees such as swamp chestnut oak (*Quercus michauxii*), river birch, black walnut (*Juglans nigra*), and shagbark hickory (*Carya ovata*) release enormous amounts of pollen from conspicuous, drooping male catkins. Because their pollen is generally dispersed by wind prior to leaf expansion, pollination success is enhanced. Some insect-pollinated plants also flower before their leaves emerge, including pawpaw, with its nodding, purple, bell-shaped flowers, and spicebush, with its tiny yellow male and female flowers (on separate plants). One of the first woody plants to leaf out (and flower) in early spring is painted buckeye—its upright clusters of elongate flowers vary in color from yellowish green to pinkish red. Spring-flowering vines include the red tubular flowers of crossvine and the fragrant white (fading to yellow) flowers of Japanese honeysuckle (*Lonicera japonica*). Poison ivy and Virginia creeper, in contrast, have clusters of tiny flowers that often go unnoticed.

Spring ephemerals such as dimpled trout lily (*Erythronium umbilicatum*) and spring beauty (*Claytonia virginica*) produce leaves and flowers in late winter and early spring, then die back and go dormant before the canopy trees leaf out. In summer, New York ironweed's purplish flower heads on tall stalks are popular food-gathering spots for butterflies, bees, and beetles.

Plants bearing conspicuous fruits in late summer and fall, whose seeds are dispersed by animals, include spicebush, with its bright red berry-like fruits; red mulberry (*Morus rubra*), with its elongate blackberry-like fruits; and silky dogwood, with its bluish white fruits. Seeds dispersed by wind include the winged seeds of box elder, the woolly seeds of black willow (*Salix nigra*), and the seeds within the ball-like fruiting structures of sweetgum and sycamore. Trees such as shagbark hickory, river birch, and sycamore are easily identified (even in winter) by their distinctive peeling bark.

Distribution

Alluvial forest occurs throughout the piedmont and lower mountains. At higher elevations, alluvial forest is often dominated by montane species such as yellow birch and sweet birch (*Betula alleghaniensis* and *B. lenta*), with a dense understory of heath shrubs, including rosebay (*Rhododendron maximum*) and mountain doghobble (*Leucothoe fontanesiana*).

Dynamics

Flooding, deposition and loss of alluvial material, and windthrow result in a constantly changing environment. Floods disturb vegetation by washing away plants and soil. In more severe floods, small parts of the forest may be eroded or completely washed away. The tendency of streamside trees to lean toward the river has both positive and negative consequences. Leaning trees gain access to higher light levels that potentially increase growth rates, but because a greater part of their trunks are immersed in fast running water during heavy floods, they are particularly susceptible to being uprooted and washed away. Prolonged flooding can also stress or kill floodplain trees. Most floodplain trees can tolerate short periods of flooding, but few species can tolerate prolonged flooding during the growing season.

Floodplains are in a continually dynamic state with the building of new substrate and the loss of old substrate. Sandbars and mudflats form on the inside curves of rivers, and regular flooding deposits alluvial materials. Floodplain soils consist of alluvial material (alluvium) that can range from 15 to 250 ft. thick. Heavy mud deposition during the growing season kills herbaceous plants and the seedlings and saplings of woody plants. Degradation, or the loss of substrate, results from erosion during heavy flooding, a shift in climate, the construction of upstream dams, and other forms of human disturbance.

Storms, tornadoes, and occasional hurricanes can cause considerable wind damage. Shallow root systems allow floodplain trees to use the uppermost soil region, where anaerobic conditions are less likely, but make them more vulnerable to windthrow (in evidence of this, trunks of wind-toppled trees often lie scattered across floodplains). The openings created by downed trees increase the abundance and diversity of herbaceous plants and facilitate forest regeneration.

> *Beavers impact plants and other organisms.* Beavers build dams on small floodplain streams with sticks and mud, flooding some of the surrounding alluvial forest. They adversely impact floodplain forests by felling trees for food and dam building. By feeding on the base of trees, beavers girdle and kill even large, established trees. Their greatest impact comes when trees die in flooded areas. Persistent flooding, and the resulting loss of trees and increased light, can change a floodplain forest into a marsh containing wetland shrubs and herbs. By building dams and creating ponds, beavers alter the vegetation and provide habitat for a number of animals, including fish, waterfowl, reptiles, and amphibians.
>
> But beaver dams are also susceptible to various kinds of disturbance. For example, dams can break or deteriorate and temporarily or permanently drain their ponds. A free-flowing stream in a forested floodplain can take over 30 years to develop into a mature beaver pond. In the absence of major disturbance, beaver ponds slowly fill with sediment, trees invade, and eventually the pond returns to forest.

Conservation Aspects

Narrow bands of alluvial forest persist along the thousands of streams and creeks that flow through the piedmont and lower mountains. These wetland forests are important reservoirs of biodiversity as they are frequently the last contiguous woodland habitats for plants and animals in heavily populated piedmont areas. Also, because alluvial forest occurs where aquatic and terrestrial systems interface, species diversity and abundance can be high. Diversity in a particular area reflects forest age, the degree of flooding, soil composition, and disturbance history.

Streamside forests provide corridors (greenways) for the travel and migration of many animals. The forest canopy shades streams, plant roots stabilize streambanks, and decomposing leaves add essential nutrients to soils, all of which contributes to a greater diversity of aquatic life. Forested floodplains are also a buffer against damaging floods, and they improve water quality by trapping and filtering pollutants washed from roads and urban areas, as well as the excess fertilizers and pesticides in farm run-off.

There is a long history of human impact on piedmont alluvial forests. Floodplain forests were the first areas in the Southeast to be converted to croplands by Native Americans. By about 1,000 AD, Native Americans throughout the Southeast had developed a system of intensive agriculture based on corn, a crop that rapidly depletes the soil of nutrients. To avoid crop failure due to nutrient-depleted soils, corn was planted in floodplains where periodic flooding deposited nutrient-rich alluvium. Villages were frequently located along rivers and major streams that were also used for transportation. As Native American populations declined, Europeans continued to convert tracts of forested floodplains into cropland and pasture. By the early 1800s, cotton was widely planted in floodplains. Logging of the remaining forest began later that century. Today, piedmont floodplain forests exist in various stages of succession following tree removal. Only a few alluvial forest tracts of great age remain, and these are usually small, inaccessible patches on steep slopes that make farming or timbering difficult.

Habitat loss due to cropland conversion, logging, urbanization, and industrial development continues to be a major threat to floodplain forests. The construction of dams on the upper portions of large rivers and the channelization of small streams change the dynamics of flooding and sediment deposition, which in turn severely alters the ecology and composition of floodplain communities.

Alluvial forests are particularly susceptible to invasion by exotic plants. Heavy infestations of nonnative species such as Chinese privet (*Ligustrum sinense*), Japanese honeysuckle (*Lonicera japonica*), and Japanese stilt grass (*Microstegium vimineum*) dramatically reduce the diversity and abundance of native plants.

Public concern over the loss of floodplain forests, along with a greater awareness of their many benefits, have increased in recent years, resulting in increased regulation and protection of forested wetlands by various state and federal agencies.

SUGGESTED READING

Blom, C. W. P. M., and L. A. C. J. Voesenek. 1996. Flooding: The Survival Strategies of Plants. *Trends in Ecology and Evolution* 11:290–95.

Brown, M. J. 1997. Distribution and Characterization of Forested Wetlands in the Carolinas and Virginia. *Southern Journal of Applied Forestry* 21:64–70.

Sharitz, R., and W. J. Mitsch. 1993. Southern Floodplain forests. In Martin, W. H., S. G. Boyce, A. C. Echternacht, eds., *Biodiversity of the Southeastern United States: Lowland Terrestrial Communities*, 311–72. New York: Wiley and Sons.

ALLUVIAL FOREST: CHARACTERISTIC PLANTS

Trees

ABUNDANT SPECIES

Acer negundo	Box elder	pp. 220–21
Acer rubrum	Red maple	p. 222
Betula nigra	River birch	p. 228
Carpinus caroliniana	Ironwood, Musclewood	pp. 228–29
Liquidambar styraciflua	Sweetgum	p. 242
Liriodendron tulipifera	Tulip tree, Yellow poplar	pp. 242–43
Platanus occidentalis	Sycamore	p. 253

OCCASIONAL TO LOCALLY ABUNDANT SPECIES

Carya ovata	Shagbark hickory	p. 230
Celtis laevigata	Hackberry, Sugarberry	pp. 232–33
†*Fraxinus pennsylvanica*	Green ash	
Ilex opaca	American holly	pp. 239–40
Juglans nigra	Black walnut	pp. 240–41
Morus rubra	Red mulberry	p. 245
†*Quercus michauxii*	Swamp chestnut oak	
Ulmus alata	Winged elm	p. 266
†*Ulmus americana*	American elm	

Shrubs and Woody Vines

ABUNDANT SPECIES

Aesculus sylvatica	Painted buckeye	p. 269
Arundinaria gigantea	Giant cane, River cane	pp. 273–74

Asimina triloba	Pawpaw	p. 274
Bignonia capreolata	Crossvine	p. 275
Cornus amomum	Silky dogwood	p. 280
Euonymus americanus	Strawberrry bush	pp. 283–84
Parthenocissus quinquefolia	Virginia creeper	pp. 296–97
Salix nigra	Black willow	pp. 311–12
Toxicodendron radicans	Poison ivy	pp. 315–16

OCCASIONAL TO LOCALLY ABUNDANT SPECIES

Alnus serrulata	Tag alder	pp. 269–70
Itea virginica	Virginia willow	pp. 289–90
Leucothoe fontanesiana	Mountain doghobble	p. 292
Lindera benzoin	Spicebush	pp. 293–94
Sambucus canadensis	Common elderberry	pp. 312–13
Viburnum acerifolium	Mapleleaf viburnum	pp. 319–20
Xanthorhiza simplicissima	Yellowroot	pp. 322–23

Herbs

OCCASIONAL TO LOCALLY ABUNDANT SPECIES

Arisaema triphyllum	Jack-in-the-pulpit	p. 335
Chasmanthium latifolium	River oats	p. 347
Claytonia virginica	Spring beauty	pp. 351–52
Erythronium umbilicatum	Dimpled trout lily	pp. 370–71
Galium aparine	Catchweed bedstraw	p. 376
Osmunda cinnamomea	Cinnamon fern	pp. 412–13
Pleopeltis polypodioides	Resurrection fern	pp. 425–26
Polystichum acrostichoides	Christmas fern	p. 429
Stellaria pubera	Giant chickweed	p. 447
Vernonia noveboracensis	New York ironweed	p. 465
Zephyranthes atamasca	Atamasco lily	pp. 469–70

Invasive Exotic Plants

Ligustrum sinense	Chinese privet	pp. 292–93
Lonicera japonica	Japanese honeysuckle	pp. 294–95
Microstegium vimineum	Japanese stiltgrass	pp. 403–4

† = *plant not included in the species profiles (Part IV)*

BASIC MESIC FOREST

Distinguishing Features

Mesophytic (moisture-loving) trees such as tulip tree, American beech, and northern red oak and an extremely species-rich and abundant herbaceous layer characterize basic mesic forest.

Introduction

Basic mesic forest is one of the most species-rich communities in the Southeast. A key factor contributing to this diversity is its moist, relatively basic soil. A high concentration of bases, especially calcium and magnesium, makes the soil pH of basic mesic forest higher than that of most piedmont soils. The moist conditions that characterize basic mesic forest are due to its occurrence on north-facing slopes, the lower slopes of ravines, and other topographic positions that are sheltered from direct sunlight and drying winds.

Vegetation

Mesophytic trees such as tulip tree (*Liriodendron tulipifera*), American beech (*Fagus grandifolia*), and northern red oak (*Quercus rubra*) are canopy dominants. Two of the more characteristic understory species are hop hornbeam (*Ostrya virginiana*) and ironwood (*Carpinus caroliniana*). Southern sugar maple and chalk maple (*Acer floridanum* and *A. leucoderme*), as well as slippery elm (*Ulmus rubra*), are good indicators of the calcium-rich soils associated with this community. Other common understory trees include flowering dogwood (*Cornus florida*), eastern redbud (*Cercis canadensis*), and red maple (*Acer rubrum*). Among the various shrubs are painted buckeye (*Aesculus sylvatica*), pawpaw (*Asimina triloba*), and hoptree (*Ptelea trifoliata*).

The rich diversity and abundance of herbaceous plants is this community's most distinctive feature. Mountain disjuncts such as doll's eyes (*Actaea pachypoda*), Dutchman's breeches (*Dicentra cucullaria*), and blue cohosh (*Caulophyllium thalictroides*) occur, as do floodplain species such as wild ginger (*Asarum canadense*) and moonseed (*Menispermum canadense*). In contrast, species such as green violet (*Hybanthus concolor*) and shooting star (*Primula meadia*) are largely restricted to basic mesic forest. Rare species include bigleaf magnolia (*Magnolia macrophylla*), mock orange (*Philadelphus inodorus*), and yellow lady's slipper (*Cypripedium parviflorum*). Two federally listed (endangered) species associated with basic mesic forest are Miccosukee gooseberry (*Ribes echinellum*) and relict trillium (*Trillium reliquum*). Miccosukee gooseberry is known from only 2 sites on earth, one of which is Stevens Creek Heritage Preserve in McCormick County, South Carolina, considered to be the best remaining example of basic mesic forest in the Southeast.

Seasonal Aspects

The best time to visit a basic mesic forest is in early spring (mid-March through late April) when the woodland herbs are in peak bloom. Among the first plants to bloom are spring beauty (*Claytonia virginica*), dimpled trout lily (*Erythronium umbilicatum*), and acute-lobed hepatica (*Hepatica acutiloba*). Trilliums such as sweet Betsy (*Trillium cuneatum*) often form dense carpets of plants bearing 3 whorled leaves and a single terminal flower. Shooting star is aptly named as its nodding white flowers (with strongly recurved petals) are clustered on leafless flower stalks above a basal rosette of large leaves. Look for bumblebees actively collecting pollen from its nectarless flowers.

In early spring, the purplish pink flowers of red bud (*Cercis canadensis*) and the white petal-like bracts of flowering dogwood (*Cornus florida*) light up the forest understory. The greenish yellow bowl-shaped flowers of tulip tree (*Liriodendron tulipifera*) and cucumber tree (*Magnolia acuminata*) are less conspicuous as they blend in with the canopy foliage. Spring-flowering shrubs include painted buckeye, with its variably colored flowers; wild hydrangea (*Hydrangea arborescens*), with its tiny flowers packed densely in round clusters; and sweet shrub (*Calycanthus floridus*), with its pleasantly fragrant maroon flowers.

One of the most striking plants of late summer and fall is doll's eyes (*Actaea pachypoda*)—its waxy white berries with a prominent black spot look like the porcelain eyes once used in dolls. Other plants producing conspicuous fruits in summer and fall are pawpaw, with its irregularly shaped yellowish green fruits; cucumber tree (*Magnolia acuminata*), with its elongate fruits that turn from green to red to brown as they ripen; and flowering dogwood and spicebush (*Lindera benzoin*), with their small clusters of red berry-like fruits.

In winter, look for the reddish blush formed in the subcanopy by hanging clusters of red maple flowers (later forming winged fruits). Red maple's wind-pollinated flowers appear on leafless plants as early as January.

Seasonal change. Most trees and shrubs of deciduous forest are leafless and dormant during the winter months. The forest floor is brown and mostly quiescent in winter, except for a few wintergreen herbaceous plants such as Christmas fern (*Polystichum acrostichoides*), pipsissewa (*Chimaphila maculata*), and the cranefly orchid (*Tipularia discolor*) that actively photosynthesize in winter, particularly on sunny days with moderate temperatures. As spring approaches, the days get longer, the sun's angle is higher in the sky, and more sunlight reaches the forest floor. As soil temperatures gradually increase, some plants begin to emerge. The earliest emerging species are woodland herbs. By appearing early in the season, they take advantage of high light levels before the canopy leafs out.

Because species respond differently to temperature, canopy and understory species begin growing at various times over a period of a month or more. As temperatures continue to warm, water and dissolved nutrients (present in sap) flow upward from the roots to the dormant buds of shrubs and trees, triggering bud expansion and leaf emergence. By mid- to late spring, depending on elevation, leaves of canopy and understory trees and shrubs have fully expanded, and the forest floor, which had received nearly full sunlight in early spring, is now deeply shaded. Low light levels dramatically slow the growth of herbaceous plants on the forest floor and many species drop their leaves and go dormant, including spring beauty, Dutchman's britches (*Dicentra cucullaria*), and dimpled trout lily. Known as spring ephemerals, these species have a growing season of just 3–4 weeks, remaining underground as dormant plants the rest of the year. Other herbaceous plants persist through spring (or summer) in spite of their deeply shaded environment. Some of these persistent species have relatively large, horizontally oriented leaves that efficiently capture available light.

Green is the dominant color of summer as millions of leaves in the various layers of the forest actively produce sugars through photosynthesis. Some of this food supports reproduction (flowers, fruits, and seeds), some goes into vegetative growth (new leaves, stems, and roots) and some is stored over winter. As days shorten in fall, the forest changes from a mass of green to a brilliant array of colors as the green pigment in leaves (chlorophyll) breaks down and the yellow (carotenoid) and red to purple pigments (anthocyanin) become visible. Because each type of tree displays a distinctive color, the rich diversity of trees is most apparent in autumn. Before autumn colors fade and leaves begin to fall, most plants have already produced the first leaves of spring—diminutive structures tightly wrapped and protectively enclosed in buds that can withstand the extremes of winter.

Distribution

Basic mesic forest is patchily distributed from Virginia south to Georgia. It's similar to rich cove forest in that it has moist, relatively basic soils and high plant species diversity. But cove forest occurs primarily in the mountains where large concave landscapes have been carved out by rivers, whereas basic mesic forest occurs on slopes or flats in the piedmont region.

Dynamics

On relatively undisturbed sites, the canopy trees represent various age classes with at least some old trees present. Disturbed areas typically have more pines and opportunistic hardwoods such as tulip tree and sweetgum (*Liquidambar styraciflua*). Fires occur infrequently and at low intensities, due to moist soils.

Conservation Aspects

Basic mesic forest is a fairly rare community because acidic soils are generally much more common than basic soils in the piedmont and the sheltered sites necessary for maintaining moist conditions are narrowly distributed across the landscape. Land clearing and other forms of human-influenced disturbance have also reduced the area covered by this community type. On steep slopes, and other less accessible sites, one can find relatively intact basic mesic forest with large trees, some of which are quite old. Wildflower enthusiasts are attracted to this community because of its lush herbaceous layer, including a number of rare and disjunct species. The main threat to basic mesic forests is timber harvesting, because the loss of the canopy results in drier soils that eliminate the rich herbaceous layer that characterizes this community. Openings in the forest also allow exotic invasives such as Chinese privet (*Ligustrum sinense*) and Japanese honeysuckle (*Lonicera japonica*) to get established and spread.

SUGGESTED READING

Hill, S. R. 1992. Calciphiles and Calcareous Habitats of South Carolina. *Castanea* 57:25–33.
Radford, A. E. 1959. A Relict Plant Community of South Carolina. *Journal of the Elisha Mitchell Society* 75:33–34.
Shafale, M. P., and A. S. Weakley. 1990. Basic Mesic Forest. In *Classification of the natural communities of North Carolina*, 49–56. Third Approximation. Raleigh: North Carolina Natural Heritage Program, Division of Parks and Recreation, North Carolina Department of Environment, Health and Natural Resources.

BASIC MESIC FOREST: CHARACTERISTIC PLANTS

Trees

OCCASIONAL TO LOCALLY ABUNDANT SPECIES

Acer floridanum	Southern sugar maple	pp. 219–20
Acer rubrum	Red maple	p. 222
Carpinus caroliniana	Ironwood, Musclewood	pp. 228–29
Celtis laevigata	Sugarberry, Hackberry	pp. 232–33
Cercis canadensis	Eastern redbud	pp. 233–34
Cornus florida	Flowering dogwood	pp. 235–36
Fagus grandifolia	American beech	pp. 237–38
Juglans nigra	Black walnut	pp. 240–41
Liriodendron tulipifera	Tulip tree, Yellow poplar	pp. 242–43
Magnolia acuminata	Cucumber tree	pp. 243–44

Ostrya virginiana	Hop hornbeam	pp. 246–47
Quercus rubra	Northern red oak	pp. 259–60
Ulmus rubra	Slippery elm	pp. 266–67

Shrubs

OCCASIONAL TO LOCALLY ABUNDANT SPECIES

Aesculus sylvatica	Painted buckeye	p. 269
Asimina triloba	Pawpaw	p. 274
Calycanthus floridus	Sweet shrub	pp. 275–76
Hydrangea arborescens	Wild hydrangea	p. 287
Lindera benzoin	Spicebush	pp. 293–94
Ptelea trifoliata	Hoptree, Wafer ash	p. 298

Herbs

OCCASIONAL TO LOCALLY ABUNDANT SPECIES

Actaea pachypoda	Doll's eyes, White baneberry	pp. 325–26
Actaea racemosa	Black cohosh, Bugbane	pp. 326–27
Adiantum pedatum	Maidenhair fern	p. 327
Asarum canadense	Wild ginger	pp. 336–37
Asplenium rhizophyllum	Walking fern	pp. 339–40
Claytonia virginica	Spring beauty	pp. 351–52
Dicentra cucullaria	Dutchman's britches	pp. 362–63
Erythronium umbilicatum	Dimpled trout lily	pp. 370–71
Hepatica acutiloba	Acute-lobed hepatica	pp. 384–85
Podophyllum peltatum	Mayapple	p. 426
Polystichum acrostichoides	Christmas fern	p. 429
Primula meadia	Shooting star	pp. 430–31
Sanguinaria canadensis	Bloodroot	p. 435
Tiarella cordifolia	Foamflower	pp. 452–53
Trillium cuneatum	Sweet Betsy, Purple toadshade	pp. 455–56

Invasive Exotic Plants

| *Lonicera japonica* | Japanese honeysuckle | pp. 294–95 |

Rare Plants

Cypripedium parviflorum	Yellow lady's slipper	pp. 358–59
[†]*Magnolia macrophylla*	Bigleaf magnolia	
Panax quinquefolius	American ginseng, Sang	p. 417
Ribes echinellum	Miccosukee gooseberry	pp. 307–8
Trillium discolor	Pale yellow trillium	pp. 456–57
Trillium reliquum	Relict trillium	p. 459

[†] = *plant not included in the species profiles (Part IV)*

Dry Communities

OAK-HICKORY FOREST

Distinguishing Features

A mixture of oaks and hickories characterizes this community. White oak is often the most common canopy tree.

Introduction

Oak-hickory forest consists of a mixture of oaks (*Quercus*) and hickories (*Carya*). Because pines are often common (particularly on disturbed sites), this community is sometimes referred to as oak-hickory-pine forest. While oaks and hickories generally grow in dry, well-drained habitats, they can also occur on relatively moist lower slopes and upland flats. Often associated with acidic soils, oak-hickory forest also occurs on calcium or magnesium-rich soils that are more basic. Differences among sites in their soil types, moisture levels, and disturbance histories result in vegetation that is both complex and variable.

Vegetation

Oaks dominate this community. White oak (*Q. alba*) is particularly common as it tolerates a wide range of soil types, moisture levels, and exposures. Other common oaks include southern red (*Q. falcata*), post (*Q. stellata*), and scarlet oak (*Q. coccinea*) on dry sites, and northern red (*Q. rubra*) and black oak (*Q. velutina*) on more mesic sites. Mockernut (*C. tomentosa*) and pignut hickory (*C. glabra*), both of which occur in dry to fairly moist upland woods, are the two most frequently encountered hickories. Common pines include shortleaf (*Pinus echinata*), loblolly (*P. taeda*), Virginia (*P. virginiana*), and eastern white pine (*P. strobus*). A well-developed understory includes sourwood (*Oxydendrum arboreum*), red maple (*Acer rubrum*), black gum (*Nyssa sylvatica*), and flowering dogwood (*Cornus florida*). The shrub layer varies from sparse to dense. Members of the heath family (Ericaceae) are particularly common, including sparkleberry (*Vaccinium arboreum*), deerberry (*V. stamineum*), and lowbush blueberry (*V. pallidum*). Where the soil is relatively basic, species diversity increases and hickories increase in abundance, but heath shrubs and other acid-loving plants are rare.

Herbaceous plants are generally sparse, particularly on more xeric sites and where understory trees and shrubs are denser. With increasing moisture (along small creeks and on north-facing slopes), and on less acidic soils, a more diverse and abundant herbaceous layer occurs.

Seasonal Aspects

Wind-pollinated oaks and hickories release enormous amounts of pollen in spring from yellow-green male flowers in slender, drooping catkins. Other early spring flowers include the pinkish purple flowers of redbud (*Cercis canadensis*) and the bright yellow flowers of Carolina jessamine (*Gelsemium sempervirens*), both pollinated by large bees (bumblebees and carpenter bees). Small bees pollinate the numerous tiny white flowers of sparkleberry (*Vaccinium arboreum*), whereas evening-flying moths imbibe nectar and pollinate the fragrant white to yellow tubular flowers of Japanese honeysuckle (*Lonicera japonica*).

Spring-blooming woodland herbs include the spectacular scarlet flowers of Indian pink (*Spigelia marilandica*), the nodding white (fading to pink) flowers of Catesby's trillium (*Trillium catesbaei*), and squawroot (*Conopholis americana*), a yellowish brown root parasite that looks like small ears of corn popping up through the leaf litter. The federally endangered smooth coneflower (*Echinacea laevigata*) produces showy flower heads with drooping, pink to purplish ray flowers in late spring and early summer.

Hickory nuts, acorns, and sweet gum balls ripen in summer and fall, as do the fleshy fruits of muscadine grapes, blueberries, and sassafras. Autumn leaf color varies from the butter yellow of tulip tree (*Liriodendron tulipifera*), the golden brown of hickories, to the brilliant reds and purples of black gum, sourwood, and flowering dogwood.

American mistletoe (*Phoradendron serotinum*), an evergreen parasitic plant that usually grows in the canopy, stands out in winter on leafless trees. If you can get close to one, look for dense clusters of small white berries in the fall. Birds feed on the fruits and spread the sticky seeds in their droppings. Other birds wipe regurgitated seeds that stick to their beaks onto branches where germination and seedling establishment can occur.

Distribution

Oak-hickory forest has a broad u-shaped distribution pattern that extends from Massachusetts south to Georgia, west to eastern Texas, and north to central Michigan. It occurs in both the piedmont and mountains at elevations up to 5,000 ft. In mountain oak-hickory forest, common canopy trees include white oak, northern red oak, chestnut oak (*Q. montana*), mockernut hickory, pignut hickory, red maple, tulip tree (*Liriodendron tulipifera*), eastern white pine, and yellow birch (*Betula alleghaniensis*), as well as root sprouts of American chestnut (*Castanea dentata*).

> *Oaks and hickories.* With about 500 species, *Quercus* is the most widespread and species-rich tree genus in the temperate zone, with more than 30 species in the Southeast. Ecologically, oaks are the predominant tree of the piedmont and mountain regions, with one or more species represented in the canopy of most forested communities. Acorns and the cups that hold them are a distinctive feature of oaks. Most of our oaks occur on dry to mesic sites and are drought tolerant. Their deep taproots provide access to soil moisture, their thick leaves minimize water loss from transpiration, and they maintain relatively high rates of photosynthesis, even when soil moisture is limited. Most have thick, fire-resistant bark and depend on periodic fires for successful regeneration and persistence.
>
> The hickory genus (*Carya*) is also a relatively large genus, with 18 species in eastern North America and Asia, including 10 species in the Southeast. The hickory genus is easily identified by its compound leaves, but when a tree is without fruits, it can be difficult to distinguish species. Hickories are most abundant on dry or dry-mesic sites with fairly basic soils. Oaks and hickories often co-occur. They also share many common traits: wind pollination, separate male and female flowers on the same plant (monoecy), unusually large seeds, masting behavior (good seed production years interspersed with poor years), seed predation and dispersal by small mammals, and generally low to intermediate shade tolerance.

Dynamics

Historically, oak forests were maintained by fires, as rural agricultural populations used fire much as Native Americans had before them. By 1940, fire suppression became commonplace, dramatically decreasing the frequency and size of fires, which gradually altered the species composition of oak forests.

Frequent fires favored oaks over most other hardwoods because oaks have thick bark and a tenacious ability to resprout after their tops are killed by a fire. Frequent fires also favored oak regeneration because competition from understory and midstory species that are tolerant of shade but not fire was reduced. The reduction in the frequency of fires over the past century has allowed shade-tolerant, fire-sensitive species such as American beech (*Fagus grandifolia*) to replace oaks in many previously oak-dominated forests in the Southeast. Oak forests are now less open than in the past, due to less frequent fires.

The lack of oak regeneration, particularly on moist sites, is a major concern to conservationists. Here the density of mesophytic (moisture-loving) species in the understory prevents the establishment of young oaks as the overstory oaks die or are cut. On drier sites, the understory is more open, and oaks are able to regenerate and maintain themselves.

A combination of prescribed burns and selective removal (by mechanical or chemical means) can open up the understory and facilitate oak regeneration, thereby helping to restore a forest that historically has been dominated by oaks.

Conservation Aspects

Once one of the most common piedmont forest types, extensive clearing for agriculture, logging, and urbanization have reduced, altered, and fragmented oak-hickory forests across the region. Successional pines have often replaced abandoned farms and logged areas that once supported oak-hickory forest. Grazing by cattle, goats, sheep, and hogs in the eighteenth and nineteenth centuries also impacted oak-hickory forest as the abundant supply of acorns and other nuts were used to help fatten livestock for winter. Hogs, by rooting in the soil, also had a major effect on the herbaceous layer of the forest.

Surviving stands of relatively intact oak-hickory forest are generally small and scattered. Oak-hickory forest is fairly common near piedmont rivers and creeks, but large, intact stands are best represented in the mountains.

Like many forest types, oak-hickory forest provides benefits such as watershed protection, wildlife habitat, recreational opportunities, wilderness areas, and timber. Fragmentation of oak-hickory forest has resulted in significant reductions in populations of migrant neotropical birds. Urban sprawl, industrial growth, conversion to pine plantations, fire suppression, and expansion of transportation corridors currently threaten piedmont forest communities, including oak-hickory forest.

SUGGESTED READING

Abrams, M. D. 1992. Fire and the Development of Oak Forests. *Bioscience* 42:346–53.
McShea, W. J., and W. M. Healy. 2002. *Oak Forest Ecosystems: Ecology and Management for Wildlife*. Baltimore: Johns Hopkins University Press.
Skeen, J. N., P. D. Doerr, D. H. VanLear. 1993. Oak-Hickory-Pine Forests. In W. H. Martin, S. G. Boyce, A. C. Echternacht, eds., *Biodiversity of the Southeastern United States: Upland Terrestrial Communities*, 1–33. New York: Wiley and Sons.

OAK-HICKORY FOREST: CHARACTERISTIC PLANTS

Trees

OCCASIONAL TO LOCALLY ABUNDANT SPECIES		
Acer rubrum	Red maple	p. 222
Carya glabra	Pignut hickory	pp. 229–30
Carya ovata	Shagbark hickory	p. 230
Carya tomentosa	Mockernut hickory	p. 231
Cercis canadensis	Eastern redbud	pp. 233–34
Cornus florida	Flowering dogwood	pp. 235–36
Liquidambar styraciflua	Sweetgum	p. 242

Liriodendron tulipifera	Tulip tree, Yellow poplar	pp. 242–43
Nyssa sylvatica	Black gum	pp. 245–46
Oxydendrum arboreum	Sourwood	p. 247
Pinus echinata	Shortleaf pine	pp. 248–49
Pinus strobus	Eastern white pine	p. 251
Pinus virginiana	Virginia pine	pp. 252–53
Quercus alba	White oak	pp. 255–56
Quercus falcata	Southern red oak	p. 257
Quercus stellata	Post oak	p. 260
†*Quercus velutina*	Black oak	
Sassafras albidum	Sassafras	pp. 261–62

Shrubs and Woody Vines

OCCASIONAL TO LOCALLY ABUNDANT SPECIES

Arundinaria appalachiana	Hill cane	pp. 272–73
Gelsemium sempervirens	Carolina jessamine, Yellow jessamine	p. 285
Phoradendron serotinum	American mistletoe	pp. 297–98
Smilax glauca	Whiteleaf greenbrier	p. 314
Toxicodendron radicans	Poison ivy	pp. 315–16
Vaccinium arboreum	Sparkleberry	p. 316
Vaccinium stamineum	Deerberry	p. 319
†*Viburnum rafinesquianum*	Downy arrowwood	
Vitis rotundifolia	Muscadine, Scuppernong	p. 322

Herbs

OCCASIONAL TO LOCALLY ABUNDANT SPECIES

Amphicarpaea bracteata	Hog peanut	pp. 331–32
Aureolaria laevigata	Appalachian oak leach	p. 341
Chimaphila maculata	Pipsissewa, Striped wintergreen	p. 349
Conopholis americana	Squawroot, Cancer root	p. 355
Cypripedium acaule	Pink lady's slipper	pp. 357–58
Desmodium nudiflorum	Beggar's ticks	p. 361
Diphasiastrum digitatum	Running cedar	p. 364
Goodyera pubescens	Rattlesnake orchid	pp. 379–80
Hexastylis arifolia	Little brown jugs	pp. 386–87
†*Hieracium venosum*	Rattlesnake weed	
Monotropa uniflora	Indian pipe, Ghost flower	pp. 408–9
Pityopsis graminifolia	Grassleaf golden aster	pp. 423–24
Spigelia marilandica	Indian pink	pp. 445–46
Tipularia discolor	Cranefly orchid	p. 453
Trillium catesbaei	Catesby's trillium	p. 455

Invasive Exotic Plants

Lonicera japonica	Japanese honeysuckle	pp. 294–95
Pueraria montana	Kudzu	pp. 298–99

Rare Plants

Echinacea laevigata	Smooth coneflower	p. 367
†*Monotropsis odorata*	Sweet pinesap	

† = *plant not included in the species profiles (Part IV)*

XERIC HARDPAN FOREST

Distinguishing Features

Xeric hardpan forest can be distinguished from other piedmont forests by its fairly open canopy of stunted trees dominated by blackjack oak (*Quercus marilandica*) and post oak (*Q. stellata*).

Introduction

Xeric hardpan forest occurs on upland flats and gentle slopes of the piedmont region where a clay hardpan or shallow rock layer impedes water movement and root growth. The scattered boulders and shallow rocks associated with this community are usually gabbro, a dark gray to black rock that contains calcium-rich feldspars that weather to form a nearly basic (circumneutral) soil that is dark in color, unlike the typical red clay soils of the piedmont. The clay hardpan or rock near the surface of the forest floor results in moisture conditions so variable that the soil can be a gummy paste during wet periods and a brick-like substrate during dry periods. In spite of high amounts of magnesium, calcium, and iron, the soil is fairly infertile. With its shallow, nutrient-poor soil and highly variable moisture conditions, xeric hardpan forest is unproductive and even mature stands are typically stunted. A local name for xeric hardpan forest is "blackjack lands," reflecting the common occurrence of blackjack oak.

Vegetation

The canopy is dominated by blackjack oak and post oak. Other canopy species include Carolina shagbark hickory (*Carya carolinae-septentrionalis*), pignut hickory (*C. glabra*), American ash (*Fraxinus americana*), Virginia pine (*Pinus virginiana*), shortleaf pine (*P. echinata*), and other oaks such as white oak (*Q. alba*) and willow oak (*Q. phellos*). Due to the stunted nature of the forest, it can be difficult to separate the overstory from the understory. Eastern red cedar (*Juniperus virginiana*) and eastern redbud (*Cercis canadensis*) are dominant subcanopy trees. Other understory species include winged elm (*Ulmus alata*), persimmon (*Diospyros virginiana*), and fringetree (*Chionanthus virginicus*). The shrub layer is often sparse and includes species such as blackhaw (*Viburnum prunifolium*), sparkleberry (*Vaccinium arboreum*), deerberry (*V. stamineum*), Saint Andrew's cross (*Hypericum hypericoides*), and fragrant sumac (*Rhus aromatica*).

On shallow soils associated with exposed bedrock, or where the canopy is kept open by artificial means, the herbaceous layer is often abundant and diverse. In these prairie-like habitats, grasses such as poverty grass (*Danthonia spicata*) and various species of broomsedge (*Andropogon* spp.) are dominant. Other interesting and unusual herbs include curlyheads (*Clematis ochroleuca*), butterfly weed (*Asclepias tuberosa*), rattlesnake master (*Eryngium yuccifolium*), and prairie dock (*Silphium terebinthinaceum*). While a number of these species have midwestern prairie affinities (discussed below), others are primarily associated with granitic outcrops, including erect dayflower (*Commelina erecta*) and Appalachian rock pink (*Phemeranthus teretifolius*). Small depressions fill with water in winter and dry out in summer. In these ephemeral pools, wetland species such as quillwort (*Isoetes* spp.) occur adjacent to drought-adapted species. Variability in factors such as soil moisture, soil depth, amount of sunlight, and disturbance history result in a mosaic of environments that contribute to a rich diversity of herbaceous plants.

Seasonal Aspects

A strong sweet fragrance in spring may indicate that fringetree, autumn olive (*Elaeagnus umbellata*), or Japanese honeysuckle (*Lonicera japonica*) is in bloom. Most fragrant in evening, their odor attracts evening flying moths that function as pollinators. Other spring-flowering plants include the solitary nodding flowers of curlyheads and the bicolored pea-like flowers of goat's rue (*Tephrosia virginiana*). From late spring through summer, numerous butterflies, bees, and other insects harvest nectar from the orange-red flowers of butterfly weed. The bright yellow bee-pollinated flowers of sundrops (*Oenothera fruticosa*) have a similarly long flowering season. The showy pink to purple flowers of purple gerardia (*Agalinis purpurea*) and the greenish white heads of rattlesnake master bloom in summer, as do the yellow composite flowers of roughleaf sunflower (*Helianthus strumosus*), Schweinitz's sunflower (*H. schweinitzii*), and prairie dock. Some sunflowers track the sun during the day, facing east in the morning and west in the afternoon.

The conspicuous reddish-orange fruits of Carolina rose (*Rosa carolina*), the bluish berry-like cones of eastern red cedar (*Juniperus virginiana*), and the long, flat seedpods of eastern redbud (*Cercis canadensis*) persist well into winter. In contrast, birds and mammals often eat the fleshy, sweet fruits of lowbush blueberry (*V. pallidum*) soon after ripening.

Distribution

Xeric hardpan forest is a relatively rare community restricted to small, widely scattered sites in the piedmont region from Virginia south to Georgia.

Dynamics

Historically, fires played an important role in maintaining this community. With frequently dry conditions and a grassy herbaceous layer, such sites were susceptible to fire. The routine use of fire by Native Americans, coupled with periodic lightning-induced fires, reduced the growth and reproduction of woody plants, resulting in an open canopy of widely spaced trees and a conspicuously dense herbaceous layer. Over the last century, fire suppression has promoted the growth and regeneration of trees such that xeric hardpan forest today typically has a more closed canopy and a less developed herbaceous layer than in the past.

> *Piedmont prairie remnants.* Prairies are dominated by grasses and other herbaceous plants, rather than by trees and shrubs. While generally associated with Midwestern states such as Kansas and Illinois, prairies were once widely scattered throughout the piedmont (as well as in the black belt region from eastern Alabama to northern Mississippi). Evidence for historic piedmont prairies comes from literary accounts of European explorers (such as John Bartram) as well as early maps of the region. Historic piedmont prairies were kept open largely because of the frequent use of fire by Native Americans to improve game hunting. Because of fire suppression and the extirpation of large grazing animals such as elk and bison, the piedmont prairie ecosystem has largely disappeared from the southeastern landscape. Not all is lost, however, as remnants of the prairie flora persist in open areas of xeric hardpan forest, in disturbed areas such as roadsides and unsprayed power line corridors, and in various preserves. For example, the Rock Hill Blackjack Heritage Preserve of South Carolina harbors more than 172 North American prairie species, most of which occur in open, grassy areas adjacent to xeric hardwood forest. Among the many interesting prairie species that persist in piedmont habitats are obedient plant (*Physostegia virginiana*), prairie dock, Indiangrass (*Sorghastrum nutans*), and rattlesnake master.

Conservation Aspects

The unusual geology and soils associated with this community occupy a very small percentage of the piedmont landscape. As a result, good examples of the community are rare. The species-rich herbaceous layer of high-quality sites includes a number of rare plants, even some federally listed (endangered) species such as smooth coneflower (*Echinacea laevigata*), Schweinitz's sunflower, Carolina prairie-trefoil (*Lotus helleri*), and Georgia aster (*Symphyotrichum georgianum*). One of the biggest threats to xeric hardpan forest is fire exclusion, which has resulted in an increase in the density of trees and a reduction in the abundance and diversity of herbaceous species. Sites are also vulnerable to development, logging, and rock quarries. Given its unusual substrate, and its diverse and unusual flora, more attention should be given to preserving and restoring examples of this threatened community.

SUGGESTED READING

Barden, L. S. 1997. Historic Prairies in the Piedmont of North and South Carolina, USA. *Natural Areas Journal* 149:149–52.

Nelson, J. 1992. The Vanishing Blackjacks. *South Carolina Wildlife* 39:34–39.

Schmidt, J. M., and J. A. Barnwell. 2002. A Flora of the Rock Hill Blackjacks Preserve, York County, South Carolina. *Castanea* 67:247–79.

XERIC HARDPAN FOREST: CHARACTERISTIC PLANTS

Trees

ABUNDANT SPECIES
Cercis canadensis	Eastern redbud	pp. 233–34
Juniperus virginiana	Eastern red cedar	pp. 241–42
Quercus marilandica	Blackjack oak	pp. 257–58
Quercus stellata	Post oak	p. 260

OCCASIONAL TO LOCALLY ABUNDANT SPECIES
†*Carya carolinae-septentrionalis*	Carolina shagbark hickory	
Carya glabra	Pignut hickory	pp. 229–30
Chionanthus virginicus	Fringetree, Old man's beard	p. 234
Diospyros virginiana	Persimmon	p. 237
Fraxinus americana	White ash	pp. 238–39
Liquidambar styraciflua	Sweetgum	p. 242
Pinus echinata	Shortleaf pine	pp. 248–49
Pinus virginiana	Virginia pine	pp. 252–53
Quercus alba	White oak	pp. 255–56
†*Quercus phellos*	Willow oak	
Ulmus alata	Winged elm	p. 266

Shrubs

ABUNDANT SPECIES
Vaccinium pallidum	Lowbush blueberry	p. 318
Vaccinium stamineun	Deerberry	p. 319
†*Viburnum prunifolium*	Blackhaw	
†*Viburnum rafinesquianum*	Downy arrowwood	

OCCASIONAL TO LOCALLY ABUNDANT SPECIES
¯*Hypericum hypericoides*	Saint Andrew's cross	
¯*Rhus aromatica*	Fragrant sumac	
Rosa carolina	Carolina rose	pp. 308–9
Vaccinium arboreum	Sparkleberry	p. 316

Herbs

ABUNDANT SPECIES
†*Danthonia spicata*	Poverty grass	
Schizachyrium scoparium	Little bluestem	pp. 436–37

OCCASIONAL TO LOCALLY ABUNDANT SPECIES
Agalinis purpurea	Purple gerardia	p. 328
Andropogon virginicus	Broomsedge, Broomstraw	pp. 332–33
Asclepias tuberosa	Butterfly weed	p. 338
†*Clematis ochroleuca*	Curlyheads	

Commelina erecta	Erect dayflower	p. 354
Coreopsis major	Whorled coreopsis	pp. 355–56
Eryngium yuccifolium	Rattlesnake master	p. 370
Helianthus strumosus	Roughleaf sunflower	pp. 382–83
†*Liatris pilosa*	Shaggy blazing star	
Oenothera fruticosa	Sundrops	pp. 410–11
Polygonatum biflorum	Solomon's seal	pp. 428–29
Rudbeckia hirta	Black-eyed Susan	pp. 432–33
Sorghastrum nutans	Indiangrass	p. 444
Tephrosia virginiana	Goat's rue	pp. 449–50

Invasive Exotic Plants

Elaeagnus umbellata	Autumn olive	pp. 282–83
†*Lespedeza bicolor*	Shrubby lespedeza	
Lonicera japonica	Japanese honeysuckle	pp. 294–95
Microstegium vimineum	Japanese stiltgrass	pp. 403–4

Rare Plants

Echinacea laevigata	Smooth coneflower	p. 367
Helianthus schweinitzii	Schweinitz's sunflower	p. 382
†*Lotus helleri*	Carolina prairie-trefoil	
Silphium terebinthinaceum	Prairie dock	p. 440
†*Symphyotrichum georgianum*	Georgia aster	

† = *plant not included in the species profiles (Part IV)*

GRANITE OUTCROP

Distinguishing Features

Piedmont granite outcrops are characterized by smooth (exfoliating) rock with scattered vegetation mats on shallow soils dominated by herbaceous plants.

Introduction

Scattered across the piedmont are islands of exposed rock that vary in size, shape, and topography. Most occur on granite (or gneissic rocks) that have a smooth exfoliating (peeling) surface that weathers unevenly, resulting in shallow depressions that accumulate soil and provide habitat for an interesting assemblage of plants. Granite outcrops that are level or gently sloping and occur at about the same level as the surrounding land are called flatrocks. Other granite outcrops rise hundreds of feet above the surrounding landscape (as Stone Mountain, Georgia, does), forming isolated peaks or ridges called monadnocks.

The environmental conditions associated with granite outcrops differ markedly from those of the surrounding forests and fields. High solar radiation and the absorption of heat by the rock surface result in summer temperatures that commonly exceed 120°F. The soils are generally shallow with very low water-holding capacity. While the soil typically remains moist during winter and early spring, it quickly dries out as temperatures increase in late spring. Sporadic rainfall and high evaporative water loss in summer result in widely fluctuating soil moisture levels, with frequent periods when soils are parched. Adjoining forests, in contrast, have deeper soils and more constant supplies of soil moisture. Highly specialized plants adapted to cope with these desert-like microenvironments occur on rock outcrops. While trees dominate adjoining forests, annuals and herbaceous perennials are the dominant life form on outcrops, including some of the rarest and most unusual plants in the piedmont region.

Vegetation

From a distance, granite outcrops appear to consist of mostly bare rock with scattered mats of vegetation and an occasional tree or shrub. Up close, however, the rock surface isn't bare, but is covered by an array of lichens and mosses. The most prolific colonizers of bare rock are crustose lichens, which, like blobs of paint, closely adhere to the rock surface, gradually expanding outward with age. Dry rock moss (*Grimmia laevigata*) is another common colonizer of bare rock. Moss mats are key species, building up organic matter and trapping soil particles, gradually creating a soil base that can be invaded by other plants.

Natural depressions with a thin layer of soil harbor many of the unusual plants that characterize granite outcrops. The shallowest soils are dominated by elf orpine (*Diamorpha smallii*), a tiny annual plant whose red succulent stems and leaves and bright white flowers form colorful mats. Elf orpine persists in areas with thin soils because it can tolerate low moisture levels and is largely free of competition from other plants. On slightly deeper soils, other annuals such as Appalachian sandwort (*Minuartia glabra*), toadflax (*Nuttallanthus canadensis*), and pineweed (*Hypericum gentianoides*) occur, as do reindeer lichens (such as *Cladina rangiferina*). A gradual buildup of soil, accompanied by an increase in organic matter and moisture-holding capacity, supports a greater diversity of plants, including conspicuous perennials such as woolly ragwort (*Packera tomentosa*), hairy spiderwort (*Tradescantia hirsuticaulis*), and broomsedge (*Andropogon virginicus*). Various shrubs and stunted trees (including eastern red cedar and pines) also occur, but a lack of moisture due to limited rainfall, competition, and shallow soils limits their occurrence.

Rock-rimmed depressions deep enough to hold water for several weeks in early spring, before completely drying out in summer, harbor several rare aquatic plants, including pool sprite (*Gratiola amphiantha*) and several species of quillwort (*Isoetes* spp.). Quillworts sometimes form dense carpets of bright green quill-like leaves in vernal pools that look like well-groomed lawns. Seepage areas are another favorable microenvironment in what is largely an exceptionally hot, dry environment. The slow release of water from adjoining forest onto the rock surface creates a continuously wet substrate that results in more robust plant growth and provides habitat for wetland species such as insectivorous bladderworts (*Utricularia* spp.) and sphagnum moss.

Called glades, the marginal zone between exposed rock and adjacent forest or field usually consists of a mixture of herbaceous and woody species. Eastern red cedars grow slowly and are seldom straight (or very tall) but those that reach old age exhibit majestic shapes. High light levels coupled with deeper (more mesic) soils enable species such as fringetree (*Chionanthus virginicus*), painted buckeye (*Aesculus sylvatica*), and Carolina jessamine (*Gelsemium sempervirens*) to produce spectacular floral displays. Look for puck's orpine (*Sedum pusillum*), a rare granite outcrop endemic under the sparse canopy of eastern red cedar (it resembles elf orpine but its tiny succulent leaves and stems are usually green, rather than red).

Coping in hot, dry microenvironments. How do rock outcrop species survive in microenvironments with shallow soil, scarce water, and intense heat? Some species escape the hot, dry summers by having a compressed life cycle. The seeds of winter annuals such as elf orpine, Appalachian sandwort, and pool sprite germinate in the fall, overwinter as frost-resistant rosettes, and then flower, produce seeds, and die in spring before the shallow soil dries out. Winter annuals survive hot, dry summers as dormant populations of drought-resistant seeds. In contrast, perennial herbs such as prickly pear cactus and Appalachian rock pink tolerate prolonged drought by collecting and storing water in succulent stems or leaves.

Other plants have adaptations that markedly reduce evaporative water loss. For example, hairy spiderwort, woolly ragwort, and hairy lip fern (*Cheilanthes lanosa*) have densely hairy leaves. By reflecting sunlight, the hairs keep leaves fairly cool, which in turn reduces evaporative water loss. The densely hairy leaves of woolly ragwort have a vertical (rather than horizontal) orientation. Because the sun's rays are parallel to these leaves during the hottest part of the day, heat load and evaporative water loss are further reduced (try touching woolly ragwort's leaves on a hot day—you'll be surprised at how cool they feel). Another way plants reduce water loss is by having small leaves. Pineweed takes this to an extreme: it has tiny scale-like leaves and thin, wiry photosynthetic stems, traits that apparently serve it well as it grows, flowers, and sets seeds in the extreme heat of summer.

Other species endure hot, dry summers through their remarkable ability to tolerate extreme water stress. These species become desiccated during dry periods and then quickly rehydrate and become metabolically active after rain. Many lichens have this ability, as do some mosses, ferns, and a small number of flowering plants. A good example is dry rock moss, a common mat-forming species that turns black and goes dormant during droughts, and quickly greens up and resumes growth when moisture returns.

A number of outcrop species are members of genera that are most abundant and diverse in southwestern deserts, including *Yucca*, *Opuntia*, and *Portulaca*.

Seasonal Aspects

Peak flowering is from late February though April. Many of the conspicuous flowering plants of early spring are ephemeral, not because of diminishing light resulting from the canopy leafing out, but because the shallow soil dries out as temperatures increase in spring. Among the first plants to bloom are 3 winter annuals—elf orpine, Appalachian sandwort, and pool sprite. Elf orpine's tiny red stems and bright white flowers form dense patches on the outer edge of vegetation mats. Often interior to elf orpine (and on slightly deeper soils) are the delicate white flowers and wiry stems of Appalachian sandwort. Pool sprite produces tiny leaves and flowers on thread-like stems that float on the surface of shallow pools of water. Other spring-flowering plants include the showy blue to rose-colored flowers of hairy spiderwort, the bright yellow flowers of eastern prickly pear (*Opuntia humifusa*), and the bell-shaped, creamy white flowers of beargrass (*Yucca filamentosa*). Woolly ragwort forms dense mats with large, upright hairy leaves contrasting with the numerous finely divided leaflets of the rare Blue Ridge ragwort (*Packera millefolium*). Other spring-flowering plants include fringetree (*Chionanthus virginicus*), with its fragrant white flowers; Carolina jessamine, with its yellow funnel-shaped flowers; and crossvine (*Bignonia capreolata*), with its tubular red (yellow within) hummingbird-pollinated flowers.

Although drought and high temperatures make summer the least favorable season for flowering, there usually are a few flowers in bloom, including the pale blue flowers of erect dayflower (*Commelina erecta*), the tiny yellow star-shaped flowers of pineweed, and the deep pink flowers of Appalachian rock pink (*Phemeranthus teretifolius*). Rock pink flowers are open for just a few hours each day, usually opening by 3:00 in the afternoon and closing by 7:00 the same evening. Carolina Jessamine, hairy spiderwort, and a few other species flower in spring and again in fall when temperatures drop and soil moisture increases. Confederate daisy (*Helianthus porteri*) and blazing star (*Liatris microcephala*) flower in late summer and fall.

Distribution

Piedmont granite outcrops occur from Virginia through the Carolinas and Georgia to Alabama. Granite outcrops vary in size from small boulders to large outcrops covering hundreds of acres. From above, they appear as islands within a landscape that is otherwise dominated by forests, successional fields, and development.

Dynamics

Outcroppings of granite reflect the gradual wearing away of less resistant surrounding rock by the erosive forces of wind and water over a period of millions of years. Soil accumulates and vegetation develops very slowly on exposed granite. As soil depth gradually increases, there's an increase in species richness, plant biomass, and the number of woody plants. Soil erosion, drought, and other natural disturbances prevent the development of continuous soil or vegetation on outcrops. In dry summers and falls, woody plants are susceptible to drought-induced mortality, resulting in dead skeletons of trees and shrubs, some standing, others toppled over. Because outcrop trees typically have shallow root systems, living trees can also be blown over, causing other plants in the mat to be uprooted and die. Trees that reach old age typically occur on deeper soils (such as those accumulating on glades or in crevices).

Conservation Aspects

Granite outcrops are extreme environments that harbor unique assemblages of plants, including a number of rare species that are entirely restricted to rock outcrops. One of the biggest threats to the community is quarrying. Urban sprawl into rural areas containing outcrops is another concern, as is recreational use (trampling by hikers and off-road vehicles can severely damage outcrop plants). Outcrops are sometimes used as dumping grounds for household appliances and other refuse, as loading areas for logging, and as pathways for moving heavy equipment. Because outcrops are relatively open habitats, they are often invaded by weedy species, including Chinese privet (*Ligustrum sinense*) on deeper soils. Some outcrops are now protected (e.g., Panola Mountain in Georgia, Forty Acre Rock in South Carolina, and Mitchell's Mill in North Carolina), but there is a need to preserve additional land containing outcrops of special significance.

SUGGESTED READING

Murdy, W. H., and M. E. Brown Carter. 2000. *Guide to the Plants of Granite Outcrops*. Athens: University of Georgia Press.

Shure, D. J. 1999. Granite Outcrops of the Southeastern United States. In R. C. Anderson, J. S. Fralish, and J. M. Baskin, eds., *Savannas, Barrens, and Rock Outcrop Plant Communities of North America*, 99–118. Cambridge: Cambridge University Press.

Wyatt, R., and J. R. Allison. 2000. Flora and Vegetation of Granite Outcrops in the Southeastern United States. In S. Porembski and W. Barthlott, eds., *Inselbergs: Biotic Diversity of Isolated Rock Outcrops in Tropical and Temperate Regions*, 408–33. New York: Springer-Verlag.

GRANITE OUTCROP: CHARACTERISTIC PLANTS

Trees

OCCASIONAL TO LOCALLY ABUNDANT SPECIES

Chionanthus virginicus	Fringetree, Old man's beard	p. 234
Diospyros virginiana	Persimmon	p. 237
Juniperus virginiana	Eastern red cedar	pp. 241–42
Pinus echinata	Shortleaf pine	pp. 248–49
Pinus taeda	Loblolly pine	pp. 251–52
Pinus virginiana	Virginia pine	pp. 252–53
Ulmus alata	Winged elm	p. 266

Shrubs and Woody Vines

OCCASIONAL TO LOCALLY ABUNDANT SPECIES

Aesculus sylvatica	Painted buckeye	p. 269
Bignonia capreolata	Crossvine	p. 275
Gelsemium sempervirens	Carolina jessamine, Yellow jessamine	p. 285
Ptelea trifoliata	Hoptree, Wafer ash	p. 298
Rhododendron minus	Gorge rhododendron, Punctatum	p. 303
Rhus copallinum	Winged sumac	p. 306
Vaccinium arboreum	Sparkleberry	p. 316

Herbs

ABUNDANT SPECIES

Andropogon virginicus	Broomsedge, Broomstraw	pp. 332–33
Diamorpha smallii	Elf orpine	pp. 361–62
Grimmia laevigata	Dry rock moss	p. 381

Hypericum gentianoides	Pineweed	p. 389
Minuartia glabra	Appalachian sandwort	pp. 404–5
†*Polytrichum commune*	Haircap moss	
Schizachyrium scoparium	Little bluestem	pp. 436–37
†*Selaginella rupestris*	Rock spikemoss	
Yucca filamentosa	Beargrass	pp. 468–69

OCCASIONAL TO LOCALLY ABUNDANT SPECIES

Aquilegia canadensis	Eastern columbine	pp. 334–35
Castilleja coccinea	Indian paintbrush	p. 345
†*Cheilanthes lanosa*	Hairy lip fern	
Commelina erecta	Erect dayflower	p. 354
†*Crotonopsis elliptica*	Rushfoil	
Erythronium umbilicatum	Trout lily	pp. 370–71
†*Helianthus porteri*	Confederate daisy	
†*Isoetes piedmontana*	Piedmont quillwort	
†*Liatris microcephala*	Blazing star	
Oenothera fruticosa	Sundrops	pp. 410–11
Opuntia humifusa	Eastern prickly pear	p. 412
Packera tomentosa	Woolly ragwort	pp. 416–17
Phemeranthus teretifolius	Appalachian rock pink	pp. 420–21
Tradescantia hirsuticaulis	Hairy spiderwort	pp. 453–54

Lichens

Cladina rangiferina	Gray reindeer lichen	p. 350

Invasive Exotic Plants

Ligustrum sinense	Chinese privet	pp. 292–93

Rare Plants

Gratiola amphiantha	Pool sprite	pp. 380–81
Packera millefolium	Blue ridge ragwort	pp. 415–16
Portulaca smallii	Small's portulaca	p. 430

† = *plant not included in the species profiles (Part IV)*

Roadside and Field

Distinguishing Features

Roadside and field habitats are disturbed areas in various stages of succession. Where there isn't bare soil, the vegetation varies from scattered patches of herbaceous plants to meadow-like areas and thickets that without continued disturbance are gradually replaced by forest.

Introduction

The plants found in roadsides and fields vary due to differences in disturbance history, seed availability, soil type, and climate. Many initial colonizers come from dormant seeds in the soil. Others emerge from seeds from outside sources, blown by wind, transported by animals (or vehicles), or in soil brought from elsewhere. Others emerge from dormant buds on persistent roots or stems. Some species are annuals, others are perennials; some are herbaceous, others are woody; some are native, others are introduced. Many are considered to be weeds because of their association with disturbed areas.

The first species to colonize roadsides and fields (called pioneers) are mostly annuals and short-lived perennials that grow rapidly and produce abundant, widely dispersed seeds, important attributes for plants associated with ephemeral habitats. These early invaders are soon replaced by larger, more competitive species. Within 5 years, fields often consist of a mix of herbaceous plants, shrubs, sprawling vines, and young trees. Roadsides and fields undergo succession to forest, unless continued disturbance (e.g., mowing, grazing, or fires) halts the process.

Vegetation

Numerous annual plants thrive in the open, sunny habitats associated with abandoned, formerly cultivated fields along roadsides and hayfields and pastures in disuse. Many annuals aren't native to North America but were either accidentally or intentionally introduced from Europe or Asia, including camphorweed (*Heterotheca latifolia*), common chickweed (*Stellaria media*), and henbit (*Lamium amplexicaule*). Native annuals include daisy fleabane (*Erigeron annuus*), horseweed (*Conyza canadensis*), and common ragweed (*Ambrosia artemisiifolia*). After several years, herbaceous perennials outcompete the annuals, which aren't able to germinate and grow under a dense cover of herbaceous plants. Common perennials include goldenrods (*Solidago* spp.), milkweeds (*Asclepias* spp.), yarrow (*Achillea millefolium*), big root morning glory (*Ipomoea pandurata*), white clover (*Trifolium repens*), common dandelion (*Taraxacum officinale*), and bracken fern (*Pteridium aquilinum*). Goldenrods grow intermixed with other species or completely dominate roadsides and fields. One of the largest nonwoody plants is pokeweed (*Phytolacca americana*); its widely branched purplish stems grow up to 10 ft. tall. Perennial grasses are also common, including sod-forming species such as Kentucky blue grass (*Poa pratensis*), and bunch grasses such as broomsedge (*Andropogon virginicus*). On poor soils, dense clumps of broomsedge can persist for years.

Among the first woody plants to colonize fields and roadsides are various shrubs and vines, including many nonnatives. As they increase in size and number they shade the soil, thereby reducing the density of herbaceous plants. Blackberry (*Rubus* spp.), multiflora rose (*Rosa multiflora*), autumn olive (*Elaeagnus umbellata*), and Chinese privet (*Ligustrum sinense*), along with woody vines such as kudzu (*Pueraria montana*), greenbriers (*Smilax* spp.), and Japanese honeysuckle (*Lonicera japonica*) form nearly impenetrable thickets in overgrown fields.

Various trees colonize fields and roadsides, including eastern red cedar (*Juniperus virginiana*), Virginia pine (*Pinus virginiana*), shortleaf pine (*P. echinata*), and loblolly pine (*P. taeda*). These shade-intolerant conifers are replaced by species such as sweet gum (*Liquidambar styraciflua*), tulip tree (*Liriodendron tulipifera*), and black cherry (*Prunus serotina*) as succession proceeds. Later colonizing trees such as oaks (*Quercus* spp.) and hickories (*Carya* spp.) eventually dominate the forest, which can take upwards of 100 years to reach maturity.

Seasonal Aspects

The pinkish purple flowers of henbit, the bright yellow flower heads of common dandelion (*Taraxacum officinale*), and the small white flowers of common chickweed are among the first flowers to bloom each year. Amazingly, the flower heads of common dandelion can be seen virtually any month of the year. Common blue violet (*Viola sororia*), a low growing plant with showy blue-violet flowers, and the white bowl-shaped flowers of wild strawberry (*Fragaria virginiana*) bloom in late winter and early spring. Wild strawberry ripens sweet red fruits with tiny seeds that are dispersed by various birds and mammals in late spring. Mimosa (*Albizia julibrissin*), a weedy roadside tree, produces showy white to pink flowers from late spring through summer.

Common vines include native species such as maypops (*Passiflora incarnata*) and trumpet vine (*Campsis radicans*) and exotic invasives such as Japanese honeysuckle and kudzu. Bumblebees and carpenter bees actively visit the fragrant purplish flowers of maypops in summer and fall. Maypop flowers, which open midday and have a distinctive circular fringe, develop into oval-shaped fleshy fruits, whose numerous seeds have a gelatinous covering with a distinctive sweet and sour taste. Evening-flying moths and long-tongued day-flying bees pollinate the sweet-smelling tubular flowers of Japanese honeysuckle whose color fades from white to yellow with age. The summer-flowering, hummingbird-pollinated red tubular flowers of trumpet vine develop into long, narrow seedpods that persist through winter. Kudzu vines dangling from trees produce numerous clusters of sweet-smelling purplish flowers in summer and fall. Historically, most kudzu flowers in the Southeast have failed to mature fruit, and those that did often produced few viable seeds. As a result, kudzu has spread primarily by vegetative growth (stolons rooting at nodes) and by humans intentionally planting it. The accidental introduction of the Asian giant resin bee in the 1990s has increased pollination success and subsequent seed production in kudzu, thereby enhancing its potential to spread into new areas.

The conspicuous yellow anthers in the center of horse nettle's (*Solanum carolinense*) star-shaped purple to white flowers attract numerous pollen-collecting bees. Other summer-flowering species include the bright orange-red flowers of butterfly weed (*Asclepias tuberosa*) and the yellow flowers on the tall stems of woolly mullein (*Verbascum thapsus*) and common evening primrose (*Oenothera biennis*). Goldenrod's dense yellow flower heads are particularly conspicuous along roadsides and fields in late summer through fall. Less conspicuous are the wind-pollinated flowers of common ragweed; its dust-like pollen is a primary cause of late summer and fall hay fever. The straw-colored upright stems of broomsedge form dense clumps that add winter color to roadsides and fields.

Distribution

Roadsides and fields are abundant across the piedmont and mountain landscape.

Dynamics

The process of vegetation change, whereby species (and communities) are replaced by other species (and communities) over time is called ecological succession. The initial colonizers of roadsides and fields are generally annuals, followed by herbaceous perennials, then woody perennials. Larger, longer-lived species generally replace smaller, shorter-lived ones. Successional change can be rapid—bare soil is often covered by herbaceous plants the first year, and by woody plants within 10 years. Mowing, which cuts back woody plants, frequently interrupts succession, leaving herbaceous plants as the dominant growth form in many fields and roadsides. In the absence of disturbance, succession typically results in the regrowth of the dominant vegetation of the area. If, for example, a piedmont field was once oak-hickory forest, it will likely eventually return to oak-hickory forest, if succession is allowed to run its course.

Using native plants along roadside corridors. Roadside views are some of the most frequently experienced landscapes in the Southeast. Encouraging regionally recognizable vegetation along roadside right-of-ways enhances the public's understanding and appreciation for a sense of place. For this and other reasons, the Federal Highway Administration encourages the use of native plants along roadside corridors. Doing so makes sense not only because of the more interesting (and colorful) landscapes created, but because an ecologically diverse, species-rich landscape is often cheaper to maintain and is more environmentally friendly than a conventional grass monoculture (due to the reduced need for mowing and herbicides).

Roadside corridors provide an opportunity to support a diversity of natural and seminatural communities. For example, roadside right-of-ways provide an excellent opportunity to restore historic piedmont prairies, a community of diverse grasses and colorful wildflowers that was once widely scattered throughout the piedmont. Common prairie species such as Indiangrass (*Sorghastrum nutans*), little bluestem (*Schizachyrium scoparium*), and rattlesnake master (*Eryngium yuccifolium*) grow well along less disturbed roadsides (and unsprayed power line corridors), as do rare species such as smooth coneflower (*Echinacea laevigata*), Schweinitz's sunflower (*Helianthus schweinitzii*), and prairie dock (*Silphium terebinthinaceum*).

Conservation Aspects

Planting and maintaining patches of native vegetation along roadside corridors provides habitat for rare plants and animals. By protecting native plant remnants, highway managers help maintain biological diversity and may inadvertently protect unknown localities of rare species. Preserved or planted native vegetation along roadsides and fields benefits wildlife by providing food and shelter for small mammals, songbirds, and insects. For example, a diversity of native fruiting shrubs and vines in roadsides and fields provides an important food resource for fall-migrating birds. Similarly, monarch butterflies depend on nectar plants and larval host plants (such as milkweeds) in fields and roadsides as they migrate south to Mexico in the fall and return the following spring. Threats to native plants along roadsides and utility corridors include indiscriminate use of herbicides, excessive disturbance, and nonnative species.

SUGGESTED READING

Godfrey, M. A. 1997. *Field Guide to the Piedmont.* Chapel Hill: University of North Carolina Press.

Harper-Lore, B., and M. Wilson, eds. 2000. *Roadside Use of Native Plants.* Washington, D.C.: Island Press.

Keever, C. 1950. Causes of Succession on Old Fields of the Piedmont, North Carolina. *Ecological Monographs* 20:229–50.

ROADSIDE AND FIELD: CHARACTERISTIC PLANTS

Trees

OCCASIONAL TO LOCALLY ABUNDANT SPECIES

Diospyros virginiana	Persimmon	p. 237
Juniperus virginiana	Eastern red cedar	pp. 241–42
Liquidambar styraciflua	Sweetgum	p. 242
Liriodendron tulipifera	Tulip tree, Yellow poplar	pp. 242–43
Pinus taeda	Loblolly pine	pp. 251–52
Pinus virginiana	Virginia pine	pp. 252–53
Prunus serotina	Black cherry	pp. 254–55

Shrubs and Woody Vines

OCCASIONAL TO LOCALLY ABUNDANT SPECIES

Campsis radicans	Trumpet vine, Trumpet creeper	pp. 276–77
Parthenocissus quinquefolia	Virginia creeper	pp. 296–97
Rhus copallinum	Winged sumac	p. 306
Rhus glabra	Smooth sumac	pp. 306–7
Smilax rotundifolia	Common greenbrier	pp. 314–15
Toxicodendron radicans	Poison ivy	pp. 315–16
Vitis rotundifolia	Muscadine, Scuppernong	p. 322

Herbs

OCCASIONAL TO LOCALLY ABUNDANT SPECIES

Achillea millefolium	Yarrow	p. 325
Ambrosia artemisiifolia	Common ragweed	pp. 330–31
Andropogon virginicus	Broomsedge, Broomstraw	pp. 332–33
Asclepias tuberosa	Butterfly weed	p. 338
Coreopsis major	Whorled coreopsis	pp. 355–56
Fragaria virginiana	Wild strawberry	pp. 373–74
Galium aparine	Catchweed bedstraw	p. 376
Ipomoea pandurata	Bigroot morning glory	pp. 392–93
Oenothera biennis	Common evening primrose	pp. 409–10
Passiflora incarnata	Maypops, Passion vine	pp. 418–19
Phytolacca americana	Pokeweed	pp. 422–23
Pteridium aquilinum	Bracken fern	p. 432
Rudbeckia hirta	Black-eyed Susan	pp. 432–33
Solanum carolinense	Horse nettle	pp. 441–42
Solidago altissima	Tall goldenrod	p. 442
Viola sororia	Common blue violet	p. 467

Nonnative Plants

Hypericum perforatum	Common St. John's wort	p. 390
Lamium amplexicaule	Henbit	pp. 394–95
†*Stellaria media*	Common chickweed	
Taraxacum officinale	Common dandelion	pp. 448–49
Trifolium repens	White clover	pp. 454–55
Verbascum thapsus	Woolly mullein	p. 464

Invasive Exotic Plants

Albizia julibrissin	Mimosa, Silktree	p. 225
Elaeagnus umbellata	Autumn olive	pp. 282–83
Ligustrum sinense	Chinese privet	pp. 292–93
Lonicera japonica	Japanese honeysuckle	pp. 294–95
Pueraria montana	Kudzu	pp. 298–99
Rosa multiflora	Multiflora rose	pp. 309–10

† = *plant not included in the species profiles (Part IV)*

PART IV

The plants profiled here are arranged alphabetically by scientific name within three categories: trees, shrubs and woody vines, and herbaceous plants. The 340 entries comprise 65 species of trees, 75 species of shrubs and woody vines, and 200 species of herbaceous plants. In addition to flowering plants, about 20 ferns, mosses, and lichens are profiled among the herbaceous species. An asterisk before a scientific name indicates that the species is introduced (nonnative).

Species Profiles

1 : Trees

Abies fraseri (Pursh) Poir.
FRASER FIR
Pinaceae (Pine family)

Description: Small to medium-sized evergreen tree with erect cones and flat needle-like leaves, shiny green above, whitish below. Nearly smooth gray or brown bark has numerous resin blisters, often with a dense cover of lichens and mosses. Female cones mostly in top few feet of crown and on outer ends of branches; seeds shed Sept.–Nov.

Habitat/range: Cool, moist sites at high elevations (above 5,000 ft.) on shallow, rocky, acidic soils. Spruce-fir forests and balds. Uncommon but locally dominant. A southern Appalachian endemic, it occurs in Virginia, North Carolina, and Tennessee.

Taxonomy: Fraser fir is very similar to balsam fir (*A. balsamea*), a species that occurs in the Appalachians as far south as northern Virginia. Seed cones distinguish these 2 species: the bracts extend well beyond the cone scales in Fraser fir, but are shorter or only slightly longer than the cone scales in balsam fir.

Ecology: Fraser fir forms a dense "sapling bank" under the forest canopy. In deep shade, individuals persist for many years, growing very slowly. When the canopy opens up and light levels increase, growth can be rapid. Once plants reach reproductive maturity, good seed crops are produced every 2–3 years. Seedling establishment typically occurs on persistently moist substrates such as moss, peat, or decaying logs. Adult trees are susceptible to damage by fires and toppling by wind. The biggest threat by far, however, is the balsam woolly adelgid, an aphid-like insect inadvertently introduced from Europe that has devastated adult Fraser fir trees in the southern Appalachians over the past 50 years and could eventually eradicate the species.

Wildlife: Fraser fir's dense evergreen foliage provides shelter for wildlife.

Uses: Fraser fir is a highly sought-after Christmas tree due to its soft, fragrant foliage, persistent needles, and attractive shape. The species is widely grown in commercial tree farms at higher elevations.

Acer floridanum (Chapm.) Pax
SOUTHERN SUGAR MAPLE
Sapindaceae (Soapberry family)

Description: Small to medium-sized deciduous tree with simple, opposite, leaves with 3–5 lobes, the upper surface dark green, the lower surface whitish, hairy. Small, drooping clusters of greenish yellow bell-shaped flowers, usually on separate male and female plants, but some flowers hermaphrodite. Paired samaras, green to brown. Flowers Apr.–May; Fruits June–Oct.

Habitat/range: On moist, rich soils along streams and rivers and in low, wet woodlands, especially common over mafic or calcareous rocks. Communities include alluvial forests, basic mesic forests, river bluff forests, and rich oak-hickory forests. Common in piedmont, rare in mountains. Widespread in Southeast, west to Texas.

Taxonomy: Southern sugar maple is similar to chalk maple (*A. leucoderme*) but has a single trunk, whitish leaf undersides, and the terminal lobes of some leaves are broader toward the apex than toward the base. In contrast, chalk maple typically has multiple trunks, a greenish yellow lower leaf surface, and a terminal lobe that is narrower toward the apex than the base.

Ecology: Southern sugar maple is a slow-growing shade-tolerant understory tree usually less than 25 ft. tall. A characteristic feature of maples is their winged seeds (samaras). When they drop from a tree, samaras begin spinning, which prolongs their descent and increases the distance the seed is dispersed from the parent plant. When seeds occur singly or in low densities, rather than in clumps beneath the parent plant, they are less likely to be discovered and eaten. Thus, one of the benefits of seed dispersal is to evade seed predators such as rodents.

Wildlife: Maples are a favorite tree of yellow-bellied sapsuckers, which drill small holes (pits) in regular horizontal rows in the bark, from which they lick up exuded sap and eat insects attracted to the sugary liquid. Ruby-throated hummingbirds opportunistically lap up sap and eat insects from these same pits.

Uses: Southern sugar maple is sometimes planted as a small shade tree due to its attractive (yellow to red) fall foliage. Unlike sugar maple, it's not tapped commercially for syrup.

Synonym: Acer saccharum ssp. *floridanum*

Acer negundo L.
BOX ELDER
Sapindaceae (Soapberry family)

Description: Small to medium-sized deciduous tree with opposite pinnately compound leaves consisting of 3–7 pointed leaflets. Small, pale green to yellowish unisexual flowers in clusters, the male and female flowers on separate trees. Fruit a paired samara with long wings in drooping clusters. Flowers Mar.–Apr.; fruits May–Oct., persisting through winter.

Habitat/range: Moist habitats, including alluvial forests and streambanks, occasionally on relatively dry upland sites. Common in piedmont, infrequent in mountains. Extends across North America from Canada south to Guatemala.

Taxonomy: Box elder is the only maple in North America with compound leaves. It's easily confused with ash (*Fraxinus*) but ashes have smooth or finely serrate leaflet margins and fruits with only 1 wing. Its 3-parted leaves also resemble those of poison ivy (*Toxicodendron radi-*

cans), but poison ivy has alternate, rather than opposite, leaves.

Ecology: Box elder's unusually wide distribution indicates that it can tolerate a variety of climatic conditions. A fast-growing but short-lived tree, it has fairly weak wood, making it susceptible to wind and ice damage. Most commonly, box elder grows on deep, moist soils near streams, but it occasionally grows on relatively dry upland sites. On riverbanks, trees often lean out sharply over the water, gaining access to additional light, but becoming increasingly vulnerable to being swept away by floodwaters. A wind-pollinated species, female trees produce large fruit crops nearly every year. The winged samaras are dispersed by wind, but birds and small mammals eat the seeds and can play a minor role as dispersers. The seeds germinate readily on moist soil.

Wildlife: Various insects eat the leaves, including caterpillars, leafrollers, gall midges, mites, and aphids. Look for huge masses of box elder bugs (blackish with red markings) on female trees in autumn; in winter they aggregate in sheltered places, including houses.

Uses: Box elder's fibrous root system helps bind the soil, reducing erosion and siltation along streams and rivers.

Acer pensylvanicum L.
STRIPED MAPLE
Sapindaceae (Soapberry family)

Description: Large shrub or small tree with a short trunk, the bark on twigs and young stems green to brown with vertical white stripes. The large 3-lobed leaves with serrate margins resemble a goose's foot. Small, bell-shaped, yellow to green flowers hang in clusters. Pairs of single-seeded winged fruits (samaras), reddish-brown at maturity. Flowers May; fruits June–Sept.

Habitat/range: Cool, moist sites, mainly northern hardwood forests and cove forests. Common in mountains. Widely distributed in northeastern United States and southeastern Canada, south in mountains to Georgia.

Taxonomy: Mountain maple (*A. spicatum*) has somewhat similar foliage but lacks the conspicuous vertical white stripes that characterize the young stems of striped maple.

Ecology: Largely an understory species, striped maple also colonizes forest openings where its growth rate and flowering increase markedly due to increased light levels. Shallow, wide-spreading roots enhance its competitiveness for soil moisture and nutrients. One of the smallest maples in North America, its leaves are the largest of any maple east of the Rockies. Striped maple's small, bell-shaped flowers are also unique among eastern maples. Sex expression is highly variable: some individuals have separate male and female flowers on the same tree, whereas others have only male or female flowers. Individual plants can also switch gender from one year to the next.

Wildlife: White-tailed deer browse the twigs and leaves. A favorite food of moose further north, striped maple is also called moosewood. Chipmunks and squirrels collect the seeds in autumn for immediate consumption or cache them for later use. More than 30 species of butterfly and moth caterpillars feed on the leaves. The nectar in the flowers is an important food for bees and flies in spring.

Uses: The white-striped stems, interesting flowers, and yellow fall foliage make it an attractive ornamental. The large, tear-resistant leaves make a good "emergency" toilet paper.

Acer rubrum L.
RED MAPLE
Sapindaceae (Soapberry family)

Description: Medium to large deciduous tree with slender bright red to dark brownish red, glabrous twigs. Opposite leaves with 3–5 lobes, coarsely toothed margins, and reddish leaf stalks. Small red (to yellowish orange) flowers in clusters appear well before the leaves; male and female flowers often on separate trees. Fruit a double-winged samara. Flowers Jan.–Mar.; fruits Mar.–July.

Habitat/range: Upland deciduous forests, moist bottomlands, and slopes, including river bluff forests, alluvial forests, mountain bogs, oak-hickory forests, pine-mixed hardwood forests, and forest edges. Common. Widespread in eastern North America.

Taxonomy: Aptly named, there is something red about this tree year-round. It has red twigs, buds, and flowers in winter, reddish new leaves in spring, red leaf stalks and seeds in summer, and reddish (or yellow) foliage in autumn.

Ecology: A highly adaptable species, red maple is one of the most abundant and widely distributed trees in eastern North America. It grows in habitats as diverse as mountain bogs and dry ridges, on soil textures ranging from sands to clays, on highly acidic to nearly neutral soils, in open areas with full sunlight to shaded sites in the forest understory, and at elevations ranging from sea level in the coastal plain to nearly 6,000 ft. in the southern Appalachians. Its abundance has increased markedly since presettlement times due to its ability to rapidly colonize disturbed areas. Fire suppression over the past century has also benefited this species. One of our first native trees to bloom in the new year, it flowers long before spring, when nighttime temperatures are often below freezing. A good seed crop is produced nearly every year and the wind-dispersed seeds germinate readily shortly after dispersal.

Wildlife: White-tailed deer and rabbits browse twigs, beavers gnaw bark, and rodents and songbirds consume seeds of red maple. The bright red spots with halos often seen on leaves are flat galls of the maple leafspot midge, a larval fly.

Uses: Red maple is a widely planted landscape tree due to its brilliant fall colors and tolerance of a wide range of conditions.

Acer saccharum Marsh.
SUGAR MAPLE
Sapindaceae (Soapberry family)

Description: Medium to large deciduous tree with a dense elliptical crown. Leaves opposite, simple, palmately veined and lobed, the 5 (rarely 3) lobes sharply pointed with smooth margins. Small, greenish yellow, male and female flowers in drooping clusters. Fruit a horseshoe-shaped pair of winged samaras about 1 in. long. Flowers Apr.–June; fruits June–Sept.

Habitat/range: Moist, well-drained soils, especially on magnesium-rich substrates with elevated soil pH. Northern hardwood forests and cove forests. Common in mountains. Widespread in northeastern North America, south in mountains to Georgia.

Taxonomy: Southern sugar maple (*A. floridanum*), chalk maple (*A. leucoderme*), and sugar maple are closely related and have a similar appearance. Southern sugar maple is shorter in stature, has smaller leaves that are pale on their lower surface, and occurs at lower elevations than sugar maple. The leaves of chalk maple are also smaller than sugar maple, with a green, pubescent lower leaf surface and multiple trunks with chalky white bark.

Ecology: Fire suppression over the past century has favored sugar maple because light surface fires damage its thin bark. The wind-pollinated flowers usually open 1–2 weeks before the leaves emerge. The seeds mature in summer and germinate the following spring, often carpeting the forest floor with seedlings. Some seedlings die because they occupy a poor microsite; rabbits and deer eliminate others; but many survive, growing very slowly until windfall or some other disturbance opens up the dense forest canopy. Shade-suppressed seedlings typically respond to increased light by vigorously growing upward as they race to fill openings in the canopy.

Wildlife: Red squirrels chew the bark of branches and twigs to create wounds that they subsequently visit to lap up sugary sap.

Uses: Sugar maple is the primary source of maple sugar and commercial sugaring, an activity occasionally still practiced in the mountains of Virginia and North Carolina. Widely planted as a landscape tree.

Acer spicatum Lam.
MOUNTAIN MAPLE
Sapindaceae (Soapberry family)

Description: Small understory tree or large shrub with a short, often crooked, trunk. Leaves deciduous, opposite, and simple, with 3–5 lobes and coarsely toothed margins. Small, yellowish green, unisexual flowers appear after leaf expansion in upright terminal clusters. Fruits a double samara that hangs in clusters. Flowers May–June; fruits Sept.–Oct.

Habitat/range: Found on cool, moist sites at higher elevations. Spruce-fir forests, northern hardwood forests, mountain bogs, and boulder fields. Locally abundant. Southeastern Canada, northeastern United States, south in mountains to Georgia.

Taxonomy: Mountain maple differs from striped maple (*A. pensylvanicum*) in that its leaves have a wrinkled texture and it lacks the white-striped bark that characterizes the young stems of striped maple.

Ecology: Mountain maple grows best in open, sunny areas associated with forest openings, but tolerates deep shade in the forest understory. It generally occurs as scattered clumps, but dense thickets sometimes form, particularly after disturbance. Once established, it spreads vegetatively by sprouting from underground stems (rhizomes) and by layering (forming low branches that come in contact with the ground form roots and shoots). Separate male and female flowers generally occur on the same plant. The first flowers to open within an inflorescence are male, followed by female flowers, then more male flowers. Unlike the flowers of most maples, the flowers of mountain maple are insect pollinated, rather than wind pollinated. Primary pollinators are bees, but flies, beetles, and moths also visit and occasionally pollinate the flowers. The winged seeds are dispersed by wind and require an overwintering period for good germination.

Wildlife: Deer actively browse the leaves and twigs of mountain maple. Birds and small to midsize mammals eat the seeds.

Uses: Mountain maple's sap can be tapped for syrup, but because its sugar content is considerably less than that of sugar maple, much more sap has to be boiled to produce the same volume of syrup.

Aesculus flava Aiton
YELLOW BUCKEYE
Sapindaceae (Soapberry family)

Description: Medium to large tree with opposite, palmately compound leaves, each with 5 (rarely 7) toothed leaflets. Yellow tubular flowers (often streaked with red) in elongate clusters near branch tips, the stamens shorter than the petals. Fruit a large round leathery pod containing 1–3 shiny brown seeds. Flowers Apr.–June; fruits Aug.–Sept.

Habitat/range: Moist, fertile soils on mountain slopes, coves, and along streams. Mainly in northern hardwood forests and cove forests, occasionally in spruce-fir forests and red oak forests. Common in mountains, rare in piedmont. Eastern United States.

Taxonomy: The genus *Aesculus* contains about 13 species in eastern Asia, North America, and Europe, including 5 species in our region. Yellow buckeye and Ohio buckeye (*A. glabra*) are our only native buckeyes that develop into large trees. Ohio buckeye has distinctive spiny fruits and is restricted (in our region) to a small area in northwest Georgia and Tennessee.

Ecology: Yellow buckeye is one of the largest and most common trees in northern hardwood and cove forests of the southern Appalachians. It's one of the first trees to leaf out in early spring and drop its leaves (in midsummer). Bumblebees are the primary pollinators but hummingbirds also visit and occasionally pollinate the tubular flowers. Each inflorescence has many flowers, but relatively few develop into fruits because most flowers are staminate (only produce pollen). The unusually large seeds (largest in our flora) give rise to large first-year seedlings with deep taproots. Seeds exposed to direct sunlight or dry conditions quickly lose viability, thereby limiting seedling establishment (and plant distribution) to moist, shaded sites.

Wildlife: The young shoots and mature seeds contain a poisonous glycoside (aesculin) that is toxic to humans and most animals. Squirrels, however, are known to consume the starch-rich seeds, and young seedlings are vulnerable to predation by rodents.

Uses: Yellow buckeye is sometimes grown as a landscape tree and the smooth seeds are considered a good-luck charm.

Synonym: Aesculus octandra Marsh

Albizia julibrissin Durazz.
MIMOSA, SILKTREE
Fabaceae (Legume family)

Description: A small, flat-topped deciduous tree with large, finely divided fern-like leaves. The showy white to pink flowers form compound clusters that resemble pom-poms. Fruit a dangling flattened pod, 3–7 in. long. Flowers May–Aug.; fruits July–Nov.

Habitat/range: Roadsides and other disturbed sites, woodlands, and forest edges and openings. Common in piedmont, occasional in mountains. Introduced from Asia, now widespread in Southeast.

Taxonomy: A genus of about 100 species of trees, shrubs, and vines in warm climates of Asia, Africa, and America. Honey locust (*Gleditsia triacanthos*) is similar, but it has stout thorns.

Ecology: This fast-growing but short-lived tree grows best in full sun. While it can tolerate partial shade, it rarely persists under a dense forest canopy or at elevations greater than 3,000 ft. due to its sensitivity to low temperatures. Its leaves and leaflets droop on cloudy days and close at night. Introduced to the United States in the mid-eighteenth century by famous French botanist André Michaux, it has escaped from cultivation and persists along roadsides, forest edges, in woodlands, and in forest openings. Its invasive properties are facilitated by its ability to thrive in a variety of soil types, to tolerate both wet and dry conditions, to quickly resprout following topkill, and to produce abundant fruits with hard-coated seeds that persist in the soil for many years. Mimosa is a strong competitor with native trees and shrubs in forest edges and other open areas. By fixing nitrogen, it can disrupt the nutrient status of naturally nutrient-poor soils.

Wildlife: Bees and butterflies are attracted to the showy, fragrant flowers that appear in abundance from late spring through summer.

Uses: Mimosa is a popular ornamental due to its wide-spreading crown, showy flowers, and fern-like leaves. Given its invasive properties, native trees such as redbud (*Cercis canadensis*), serviceberry (*Amelanchier arborea*), and sourwood (*Oxydendrum arboreum*) make excellent alternatives.

Amelanchier laevis Wiegand
SMOOTH SERVICEBERRY
Rosaceae (Rose family)

Description: A shrub or small deciduous tree up to 30 ft. tall with smooth gray bark (much like the bark of American beech) when young, with long, narrow, sharply pointed winter buds. Alternate, pinnately veined leaves with finely serrate margins. Showy clusters of white flowers emerge before the leaves. Fruit a berry-like pome, sweet and edible, initially red, ripening to dark purple or black. Flowers Apr.–May; fruits June–July.

Habitat/range: High-elevation rock outcrops, balds, red oak forests, and forest edges. Common in mountains, uncommon in piedmont. Eastern North America.

Taxonomy: The genus *Amelanchier* includes 40 species of shrubs and trees of north temperate regions. *A. laevis* and *A. arborea* (downy serviceberry) are similar species with overlapping distributions. *A. laevis* has smooth, coppery purple, newly emerged leaves and sweet, juicy fruits, whereas *A. arborea* has hairy emerging leaves and drier ripe fruits. In some areas, hybridization obscures these differences, making it difficult to tell them apart.

Ecology: From afar, serviceberry trees resemble white clouds against a backdrop of mostly leafless trees in early spring. In spite of the showy white flowers and their potential to attract pollinators, the seeds of serviceberry are generally produced asexually (without fusion of eggs and sperm, much like dandelions). Fruits with more seeds develop more rapidly and ripen earlier than fruits with fewer seeds. Variation in fruit rate ripening extends the fruiting season, which in turn increases the number and diversity of birds and mammals that harvest fruits and disperse the seeds. Widespread seed dispersal enables serviceberry to be one of the first and most common woody plant invaders of grassy balds.

Wildlife: Smooth serviceberry's early spring flowers provide an important source of nectar and pollen for bees and other insects, while the fruits are consumed by various birds and mammals, including bears, skunks, and chipmunks.

Uses: Showy early spring flowers, many wildlife benefits, and tolerance of a wide range of conditions make smooth serviceberry an appealing landscape plant.

Synonym: Amelanchier arborea (Michx. f.) var. *laevis* (Wiegand) H. E. Ahles

Betula alleghaniensis Britton
YELLOW BIRCH
Betulaceae (Birch family)

Description: A medium to large deciduous tree. The yellowish or silvery bark on young trunks and branches peels horizontally into thin, curly papery strips. Twigs have a faint wintergreen odor when cut. Leaves alternate, simple, ovate with doubly serrate margins. Male and female flowers in catkins near tips of twigs. Small oval cones contain many small, winged seeds (nutlets). Flowers Mar.–May; fruits June–Aug.

Habitat/range: Moist, well-drained soils northern hardwood forests, spruce-fir forests, red oak forests, cove forests, and boulder fields. Common at medium to high elevations in mountains. Canada south to Georgia in mountains, west to Great Lakes region.

Taxonomy: Betula is a genus of about 35 species of trees and shrubs of North America, Asia, and Europe, including 6 species in the mountains and piedmont.

Ecology: Yellow birch is a relatively long-lived species that requires gaps in the forest canopy for successful establishment and growth. A prolific seed producer, its tiny wind-dispersed seeds germinate mostly on surfaces free of leaf litter, such as exposed mineral soil, rotting logs, and boulders. Seeds that germinate on decomposing logs produce seedlings whose roots grow down over the side of the log and through it to reach the soil. When the "nurse" log decays, the elevated tree is left standing, as if on stilts. Seeds of yellow birch can also germinate and establish new plants on boulders, making it a common tree in boulder fields. Its shallow, wide-spreading roots make it susceptible to both windthrow and drought and its thin bark makes it vulnerable to fire.

Wildlife: Yellow birch is a favorite tree of birds that glean insects from leaves, as its foliage is a particularly rich source of prey. Look for spider webs in the foliage in early spring when birch pollen is dispersed by the wind. Certain orb spiders, when young, catch pollen in their webs, after which they eat the webs, including the highly nutritious pollen grains.

Uses: The papery bark curls are highly flammable and can be used to start a campfire, even when wet.

Synonym: Betula lutea Michx.

Betula lenta L.
SWEET BIRCH, CHERRY BIRCH
Betulaceae (Birch family)

Description: A medium-sized deciduous tree with reddish brown to almost black bark with horizontally elongate lenticels, the leaves and twigs produce a strong wintergreen odor. Leaves simple, alternate with a cordate base and toothed margins. Male flowers in slender drooping catkins near tip of twigs, female flowers in short, erect catkins. Fruit an apically winged seed. Flowers Mar.–Apr; fruits June–July.

Habitat/range: Mostly in rich, moist woods, occasionally on drier rocky soils. Common in mountains, uncommon in upper piedmont. From Maine west to Ohio, south in mountains to Georgia.

Taxonomy: Sweet birch and yellow birch (*B. alleghaniensis*) are closely related species with overlapping distributions that occasionally form hybrids. The 2 species are readily distinguished by their bark: sweet birch has reddish brown to nearly black bark, whereas yellow birch has shiny yellowish or silvery bark that separates into thin, curly, horizontal strips.

Ecology: Sweet birch is a shade-intolerant tree that depends on forest gaps and areas with a more open canopy for successful regeneration. Fire suppression over the last century has led to an increase in sweet birch, as its thin bark makes it highly vulnerable to low-intensity surface fires. Like the flowers of many deciduous trees, the flowers of sweet birch are wind-pollinated, with male flowers releasing huge amounts of pollen before the leaves emerge. Abundant seeds are widely dispersed by wind, increasing the chance that some seeds will end up in forest openings where seedling establishment and growth can occur.

Wildlife: Deer feed on twigs and young leaves and birds eat catkins, buds, and seeds.

Uses: Sweet birch was once a primary source of the wintergreen flavoring used in medicines and confections, but most flavoring is now produced synthetically.

Betula nigra L.
RIVER BIRCH
Betulaceae (Birch family)

Description: Small to medium-sized deciduous tree with reddish brown or pinkish bark peeling into thin shaggy sheets. Leaves alternate with a wedge-shaped base and double-toothed margins. Tiny unisexual flowers in catkins; male catkins elongate and drooping, female catkins upright. Small nutlets in narrow cone-like clusters near branch tips. Flowers Mar.–Apr.; fruits May–June.

Habitat/range: Periodically wet areas such as riverbanks, streambanks, sandbars, and alluvial forests. Common in piedmont, uncommon in mountains. Throughout eastern United States.

Taxonomy: River birch can be distinguished from yellow birch (*Betula alleghaniensis*) and sweet birch (*B. lenta*) by reddish brown or pink bark peeling into thin, paper-like layers, wedge-shaped leaf bases, and a lack of a wintergreen odor in crushed leaves and cut twigs.

Ecology: A characteristic floodplain species, river birch can tolerate frequently waterlogged soils. The conspicuously peeling bark benefits the plant as it provides a mechanism to "shed" vines that might otherwise grow up into the canopy and shade out its leaves. Large seed crops are produced almost every year. The winged seeds are dispersed by wind and by water; water is probably the more important dispersant, as it is more likely to deposit seeds in a favorable site for germination and seedling establishment, which for river birch is a site with soil high in moisture and sunlight (as is found along river margins). Unlike the seeds of our other birches, its seeds are dispersed in early summer (rather than in fall), a time when the surrounding landscape is less likely to be flooded. The seeds germinate almost immediately after dispersal, as they lose viability within 3 days. On moist, open alluvial soils such as river sandbars, large numbers of seedlings can establish, forming dense thickets of river birch.

Wildlife: White-tailed deer browse the foliage and various birds consume the seeds.

Uses: River birch is a widely planted landscape tree because of its attractive peeling bark, adaptability, and drought tolerance. River birch helps reduce erosion and siltation along waterways, but produces abundant wind-dispersed pollen in early spring, which can be allergenic.

Carpinus caroliniana Walter
IRONWOOD, MUSCLEWOOD
Betulaceae (Birch family)

Description: A small deciduous tree with smooth gray bark with muscle-like ridges. Leaves alternate, simple, elliptic to ovate, margins doubly toothed. Male and female flowers in separate catkins on same tree. Nutlets subtended by a

3-lobed leaf bract, in loose droopy clusters 2–4 in. long. Flowers Mar.–Apr.; fruits Sept.–Oct.

Habitat/range: Moist forests, including along streambanks, in alluvial forests, basic mesic forests, and rich cove forests. Common in piedmont and lower elevations of mountains. Widespread in eastern North America.

Taxonomy: Of the 26 species in the genus, ironwood is the only species native to North America. Its leaves resemble hop hornbeam (*Ostrya virginiana*) but its bark is smooth and ridged, unlike the shredding bark of hop hornbeam.

Ecology: Ironwood is a small, slow-growing tree that reaches an average height of 8–10 ft. after about 10 years. Like most shade-tolerant trees, its growth rate increases in response to the increased light associated with canopy gaps. A moisture-loving (mesophytic) species, it grows best in areas with abundant moisture such as floodplains, coves, and lower slopes, but its shallow roots can't tolerate the poor aeration associated with soils saturated for prolonged periods. Its maximum elevation is about 3,000 ft. in the southern Appalachians, but is more common at lower elevations where it's largely restricted to communities that infrequently experience fires, since its thin bark makes it vulnerable. A masting species, ironwood produces large seed crops at 3- to 5-year intervals. The seeds are dispersed by birds and by wind. When nutlets fall from a tree, their associated leaf-like bracts function as sails, carrying the seeds away from the parent plant in the direction of the prevailing wind. Established trees can spread laterally by root sprouts.

Wildlife: Beavers fell ironwood trees for food and lodging material, white-tailed deer and rabbits browse the twigs and foliage, and birds and small mammals eat the nutlets.

Uses: The extremely hard wood was once used for mallets, tool handles, and golf club heads. Ironwood is occasionally planted as a landscape tree.

Carya glabra (Mill.) Sweet
PIGNUT HICKORY
Juglandaceae (Walnut family)

Description: A medium-sized deciduous tree with alternate pinnately compound leaves with 5 (sometimes 7) leaflets, the leaflets and rachis glabrous, the foliage fragrant when crushed. Yellowish green male flowers in drooping catkins, female flowers inconspicuous in small, erect clusters at shoot tips. Nut roundish to egg- or pear-shaped, about 1 in. long with a thick husk, turning brown to brownish black while ripening. Flowers Apr.–May; fruits Oct.

Habitat/range: Dry to moist woods, including oak-hickory forests, chestnut oak forests, and xeric hardpan forests. Common in piedmont and at lower elevations in mountains. Eastern United States.

Taxonomy: There are more species of hickory in the Southeast than anywhere else in the world, including 10 species in the mountain and piedmont regions. Hickories and ash (*Fraxinus*) are similar in having pinnately compound leaves, but hickories have alternate leaves whereas ash has opposite leaves.

Ecology: Pignut hickory grows on a variety of sites but is most common on dry slopes and ridges of upland forests. Like other hickories, it produces separate male and female flowers on the same tree. The wind-pollinated flowers produce a good seed crop at 1–2 year intervals. Nuts buried by squirrels (but not recovered) have higher germination and seedling establishment rates than nuts on the soil surface. Periodic fires tend to favor oaks over less fire-resistant hickories. Hickories, like dogwoods (*Cornus*), are considered to be "soil improvers" because their decomposing leaves release relatively high amounts of calcium, which elevates soil pH and enhances nutrient availability.

Wildlife: Numerous mammals eat the bitter-tasting nuts, as do a variety of birds including blue jays, crows, and red-bellied woodpeckers. High nut predation is one reason why hickory seedlings occur at low densities in most forests.

Uses: Native Americans ground and cooked the nuts with cornmeal, threw the crushed green shells into pools to stun fish for easy capture, and made bows out of the wood. Hickory makes excellent firewood as it burns hotter than most other woods.

Carya ovata (Mill) K. Koch
SHAGBARK HICKORY
Juglandaceae (Walnut family)

Description: Medium to large deciduous tree, with bark forming long strips that curl outward at each end, giving mature trees a conspicuously shaggy appearance. Pinnately compound leaves with 5 (sometimes 7) leaflets. Male flowers in drooping catkins, female flowers inconspicuous. Fruit a nearly round nut with a thick husk that splits to the base. Flowers May; fruits Oct.

Habitat/range: Alluvial forests, moist slopes, occasionally on dry upland flats. Uncommon. Widespread in eastern North America.

Taxonomy: The common name describes the very shaggy bark of older trees. Crushed leaves have a faint apple odor rather than the astringent odor typically associated with hickory leaves.

Ecology: This slow-growing but long-lived, shade-tolerant tree can persist for many years under a forest canopy. It generally occurs with oaks, other hickories, and various other hardwoods. Periodic fires tend to favor oaks over thinner-barked, less fire-resistant hickories. Like the flowers of other hickories, its flowers are wind pollinated. Trees begin producing nuts after about 4 decades, then every 1–3 years, with little or no nut production in intervening years. A thick green husk surrounds and protects the developing nut, as does the tan-colored nutshell that encloses the sweet, edible kernel. The seeds are dispersed by gravity and by small mammals and birds. The now extinct passenger pigeon dispersed seeds of many hickory species. The seeds require exposure to a cool, moist overwintering period (stratification) prior to germinating in spring. Seedlings develop a deep taproot with minimal shoot growth; after 3 years growth, the shoots are often less than 8 in. tall with taproots 3 ft. deep.

Wildlife: The large sweet seeds are sought after by a wide variety of birds and mammals including wood ducks, blue jays, crows, squirrels, foxes, and bears. Brown creepers build their nests and bats roost under the loose bark.

Uses: Shagbark hickory's wood is highly valued for lumber, fuel, and charcoal, its sweet nuts are sometimes sold commercially, and its picturesque bark makes it an attractive landscape tree.

Carya tomentosa (Lam.) Nutt.
MOCKERNUT HICKORY
Juglandaceae (Walnut family)

Description: A medium to large deciduous tree with stout ascending branches and pinnately compound leaves with 7–9 (sometimes 5) leaflets, the petioles and lower sides of leaflets covered with dense woolly hairs, the foliage aromatic when crushed. Male flowers in yellowish green drooping catkins, female flowers inconspicuous in small, erect clusters at shoot tips. Fruit a large round to elliptical nut with a thick husk, splitting to base. Flowers Apr.–May; fruits Oct.

Habitat/range: Forests and woodlands, including oak-hickory forests, chestnut oak forests, and forest edges. Common. Widespread in eastern and central United States.

Taxonomy: A genus of 18 species of eastern North America and Asia, including 10 species in the Southeast. Mockernut hickory is readily identified by its hairy leaves and petioles, thick fruit husks, and fissured bark with interlacing ridges that form a diamond-like pattern on mature trees.

Ecology: The most common hickory in the Southeast, mockernut hickory is a long-lived (up to 500 years), shade-intolerant canopy tree. A good seed crop is produced every 2–3 years; the fall-ripened nuts are dispersed by gravity and by wildlife, especially squirrels, which bury the seeds at varying distances from the parent tree. The short-lived seeds (lasting about 1 year) germinate in spring, producing slow-growing seedlings that are vulnerable to frost damage. It takes about 50 years before a newly established tree begins producing nuts.

Wildlife: Hickory nuts are large and highly nutritious relative to the fruits and seeds of most trees. They are highly sought after by mammals (squirrels, foxes, bears, and deer), birds (wild turkeys, mallards, and wood ducks), and insect larvae (including the hickory nut weevil and the hickory shuckworm). Nuts that escape predation and emerge as seedlings are vulnerable to browsing deer and rabbits and defoliation by insects. As a result, a tiny fraction of the nuts successfully produce trees.

Uses: Hickories are highly valued for their edible nuts, exceptionally strong wood, the golden yellow to brown fall colors they produce, and the flavor their hickory chips give smoked meats.

Castanea dentata (Marsh.) Borkh.
AMERICAN CHESTNUT
Fagaceae (Beech family)

Description: A large deciduous tree, once abundant in mountains, now persists mostly as multistemmed sprouts up to 30 ft. tall. Leaves green and glabrous on both sides, 6–11 in. long, tapering to a pointed tip, each lateral vein ending in a curved, bristle-tipped tooth. Large spiny fruits enclose 2–3 flattened nuts. Flowers June–July; fruits Sept.–Oct.

Habitat/range: Mesic to xeric forests on well-drained soils, including red oak forests, northern hardwood forests, cove forests, chestnut oak forests, pine-oak-heath, and oak-hickory forests. Common in mountains, occasionally in piedmont. Ontario and Maine, west to Michigan, south to Georgia.

Taxonomy: Castanea is a genus of 8–10 species of eastern North America, Asia, and Europe.

Ecology: American chestnut was once a dominant canopy tree of eastern North America. It reached its greatest size and density in the southern Appalachians where it made up roughly 40 percent of the canopy trees in some pre-blight forests. American chestnut was severely impacted by the chestnut blight, a fungus accidentally introduced to New York from Asian nursery plants in 1904. The highly infectious spores spread rapidly by wind, insects, and migrating birds; by 1940, nearly all standing American chestnut trees in the southern Appalachians were dead. Because the pathogen can't enter root systems, many topkilled trees survived, producing new shoots from the root crown. Today, the American chestnut persists throughout much of its range as root sprouts, growing in the understory, usually as a shrub, only occasionally flowering and producing seeds. The chestnut blight fungus persists in forests and continues to infect chestnut sprouts. Lost as a major tree species in the eastern United States, American chestnut likely faces eventual extinction as a distinct species. Efforts are being made, however, to develop plants resistant to the chestnut blight fungus by hybridizing the American chestnut with blight-resistant Asian chestnuts.

Wildlife: Before the blight, chestnut trees produced a large crop of nuts each autumn, providing a reliable food source for many wildlife species, including bears, deer, and squirrels.

Uses: American chestnut was once valued more highly than any other North American tree due to its soft yet durable wood and abundant sweet nuts.

Celtis laevigata Willd.
HACKBERRY, SUGARBERRY
Cannabaceae (Hops family)

Description: Medium-sized deciduous tree with a straight trunk and smooth gray bark with conspicuous corky outgrowths. Leaves variable, usually more than twice as long as wide, long-pointed at apex, asymmetric at base. Small, unisexual yellow-green flowers lack petals. Small, round, orange-red to yellow, 1-seeded fruits with a thin layer of sweet edible pulp. Flowers Apr.–May; fruits Aug.–Oct, often persisting into winter.

Habitat/range: Moist woods, including alluvial forests and streambanks, occasionally upland forests and roadsides. Common in piedmont, uncommon in mountains. Widespread in Southeast, west to Texas.

Taxonomy: A genus of about 60 species of trees, shrubs, and woody vines of tropical and temperate regions, nearly worldwide. Of the 3 hackberry species in our region, it's the only one whose leaves are more than twice as long as wide.

Ecology: This shade-tolerant, relatively short-lived tree occurs primarily in bottomlands and on the edges of streams. Like many bottomland species, it has a shallow, spreading root system, rather than a deep taproot. The insect-pollinated flowers open before the leaves emerge in spring, and good seed crops are produced most years. Widely dispersed by birds, small mammals, and water, the seeds require an overwintering period prior to germinating in spring. Hackberries often have a thick profusion of twigs at the end of branches (most easily seen in winter). Called witches' broom, this abnormal branching pattern results from the combined effect of a powdery mildew fungus and the hackberry witches' broom gall mite.

Wildlife: The fruits provide winter food for more than 25 species of birds, including yellow-bellied sapsuckers, Northern flickers, and cedar waxwings. Nocturnal flying squirrels also consume the fleshy fruits and disperse the seeds. Hackberry is a caterpillar host plant for eastern snout and hackberry butterflies. Sap-sucking hackberry lace bugs cause the foliage to turn prematurely yellow or brown in early fall.

Uses: Hackberry makes a nice shade or street tree because it tolerates a wide range of conditions (including air pollution), but its branches are easily broken by wind and ice.

Cercis canadensis L.
EASTERN REDBUD
Fabaceae (Legume family)

Description: Small understory tree with broad, heart-shaped, palmately-veined leaves and pea-shaped, purplish pink flowers borne on leafless twigs in early spring. Fruit a flat, thin pod, 2–4 in. long. Flowers Mar.–May; fruits June–Nov., persisting into winter.

Habitat/range: Moist to dry forests and woodlands, often on calcareous soils. Basic mesic forests, oak-hickory forests, river bluff forests, alluvial forests, and xeric hardpan forests. Common in piedmont, less so in mountains. Widespread in eastern North America.

Taxonomy: A genus of 6 species of trees of North America, Asia, and Europe, with only 1 species in the mountains and piedmont.

Ecology: Redbud grows almost anywhere that's not excessively wet, dry, or strongly acidic, but does best on moist, well-drained soils in partial shade. Fast-growing but short-lived, it typically occurs as a small understory tree with a short trunk and a broad, rounded, or flat crown. Like many plants, it adjusts its leaf angle in response to the amount of sunlight received. In full sunlight, the leaves are typically slanted so that the apex is pointed toward the ground; in shade, the leaf blade is lifted to a nearly horizontal position. This is an adaptive response as the sun position intercepts less light, promoting leaf cooling, which in turn reduces transpirational water loss. In contrast, the horizontal orientation in the shade allows leaves to intercept more light, enhancing the efficiency of photosynthesis. The pea-like flowers are actively visited and pollinated by large bees, typically resulting in high fruit set. Each fruit (pod) contains from 4 to 10 seeds that can persist in the soil for several years before germinating. Unlike most members of the legume family, redbud lacks nitrogen-fixing nodules in its roots.

Wildlife: Birds and small mammals pry open the pods to feed on the seeds, and caterpillars of several moth species feed on the leaves.

Uses: Redbud is a popular landscape tree because of its showy early spring flowers and its ability to tolerate a wide range of conditions. Both the flowers and young seedpods are edible.

Chionanthus virginicus L.
FRINGETREE, OLD MAN'S BEARD
Oleaceae (Olive family)

Description: A large shrub or small tree with a spreading, rather open habit, often wider than tall, with simple, opposite, deciduous leaves on short purplish stalks. Large, drooping clusters of small, fragrant flowers with 4 linear white petals. Fruit a bluish black berry-like drupe in axillary clusters. Flowers Apr.–May; fruits July–Sept.
Habitat/range: Wide variety of habitats, including dry to moist forests, woodlands, and granite outcrops. Common. Eastern United States.
Taxonomy: A genus of more than 100 mostly tropical species. Fringetree is distinguished by its conspicuous clusters of white, fringe-like flowers in spring. At other times it can be recognized by its opposite leaves with purplish petioles, enlarged nodes, and large rough lenticels.

Ecology: Fringetree is spectacular in spring when masses of drooping, fragrant white flowers cover the plant. Mostly dioecious, individuals produce either male or female flowers but occasionally both flower types are found on the same plant. Evening-flying moths probably pollinate the strongly fragrant sweet-smelling flowers. In bloom, male plants are usually showier than females (their flowers have longer petals), but female plants compensate by producing attractive clusters of bluish black fruits from mid- to late summer.
Wildlife: Various birds and mammals eat the fleshy fruits and disperse the seeds.
Uses: Fringetree is an excellent landscape plant because of its striking clusters of fragrant flowers and its drought tolerance.

Cladrastis kentukea (Dum. Cours.) Rudd
YELLOWWOOD
Fabaceae (Legume family)

Description: Small to medium-sized deciduous tree with spreading branches and smooth, gray, often wrinkled bark. Alternate pinnately compound leaves with 5–9 mostly alternate leaflets with smooth margins, the swollen petiole enclosing the lateral buds. Pea-like, somewhat fragrant white flowers borne in hanging clusters. Fruit a thin flat pod, 2–4 in. long, persists into winter. Flowers Apr.–May; fruits July–Aug.

Habitat/range: Moist forests, especially on calcareous soil. Rich cove forests in mountains, river bluff forests in piedmont. Rare. Occurs mainly on western side of southern Appalachians and in Ozarks.

Taxonomy: Yellowwood is the only southeastern species in the genus; the other 5 species occur in eastern Asia. The pinnately compound leaves resemble ash (*Fraxinus*) but the leaves (and leaflets) of yellowwood are alternate, whereas ash leaves are opposite. Freshly-cut heartwood is a light to brilliant yellow color, providing the common name.

Ecology: Yellowwood grows in full sun to partial shade, on soil over bedrock that is usually high in calcium or magnesium. Individuals usually flower and produce good seed crops in alternate years. Each flat, brown fruit pod contains 4–6 compressed seeds with hard (impermeable) seed coats that delay germination until spring. Thin bark makes it susceptible to topkill by fire. Yellowwood, like most members of the legume family, has roots with nodules that fix nitrogen gas and convert it into biologically useful ammonia, a process mediated by bacteria in the genus *Rhizobium*. The plant uses nitrogen fixed by the bacteria; in turn, the bacteria are provided habitat and sugars derived from photosynthesis. Because the relationship between the plant and the bacteria is mutually beneficial, it is considered to be a type of mutualism.

Wildlife: Bees actively visit and pollinate the flowers and birds and rodents disperse the seeds.

Uses: Yellowwood is often planted as a landscape tree due to its showy clusters of fragrant flowers and attractive foliage. Its wood is the source of a clear yellow dye.

Cornus florida L.
FLOWERING DOGWOOD
Cornaceae (Dogwood family)

Description: A small, low-branched deciduous tree with a flat-topped, layered canopy, and a dark, irregularly checkered bark like an alligator's hide. Leaves opposite with lateral veins curving toward the tip of the blade. Flowers in small, dense clusters surrounded by 4 large, white petal-like bracts. Bright red fruits in tight clusters. Flowers Mar.–May; fruits Sept.–Oct.

Habitat/range: Dry to moist forests. Common. Widespread in eastern United States.

Taxonomy: Flowering dogwood is readily distinguished from the other 10 species of dogwood in the mountains and piedmont by the 4 large, white bracts that resemble petals, by clusters of red fruits in fall, by numerous globe-shaped terminal flower buds in winter, and by its distinctive checkered bark.

Ecology: Nearly everyone living in the South is familiar with flowering dogwood since it's planted in yards and parks. Many people, however, don't realize that flowering dogwood is a common understory tree in eastern deciduous forests. A short-lived but relatively fast-growing species, it grows in deep, moist soils along streams, as well as on upper slopes and ridges where the soil is drier. While it can tolerate high temperatures, its shallow root system makes it vulnerable to prolonged drought. The number of flowering dogwoods is declining (particularly in cool, moist, shaded habitats at higher elevations) due to an anthracnose fungus.

Wildlife: White-tailed deer and rabbits browse the foliage (and twigs), beavers eat the bark, and beetles, bees, and flies pollinate the flowers. Although bitter and mildly toxic to humans, the high-fat-content fruits are consumed by numerous birds, including fall migrants that typically consume the pulp and disperse the seeds in their droppings, sometimes long distances from the parent tree. Fruits that fall to the ground beneath the parent plant suffer high seed predation rates by squirrels and other rodents.

Uses: A tea made from the bark of roots was widely used to treat malaria in the nineteenth century. One of America's most popular landscape trees, it's the state tree (and flower) of Virginia and the state flower of North Carolina.

Crataegus macrosperma Ashe
BIGFRUIT HAWTHORN
Rosaceae (Rose family)

Description: Shrub or small deciduous tree up to 20 ft. tall with stout twigs, zigzag branching, and long sharp thorns. Leaves simple, alternate with sharply serrate margins. White to pinkish flowers in flat-topped clusters with 5 petals, 5 sepals, and numerous red anthers. Fruit a small, round, apple-like fleshy pome. Flowers Apr.–early May; fruits Sept.–Oct.

Habitat/range: Found in variety of habitats, including red oak forests, rock outcrops, mountain balds, forest edges, and abandoned fields. Common in mountains and piedmont. Virginia south to Georgia, west to Kentucky.

Taxonomy: Crataegus is a large genus of woody species with much hybridization and taxonomic uncertainty. It's fairly easy to recognize members of the genus (especially if thorns are present), but distinguishing between species can be difficult. Some experts include about 100 species in the genus; others recognize more than 500.

Ecology: Bigfruit hawthorn typically produces large numbers of fruits that persist on the tree for some time. Once the more preferred fruits of other species are consumed, hawthorn fruits are actively removed and widely dispersed by birds and mammals. A common early colonizer of grassy balds and other open habitats, bigfruit hawthorn spreads rapidly by vegetative propagation and by seed. Seeds are produced both sexually (from the fusion of egg cell and sperm cell) and asexually. Bigfruit hawthorn is one of the most common trees in the southern Appalachians.

Wildlife: Hawthorn thickets with their dense twigs and thorns provide excellent nesting cover for songbirds. Birds sometimes appear to be intoxicated when feeding on fermented hawthorn fruits in early winter. Wormy fruits in fall or winter usually indicate an infestation by codling moth caterpillars, also called apple worms, a harmful pest species found in apple orchards.

Uses: The fruits vary in both taste and texture: some are dry and mealy, others are sweet and succulent and can be used in jams and jellies. Bigfruit hawthorn isn't a good tree to plant close to people, pets, or cars because of its low branches and sharp tire-piercing thorns.

Diospyros virginiana L.
PERSIMMON
Ebenaceae (Ebony family)

Description: A small to medium-sized deciduous tree with deeply furrowed bark. Leaves alternate, simple, pointed at apex, mostly rounded at base, upper surface dark green, often with black marks, lower surface lighter green. Inconspicuous, fragrant, urn-shaped yellowish green flowers appear after the leaves. Fruit a large edible pumpkin-colored berry with large flat seeds. Flowers May–June; fruits Sept.–Dec.

Habitat/range: Dry to mesic forests, alluvial forests, fencerows, fields, and clearings. Common in piedmont, occasional in mountains. Widespread in eastern United States, but most abundant in South.

Taxonomy: A large genus of trees and shrubs found mainly in tropical and subtropical regions with only 1 species in the mountains and piedmont. Can be confused with black gum (*Nyssa sylvatica*) when flowers or fruits aren't present, but the leaves of persimmon tend to be spread along the stem (rather than clustered at the stem tips).

Ecology: This slow-growing, shade-tolerant tree grows in an exceptionally wide range of habitats—from the deep, moist soils of alluvial forests to dry, rocky hillsides. Male and female flowers occur on separate trees and bees pollinate the small but delightfully fragrant flowers. Good fruit crops are usually produced every other year, but a late freeze can damage the flowers and cause premature fruit drop. Seeds that pass through the gut of fruit-eating animals are exposed to gastrointestinal enzymes that scarify (weaken) the seed coat, allowing water uptake and subsequent germination. Persimmon spreads by seeds and vegetatively by root suckers. Trunks damaged, burned, or cut, often resprout from the base. Leaf spot disease causes black spots on the leaves and premature defoliation, but doesn't kill the tree. However, a fungal disease known as persimmon wilt kills many trees in the Southeast.

Wildlife: The sweet, pulpy fruits are relished by numerous wildlife species and the large flattened seeds are commonly seen in the droppings of raccoons, foxes, and other mammals.

Uses: Fully ripened persimmon fruits are edible, but unripe fruits are strongly astringent, causing one's mouth to pucker unpleasantly.

Fagus grandifolia Ehrh.
AMERICAN BEECH
Fagaceae (Beech family)

Description: A large deciduous tree easily recognized by its smooth, light to dark grey bark, long, slender, sharply pointed buds, and prickly fruits with

2–3 triangular nuts. Alternate coarsely toothed leaves with prominent parallel veins, some thin, tan leaves persisting through winter. Separate male and female flowers on same tree. Flowers Mar.–Apr.; fruits Sept.–Oct.

Habitat/range: Moist forests from near sea level to high mountains, including northern hardwood forests, rich cove forests, river bluff forests, and basic mesic forests. Common. Widespread in eastern North America.

Taxonomy: The genus includes 10 species worldwide, but only 1 in North America.

Ecology: This slow-growing but long-lived, very shade-tolerant tree commonly occurs in both the understory and canopy of mature forests. Its shallow, wide-spreading roots make it susceptible to drought, flooding, and soil compaction, especially when vehicles are driven near trees. Beech bark disease is caused by a scale insect (accidentally introduced from Europe) that pierces the thin bark (to suck sap), which in turn provides an entry point for bark canker fungi. This serious disease has killed numerous beech trees, particularly in stands where beech is a dominant species. Initials carved into the thin, smooth bark can also provide an entry point for disease. Thin bark and shallow roots make beech trees extremely vulnerable to fire damage. Fire suppression over the past century has resulted in a dramatic increase in the number of American beech trees. Beechdrops (*Epifagus virginiana*) often grows near beech trees; it's a small, parasitic, flowering plant that obtains all its nutrients from beech roots.

Wildlife: Beech "nuts" are an important food source for many animals, including squirrels, chipmunks, bears, and various birds. Blue jays cache the nuts and disperse the seeds. The nuts were a favorite food of the now extinct passenger pigeon.

Uses: Beeches make nice shade trees.

Fraxinus americana L.
WHITE ASH
Oleaceae (Olive family)

Description: Large, usually straight tree with grayish brown bark roughened by a network of interlacing ridges with diamond-shaped furrows between them. Leaves opposite, deciduous, pinnately compound with 5–9 leaflets, dark green on top, whitish on bottom. Separate male and female trees with small, fairly inconspicuous flowers that open before the leaves emerge. Fruit a winged samara, about 1–2 in. long, paddle-shaped, in loose, drooping clusters in leaf axils. Flowers Apr.–May; fruits Aug.–Oct.

Habitat/range: Moist, fertile, well-drained soils in a variety of upland and lowland deciduous forests. Common in mountains and piedmont. Widely distributed in eastern North America.

Taxonomy: The genus *Fraxinus* occurs in north temperate regions of North America, Asia, and Europe. Six of the more than 50 species in the genus occur in the mountains and piedmont.

Ecology: White ash is a fast-growing pioneer species most often found in early-successional to midsuccessional stages. Its seedlings and saplings can survive several years under moderately dense shade, but few individuals reach the overstory unless exposed to increased light. Mature white ash trees in dense forests typically have long trunks free of branches for much of their length as shaded branches are readily shed.

Wildlife: White-tailed deer browse the twigs and leaves, various songbirds and small mammals eat the seeds, and cavity-nesting birds such as woodpeckers, wood ducks, and owls can be found in larger trees. Fall webworms feed on the leaves and build unsightly nests in late summer.

Uses: White ash is a valuable timber tree because the wood is hard, strong, and flexible. Native Americans used white ash for making bows and arrows, and it's still the wood of choice for the legendary Louisville slugger baseball bat. A desirable shade tree, it also makes an excellent fuel wood and campfire starter due to its flammable sap.

Halesia tetraptera Ellis
CAROLINA SILVERBELL
Styracaceae (Storax family)

Description: An understory deciduous tree or large shrub with distinctive white-yellow streaks on young stems and alternate, elliptical leaves 3–6 in. long with finely toothed margins and pointed tips. White bell-shaped flowers in drooping clusters below the branches. Distinctive pod-like fruits about 2 in. long with 4 broad wings, green and fleshy in summer, dry and brown in autumn. Flowers Mar.–May; fruits Aug.–Sept.

Habitat/range: Moist, wooded slopes and fertile soils along streams, bottomlands, and cove forests. Common in mountains and upper piedmont. Eastern United States.

Taxonomy: The genus *Halesia* comprises 5 species of trees and shrubs of eastern North America and eastern Asia. *H. diptera*, a coastal plain species, is similar to Carolina silverbell, but it has 2, rather than 4, wings per fruit.

Ecology: Carolina silverbell is usually a small understory tree with a narrow trunk that is divided at the base into several spreading stems forming a rounded crown. On moist, rich soils of cove forests and north-facing slopes in the mountains, individuals up to 100 ft. tall reach the canopy. Larger trees can produce large fruit crops, but many of the seeds are sterile. The fruits persist on trees well into winter but are eventually removed by fruit-eating animals or simply fall to the ground below. The function of the 4 wings is unclear as the fruits are usually too large to be carried very far by wind.

Wildlife: Bees pollinate the bell-shaped flowers in early spring, and birds and small mammals disperse the seeds in fall and winter.

Uses: The showy flowers and interesting fruits of Carolina silverbell, along with its small to medium size, make it an attractive landscape tree.

Synonym: Halesia carolina L.

Ilex opaca Aiton
AMERICAN HOLLY
Aquifoliaceae (Holly family)

Description: Small to medium-sized evergreen tree with grayish smooth bark, sometimes roughened with warty outgrowths. Alternate, dark green, leathery leaves with sharp marginal spines. Small, greenish white flowers in axillary clusters. Fruit a bright red or orange drupe persisting through winter. Flowers Apr.–June; fruits Sept.–Oct.

Habitat/range: Occurs in variety of moist to dry forests, including river bluff forests, oak-hickory forests, acidic cove forests, and alluvial forests. Common. Widespread in eastern United States.

Taxonomy: A cosmopolitan genus of 500 species, including 12 species in the mountains and piedmont. This is our only species of native holly that is a medium-sized tree, the others are shrubs or small trees.

Ecology: American holly is a slow-growing, very shade-tolerant tree that typically occurs in the forest understory. Because its thin bark makes it vulnerable to fire, American holly is often absent from habitats subject to frequent or even occasional fires. Unlike most broad-leaved trees of the Southeast, it doesn't lose its leaves in winter. A synchronous flush of new leaves is produced each spring, followed by shedding of some of the older leaves. Individuals growing in sunny forest openings or woodland borders produce many more flowers and fruits than individuals growing in the shade of the forest understory. Male and female flowers are similar in appearance, but occur on separate plants. Bees are the primary pollinators, but beetles, wasps, and night flying moths also visit the flowers. The fruits ripen in fall but often remain on trees through most of winter, eventually being taken by winter-migrating flocks of birds (such as cedar waxwings and American robins) that consume the pulp and disperse the seeds.

Wildlife: Relatively few animals (including insects) feed on the leaves of American holly, as they're tough and spiny, contain bitter-tasting saponins, and are of low nutritional value.

Uses: This hardy plant (with numerous cultivars) is commonly used as a landscape tree because of its showy, persistent fruits and evergreen spiny leaves. The leaves and fruits are used for holiday decorations (but be careful as the fruits are toxic to humans if ingested).

Juglans nigra L.
BLACK WALNUT
Juglandaceae (Walnut family)

Description: A large tree with dark brown to almost black bark, with alternate, pinnately compound, aromatic leaves, 12–24 in. long with 10–24 leaflets, usually lacking a terminal leaflet. Male flowers in drooping catkins, female flowers less conspicuous, on same tree. Fruits round, about 2 in. across, with a thick green to dark brown husk surrounding a grooved nut with a sweet, edible seed. Flowers Apr.; fruits Sept.–Oct.

Habitat/range: Moist, nutrient-rich forests, including basic mesic and alluvial forests. Common. Eastern United States.

Taxonomy: A genus of 21 species of trees and shrubs of North, Central, and South America, Mexico, and Eurasia. The only other species in our region, butternut (*J. cinerea*) was once common but is now rare due to the butternut canker disease. The bark of black walnut is dark brown to black with long, interlacing ridges, whereas butternut has light gray bark with broad ridges.

Ecology: Black walnut grows best in rich, moist, well-drained, neutral (pH 7) to slightly alkaline soils. A shade-intolerant species, it depends on gaps (openings) in the forest canopy for successful establishment and growth. In forests, black walnut trees are usually straight and tall and often free of branches for two-thirds of their height, but in open areas the trunk usually forks within 10 ft. of the ground, forming massive spreading branches and a wide but open crown. Good nut crops are produced every 2–3 years. Ripe fruits are dispersed in fall, but an overwintering period is required to crack the nut before germination occurs in spring. Juglone, a chemical in black walnut leaves, bark, husks, and roots, inhibits the growth of some but not all plants.

Wildlife: Tent caterpillars (in spring) and fall webworms (from midsummer–fall) feed on the foliage and build communal, tent-like nests. Squirrels eat as many ripe nuts as they can and bury the rest as winter food. Most regeneration results from seeds that squirrels disperse and bury but fail to recover.

Uses: Black walnut is widely planted as a nut tree, timber tree, and landscape tree. The nuts were a staple food in the diets of Native Americans and early pioneers.

Juniperus virginiana L.
EASTERN RED CEDAR
Cupressaceae (Cypress family)

Description: Columnar to broadly pyramidal tree with thin, fibrous reddish brown bark peeling into long, narrow strips. Mostly small, opposite, scale-like evergreen leaves. Separate male and female trees; the male cones release pollen in winter (Jan.–Mar.), turning a conspicuous yellowish brown color; tiny, berry-like, waxy blue female cones ripen Oct.–Dec. and persist through winter.

Habitat/range: A wide variety of forests as well as pastures, abandoned fields, roadsides, fencerows, and rock outcrops. Common (especially in piedmont). The most widely distributed conifer in the eastern United States.

Taxonomy: Eastern red cedar is an unusual gymnosperm because of its fleshy (rather than woody) seed cones. The only other species in our region is ground juniper, *Juniperus communis* var. *depressa*, a rare, low-growing shrub, sometimes grown as a landscape plant.

Ecology: Red cedar thrives almost everywhere, except in deep shade and standing water. It grows on ridgetops, slopes, and flatlands, on deep, moist soils on the edges of swamps, and on dry, shallow soils associated with rock outcrops. Its wide elevational range (from sea level to 5,000 ft.) demonstrates its ability to grow under a wide range of climates. One of the first woody plants to invade abandoned fields, eastern red cedar is often replaced by more shade-tolerant hardwoods. In addition to shade, eastern red cedar's worst enemy is fire, as its low stature, thin bark, shallow roots, and inability to resprout make it particularly vulnerable to even low-intensity surface fires. Eastern red cedar is more common today than it was 200 years ago, due to widespread fire suppression over much of the past century. It's often parasitized by the cedar-apple rust fungus, which forms large masses of gelatinous orange tissue.

Wildlife: Birds digest the thin pulp and deposit the seeds in their droppings, thereby dispersing the seeds and facilitating germination. Flock feeders such as cedar waxwings, European starlings, and American robins can remove an entire tree's fruit crop within a couple of days.

Uses: The heartwood is used in cedar chests, the fruits flavor gin, and it's grown as a Christmas tree.

Liquidambar styraciflua L.
SWEETGUM
Altingiaceae (Sweetgum family)

Description: Large deciduous tree with deeply lobed, star-shaped leaves and corky, wing-like projections on twigs. Male and female flowers in separate round clusters on same tree. Fruits hang on long stalks in spiny ball-like clusters. Flowers Apr.–May; fruits Aug.–Sept.

Habitat/range: Moist or wet woods, fields, and disturbed areas. Common in piedmont, infrequent in mountains. Eastern United States, Mexico, and Guatemala.

Taxonomy: A genus of 4 trees of North and Central America, Asia, and the eastern Mediterranean. The common name alludes to the sweet, gummy inner bark once used as a substitute for chewing gum.

Ecology: Sweetgum grows in a wide variety of soil types, moisture conditions, and habitat types but does best on rich, moist alluvial soils in floodplains where trees can reach heights of 130 ft. and diameters of 6 ft. A prolific seed producer, sweetgum quickly invades abandoned fields and logged areas. Fast-growing and shade-intolerant, it can also persist as a canopy tree in mature forests, particularly on moist sites. Relatively thin bark makes it susceptible to topkill by fire, but it resprouts vigorously from the stump and spreads laterally from root sprouts, sometimes forming thickets. Its root system varies with site conditions. On wet sites with poor drainage, its roots are shallow and wide spreading, while on upland sites, it forms a deep taproot. Young sweetgums generally have narrow crowns, while mature trees often have round, spreading crowns. Sweetgums are self-pruning, readily dropping lower branches.

Wildlife: Beavers relish sweetgum bark, often girdling and killing the trees. Finches and other birds glean seeds from the spiny, round fruits. Sweetgum is a caterpillar host plant for luna moths (as are hickories).

Uses: Sweetgum is widely planted as a landscape tree because of its spectacular fall colors and its ability to tolerate a wide range of conditions, but its spiny fruits can be a nuisance.

Liriodendron tulipifera L.
TULIP TREE, YELLOW POPLAR
Magnoliaceae (Magnolia family)

Description: A tall deciduous tree with a straight trunk and conical crown, easily recognized by its broadly notched leaves with 4–6 lobes, greenish yellow tulip-shaped flowers, and persistent cone-shaped fruits. Flowers Apr.–June; fruits Sept.–Oct.

Habitat/range: Common on moist, rich soils but also present on drier sites such as fields and roadsides. Many forest types, including cove forests, chestnut oak forests, river bluff forests, alluvial forests, oak-hickory forests, and forest edges. Common. Widespread in eastern North America.

Taxonomy: The genus *Liriodendron* has just 2 species, 1 in eastern North America, the other in Asia.

Ecology: Tulip tree is a shade-intolerant species that depends on open, sunny areas for successful growth and reproduction. Once established, trees grow rapidly and frequently reach the canopy before competing species. Tulip tree is unusual because it's a pioneer species that invades open, disturbed sites and it persists in mature or old-growth forests, reaching ages of 200–250 years or more. In forests, the trunk is typically very straight, tall, and free of lateral branches for a considerable height. Seedlings and saplings with their thin bark are highly susceptible to fire. In contrast, trees with stems greater than 3–4 in. in diameter have a thicker bark that insulates the cambium, enabling larger trees to survive moderately hot fires. The large number of wind-dispersed seeds produced nearly every year allows tulip tree to rapidly colonize forest openings, fields, and other disturbed sites.

Wildlife: White-tailed deer heavily browse the leaves, twigs, and branches, and beavers chew down young tulip trees growing near water. Tulip tree's flowers provide an important nectar source for bees in spring, and birds and small mammals eat the seeds in autumn.

Uses: Native Americans made canoes from the trunks, and the soft, easily worked wood is widely used in furniture. One of our tallest and most attractive trees, tulip tree is often planted as a shade tree due to its rapid growth, interesting foliage, and yellow fall color. It's the state tree of Tennessee.

Magnolia acuminata (L.) L.
CUCUMBER TREE
Magnoliaceae (Magnolia family)

Description: A medium-sized deciduous tree with a single trunk and large silky-white terminal buds. Large (6–10 in. long) leaves spread along twigs, are pointed at apex, wedge-shaped or rounded at base. Slightly fragrant, yellowish green, 2–4 in. long flowers with numerous spirally arranged stamens and pistils. Fruits 2–4 in. long, initially green, later turning red, then dark brown, shaped like a cucumber, hence the common name. Flowers Apr.–May; fruits July–Aug.

Habitat/range: Usually on moist, fertile soils, including northern hardwood forests, cove forests, and floodplain forests. Common in mountains, uncommon in piedmont. Eastern North America.

Taxonomy: A genus of about 130 species of trees and shrubs of east Asia and North, Central, and South America, including 6 species in the mountains and piedmont. Cucumber tree differs from umbrella magnolia (*M. tripetala*) in having distinctly alternate leaves, rather than a whorl-like cluster of leaves, at the stem tip.

Ecology: This widely distributed but seldom abundant tree grows in full sun or partial shade on cool, moist sites. One of our fastest growing magnolias, its large leaves cast a deep shadow on the forest below. The yellowish green flowers often go unnoticed as they generally occur high in the tree and blend in with the foliage. All other magnolias native to the United States have white flowers. Because magnolia flowers generally don't produce ripe pollen until after the stigmas have lost receptivity, a pollinator is needed to transfer pollen from a male (pollen) phase flower to a female phase flower. A good seed crop is produced every 4–5 years. Seeds lose viability if exposed to long periods of hot, dry conditions. A wide-spreading but relatively shallow root system makes it susceptible to windthrow, particularly on steep slopes.

Wildlife: White-tailed deer browse the twigs and leaves, various birds and small mammals consume the seeds, and sapsuckers commonly make holes in the bark to feed on the sap.

Uses: Cucumber tree is a hardy landscape tree that has interesting leaves, flowers, and fruits.

Magnolia fraseri Walter
FRASER MAGNOLIA
Magnoliaceae (Magnolia family)

Description: Small to medium-sized deciduous tree, often with multiple stems and slender, sharply pointed terminal buds. Leaves alternate, simple, entire, 8–12 in. long with 2 prominent lobes at base, often crowded near tips of twigs. Flowers creamy white, 8–10 in. across with a pleasant fruity odor. Fruit a large cone-like aggregate of follicles from which dangle bright red "seeds." Flowers Apr.–May; fruits July–Aug.

Habitat/range: Common in cove forests and other moist forests in mountains and upper piedmont. Restricted to southern Appalachians from Virginia south to Georgia.

Taxonomy: Six of the 130 species of *Magnolia* occur in the mountains and piedmont.

Ecology: A relatively fast-growing understory tree, Fraser magnolia grows best in small openings in the forest canopy where light levels are elevated. Seedlings and saplings are most commonly observed in open, mesic sites near seed-bearing trees. Fraser magnolia's thin bark makes it vulnerable to fire and damage by logging operations, but it often "bounces back" following disturbance by resprouting from its base. The large, showy flowers are typical of magnolias, each with an elongated axis surrounded by a basal cluster of spirally arranged stamens terminated by spirally arranged pistils, each pistil bearing a single recurved stigma lobe at its tip. Because the stigma lobes are receptive before the anthers open and release pollen, cross-pollination is promoted. Beetles are the primary pollinators of Fraser magnolia, although bees and flies also visit the flowers. Magnolia flowers, with their white petals, heavy fragrance, and well-protected ovules (potential seeds) are well adapted to beetle pollination, since beetles have a better developed sense of smell than vision and their chewing mouthparts can seriously damage more vulnerable flowers.

Wildlife: Deer browse the basal sprouts, birds and small mammals eat the seeds, and flying squirrels nest in both cavities and leaf nests.

Uses: Fraser magnolia is an attractive tree in woodland gardens due to its large showy flowers, red cone-like fruits, and interesting foliage.

Morus rubra L.
RED MULBERRY
Moraceae (Mulberry family)

Description: Small to medium-sized tree with a short trunk and spreading, rounded crown. Leaves heart-shaped with long acuminate tips and coarsely serrate margins, often with unlobed and deeply lobed leaves on same plant. Small male and female flowers usually on separate trees. Red to purple-black fruits look like elongated blackberries, sweet, juicy, edible. Flowers Apr.–May; fruits May–June.

Habitat/range: Moist forests, including alluvial forests, cove forests, forest edges, suburban woodlands, and disturbed areas. Common. Widespread in eastern North America.

Taxonomy: A genus of 10 species of trees, widespread in temperate and tropical regions of North America, Europe, and Asia. Differs from white mulberry (*M. alba*), an introduced species, in having larger leaves with a rough upper and smooth lower leaf surface; white mulberry leaves are usually smooth on both sides but the 2 species hybridize and intermediate forms occur.

Ecology: A shade-tolerant species, red mulberry most often grows as an understory tree. Like many plants, red mulberry adjusts its leaf angle in response to the amount of sunlight received. Leaves are typically slanted (some nearly vertical) in full sunlight and are more horizontal in shade. An adaptive response, the vertical leaves reduce heat gain and transpirational water loss, while leaves in the horizontal shade position capture more sunlight, increasing photosynthesis. Leaves that develop in the sun tend to have deep lobes, while shade leaves often lack lobes. This is also adaptive, as lobed leaves reduce heat gain, a favorable trait for leaves exposed to high light levels.

Wildlife: White-tailed deer browse the foliage, beavers and rabbits consume the bark, and woodchucks occasionally climb trees to feed on leaves. A wide variety of birds and mammals seek out the fruits.

Uses: Mulberry is sometimes considered a nuisance in urban landscapes as its abundant fruit stains sidewalks and cars. However, a female mulberry tree is hard to beat for attracting summer birds to gardens.

Nyssa sylvatica Marsh.
BLACK GUM
Nyssaceae (Tupelo family)

Description: Usually an understory tree, with very rough, deeply furrowed bark on older individuals. Leaves alternate, usually broadest above middle, abruptly pointed at tip, wedge shaped at base. Small, greenish yellow, male and female flowers borne on separate plants. Fruits dark blue with thin pulp surrounding a single seed. Flowers Apr.–June; fruits Aug.–Oct.

Habitat/range: Dry to mesic upland forests, less common in alluvial forests. Common. Widespread in eastern United States.

Taxonomy: A genus of 8 species of trees and shrubs of eastern North America, Asia, and Central America, with 2 species in the mountains and piedmont. The common name "black gum" is a misnomer, as it doesn't produce gum or latex.

Ecology: The inconspicuous yellow-green flowers attract more than 45 species of bees and other insects with spherical droplets of nectar that sparkle in the sunlight. Female trees don't usually flower and bear fruit in successive years, due to resource depletion associated with the high energy cost of reproduction. Male trees expend much less energy on reproduction and flower in most years. Individual trees form clones by producing multiple stems from root sprouts. The thick bark on older trees provides protection from the heat of fire, but fire scars at the base of a tree can provide an entry point for heart rot fungi, which can eventually kill the tree.

Wildlife: The flowers are a good source of nectar for bees and other insects, small mammals and birds consume the fruits (despite their sour taste), and young foliage is consumed by deer.

Uses: An excellent landscape tree due to its dense green foliage, brilliant orange-red autumn colors, and drought tolerance.

Ostrya virginiana (Mill.) K. Koch
HOP HORNBEAM
Betulaceae (Birch family)

Description: A small deciduous tree with brown, furrowed, shredding bark (young trees have smooth bark). Leaves simple, alternate, oval in shape with doubly serrate margins and long, pointed tips. Tiny male and female flowers borne on separate catkins on the same tree. Fruit a distinctive cone-like cluster of 10–20 inflated paper sacs, each enclosing a tiny flattened seed (nutlet). The sacs resemble hops, hence the common name. Flowers Apr.–May; fruits Aug.–Oct.

Habitat/range: Moist to dry woods, particularly on calcium-rich soils. Occurs in many forest types, including northern hardwood forests, cove forests, floodplain forests, basic mesic forests, and oak-hickory forests. Common. Widespread in eastern North America.

Taxonomy: The genus *Ostrya* includes 7 species of trees of North America, Europe, and Asia, only 1 of which occurs in the mountains and piedmont. Hop hornbeam resembles ironwood (*Carpinus caroliniana*), but its bark is flaky, unlike the smooth, fluted (muscle-like) trunk of ironwood.

Ecology: Hop hornbeam is a slow-growing but relatively long-lived, shade-tolerant tree, with many horizontal or drooping branches forming open crowns. Loosely scattered in the forest understory, hop hornbeam rarely if ever forms pure stands. This tough tree is highly resistant to damage by wind, snow, or ice and can tolerate heat, drought, dense shade, and a wide range of climates. Good seed crops are produced most years and the inflated papery sac that surrounds each seed provides buoyancy that facilitates wind dispersal. The seeds are typically dispersed in autumn and germinate in spring after exposure to cold, moist conditions over winter.

Wildlife: Birds and squirrels eat the small nut-like seeds in autumn and the buds and catkins in winter and early spring. Deer and rabbits occasionally browse the twigs and foliage.

Uses: Native Americans used hop hornbeam's dense, tough wood for bows and as handles for their stone war clubs. The wood was later used for tool handles, mallets, and fence posts.

Oxydendrum arboreum (L.) DC.
SOURWOOD
Ericaceae (Heath family)

Description: A small to medium-sized deciduous tree with a slender crown, leaning trunk, and deeply furrowed bark on mature trees. Leaves alternate, 3–5 in. long, elliptical with finely toothed margins, greenish yellow turning scarlet in autumn. Small, white bell-shaped flowers in drooping curved racemes. Fruit a small, woody, erect capsule in 1-sided, drooping clusters. Flowers June–July; fruits Sept.–Oct., persisting through winter.

Habitat/range: Moist to dry deciduous forests and open areas, including oak-hickory forests, chestnut oak forests, forest edges, fields, and roadsides. Common. Eastern United States.

Taxonomy: The only species in the genus *Oxydendrum*, its common name reflects the sour taste of its leaves.

Ecology: Primarily an understory tree, sourwood can reach the canopy when disturbance removes overtopping vegetation. In the mountains, sourwood commonly grows on dry, open slopes and ridges with various oaks, including chestnut oak, scarlet oak, and white oak; less often, it grows in more sheltered mesic sites such as cove forests. Sourwood also occurs in upland forests and in lowland areas in the piedmont not subject to flooding. Like most members of the heath family, sourwood is restricted to acidic soils. Dense clusters of small, nectar-producing flowers are actively visited and pollinated by various bees, and the tiny seeds are gradually dispersed from the persistent capsules by wind and gravity. Low-intensity fires typically topkill sourwood, but individuals often resprout from root crowns.

Wildlife: White-tailed deer browse the foliage. Standing dead trees (snags) are frequent cavity-nesting sites for birds. Fall webworms (actually the larvae of moths) enclose leaves and small branches in their gray silken webs, which protect the larvae (caterpillars) as they feed on the foliage. While the webs are unsightly, damage to the tree is minor as the leaves are consumed late in the growing season, shortly before fall leaf drop.

Uses: Sourwood is an attractive landscape plant due to its drooping white flower clusters, dangling persistent fruits, and brilliant fall colors. Honeybees harvest nectar from the flowers and produce highly prized sourwood honey.

Picea rubens Sarg.
RED SPRUCE
Pinaceae (Pine family)

Description: A medium to large evergreen tree with stiff, sharply pointed, round, needle-like leaves that radiate from all sides of the branch. Small (1–2 in. long) downward-hanging seed cones with thin, rounded scales mature in Oct.; cones usually fall shortly after seeds disperse.

Habitat/range: Common in spruce-fir forests at high elevations, loosely scattered in northern hardwood forests, balds, boulder fields, bogs, and cold-air drainage valleys at elevations down to about 3,000 ft. Occurs from southeastern Canada and northeastern United States south in mountains to Virginia, North Carolina, and Tennessee.

Taxonomy: One can readily differentiate red spruce from Fraser fir by "shaking hands" with the tip of a branch. The foliage of Fraser fir is soft to the touch, whereas the sharp, stiff needles of red spruce are prickly.

Ecology: In the southern Appalachians, red spruce typically occurs in isolated patches at elevations from about 4,500 to 6,200 ft., above which it's usually replaced by Fraser fir. Red spruce is an unusually shade-tolerant conifer. Large numbers of seedlings and saplings often form a persistent "sapling bank" under the forest canopy. These shade-suppressed "saplings" can be more than 50 years old and just 4–5 ft. tall. If the canopy opens up, growth rates increase rapidly in response to higher light levels. Once established, red spruce trees are potentially long-lived, often reaching ages greater than 350 years. The total acreage of red spruce is only a fraction of what it was just a century ago. This reflects widespread clear-cutting and catastrophic crown fires early in the twentieth century. Moreover, the vigor of red spruce trees has declined throughout much of the Appalachians. While the specific cause of the decline hasn't been identified, air pollution (acting alone or in combination with insect and disease factors) and increased exposure due to the loss of adult Fraser firs are primary suspects.

Wildlife: Mice and voles consume and store large numbers of red spruce seeds, and red squirrels clip twigs and eat both the reproductive and vegetative buds.

Uses: In the colonial period, settlers added molasses, honey, or maple syrup to needles and fermented it, creating spruce beer, one of North America's earliest alcoholic beverages.

Pinus echinata Mill.
SHORTLEAF PINE
Pinaceae (Pine family)

Description: A medium to large tree generally with a straight trunk and reddish brown bark with small (pencil point) resin holes and a conical crown. Soft, flexible needles, 3–5 in. long, usually in bundles of 2 (sometimes 3), not twisted. Egg-shaped seed cones about 2 in. long with weak, slender prickles. Pollen released Mar.–Apr.; seed cones mature Sept.–Oct.

Habitat/range: Mostly on dry sites but also present in mesic and even wet areas. Occurs in a variety of communities, including oak-hickory forests, chestnut oak forests, pine-oak-heath, alluvial forests, and fields. Common. Eastern United States.

Taxonomy: A genus of 110 species of the Northern Hemisphere, south to Central America, including 9 species in the mountains and piedmont.

Ecology: A highly adaptable species, shortleaf pine grows on a wide variety of sites and soils but does best on well-drained, acidic soils in open, sunny habitats. It commonly colonizes fields, forming a dense canopy after 10–15 years. Periodic low-intensity fires benefit this species because fires create conditions favorable for seedling establishment and prevent hardwoods (such as oaks) from taking over. Adult shortleaf pines are generally resistant to crown fires because of their moderately high, open crowns and because stands are typically rather open. Unlike most pines, individuals (up to about 30 years of age) resprout vigorously from the base if topkilled by fire or cut down. Acid rain reduces its growth, severe ice storms cause large branches and twigs to break, and prolonged drought weakens or kills trees (and makes them more susceptible to southern pine beetle infestations).

Wildlife: Birds and small mammals eat seeds within the cones and after they have fallen to the ground. Older trees provide habitat for cavity dwellers such as woodpeckers.

Uses: Shortleaf pine is an important lumber and pulp-producing tree in the Southeast; it's also used as a landscape tree.

Pinus pungens Lamb.
TABLE MOUNTAIN PINE
Pinaceae (Pine family)

Description: A small to medium-sized tree with a straight to crooked trunk, stout branches, and a round to flattened crown. The rigid, sharp-pointed, twisted needles occur in groups of 2. Seed cones sessile, broadly egg-shaped, about 3 in. long with sharp upward-curved prickles, mature Sept.–Oct. and persist on tree for many years.

Habitat/range: Open forests on dry ridges, cliffs, and steep southwest-facing slopes, mostly at elevations between 1,000 and 4,000 ft., but as high as 5,800 ft. Common in mountains, with rare outlying populations on monadnocks in upper piedmont. A central and southern Appalachian endemic, from New Jersey to Georgia.

Taxonomy: Table mountain pine is distinguished from other southern pines by its large, persistent seed cones with thickened scales, each armed with a stout, curved prickle.

Ecology: Table mountain pine occurs as a scattered upland tree with oaks and other hardwoods and in pure or mixed stands with pitch pine (*Pinus rigida*). It's a slow-growing, often stunted tree, intolerant of both shade and competition. On most sites, fire plays a key role in the regeneration and persistence of table mountain pine. On soils with a thick leaf litter layer, or where a dense shrub layer is present, fire is needed for successful seedling establishment. The closed (serotinous) cones release their seeds following a fire, when conditions are most favorable for seedling establishment and growth. On thin, dry, rocky soils, such as those on exposed ridgetops where few trees can survive, table mountain pine can persist without periodic fires. On slightly more favorable sites, oaks and other hardwoods typically replace table mountain pine in the absence of fire.

Wildlife: The seeds stored in the cones of table mountain pine provide food for wildlife, including red squirrels that sometimes harvest an entire tree's seed crop. Southern pine beetle outbreaks periodically kill large numbers of table mountain pine, particularly in drought years.

Uses: Table mountain pine is too small and knotty to have much commercial value except as pulpwood and firewood.

Pinus rigida Mill.
PITCH PINE
Pinaceae (Pine family)

Description: A scraggly pine with stiff, somewhat twisted, yellowish green needles in groups of 3. Seed cones 1 ½ –3 in. long, with slender, sharp prickles, mature Sept.–Oct.

Habitat/range: Mostly on dry slopes and ridges on thin, nutrient-poor soils at moderate elevations. In pine-oak-heath, chestnut oak forests, rock outcrops, and occasionally mountain bogs. Fairly common in mountains, less so in piedmont. Southern Canada, south to Georgia.

Taxonomy: Pitch pine has unusual tufts of needles growing directly from the trunk. Shortleaf pine (*P. echinata*) superficially resembles pitch pine but has straight (rather than twisted) needles in groups of 2 (sometimes 3), with numerous small pits in bark.

Ecology: A poor competitor, pitch pine depends on frequent fires and poor soils to persist as a dominant species. Its highly resinous wood and needles make it vulnerable to topkill by fire, but unlike most pines, it can regenerate from stump sprouts. Individuals in some populations produce cones that open and disperse their seeds soon after maturity, but in regions with long histories of periodic fires, individuals typically produce cones that remain closed on trees for years, eventually opening and releasing their seeds in response to the heat of a fire (serotinous cones). Because fires remove competing vegetation, consume leaf litter, and expose bare mineral soil, the release of seeds following a fire ensures that seeds are exposed to ideal conditions for seedling establishment and growth. In fire-suppressed areas, prescribed burns can create conditions favorable for the regeneration of pitch pine, preventing oaks and other hardwoods from overtopping and eventually replacing it.

Wildlife: White-tailed deer and rabbits browse young shoots, and southern pine beetles drill into trees to feed on the phloem.

Uses: Pitch pine is currently of minor economic importance, but in colonial times, its resin was cooked into a thick tar used to preserve ropes and caulk the seams of wooden ships. The pitch-filled stumps can be used for starting fires.

Pinus strobus L.
EASTERN WHITE PINE
Pinaceae (Pine family)

Description: A large tree with whorled branches and soft, needle-like leaves in bundles of 5. Seed cones pendant, narrowly cylindrical, 5–8 in. long, lacking prickles, mature in Aug.–Sept.

Habitat/range: Moist to dry forests ranging from mountain bogs to dry, rocky ridges. Common in mountains and upper piedmont. Widespread in eastern North America.

Taxonomy: Eastern white pine is our only native conifer that has needles in groups of 5.

Ecology: Eastern white pines 250–300 years old and 150–175 ft. tall were common in forests during colonial times. Today, trees older than 80 years and taller than 100 ft. are rare due to their commercial value. One can conservatively estimate an individual's age by counting the number of whorled branches (since 1 whorl is produced each year). Eastern white pine readily colonizes burned over, cutover, and storm-damaged forests but rarely regenerates under an intact canopy, as its seedlings require nearly bare soil, adequate light, and little competition from other trees. Mature trees survive low-intensity fires, due to their thick bark, branch-free lower trunks, and moderately deep root systems.

Wildlife: Eastern white pine is host to a wide variety of insects including caterpillar-like sawfly larvae that feed in groups and devour large numbers of needles. The larvae of clear-winged moths (known as pitch mass borers) excavate tunnels into the wood causing 3–4 in. swaths of resin to exude from the trunk. Hawks, owls, and woodpeckers use pines as nesting sites and black bears utilize large hollows as cavity dens.

Uses: Eastern white pine's tall, straight trunks were frequently made into masts for large sailing ships during the seventeenth and eighteenth centuries. It continues to be a valuable timber tree and is a widely planted shade tree but is susceptible to drought, strong winds, ice damage, and white pine blister rust (an introduced fungus that causes tree mortality).

Pinus taeda L.
LOBLOLLY PINE
Pinaceae (Pine family)

Description: One of our largest southern pines, with long, straight trunks, reaching heights of 90–100 ft. Dark green, stiff needles, 6–9 in. long, in bundles of 3. Seed cones longer than they are broad, about 4–5 in. long, each cone scale tipped with a stout, sharp prickle. Seeds mature Oct.–Nov.

Habitat/range: Occurs in wide range of habitats, from moist alluvial forests to drier upland forests, fields, and granite outcrops. Common in piedmont. Eastern United States.

Taxonomy: Loblolly pine differs from slash pine (*P. elliottii*) in that its seed cones have very sharp prickles and its needles occur in bundles of 3 (slash pine has needles in bundles of 2 or 3).

Ecology: Loblolly pine commonly invades and dominates old fields, clearcuts, and other disturbed piedmont sites. More shade-tolerant hardwoods such as oak, hickory, and sweetgum often invade the understory, eventually replacing loblolly pine. In contrast, where fires occur every 10 years or so, loblolly pine usually persists because its relatively thick bark and tall crowns are more resistant to the heat of fire than the bark and crowns of young hardwoods in the forest understory. Due to extensive lateral root spread (often wider than their crowns!), root grafting among neighboring trees is common. In a good year, a mature tree can produce more than 10,000 seeds. Successful seed germination and seedling establishment are enhanced by bare mineral soil, such as occurs after a fire. High temperatures and droughts cause widespread seedling mortality as well as increased stress and reduced growth in larger trees, making them more vulnerable to insect infestations and disease. In pine plantations and woodland borders, kudzu vines can overtop, shade out, and eventually kill large pines.

Wildlife: Loblolly pine is a preferred host of the southern pine beetle. Most infestations originate in stands that are stressed by droughts, fires, or competition due to high density.

Uses: Loblolly pine is one of the most important commercial timber species in the Southeast.

Pinus virginiana Mill.
VIRGINIA PINE
Pinaceae (Pine family)

Description: A small to medium-sized tree, often scrubby in appearance due to its persistent dead lower branches. Needles in bundles of 2, short, twisted, rather stiff. Seed cones small with slender, sharp prickles, opening at maturity to release seeds but cones remaining on tree for years. Pollen released Mar.–May; seeds mature Sept.–Nov.

Habitat/range: Dry forests and woodlands, especially on slopes, ridges, and abandoned fields, including oak-hickory forests, chestnut oak forests, xeric hardpan forests, granite outcrops, and forest edges. Common in piedmont and lower mountains. Widespread in eastern United States.

Taxonomy: Virginia pine is most easily confused with shortleaf pine (*P. echinata*), but it has short, twisted needles, flaky bark, and numerous dead lower branches.

Ecology: This scrubby pine, rarely over 60 ft. tall, often grows in dense, pure stands, usually as a pioneer species in old fields, cutover areas, and other disturbed sites. Because the species is shade-intolerant, young plants can't grow under existing trees. This allows shade-tolerant hardwoods to invade the understory and gradually overtop and replace Virginia pine. Its thin bark and shallow roots make Virginia pine vulnerable to fire; however, it rapidly colonizes sites following a fire. In open, sunny areas, individuals can produce seed cones at as early as 5 years of age, but cone production can be delayed for as many as 50 years in dense stands. Once reproductive maturity is reached, some seeds are produced each year, with heavy seed cone crops produced every 3 years or so. The large number of seeds produced enhances Virginia pine's ability to rapidly colonize disturbed areas. Successful seeding establishment requires bare mineral soil and lots of sunlight.

Wildlife: Virginia pine provides good nesting sites for woodpeckers because the wood of older trees is often softened by fungal decay. Trees weakened by drought stress or fires, are particularly susceptible to southern pine beetles.

Uses: Virginia pine is used for pulpwood and is widely cultivated in the Southeast for Christmas trees.

Platanus occidentalis L.
SYCAMORE
Platanaceae (Plane tree family)

Description: A massive deciduous tree with stout, spreading branches, zigzag twigs, and a thin, peeling outer bark that exposes a greenish gray to creamy white inner bark. Large (4–8 in. diameter) maple-like leaves with 3–5 coarsely toothed lobes. Numerous tiny male and female flowers in separate, round, drooping heads. Fruit a round head containing numerous achenes. Flowers Apr.–May; fruits Sept.–Nov., persisting through winter.

Habitat/range: Alluvial forests, riverbanks, rocky streamsides, fields, and roadsides. Common in piedmont, uncommon in mountains. Widespread in eastern North America.

Taxonomy: A genus of 7 species of trees of North and Central America and Asia; this is the only species in the mountains and piedmont.

Ecology: Fast-growing and relatively long-lived, sycamore is one of the largest and most ancient trees in eastern North America, with fossils identical to today's trees dating back about 100 million years. Most abundant along streams and rivers and in bottomland forests, it also colonizes fields and drier upland slopes. Abundant fruits are produced most years, but late frosts can kill flowers, reducing seed production for that year. Seeds are widely scattered by wind (hairs on the seed act as a parachute) and by water as the fruit balls break up in spring. Freshly dispersed seeds germinate readily. Under favorable conditions (high light and moist soils) the seedlings grow rapidly, as much as 3–4 ft. in their first year. Plants are typically sparse beneath sycamore trees as chemicals leaching into the soil after leaf fall inhibit their growth.

Wildlife: Cavities and hollows in older trees are used by hole-nesting birds such as wood ducks and owls, as den sites by raccoons and opossums, and as roosting sites by bats. Goldfinches and other birds feed on the seeds, as do squirrels.

Uses: Native Americans made enormously heavy dugout canoes from hollowed-out trunks. Sycamores are widely planted shade trees.

253

Prunus pensylvanica L.
FIRE CHERRY, PIN CHERRY
Rosaceae (Rose family)

Description: A small deciduous tree with reddish brown bark, distinct horizontal lenticels, and narrow leaves that taper to a long, slender, pointed tip. Small flowers with 5 white petals emerge as leaves unfold, forming dense clusters at tips of twigs. Fruit a bright red drupe with a thin sour pulp and poisonous pit. Flowers Apr.–May; fruits Aug.–Sept.

Habitat/range: Moist to dry, open forests or clearings at high elevations, often after fire or other kinds of disturbance. Most abundant in spruce-fir forests and heath balds. Common. Widespread in Canada and northern United States, south in mountains to Georgia.

Taxonomy: Fire cherry most closely resembles black cherry (*P. serotina*) but has flowers in umbels and glabrous leaves, whereas black cherry has flowers in racemes and wider leaves with the midrib on the lower leaf surface pubescent.

Ecology: Fire cherry rapidly colonizes areas denuded of vegetation by wildfire, clearcuts, and other major disturbances. A shade-intolerant species, it flourishes wherever there is full sunlight, including roadsides, woodland borders, abandoned fields, and forest openings. A fast-growing but short-lived tree, fire cherry rarely persists more than 30 years. The key to its success is the production of large numbers of seeds that remain viable in the soil for many (50–150) years until the canopy opens up following disturbance. Following canopy removal, increased temperature fluctuations at or near the soil surface trigger germination of the long-dormant seeds. In disturbed areas with large soil seed banks, dense stands of pin cherry frequently establish and persist for 2–3 decades until shaded out by competing vegetation.

Wildlife: Birds such as cedar waxwings, thrushes, robins, and grosbeaks, along with mammals such as deer, bears, skunks, and raccoons, are among the many animals that feed on the fruits. Frugivores typically consume the pulp and either regurgitate or pass the seeds, thereby dispersing the plant.

Uses: The shallow roots of fire cherry penetrate and bind the soil, thereby reducing erosion and nutrient loss following disturbance. While the fruits can be used to make jam or syrup, the leaves, bark, and seeds are poisonous due to the presence of cyanogenic glycosides.

Prunus serotina Ehrh.
BLACK CHERRY
Rosaceae (Rose family)

Description: Medium to large tree with simple alternate deciduous leaves, tapered at both ends, with finely serrate margins. Small white flowers in long clusters terminating short, leafy twigs. Thick-skinned, dark purple fruits with bittersweet pulp contain a single seed. Flowers Apr.–June; fruits July–Sept.

Habitat/range: Rich cove forests, northern hardwood forests, alluvial forests, oak-hickory forests, and disturbed areas. Common. Widely distributed in eastern North America, south to Guatemala.

Taxonomy: A genus of about 200 species, including plum, cherry, peach, and apricot. Excluding cultivars, 13 species occur in our region.

Ecology: This fast-growing opportunistic tree native to North America has become a serious weed in parts of Europe. Rapid growth, high reproductive output, widely dispersed seeds, and the ability to tolerate a wide range of environmental conditions enhance its invasive capacity. Thin bark makes it vulnerable to fire, but individuals quickly resprout following a fire (or cutting). Bees, flies, and beetles visit the flowers for nectar and pollen. Ants feed on droplets of nectar produced by glands on the leaf stalks (extra floral nectaries); by attacking caterpillars and other plant-feeding insects, the ants benefit the plant. Eastern tent caterpillars, which can completely defoliate trees in a bad infestation, protect themselves from ants by regurgitating fluid that contains cyanogenic compounds derived from eating young black cherry leaves.

Wildlife: White-tailed deer and other mammals apparently eat fresh leaves without harm; in contrast, wilted leaves (which contain higher concentrations of cyanogenic glycosides than fresh leaves) are harmful or fatal if ingested in quantity. Numerous animals consume the fruits and disperse the seeds. Birds sometimes become intoxicated from eating too many overripe, slightly fermented cherries late in the fruiting season.

Uses: Wild cherry cough syrup is made from extracts of the bark, the fruits make a fine jelly, and the reddish brown wood is prized for furniture. Break off a twig and smell the broken end to detect the bitter, almond-flavored cyanogenic glycosides that make this plant toxic.

Quercus alba L.
WHITE OAK
Fagaceae (Beech family)

Description: A large, long-lived deciduous tree with whitish gray bark separating into long, broad, scaly plates. Alternate leaves divided into 7–10 shallow to deeply rounded lobes without bristle tips, turning brown in autumn with some leaves persisting through winter. Male flowers in hanging catkins, female flowers inconspicuous. Fruit an acorn about three-quarters of an in. long with a shallow cup. Flowers Apr.; fruits Sept.–Nov.

Habitat/range: Moist to dry forests and woodlands, including oak-hickory forests, chestnut oak forests, and xeric hardpan forests. Common. Widespread in eastern North America.

Taxonomy: A genus of about 500 species of trees and shrubs of temperate, subtropical, and rarely tropical regions of the Northern Hemisphere, including nearly 30 species in the mountains and piedmont.

Ecology: One of our most common trees, white oak occurs in a wide variety of sites but doesn't grow on extremely dry ridges, in poorly drained flats, or in bottomland forests. In a good year (when masting occurs), a mature tree typically produces more than 10,000 acorns, but good acorn crops occur sporadically. Even though white oak acorns germinate almost immediately after falling to the ground, the vast majority are consumed or damaged by seed predators. Those that escape predation produce a thick taproot in the fall, but a green shoot doesn't emerge until the following spring. The rough, scaly bark is more fire-resistant than the smooth bark of many other oaks. Fire benefits white oak by opening up the canopy and reducing competition, which facilitate seedling establishment and growth.

Wildlife: White oak acorns are sweet, rather than astringent, and at least 36 different kinds of birds (including several types of woodpeckers) consume the acorns, as do a variety of mammals and insects. Cotton candy–like structures (known as wool sower galls) are sometimes present on twigs in early spring.

Uses: White oak was a vital source of wood for shipbuilding in North America prior to the use of steel, as it's impervious to water and resistant to rot. The hard, strong wood is currently used in flooring, furniture, and whiskey barrels. Its broad crown and dense foliage make it an attractive shade tree.

Quercus coccinea Munchh.
SCARLET OAK
Fagaceae (Beech family)

Description: A medium to large deciduous tree with an open, rounded crown and brilliant scarlet-red fall foliage. Alternate leaves deeply divided into 5–9 bristle-tipped lobes, male flowers in drooping catkins, female flowers in spikes in leaf axils. Flowers Apr.; fruits Sept.–Nov.

Habitat/range: Dry upland forests, including pine-oak heath, chestnut oak forests, and oak-hickory forests. Common. Eastern United States.

Taxonomy: Scarlet oak can be distinguished from our other oaks by its very deeply lobed leaves (the sinuses extend more than half the distance to the midrib and resemble the letter "C").

Ecology: A very shade-intolerant species, scarlet oak does best in forests that are exposed to periodic fires or other disturbance that open up the canopy and provide an opportunity for it to regenerate and persist as a canopy tree. Due to its thin bark, even low-intensity surface fires can topkill scarlet oak, but it readily resprouts after a fire, producing numerous new shoots, of which only 1 or 2 survive. Trees begin producing acorns after about 20 years with maximum production at about age 50. Like most oaks, scarlet oak is a masting species, producing good acorn crops every several years. Insect larvae (primarily nut weevils, moth larvae, and cynipid gall wasps) destroy most acorns after they fall from the tree. The proportion of acorns that escape predation by insects is usually highest in years when abundant acorns are produced.

Wildlife: Gray squirrels, chipmunks, wild turkeys, white-tailed deer, bears, blue jays, and redheaded woodpeckers relish the acorns; small mammals and birds nest in the canopy and in cavities.

Uses: A desirable landscape tree since it can be grown in a wide variety of soils, tolerates drought, and its foliage turns scarlet red in autumn.

Quercus falcata Michx.
SOUTHERN RED OAK
Fagaceae (Beech family)

Description: A medium to large deciduous tree usually with a long, straight trunk and an open, rounded crown. Leaves alternate, variably shaped with 3–5 bristle-tipped lobes, the terminal lobe usually long and narrow with a conspicuously U-shaped leaf base. Male flowers in drooping catkins, female flowers in short spikes in leaf axils, appearing with the leaves. Fruit a solitary or paired, nearly round acorn about one-half in. long, the cup enclosing about one-third of the nut. Flowers Apr.; fruits Sept.–Nov.

Habitat/range: Mostly on drier, less fertile upland soils, including oak-hickory forests and chestnut oak forests. Common in piedmont, uncommon in mountains. Widespread in eastern United States.

Taxonomy: Easily recognized by its conspicuously U-shaped leaf base and the droopy (wilted) appearance of the leaves throughout the growing season.

Ecology: Southern red oak usually grows on dry ridgetops and upper slopes facing south and west, rather than on more mesic lower slopes or north and east facing slopes. It occasionally occurs along streams in fertile bottomlands where trees reach a large size. The droopy, vertically oriented leaves absorb less direct sunlight during the hottest part of the day; at this angle, the leaves remain cooler and lose less water through transpiration. Good seed crops are produced at intervals of 1–2 years. Acorns mature in autumn in the second year after flowering, and germinate the following spring. Acorn dispersal by gravity is important on steep slopes. Its thin bark makes southern red oak vulnerable to fire, and fire damage on surviving trees provides entry points for numerous fungi that cause cankers and heart rot, which can eventually kill the trees.

Wildlife: Gray squirrels and blue jays function as both acorn predators and dispersers as they cache (bury) acorns at varying distances from the parent tree, some of which aren't recovered. Southern red oak acorns are preferred by jays because their relatively small size makes them easier to transport and their shells are easier to crack than most.

Uses: Southern red oak was traditionally planted as a shade tree near homes, particularly on dry, less fertile sites.

Quercus marilandica Munchh.
BLACKJACK OAK
Fagaceae (Beech family)

Description: Small to medium-sized scrubby tree with a short trunk and a round, compact crown. Thick, leathery leaves, 5–8 in. long, abruptly broaden at tip, with 3 bristle-tipped lobes, or unlobed in overall "T" or triangular shape, the leaf underside brownish and scurfy. Male flowers in drooping catkins and female flowers in leaf axils emerge after the leaves. Acorns about three-quarters of an in. long, ending in a stout point, the cup covering about half the nut. Flowers Apr.; fruits Sept.–Nov.

Habitat/range: Dry upland forests and woodlands, including oak-hickory forests and xeric hardpan forests. Common in piedmont, uncommon in mountains. Widespread in eastern United States.

Taxonomy: Readily distinguished by its scraggly appearance, broadly triangular leaf shape, and rusty-colored, densely hairy lower leaf surface.

Ecology: Grows on extremely dry, nutrient-poor soils on upper slopes and ridges, often on southerly or westerly exposures that are too dry for other oaks. On most sites, individuals are small and gnarled, rarely reaching 30 ft. in height. A slow-growing, shade-intolerant species, it's overtopped and outcompeted by faster-growing species, including most oaks, on more favorable sites. A large tuberous taproot (that absorbs and stores water) and a thick, waxy leaf cuticle (that reduces transpirational water loss) enable blackjack oak to tolerate extremely dry soils. Smaller individuals are often topkilled by fires, but larger trees can withstand most fires because their thick bark provides insulation from the heat of fire. If topkilled by a fire (or cut), new stems readily sprout from the root crown.

Wildlife: Female acorn weevils drill holes in acorns and lay eggs that hatch into grub-like larvae that feed on the acorn. The holes made by weevils are utilized by female acorn moths whose eggs hatch into larvae that feed on what's left of the acorn meat.

Uses: Its compact growth form, shiny dark green leaves, and drought tolerance make it a desirable landscape tree. The wood has been used for fence posts, railroad ties, and fuel.

Quercus montana Willd.
CHESTNUT OAK
Fagaceae (Beech family)

Description: Deciduous tree to 100 ft. tall with dark grey, deeply furrowed bark. Leaf margins with broad round teeth that lack bristles. Male flowers in drooping catkins, female flowers in leaf axils. Acorns 1–1 ½ in. long, cups bowl-shaped, enclosing about one-third of the nut. Flowers Apr.; fruits Sept.–Nov.

Habitat/range: Dry upland forests and rocky ridges, including chestnut oak forests, pine-oak-heath, dry oak-hickory forests, and monadnock forests. Common in mountains and upper piedmont. Widespread in eastern United States.

Taxonomy: Swamp chestnut oak (*Q. michauxii*) resembles chestnut oak but has scaly bark and occurs in bottomland, rather than upland forests.

Ecology: Chestnut oak is a slow-growing but long-lived tree that commonly occurs on ridgetops and upper slopes on dry, rocky, acidic soils. It's outcompeted by faster-growing species such as tulip tree, red maple, and red oak on more mesic or fertile sites. More drought-tolerant species such as scarlet oak, post oak, and pitch pine occur on the most xeric sites. Large chestnut oaks have fairly thick bark and survive most ground fires. A masting species, good acorn crops are generally produced every 4–5 years. The sweet-tasting acorns germinate in autumn shortly after dispersal. Most acorns buried under the leaf litter by squirrels, chipmunks, and blue jays are retrieved and eaten; those that aren't consumed germinate and establish seedlings at a higher rate than acorns on the soil surface. An unusually thick parenchyma layer helps acorns of this species absorb and retain moisture, which enhances germination and seedling establishment on dry sites.

Wildlife: Adult weevils lay eggs inside acorns where the larvae feed and eventually pupate. While germination is usually not affected, acorns with weevils produce smaller seedlings with higher mortality than acorns without weevils. In mast years, abundant acorn crops satiate weevil populations, resulting in more weevil-free acorns. Few acorns escape weevil infestation in non-mast years.

Uses: The wood of chestnut oak was once used for railroad cross ties and fence posts.

Synonym: Quercus prinus L.

Quercus rubra L.
NORTHERN RED OAK
Fagaceae (Beech family)

Description: Medium to large, moderately fast-growing deciduous tree. Leaves alternate with 7–11 bristle-tipped lobes, the lobes pointing forward and often toothed. Male flowers in clusters of hanging catkins, female flowers inconspicuous. Large egg-shaped, bitter-tasting acorns with shallow cups, mature in 2 years. Flowers Apr.–May; fruits Aug.–Oct.

Habitat/range: Moist to fairly dry upland forests, including red oak forests, cove forests, chestnut oak forests, oak-hickory forests, river bluff forests, basic mesic forests, and forest edges. Common. Widespread in eastern North America.

Taxonomy: The genus *Quercus* consists of about 500 species of trees and shrubs of temperate, subtropical, and, rarely, tropical regions of the Northern Hemisphere.

Ecology: Northern red oak grows on a variety of soils and moisture regimes but does best on moist, somewhat fertile, well-drained sites. It's less tolerant of shade than co-occurring trees such as chestnut oak, white oak, and hickory but is more shade-tolerant than tulip tree, white ash, and black cherry. In good acorn years, mammals, birds, and insects eat up to 80 percent of the acorns produced. In poor years, virtually the entire acorn crop is consumed. Of the few acorns that escape predation and become seedlings, even fewer survive more than a few years or grow more than 6–8 in. tall due to shade, drought stress, competition with herbaceous plants, and browsing by herbivores such as white-tailed deer.

Wildlife: Oaks are an important food source for a wide variety of wildlife, including more than 1,000 species of insects. Three common leaf-feeding insects are the spiny, striped caterpillars known as oakworm moths, walking sticks (whose body shape mimics a twig), and the nocturnal, buzzing insects known as June beetles that eat circular holes in leaves.

Uses: Native Americans leached the bitter-tasting tannins from acorns and ground them into a meal to make bread. Northern red oak is often used as a landscape tree due to its symmetrical growth form and deep scarlet-colored leaves in autumn.

Quercus stellata Wangenh.
POST OAK
Fagaceae (Beech family)

Description: Small to medium-sized deciduous tree with a dense round crown of large, gnarled, horizontal branches. Leaves leathery, shiny dark green above, light green and densely hairy below, 3–5 lobed, the middle pair of lobes largest, suggesting a cross. Male flowers yellow-green, in hanging catkins, female flowers in short spikes in leaf axils, appearing with the leaves. Acorns one-half to 1 in. long, broadest at base, with shallow cups enclosing about one-third of the nut. Flowers Apr.; fruits Sept.–Nov.

Habitat/range: Dry upland woodlands and forests, including dry oak-hickory forests and xeric hardpan forests. Common in piedmont, uncommon in mountains. Widespread in eastern United States.

Taxonomy: The cross-like leaf shape and dense covering of star-shaped hairs on the lower leaf surface characterize this species.

Ecology: Post oak typically grows on dry sites with shallow, nutrient poor soils. On more favorable sites, neighboring trees often overtop it because of its slow growth rate. On poor sites, it tends to persist because it's more drought resistant than most other trees. Individuals can live for 300–400 years. Like many shade-intolerant species, it benefits from periodic fires opening up the canopy. Smaller trees are easily topkilled by fires, but vigorously resprout from dormant buds at the base. Fire scars on surviving trees provide an entry point for fungi that can cause heart rot and eventual tree death. Individuals begin producing acorns after about 25 years. A masting species, good acorn crops are produced every 2–3 years. Acorns ripen and fall from the tree in autumn and germinate shortly thereafter.

Wildlife: In good acorn-producing years, mammals such as squirrels, black bears, and white-tailed deer fatten quickly, and are more likely to produce healthy young the following year. Cavities provide nests and dens for various birds and small mammals.

Uses: Post oak makes a good landscape tree on dry sites but is slow growing and occasionally succumbs to chestnut blight.

Robinia pseudoacacia L.
BLACK LOCUST
Fabaceae (Legume family)

Description: Medium-sized, fast-growing but relatively short-lived tree with deeply furrowed bark and stout, paired spines at nodes. Leaves alternate, deciduous, pinnately compound with 7–19 leaflets. White, fragrant, pea-like flowers in drooping clusters. Flat brown pods (legumes) 2–4 in. long often hang from branches through winter. Flowers Apr.–June; fruits July–Nov.

Habitat/range: Forests, woodlands, and disturbed areas, including roadsides, clear cuts, and abandoned fields. Common. Native to central and southern Appalachians from Pennsylvania south to Georgia.

Taxonomy. Robinia is a small genus of 8 species of shrubs and trees native to eastern and southwestern North America, 5 of which occur in the mountains and piedmont.

Ecology: Black locust has been introduced and subsequently naturalized over a wide geographic area, including parts of Canada, Europe, and Asia. Its success reflects an ability to tolerate a wide range of environments, grow rapidly, reproduce at an early age, produce large seed crops, and to spread rapidly by root sprouts, forming clones.

Wildlife: Black locust is susceptible to various insects and pathogens, including the locust leafminer, which causes the leaves to turn gray or brown, suggesting an early fall color change. A more destructive insect is the locust borer, a black, yellow-lined longhorn beetle whose larvae build feeding tunnels throughout the wood. The tunnels provide entry points for heart rot fungi that cause extensive wood decay, sometimes leading to tree death. A sap-sucking insect known as the locust treehopper mimics the thorns of black locust, thus hiding from predators. If a thorn appears to be moving, this insect may be playing hide and seek with you. Because of its susceptibility to insects and rots, black locust is a good nest-cavity tree, particularly for woodpeckers.

Uses: As a nitrogen fixer, black locust can grow on nutrient-poor soils and is often planted on reclamation sites for soil improvement and erosion control. Its wood is used for split rail fence posts, as seen along the Blue Ridge Parkway.

Sassafras albidum (Nutt.) Nees
SASSAFRAS
Lauraceae (Laurel family)

Description: Small to medium-sized deciduous tree with dark green twigs on young branches. Leaves variable in size and form with distinctive 2-lobed, 3-lobed, or unlobed margins. Male and female flowers on separate plants appear before the leaves emerge. Fruit a dark blue drupe on a red club-shaped stalk. Flowers Mar.–Apr.; fruits June–July.

Habitat/range: Wide variety of forests, fields, and woodland borders. Common. Widespread in eastern United States.

Taxonomy: Sassafras is a genus of 3 species, 2 in east Asia, 1 in eastern North America. Red mulberry (*Morus rubra*) also has variably lobed leaves but differs in having sharply toothed (rather than smooth) leaf margins.

Ecology: Sassafras is an early successional species that frequently colonizes abandoned fields and woodland borders. A shade-intolerant species, sassafras grows quickly in full sun, but often dies early after being overtopped by competing vegetation. Fires and other types of disturbance that maintain an open canopy benefit sassafras. Flies, wasps, and other insects visit and pollinate the dense clusters of small, yellowish green flowers in early spring. A good seed crop is produced every 2–3 years. Birds quickly remove the ripe, high-fat-content (and high-energy) fruits. The seeds typically require an overwintering period (stratification) before germinating in spring. Spreads vegetatively by root sprouts.

Wildlife: Sassafras is one of several larval host plants for spicebush swallowtail butterflies. Female spicebush swallowtails choose smooth-leaved sassafras plants over pubescent-leaved plants to lay their eggs on. Larvae (caterpillars) fed pubescent leaves have slower growth rates and a higher mortality than larvae fed smooth leaves. Thus, leaf pubescence in sassafras likely reduces herbivore damage by caterpillars of spicebush swallowtails.

Uses: Oil of sassafras is no longer used to flavor root beer, tobacco, chewing gum, and perfumes because one of its constituents, safrole, is a suspected carcinogen. Sassafras is an attractive landscape plant in open, sunny areas, but is sensitive to ozone.

Sorbus americana Marsh.
MOUNTAIN ASH
Rosaceae (Rose family)

Description: Small to medium-sized deciduous tree recognizable by its large, pinnately compound leaves, flat-topped inflorescences of densely packed small white flowers, and striking clusters of orange-red fruits that persist into winter. Flowers June–July; fruits Sept.–Oct.

Habitat/range: Forest openings, woodland borders, and roadsides at high elevations. Spruce-fir forests, balds, and high-elevation rock outcrops. Common. Newfoundland west to Minnesota, south in mountains to Georgia.

Taxonomy: Mountain ash is the only species of the genus *Sorbus* in the mountains and piedmont. Despite its common name, it's not a member of the ash (Oleaceae) family, but is in the rose family along with trees such as apples, peaches, plums, and cherries.

Ecology: Mountain ash is a slow-growing, short-lived, shade-intolerant tree that is most abundant in forest openings and other early successional habitats. Over the last half-century, mountain ash has become more abundant in spruce-fir forests due to openings created by the large-scale dieback of Fraser fir. In good fruiting years, dense clusters of orange-red fruits cover the tree.

Wildlife: Deer feed on the leaves in summer and browse the twigs and buds in winter (as do moose at more northerly latitudes). The fruits are a favorite of black bears and red squirrels. Songbirds, such as evening grosbeaks, American robins, and cedar waxwings, feast on the fruits, occasionally getting a "buzz" from fermented fruit. Because the seeds quickly pass through the guts of birds (often within 30 minutes), most are probably dispersed fairly short distances. Fruits tend to persist on mountain ash well into winter, making them an important food source for year-round residents at high elevations.

Uses: Native Americans used the fruits, rich in vitamin C, as a tea to prevent scurvy. The pectin-rich fruits also make a good jelly. Prior to ripening, the fruits are high in tartaric acid and are unpalatable, but after a few frosts, they become less bitter and are edible.

Symplocos tinctoria (L.) L'Her.
HORSE SUGAR, SWEETLEAF
Symplocaceae (Sweetleaf family)

Description: A tardily deciduous shrub or small tree up to 30 ft. tall with a smooth to slightly furrowed gray to light brown bark, often with small, warty outgrowths. Leaves alternate, leathery, dark green above, sometimes tinged with purple, 2–4 in. long, margins minutely serrate, pointed at tip, wedge-shaped at base, often crowded towards stem tip. Flowers fragrant, cream to yellow with long stamens in dense showy clusters that open before the new leaves emerge. Fruit cylindrical, green when young, becoming dry and brownish with a thin pulp and single seed. Flowers Mar.–May; fruits Aug.–Sept.

Habitat/range: An understory tree of moist deciduous woods, including river bluff forests, alluvial forests, oak-hickory forests, pine-oak heath, and ridgetop forests. Common in piedmont, uncommon in mountains. Eastern United States.

Taxonomy: A genus of 300 species of Asia, Australia, and the Americas, with only 1 species in North America. The leaves of horse sugar can be confused with mountain laurel (*Kalmia latifolia*) but its sweet-tasting leaves (with a flavor similar to green apples) and clusters of cylindrical fruits are distinguishing characteristics.

Ecology: Horse sugar is easily topkilled by fires, due to its thin bark but can grow quite tall in habitats protected from fire. The fragrant flowers, with numerous long stamens, are actively visited and pollinated by bumblebees.

Wildlife: White-tailed deer, horses, cattle, and various insects relish the sweet-tasting leaves, hence the common names "horse sugar" and "sweetleaf." It's a larval (caterpillar) host plant of king's hairstreak butterflies.

Uses: Pioneers boiled the leaves and inner bark to obtain a yellow dye. The leaves can be chewed as a trailside snack, but their sweetness varies among plants, seasons, and tasters.

Tilia americana L.
WHITE BASSWOOD
Tiliaceae (Basswood family)

Description: A medium to large deciduous tree usually with a straight trunk and slender, spreading branches. Large heart-shaped leaves with toothed margins, a pointed tip and asymmetrical base. Small, yellowish green flowers and round pea-sized fruits hang from slender stalks attached to a distinctive, narrow leaf-like bract. Flowers June; fruits July–Aug.

Habitat/range: Moist, fertile, well-drained slopes and stream bottoms. Northern hardwood forests, cove forests, river bluff forests, floodplain forests, and oak-hickory forests. Common in mountains, uncommon in piedmont. Widely distributed in eastern North America.

Taxonomy: The genus *Tilia* comprises about 25 species of trees in temperate regions of North America, Europe, and Asia. Species of basswood can be distinguished from all other trees by the attachment of its flower and fruit clusters to a leaf-like bract.

Ecology: White basswood is a shade-tolerant tree that usually occurs in the understory but occasionally reaches the canopy. Vulnerable to fire because of its thin bark, white basswood has become more abundant over the last century due to fire suppression. Its decaying leaves improve the soil by providing a rich source of calcium and magnesium as well as nitrogen, potassium, and phosphorous. Bees pollinate the creamy yellow nectar-rich flowers in the day, whereas moths function as nighttime pollinators. Moths are attracted to the flowers' sweet odor, which is strongest at night. The leaf-like bracts from which the flowers and fruits hang also attract pollinators. Later in the season, the bracts catch the wind, thereby facilitating seed dispersal.

Wildlife: Chipmunks, squirrels, and mice eat the seeds, rabbits and other grazers consume the seedlings, and a wide array of insects feed on the leaves. Various birds, mammals, and insects (including wild honeybees and black bears) nest or den in hollow old basswoods.

Uses: Native Americans used the long, strong fibers from the inner bark of basswood to make rope. The soft, easily worked wood can be carved into various pieces, including musical instruments.

Synonym: Tilia heterophylla Vent.

Tsuga canadensis (L.) Carriere
CANADA HEMLOCK, EASTERN HEMLOCK
Pinaceae (Pine family)

Description: A medium to large evergreen tree with a dense, conical crown and pendulous, graceful branches. Needles flattened, shiny green above with 2 white lines below. Mature seed cones one-half to three-quarter in. long, reddish brown, hang from branch tips usually until the following spring. Pollen dispersed Mar.–Apr.; seeds mature Sept.–Nov.

Habitat/range: Primarily in cool, moist ravines and valleys and along streams and lower slopes of cove forests, but also in mountain bogs, spray cliffs, dry rocky gorges, and river bluff forests. Prior to the woolly adelgid infestation, Canada hemlock was common in mountains, rare in piedmont (south of Virginia), and widespread in eastern North America.

Taxonomy: The genus *Tsuga* consists of 2 species in eastern North America, 2 in western North America, and 10 in east Asia. Carolina hemlock (*T. caroliniana*) resembles Canada hemlock, but its needles are arranged all around the twigs, rather than more or less in a single plane.

Ecology: Canada hemlock is a slow-growing but long-lived tree with a potential life span of 400–600 years, commonly reaching heights in excess of 100 ft. One of our most shade-tolerant trees, individuals can persist in the understory for 100 years or more before reaching the canopy. Canada hemlock's shallow root system makes it vulnerable to drought, windthrow, ground fires, and human intrusion (such as nearby roads and footpaths). Both of our native hemlocks are currently threatened by the hemlock woolly adelgid, an aphid-like insect that sucks sap from twigs, causing needle loss and tree death within several years of infestation. This tiny insect introduced from Asia has left a trail of dead hemlocks throughout the Appalachians and beyond.

Wildlife: Many wildlife species find shelter in Canada hemlock's dense evergreen foliage.

Uses: The bark was widely used as a source of tannins for making leather. Canada hemlock is planted as a landscape tree, and trimmed into a hedge.

Tsuga caroliniana Engelm.
CAROLINA HEMLOCK
Pinaceae (Pine family)

Description: A medium-sized evergreen tree with a slender trunk and narrow crown with slightly drooping branches. The needle-like leaves, shiny green above, whitish below, radiate out at different angles along twigs. Seed cones up to 1 ½ in. long, elliptical, with yellow to light brown spreading cone scales. Pollen released Mar.–Apr., seed cones mature Aug.–Sept., persisting on tree through spring.

Habitat/range: Mostly on dry, exposed sites with rocky, acidic, nutrient-poor soils, occasionally on moister sites. High-elevation rock outcrops and open forests in small, pure stands or with mixed hardwoods. Uncommon. A southern Appalachian endemic with rare outlier populations in the upper piedmont.

Taxonomy: Carolina hemlock resembles Canada hemlock (*T. canadensis*), but its needles spread in all directions along the twigs, rather than being more or less flattened in a single plane along the twigs, as occurs in Canada hemlock. Carolina hemlock also has larger cones than Canada hemlock and tends to occur on more exposed sites with drier, rockier soils.

Ecology: Carolina hemlock grows with hardwoods such as chestnut oak and red maple and understory species such as rhododendron and mountain laurel. Never abundant, it sometimes occurs in nearly pure stands, particularly on dry, rocky soils where most trees can't survive. Carolina hemlock is tolerant of both drought and deep shade. Its slow growth and small evergreen leaves help it cope with nutrient-poor soils. Its ability to grow and reproduce in shaded environments, coupled with its long lifespan, eventually enable it to replace earlier established trees. The dense foliage of Carolina hemlock shades the understory, making it difficult for other species to overtop it. Carolina hemlock is currently threatened throughout its range by the hemlock woolly adelgid.

Wildlife: Birds and small mammals consume the seeds and the dense evergreen foliage provides food and cover for wildlife in winter.

Uses: Carolina hemlock was used as a source of tannin for processing leather.

***Ulmus alata* Michx.**
WINGED ELM
Ulmaceae (Elm family)

Description: Small to medium-sized tree often with corky, wing-like projections on twigs. Leaves small, narrowly elliptical with doubly serrate margins, long-pointed at apex, rounded at base. Tiny reddish flowers in pendulous clusters develop into small, flattened, winged samaras with dense white hairs on margins. Flowers Feb.–Mar.; fruits Mar.–Apr.

Habitat/range: Dry and mesic forests, along streams and floodplains, woodlands, forest edges, rock outcrops, fields, disturbed areas. Common in piedmont, rare in mountains. Widespread in Southeast and southern Midwest.

Taxonomy: A genus of 25 species of trees, rarely shrubs, of temperate and boreal regions of the Northern Hemisphere with 4 native and 3 introduced species in the mountains and piedmont.

Ecology: Winged elm grows on a variety of sites, including rich, moist soils of floodplains and dry, nutrient-poor soils associated with rock outcrops. On poor, dry sites, it typically has a stunted, gnarled growth form. While it can persist under a forest canopy, its growth rate and flower and fruit production are markedly reduced relative to open areas with abundant sunlight. One of the earliest trees to bloom, both the flowers and fruits mature before the leaves emerge. Wind-pollinated flowers develop into winged seeds that are dispersed by wind and water. Like all native elms, it's susceptible to Dutch elm disease. Although the introduced fungus that causes this disease can kill trees, its effect has been less in the southern than northern United States.

Wildlife: Wood ducks, rose-breasted grosbeaks, purple finches, and squirrels are among the many birds and small mammals that seek out the early ripening seeds. Numerous butterfly and moth caterpillars feed on the leaves.

Uses: Winged elm is frequently planted as a street or shade tree because it grows rapidly and is drought tolerant.

***Ulmus rubra* Muhl.**
SLIPPERY ELM
Ulmaceae (Elm family)

Description: Medium-sized deciduous tree with alternate simple leaves 4–6 in. long, abruptly short to long-pointed at apex, usually asymmetrical at base, the upper surface very rough (like sandpaper) with doubly toothed leaf margins. Inconspicuous dark red flowers in dense clusters form round, flat-winged samaras before the leaves emerge. Flowers Feb.–Mar.; fruits Mar.–Apr.

Habitat/range: Moist forests on lower slopes, floodplains, occasionally on drier upland sites, particularly on limestone soils. Alluvial forests, basic mesic forests, and cove forests. Common in piedmont and lower mountains. Widespread in eastern North America.

Taxonomy: The common name alludes to its slimy inner bark. Several elms in the region are introduced from Asia, including the Chinese or lacebark elm (*U. parviflora*), a widely planted landscape tree that can escape and become a problem weed.

Ecology: Slippery elm grows primarily in bottomlands and moist upland forests. Its presence on drier upland sites is a good indicator of calcium-rich (limestone) soil. It can persist on poorly drained soils that are occasionally flooded, but not on sites where frequent or prolonged flooding occurs. Like the blooms of most wind-pollinated plants, the flowers are inconspicuous, lack odor, and don't produce nectar (as they don't need to attract or reward pollinators). Flowering occurs before the leaves emerge, thereby enhancing pollen dispersal and increasing the likelihood of successful pollination. Like other elms, it's susceptible to Dutch elm disease.

Wildlife: Various birds, including wood ducks, rose-breasted grosbeaks, and purple finches eat the seeds, as do squirrels. White-tailed deer and rabbits browse the foliage and twigs, and many butterfly and moth caterpillars feed on the leaves. The elm leaf beetle can defoliate entire trees—look for the olive-green beetles on the underside of leaves along with the yellowish, slug-like larvae that strip the leaves.

Uses: The slimy inner bark (which has a licorice-like taste) was once chewed to prevent scurvy and ground into a nutritious flour. Slippery elm lozenges are still available in some drugstores.

2 : Shrubs and Woody Vines

Aesculus sylvatica Bartram
PAINTED BUCKEYE
Sapindaceae (Soapberry family)

Description: Shrub or small deciduous tree 3–16 ft. tall with palmately compound leaves with 5 (rarely 7) leaflets. Yellowish green, cream, pink, or red petals form a tubular corolla. Fruit a light brown leathery pod with 1–3 large, shiny brown seeds. Flowers Mar.–May; fruits July–Aug.

Habitat/range: Mesic, nutrient-rich forests, including cove forests, alluvial forests, basic mesic forests, and riverbanks. Common in piedmont and low mountains. From Virginia south to Georgia.

Taxonomy: A genus of 13 species of trees and shrubs of North America, Mexico, Asia, and Europe, including 6 species in the mountains and piedmont. Similar to yellow buckeye (*A. flava*) but smaller in size. The common name alludes to the conspicuous light brown scar on the seeds (the "buck's eye").

Ecology: One of the first woody plants to leaf out in spring (in March) and to lose its leaves in summer (beginning in early June). By leafing out early, it takes advantage of the short period in spring when daytime temperatures are favorable for growth and light levels are high because canopy trees have yet to leaf out. Bumblebees are the most common pollinators, but ruby-throated hummingbirds also visit and pollinate the tubular flowers. The reddish color sometimes seen in the flowers of painted buckeye (as well as in the flowers of yellow buckeye) is thought to reflect hybridization with red buckeye (*A. pavia*), a coastal plain species. Migrating hummingbirds moving from coastal areas into the piedmont and mountains in spring and early summer are the most likely candidates for introducing red buckeye pollen into populations of painted and yellow buckeye.

Wildlife: Most wildlife species avoid buckeyes as both the leaves and seeds contain a poisonous glycoside called aesculin.

Uses: Native Americans threw crushed buckeye seeds into streams to stun fish. Toxins in the seeds destabilized the fish's nervous systems, causing them to float to the surface, where they were easily scooped into baskets. Painted buckeye makes a nice addition to woodland gardens.

Alnus serrulata (Aiton) Willd.
TAG ALDER
Betulaceae (Birch family)

Description: A deciduous shrub or small tree with simple, alternate leaves, obovate to elliptical, 2–4 in. long, pinnately veined. Male flowers in long, slender, pendulous catkins, female flowers in short, erect cones. Fruit a nutlet in small, woody cones that persist through winter. Flowers Feb.–Mar.; fruits Aug.–Oct.

Habitat/range: Moist to wet places, including rocky streamsides, mountain bogs, and alluvial forests. Common. Widely distributed in eastern North America.

Taxonomy: The genus *Alnus* includes about 25 species of shrubs and trees widely distributed in North America, Europe, and Asia. Alders can be recognized by their clusters of small, persistent woody seed cones at the tips of branches.

Ecology: In late winter, male catkins hang like long tassels, releasing a little pollen at a time into cup-like sections of the flower before the pollen is picked up and dispersed into the wind. A tiny fraction of this pollen is "caught" by small, reddish, hair-like structures (stigmas) that project from young female catkins. The abundantly produced pollen helps ensure pollination success but contributes to hay fever. Alders spread vegetatively via underground stems and by layering, sometimes forming dense thickets. Alder roots, in association with certain bacteria, absorb atmospheric nitrogen and convert it into a form the plant can use. The leaves of alder are especially rich in nitrogen, and with fall leaf drop, substantial amounts of nitrogen are released into the soil, which can be used by neighboring plants. Based on fossil pollen, research shows alders have been in North America for at least 65 million years.

Wildlife: Dense alder thickets provide valuable wildlife cover. Various songbirds consume the seeds, and beavers eat the bark and use the stems for constructing dams. Conspicuous clumps of "woolly" aphids commonly occur on alder stems from late summer through fall. These aphids look like sticky masses of white cotton as they ingest and modify sap from the plant and secrete it through pores on their backs.

Uses: The dense mats of roots associated with alder thickets help hold soil in place, reducing erosion along streams and lakeside margins.

Aralia spinosa L.
DEVIL'S WALKINGSTICK
Araliaceae (Ginseng family)

Description: An erect deciduous shrub or small tree with sharp pointed prickles on the trunk, branches, and leaves. The large (up to 4 ft. long and 2–3 ft. wide), highly divided leaves can have as many as 100 leaflets. Small, greenish white flowers in large, showy, terminal clusters 2–4 ft. long develop into purple-black juicy fruits in large, drooping clusters. Flowers June–Sept.; fruits Sept.–Oct.

Habitat/range: Moist to dry woods, along streams and bottomlands, forest edges, and road banks. Common. Widespread in eastern United States.

Taxonomy: The 30 species of *Aralia* occur mainly in eastern North America and east Asia. Of the 4 species of *Aralia* in the region, Devil's walkingstick is unique in having stout spines, large, highly divided leaves, and woody stems.

Ecology: This is a plant that you don't want to brush against, grab, or use as a walking stick as its stems and leaves are covered with sharp spines. The spines help protect the plant from physical damage caused by larger animals, and deter smaller animals and some insects from landing, crawling, or feeding on its tissues. In winter, the tips of the leafless stems end in a large terminal bud containing all of the plant's leaves for the upcoming year. A very fast-growing species, devil's walkingstick can grow more than 10 ft. in a single year. It also spreads vigorously by root sprouts, sometimes forming dense thickets.

Wildlife: Bees, wasps, and butterflies actively visit the flowers for nectar, pollen, or both. Numerous birds and small mammals consume the fruits and disperse the seeds, and white-tailed deer browse the young foliage.

Uses: Early settlers used the berries for toothaches and rheumatic pain. The huge leaves, showy inflorescences, and large clusters of purple fruit make it an attractive plant in woodland borders, but it can form thickets.

Aristolochia macrophylla Lam.
PIPEVINE, DUTCHMAN'S PIPE
Aristolochiaceae (Birthwort family)

Description: Woody vine with large, heart-shaped deciduous leaves and inconspicuous brown-purple flowers that resemble an old-fashioned smoking pipe. Fruit a pod 2–3 in. long with thin, flat seeds stacked like coins. Flowers May–June; fruits Aug.–Sept.

Habitat/range: Northern hardwood forests, cove forests, and forest edges. Common in mountains. An Appalachian endemic, from Pennsylvania south to Georgia.

Taxonomy: Aristolochia macrophylla is nearly glabrous and has purple-brown flowers, whereas *A. tomentosa* (woolly pipevine) has pubescent foliage and yellow flowers. These two species are sometimes placed in the genus *Isotrema*.

Ecology: Pipevine flowers have a trap-and-release pollination mechanism whereby small flies enter flowers when the stigmas are receptive and are trapped inside until the anthers dehisce and the downward-pointing hairs that block the opening wilt, allowing flies (which are likely to be carrying pollen on their bodies) to exit. Flies are fooled into visiting additional flowers by a floral odor that mimics fungi, carrion, or feces, depending on the particular species of pipevine. In trying to escape, trapped flies inadvertently rub pollen onto the stigmas, cross-pollinating the flowers.

Wildlife: Toxins (aristolochic acids) in the leaves prevent most animals from feeding on pipevines. An exception is the pipevine swallowtail butterfly whose larvae (caterpillars) feed on the leaves and use the aristolochic acids in the plant as a chemical defense mechanism against potential predators (just as monarch butterflies employ toxins from milkweed plants). Adult female butterflies utilize the odor of aristolochic acids to identify appropriate host plants for egg laying, as the caterpillars can only feed on pipevine and other members of the birthwort family. Black with iridescent blue-green hind wings, pipevine swallowtails fly slowly and are long-lived, characteristics of butterflies unpalatable to predators.

Uses: Pipevine's woody stems are collected to make "rustic" hanging baskets, a practice that threatens wild populations.

Aronia melanocarpa (Michx.) Elliott
BLACK CHOKEBERRY
Rosaceae (Rose family)

Description: A small, deciduous, multi-stemmed shrub with alternate, elliptical leaves with finely toothed margins, glabrous except for small, reddish brown hairs scattered on the upper midrib. Small white to light pink flowers in flat-topped terminal clusters. Fruit a small, berry-like pome, dark purple to black. Flowers May–June; fruits Aug.–Sept.

Habitat/range: Heath balds, rock outcrops, mountain bogs, and forest openings, mostly at high elevations. Common in mountains, rare in piedmont. Widespread in northeastern North America, extending south into Georgia and Alabama.

Taxonomy: The genus *Aronia* comprises 65 species of east Asia and eastern North America, south into Central America, including 3 species in the mountains and piedmont. Black chokeberry and red chokeberry (*A. arbutifolia*) are morphologically and ecologically very similar, sometimes occurring in the same habitat. The best way to distinguish between them is by fruit color—black or red—as is indicated by their common names. When fruits are absent, check the lower surfaces of the leaves—black chokeberry is mostly smooth whereas red chokeberry is densely hairy.

Ecology: Black chokeberry grows on substrates that range from dry to swampy. A sun-loving plant, it does best in open, rocky areas and other early successional habitats. In the forest understory, plants are typically more scattered and produce fewer flowers and fruits. The flowers are actively visited and pollinated by bees. Fruit set is higher when flowers are cross-pollinated, rather than self-pollinated. The fruits are about the size of blueberries but are far less sweet and much chewier. Plants spread by seeds as well as vegetatively through suckering.

Wildlife: Birds generally ignore black chokeberry fruits until late fall or early winter when more desirable fruits are less available.

Uses: The red fall color, persistent fruits, and tolerance to a wide range of conditions make black chokeberry a desirable plant for landscape use.

Synonym: Sorbus melanocarpa (Mich.) Heynh.

Arundinaria appalachiana Triplett, Weakley, Clark
HILL CANE
Poaceae (Grass family)

Description: Aboveground stems usually 1 ½–3 ft. tall but sometimes reaching heights of 5 ft. Individuals consist of multiple stems with alternate grass-like leaves arising from a rhizome. Inconspicuous reddish purple flowers in small clusters, 1–2 in. long. Flowering and fruiting characteristics largely unknown as individuals rarely flower.

Habitat/range: Dry to moist forests on upland slopes, including oak-hickory forests, chestnut oak forests, pine-oak-heath, river bluff forests, and forest edges. Common in mountains and upper piedmont. From North Carolina south to Georgia.

Taxonomy: Hill cane is one of only 3 temperate species of bamboo native to North America, all of which occur in the Southeast. Giant cane (*A. gigantea*) commonly occurs in floodplains and swamps, occasionally reaching heights of 20 ft. or more, while switch cane (*A. tecta*) grows in swamps and other very wet habitats in the coastal plain and piedmont. A distinctive trait of hill cane is that it drops its leaves in autumn, an unusual trait in bamboos. The closest relatives of these 3 native species are in east Asia where about 500 species of bamboo occur.

Ecology: While hill cane typically occurs on dry to somewhat moist upland slopes, it sometimes occurs on moister soils associated with seeps and well-drained streambanks. Although somewhat shade-tolerant, hill cane grows best in relatively open forests where light levels are higher. Because it is slow growing and long lived, hill cane can persist for decades, possibly centuries. Individuals rarely flower, but spread vegetatively from rhizomes. Large nutrient reserves stored underground in rhizomes facilitate rapid resprouting following a fire.

Wildlife: The dense foliage provides both food and cover for various wildlife, including several kinds of warblers that forage, roost, and nest in dense stands of cane.

Uses: Hill cane is a good forage plant for livestock; the tender shoots can be eaten by humans, just as bamboo shoots are in Asia.

Synonym: Arundinaria gigantea (Walter) Muhl.

Arundinaria gigantea (Walter) Muhl.
GIANT CANE, RIVER CANE
Poaceae (Grass family)

Description: Upright, woody grass 3–6 ft. tall (possibly reaching 30 ft. tall) with multiple stems from a thick rhizome. Leaves alternate with long, tapering tips. Flowers in dense terminal clusters of separate male and female flowers. Rarely flowers; like most bamboos, individuals usually die after fruiting. Fruit a brown grain. Flowers Apr.–May.

Habitat/range: Alluvial forests and swamps. Common. Widespread in Southeast.

Taxonomy: A genus of 3 species of woody grasses (bamboos) native to the Southeast. All other bamboos in the region are introduced.

Ecology: The term "canebrake" refers to large areas covered by dense stands of cane (*Arundinaria* ssp.). Historic accounts by European explorers and early settlers frequently mention large canebrakes along riverbanks. For example, William Bartram made reference to "widespread cane swamps" and "an endless wilderness of canes." Periodic burnings by Native Americans encouraged the persistence and expansion of canebrakes, as fires opened up the canopy and increased the amount of light reaching the forest floor. Following European settlement, canebrakes declined rapidly due to overgrazing and land clearing. Cane, a highly desirable forage plant, was particularly sensitive to continuous grazing. Overgrazing by cows, coupled with pigs consuming the carbohydrate-rich rhizomes, destroyed canebrakes. Settlers intending to farm the land understood the presence of canebrakes as an indicator of fertile soil; as a result, canebrakes were frequently cleared for growing crops. Over the last century, fire suppression has increased the density of woody plants at the expense of cane. While cane continues to persist as an understory species throughout much of its historic range, large canebrakes have virtually disappeared.

Wildlife: Giant cane provides food and cover for a number of wildlife species.

Uses: Native Americans made fishing poles from the stems and mats and baskets from the leaves.

Asimina triloba (L.) Dunal
PAWPAW

Annonaceae (Custard apple family)

Description: Large shrub or small deciduous tree, the twigs covered with rust-colored hairs. Leaves 6–12 in. long, widest above the middle, gradually tapering toward the base. Flowers 1–2 in. wide with 6 maroon petals in 2 whorls appearing before the leaves emerge. Large (2–5 in. long) fleshy fruits with yellowish green to brown skin enclose a custard-like pulp with several large, flat seeds. Flowers Mar.–May; fruits Aug.–Oct.

Habitat/range: Moist, fertile sites, including alluvial forests, cove forests, and northern hardwood forests. Common. Eastern and central United States.

Taxonomy: A genus of 8 species of shrubs and small trees in eastern North America, including 2 species in the mountains and piedmont. Small-flowered pawpaw (*A. parviflora*) is a similar but shorter shrub with smaller leaves, flowers, and fruits.

Ecology: Walking through a grove of pawpaws is almost like being in the tropics. The large leaves produce heavy shade that inhibits the growth of shade-intolerant plants. Newly opened flowers have shiny stigmas receptive to pollen. After 6 days, stigmas turn brown, anthers release pollen, and flowers become functionally male. Cross-pollination is necessary for successful fruit set, as self-pollen is incompatible. The flowers produce a yeasty odor that attracts flies and beetles, but lack of compatible (outcrossed) pollen reaching stigmas often results in low fruit set. Plants spread locally by root sprouts, forming thickets with progressively younger trees towards the periphery.

Wildlife: Few herbivores feed on pawpaws, due to the presence of toxic compounds unique to the custard apple family. A notable exception is the zebra swallowtail butterfly; pawpaws are their sole larval food source. As caterpillars feed on pawpaw leaves, they store the plant defense compound in their own tissues, which protects both the larvae (caterpillars) and adult zebra swallowtails from predators.

Uses: Pawpaws are an interesting landscape plant with sweet, edible fruits.

Bignonia capreolata L.
CROSSVINE
Bignoniaceae (Bignonia family)

Description: High-climbing woody vine with opposite, pinnately compound leaves with just 2 leaflets per leaf (and a long, slender corkscrew-like tendril between them). Clusters of 2–5 tubular flowers, red to orange on the outside, yellow or red within. Fruit a slender, flat seedpod about 6–8 in. long with numerous winged seeds. Flowers Apr.–May; fruits July–Aug.

Habitat/range: Mostly wet to moist forests and woodlands, occasionally drier forests, disturbed areas. Alluvial forests, swamp forests, river bluff forests, oak-hickory forests, forest edges, and granite outcrops. Common in piedmont, rare in mountains. Eastern United States.

Taxonomy: This is the only temperate species in the genus (the other 28 species occur in the tropics). Crossvine is similar to trumpet creeper (*Campsis radicans*) but it typically has only 2 leaflets per leaf, climbs by tendrils (instead of aerial roots), and blooms in spring (rather than in summer). Both are members of the bignonia family.

Ecology: This fast-growing, semi-evergreen to evergreen vine often occurs high up in the canopy where light levels are highest. It climbs by its curly tendrils attaching to the bark and twigs of trees; also, small adhesive disks at the tips of the tendrils collectively "cement" the vine to trees, fence posts, and even buildings. Hummingbirds pollinate the reddish tubular flowers. In favorable sites, abundant flowers, fruits, and seeds are produced. It spreads locally from root sprouts, and its winged seeds are widely dispersed by wind.

Wildlife: Crossvine begins flowering from early to mid-April, which usually coincides with the return of ruby-throated hummingbirds from their overwintering in Mexico or Central America.

Uses: Crossvine makes a striking plant for garden trellises, and has the added benefit of attracting ruby-throated hummingbirds.

Synonym: Anisostichus capreolata (L.) Bureau

Calycanthus floridus L.
SWEET SHRUB
Calycanthaceae (Sweet shrub family)

Description: A 3–6 ft. tall deciduous, aromatic shrub that forms dense thickets from root sprouts. Leaves opposite, simple, oval to elliptical, 3–6 in. long with smooth margins. Twigs enlarged and flattened at nodes. Flowers showy, with numerous maroon to brown sepals and petals with a spicy fragrance. Leathery pod-like fruits, 1 ½ –3 in. long, green in summer, dark brown to black in winter with large brown seeds. Flowers Mar.–June; Fruits July–Sept.

Habitat/range: Moist to somewhat dry forests and streambanks. Cove forests, rocky streamsides, forest edges, basic mesic forests, and oak-hickory forests. Common. Eastern United States.

Taxonomy: A genus of 4 species of North America and China, 2 of which occur in the mountains and piedmont.

Ecology: Sweet shrub's nectarless flowers have a strong fruity odor that attracts small beetles that become trapped in the flowers. When a flower first opens, a few of the outer petal-like sepals open while the innermost petals curl inward, creating a passageway down to the stigmas. Beetles that crawl down this corridor get trapped inside the flower, and as they struggle to find an exit, they brush pollen (deposited on their bodies from a previously visited flower) onto the receptive stigmas. After 1–2 days, the anthers open, the trapped beetles get dusted with fresh pollen and the inner petals reflex, releasing the beetles to visit other flowers. At this point, the flower turns brown and loses its scent. The temporal separation of the female and male phases of the flower promotes cross-pollination, and the trapping of pollinators is similar to that of Dutchman's pipe (*Aristolochia macrophylla*).

Wildlife: White-tailed deer browse the foliage and mice chew holes in the pods to get at the seeds. Seeds eaten in large quantities are toxic to humans and livestock, due to the presence of calycanthine, an alkaloid similar to strychnine.

Uses: Sweet shrub is a highly desirable landscape plant, due to its showy, fragrant flowers, unusual fruits, and yellow fall foliage.

Campsis radicans (L.) Seem. ex Bureau
TRUMPET VINE
Bignoniaceae (Bignonia family)

Description: Fast-growing, high-climbing woody vine with straw-colored stems and opposite, pinnately compound leaves with 7–15 leaflets. The 3–4 in. long, trumpet-shaped, orange-red flowers readily distinguish this species. The long, narrow, pod-like capsules often hang on the vine through winter. Flowers June–July; fruits Sept.–Oct.

Habitat/range: Alluvial forests, woodlands, fencerows, roadsides, fields, and disturbed areas. Common. Most of eastern United States.

Taxonomy: A member of a mostly tropical family, the genus contains just 2 species, 1 in eastern North America, the other in east Asia.

Ecology: Trumpet vine is sometimes sprawling or shrubby but usually climbs by aerial rootlets to heights of 30 ft. or more, with many leafy branches curving outward to capture more sunlight. One typically finds this native shade-intolerant vine growing in open, disturbed areas created by humans, but its precolonial habitat was probably woodlands and along the margins of alluvial forests and swamps. Trumpet vine is a classic hummingbird-pollinated plant—the tubular orange-red flowers produce abundant nectar, have no scent, and attract numerous hummingbirds. Hummingbirds visiting trumpet vine flowers often have a yellow cap of pollen on their heads and regularly deposit large amounts of pollen on stigmas, indicating they are effective pollinators of this species. The amount of nectar produced per trumpet vine flower is among the highest of any known temperate species. Because hummingbirds have high energy demands, only plants producing abundant nectar regularly attract them as pollinators. Worldwide, there are more than 1,600 nectar-feeding birds that pollinate plants, most of which occur in the tropics. In eastern North America, there is only one, the ruby-throated hummingbird, although other hummingbird species are occasionally sighted as vagrants.

Wildlife: The fruit pods have numerous nectaries that secrete droplets of sugary fluid that attract ants. The ants in turn defend the developing fruits from seed-eating insects.

Uses: This easy-to-grow vine is one of our best native plants for attracting hummingbirds.

*Celastrus orbiculatus Thunb.
ORIENTAL BITTERSWEET
Celastraceae (Bittersweet family)

Description: A twining woody vine with ovate to nearly round glossy leaves with finely toothed margins. Small, yellowish green flowers form clusters in leaf axils. Round yellow capsules open at maturity, revealing reddish-orange arils surrounding the seeds within. Flowers May; fruits Aug.–Sept., persisting through winter.

Habitat/range: Woodlands, thickets, floodplains, forest edges, and roadsides, often associated with disturbance. Common. Eastern United States.

Taxonomy: Two of the 30 species in the genus occur in the mountains and piedmont, 1 introduced, the other native. American bittersweet (*C. scandens*) differs from oriental bittersweet by having leaves nearly twice as long as wide, with flowers and fruits in terminal clusters.

Ecology: Introduced from Asia as an ornamental, oriental bittersweet quickly escaped into surrounding natural areas in the eastern United States. Though attractive, it has become a harmful weed. Much like kudzu, this fast-growing, woody vine climbs over and smothers native vegetation, forming dense monocultures. When vines climb high up in trees, the increased weight in the crown makes the tree more susceptible to windthrow and ice damage. Vines also provide a "ladder fuel" that can carry fire into the canopy, potentially increasing the frequency of destructive crown fires. While oriental bittersweet grows best in open, sunny areas, it can establish, grow slowly, and persist under a dense forest canopy. When disturbance opens the canopy, increasing the amount of light reaching the understory, rapid growth enables oriental bittersweet to overtop and shade out neighboring plants. In addition to growing upward, oriental bittersweet spreads horizontally via root suckering, often forming dense thickets.

Wildlife: Birds relish the fruits and disperse the seeds widely, thereby contributing to its invasiveness.

Uses: Although still available commercially as an ornamental vine, oriental bittersweet shouldn't be planted, due to its invasive properties.

Cephalanthus occidentalis L.
BUTTONBUSH
Rubiaceae (Madder family)

Description: Densely branching deciduous shrub or small tree, 3–12 ft. tall with mostly opposite, sometimes whorled, elliptical leaves 2–5 in. long, with pointed tips and entire margins. Numerous small, white tubular flowers in dense, round, pin-cushion-like heads with protruding styles. Fruit a dense head of nutlets, reddish brown, persisting through winter. Flowers June–Aug.; fruits Aug.–Sept.

Habitat/range: Occurs along margins of streams, rivers, ponds, lakes, marshes, wet meadows, and ditches. Common in piedmont, occasional in mountains. Widespread in eastern North America.

Taxonomy: The genus *Cephalanthus* includes 6 species of tropical and temperate North America, Asia, and Africa, but this is the only species in the mountains and piedmont.

Ecology: Buttonbush is a fast-growing but short-lived species that often forms dense thickets in moist areas where there is standing water for part or most of the year. With rising water levels, it produces roots on the lower stem, thereby keeping some roots close to the surface where oxygen is more readily available. Buttonbush spreads by seed and vegetatively by new stems arising from lateral roots. Flowers generally last 4 days. On the first day, flowers are in the male phase (the anthers release pollen); then on days 2–4, flowers are functionally female (the stigmas are receptive to pollen). Successful seed set depends on cross-pollination as plants are self-incompatible. Long-tongued insects, mainly bumblebees and butterflies, are the main pollinators.

Wildlife: Buttonbush thickets provide good resting and roosting sites for birds, and the seeds are eaten by various birds. Deer and beavers eat the leaves, twigs, and bark, and the fragrant nectar-rich flowers attract a rich diversity of butterflies. In seasonal pools, the submerged stems are commonly used for egg attachment sites by frogs and salamanders.

Uses: Buttonbush makes an interesting garden addition in wet sites.

Clethra acuminata Michx.
MOUNTAIN SWEET PEPPERBUSH
Clethraceae (Clethra family)

Description: Multistemmed shrub or small tree with cinnamon-like, reddish brown, smooth to peeling bark. Alternate deciduous leaves up to 8 in. long, mostly clustered toward stem tips, elliptic to oblong, long-pointed at tip, with finely serrate margins. Fragrant white flowers in terminal racemes develop into small, hairy capsules in upright clusters that persist through winter. Flowers July–Aug.; fruits Sept.–Oct.

Habitat/range: Mostly on rich, moist, acidic soils at high elevations. Heath balds, margins of rock outcrops, acidic cove forests, and rocky streamsides. Common in mountains. Restricted to Appalachians from Pennsylvania south to Georgia.

Taxonomy: The family Clethraceae consists of a single genus, *Clethra*, which has about 65 species of shrubs and small trees, only 2 of which occur in North America (most other species occur in Asia). The flowers, fruits, and branching pattern of mountain sweet pepperbush are similar to those of sweet pepperbush (*C. alnifolia*), a species usually found in the coastal plain.

Ecology: Mountain sweet pepperbush reproduces sexually by producing enormous numbers of tiny seeds that germinate readily. Once established, individuals often form clumps by suckering. The reddish brown trunks and their exfoliating bark are useful for identifying this plant. But how might peeling bark actually benefit the plant? One hypothesis is that as the outer bark peels away, it sheds vines that might otherwise grow up the trunk and shade the leaves.

Wildlife: The fragrant white flowers attract bees and butterflies and various birds consume the tiny seeds.

Uses: Mountain sweet pepperbush is a desirable garden plant, due to its fragrant flowers and interesting bark.

Cornus alternifolia L.
ALTERNATE LEAF DOGWOOD, PAGODA DOGWOOD
Cornaceae (Dogwood family)

Description: Multistemmed deciduous shrub or small tree with widely spreading, nearly horizontal branches. Leaves simple, alternate (usually clustered at ends of twigs, appearing to be whorled), pointed at tip, wedge-shaped at base. Small, malodorous white flowers in showy, flat-topped clusters. Fruits in loose clusters of dark blue berry-like drupes on red stalks. Flowers May–June; fruits Aug.–Sept.

Habitat/range: Moist forests, margins of woodlands, and streambanks, including red oak forests, northern hardwood forests, and cove forests. Common in mountains, rare in piedmont. Widespread in eastern North America.

Taxonomy: This is the only North American dogwood that has alternate leaves (the others have opposite leaves).

Ecology: There are 2 main groups of dogwoods: species with blue (less commonly white) fruits that lack showy bracts (such as alternate leaf dogwood), and red-fruited species that have large, showy bracts surrounding the flower clusters, such as flowering dogwood (*C. florida*). Most dogwood species depend on cross-pollination by insects for fruit and seed development. Alternate leaf dogwood's showy white flower clusters attract a wide range of potential pollinators, including beetles, bees, flies, and butterflies. Its spreading branches are arranged in horizontal tiers that decrease in size from the bottom upward, as do the branches of many conifers. This branching pattern is thought to be particularly efficient at capturing the reduced light in the forest understory.

Wildlife: Although dogwood fruits taste dry and bitter to humans, numerous birds, including fall migrants, consume the lipid-rich fruits, as do white-tailed deer, black bears, and small mammals. Germination is enhanced when fruit-eating animals remove the pulp surrounding dogwood seeds.

Uses: Native Americans scraped and dried the bark of dogwood trees and mixed it with tobacco to form a pipe blend they called kinnikinnik.

Cornus amomum Mill.
SILKY DOGWOOD
Cornaceae (Dogwood family)

Description: Multistemmed deciduous shrub to about 15 ft. tall, the twigs dark red with dense rusty or silky gray hairs. Leaves opposite, 2–4 in. long, pointed at apex, green and glabrous above, with parallel curved veins. Small, white flowers in flat-topped clusters about 2 in. across. Fruit a berry-like drupe, bluish with white blotches. Flowers May–June; fruits Aug.–Sept.

Habitat/range: Moist to wet woods and streambanks, including alluvial forests and borders of swamps. Common. Eastern United States.

Taxonomy: A genus of 60 species of trees, shrubs, and subshrubs, including 11 species in the mountains and piedmont. The dome-shaped clusters of creamy white flowers and leaves are similar to those of viburnums, but dogwood flowers have 4, rather than 5, petals.

Ecology: Silky dogwood is a sprawling shrub commonly found along the banks of streams, lakes, and swamps. It spreads by seeds and vegetatively by layering (its lower branches readily root in the soil and send up new shoots).

Wildlife: Flocks of migrating robins, starlings, and grackles strip plants of their fruits in autumn. White-footed mice climb up the branches to harvest the fruits, which they store and use as a winter food source. Female tephritid flies lay a single egg under the skin of a ripening fruit and mark it with a pheromone that deters other flies from ovipositing in the fruit. After hatching, the fly larva feeds on the pulp. The puncture wound associated with egg laying enables microbes to access the pulp, which in turn causes the fruit to turn brown and produce a vinegar-like odor that is easily detected in heavily infested plants. Because parasitized fruits fall off the plant prematurely, and because birds prefer undamaged fruits, tephritid flies decrease the number of seeds dispersed.

Uses: The multiple stems and shallow roots of silky dogwood help stabilize mudbanks along rivers and lakes, thereby reducing erosion and siltation.

Corylus cornuta Marsh.
BEAKED HAZELNUT
Betulaceae (Birch family)

Description: A dense thicket-forming shrub with coarsely toothed oval leaves, rounded or heart-shaped at base, long-pointed at tip. Wind-pollinated flowers appear in winter, long before the leaves emerge in spring. Fruit an edible brown nut enclosed within 2 leafy bracts that form a long, protruding, tube-like beak. Flowers Feb.–Mar.; fruits Aug.–Oct.

Habitat/range: Forms dense thickets in dry rocky woodlands, high-elevation forests, and clearings, including red oak forests, chestnut oak forests, oak-hickory forests, and forest edges. Common. Eastern North America.

Taxonomy: The genus *Corylus* consists of 15 species of shrubs and trees of North America, eastern Asia, and Europe, of which 2 species occur in the mountains and piedmont. Beaked hazelnut can be distinguished from American hazelnut (*C. americana*) by its green leafy bracts that form a slender beak around the nut.

Ecology: Beaked hazelnut occurs in the forest understory as well as in forest openings and woodland borders, where it forms dense clumps or thickets. A thick mat of roots and rhizomes below the surface and a dense stand of stems above the surface can choke out tree seedlings and slow the process of reforestation. A light surface fire can topkill beaked hazelnut, but it resprouts readily if the shallow roots and rhizomes are not killed.

Wildlife: In good fruiting years (occurring about every 2–3 years), hazelnut's protein-rich nuts are an important food source for squirrels, chipmunks, mice, and blue jays, as well as for a specialist weevil, whose larvae can infest more than 70 percent of developing fruits. Rodents and blue jays cache (bury) some nuts, of which a small number escape predation and establish new plants.

Uses: Wild hazelnuts are smaller in size but just as tasty as hazelnuts (filberts) sold in stores.

Decumaria barbara L.
CLIMBING HYDRANGEA
Hydrangeaceae (Hydrangea family)

Description: A semi-evergreen woody vine with slender stems that climbs by numerous aerial rootlets. Leaves opposite, ovate, 2–5 in. long, somewhat fleshy in texture, shiny green above, paler beneath, the margins entire or barely toothed. Small, fragrant, creamy-white flowers in dense terminal clusters. Fruit a small urn-shaped capsule. Flowers May–June; fruits July–Oct.

Habitat/range: Moist woods on acidic soils. Acidic cove forests, floodplain forests, and river bluff forests. Common in piedmont, rare in mountains. Widespread in Southeast.

Taxonomy: The genus consists of 2 species of vines, 1 in eastern North America, the other in eastern Asia.

Ecology: Climbing hydrangea initiates growth as a seedling on the forest floor and remains connected to the forest floor even as it climbs high up into the canopy of trees. Like poison ivy, English ivy, and Virginia creeper, it can climb straight up a tree, using numerous aerial rootlets that attach firmly to the trunks of trees. The branches that extend horizontally away from the tree trunk form flowers and fruits but don't produce roots. As a result, root-climbing vines such as climbing hydrangea are generally unable to spread from the canopy of one tree to another. Root climbers, however, typically produce lateral stems and roots on the forest floor that "search" for trees to climb, thereby gaining access to additional light.

Wildlife: The flowers attract bees, flies, and butterflies that probe between the stamens for nectar secreted by a disk on the upper surface of the ovary.

Uses: Underused by gardeners, climbing hydrangea is an attractive climber in trees and provides cover for ledges and rock outcrops.

Diervilla sessilifolia Buckley
SOUTHERN BUSH HONEYSUCKLE
Diervillaceae (Bush honeysuckle family)

Description: Sprawling soft-wooded shrub 2–6 ft. tall. Leaves opposite, sessile, long-pointed at apex with rounded base, margins finely toothed, not ciliate. Small, yellow, mildly fragrant, trumpet-shaped flowers occur in clusters at branch tips and in leaf axils. Fruit a slender, long-beaked, woody capsule, persisting into winter. Flowers June–Aug.; fruits Aug.–Oct.

Habitat/range: Rock outcrops, ridges, landslide scars, trail margins, other rocky open places, including streambanks, at moderate to high elevations. Locally common in mountains. From North Carolina south to Georgia.

Taxonomy: A genus of 3 very similar shrubs, all of which grow on high-elevation rock outcrops in the mountains. Southern bush honeysuckle differs from northern bush honeysuckle (*D. lonicera*) in that it has sessile leaves that lack cilia on their margins, and its twigs are more or less square (rather than round) when seen in cross section.

Ecology: Southern bush honeysuckle spreads vegetatively by underground stems (rhizomes), forming large clumps or patches. Because the plants are self-incompatible, successful seed set depends on insects carrying pollen from one patch (clone) to another. The main pollinators are bumblebees and a bee-like moth known as the bumblebee hawkmoth. After about 3 days, the flower color changes from yellow to red in the flowers' interior, after which bumblebees infrequently visit red flowers. By learning to associate the color change with older, less rewarding flowers, bumblebees increase their nectar foraging efficiency. The seeds, dispersed in late summer, don't germinate until spring, as embryo maturation requires an overwintering period.

Wildlife: Southern bush honeysuckle is the larval host plant of the bumblebee hawkmoth. In this plant-insect interaction, the larvae (caterpillars) feed on the leaves and the adults pollinate the flowers. Whereas most moth species are active in the evening or night, bumblebee hawkmoths hover in front of the flowers from morning to late afternoon sucking up nectar with their unrolled tongues.

Uses: Southern bush honeysuckle makes a nice addition to woodland gardens.

*Elaeagnus umbellata Thunb.
AUTUMN OLIVE
Elaeagnaceae (Oleaster family)

Description: A bushy deciduous shrub, 3–20 ft. tall, often with thorny branches. Alternate, lanceolate leaves, dull green and scaly above, silvery and scaly below. Small, funnel-shaped, yellowish white flowers in axillary clusters with a strong sweet fragrance. Berry-like fruits, silvery or silvery brown, turn red when ripe. Flowers Feb.–May; fruits Aug.–Sept.

Habitat/range: Abandoned fields, pastures, roadsides, early successional forests, and forest openings. Common in piedmont, occasional in mountains. Widespread in eastern North America.

Taxonomy: Introduced from Asia, autumn olive is the most common of the 4 species of *Elaeagnus* that occur in the mountains and piedmont. Silverthorn (*E. pungens*) is similar but flowers in autumn and fruits in spring.

Ecology: This large, moderately shade-tolerant shrub can grow 12–20 ft. tall and nearly as wide. It tolerates a wide range of soils, and its ability to fix atmospheric nitrogen by using bacteria housed within its root nodules allows autumn olive to enhance nutrient-poor soils and thrive. Individuals begin producing fruit within 3–5 years; a large mature plant in full sun can produce about 60,000 seeds. Its seeds are widely dispersed by birds and to a lesser extent by mammals. Due to its rapid growth, prolific fruiting, widely dispersed seeds, and ability to adapt to a wide range of conditions, autumn olive has become one of the most invasive shrubs in the eastern United States. It spreads readily into native plant communities where it can displace native vegetation. Autumn olive plants that are cut, mowed, or burned, quickly resprout, making them difficult to eradicate.

Wildlife: The persistent fruits provide a source of food for mammals and birds from fall through winter, white-tailed deer browse the foliage, and the plant provides cover and nesting sites for songbirds.

Uses: Formerly planted along roadsides and as a wildlife food plant, autumn olive escapes plantings and spreads by bird-dispersed fruits, becoming a pest species.

Euonymus americanus L.
STRAWBERRY BUSH, HEART'S-A-BUSTIN'
Celastraceae (Bittersweet family)

Description: An erect or straggling deciduous shrub, generally 2–6 ft. tall, with smooth, slender, 4-sided green stems. Leaves opposite, lanceolate to narrowly ovate with finely toothed margins. Small, flat, greenish cream flowers on long stalks from leaf axils. Fruit a warty red capsule that splits at maturity revealing orange-red seeds. Flowers May–June; fruits Sept.–Oct.

Habitat/range: Variety of moist to dry forests, including river bluff forests, alluvial forests, cove forests, and oak-hickory forests. Common. Widespread in eastern United States.

Taxonomy: A genus of about 129 species of trees, shrubs, and woody vines of temperate and tropical areas. Three of the 6 species in the mountain and piedmont region are introduced from Asia. Strawberry bush is by far the most common native species in the region. The common names of this plant reflect the deep red, warty fruits that split open.

Ecology: Strawberry bush is a relatively shade-tolerant shrub with slender green (photosynthetic) stems. The plants flower and fruit best in partial to full sun. Although the flowers are hermaphroditic, the male and female parts mature at different times (the anthers release pollen before the stigmas are receptive), requiring a pollinator to transfer pollen from male- to female-phase flowers. Short-tongued bees and flies foraging for nectar in the center of the small, inconspicuous flowers function as pollinators. Ants also lap up droplets of nectar from the flowers but are less effective pollinators. Strawberry bush spreads by seeds and by root suckers.

Wildlife: White-tailed deer frequently browse the stems and twigs, especially in winter, often reducing plant size. Various songbirds, wild turkeys, and white-tailed deer eat the fruits and disperse the seeds. Clusters of small-scale insects feed on the green stems, their waxy coverings resembling tiny oyster shells.

Uses: Strawberry bush makes a striking landscape plant, although the fruits, seeds, and bark are toxic if eaten.

Gaylussacia ursina (M. A. Curtis) Torr. & A. Gray ex A. Gray
BEAR HUCKLEBERRY
Ericaceae (Heath family)

Description: Low-growing deciduous shrub, often forming dense colonies. Leaves alternate, entire, pointed at apex with characteristic minute resinous glands on the lower leaf surface. Small, pendant white (tinged with red) flowers in short racemes form small, berry-like fruits that vary from sweet to tasteless. Flowers May–June; fruits July–Sept.

Habitat/range: Forests on upper slopes and ridgetops, including high-elevation red oak forests, pine-oak heath, chestnut oak forests, oak-hickory forests. Common in mountains. From North Carolina south to Georgia.

Taxonomy: Bear huckleberry is similar to black huckleberry (*G. baccata*) but has tiny resinous glands only on the lower leaf surface, rather than on both leaf surfaces.

Ecology: On upper slopes and ridgetops where the soil is generally shallow, nutrient poor, and acidic, bear huckleberry is often the dominant shrub, forming large clonal patches. Fires typically kill aboveground shoots, but plants resprout from dormant buds at the base of shoots. Bees foraging for nectar, pollen, or both, pollinate the flowers, and as the fruits ripen, they change from inconspicuous green to red to black. With this color change, the fruits become softer, and nutritious sugars replace the bitter compounds that give unripe fruits an unpleasant taste.

Wildlife: Various songbirds, gray squirrels, raccoons, white-footed mice, and black bears consume the fruits and disperse the tiny seeds. Huckleberry thickets provide good cover for wildlife.

Uses: Closely related to blueberries, the fruits of huckleberries are sometimes collected and eaten, but commercial varieties have yet to be developed.

Gelsemium sempervirens (L.) W. T. Aiton
CAROLINA JESSAMINE, YELLOW JESSAMINE
Gelsemiaceae (Jessamine family)

Description: Twining evergreen, climbing, or trailing vine with thin, wiry reddish stems up to 30 ft. long. Leaves opposite, lanceolate to elliptical with short petioles. Bright yellow, generally fragrant, funnel-shaped flowers with 5 broad lobes. Fruit a small brownish capsule with numerous winged seeds. Flowers Feb.–May (sporadically in fall); fruits Sept.–Nov.

Habitat/range: Found in a variety of habitats, including oak-hickory forests, river bluff forests, forest edges, roadsides, and rock outcrops. Common in piedmont, uncommon in mountains. Southeastern United States, disjunct in Guatemala and Mexico.

Taxonomy: A genus of 3 species of vines of North America and Asia, only 1 of which occurs in the mountains and piedmont.

Ecology: Carolina Jessamine clambers over shrubs, trees, fences, rock piles, and other structures. It's most conspicuous in spring when covered with showy, tubular, yellow flowers. The sweet-smelling flowers come in 2 forms—one with short styles bearing stigmas below the stamens, the other with long styles with stigmas above the stamens. The flowers depend on bees (including bumblebees, carpenter bees, and blueberry bees) for cross-pollination and subsequent seed set. Carpenter bees sometimes "rob nectar" from the flowers by making a slit near the base of the flower tubes, from which they imbibe nectar. Nectar-robbing bees generally don't transfer pollen, as their body parts are unlikely to contact the sexual organs of the flower.

Wildlife: Toxic alkaloids (gelsemine) deter most herbivores from feeding on the plant. The toxic alkaloid gelsemine is present in the flower's nectar, as an apparently unavoidable byproduct of its production in other tissues. Bees visiting Carolina Jessamine will switch to flowers with lower levels of alkaloids when available, which can result in a reduction in pollination success and subsequent seed production.

Uses: Carolina Jessamine is a popular landscape plant, due to its long-lasting colorful flowers, shiny evergreen leaves, and its ability to tolerate drought. It's the state flower of South Carolina.

Hamamelis virginiana L.
WITCH HAZEL
Hamamelidaceae (Witch hazel family)

Description: A deciduous shrub or small tree with large, oval to nearly round leaves, often asymmetrical at the base with scalloped leaf margins. Flowers in small, showy axillary clusters with 4 twisted, ribbon-like yellow petals. Fruit a woody 2-beaked capsule. Flowers Oct.–Dec.; fruits develop the following year (Oct.–Nov.).

Habitat/range: Moist woods, ravines, stream banks, and forest openings, including red oak forests, northern hardwood forests, cove forests, and forest edges. Common in mountains and piedmont. Widespread in eastern North America.

Taxonomy: Hamamelis is a genus of 5 species of shrubs and small trees of eastern North America and eastern Asia. Witch hazel is the only species represented in the mountains and piedmont.

Ecology: In mid- to late fall, when most other plants are dropping their leaves and going dormant, witch hazel is in full flower. The showy yellow flowers depend on insects for pollination, but frequent low temperatures limit insect activity. Witch hazel is opportunistic in that it uses whatever potential pollinators are available (including bees, flies, and moths) and its long flowering period enables it to take advantage of temperatures sporadically favorable for insect flight. Nonetheless, a lack of successful pollination often limits fruit set. When pollination occurs, fertilization is delayed until the following spring, causing fruits to mature in the fall, one year after flowering. When temperature and humidity are just right, ripe fruits suddenly split open, often with an audible pop, shooting small black seeds up to 15 ft. from the parent plant.

Wildlife: Two galls, both caused by aphids, commonly occur on witch hazel. One type, shaped like a witch's hat (hence the plant's common name) occurs on the upper leaf surface. The other common gall occurs on the twigs and resembles a small bur.

Uses: Native Americans first used an extract of the leaves, twigs, or bark to treat muscle aches and bruises. Witch hazel liniment, as it's currently called, is still on the market.

Hudsonia montana Nutt.
MOUNTAIN GOLDEN HEATHER
Cistaceae (Rockrose family)
Federally Threatened

Description: Low-growing perennial subshrub with needle-like evergreen leaves and solitary yellow flowers with 5 petals and numerous stamens. Plants generally grow in small clumps 4–8 in. across and about 6 in. tall. Vegetative plants superficially resemble a large moss or small juniper. Flowers May–July; fruits July–Sept.

Habitat/range: Occurs on ledges and cliffs of high mountain peaks and ridges on thin sandy soils in the sparsely vegetated ecotone between bare rock and heath balds dominated by sand myrtle (*Kalmia buxifolia*). A rare, narrow endemic in mountains of western North Carolina.

Taxonomy: The genus *Hudsonia* consists of 3 species of dwarf shrubs restricted to North America.

Ecology: Mountain golden heather is a species at risk. Of the 7 known populations, 5 occur within a single Blue Ridge Escarpment gorge, Linville Gorge. Population estimates suggest a total population size of only 2,000–2,500 plants. Currently, populations are declining due to suppression of natural fires, trampling by hikers and campers, drought, and encroachment by taller woody species. Its main competitor, sand myrtle (ironically also a regionally rare species) invades and overtops *Hudsonia* populations. Periodic fires benefit golden mountain heather by knocking back the foliage of encroaching shrubs. Also, by burning away the leaf litter and exposing bare mineral soil, fires facilitate seedling establishment.

Wildlife: Small bees pollinate the flowers and an unknown insect feeds on seeds within developing fruits.

Hydrangea arborescens L.
WILD HYDRANGEA
Hydrangeaceae (Hydrangea family)

Description: A deciduous shrub with soft wood and peeling bark on older stems. Leaves opposite, pointed at apex with fine-toothed margins. Small white flowers in flat-topped or rounded clusters, the outer flowers sometimes larger but sterile. Numerous small, dry capsules persist into winter. Flowers May–July.

Habitat/range: Moist wooded cliffs and ravines, along streams, moist road banks, and forest edges. Common. Widely distributed in eastern United States.

Taxonomy: A genus of 25 species of shrubs found in eastern North America and east Asia, including 5 species in the mountains and piedmont. Silverleaf hydrangea (*H. radiata*) and ashy hydrangea (*H. cinerea*) are similar but have a bright white or gray (rather than green) lower leaf surface.

Ecology: Wild hydrangea is a low-growing, rounded shrub that's often broader than high, spreading laterally by root suckers. While typically growing in shaded sites, plants can survive full sun if soil moisture levels are sufficient. Flowers are produced on new growth. The small flowers in the center of the inflorescence are fertile, producing both pollen and seeds. The showy marginal flowers, with 3–4 petal-like calyx lobes, help attract pollinators, but are sterile. The tiny, dust-like seeds are dispersed by wind.

Wildlife: White-tailed deer browse the foliage.

Uses: Various cultivars are grown in gardens. The bark, leaves, and flower buds are poisonous if ingested in quantity.

Hypericum buckleyi M. A. Curtis
GRANITE DOME ST. JOHN'S WORT
Hypericaceae (St. John's wort family)

Description: A mat-forming shrub with numerous slender stems up to 12 (rarely 20) in. tall with mostly sessile, elliptic to obovate leaves, about twice as long as wide. Bright yellow flowers solitary or in small, flat-topped inflorescences, 5 sepals and petals, petals about twice as long as sepals, stamens numerous, clustered. Fruit a pointed capsule. Flowers June–Aug.; fruits July–Sept.

Habitat/range: Rock outcrops at moderate to high elevations in mountains. A rare but locally common southern Appalachian endemic restricted to North Carolina, South Carolina, and Georgia.

Taxonomy: Hypericum is a large genus of almost 400 species of trees, shrubs, and herbs, primarily of temperate regions.

Ecology: Granite dome St. John's wort is a narrow endemic with striking flowers and fruits. It occurs on shallow soils over rocky surfaces where seepage water flows, as well as in cracks in rocks where roots have access to deeper soil with increased moisture. It's a classic example of a "pollen flower" in that there are numerous stamens but no nectar. The readily available and abundant pollen attracts a variety of potential pollinators, including bees, flies, and beetles. Pollen is a rich source of nutrients, especially proteins, and is eaten directly by beetles and flies. Pollen is also the primary larval food source of bees. Bees collect and transport huge quantities of pollen to provision broods. Some bees carry pollen internally in a "crop," but most carry pollen externally between stiff abdominal hairs or on their extremities. In many plants, pollen serves as an attractant for pollinators and carries the male gametes necessary for sexual reproduction. Because these 2 functions are mutually exclusive (a pollen grain eaten is lost for reproduction), only the production of abundant pollen allows both to be carried out.

Uses: Granite dome St. John's wort is an attractive alpine or rock garden plant, due to its interesting foliage, golden yellow flowers, and low growth form.

Ilex montana Torr. & A. Gray ex A. Gray
MOUNTAIN HOLLY
Aquifoliaceae (Holly family)

Description: A deciduous shrub or small tree with multiple stems, commonly to 20 ft. tall. Alternate leaves often clustered at tips of spur shoots, elliptical or ovate, with acuminate tips and sharply toothed margins. Small greenish white flowers on short stalks, usually in clusters. Fruit a round, orange to red drupe. Flowers Apr.–June; fruits Aug.–Sept.

Habitat/range: Mesic forests, including red oak forests, northern hardwood forests, cove forests, oak-hickory forests, and mountain bogs. Common in mountains, occasional in upper piedmont. Largely restricted to Appalachians from New York to Georgia.

Taxonomy: Mountain holly can be distinguished from our other deciduous hollies by its large (more than 4 in. long) leaves and one-half in. wide fruits.

Ecology: When you mention hollies, most people think of American holly (*I. opaca*), a common native (and widely planted) tree of eastern North America characterized by prickly evergreen leaves and persistent orange-red fruits. But many native species of holly occur in eastern North America, including 12 species in our region. Most of our native hollies are deciduous, some are shrubs, and others are trees. All hollies have male and female flowers on separate individuals. If a male (pollen donor) is nearby, females produce fruits that are either orange-red or black, depending on the species. Insects transfer pollen from male to female trees, rewarded by nectar, pollen, or both.

Wildlife: White-tailed deer browse the foliage and numerous birds eat the brightly colored fruits in winter.

Ilex verticillata (L.) A. Gray
WINTERBERRY
Aquifoliaceae (Holly family)

Description: A multistemmed deciduous shrub with alternate, toothed leaves, pointed at tip, wedge-shaped at base. Small greenish white flowers, usually in dense clusters, form bright red berries on short stalks. Flowers Apr.–May; fruits Sept.–Nov.

Habitat/range: Bogs, wet thickets, streambanks. Occasional. Eastern North America.

Taxonomy: A genus of about 500 species, mostly trees and shrubs of temperate and tropical areas, especially North America and Asia, including 12 species in the mountains and piedmont.

Ecology: Like the flowers on other hollies, winterberry's male and female flowers occur on separate plants. In good years, female plants produce abundant fruits that turn from green to orange to red as they ripen. The fruits ripen in fall but are typically not taken by birds until winter when other foods are scarce. Fruits not removed by frugivores fall to the ground, usually directly beneath the parent plant. Seeds in undispersed fruits are unlikely to successfully establish new plants as the parent plant already occupies the site and seedlings are inferior competitors. In addition, when many seeds drop beneath the parent plant, their high concentration attracts seed predators such as insects and small mammals that often digest or damage the seeds, preventing germination. So, fruits that successfully attract seed-dispersing animals benefit both from dispersal away from the parent plant and from the reduced risk of the seeds being discovered and destroyed by seed predators. Winterberry also spreads by root suckers, often forming dense, spreading thickets.

Wildlife: A variety of birds consume the fruits and disperse the seeds of winterberry, including winter-flocking birds such as cedar waxwings and robins.

Uses: This hardy, easy-to-grow shrub can thrive in moist and drier soils; its dense clusters of red fruits provide striking color in winter.

Itea virginica L.
VIRGINIA WILLOW
Iteaceae (Sweetspire family)

Description: An upright, multistemmed deciduous shrub with slender, arching branches. Leaves elliptic to obovate, 2–4 in. long, pointed at tip, usually wedge-shaped at base. Numerous small white flowers in droopy to upright, showy racemes 2–6 in. long. Fruit a small, 2-parted woody capsule in terminal clusters that persist into winter. Flowers May–June; fruits July–Aug.

Habitat/range: Common along streambanks, swamps, and floodplains. Widespread in eastern United States.

Taxonomy: Only 1 of 20 species in the genus *Itea* occurs in North America; the others are native to Asia.

Ecology: Dense clusters of fragrant white flowers provide a rich nectar source for pollinators such as bees and butterflies. A recent study demonstrated an interesting interaction whereby fish indirectly benefit some plants by facilitating pollinator availability. Fish prey on dragonfly larvae in streams, which in turn reduces the number of adult dragonflies in the local area. Because dragonfly adults prey on insects, including bees and butterflies, plants near streams with fish may receive more pollinator visits than plants near streams where few or no fish are present. Having fish nearby can benefit streamside plants that produce fewer (or lower-quality) seeds when pollinators are absent or less abundant. Virginia willow spreads by seeds and by root sprouts, forming dense colonies. Although shade-tolerant, it flowers most prolifically and has more colorful fall foliage when growing in sunny habitats.

Wildlife: White-tailed deer browse the foliage, bees and butterflies visit the fragrant nectar-rich flowers, and birds forage on the small seeds within capsules.

Uses: Showy, long-lasting flowers, attractive fall foliage, and the ability to tolerate both wet and relatively dry soils makes Virginia willow an attractive landscape plant.

Kalmia buxifolia (Burg.) Gift, Kron, & Stevens
SAND MYRTLE
Ericaceae (Heath family)

Description: A low-growing, widely branched evergreen shrub seldom over 3 ft. tall with shredding bark on older stems and small, shiny elliptical leaves crowded toward the stem tips. Small white to light pink flowers in dense clusters within the upper leaf axils. Fruit a small, pointed capsule with many tiny seeds. Flowers Mar.–June (sporadically to Oct.); fruits Sept.–Oct.

Habitat/range: Sand myrtle has a curious distribution. It's rare but locally common on rock outcrops at high to moderate elevations in North Carolina, South Carolina, and Georgia. It occurs on a few isolated rock outcrops (monadnocks) in the piedmont of North Carolina, and it grows in sandy, acidic soils in the coastal plain of North and South Carolina, and in the pine barrens of New Jersey.

Taxonomy: Recent studies have incorporated members of the genus *Leiophyllum*, of which sand myrtle was a member, into the genus *Kalmia*. The specific epithet "*buxifolia*" refers to the similar foliage of sand myrtle and ornamental boxwoods (genus *Buxus*).

Ecology: Sand myrtle tolerates a remarkably wide range of environments. For example, populations cope with low temperatures, high winds, shallow soils, and a relatively short growing season at high elevations. In contrast, populations are exposed to high temperatures, deep, dry soils, and a relatively long growing season in the sandhills and coastal plain. How do species such as sand myrtle cope with such dramatically different environments? One mechanism is genetically based local adaptations. For example, mountain and coastal populations likely differ in their response to temperatures, making mountain plants more tolerant of low temperatures (including growing season frosts) than coastal plain plants. Conversely, plants in the coastal plain likely photosynthesize more efficiently at high temperatures than do plants from the mountains. In other words, populations of a species can evolve characteristics that best match local conditions, which allows a species to occupy a wider range of environments.

Wildlife: Small bees and flies pollinate the flowers.

Synonym: Leiophyllum buxifolium (Bergius) Elliot

Kalmia latifolia L.
MOUNTAIN LAUREL
Ericaceae (Heath family)

Description: A medium to large evergreen shrub with a rounded crown and crooked branches with thick, leathery leaves 2–4 in. long, mostly crowded near twig tips. White to pink bowl-shaped flowers in showy clusters 4–6 in. across. Fruit a rounded capsule with numerous wind-dispersed seeds. Flowers Apr.–June; fruits Sept.–Oct., persisting into winter.

Habitat/range: Acidic cove forests, heath balds, river bluffs, and mountain bogs, nearly ubiquitous in mountains, less common in piedmont. Widespread in eastern United States.

Taxonomy: When flowers aren't present, mountain laurel superficially resembles rosebay (*Rhododendron maximum*) and gorge rhododendron (*R. minus*), but rosebay has much larger drooping leaves with rolled edges, and gorge rhododendron has dotted glands on its lower leaf surface.

Ecology: Dense thickets of mountain laurel are sometimes referred to as "laurel hell" because the stout, spreading branches are difficult to walk through. Individuals reproduce vegetatively from a spreading root system that grows new shoots, and by layering (low-growing branches buried in leaf litter form roots and additional shoots). Fires typically kill the aboveground plants, but dormant buds on root crowns or rhizomes give rise to new shoots. Mountain laurel grows in full sun to deep shade but flowers best in well-lit areas. The bowl-shaped flowers have tiny pouches enclosing each anther, their bent filaments held under tension. When touched by a large bee, the stamens suddenly spring forward, showering the insect with sticky strands of pollen, which subsequently may be deposited on another flower's stigma, resulting in cross-pollination. If no pollinator visits the flower, the anther filaments will spring as the flower senesces, thereby flinging pollen onto the flower's own stigma, providing a backup mechanism should insect-mediated pollination fail to occur.

Wildlife: Mountain laurel provides good cover for wildlife but has limited value as a food plant because toxic compounds diminish the palatability of its foliage and its fruits are dry.

Uses: Widely used as an ornamental, due to its striking flower clusters and attractive evergreen foliage.

Leucothoe fontanesiana (Steud.) Sleumer
MOUNTAIN DOGHOBBLE
Ericaceae (Heath family)

Description: Sprawling evergreen shrub to 5 ft. tall with arching branches and alternate leathery leaves 3–6 in. long, pointed at tip with sharply toothed margins. White urn-shaped flowers in dense drooping clusters (racemes) from leaf axils. Fruit a persistent capsule with many tiny seeds. Flowers Apr.–May; fruits Sept.–Oct.

Habitat/range: Moist, acidic soils usually along streams and in ravines, including rocky streamsides and acidic cove forests. Common in mountains, rare in upper piedmont. A southern Appalachian endemic from Virginia south to Georgia.

Taxonomy: Leucothoe is a genus of 6 species of shrubs of eastern North America and east Asia, 2 of which occur in the mountains and piedmont. Coastal doghobble (*L. axillaris*) is similar to mountain doghobble but is rare in our region.

Ecology: Mountain doghobble forms dense thickets that are difficult to walk through, hence the common name. The shiny evergreen leaves have a waxy coating that reduces water loss, a beneficial trait, as doghobble is sensitive to drought stress. Individuals reproduce by seed as well as vegetatively by rooting at the shoot tips. In late summer, small flower buds are produced in the leaf axils, which expand early the following spring into dense clusters of small, urn-shaped flowers that vary in odor from pleasantly sweet to musky. The potential benefit of these floral scent morphs (do they attract different suites of pollinators?) has yet to be explored.

Wildlife: Dense thickets of mountain doghobble provide good wildlife cover for small mammals and amphibians.

Uses: Mountain doghobble's gracefully arching stems, dark green evergreen foliage, and waxy white flowers make a great addition to gardens. Highly toxic if ingested.

Synonym: Leucothoe axillaris var. *editorum* (Fern. and Schub.) H. E. Ahles

*Ligustrum sinense Lour.
CHINESE PRIVET
Oleaceae (Olive family)

Description: Thicket-forming evergreen to semi-evergreen shrub with opposite, mostly elliptical leaves on short stalks. Numerous fragrant, small white flowers in terminal and axillary clusters form berry-like drupes, pale green in summer, bluish black in fall. Flowers Apr.–June;

fruits Sept.–Nov., persisting through winter.

Habitat/range: Moist forests and thickets, including alluvial forests, forest edges, fields, home sites, borders of rock outcrops, disturbed areas. Common. Naturalized throughout the eastern United States.

Taxonomy: A genus of about 40 species of shrubs and trees. Seven of the 8 species in the mountains and piedmont are introduced from Asia. Japanese privet (*L. japonicum*) is similar, but has larger, leathery, shiny leaves with nearly smooth, rather than distinctly hairy, twigs.

Ecology: Chinese privet occurs in a variety of habitats and can tolerate a wide range of light and soil conditions but grows best in moist soils with abundant light. Abundant in disturbed areas, it also spreads into intact forests, especially in floodplains. Introduced into the United States from China as an ornamental shrub in the mid-nineteenth century, it was widely planted, primarily as a hedge in landscaping. Chinese privet readily escapes cultivation as it produces abundant fleshy fruits whose seeds are widely dispersed by birds. Established plants spread clonally by root sprouts, forming dense thickets that reduce the densities of trees, shrubs, and herbaceous plants. By choking out native species, biological diversity is reduced. Once established, it's difficult to eradicate because topkilled privet readily resprouts and it has a large, persistent soil seed bank. Chinese privet is an example of an invasive species because it spreads into natural areas and dominates or degrades the native vegetation.

Wildlife: Dense thickets of privet provide cover for various wildlife species and beavers feed on the leaves, stems, and bark. The persistent fruits provide food for birds in winter and early spring.

Uses: Chinese privet is one of our most noxious and invasive weeds; its continued use as a landscape plant should be discouraged.

Lindera benzoin (L.) Blume
SPICEBUSH
Lauraceae (Laurel family)

Description: A deciduous, much-branched, aromatic shrub usually 5–9 ft. tall. Leaves alternate, simple, ovate in shape, decreasing in size toward base of twig. Tiny, fragrant yellow flowers in dense clusters in early spring, before the leaves emerge. Bright red, strongly aromatic, single-seeded fleshy fruits. Flowers Mar.–Apr.; fruits Aug.–Sept.

Habitat/range: Moist forests and bottomlands, including cove forests, river bluff forests, alluvial forests, and basic mesic forests. Common. Widespread in eastern North America.

Taxonomy: The genus includes about 100 species of trees and shrubs of tropical and temperate Asia, Australia, and eastern North America, including 3 species in the mountains and piedmont.

Ecology: One of the first shrubs to bloom in early spring, spicebush flowers before most plants leaf out. Flies and small bees pollinate the dense clusters of tiny unisexual flowers. A low proportion of the female flowers mature fruit because of a lack of successful pollination. The availability of resources can also limit fruit set. Individuals in forest openings (gaps) typically set more fruit than plants in the shaded understory because their higher photosynthetic rates result in more resources available for reproduction. Because the energetic costs associated with reproduction are much higher for female (fruit-bearing) plants than male (pollen-producing) plants, female plants grow more slowly than do their male counterparts.

Wildlife: The lipid-rich, high-energy fruits of spicebush are an important food source for fall migrants. In addition to dispersing the seeds, fruit-eating birds benefit the plant by eating the pulp surrounding the seeds, thereby markedly improving the germination rate. Spicebush is an important food plant for butterfly larvae, including the spicebush swallowtail and eastern tiger swallowtail. It takes about 3 leaves for a spicebush swallowtail caterpillar to complete larval development; when not feeding, the smooth green caterpillars with 4 eyespots hide under curled leaves.

Uses: The aromatic leaves, twigs, and bark can be steeped to make a spicy tea. Spicebush is a desirable landscape plant that provides food and cover for wildlife.

*___Lonicera japonica___ Thunb.
JAPANESE HONEYSUCKLE
Caprifoliaceae (Honeysuckle family)

Description: A sprawling or climbing woody vine, often forming dense tangles in shrubs and trees and extensive mats on the ground. Opposite, mostly evergreen leaves and fragrant, white (fading to yellow) tubular flowers form round, shiny black berry-like fruits. Flowers Apr.–June (and sporadically into Sept.); fruits Aug.–Oct.

Habitat/range: Occurs in almost any disturbed habitat, including fields, woodlands, forest edges, and alluvial forests. Common (especially in piedmont). Introduced from Japan and widely planted across North America, it frequently escapes cultivation.

Taxonomy: Of the 13 species of honeysuckle (*Lonicera*) in our region, both native and introduced, Japanese honeysuckle is by far the most common. It can be distinguished from other honeysuckles by its black fruits in lateral, rather than terminal, branches.

Ecology: Japanese honeysuckle is a twining vine that can densely cover the ground surface or climb high into the canopy. It grows most vigorously in open habitats, but can spread extensively within forests, persisting in the understory until disturbance creates an opening in the canopy. Most common in areas previously planted (for erosion control, wildlife habitat, or as an ornamental), it subsequently invades openings in surrounding vegetation with bird-dispersed seeds as well as by vegetative spread (a single plant can produce 30 ft. of stem growth per year). Once established, it can overtop small trees and shrubs, blocking light by its dense canopy, eventually pulling down dead host plants with its weight. Its tightly twining vines can also girdle the stems and trunks of host plants, and dense thickets of Japanese honeysuckle can eliminate the herbaceous layer and inhibit regeneration (by seedlings and saplings) of woody plants. By outcompeting native plants for light and belowground resources (water and nutrients), Japanese honeysuckle reduces species diversity in many communities.

Wildlife: Evening-flying sphinx moths and long-tongued bees pollinate the sweet-smelling tubular flowers, and birds and mammals consume the fruits and spread the seeds.

Uses: Once promoted and planted as a beneficial wildlife species, emphasis has now focused on efforts to control its spread.

Lonicera sempervirens L.
CORAL HONEYSUCKLE
Caprifoliaceae (Honeysuckle family)

Description: Climbing or trailing twining vine up to 16 ft. tall with older bark shredding into long, fibrous strips. Opposite, partially evergreen leaves, green on upper side, whitish green below, mostly oval with the uppermost pairs joined at base. Long, slender, trumpet-shaped flowers in clusters at stem tips, red outside, yellow within. Fruit a bright red berry. Flowers Mar.–July (sporadically to Nov.); fruits July–Sept.

Habitat/range: Dry to moist forests, woodlands, and thickets, including river bluff forests, oak-hickory forests, and forest edges. Common in piedmont, uncommon in mountains. Widespread in eastern United States.

Taxonomy: A genus of 180 species of shrubs and vines. Most of the 13 species in the mountains and piedmont are introduced from Asia.

Ecology: This native species isn't aggressive and weedy like the introduced Japanese honeysuckle (*L. japonica*) that chokes out native plants in fields, woodlands, and floodplains. Coral honeysuckle produces upright shoots that climb up support plants (by twining from left to right) as well as prostrate shoots that root wherever a leaf node touches the ground, thereby allowing both vertical and lateral spread. The flowers of coral honeysuckle lack fragrance and are pollinated by hummingbirds, whereas the very fragrant flowers of Japanese honeysuckle are pollinated by evening-flying moths and long-tongued bees.

Wildlife: The nectar-rich flowers help sustain hummingbirds as they migrate north in early spring; caterpillars of the spring azure butterfly feed on the leaves.

Uses: Coral honeysuckle is an excellent vine in gardens as it flowers abundantly in full sun, has a long blooming season, attracts hummingbirds, and is drought tolerant.

Menziesia pilosa (Mich. ex Lam.) Juss. ex Pers.
MINNIEBUSH
Ericaceae (Heath family)

Description: A 3–6 ft. tall shrub with alternate deciduous leaves with a characteristic, small whitish spur at leaf tip. Small, urn-shaped flowers in clusters, the corolla greenish white, often with a reddish tinge. Fruit a small, erect capsule on a long, slender stalk. Flowers May–July; fruits Aug.–Oct.

Habitat/range: Heath balds, mountain bogs, high-elevation rock outcrops, and moist woodlands, mostly at high elevations. Common in mountains, rare in piedmont. Restricted to Appalachians, from Pennsylvania south to Georgia.

Taxonomy: Minniebush is a member of the heath family (Ericaceae), a widespread family consisting of about 3,500 species of trees, shrubs, and herbs that range from the tropics to the polar regions of both hemispheres. The genus *Menziesia* has just 10 species, 8 in Japan, and 2 in North America, with only 1 species in the mountains and piedmont. "Bumps" on the midrib of the lower leaf surface distinguish minniebush from similar azaleas (*Rhododendron* spp.) when flowers aren't present.

Ecology: Members of the heath family almost always have mycorrhizal associations with certain fungi that live in or on their roots. This root-fungus association is considered to be mutually beneficial since the fungus provides the plant with dissolved mineral elements and soil water, while the plant provides carbohydrates (obtained through photosynthesis) to the fungus. Plants with mycorrhizae can obtain several times the phosphorous of non-mycorrhizal plants, boosting growth on soils low in this important nutrient. Interestingly, mycorrhizae can also protect the host plant from bacterial and fungal plant diseases by secreting pathogen-killing chemicals into the root-soil interface or by stimulating the root to produce such compounds. Mycorrhizae are essential to the survival of minniebush and other heath shrubs such as rhododendron, blueberry, and mountain laurel, which characteristically occur on acidic, nutrient-poor soils.

Uses: Minniebush makes a nice addition to gardens.

Parthenocissus quinquefolia (L.) Planch.
VIRGINIA CREEPER
Vitaceae (Grape family)

Description: A high-climbing or trailing woody vine with alternate, palmately compound leaves with 3–7 (usually 5) leaflets and numerous branched tendrils. Tiny greenish flowers in clusters. Fruit a dark blue to black berry, resembling a small grape but inedible. Flowers May–July; fruits July–Aug.

Habitat/range: Dry to moist woods, alluvial forests, thickets, rock outcrops, and forest edges. Common. Widely distributed in eastern and central United States.

Taxonomy: A genus of 10 species of vines of Asia and North America, with only 1 species in our region. Sometimes mistaken for poison ivy (*Toxicodendron radicans*), Virginia creeper typically has 5, rather than 3, leaflets and its fruits are dark blue-black, rather than whitish.

Ecology: Virginia creeper occurs in many habitats but grows best in open places with lots of sunlight, including fencerows, streambanks, and forest edges. Trailing along the ground or climbing high into trees, its stems can elongate as much as 6–10 ft. in a single season. Instead of climbing by tendrils as grapes and greenbriers do, or twining as pipevine and wisteria do, Virginia creeper climbs with small, branching tendrils that form adhesive disks at their tips. Each disk secretes a cement-like substance that effectively adheres the vine to tree trunks, walls, and rock faces. Bees pollinate the tiny green flowers and birds spread the plant by dispersing its seeds. When growing on the ground, it spreads and persists by rooting at the nodes. Its thin bark and shallow roots make it susceptible to fire.

Wildlife: The combination of colors created by the deep blue-black fruits on red stalks subtended by purple-red to crimson autumn leaves help attract numerous fruit-feeding birds and small mammals.

Uses: Virginia creeper can be used as an attractive low-maintenance cover plant for walls, trellises, and tree trunks. The "ivy covered walls" of many Universities are covered with creeper, rather than ivy.

Phoradendron serotinum (Raf.) M. C. Johnst.
AMERICAN MISTLETOE
Viscaceae (Mistletoe family)

Description: Evergreen hemiparasite on a variety of broadleaf, deciduous trees. Greenish branches with opposite, oblong, leathery leaves and small, inconspicuous male and female flowers on separate plants. Fruit a small white berry. Flowers Oct.–Nov. (less often in Mar.); fruits Nov.–Jan. (less often in May).

Habitat/range: Grows on woody stems of deciduous trees in a variety of habitats. Common in piedmont, uncommon in mountains. Widespread in eastern United States.

Taxonomy: A genus of 235 species of epiphytic hemiparasites mostly of tropical regions, with only 1 species in the mountains and piedmont.

Ecology: American mistletoe is one of more than 4,000 species of parasitic flowering plants, whose highly modified roots grow into and connect with their host's vascular tissue, from which they take up water and nutrients. Mistletoes are considered to be hemiparasites because in addition to obtaining water and nutrients from their host tree, they manufacture their own sugars from photosynthesis (both the stems and leaves of American mistletoe have an abundance of chlorophyll and are photosynthetically active). Efficient photosynthesis in this species depends on a constant supply of water and nitrogen from the host tree. Mistletoe infections are most common high up in trees and along the outer edges of tree crowns, where light levels are relatively high. Shoots that break off in wind or ice storms provide an opportunity to examine this interesting plant up close.

Wildlife: Various birds feed on the fruits and spread the seeds in their droppings or by wiping regurgitated seeds that stick to their beaks onto branches. In either case, some of the sticky seeds adhere to the bark of a potential host tree where germination and subsequent establishment can occur.

Uses: This is the common mistletoe used in Christmas decorations. The berries are toxic to humans, if ingested.

Ptelea trifoliata L.
HOPTREE, WAFER ASH
Rutaceae (Citrus family)

Description: Deciduous aromatic shrub or small tree to 15 ft. tall with trifoliate leaves on long stalks. Small greenish white flowers in flat-topped, terminal clusters. The large, round, flattened fruits resemble wafers. Flowers Apr.–June; fruits June–Aug.

Habitat/range: Rocky bluffs, granitic domes and calcareous outcrops, stream terraces, and open woodlands. Uncommon. Loosely scattered populations in eastern United States.

Taxonomy: Hoptree can be identified by its fragrant trifoliate leaves and clusters of large, round, flattened fruits.

Ecology: Individuals generally produce either male or female flowers. The small, strongly scented, greenish white flowers depend on insects to transfer pollen from male to female plants for successful fruit set. A variety of insects harvest nectar from female flowers and nectar, pollen, or both from male plants, although flies are thought to be the primary pollinator. Like the fruits of maples, ashes, and elms, the samaras of hoptree twirl as they fall, effectively slowing their descent and facilitating dispersal. When hoptree grows near streams and lakes, its seeds are also dispersed by water, as the fruits remain buoyant for days. The summer-ripened seeds germinate in spring after exposure to an overwintering period.

Wildlife: Most herbivores avoid feeding on the foliage because it contains alkaloids and other toxic chemicals. Certain grasshoppers, however, not only utilize the leaves as a food source, they regurgitate the partially digested leaves to deter attacking lizards and other predators. Thus, grasshoppers utilize a plant-based defense compound as protection against predators. Hoptree is a larval (caterpillar) host plant for giant and eastern tiger swallowtails.

Uses: The bitter-tasting fruits have been used as a substitute for hops in making beer, hence the common name. This attractive but underused landscape plant has interesting fruits and foliage and tolerates a wide range of conditions, including drought.

*Pueraria montana (Lour.) Merr.
KUDZU
Fabaceae (Legume family)

Description: A trailing or climbing woody vine with rope-like stems up to 100 ft. long, compound leaves with 3 large leaflets, and fragrant, purple pea-like flowers in long-drooping clusters. Fruit a flattened pod covered with golden-brown hairs. Flowers July–Oct.; fruits Aug.–frost.

Habitat/range: Roadsides, fields, and forest edges. Common. Widespread in eastern United States.

Taxonomy: A genus of 15 species of vines of tropical and subtropical Asia, with only 1 species in the mountains and piedmont.

Ecology: Intentionally introduced from east Asia, the primary cause of its spread in the Southeast was a government-aided program in the first half of the twentieth century to plant kudzu to reduce soil erosion. In 1953, the USDA designated kudzu as a pest species and stopped encouraging its use. It grows best in open, sunny habitats in regions with mild winters, warm summers, and annual rainfall exceeding 40 in. A fast-growing species, the stems elongate as much as 1 ft. per day or over 60 ft. in a growing season. The stems climb vertically by twining around other vines and smaller-diameter trunks, often overwintering in the canopy and resuming growth the following spring. Kudzu eliminates native species and reduces species diversity by smothering other plants under a dense cover of leaves. Fortunately, kudzu generally doesn't invade intact vegetation, as it can't tolerate deep shade. It spreads mainly by horizontal stems rooting at the nodes along the ground. The large, tuberous roots can reach depths of 3–15 ft. and weigh up to several hundred pounds. The foliage is usually killed by the first fall frost, and plants are dormant until late April or May.

Wildlife: White-tailed deer browse the foliage and woodchucks sometimes build dens under kudzu thickets. The recently introduced Asian giant resin bee facilitates pollination success and subsequent seed production, thereby contributing to kudzu's spread.

Uses: The rhizome is used as a source of starch in Asia.

Pyrularia pubera Michx.
BUFFALO NUT
Santalaceae (Sandalwood family)

Description: A deciduous shrub to 10 ft. tall with highly branched, arching stems. Leaves alternate, simple, prominently veined, long-pointed at apex. Inflorescence an erect terminal spike with greenish, unisexual, apetalous flowers. Fruit a pear-shaped fleshy drupe about 1 in. long. Flowers Apr.–May; fruits July–Oct.

Habitat/range: Variety of moist to dry forests. Common. An Appalachian endemic, from Pennsylvania south to Georgia.

Taxonomy: Pyrularia is a genus of 4 species, 3 in east Asia, 1 in eastern North America.

Ecology: Buffalo nut is one of more than 4,000 species of parasitic flowering plants. Plants such as dodder (*Cuscuta*) lack chlorophyll and are completely parasitic. Other plants, called hemiparasites, have chlorophyll and can manufacture much of their own food, deriving mainly water and mineral nutrients from their host plants. Buffalo nut is a hemiparasite whose roots parasitize a wide range of plants, including both woody and herbaceous species. Like other root parasites, it has specialized structures called haustoria that function as vascular bridges through which water, minerals, and perhaps carbohydrates pass from the host plant into the parasite. The green leaves and young stems of hemiparasites such as buffalo nut belie their parasitic nature, and they're often overlooked as pathogens of other plants. Yet buffalo nut is an obligate parasite: if its roots don't attach to a host plant, it won't survive. Individual plants produce either male or female flowers. Male flowers have a sterile pistil and female flowers have sterile stamens. Female plants commonly produce hundreds of flowers, but relatively few fruit. Low fruit set reflects unsuccessful pollination or resource limitations as the large, fleshy fruits are energetically expensive to produce.

Wildlife: Toxic proteins (thionins) in the leaves and fruits of buffalo nut deter most herbivores as well as bacteria and fungi. Tasting just a single seed causes severe mouth irritation in humans.

Uses: Native Americans made a salve from buffalo nut to treat sores.

Rhododendron arborescens (Pursh) Torr.
SWEET AZALEA
Ericaceae (Heath family)

Description: A deciduous shrub or small tree with slender glabrous twigs, the leaves entire, glabrous, obovate (widest above the middle). Very fragrant white or pinkish, tubular, funnel-shaped flowers, about 2 in. long, open after the leaves expand. Bright red stamens and stigma protrude well beyond the petals. Fruit a capsule. Flowers late May–July; fruits July–Oct.

Habitat/range: Mostly along streams and in wet woods, including rocky streamsides, mountain bogs, swamps, and shrub balds. Common in mountains, occasional in piedmont. Mostly in the Appalachian Mountains from Pennsylvania south to Georgia.

Taxonomy: Rhododendron is a large genus of more than 800 species that is widely distributed across North America, Asia, Europe, and tropical Australasia. The largest number of species occurs in the Himalayas. A surprising diversity of growth forms are represented, including tropical rhododendrons growing as epiphytes on trees, diminutive high-mountain species only a few inches tall, and trees nearly 100 ft. tall. Sixteen species of rhododendron occur in the mountains and piedmont, representing a mix of evergreen and deciduous shrubs and small trees.

Ecology: Sweet azalea tolerates a wide range of conditions as populations range from near sea level to elevations approaching 4,500 ft. Individuals at higher altitudes typically have smaller leaves and shorter statures than mid- to low-elevation plants. It hybridizes readily with other deciduous azaleas.

Wildlife: Dense clumps of sweet azalea provide good cover for wildlife.

Uses: Rhododendrons are one of the most important and diverse groups of ornamental shrubs, with over 25,000 cultivars, most of which have been bred for their showy flowers. Sweet azalea is a prized garden plant for its showy white flowers, red stamens, and wonderful fragrance.

Rhododendron calendulaceum (Michx.) Torr.
FLAME AZALEA
Ericaceae (Heath family)

Description: Deciduous erect shrub with numerous spreading branches. Leaves 2–4 in. long, pointed at apex, wedge-shaped at base, whitish-hairy beneath. Tubular flowers in terminal clusters of 5–15, bright orange, yellow, or red with 5 spreading lobes, scarcely scented. Fruit a persistent capsule. Flowers late Apr.–July; fruits June–Sept.

Habitat/range: Dry-to-moist slopes of oak-dominated forests and grassy balds. Common in mountains, rare in piedmont. Mostly Appalachian Mountains, from Pennsylvania south to Georgia.

Taxonomy: Flame azalea is one of about 12 native azaleas (deciduous rhododendrons) in the mountains and piedmont. The common name, "flame," alludes to the fiery color of the open flowers as well as the resemblance of the expanded flower buds to the flame of a candle.

Ecology: Flame azalea grows best in well-drained soils of open woods. Periodic fire benefits the species by maintaining an open canopy. Flame azalea flowers in late April and May at lower elevations and in June and July at higher elevations. The showy flowers open with or before the expanding leaves and usually last several weeks. The wide spectrum in flower color is influenced by past hybridization with other azaleas. Flame azalea is susceptible to a fungus that causes the plant to produce large, tumor-like, fleshy galls. The green succulent galls often appear on the tips of shoots in early spring as the leaf and flower buds are expanding. By mid- to late summer, a white layer of spores appears on the outer surface of the gall. After about a week of sporulation, the gall darkens and shrinks in size, and a hard, dry mass remains attached to the shrub. Galls often have a negative effect on their host plants by diverting resources away from reproductive and photosynthetic structures on affected twigs. For example, gall-infected branches of flame azalea are 4 times less likely to mature fruit as uninfected branches, and about 90 percent of infected branches die by the following year.

Wildlife: Swallowtail butterflies, bumblebees, honeybees, and solitary bees visit flame azalea's flowers for nectar, pollen, or both, many functioning as pollinators.

Uses: A widely cultivated species, flame azalea is one of our most attractive native azaleas.

Rhododendron catawbiense Michx.
CATAWBA RHODODENDRON
Ericaceae (Pink family)

Description: Evergreen thicket-forming shrub or small tree with a broad, rounded crown and large, showy clusters of deep pink to purple flowers at branch tips. Thick, leathery elliptical leaves, 3–6 in. long, rounded at base, blunt at tip. Fruit an elongate capsule, densely covered with reddish brown hairs with a persistent style at tip. Flowers Apr.–June; fruits July–Oct.

Habitat/range: Heath balds, high-elevation rock outcrops, spruce-fir forests, northern hardwood forests, and river bluff forests. Common in mountains, rare in piedmont. A southern Appalachian endemic from Virginia south to Georgia, disjunct in the lower piedmont and upper coastal plain of North Carolina.

Taxonomy: The common and scientific names refer to the Catawba tribe. Catawba rhododendron can be distinguished from both rosebay and gorge rhododendron (*R. maximum* and *R. minus*) by its round, rather than wedge-shaped, leaf base.

Ecology: Surprisingly little is known about the ecology of this common and highly visible shrub of mountain peaks, ridges, balds, and roadside embankments. A long-time favorite of plant enthusiasts, Catawba rhododendron is especially striking in spring when large, showy clusters of purple flowers are produced amid the dark green foliage. Plants are showiest in areas that get ample sun; on shaded slopes, plants are taller but flower less. The flowers develop into elongated capsules that split into 5 parts, each part opening first at the tip and curling backward, releasing the tiny seeds within. Newly dispersed seeds germinate right away if exposed to light, moisture, and suitable temperatures.

Wildlife: Catawba rhododendron's dense thickets and evergreen foliage provide good cover for wildlife.

Uses: The spectacular floral display of Catawba rhododendron attracts thousands of visitors to the southern Appalachians each year. It's widely grown as an ornamental and has often been used as a parent species in forming hybrids with other (mostly Himalayan) species of rhododendron.

Rhododendron maximum L.
ROSEBAY

Ericaceae (Heath family)

Description: An evergreen thicket-forming shrub or small tree up to 20 ft. tall with thick, leathery leaves, sharply pointed at apex, wedge-shaped at base, 4–10 in. long. Flowers in dense, showy clusters at branch tips, white to pale pink with 5 rounded petal lobes, the largest spotted with greenish yellow or orange spots. Fruit a cylindrical capsule with a persistent sticky style. Flowers June–Aug.; fruits Sept.–Oct.

Habitat/range: Moist to wet acidic slopes, streambanks, ravines, and flats. Heath balds, red oak forests, cove forests, mountain bogs, chestnut oak forests, pine-oak-heath, spray cliffs, rocky streamsides, and river bluff forests. Common in mountains, rare in piedmont. Southern Canada and the northeastern United States, extending south mainly in mountains to Georgia.

Taxonomy: Catawba rhododendron (*R. catawbiense*) is similar to rosebay but has smaller leaves with a rounded base and rose-pink to purple flowers.

Ecology: Rosebay is our largest and most common rhododendron, forming dense colonies in the understory of many forest types. Rosebay thickets became more widespread following large-scale logging in the early 1900s and again after the forest opened up following the chestnut blight in the mid-1900s. Once established, plants spread laterally by root sprouts and stem layering, forming large thickets that persist for decades. Rosebay thickets inhibit tree regeneration and reduce shrub and herbaceous plant diversity due to a combination of factors including increased soil acidity, a thick leaf litter layer, and a reduction in light, water, and soil nutrients.

Wildlife: Rosebay thickets provide excellent cover for wildlife. The foliage is said to be highly toxic to livestock (and humans) but is occasionally browsed by white-tailed deer.

Uses: Rosebay provides watershed protection and erosion control on steep slopes and makes an attractive shrub in cool, moist woodland gardens.

Rhododendron minus Michx.
GORGE RHODODENDRON, PUNCTATUM
Ericaceae (Heath family)

Description: An evergreen shrub 3–10 ft. tall with thick, leathery elliptical leaves sharply pointed at apex, wedge-shaped at base with dense brown scales on the underside. The leaves curl up and hang down during times of drought and extreme cold. Flowers pink to white, often spotted with green, in terminal clusters. Fruit a 5-parted capsule. Flowers Apr.–June; fruits Sept.–Oct.

Habitat/range: Streambanks, wooded slopes, high ridges, including high-elevation rock outcrops, acidic cove forests, chestnut oak forests, oak-hickory forests, and river bluff forests. Common in mountains, occasional in piedmont.

Taxonomy: Gorge rhododendron can be distinguished from our other 3 evergreen rhododendrons by its smaller leaves (up to 4 in. long) and dense brown scales on the lower leaf surface.

Ecology: Rhododendrons have tubular flowers with a pistil and stamens that project beyond the tip of the petals. While flower color and corolla tube length vary among species, the pollination mechanism is basically the same. The tip of the pistil (the stigma) extends beyond the anthers so that a potential pollinator is likely to first contact the stigma when approaching the flower. As an insect pollinator enters the flower to harvest nectar at its base, it may brush against the anthers, which, when jostled, expel pollen from their pores onto the pollinator. When visiting other flowers, the insect again touches the pistil first, potentially brushing pollen from its body onto the stigma. Cross-pollination, rather than self-pollination, is promoted by this behavior.

Wildlife: Most animals avoid eating gorge rhododendron because of its thick, leathery leaves and toxic properties.

Uses: Some rhododendrons have a toxin called grayanotoxin in their nectar. People that eat honey made by bees that forage on nectar from rhododendron flowers may become ill.

Rhododendron periclymenoides (Michx.) Shinners
WILD AZALEA, PINXTERFLOWER
Ericaceae (Heath family)

Description: Erect deciduous shrub to 6 ft. tall. Leaves simple, elliptical, 2–4 in. long, tightly clustered at twig tips. Pleasantly fragrant, pink to white, funnel-shaped flowers in small terminal clusters, appearing with or before the leaves. Fruit a capsule. Flowers Mar.–May; fruits Sept.–Oct.

Habitat/range: Moist to dry forests, including rocky streamsides, mountain bogs, river bluff forests, and oak-hickory forests. Common in mountains, uncommon in piedmont. Widespread in eastern United States.

Taxonomy: Deciduous species of *Rhododendron* are commonly called azaleas. Wild azalea (*R. periclymenoides*) can be distinguished from the similar mountain azalea (*R. canescens*) by its mostly smooth, rather than woolly, lower leaf surface.

Ecology: Species of *Rhododendron* are generally highly interfertile and hybridize frequently where the distribution and flowering periods of species overlap. In such areas, identifying species of individual plants can be difficult as the differences between species are obscured.

Uses: Horticulturists have taken advantage of the interfertility among *Rhododendron* species by producing thousands of hybrid plants, many of which have been introduced into the horticultural trade. Over 25,000 cultivars of *Rhododendron* have been developed through controlled crosses between parent species with desirable characteristics. Hybrid rhododendron cultivars first appeared about 1825, with some of the earliest hybrids produced between 2 species native to our mountains—Catawba and rosebay rhododendron (*R. catawbiense* and *R. maximum*).

Synonym: *Rhododendron nudiflorum* (L.) Torr.

Rhododendron vaseyi A. Gray
PINKSHELL AZALEA
Ericaceae (Pink family)

Description: A deciduous shrub up to 15 ft. tall with erect branches and a shallow root system. Leaves alternate, elliptical, 1 ½–5 in. long, widest near middle, tapering to a pointed tip. Deep pink funnel-shaped flowers, with slender, exerted stamens and style and a short (one-quarter in. long) corolla tube. Flowers emerge before the leaves unfold. Fruit a narrowly oblong capsule. Flowers May–June; fruits Aug.–Oct.

Habitat/range: High-elevation rock outcrops, heath balds, mountain bogs, and spruce-fir forests. Rare. Its natural distribution restricted to about 10 counties in the mountains of western North Carolina.

Taxonomy: The genus *Rhododendron* is distributed across North America, Europe, Asia, and tropical Australia. Some alpine species grow as groundcovers only a few inches tall, while some Asian species are trees almost 100 ft. tall. In the tropics, many rhododendrons grow as epiphytes on the trunks and branches of trees. In our region, rhododendrons grow as shrubs or small trees.

Ecology: Pinkshell azalea prefers rich, moist, acidic soils and the cooler temperatures associated with higher elevations. It colonizes disturbed areas, including roadside embankments along the Blue Ridge Parkway of North Carolina, where leafless plants covered with pink flowers are quite striking in mid- to late spring. The flower is intermediate in corolla shape between evergreen rhododendrons and deciduous azaleas. Very little is known about the ecology of this rare shrub.

Wildlife: Bees and butterflies function as pollinators while seeking nectar, pollen, or both.

Uses: First introduced into cultivation by the Arnold Arboretum in 1880, pinkshell azalea is now widely grown in gardens in the United States and Europe.

Rhododendron viscosum (L.) Torr.
SWAMP AZALEA, CLAMMY AZALEA
Ericaceae (Heath family)

Description: Deciduous shrub with hairy twigs, 6 ft. tall or more. Leaves wedge-shaped at base, shiny dark green above, lighter green with hairy midrib below. White or sometimes pinkish flowers with a long, slender tube covered with glandular hairs, sticky to the touch, very fragrant. Flowers in clusters of 4–9, appearing after the leaves emerge. Fruit a capsule with bristly hairs. Flowers late May–July; fruits July–Oct.

Habitat/range: Moist habitats, including rocky streamsides, bogs, and shrub balds. Common in mountains, rare in piedmont. Widespread in eastern United States.

Taxonomy: Swamp azalea is one of about a dozen native species of deciduous *Rhododendron* in the mountains and piedmont. It's most similar to sweet azalea (*R. arborescens*) but lacks red stamens and rounded leaf tips.

Ecology: Flower scent reflects a complex mixture of volatile organic compounds that readily turn to gases and float through the air. Insect pollinators have the ability to detect floral odors and discriminate among them. Fragrant flowers such as those of swamp azalea attract bees and other long-distance pollinators. Nectar and pollen, the food rewards of flowers, are often marked by more intense or different scents than elsewhere in the flower. Pollinators learn to associate particular scents with a food reward, which enhances flower fidelity and increases the likelihood of pollen transfer between flowers of the same type. Pollinators can be picky about floral scents: bees prefer sweet scents; beetles are partial to flowers with a fruity or spicy fragrance (such as magnolias); and some flies are attracted to flowers that mimic the odor of carrion or dung. The timing of scent production is also important. Snapdragons are 4 times more fragrant during the day, when their bee pollinators are active, than at night. The flowers of swamp azalea, in contrast, are most fragrant in the evening, when their moth pollinators are active, although bees and butterflies also visit and pollinate the flowers during the day.

Uses: Swamp azalea's showy, pleasantly fragrant flowers make a nice addition to gardens.

Rhus copallinum L.
WINGED SUMAC
Anacardiaceae (Cashew family)

Description: A deciduous shrub or small tree that forms dense thickets from root sprouts. Alternate, pinnately compound leaves with a winged stalk; leaflets shiny green above, turning scarlet in fall. Terminal clusters of small yellowish flowers form dense clumps of small, dark red fruits. Flowers July–Sept.; fruits Aug.–Oct.

Habitat/range: Dry woods, forest edges, fields, and roadsides. Common. Widespread in eastern United States.

Taxonomy: A genus of 25 species of trees, shrubs, and woody vines of Eurasia, North America, and Central America. Of our 5 species of sumac (*Rhus*), winged sumac is the only one that has a winged leaf stalk (rachis), hence the common name.

Ecology: Winged sumac is a native species that exploits disturbed habitats. Established plants spread by lateral root sprouting, forming dense compact islands along roadsides and fields. An early successional species, it persists in the understory until the canopy fills in. Fires benefit sumac because they keep the habitat open; the heat of fire also enhances seed germination, and individuals readily resprout from the root crown following topkill by a fire. Bees pollinate the small yellowish flowers which develop into small, berry-like fruits. Although the fruits are relatively high in lipids (more than 20 percent fat), the energy content per fruit is low because a thin layer of pulp surrounds a relatively large seed. The relatively low-quality fruits of winged sumac tend to persist on the plant well into winter. In contrast, lipid-rich fruits that have a relatively high pulp to seed ratio (high quality fruits) such as those of flowering dogwood (*Cornus florida*), black gum (*Nyssa sylvatica*), and spicebush (*Lindera benzoin*) are usually quickly eaten following fruit ripening.

Wildlife: Sumac thickets provide cover for a variety of birds and mammals and the fruits are an important food source in winter, when other foods are in short supply.

Uses: Crushed fruits mixed with sugar make a pinkish, lemonade-like beverage.

Rhus glabra L.
SMOOTH SUMAC
Anacardiaceae (Cashew family)

Description: Thicket-forming shrub or small tree with smooth stems covered with a whitish waxy bloom. Pinnately compound alternate leaves with numerous 2–4 in. long leaflets with serrate margins, the upper surface green, the lower surface white with exposed veins. Small greenish white flowers in dense terminal panicles. Numerous dark to bright red fruits in compact terminal clusters 8–12 in. long persist over winter. Flowers late May–July; fruits June–Oct.

Habitat/range: Along roadsides, fields, thickets, forest edges, and other disturbed areas. Common. Widespread in North America.

Taxonomy: Similar to winged sumac (*R. copallinum*), but it lacks a winged leaf stalk (rachis) and its stems are smooth with a whitish bloom.

Ecology: This fast-growing, shade-intolerant species quickly colonizes disturbed areas but seldom occurs in the understory of closed forest canopies. Widespread in the mountains and piedmont on drier sites, it has been described as the most widespread woody species in the United States, occurring in all lower 48 states as well as in Canada and Mexico. Female plants typically produce abundant fruits, some of which are eaten by fall-migrating birds; most, however, persist until late winter or early spring when they're eaten by winter resident birds. Like other sumacs, it spreads by seeds as well as by underground stems (rhizomes) forming large, dense thickets. Fires stimulate seed germination (dormant viable seeds can persist in the soil for years) and topkilled plants readily resprout from dormant underground buds.

Wildlife: A variety of birds and small mammals consume the fleshy pulp of the fruit and then disperse the seeds in a viable condition by either regurgitating or defecating them. White-tailed deer browse the twigs and foliage and the larvae of the tiny (chalcid) wasp feed on developing seeds.

Uses: In the southern Appalachians, the leaves are sometimes rolled and smoked to treat asthma. Sumac is an attractive plant in natural openings because of its bright red autumn foliage and persistent red fruits.

Ribes echinellum (Coville) Rehder
MICCOSUKEE GOOSEBERRY
Grossulariaceae (Currant family)
Federally Threatened

Description: Low-growing spiny shrub with shredding bark and alternate, palmately lobed leaves. Greenish flowers with 5 small petals, 5 spreading sepals, and long, exerted stamens. Fruit a spiny berry. Flowers Mar.–Apr.; fruits June–Sept.

Habitat/range: Basic mesic forest. Very rare, but locally abundant at a single site in the piedmont (Stephens Creek, McCormick County, South Carolina). Its only other known location is near Lake Miccosukee (Jefferson County, Florida).

Taxonomy: A genus of about 150 species found in temperate regions of the northern hemisphere and the mountains of South America.

Ecology: This rare species was first discovered near Lake Miccosukee, Florida, in 1924. The only other known population was discovered more than 30 years later at Stephens Creek, South Carolina. Both locations harbor an unusually large number of disjunct species (species more common in the mountains or Midwest than in the piedmont and coastal plain). Miccosukee gooseberry is unusual in that it apparently takes advantage of the higher light levels associated with a nearly leafless canopy in winter by producing a new flush of leaves in December. In early spring, bumblebees visit the pendant flowers, grasping the sepals and petals with their hind legs and the stamens and style with their front legs. As they probe the flower tube for nectar, pollen that has accumulated on the underside of their thoraxes and abdomens may be picked up by the stigmas, resulting in pollination. In addition to seeds, it spreads by layering (rooting where stem tips touch the ground), forming small thickets.

Wildlife: White-tailed deer browse the foliage and twigs of gooseberries and various insect species feed on the leaves, stems, and fruits. Birds and small mammals consume the fleshy fruits and disperse the seeds. By passing through the digestive tracts of frugivores, the seeds are more likely to germinate.

Habitat/range: Moist woods and open slopes, mostly above 4,500 ft. Balds, boulder fields, northern hardwood forests, and red oak forests. Common in mountains, rare in piedmont. Eastern United States.

Taxonomy: Ten of the 150 species in the genus occur in the mountains and piedmont.

Ecology: Species of *Ribes* harbor a stage of white pine blister rust, a fungal disease that infects and kills its alternate host, eastern white pine (*Pinus strobus*). The presence of orange-yellow pustules on the underside of gooseberry leaves from late summer–fall is an indication of the fungus.

Wildlife: Many kinds of insects feed on gooseberry leaves, stems, and fruits. Moth caterpillars such as the currant spanworm defoliate entire plants, and maggots of the currant fruit fly cause fruits to turn red and drop prematurely. Various birds and small mammals consume whole fruits and pass intact seeds through their digestive tracts, thereby helping to disperse the plant.

Uses: Appalachian gooseberry is sometimes cultivated for its edible sweet to tart fruits, which make excellent jellies and pies.

Ribes rotundifolium Michx.
APPALACHIAN GOOSEBERRY
Grossulariaceae (Currant family)

Description: Small to medium, erect or spreading shrub 2–5 ft. tall, short spines present or absent at nodes with finely peeling bark. Leaves alternate, simple, deciduous, roundish in general outline, 1–2 in. across, palmately veined and lobed. The small flowers occur singly or in clusters of 2–3 with green to reddish sepals and white to pinkish petals with protruding stamens. Smooth, round, edible berries contain numerous seeds. Flowers Apr.–May; fruits June–Sept.

Rosa carolina L.
CAROLINA ROSE
Rosaceae (Rose family)

Description: Deciduous shrub seldom over 2–3 ft. tall with smooth green to reddish stems and slender, nearly straight prickles. Alternate compound leaves with 5–9 narrowly elliptic to ovate, coarsely toothed leaflets. Solitary pink flowers, about 2 in. across, with numerous bright yellow stamens and 5 reflexed sepals. Fruit an orange to red hip. Flowers May–June (and sporadically thereafter); fruits Aug.–Sept., often persisting into winter.

Habitat/range: Upland forests, woodlands, pastures, including xeric hardpan forests, forest edges, fields, and roadsides. Occasional. Widespread in eastern North America.

Taxonomy: The genus consists of more than 100 species of shrubs and woody vines, primarily in north-temperate regions. Only 3 of the 16 species in the mountains and piedmont are native, including Carolina rose. The invasive multiflora rose (*Rosa multiflora*) is similar but is a larger plant with downward-curving (rather than straight) prickles.

Ecology: Unlike many cultivated roses, wild roses are usually fragrant. Bees and other insects can detect some floral odors that humans can't. The floral scent of Carolina rose probably helps attract potential pollinators to the golden yellow pollen, as the flowers lack nectar. Bumblebees actively harvest pollen from early morning until the supply is exhausted, usually by midday. By rapidly vibrating their wings, bumblebees sonically dislodge pollen from the anthers, which adheres to their body hairs; the pollen is then groomed and deposited in pollen baskets on bees' hind legs for transport to the nest. Cryptically camouflaged crab spiders with enlarged front legs used for capturing prey sit and wait in the flowers to ambush flower-visiting insects. Bumblebees apparently recognize the danger (perhaps by detecting the scent of previously killed bees), as flower patches harboring crab spiders receive fewer bee visits than patches lacking spiders.

Wildlife: White-tailed deer browse the foliage (in spite of the prickles), caterpillars of various moths feed on the foliage, and birds and small mammals eat the fruits and disperse the seeds.

Uses: Carolina rose makes a nice addition to gardens on well-drained soils with lots of sunlight.

*Rosa multiflora Thunb.
MULTIFLORA ROSE
Rosaceae (Rose family)

Description: A thicket-forming shrub with slender, arching, hairless stems armed with curved prickles. Pinnately compound leaves with 7–9 sharply toothed leaflets, each less than 1 ½ in. long. Clusters of fragrant, showy, white to pinkish flowers form bright red fruits that become leathery and persist into winter. Flowers May–June; fruits Sept.–Oct.

Habitat/range: Roadsides, fencerows, pastures, forest edges, thin woods, and alluvial forests. Common. Introduced from Asia, occurs throughout the eastern and central United States, and along the west coast.

Taxonomy: Most wild roses have prickly stems, compound leaves, winged leafstalk bases, flowers with 5 showy petals, and red fleshy fruits called rose hips.

Ecology: Multiflora rose occurs abundantly in disturbed habitats but also invades many natural communities, due to its ability to grow in various soil types, moisture regimes, and light levels. First introduced in the late

1700s as a garden plant and rootstalk for ornamental roses, it was later promoted as a "living fence" to confine livestock and to provide food and cover for native wildlife. It subsequently escaped into pastures, fields, and natural communities. A single large plant can produce up to half a million seeds per year, which persist in the soil for 10–20 years. Once established, individuals grow rapidly, forming dense impenetrable thickets from root sprouts and by layering (rooting from tips of arching stems that touch the ground). This noxious weed now covers more than 45 million acres in the eastern United States.

Wildlife: The stems and foliage are a favorite food of sap-sucking aphids. Ants feed on honeydew expelled by the aphids; in turn, the ants protect the aphids from predators.

Uses: Three rose hips (fruits) are said to contain as much vitamin C as a single orange. Given its invasive properties, it's best not to use this species as a landscape plant.

Rubus allegheniensis Porter
ALLEGHENY BLACKBERRY
Rosaceae (Rose family)

Description: A non-woody thicket-forming shrub with erect or arching stems. Young stems reddish to purplish, covered with glandular hairs (at least near tip) with many large thorns. Leaves palmately compound, mostly with 5 leaflets, serrated margins and prickles on petioles. Showy white flowers in elongated clusters mature into berry-like aggregates of black drupelets containing single seeds. Flowers May–June; fruits July–Aug.

Habitat/range: Occurs mostly in open woods and thickets at high elevations. Spruce-fir forests, grassy balds, and red oak forests. Common. From Nova Scotia south to Georgia.

Taxonomy: The more than 250 species of *Rubus* are sometimes difficult to distinguish because hybridization between species is common. Smooth blackberry (*R. canadensis*) also occurs in openings at high elevations and is similar to Allegheny blackberry but lacks or has only a few weak prickles.

Ecology: Allegheny blackberry is a shade-intolerant species that quickly colonizes disturbed areas but which is shaded out as taller plants establish. Widespread dieback of Fraser fir has resulted in a marked increase of blackberry thickets in spruce-fir forests. Abundant nectar attracts various kinds of insects to the flowers. Bumblebees are the most important pollinators. As the fruits mature, they change color from green to red to black, becoming sweeter as they darken. Ripe fruits, if uneaten, dry on the plant. Bright orange spots on the lower surfaces of leaves, coupled with stunted shoots, indicate orange rust, a fungus that is blackberry's most serious plant disease.

Wildlife: Allegheny blackberry's dense thickets and stout prickles provide excellent cover for birds, rabbits, and other animals. Rabbits and deer heavily browse the prickly stems and numerous birds, mammals (and even turtles) consume the fruits and disperse the seeds.

Uses: Commercially grown varieties of Allegheny blackberry and other *Rubus* species have been genetically selected for large fruits and high yields. The fruits provide a rich source of vitamin C and are used in jams, jellies, pies, and wines.

Rubus odoratus L.
FLOWERING RASPBERRY
Rosaceae (Rose family)

Description: Widely branching shrub with soft woody stems densely covered with red or purplish glandular hairs, thorns lacking. Leaves simple, maple-like, 3–5 lobed, 4–12 in. across. Open, bowl-shaped flowers with 5 deep pink to purplish petals, about 1–2 in. across. Dense, flattened clusters of small, single-seeded fleshy fruits (drupes). Flowers June–Aug.; fruits July–Oct.

Habitat/range: Moist forests, woodlands, streambanks, and roadsides, including northern hardwood forests and forest edges. Occasional in mountains. Northeastern North America, south in mountains to Georgia.

Taxonomy: Nearly worldwide in temperate regions, the genus *Rubus* consists of about 250 species, including 11 native and several introduced species in the mountains and piedmont. Flowering raspberry differs from other raspberry species in the region by having simple, palmately lobed leaves, and deep pink to purplish flowers.

Ecology: Flowering raspberry's open, bowl-shaped flowers are a good example of a generalist flower in that almost any kind of potential pollinator can access the nectar and pollen. In contrast, specialist flowers have more complex shapes and the nectar and pollen are often concealed, limiting access to a select pool of pollinators. The earliest (most primitive) flowering plants, such as magnolias, have generalist flowers, whereas more recently evolved groups, such as the orchids, have highly specialized flowers.

Wildlife: Dense raspberry thickets provide nesting sites and protective cover for many birds and small mammals that also consume the fruits and disperse the seeds. Insects feed on virtually all parts of the plant, some doing serious damage. For example, a long-horned black beetle, known as the raspberry cane borer, tunnels into stems causing them to wilt, droop, or die. The raspberry aphid sucks juices from the growing tips and young leaves; its most damaging effect is spreading the raspberry mosaic virus from plant to plant.

Uses: Flowering raspberry's fruits are edible but rather dry and seedy.

Salix nigra Marsh.
BLACK WILLOW
Salicaceae (Willow family)

Description: Deciduous shrub or tree, often with more than one trunk, leaves lance-shaped. Male and female flowers in catkins, on separate plants, male catkins erect, female catkins pendulous. Fruit a capsule with many small seeds, each with a tuft of white hairs. Flowers Mar–Apr.

Habitat/range: Moist to wet places such as margins of streams, rivers, swamps, lakes, and ponds, including rocky streamsides and floodplain forests. Common. Widespread in eastern North America.

Taxonomy: Salix is a widespread genus of more than 400 species of woody plants that occur in wet habitats. The large number of species, the high variability within species, and the tendency of species to interbreed and hybridize regularly can make willow identification difficult.

Ecology: Willows are unusual because they are both insect- and wind-pollinated. The presence of nectar and floral scent attracts insect pollinators, whereas the inconspicuous flowers with exposed anthers and stigmas and abundant nonsticky pollen facilitate wind pollination. The production of numerous widely dispersed seeds facilitates rapid colonization of large areas of newly exposed, wet sites. Willow seeds germinate within hours of landing on moist soil, but lose viability within days if the soil is dry. Established plants sucker easily, sometimes forming large clones with multiple stems. Based on the fossil record, research shows willows have existed in North America for at least 65 million years. Back then, dinosaurs likely browsed willow shoots, much the way deer and other wildlife do today.

Wildlife: Willows overhanging mountain streams help keep the water temperature cool for fish such as trout and provide cover for waterfowl. Beavers collect and store willow branches in their underwater dens prior to winter.

Uses: All species of willow contain salicin, now synthesized as acetylsalicylic acid, and marketed as aspirin. Willows are frequently used in streambank restoration and erosion control because their wide-spreading, shallow, fibrous roots stabilize the soil.

Sambucus canadensis L.
COMMON ELDERBERRY
Adoxaceae (Moschatel family)

Description: Soft-wooded deciduous shrub with multiple stems, a smooth bark with warty lenticels, and brittle twigs with white pith. Leaves opposite, pinnately compound, usually with 7 leaflets and serrate margins. Numerous small, fragrant white flowers in flat-topped to convex clusters, 4–10 in. across. Fruit a shiny black to purple berry-like drupe in terminal, drooping clusters. Flowers Apr.–July; fruits July–Aug.

Habitat/range: Moist forests, streambanks, clearings, and roadsides. Common. Eastern North America, Mexico, and the Caribbean.

Taxonomy: The genus *Sambucus* consists of 9 species of shrubs and small trees of temperate and subtropical regions, including 2 species in the mountains and piedmont. Red elderberry (*S. racemosa*) resembles common elderberry but has a long pyramidal inflorescence, bright red fruits, and a brown pith.

Ecology: Common elderberry grows best in open, sunny areas such as woodland borders and streamsides, where it spreads vegetatively by rhizomes, often forming dense thickets of arching stems.

The conspicuous wart-like bumps on the stems are lenticels, corky tissue with numerous intercellular spaces that allow gas exchange to inner stem cells. Bees and syrphid flies pollinate the pleasant but somewhat musk-scented flowers.

Wildlife: Numerous birds and small mammals forage on the fruits, often stripping plants of berries within a few days of fruit ripening. Catbirds and indigo buntings nest in elderberry, and dead stems are often hollowed out and used as nesting chambers by small bees.

Uses: Hollowed-out stems of elderberry were once used for whistles and blowguns, and the unpleasant odor of crushed stems and leaves (due to cyanogenic acid) is said to be an effective insect repellent. The fruits are occasionally used for making jelly, pies, and wine. Elderberry makes a nice addition to gardens, due to its luxuriant display of white flowers and large fruit crops that attract numerous songbirds.

Sambucus racemosa L.
RED ELDERBERRY

Adoxaceae (Moschatel family)

Description: A multistemmed, 8–20 ft. tall deciduous shrub with opposite, pinnately compound leaves with serrate margins and 5–7 leaflets. Stems covered with abundant raised lenticels, the interior filled with soft, spongy pith. Small creamy white flowers in pyramidal clusters develop into bright red berry-like drupes. Flowers Apr.–early June; fruits late June–Aug.

Habitat/range: Cool, moist sites at higher elevations, such as wooded ravines, mountain streambanks, moist thickets, boulder fields, and roadsides, including spruce-fir forests and northern hardwood forests. Uncommon. From Newfoundland west to Alaska, south in mountains to Georgia.

Taxonomy: Red elderberry differs from common elderberry (*S. canadensis*) in that it has a pyramidal inflorescence, bright red berries, and occurs primarily at higher elevations.

Ecology: Red elderberry grows best in open, well-lit areas such as forest gaps and woodland borders where new shoots grow rapidly (up to 12 ft. in a single year) and good fruit crops are produced most years. In contrast, plants develop slowly, are shorter in stature, and fruit sparingly in shaded areas under forest canopies. Individuals reproduce sexually by seed and vegetatively by sprouts, rhizome suckers, and layering. The strongly scented flowers are insect-pollinated. Seeds ripen in late summer and germinate the following spring. All parts of the plant (except the ripe fruits) are toxic to most animals (including humans), due to the release of cyanide when tissue is damaged. The roots are said to be toxic enough to kill a wild hog.

Wildlife: Many birds and other animals swallow elderberry fruits whole, digest the pulp, and disperse intact seeds in their droppings. Grosbeaks crack open the seeds in their beaks, thereby functioning as seed predators, rather than dispersers. Small carpenter bees and spider and potter wasps hollow out the soft pith in broken twigs to construct nesting chambers.

Uses: Red elderberry is an attractive landscape plant with colorful fruits that attract birds.

Synonym: Sambucus racemosa L. var. *pubens* (Mich.) Koehne

Smilax glauca Walter
WHITELEAF GREENBRIER
Smilacaceae (Greenbrier family)

Description: Slender-stemmed woody vine from underground runners with knotty, tuberous thickenings. Stem densely white, waxy, becoming smooth green or brown with age, the lower portion with numerous slender prickles, upper portion with fewer flattened thorns, often forming dense tangles. Leaves alternate, broadly ovate to lanceolate, distinctly whitish or bluish beneath and shiny green above, turning reddish to purple in fall. Small yellowish green flowers in flat-topped clusters in upper leaf axils, male and female flowers on separate plants. Fruit a green waxy berry ripening to shiny bluish black with whitish covering, 1–3 seeds in sticky pulp. Flowers late Apr.–early June; fruits Sept.–Nov., persisting into winter.

Habitat/range: Wide variety of upland and wetland habitats, including oak-hickory forests, alluvial forests, forest edges, fields, roadsides. Common. Eastern United States, south to Mexico.

Taxonomy: A genus of about 300 species of herbs and slightly woody vines widely distributed in temperate and tropical regions of the world, including 15 species in the mountains and piedmont. Whiteleaf greenbrier is easily identified by its whitish lower leaf surfaces.

Ecology: Whiteleaf greenbrier is a common vine of fields, woodlands, and open, mature forests in both dry and seasonally wet habitats. A sun-loving plant, it's often associated with openings created by past disturbance. Once established, individuals grow vigorously from the forest floor into the shrub and tree layers, climbing by paired tendrils (modified stipules) that coil around twigs and other slender supports with which they make contact. While the small, light green, fly-pollinated flowers of spring are easily missed, the bluish black berries form dense spherical clusters that contrast vividly with its reddish to purplish foliage from fall through much of winter. Most greenbriers are unpleasant to brush against because of numerous prickles and thorns. If cut down, greenbriers quickly send up new shoots.

Wildlife: The blue-black berries are an important winter food for various birds and mammals; wild hogs devour the nutrient-rich tuberous rhizomes.

Uses: Native Americans used the seeds as beads for necklaces.

Smilax rotundifolia L.
COMMON GREENBRIER
Smilacaceae (Greenbrier family)

Description: A climbing woody vine with numerous tendrils and stout, flattened prickles. Thin, narrowly ovate to almost round leaves, green and shiny on both sides, 2–4 in. long, the main veins curving and nearly parallel. Small greenish yellow flowers in small, round clusters in leaf axils. Fruit a roundish bluish black berry with white coverings in dense clusters. Flowers Apr.–May; fruits Sept.–Nov., persisting through winter.

Habitat/range: Occurs in a variety of moist to dry habitats, including open woods, alluvial forests, forest edges, and roadsides. Common. Widespread in eastern North America.

Taxonomy: Common greenbrier is similar to whiteleaf greenbrier (*S. glauca*), but with a green lower leaf surface.

Ecology: Common greenbrier occurs in a wide variety of sites, including dry, south-facing slopes and ridges in the mountains and moist, alluvial forests in the piedmont. It grows best in areas with abundant sunlight but can tolerate partial shade. It sometimes forms dense thickets that are nearly impenetrable, almost like green barbed wire. Like most vines, it uses other plants for support. By not having to produce its own thick support stems, it has more resources available for other purposes, including growth, reproduction, and food storage. Greenbriers climb with paired tendrils (modified stipules) attached near the base of leaf stalks. Once a tendril curls around a support, it becomes very tough and rigid; in contrast, tendrils that don't find a support to wrap around usually wither. Common greenbrier spreads by seeds and by new shoots emerging from long, slender rhizomes.

Wildlife: Greenbrier patches provide cover and nesting sites for various birds and mammals, and white-tailed deer browse the foliage, stimulating new shoots to form, making thickets even thicker. Small flies pollinate the flowers and the persistent fruits are an important food source for both overwintering birds and early spring migrants.

Uses: Young shoots and leaves can be eaten fresh or steamed like asparagus (they're tasty!).

Toxicodendron radicans (L.) Kuntze
POISON IVY
Anacardiaceae (Cashew family)

Description: A woody vine, small shrub, or trailing herb that climbs by aerial roots. Leaves pinnately compound with 3 highly variable shiny leaflets, the margin entire with a few irregular teeth or shallow lobes, the terminal leaflet long-stalked, the laterals nearly sessile. Clusters of small creamy white flowers in leaf axils, fruit a small, whitish, berrylike drupe that persists into winter. Flowers late Apr.–May; fruits Aug.–Oct.

Habitat/range: Occurs in a wide range of habitats, including mesic to dry forests, woodlands, forest edges, fields, and roadsides. Common. Widespread in eastern North America.

Taxonomy: A genus of 10 species of trees, shrubs, and vines of North and South America and Asia, including 4 species in the mountains and piedmont. Poison oak (*T. pubescens*) is similar but is usually a low shrub, rather than a vine, with leaflets more lobed and rounded, and occurring on drier sites.

Ecology: This ubiquitous plant is particularly abundant on fertile soils, such as floodplain and calcium-rich soils. It can grow as a prostrate ground cover, a low shrub, or high-climbing vine. Tree-climbing vines can be recognized by their dense aggregate of fibrous, hair-like rootlets attached to tree bark. Flowers and fruits are produced on horizontal branches that extend outward from the trunks and large branches of host trees. The leaves turn a brilliant red in autumn.

Wildlife: Few animals appear to suffer ill effects from eating this plant. Black bears, white-tailed deer, and rabbits feed on the foliage, and birds consume the fruits and spread the seeds.

Uses: All parts of the plant contain a resin called urushiol that causes severe dermatitis in most humans. Applying crushed jewelweed (*Impatiens*) to the skin helps alleviate the symptoms. Increasing atmospheric CO_2 associated with global climate change promotes larger plants with higher urushiol concentrations, thereby increasing the abundance and itchiness of poison ivy.

Synonym: Rhus radicans L.

Vaccinium arboreum Marsh.
SPARKLEBERRY
Ericaceae (Heath family)

Description: A large shrub or small tree with a short trunk and many crooked branches with flaking reddish brown bark. Small, glossy, dark green leaves with an oval to elliptical shape. Abundant small, bell-shaped white flowers form small black berries. Flowers late Apr–June; fruits Sept.–Oct.

Habitat/range: Dry rocky woodlands, bluffs, and cliffs, including oak-hickory forests, chestnut oak forests, pine-oak-heath, granite outcrops, and forest edges. Common in piedmont, rare in mountains. Widely distributed in Southeast.

Taxonomy: A genus of about 140 species of shrubs, vines, and small trees, widely distributed from the tropics to north of the Arctic Circle, including about 17 species in the mountains and piedmont. Sparkleberry can be distinguished from other species of *Vaccinium* by its larger size, dark green, glossy leaves, and crooked, twisted branches.

Ecology: Sparkleberry is the only member of the blueberry genus (*Vaccinium*) in the United States that reaches tree size. It's also a very unusual blueberry in that it can tolerate and grow quite well on neutral to slightly alkaline soils, although it thrives on acidic soils, too. The leaves tend to persist well into winter in the Southeast, turning purplish red in autumn. Individuals growing in full sun typically produce dense masses of small, bell-shaped white flowers. The small, dry fruits, like the leaves, tend to persist into winter. Because the tiny seeds require light to germinate, they must be on or very close to the soil surface to germinate.

Wildlife: The abundant flowers are a good source of nectar for bees. The fruits, while mealy and largely unpalatable to humans, are actively consumed by birds, deer, bears, and various small mammals, particularly in winter. Because the tiny seeds generally pass through the gut intact, viable seeds are widely dispersed by animals.

Uses: Its glossy foliage, dense clusters of white flowers and fruits, and ability to tolerate drought make sparkleberry an attractive plant for woodland gardens.

Vaccinium corymbosum L.
HIGHBUSH BLUEBERRY
Ericaceae (Heath family)

Description: A multistemmed medium to large deciduous shrub with alternate, simple, elliptical leaves 1–3 in. long. Flowers small, white or pinkish, cylindrical in shape, minutely 5-lobed, in pendulous clusters that open as the leaves emerge. Fruit a dark blue berry with whitish waxy covering, sweet and edible. Flowers Apr.–May; fruits July–Aug.

Habitat/range: Heath balds, mountain bogs, and open forests at high elevations and monadnocks in the piedmont. Common in mountains, rare in piedmont. Widespread in eastern North America.

Taxonomy: The Southeast is a center of biodiversity for blueberries as more species occur here than any other region of comparable size in North America. Distinguishing between our 17 species of *Vaccinium*, however, can be confusing because hybridization between species is common, resulting in much variation and taxonomic uncertainty.

Ecology: Highbush blueberry occurs in open, sunny habitats such as heath balds, mountain bogs, and open woods. Insects, especially bees, are generally required for successful pollination in blueberries. In one study, 42 different species of bees were observed visiting highbush blueberry flowers. Bees visiting blueberry flowers sometimes function as nectar "robbers," rather than pollinators. This occurs when bees chew small holes at the base of petals to access floral nectar, as well as when other bees use these holes to obtain nectar without benefiting the plant.

Wildlife: Blueberry fruits are an important food for many species of birds, bears, and small mammals, which digest the pulp and disperse the tiny hard-coated seeds in their droppings.

Uses: More than 50 highbush blueberry cultivars have been developed since the 1920s, making it one of the most agriculturally important blueberries in North America. Highbush blueberry is also an attractive, trouble-free landscape plant.

Vaccinium macrocarpon Aiton
CRANBERRY
Ericaceae (Heath family)

Description: Low-creeping subshrub up to 1–2 ft. tall with slender, wiry stems covered with small evergreen leaves. Solitary, white to pink pendulous flowers with 4 reflexed petals borne on short vertical shoots. Fruit a tart red berry, often persisting over winter. Flowers May–July; fruits Aug.–Nov.

Habitat/range: Mountain bogs of Virginia and North Carolina. Rare. Primarily northeastern North America, with disjunct populations south to North Carolina.

Taxonomy: Cranberry can be distinguished from most species of *Vaccinium* (blueberries) by its creeping growth form, reflexed petals, and red fruits.

Ecology: A shade-intolerant species, cranberry grows in open, poorly drained, acidic soils, often in close proximity to sphagnum moss, within which its seeds readily germinate and form new plants. Once established, plants send out slender horizontal stems that root at the leaf nodes. Under favorable conditions, a dense mat of spreading shoots develops with solitary flowers on short vertical shoots. Bees, particularly bumblebees, actively harvest nectar and pollen from the flowers and are the primary pollinators.

Wildlife: Mammals, birds, and possibly turtles consume the fleshy fruits and disperse the hard seeds. The name cranberry alludes to the fruits being a favorite food of cranes.

Uses: This species is the source of commercial cranberries grown in artificially created bogs. The fruits are used medicinally to treat urinary tract infections, as a source of antioxidants to help prevent cardiovascular disease, and to help boost the immune system.

Vaccinium pallidum Aiton
LOWBUSH BLUEBERRY
Ericaceae (Heath family)

Description: Low-growing deciduous shrub (1–2 ft. tall) with slender, green to somewhat reddish stems, forming dense colonies from rhizomes. Leaves alternate, longer than wide, the midrib protruding beyond the apex as a stiff, slender point. Small, white or greenish, urn-shaped flowers in short, hanging clusters. Fruit a small blue-black berry with white bloom, sweet and edible. Flowers Mar.–Apr.; fruits June–July.

Habitat/range: Mostly dry, forested slopes, including pine-oak-heath and oak-hickory forests. Common. Widespread in eastern United States.

Taxonomy: A center of diversity for the heath family (Ericaceae), the mountain and piedmont region includes representative species in genera such as *Rhododendron*, *Gaylussecia*, *Vaccinium*, *Kalmia*, *Oxydendrum*, and *Chimaphila*, almost all of which are associated with nutrient-poor, acidic soils.

Ecology: Lowbush blueberry spreads vegetatively by underground stems (rhizomes), often forming large, dense colonies. The green stems indicate the presence of chlorophyll, allowing both stems and leaves to harvest energy from the sun through photosynthesis. Well adapted to fire, lowbush blueberry readily regenerates from rhizomes, root crowns, and surviving branches.

Wildlife: Blueberries are eaten by numerous species of small birds and mammals, including black bears, which consume mouthfuls of leaves and twigs along with the berries.

Uses: Blueberries were an important food plant for Native Americans. They dried berries and added strips of dried venison to make pemmican, a winter staple. Today, the fruits are eaten fresh or used to make pies, jellies, and blueberry pancakes.

Synonym: *Vaccinium vacillans* Kalm ex Torr.

Vaccinium stamineum L.
DEERBERRY
Ericaceae (Heath family)

Description: Small to medium (2–6 ft. tall), much-branched deciduous shrub generally with 2 leaf forms—larger leaves on vegetative twigs with bluish white beneath and smaller leaf-like bracts on flowering stems. Numerous open, bell-shaped, whitish flowers with protruding yellow-orange stamens. Berries yellowish pink or greenish to blue with whitish covering, often tart and early deciduous. Flowers Apr.–June; fruits Aug.–Oct.

Habitat/range: Dry to somewhat moist woodlands, forests, rock outcrops, including oak-hickory forests, pine-oak-heath, and chestnut oak forests. Common. Widespread in eastern North America.

Taxonomy: Two characteristics distinguish this species from other blueberries—the leaf-like bracts on the flowering stems and the open, bell-shaped flowers with exerted stamens and stigmata. This highly variable species is divided into several varieties.

Ecology: Like the flowers of other blueberries, the flowers of deerberry depend on bees for successful fruit set. Bees visiting flowers grab the anthers, and rapidly move their flight muscles to produce a high-pitched, audible sound that resonates within the hollow pollen-containing anthers, causing pollen to be sonically dislodged in an explosive cloud. Bees use a single buzz on flowers with relatively little pollen and a sequence of multiple buzzes on previously unvisited flowers with pollen-rich anthers. This process, called buzz pollination, allows pollen-harvesting female bees to harvest the protein-rich pollen. They gather pollen on their hind legs and mix it with nectar to provision their brood cells. In the process of collecting pollen, bees inadvertently brush pollen against a flower's stigma, resulting in pollination. Most buzz-pollinated plants have large tubular anthers that contain thousands of dry (rather than oily) pollen grains with a single pore-like opening at the tip. Other buzz-pollinated plants include cranberries (*Vaccinium*), tomatoes and eggplants (*Solanum*), and shooting stars (*Primula*).

Wildlife: Birds and mammals eat the fruits and disperse the tiny seeds in their droppings.

Uses: Deerberry is an attractive low-maintenance shrub that is underused in gardens.

Viburnum acerifolium L.
MAPLELEAF VIBURNUM
Adoxaceae (Moschatel family)

Description: Low, deciduous clump-forming shrub, 3–6 ft. tall with opposite, 3-lobed maple-like leaves with coarsely toothed margins. Numerous small white flowers in showy, flat-topped clusters well above the leaves. Fruit fleshy, 1-seeded, purple-black when ripe. Flowers late Apr.–early June; fruits Aug.–Oct.

Habitat/range: Moist to dry woods, including cove forests, oak-hickory forests, and river bluff forests. Fairly common. Widely distributed in eastern North America.

Taxonomy: The genus *Viburnum* consists of about 150 species of shrubs and small trees with opposite leaves and mostly small white flowers with fleshy single-seeded fruits in flat-topped terminal clusters. Mapleleaf viburnum can be distinguished from true maples (*Acer*) by its showy clusters of white flowers and fleshy berry-like fruits.

Ecology: Mapleleaf viburnum occurs on moist to dry sites and in both open and shady habitats but grows best on well-drained, moist soils in partial shade. Plants reach sexual maturity quickly, flowering as early as their second year. Established plants spread vegetatively from rhizomes, often forming dense colonies. Low to moderately hot fires topkill mapleleaf viburnum. Although it can resprout, the underground stems are shallow and easily damaged, so the species declines in areas exposed to hot or repeated fires.

Wildlife: Dense patches of mapleleaf viburnum provide good nesting sites and escape cover for wildlife. In spring, butterflies perch on the flat-topped inflorescences, imbibing nectar while birds and mammals feed on the small, juicy fruits in autumn. Rose-tinted, slug-like caterpillars tended by ants are most likely the larvae of spring azure butterflies, one of the first adult butterflies to emerge in spring, and known to feed on the leaves of mapleleaf viburnum.

Uses: To the human palate, some viburnum fruits are edible straight from the plant, some require boiling and lots of sugar, whereas others are so bitter, they are best left alone.

Viburnum cassinoides L.
WILD RAISIN
Adoxaceae (Moschatel family)

Description: An upright, deciduous, multistemmed shrub 3–12 ft. tall with opposite, pinnately veined leaves. Small creamy white flowers with a slightly unpleasant odor in large, terminal, flat-topped clusters. Fruit a berry-like drupe with a single seed and generally sweet edible pulp, becoming bright pink, then bluish black with a whitish-waxy bloom, wrinkling with age, hence the common name. Flowers late May–June; fruits Aug.–Oct.

Habitat/range: Moist to wet open woods, thickets, outcrops, including mountain bogs, high-elevation red oak forests, and heath balds. Fairly common in mountains, mostly above 4,500 ft. Eastern North America.

Taxonomy: Viburnums have opposite leaves, umbrella-shaped inflorescences, flowers with 5 petals and stamens, and fleshy berry-like fruits. Dogwoods (*Cornus*) are similar in having opposite leaves with berry-like fruits, but viburnums typically have a toothed or lobed leaf margin, while dogwoods have smooth margins.

Ecology: Like the fruits of many plants, the fruits of viburnums change color as they age. With their excellent vision, birds detect this color change and use it as an indicator of fruit ripening. Fruit-eating birds are generally only attracted to fruits after the seeds have ripened, as immature fruits are usually inconspicuous (green in color), hard, bitter, and sometimes astringent, as are unripe persimmons. Mature fruits, in contrast, are generally brightly colored, soft, and flavorful (note that fruits eaten by animals aren't necessarily edible for humans). Birds typically don't crush the seeds; instead, they digest the nutritious pulp and pass the seeds in a viable condition, often some distance from the parent plant.

Wildlife: White-tailed deer frequently browse the leaves and twigs, sometimes ingesting ripe fruits and dispersing the seeds in their droppings.

Uses: Like most viburnums, wild raisin is easy to grow, and its large, showy flowers, colorful fruits, and attractive foliage (which turns red in autumn) make it an excellent landscape plant, particularly in moist to poorly drained sites.

Viburnum lantanoides Michx.
WITCH HOBBLE, HOBBLEBUSH
Adoxaceae (Moschatel family)

Description: A sprawling deciduous shrub up to 10 ft. tall with broadly ovate to heart-shaped opposite leaves, coarsely textured, with sunken veins and toothed margins. Inflorescence a large, flat-topped, terminal cluster about 4 in. wide, with many small whitish to pink fertile flowers surrounded by a ring of larger showy, sterile flowers. Small, berry-like drupes change color from greenish red to purplish black as they ripen. Flowers May–June; fruits Aug.–Sept.

Habitat/range: Cool, moist woods, shaded ravines, and woodland borders at high elevations. Spruce-fir forests, northern hardwood forests, and boulder fields. Common. Northeastern United States and Canada, south in mountains to Georgia.

Taxonomy: Of the 150 species of *Viburnum*, 12 occur in the mountains and piedmont. The common names of this species allude to its drooping branches, which hinder passage.

Ecology: The leaves of witch hobble emerge in early spring, providing several weeks of high light before canopy trees leaf out. During this short period of time, the leaves of witch hobble have an unusually high rate of photosynthesis, contributing almost 40 percent of the plant's net annual photosynthetic gain. With canopy closure, the leaves continue to be photosynthetically active, but at a much lower rate. Witch hobble has an unusual dual strategy, exploiting early season high light, as ephemeral herbs do, as well as maintaining low photosynthetic rates throughout the summer under a dense canopy, much the way shade-tolerant species do. Its reproductive system is also quite flexible. Sexual reproduction involves pollination by insects but because seed set is often low, asexual reproduction by layering provides an important mechanism for spreading into new areas. Layering involves lower branches, weighed down by snow or fallen branches, coming in contact with the ground, forming roots and new shoots, which in time separate from the parent plant, forming separate clones.

Wildlife: Birds consume the fleshy fruits and disperse the seeds.

Uses: Witch hobble's ripe fruits are tasty, but a low pulp to seed ratio means lots of gathering but not much eating.

Vitis rotundifolia Michx.
MUSCADINE, SCUPPERNONG
Vitaceae (Grape family)

Description: High-climbing or trailing woody vine with unbranched tendrils, the leaves much smaller than those of other wild grapes, up to 3 in. wide, nearly circular to broadly ovate, coarsely toothed, green and glossy on both sides. Inconspicuous greenish white flowers in axillary clusters. Fruit a large berry (a grape) ½–1 in. across, initially green, turning red to purple to black (occasionally bronze), the pulp sweet and edible within a thick skin. Flowers May–June; fruits Aug.–Sept.

Habitat/range: Wide variety of habitats. Oak-hickory forests, alluvial forests, forest edges, and roadsides. Common in piedmont, occasional in mountains. Widely distributed in eastern United States.

Taxonomy: A genus of 65 species of vines of temperate regions of Eurasia and North America, including 6 species in the mountains and piedmont. Muscadine differs from our other wild grapes in having unbranched tendrils.

Ecology: The stems of this high-climbing woody vine can be over 6 in. thick and reach the tops of trees more than 100 ft. tall. It clambers over shrubs and climbs up trees with coiled tendrils that wrap tightly around anything they contact. When climbing structures aren't available, it can spread along the ground, rooting at the nodes, sometimes forming a dense ground cover. Individuals grow best and yield the most fruits when they receive abundant sunlight. Grapevines can damage young trees by breaking branches and tops and shading out foliage, and vines can worsen winter storm damage by accumulating ice and snow. The visually inconspicuous but very fragrant flowers attract various insect pollinators. The fruits vary in tartness, as does the annual yield.

Wildlife: Many kinds of birds and mammals consume the fruits and disperse the seeds (look for the pear-shaped seeds in mammal scat in autumn).

Uses: Cultivars include plants with bronze fruits (called scuppernongs), and those with purple fruits (called muscadines). The fruits are a rich source of vitamins B and C, iron, and antioxidants, and can be eaten plain or made into wine, juice, jelly, or pies.

Xanthorhiza simplicissima Marsh.
YELLOWROOT
Ranunculaceae (Buttercup family)

Description: Low-growing deciduous shrub with bright yellow rhizomes, the leaves clustered towards stem tips, pinnately compound with 3–5 sharply toothed leaflets. Flowers small, lacking petals, with brownish purple (to yellowish green) sepals, in terminal, drooping racemes to 5 in. long. Fruit a small, dry, single-seeded pod (follicle) in drooping clusters. Flowers Mar.–May; fruits May–June.

Habitat/range: Shaded streambanks and wet, rocky ledges. Common. Widely distributed in eastern United States.

Taxonomy: The Latin name *Xanthorhiza* aptly describes the roots, as *xantho* means "yellow" and *rhiza* means "root." This is the only species in the genus.

Ecology: Yellowroot thrives in moist, cool, acidic soils in streamside habitats where it spreads from rhizomes to form dense thickets. The upright stems that make up a particular patch are often part of one large individual plant connected by belowground stems. Yellowroot is rarely washed away during floods because its well-developed underground stems anchor plants to the substrate and its short stature and flexible, unbranched stems reduce resistance to the force of flowing water. Its buoyant seeds, however, readily disperse downstream. All leaves on a given stem emerge from a single terminal bud each spring. The pinnately compound leaves are arranged in a circular pattern, resembling a rosette, a pattern that maximizes the amount of light received by each leaf, thereby increasing photosynthesis and growth. The small flowers in dense pendulous racemes lack fragrance and appear to receive few visitors.

Wildlife: Birds and small mammals eat the seeds and dense colonies provide cover for small mammals and amphibians.

Uses: Yellowroot's rhizomes contain a bright yellow, bitter-tasting alkaloid that yields a dye. Its wide-spreading roots and dense cover help prevent streambank erosion.

3 : Herbaceous Plants

Achillea millefolium L.
YARROW
Asteraceae (Sunflower family)

Description: Aromatic herbaceous perennial, 1–3 ft. tall. Finely dissected grayish green leaves with a feathery appearance occur as basal rosettes and on stems. Numerous small white flowers in flat or round-topped terminal clusters. Fruit a flattened achene. Flowers Apr.–Nov.

Habitat/range: Grassy balds, roadsides, disturbed areas. Common. Widely distributed throughout Northern Hemisphere.

Taxonomy: Yarrow includes both native and introduced plants that have hybridized, forming a highly variable species. The genus name honors the Greek hero Achilles, who is said to have saved the lives of numerous soldiers by applying this plant to their wounds.

Ecology: Yarrow tolerates a wide variety of climates, from mild coastal areas up to high elevations and latitudes in both North America and Europe. Often an invader of disturbed habitats, its deep and extensive root system enables it to withstand long periods of drought. While many sunflowers have a few large flower heads composed of many disk and ray flowers, yarrow has many small flower heads, each composed of a few small disk and ray flowers. The flowering season is unusually long, extending from April to November. The small, flat achenes allow a relatively large part of the seed to be in direct contact with the soil, facilitating water uptake and germination on drier substrates. In addition to spreading by seeds, yarrow spreads vegetatively from a much-branched rhizome system, forming dense, spreading mats of lacy, grayish green leaves.

Wildlife: Most grazers avoid yarrow because of its bitter-tasting foliage.

Uses: Best known as a plant that stops bleeding, it was used widely in the American Civil War to treat wounds, and became known as "soldiers woundwort." Yarrow is a frequently used garden plant.

Actaea pachypoda Elliott
DOLL'S EYES, WHITE BANEBERRY
Ranunculaceae (Buttercup family)

Description: An aromatic perennial herb up to 3 ft. tall. Leaves large, 2–3 times compound on long stalks with sharply lobed margins. Small white flowers in compact racemes extend above leaves. Round white fruits with a prominent black spot on bright red stalks. Flowers Apr.–May; fruits Aug.–Oct.

Habitat/range: Rich woods and bottomlands, including cove forests, floodplain forests, and basic mesic forests. Common in mountains, rare in piedmont. Widespread in eastern North America.

Taxonomy: The waxy berries resemble the porcelain eyes once used in dolls, hence the common name "doll's eyes."

Ecology: This plant catches your eye both in spring when feathery clusters of white flowers are present and in late summer and fall when colorful white berries appear on stout red stalks. The numerous stamens give the apetalous flowers a distinctly feathery appearance. Doll's eyes flowers lack nectar but have a citrus-like odor that attracts pollen-collecting bees, syrphid flies, and beetles that function as pollinators when they inadvertently brush pollen onto receptive stigmas while foraging. The European snout beetle uses the flowers as a mating site (rather than as a food source), and as it scrambles over the flowers, pollination occurs. The opportunity for cross-pollination is enhanced by the stigmas being receptive for several days before the anthers release pollen.

Wildlife: Pollen-foraging insects pollinate the flowers in spring, deer browse the foliage in summer, and birds and rodents consume the fleshy fruits and disperse the seeds from late summer–fall.

Uses: Native Americans used doll's eyes for a variety of ailments, including heart problems, and as an aid in childbirth. The fruits and all other parts of the plant are poisonous, as suggested by the common name "white baneberry."

Actaea racemosa L.
BLACK COHOSH, BUGBANE
Ranunculaceae (Buttercup family)

Description: Herbaceous perennial with large 2–3 times compound leaves with 20 or more sharp-pointed, coarsely toothed leaflets. Flower stalks 3–8 ft. tall with tassel-like white flowers in long, narrow, arching racemes. Fruit a follicle with several seeds. Flowers May–Aug.; fruits July–Sept.

Habitat/range: Moist, rich forests, wooded slopes, ravines, and creek margins. Northern hardwood forests, cove forests, rocky streamsides, forest edges, river bluff forests, and basic mesic forests. Common. Moderately widespread in eastern North America.

Taxonomy: It's sometimes difficult to distinguish cove forest genera such as *Actaea*, *Astilbe*, *Aruncus*, *Caulophyllum*, and *Aralia* when only vegetative parts are present because of the similarity of their pinnately compound leaves.

Ecology: If you look closely at the tassel-like flowers of black cohosh, you'll discover that the flowers lack petals and the sepals fall off as the flower opens (much the way they do on doll's eyes, *A. pachypoda*). As such, the numerous stamens within each flower give the long, narrow inflorescences their fuzzy appearance. Carrion flies and beetles, attracted, rather than repelled, by the flowers fetid odor, are the primary pollinators.

Wildlife: The plant's unpleasant odor is thought to repel most insects (and perhaps vertebrates as well), hence the common name "bugbane."

Uses: Rubbing the fetid-smelling flowers on skin repels biting bugs (but may attract a few carrion flies and beetles looking for dead meat). Black cohosh has become a popular herbal remedy in treating menopausal symptoms, particularly "hot flashes." Because most black cohosh used in the pharmaceutical industry is collected from wild populations, overcollecting is a potential threat.

Synonym: Cimicifuga racemosa (L.) Nutt.

Adiantum pedatum L.
MAIDENHAIR FERN
Pteridaceae (Maidenhair fern family)

Description: Semicircular or fan-shaped leaf with a shiny, dark brown to black stalk, the leaves generally flat (horizontal to ground) on an erect stalk. Spore clusters (sori) oblong, on underside of recurved leaf margin. Spores released June–Aug.

Habitat/range: Moist forests and cliffs, often on calcium-rich soil derived from calcareous or mafic rock. Rich cove forests, basic mesic forests, and seepage slopes. Common in mountains, uncommon in piedmont. Widespread in eastern North America.

Taxonomy: A nearly worldwide genus of about 150 species that is most diverse in the Andes of South America. Maidenhair fern differs from Venus' hair fern (*A. capillus-veneris*) in that its leaflets are longer than broad.

Ecology: Ferns make up about 3 percent of the vascular plants of North America, most of which occur in rich, moist forests. Ferns disperse by spores, rather than by seeds. The spores of most ferns develop on the undersides of leaves; other species, such as cinnamon fern (*Osmunda cinnamomea*) and rattlesnake fern (*Botrypus virginianus*) have separate spore stalks (fertile leaves). Still others, like interrupted fern (*Osmunda claytoniana*), develop modified portions of their regular leaves for spore production. Because fern spores are tiny (dust-like), they can be carried long distances by wind, which partially explains the wide geographic distribution of many ferns. Spores that land in suitable places, such as on moist soil or in rock crevices, germinate and develop into thumbnail-sized gametophyte plants that produce eggs and flagellate swimming sperm (ferns don't need pollinators, but they do require water for fertilization to occur). If all goes well, the fertilized egg (zygote) develops into a mature fern plant (the sporophyte).

Uses: An attractive fern on moist sites in woodland gardens.

Agalinis purpurea (L.) Pennell
PURPLE GERARDIA

Orobanchaceae (Broomrape family)

Description: Slender-stemmed, branching annual with dark green or purplish opposite linear leaves, 1–2 in. long, with a prominent midvein. Pink to purplish tubular flowers with 5 spreading lobes, the throat hairy within and striped with yellow. Fruit a small, roundish capsule. Flowers Aug.–frost; fruits Sept.–Nov.

Habitat/range: Moist openings, including roadsides, fields, woodlands, and mountain bogs. Common in piedmont, less so in mountains. Widely distributed in eastern United States.

Taxonomy: A genus of 40 species of hemiparasitic herbs of tropical and temperate regions of America, including 10 species in the mountains and piedmont. Fascicled purple gerardia (*A. fasciculata*) is similar except that its leaves are in fascicles (small clusters) and it has rough, rather than smooth, stems.

Ecology: Like all members of the genus *Agalinis*, this species is a root hemiparasite—individuals are green and produce their own carbohydrates through photosynthesis and obtain dissolved nutrients by penetrating the roots of neighboring plants with specialized structures called haustoria. Appearing as bumps on host roots, each haustorium forms a bridge that carries water, mineral elements, and in some cases, carbohydrates, from the host to the parasite. While purple gerardia often parasitizes grasses, its roots can parasitize a wide range of host plants. The showy flowers are actively visited and pollinated by bumblebees and other long-tongued bees. The yellow stripes inside the tubular flower function as nectar guides, directing bees to where the nectar is located, much like runway lines direct a pilot landing a plane. Cross-pollination, rather than self-pollination, is promoted, since a bee approaching a flower is likely to contact the exserted stigma before the anthers. When ripe, capsules split open at the top, and gusts of wind disperse the tiny seeds varying distances from the parent plant.

Wildlife: Purple gerardia is the preferred larval (caterpillar) host plant of the common buckeye butterfly. Caterpillars of the orange sallow moth consume developing seeds within the fruits.

Uses: Purple gerardia provides a splash of color in open, sunny areas of gardens.

Ageratina altissima (L.) King & H. Rob.
WHITE SNAKEROOT

Asteraceae (Sunflower family)

Description: Robust perennial herb usually 3–4 ft. tall, often forming dense colonies. Leaves ovate to heart-shaped with an acuminate tip and sharply toothed margins, the leaf stalk (petiole) more than 1 in. long. Flower heads have a fuzzy appearance because the stamens extend beyond the corolla tube; ray flowers absent. Fruit an achene with a tuft of whitish, hair-like bristles. Flowers late July–Oct.

Habitat/range: Moist forests, including spruce-fir forests, high-elevation red oak forests, northern hardwood forests, rich cove forests, oak-hickory forests, and forest edges. Common. Widely distributed in eastern North America.

Taxonomy: This genus of about 250 species occurs in North, Central, and South America, including 2 species in the mountains and piedmont. Small white snakeroot (*A. aromatica*) is similar, but its leaves are smaller with blunt (rather than sharp) teeth.

Ecology: White snakeroot frequently occurs along forest margins and clearings where light levels are relatively high. Plant size, density, and the number of flowers produced are typically greater in relatively open areas than under a dense forest canopy. Soil compaction, such as occurs along roadsides and recently logged areas, results in a marked reduction in plant size and a relatively shallow root system, making the plant susceptible to desiccation. One of the last species to bloom in autumn, the fragrant flowers are visited by a variety of insects, including bees, wasps, flies, butterflies, and moths. On favorable sites, colonies increase rapidly from seeds and spreading rhizomes.

Wildlife: Deer and other mammalian herbivores generally avoid this plant, as the foliage is bitter tasting and toxic. In overgrazed areas, cows and other livestock sometimes eat it, which can cause them to tremble, lose weight, and eventually die. The toxins from this plant can pass from cattle to humans through milk, causing "milk sickness," a disease that killed thousands of pioneers settling in the Appalachians in the eighteenth and early-nineteenth centuries.

Uses: The root was used to treat snakebite, hence the common name.

Synonym: Eupatorium rugosum Houtt.

Allium tricoccum Aiton
RAMPS, WILD LEEK
Alliaceae (Onion family)

Description: Bulb-forming spring ephemeral with large flat leaves, 1–2 ½ in. wide and 6–12 in. long with a reddish stalk and strong onion odor. Tiny pale yellow to cream-colored, bell-shaped flowers in hemispherical clusters (umbels). Fruit a 3-lobed capsule with shiny black seeds. Flowers June–July; fruits Aug.–Sept.

Habitat/range: Rich, moist woods, including cove and northern hardwood forests. Common in mountains. Widely distributed in eastern North America.

Taxonomy: The genus *Allium* is widely distributed in Europe, Asia, Africa, and North America with 12 of the approximately 700 species occurring in the mountains and piedmont.

Ecology: Ramps form dense patches in moist, rich soils of undisturbed forest. The leaves emerge from underground bulbs as early as late February and persist for 5–6 weeks until the canopy trees leaf out. By the time flowers are produced in summer, the leaves have long since withered and died. Ramps, like the cranefly orchid (*Tipularia*), is unusual in that it has separate vegetative and flowering phases. The bulbs of large plants reproduce vegetatively by dividing into 2 or 3 parts that give rise to new clusters of leaves. Vegetative reproduction seems to occur more frequently than reproduction by seed. This may reflect bulb offshoots being larger and more likely to survive than individuals from seed. Some reproduction by seed, however, is important both as a mechanism of dispersal and for the long-term survival of populations.

Wildlife: Mice collect and cache seeds of ramps under the leaf litter. Most are retrieved and eaten, but "forgotten" seeds can give rise to new plants.

Uses: The leaves and bulbs, with their strong onion/garlic flavor, can be cooked as a vegetable, served in salads, or, most commonly, fried and mixed with eggs. Today, many people dig ramps from wild populations, and traditional ramp festivals continue to be a popular springtime fundraising activity throughout the southern Appalachians. Unfortunately, wild populations are declining because current levels of harvesting aren't sustainable.

Ambrosia artemisiifolia L.
COMMON RAGWEED
Asteraceae (Sunflower family)

Description: Weedy annual with branched stems forming a bushy round top. Leaves deeply lobed to dissected, lower opposite, upper alternate, fragrant when crushed. Male flowers in spike-like clusters (or spikes) near top, less conspicuous female flowers in small clusters in upper leaf axils. Fruit a beaked achene. Flowers Aug–frost; fruits Sept.–Dec.

Habitat/range: Roadsides, fields, and waste areas. Common. Widespread in North America and much of the world.

Taxonomy: Of the 5 species of *Ambrosia* in the mountains and piedmont, common ragweed is the most pervasive. Giant ragweed (*A. trifida*) is similar to common ragweed but has opposite upper leaves with 3–5 palmate lobes.

Ecology: Ragweed is a disturbance-dependent species that emerges from dormant seeds in the soil. Famous for its power to induce allergic responses, ragweed pollen is the primary cause of late summer–fall hay fever. Because the flowers are pollinated by wind, huge amounts of pollen are needed to ensure successful pollination and seed set (a single plant can produce several million pollen grains). The surface of pollen grains contains proteins that cause sneezing, watery eyes, and breathing difficulties for people sensitive to ragweed pollen. Unfortunately, there is little relief in sight for hay fever sufferers as widespread disturbance continually creates habitat for ragweed; moreover, increasing atmospheric CO_2 levels associated with global climate change are causing increased pollen production in ragweed. Because ragweed grows best in open areas with full sun, plants grow vigorously the first year after disturbance, but later only stunted plants with relatively few flowers (and pollen grains) are found. One of the best controls for ragweed is to let perennial species simply crowd it out.

Wildlife: Insects are generally not attracted to the tiny wind-pollinated flowers, but numerous birds consume the small seeds; those not digested are dispersed in droppings.

Amianthium muscitoxicum (Walter) A. Gray
FLY POISON
Melanthiaceae (Bunchflower family)

Description: Herbaceous perennial 1–3 ft. tall with grass-like, mostly basal leaves and showy white flowers in dense terminal racemes. Fruit a 3-beaked, dark brown capsule. Flowers May–June; fruits July–Sept.

Habitat/range: Moist woods, especially oak forests, meadows, and bogs. Common. Widespread in eastern United States.

Taxonomy: Fly poison is the only species in the genus *Amianthium*. Turkey beard (*Xerophyllum asphodeloides*) also has dense terminal racemes of white flowers on long stalks but has long, wiry leaves and grows in dry, pine woodlands, rather than in moist woods.

Ecology: Fly poison's aboveground shoots die back in autumn and emerge each spring from a dormant bulb, producing up to 15 clusters of leaves. The number of leaf clusters corresponds to the number of lobes on the bulb, which in turn reflects the amount of energy reserves stored over winter. The number of flowers within an inflorescence is also quite variable, ranging from 25 to over 125. The flowers depend on insects for pollination and fruit set. Beetles, flies, butterflies, and bees are among the wide variety of insects that visit the flowers for nectar, pollen, or both. The most important pollinators are thought to be beetles and butterflies, including the (Eastern) tiger swallowtail (*Papilio glaucus*). Individual plants flower over a period of about 2 weeks. The white flowers don't wither following pollination but persist on the plant for 5–6 days, turning green to greenish purple as they age. Seeds ripen in autumn and usually germinate the following spring.

Wildlife: Most herbivores avoid fly poison due to its toxic alkaloids. Theridiid spiders frequently perch in inflorescences, where they ambush flower-foraging insects. Mice harvest the seeds.

Uses: Pulp from crushed bulbs mixed with honey or molasses was used to attract and kill houseflies, hence the common name "fly poison."

Amphicarpaea bracteata (L.) Fernald
HOG PEANUT
Fabaceae (Legume family)

Description: Slender, twining annual or short-lived perennial vine up to 5 ft. long, the leaves divided into 3 ovate leaflets. Pale lilac to white, pea-like flowers in nodding racemes on long stalks from the leaf axil, other flowers at base of stem or underground. Fruit a legume. Flowers July–Sept.; fruits Aug.–Oct.

Habitat/range: Dry to moist forests, including oak-hickory forests, cove forests, alluvial forests, forest edges, and roadsides. Common. Eastern North America.

Taxonomy: Amphicarpaea is a genus of 3 species—1 each in eastern North America, eastern Asia, and East Africa.

Ecology: Hog peanut is a common but often overlooked plant because of its inconspicuous flowers and habit of twining around other plants. It's 1 of only about 30 species worldwide that produces both above- and belowground flowers and fruits. The subterranean flowers don't open, are self-fertile, and produce fruits with a single large seed. In contrast, the aerial flowers open, can cross-pollinate, and produce fruits with 1–3 smaller seeds with greater potential for dispersal (the aerial fruits are ballistically dispersed). Potential advantages of producing subterranean fruits include protection from seed predators and insulation from climate extremes. Because subterranean seeds are about 15 times heavier than aerial seeds, they produce more vigorous seedlings that have higher survival rates than seedlings from aerial seeds. On the other hand, the potential for cross-pollination among aerial flowers results in more genetically variable seeds, facilitating adaptation to environmental change. Also, the greater potential for seed dispersal associated with aerial fruits facilitates the founding of new populations. The production of 2 types of flowers and 2 types of fruits/seeds is considered a bet-hedging strategy that may reap both short- and long-term benefits.

Wildlife: Birds eat the aboveground seeds and wild hogs eat the subterranean seeds.

Uses: Native Americans boiled the subterranean fruits, which are somewhat similar to garden beans.

Andropogon virginicus L.
BROOMSEDGE, BROOMSTRAW
Poaceae (Grass family)

Description: Warm-season perennial bunchgrass 2–4 ft. tall, whose dried, straw-colored basal leaves persist until the following spring. Inflorescences in (forked) paired racemes, rather than solitary, as in little bluestem (*Schizachyrium scoparium*). Fruit a slender grain tipped with a straight, hair-like awn. Flowers Sept.–Oct.

Habitat/range: Roadsides, fields, rock outcrops, open woodlands, forest edges, and disturbed sites. Common. Widespread in eastern North America, Central America, the Caribbean.

Taxonomy: A genus of 100 mostly tropical species, including 7 species in the mountains and piedmont. The common name "broomsedge" is misleading, since it's a grass not a sedge.

Ecology: Broomsedge occurs in a wide variety of habitats, in grasslands, pastures, open forests, and roadsides. It grows well on nutrient-poor soils, such as eroded, "worn out," abandoned farmlands where it often forms a continuous cover due to reduced competition. Individuals also establish and persist on the shallow soils of rock outcrops. Because individuals are both short-lived and shade-intolerant, periodic disturbance is generally necessary for successful establishment and persistence. Broomsedge responds favorably to fires, quickly regenerating from underground meristems and from wind-dispersed seeds. Some flowers self-pollinate in buds, others open and can be cross-pollinated by wind.

Wildlife: The new growth of spring and summer is sometimes heavily grazed, and the dense tufts of foliage provide cover for ground-nesting birds.

Uses: Broomsedge tied in bundles was once widely used in homemade brooms, hence the common name. The straw-colored basal leaves add winter interest to fields, roadsides, and gardens, and the dense, fibrous roots stabilize the soil, thereby reducing erosion.

Anemone quinquefolia L.
WOOD ANEMONE
Ranunculaceae (Buttercup family)

Description: A small (4–8 in.) perennial herb that emerges from a slender rhizome in early spring and dies back by early summer. Leaves on long stalks, deeply divided into 3 or 5 lobes. Flowers solitary, about 1 in. across, on long stalks with 5 or more petal-like sepals. The fruiting head is a rounded cluster of small, woolly achenes. Flowers Mar.–May; fruits Apr.–June.

Habitat/range: Rich, moist soil, open woods, clearings, and streamsides. Cove forests, northern hardwood forests, grassy balds, and forest edges. Common in mountains, rare in piedmont. Widespread in eastern North America.

Taxonomy: Wood anemone and rue anemone (*Thalicrum thalictroides*) are similar, but the latter species has multiple, rather than single, flowers and the stem leaves have 3 leaflets, each with 3 shallow, rounded lobes.

Ecology: A spring ephemeral, wood anemone emerges in early spring and dies back as canopy trees leaf out, reducing the amount of light reaching the forest floor. Canopy "leaf escapers" such as wood anemone typically have a growing season of 12 weeks or less, spending the rest of the year as a dormant underground rhizome. Interestingly, many plants emerge and flower earlier than in the past due to warmer springtime temperatures associated with climate change. A recent study found that wood anemone flowers about 15 days earlier than it did in the early 1970s. The normally wide-open flowers close in cloudy weather and at night, an adaptation that protects the delicate reproductive parts when pollinators aren't likely to be active. Wood anemone spreads by seeds and vegetatively by thin white rhizomes giving rise to upright shoots that form small colonies.

Wildlife: Pollen-harvesting bees and flies pollinate the nectarless flowers. Anemones are among the many spring woodland herbs with ant-dispersed seeds.

Uses: Handling wood anemone can cause a local skin irritation, and ingestion can cause sickness. The plant is considered toxic.

Angelica triquinata Michx.
MOUNTAIN ANGELICA, FILMY ANGELICA
Apiaceae (Carrot family)

Description: A stout, herbaceous perennial 2–5 ft. tall with smooth, purplish stems and large, highly compound leaves with coarsely toothed leaflets, the leaves progressively smaller toward stem tip, with sheaths at base of petioles partially enclosing the swollen stem. Tiny greenish yellow flowers tightly packed in large, terminal, compound umbels about 3–6 in. across. Fruits strongly flattened with 2 lateral wings. Flowers July–Sept.; fruits Sept.–Oct.

Habitat/range: Mesic forests, meadows, streambanks, and along shaded roadsides at moderate to high elevations. Grassy balds, northern hardwood forests, and red oak forests. Common. An Appalachian endemic from Pennsylvania south to Georgia.

Taxonomy: The genus *Angelica* comprises 110 species of herbaceous plants of the Northern Hemisphere. Hairy angelica (*A. venenosa*) is widespread in dry to mesic woodlands and borders; it can be distinguished from mountain angelica by its densely hairy umbels and fruits.

Ecology: Mountain angelica and other members of the parsley family (Apiaceae) have flowers arranged in umbels. The tiny, densely clumped flowers are generalist flowers with nectar and pollen readily accessible to a wide range of insects. Many insects visit the flowers for nectar or pollen, while others seek a mate or simply a place to rest. The most effective pollinators are various kinds of Hymenoptera, including bees, wasps, and hornets that apparently become intoxicated as they forage for nectar. These drunken insects can be seen sitting lethargically on flowers, bumbling into each other while crawling about the flowers, or flying erratically from one inflorescence to another. The "intoxicating" substance in the nectar has yet to be identified.

Wildlife: White-tailed deer actively feed on mountain angelica's foliage.

Uses: Numerous species in the parsley family are edible and widely used as vegetables, herbs, and spices, including carrot, fennel, and dill. Others are extremely toxic, including poison hemlock (*Conium maculatum*), the source of the poison responsible for the death of Socrates.

Aquilegia canadensis L.
EASTERN COLUMBINE
Ranunculaceae (Buttercup family)

Description: Herbaceous perennial with slender, leafy, much-branched stems 1–3 ft. tall. Stem and basal leaves divided into 3 leaflets, each mostly 3-lobed with rounded tips. Distinctive nodding flowers red outside, yellow within, a deep nectar spur at base of each petal. Numerous exserted yellow stamens. Fruit a cluster of 5 slender, curved pods (follicles). Flowers Mar.–May.

Habitat/range: Occurs in variety of moist to dry habitats, including forests, woodlands, and rock outcrops, often on high-calcium soils associated with calcareous or mafic rocks. Common. Widespread in eastern North America.

Taxonomy: Readily identified by its distinctive flowers and fruits, eastern columbine is the only member of the genus native to the eastern United States.

Ecology: Ruby-throated hummingbirds use their long beaks and tongues to lap up nectar within the red nectar spurs. Several species of long-tongued bumblebees also visit the flowers for nectar (or pollen) and function as pollinators. The tubular nectar spurs narrow just below their tips, where the nectar is secreted, which probably prevents most insects from reaching the nectar. However, some bees and wasps get around this by cutting a hole in the base of the spur to get at the nectar. Although the flowers are well adapted for cross-pollination by hummingbirds, they are fully self-compatible, so abundant seeds can be produced in the absence of pollinators. Self-fertilized seeds, however, give rise to much less vigorous plants than seeds derived from cross-pollination, suggesting that the energy expenditure associated with producing showy, nectar-rich flowers that attract pollinators is a good investment.

Wildlife: Caterpillars of the columbine dusky wing butterfly and the purplish winged skipper feed on the foliage—look for them hiding in rolled up leaves on the plant.

Uses: Easily grown from seed, eastern columbine makes a wonderful addition to wildflower gardens.

Arisaema triphyllum (L.) Schott
JACK-IN-THE-PULPIT
Araceae (Arum family)

Description: An erect perennial 1–2 ft. tall with 1–2 leaves, each divided into 3 leaflets. Tiny male or female flowers at base of fleshy spadix ("Jack") surrounded by a large green or purple-striped tubular structure (called a spathe) that resembles a hooded pulpit. Fruits form a cluster of bright red berries. Flowers Mar.–May; fruits July–Aug.

Habitat/range: Mesic forests, including alluvial forests, acidic cove forests, and river bluff forests. Common. Widespread in eastern North America.

Taxonomy: A genus of about 170 species mostly in Asia but also in eastern North America and Africa. Green dragon (*A. dracontium*) has a single leaf with 7 or more leaflets.

Ecology: Jack-in-the-pulpit is one of a number of plants that can change gender from one year to the next. The gender expressed by an individual is determined by the amount of nutrients accumulated in the corm (an underground food storage organ) during the previous year's growing season. If the corm has accumulated sufficient resources to support the development of fruits, female flowers develop. With moderate resources, male flowers develop (rarely, both male and female flowers develop within a single spathe). If resources are scant (due to shade, removal of leaves by herbivores, or other kinds of stress), no flowers are produced. This pattern is reflected in plant size—female plants are generally largest, male plants are of intermediate size, and nonreproductive plants are smallest. Depending on resource availability, a male plant may change to female; conversely, females may revert to being male (or nonreproductive) in successive years. This flexibility in gender expression benefits the plant in that it matches resource availability with the energy demands of the 2 sexes (fruits require more energy than pollen).

Wildlife: Most herbivores avoid this plant because its tissues contain numerous needle-like calcium oxalate crystals that, if ingested, cause severe burning and swelling. Birds consume the pulp and disperse the seeds in autumn.

Uses: Jack-in-the-pulpit is well suited for woodland gardens but only use nursery-propagated material.

Aruncus dioicus (Walter) Fernald
GOAT'S BEARD
Rosaceae (Rose family)

Description: Perennial herb with multiple smooth, arching stems up to 5 ft. tall arising from a common rootstock. Leaves up to 20 in. long, divided into multiple lance-shaped leaflets from 2 to 6 in. long, with toothed margins. Tiny white flowers in large feathery, terminal inflorescences, male and female flowers on separate plants. Fruit a dry capsule that splits into 3 chambers. Flowers May–June; fruits June–Sept.

Habitat/range: Moist, nutrient-rich forests, seepage slopes, forest edges. Common. Eastern and central United States.

Taxonomy: A genus of 2 species of temperate North America and Europe, 1 of which occurs in our region. Appalachian false goat's beard (*Astilbe biternata*) has similar arching plumes of flowers and occurs in similar habitats but has hairy, rather than smooth, stems with 3-lobed, rather than unlobed, terminal leaflets.

Ecology: This long-lived herbaceous perennial requires relatively cool, moist conditions, as occurs on north-facing slopes. It has a well-developed root system that holds the plant firmly in place on steep slopes and road banks. Under a forest canopy, relatively few plants flower, but along forest margins, road cuts, or on steep, eroding slopes, a fairly high proportion of plants can flower in a given year. Male plants are showier than females since male flowers include 15–20 white stamens, and their inflorescences are more upright and feathery than female inflorescences. With successful fertilization and sufficient resources, female flowers produce attractive reddish seed heads. Once established, plants spread vegetatively from rhizomes, forming dense clusters of shoots.

Wildlife: Goat's beard is the larval host plant of the rare dusky blue butterfly (*Celastrina ebenina*). Female butterflies lay their eggs on newly emerged leaves; upon hatching, the caterpillars feed on soft leaf tissue and occasionally on tiny flower buds.

Uses: Available in the nursery trade, its wispy flowers add interest to moist woodland gardens.

Asarum canadense L.
WILD GINGER
Aristolochiaceae (Birthwort family)

Description: A pair of large heart-shaped deciduous leaves arises from a creeping, horizontal stem. A solitary maroon flower with an urn-shaped calyx about 1 in. long with 3 long-pointed lobes occurs at the base of the plant, often hidden by the leaves. Fruit a fleshy capsule. Flowers Apr.–May.

Habitat/range: Moist, nutrient-rich woods, including cove forests and basic mesic forests. Common in mountains, less common in piedmont. Widespread in eastern North America.

Taxonomy: The genus *Asarum* includes 6 North American and 4 Eurasian species, with only 1 species in the Southeast. *Hexastylis* is similar and is also referred to as wild ginger but is comprised of evergreen, rather than deciduous, species.

Ecology: Flesh-eating flies seeking thawing carcasses of winter-killed insects and other animals are apparently attracted to the urn-shaped, ground hugging, carrion-colored early spring flowers. Upon entering the flower, these flies often feed on pollen, some of which may inadvertently be transferred from one flower to another. Other flower visitors and potential pollinators include fungus gnats that are fooled into thinking their eggs can hatch and their larvae can feed on the flower, but toxins in the tissue kill the gnat larvae as they feed, allowing the plant's seeds to develop unharmed. Seeds mature in early summer and germinate in fall, but only the root emerges from the seed coat. This germination behavior enables the root system to develop before the embryo leaves (cotyledons) emerge the following spring. Plants spread both by seeds and vegetatively by rhizomes, sometimes forming dense carpets of leaves.

Wildlife: Pipevine swallowtail caterpillars feed on the leaves, and rodents consume the seeds. A lipid-rich food body (elaiosome) attached to the seed coat attracts ants. By quickly dispersing ripe seeds away from the parent plant, ants reduce the risk of seed predation by rodents.

Uses: Although not related to the tropical ginger plant (*Zingiber officinale*) from which commercially marketed ginger is obtained, both the leaves and rhizomes of wild ginger (*Asarum*) emit a ginger-like aroma when broken or crushed.

Asclepias syriaca L.
COMMON MILKWEED
Apocynaceae (Dogbane family)

Description: Stout perennial herb with unbranched hairy stems 2–6 ft. tall with opposite leaves up to 8 in. long and 4 in. wide. Fragrant purple to greenish-white flowers in dense umbels, each about 3–4 in. across, in axils of upper leaves and shoot tips. Fruit a spiny, erect follicle 3–5 in. long. Flowers June–Aug.; fruits July–Sept.

Habitat/range: Roadsides, fields, and waste places. Common. Widespread in eastern North America.

Taxonomy: A genus of about 100 species of herbs of North and Central America, including 14 species in the mountains and piedmont. Common milkweed differs from most milkweeds in having spiny, rather than smooth, fruits.

Ecology: Primarily a plant of disturbed sites, it grows best in full to partial sun, rather than under a forest canopy. The fragrant flowers attract a wide variety of long-tongued bees, wasps, skippers, and butterflies seeking nectar. The amount of nectar produced is influenced by soil moisture levels—increasing substantially after rainfall and decreasing during drought. The flowers depend on pollinators (particularly bumblebees) for cross-pollination and subsequent fruit and seed development. The large fruits (follicles) contain hundreds of flat brown seeds, each with a tuft of long, silky hairs that catch the wind. It also spreads by long, creeping rhizomes, forming colonies that range from a few to several hundred stems, making it one of the most commonly seen milkweeds.

Wildlife: Few animals feed on milkweeds because their milky fluid contains high concentrations of cardenolides, a toxic alkaloid. One notable exception is the monarch butterfly, whose larvae (caterpillars) actively feed on milkweeds and in so doing accumulate cardenolides in their body tissue, which protects them (as caterpillars and as adult butterflies) from predators (mostly birds).

Uses: Milkweeds grown in wildflower gardens (as well as those that occur in fields and along roadsides) provide an important larval food source for migrating monarch butterflies—look for the conspicuously yellow, black, and white-striped caterpillars on the leaves.

Asclepias tuberosa L.
BUTTERFLY WEED
Apocynaceae (Dogbane family)

Description: Perennial herb 1–2 ft. tall, erect or ascending, with numerous broadly lanceolate, nearly sessile, alternate leaves. Orange to reddish typical milkweed flowers in terminal or axillary clusters. Seedpods tapered at both ends. Flowers May–Aug.; fruits Aug.–Sept.

Habitat/range: Roadsides, fields, open woods, and forest edges. Common. Widely distributed in eastern and central United States.

Taxonomy: Milkweeds (*Asclepias*) are easy to recognize because of their distinctive flowers and fruits. Among our 14 species, butterfly weed is unique in having brilliant orange-red flowers, clear, rather than milky, sap, and alternate leaves, rather than opposite or whorled leaves.

Ecology: Butterfly weed thrives in full sun and well-drained soils, but fewer plants occur along roadsides and rights-of-way today than in the past, due to more frequent mowing and use of chemical herbicides by maintenance crews. The nectar-rich flower heads attract numerous butterflies, including monarchs, swallowtails, fritillaries, sulphurs, coppers, and hairstreaks, as well as large bees, wasps, and ants. On average, only about 1 percent of flowers set fruit, reflecting both a lack of successful pollination and limited resources for maturing the large, energetically expensive seedpods. Plants spread locally by multiple stems arising from underground tubers. Seeds with feathery, parachute-like structures float on the slightest breeze, thereby facilitating long-distance dispersal. A thick taproot extends deep into the soil, helping the plant withstand prolonged dry periods.

Wildlife: Look closely for crab spiders hidden within the flowers—they ambush pollinators, including large bumblebees.

Uses: Butterfly weed is a striking addition to gardens due to its brightly colored, long-lasting flowers and its ability to tolerate drought.

Asplenium montanum Willd.
MOUNTAIN SPLEENWORT
Aspleniaceae (Spleenwort family)

Description: Numerous bluish green, finely cut evergreen fronds typically form drooping clumps. Elongate spore-producing clusters (sori) occur on underside of fronds. Spores released May–Oct.

Habitat/range: In crevices on moist to dry outcrops of various rock types, including gneiss, schist, quartzite, and sandstone, often associated with spray cliffs. Occasional in mountains and piedmont. Appalachian Mountains from New York south to Georgia.

Taxonomy: A genus of more than 700 species, *Asplenium* is represented on all continents except Antarctica. Hybridization among closely related species is common among some groups of ferns, including members of this genus, which has led to the formation of a number of new species.

Ecology: Most of our ferns are winter deciduous, producing new fronds each spring from long-lived underground stems (rhizomes). Unlike flowering plants, ferns reproduce sexually by spores, rather than by seeds. The dust-sized spores, produced by the millions, are widely dispersed by wind. Most ferns also reproduce vegetatively via horizontal rhizomes, sometimes forming large clones. In contrast, ferns of exposed rock cliffs, such as mountain spleenwort, typically form small, tuft-like plants with short rhizomes. Their limited lateral spread reflects a habitat confined to small crevices surrounded by larger expanses of bare rock unfavorable for growth.

Wildlife: This small, low-growing fern, often clinging to the sides of near-vertical cliffs, is probably inaccessible to most vertebrate herbivores.

Uses: Mountain spleenwort is a difficult fern to grow in gardens.

Asplenium rhizophyllum L.
WALKING FERN
Aspleniaceae (Spleenwort family)

Description: Narrow evergreen fronds 2–12 in. long with a long-pointed tip, occurring in small clusters from a short, scaly rhizome. Spore clusters (sori) scattered in linear masses on underside of fronds. Spores released May–Oct.

Habitat/range: Largely restricted to moist, calcium-rich boulders and rock crevices, including rich cove forests, spray cliffs, and basic mesic forests. Uncommon. Widely distributed in eastern North America.

Taxonomy: A large, nearly cosmopolitan genus of more than 700 species, with centers of diversity in the Appalachians, Central American mountains, Andes, and Himalayas. This very distinctive fern is easily identified.

Ecology: Walking fern grows on moist, shaded, usually moss-covered boulders and ledges, primarily on limestone and other basic rocks, but also occasionally on sandstone or other acidic rocks, and rarely on organic substrates (e.g., tree trunks). This species "walks" with its long, tapering leaf tips, arching downward, forming new "fernlets" where the tips contact the surface. In this way, large colonies sometimes carpet the surface of mossy boulders and ledges. Mature plants broadcast millions of wind-dispersed spores across the landscape, few of which land in favorable microsites for establishment and growth. Naturally occurring hybrids between walking fern and other species of *Asplenium* have resulted in the formation of new species, some fertile and others sterile. For example, the lobed spleenwort (*A. pinnatifidum*), a fertile species, is a hybrid between walking fern and mountain spleenwort (*A. montanum*). In contrast, hybridization between walking fern and ebony spleenwort (*A. platyneuron*) formed Scot's spleenwort (*A. ebenoides*), a sterile hybrid. Threats to walking fern include the removal of forest canopy (as partial shade is needed to maintain a moist microhabitat), people climbing over rock boulders, and summer drought.

Athyrium asplenioides (Michx.) A. A. Eaton
SOUTHERN LADY FERN
Woodsiaceae (Lady fern family)

Description: Upright deciduous fern with large (up to 3 ft.) lanceolate to triangular arching fronds in clusters from a thick rhizome, with highly dissected feather-like fronds. Pinnae (leaflets) up to 6 in. long and 1 in. wide, alternate, with narrow, pointed tips. Numerous dark brown, crescent-shaped spore clusters (sori) develop under fertile leaflets in 2 rows between the midvein and margin, the tiny wind-dispersed spores released May–Sept.

Habitat/range: Moist to wet forests, thickets, roadside banks, and along streams, from near sea level to over 6,000 ft. Common. Widely distributed in eastern United States.

Taxonomy: Species in the genus *Athyrium* and *Dryopteris* can be difficult to distinguish in the absence of spore-bearing structures. To tell them apart, break off a leaf and count the number of vascular bundles (which appear as thread-like strands)—*Dryopteris* has 5, *Athyrium* has 2.

Ecology: Southern lady fern tolerates a broad range of ecological conditions, as indicated by its wide elevational range. A good colonizing species, it grows in cracks in rocks and in crevices between rocks in generally moist soil. It reproduces sexually by spores and spreads vegetatively by rhizomes. Mating system studies indicate that cross-fertilization is the norm and that plants resulting from cross-fertilization grow more vigorously and have higher survival rates than plants resulting from self-fertilization.

Wildlife: The fairly large clustered fronds provide cover for small mammals, amphibians, and reptiles. Plants contain filicic acid, a toxin suspected to be harmful to some livestock, which also deters browsing by native herbivores. Earthworms facilitate local dispersal as viable spores pass through their guts.

Uses: Southern lady fern is an attractive plant in gardens with rich, moist soils.

Synonym: Athyrium filix-femina (L.) ssp. *asplenioides* (Michx.) Hulten

Aureolaria laevigata (Raf.) Raf.
APPALACHIAN OAK LEACH
Orobanchaceae (Broomrape family)

Description: Herbaceous perennial 2–5 ft. tall, generally with smooth green stems and narrowly lanceolate, 2–4 in. long, mostly unlobed leaves. Yellow trumpet-shaped flowers to 1 ½ in. long, the 5 corolla lobes shorter than the tube. Fruit a smooth capsule. Flowers Aug.–Sept.; fruits Sept.–Oct.

Habitat/range: In and along margins of oak forests and woodlands. Oak-hickory forests, chestnut oak forests, and pine-oak-heath. Common in mountains, uncommon in piedmont. From Pennsylvania south to Georgia.

Taxonomy: Aureolaria is a genus of 10 species of hemiparasitic herbs of eastern North America and Mexico, including 6 species in the mountains and piedmont. Yellow false foxglove (*A. flava*) is similar but has waxy, often purplish stems and lower leaves that are usually deeply lobed. Downy oak leach (*A. virginica*) has hairy stems and flowers in the spring, rather than in late summer and fall.

Ecology: There are more than 4,000 species of parasitic flowering plants in 22 families and 270 different plant genera. Some are holoparasites—plants that lack chlorophyll and derive all of their resources from their host; others are hemiparasites—plants that have chlorophyll and derive only some of their resources from their hosts. And, while some parasitic plants are shoot parasites, others are root parasites. The Appalachian oak leach is a hemiparasite on the roots of trees, particularly oaks. A characteristic feature of all parasitic plants is the haustorium, a unique organ that attaches to the host, establishing a xylem/phloem bridge between the parasite and its host that results in the unidirectional flow of resources to the parasite. Hemiparasites are usually xylem feeders (obtaining water and minerals), whereas holoparasites generally tap into the phloem of their host plant for sugars, amino acids, and water. The famous Harvard botanist and early southern Appalachian plant explorer Asa Gray first described root parasitism in the genus *Aureolaria* more than a century ago.

Wildlife: Bumblebees turn upside down as they visit and pollinate the large yellow flowers. Because the plant is self-sterile, bees must cross-pollinate the flowers for seeds to mature.

Avenella flexuosa (L.) Drejer
WAVY HAIRGRASS
Poaceae (Grass family)

Description: Perennial grass that forms a tight clump of narrow, wiry foliage with pale to reddish flowering stems. Loose, open inflorescences with spikelets at tips of long, flexible branches. Spikelets contain 2 fertile flowers, each with a lemma (outer bract) that has a striking bent awn. Flowers Apr.–June.

Habitat/range: Grassy balds, high-elevation rock outcrops, and woodlands. Common in mountains, uncommon in piedmont. Eastern North America and widely disjunct in other parts of world.

Taxonomy: This is the only species in the genus. Tufted hairgrass (*Deschampsia cespitosa*) is similar but is a less common and somewhat taller grass restricted to serpentine barrens and outcrops.

Ecology: Like all plants, grasses grow from regions of actively dividing undifferentiated cells called meristems. The meristems of grasses are generally located near ground level, out of the way of grazing animals' teeth. This enables grasses to rapidly regrow tissues lost to grazers (or mowing). Grasses also tend to have thick fibrous roots, which make up most of the plant's total weight. These roots not only absorb water; they store nutrients that are used for various purposes, including leaf replacement following grazing. These features enable most grasses to tolerate unusually high levels of grazing.

Uses: Wavy hairgrass is relatively easy to grow and makes a nice accent plant in gardens.

Synonym: Deschampsia flexuosa (L.) Trin

Botrypus virginianus (L.) Holub
RATTLESNAKE FERN
Ophioglossaceae (Adder's tongue family)

Description: Produces 2 types of fronds—the sterile frond triangular, like a small bracken fern, the fertile frond upright, composed of densely clustered bright yellow spore cases (sporangia) on branching segments that resemble tiny grapes. Spores released Apr.–June.

Habitat/range: Occurs in fairly dry, moist, or wet deciduous forests, including river bluff forests, cove forests, and oak-hickory forests. Widespread in North, Central, and South America, Europe, and Asia.

Taxonomy: The one species in this genus is closely related to ferns in the genus *Botrychium*. The clustered sporangia resemble a snake's rattle, hence the common name "rattlesnake fern."

Ecology: Tiny wind-blown spores facilitate long-distance dispersal, and partially explain this fern's wide distribution across Europe, Asia, and the Americas. Following dispersal, the spores settle into the soil, germinate, and give rise to subterranean gametophytes that lack chlorophyll. Gametophytes obtain carbohydrates, water, and minerals from nearby photosynthetic plants through a mycorrhizal-like association with a fungus. After eggs and sperm are produced, and following fertilization, a belowground juvenile sporophyte develops that remains underground for several years before emerging as an adult fern. Adult plants are green and photosynthetic but, since they lack root hairs, depend on the fungal associate for water and minerals. Protected from drought, fires, and other kinds of disturbance, the underground gametophytes and juvenile sporophytes function as a reserve capable of regenerating populations, much the way a soil seed bank functions in flowering plants.

Synonym: Botrychium virginianum (L.) Sw.

Campanulastrum americanum (L.) Small
TALL BELLFLOWER
Campanulaceae (Bellflower family)

Description: An erect annual or biennial 2–6 ft. tall. Alternate, lanceolate leaves with toothed margins terminate in a loose spike of pale blue flowers with a flat (rather than bell-shaped) corolla and a long, curved style. Fruit a capsule with numerous small seeds. Flowers late June–frost; fruits Aug.–Oct.

Habitat/range: Moist forests and streambanks, especially over mafic or calcareous rocks. Rich cove forests, rocky streamsides, and basic mesic forests. Common in mountains, uncommon in piedmont. Widely distributed in eastern North America.

Taxonomy: The genus consists of a single species. In spite of its common name, tall bellflower doesn't have a bell-shaped flower, as do species in the closely related genus *Campanula*.

Ecology: Tall bellflower is unusual because the timing of germination determines its life history pattern. Seeds that germinate in autumn overwinter as vegetative rosettes and flower, set seed, and die the following summer. These plants function as winter annuals because the vernalization requirement (the cold period necessary to induce flowering) is met during the winter months. Seeds that germinate in spring don't flower their first summer after germination because the vegetative plants haven't been vernalized. Instead, they complete a summer growing season prior to vernalization in winter, and then flower, set seed, and die in their second summer, thereby exhibiting a biennial life cycle. The flowers are frequently visited and efficiently pollinated by bumblebees, which typically land on the elongated style and use it as a walkway to reach the nectar that is secreted at the top of the ovary. Studies indicate that most tall bellflower seeds result from cross-pollination, rather than self-pollination, and that outcrossed seeds give rise to more vigorous offspring than those derived from self-fertilized seeds.

Wildlife: White-tailed deer nibble on the foliage.

Uses: Tall bellflower is an attractive plant in woodland gardens that persists by self-seeding.

Synonym: *Campanula americana* L.

Carex pensylvanica Lam.
PENNSYLVANIA SEDGE
Cyperaceae (Sedge family)

Description: A low-growing, grass-like sedge recognizable by its orderly, drooping stems with 2–4 long, narrow leaves. Small, inconspicuous flowers lacking petals and sepals occur in spikes. Fruit a nutlet. Flowers Apr.–June; fruits May–July.

Habitat/range: Dry to moist, well-drained soils, northern hardwood forests, red oak forests, grassy balds, rock outcrops, and forest edges. Common. Widely distributed in eastern North America.

Taxonomy: Almost worldwide in distribution, the genus *Carex* consists of approximately 2,000 species, including 122 species in the Southeast, making it the largest genus of vascular plants in the region.

Ecology: Sedges generally occur in moist to wet habitats in a wide range of environments from the tropics to the arctic. Sedges often form a major component of the forest floor in the deciduous forests of eastern North America. All species of *Carex* are perennial and have rhizomes (underground stems), some producing large clones, others forming tufts, clumps, or tussocks of various sizes. Nearly all sedges have a light requirement for germination and a persistent soil seed bank. All are wind-pollinated and some have ant-dispersed seeds. On grassy balds and in forest understories, Pennsylvania sedge forms dense patches that can slow tree and shrub establishment and thereby delay successional change. It spreads vegetatively, by long rhizomes that colonize nearby open areas and by short rhizomes that form tufts or mats. Regeneration by seed is thought to be rare. Light ground fires consume the shoots, but Pennsylvania sedge readily resprouts from underground stems. Hot fires, however, can destroy the shallow rhizomes and kill the plant.

Uses: Pennsylvania sedge is sometimes planted as a "no mow" lawn.

Carex torta F. Boott
TWISTED SEDGE
Cyperaceae (Sedge family)

Description: Clump-forming perennial herb with flat, grass-like leaves, basal sheath reddish brown. Separate male and female flowers on same plant, flowers lacking petals and sepals. Fruit a nutlet enclosed within a minute sac (perigynium). Flowers Apr.–May; fruits June.

Habitat/range: Rocky streambeds. Common. Widespread in eastern North America.

Taxonomy: Sedges are grass-like perennial herbs with inconspicuous wind-pollinated flowers. Unlike grasses, most sedges have stems that are triangular in cross-section ("sedges have edges, grasses are round") and lack nodes or joints.

Ecology: Twisted sedge is a dominant species on sand, gravel, and on rock bars in rivers and large streams in the southern Appalachians. Massive periodic floods transport and deposit large numbers of cobbles, stones, and boulders. Twisted sedge is one of the first colonizers of recently deposited rock substrates, forming large clumps (tussocks) with fibrous roots and rhizomes that trap soil and build up the substrate, thereby providing suitable habitat for later colonizing species. Species such as twisted sedge that establish and persist in flood-prone streambeds are typically tough-rooted perennials that can endure frequent inundation and flood scouring.

Wildlife: Despite their abundance, sedges generally make up a minor part of the diet of mammalian herbivores such as white-tailed deer and beavers. Numerous species of insects, however, feed on sedges, including a number of moth caterpillars. Birds such as grouse and wild turkeys forage on sedges both for their seeds and for insects on their leaves.

Uses: Sedges are sometimes used as ornamentals.

Castilleja coccinea (L.) Spreng.
INDIAN PAINTBRUSH
Orobanchaceae (Broomrape family)

Description: Annual or biennial hemiparasite up to 2 ft. tall, with a usually solitary, unbranched hairy stem arising from a rosette of basal leaves. Basal leaves oblong and mostly entire, stem leaves often deeply and irregularly lobed. Greenish yellow flowers in terminal spikes subtended by showy scarlet to crimson leaf-like bracts. Fruit an elliptic capsule with numerous tiny seeds. Flowers Apr.–May and sporadically in fall.

Habitat/range: Grows in a variety of habitats, including moist meadows, forest edges, and rock outcrops, usually over mafic rock. Uncommon. Widely distributed in eastern North America.

Taxonomy: A genus of 200 species of partially parasitic herbs primarily of western North America, this is the only species in our region.

Ecology: The vibrant colors that characterize this plant come not from its small greenish yellowish flowers, but from the brightly tipped bracts (modified leaves) associated with the flowers. The reddish bracts play an important role in attracting ruby-throated hummingbirds, the species' primary pollinator. Because hummingbirds are long-distance flyers, they can effectively transfer pollen from one population to another as they forage for nectar, which particularly benefits species such as Indian paintbrush, whose populations are typically small and widely scattered. While it produces its own food through photosynthesis, studies indicate that up to a 40-fold increase in growth occurs when nutrients are obtained from tapping into the roots of a host plant. A poor competitor, Indian paintbrush grows best in relatively open areas with high light, such as in shallow soils associated with rock outcrops.

Wildlife: Hummingbirds actively visit and pollinate the various species of paintbrush in the Americas.

Uses: Indian paintbrush is easily grown from seed in sunny gardens.

Caulophyllum thalictroides (L.) Michx.
BLUE COHOSH
Berberidaceae (Barberry family)

Description: Smooth, erect perennial herb up to 3 ft. tall, younger plants with bluish white cast. Large compound leaf on upper stem with a long stalk and many leaflets 2–3 in. long, irregularly lobed above middle; 1 (rarely 2) similar but smaller compound leaf just below the inflorescence. From 1 to 3 clusters of yellow-green to purple-green flowers terminate the stem. Blue berry-like seeds. Flowers Apr.–May; fruits July–Aug.

Habitat/range: Rich moist woods, often on calcium-rich soil. Cove forests, northern hardwood forests, and basic mesic forests. Common in mountains, rare in piedmont. Widely distributed in eastern North America.

Taxonomy: The genus *Caulophyllum* includes just 2 species, 1 in eastern North America, 1 in eastern Asia.

Ecology: New shoots emerge from a winter-dormant rhizome in early spring and die back from late summer to fall. The spring-opening flowers have 6 petal-like sepals and 6 smaller, highly modified petals. The petals form hood-like structures containing large nectar-secreting glands that attract potential pollinators, mainly flies and occasionally bees. If insects don't pollinate the flowers, self-pollination can occur, an important backup given sporadic insect visitation in the often cool, wet days of early spring. The bluish tinge of the leaves and the color of the seeds give blue cohosh its common name. The developing seeds are highly unusual in that they rupture their ovaries soon after fertilization, ripening into fully exposed blue seeds in late summer that resemble berry-like fruits. The buoyant seeds are dispersed by water as well as by birds and small mammals that perhaps mistake the blue seeds for fleshy berries.

Uses: The Cherokee used blue cohosh to treat various ailments, including fever, rheumatism, and toothache, and also used the plant to ease the pain of childbirth. Today, blue cohosh is used in homeopathic medicines and is sometimes grown in woodland gardens. Alkaloids within the seeds and roots are poisonous to humans.

Chamaelirium luteum (L.) A. Gray
FAIRYWAND, DEVIL'S BIT
Melanthiaceae (Bunchflower family)

Description: Perennial herb with a basal rosette of leaves and a single flowering stalk with either male or female flowers. Large spoon-shaped leaves at base of plant, stem leaves much smaller, reduced upward. Numerous small white flowers in a 3–9 in. long spike, male flowers turn yellowish as pollen matures. Fruit a 3-celled capsule. Flowers Mar.–May; fruits Sept.–Nov.

Habitat/range: Variety of upland and lowland forests, including river bluff forests, oak-hickory forests, cove forests, and alluvial forests. Common. Widespread in eastern North America.

Taxonomy: This is the only species in the genus. The common name "fairywand" reflects the dense, elongated cluster of small white flowers on a wand-like stalk.

Ecology: Fairywand flowers best in partially open habitats, but vegetative plants can persist for years in more shaded conditions. The flowering stalks of male plants wither and disappear shortly after flowering; in contrast, the stalks of female plants persist for months as the fruits mature. Successful fertilization and subsequent fruit and seed set depends on insects moving pollen from male to female plants. Due to the greater resource depletion associated with maturing fruits, female plants experience higher mortality rates than males. As a result, there are more male than female plants in most populations.

Wildlife: White-tailed deer browse the foliage.

Uses: An interesting addition to woodland gardens, fairywand can be purchased from a number of native plant nurseries. Native Americans used it to treat stomach ailments and indigestion.

Chasmanthium latifolium (Michx.) Yates
RIVER OATS
Poaceae (Grass family)

Description: A perennial clump-forming grass 2–5 ft. tall with lanceolate leaves 4–8 in. long and nodding clusters of flattened, oat-like seedheads, initially green, becoming tan or bronze in autumn. Flowers June–Oct.

Habitat/range: Moist forests, riverbanks, streambanks, along ditches, seepages, and glades, over mafic or calcareous rock. Common in piedmont, uncommon in mountains. Widespread in eastern and central United States.

Taxonomy: River oats is readily distinguished from the 4 other species in the genus by its nodding fruits. A closely related species, sea oats (*Uniola paniculata*) commonly occurs on coastal sand dunes.

Ecology: River oats grows best on nutrient-rich, moist (but not waterlogged) soils in partial to full sunlight. Individual plants form clumps 2–5 ft. tall with short, stout rhizomes that limit lateral spread. The wind-pollinated flowers hang gracefully on thread-like pedicels in open, nodding clusters above the leaves. Abundant wind-dispersed seeds are produced in late autumn. Once established, plants are quite drought tolerant.

Wildlife: Like tiny shards of glass, its silica-rich leaves deter most herbivores. Various birds consume the seeds.

Uses: Easily grown from seeds or rhizome cuttings, river oats makes an attractive landscape plant (but reseeds vigorously) and is used in stream restoration projects. Dried seed heads are used in floral arrangements.

Synonym: Uniola latifolia Michx.

Chelone glabra L.
WHITE TURTLEHEAD
Plantaginaceae (Plantain family)

Description: Smooth, perennial herb with several stems from a single root system, 20–36 in. tall. Opposite, relatively narrow lanceolate leaves, 4–6 in. long, short-stalked or sessile. Flowers white, often tinged with pink or purple at tip, in a dense terminal spike. Fruit a broadly ovoid capsule. Flowers Aug.–Oct.; fruits Sept.–Nov.

Habitat/range: Moist woods, seeps, and along streams, including rocky streamsides and mountain bogs. Common. Widespread in eastern North America south to Georgia.

Taxonomy: All 4 species in the genus *Chelone* occur in the mountains and piedmont. The 2-lipped corolla resembles a turtle's head, hence the common name.

Ecology: Turtleheads contain toxins called iridoid glycosides that impart a bitter taste to the plant, making it unpalatable to all but a few herbivores. Caterpillars of the checkerspot butterfly and the caterpillar-like larvae of sawflies circumvent the plant toxin by sequestering it in their body tissues, thereby becoming unpalatable to potential predators. Birds quickly learn to avoid the toxic caterpillars/larvae, which are conspicuously colored and feed non-evasively on the upper surfaces of leaves. Adult checkerspot butterflies are protected from predators in the same way as the caterpillars. The adult butterflies are conspicuously colored, slow flying, and sluggish, whereas palatable butterfly species typically fly fast and erratically to reduce predation risk. While checkerspot butterflies and sawflies gain nourishment and protection against predators from their host plant, the cost to the plant is high as individuals are often defoliated and significantly fewer fruits and seeds are produced.

Wildlife: Bumblebees squeeze between the closed lips and crawl down the tube to access nectar at the base of the flowers. In so doing, their dorsal surface gets dusted with pollen, which may be deposited onto the stigmas of subsequently visited flowers.

Uses: Turtleheads make a nice addition to pond and bog gardens as they have showy flowers and tolerate water-saturated soils.

Chelone lyonii Pursh
PINK TURTLEHEAD
Plantaginaceae (Plantain family)

Description: Perennial herb from 15 to 40 in tall with opposite, 3–5 in. long, ovate to lanceolate leaves on well-developed leaf stalks. Pink to purple 2-lipped flowers, the lower lip with a yellow beard, in short terminal spikes. Fruit a broadly ovate capsule. Flowers July–Sept.; fruits Oct.

Habitat/range: Spruce-fir forests, balds, cove forests, and streamsides. Locally common at high elevations. A southern Blue Ridge endemic found in North Carolina, South Carolina, and Tennessee. Escaped from cultivation in the northeastern United States.

Taxonomy: White turtlehead (*C. glabra*) is similar but has white flowers and generally occurs at lower elevations.

Ecology: Turtleheads usually grow in wet areas subject to periodic flooding. Plants are smaller, with fewer leaves and flowers in dry years. Individuals reproduce sexually by seed and spread vegetatively by rhizomes. As a bumblebee (the main pollinator) pushes into the 2-lipped flower, its head and thorax get dusted with pollen from the 4 fertile stamens. At the next flower it visits, the bee may inadvertently brush pollen from its body surface onto a receptive stigma, thereby pollinating the flower.

Wildlife: Leaf-feeding herbivores sometimes completely defoliate plants, and insects that specialize on turtleheads consume developing seeds within the capsules.

Uses: The large, showy flowers and perennial habit make turtleheads an attractive garden plant in cool climates.

Chimaphila maculata (L.) Pursh
PIPSISSEWA, STRIPED WINTERGREEN
Ericaceae (Heath family)

Description: A low-growing evergreen perennial with upright branches arising from creeping underground stems (rhizomes). Thick lance-shaped leaves with broad whitish green stripes along the veins, mostly crowded near stem tip. Nodding white to pink waxy flowers in loose clusters well above the leaves. Fruit a flattened spherical capsule. Flowers May–June; fruits July–Oct.

Habitat/range: Forests and woodlands mostly on dry, acidic soils, including pine-oak-heath, oak-hickory forests, chestnut oak forests, river bluff forests. Common. Widespread in eastern United States.

Taxonomy: Of the 2 species of *Chimaphila* in our region, pipsissewa (*C. maculata*) is the more common; its leaves have whitish green stripes along the major veins, whereas prince's pine (*C. umbellata*) has solid green leaves throughout.

Ecology: A common plant of the forest floor, pipsissewa grows and flowers in heavy shade under deciduous forests as well as under pines and other conifers. Its leathery leaves are replaced by a fresh set of leaves each spring. The nodding, mildly fragrant flowers depend on insects (mainly bumblebees) for successful pollination and subsequent fruit set. A nectar-secreting disc occurs at the base of the flower, and a single pistil with a large, round, sticky green stigma is located in the center of the flower. The large stigma facilitates pollination success by increasing the likelihood of flower-visiting insects brushing against it as they forage for nectar or pollen, and the stamen's sticky aspect helps pollen grains adhere to its surface. Following fertilization, the nodding flowers reflex upward 180 degrees, developing erect capsules that eventually split open and release numerous tiny seeds that are dispersed by gravity and wind. In addition to spreading by seeds, it spreads locally by creeping rhizomes, often forming small colonies.

Uses: The name pipsissewa comes from the Native American word "pipsiskeweu," which means "breaks into small pieces," a reference to the plant's use as a treatment for kidney stones.

Cladina rangiferina (L.) Nyl.
GRAY REINDEER LICHEN
Cladoniaceae (Cladonia family)

Description: Densely branched clump or mat-forming ground lichen with numerous short white to silver-gray branchlets that become greenish when wet. Small, roundish, spore-producing structures (apothecia) at branch tips.

Habitat/range: On thin soils over rock or in sandy places, usually in full sun. Granite outcrops. Common. Widely distributed in North America.

Taxonomy: The genus *Cladina* includes 14 species in North America. The gray color typically associated with *C. rangiferina* is unusual since most *Cladina* are greenish or yellow-green, but the color distinction can be difficult to see as the gray species become greener when wet.

Ecology: Lichens are unusual because they appear to be a discrete organism but are actually a composite of 2 very different kinds of organisms—a fungus and a green alga, or cyanobacteria. The close association between these 2 organisms is considered to be mutually beneficial as the fungus provides protection, helps retain moisture, and accumulates mineral nutrients; in turn, some of the carbohydrates produced by the alga through photosynthesis are used by the fungus. Because lichens are able to take up moisture directly from the air, the underlying soil isn't as important a source of moisture as it is to green plants. As a result, lichens can colonize and become dominant on bare rock and other places where there is too little soil to support larger plants. Lichens typically grow very slowly but are potentially long-lived, with some individuals estimated to be over 4,000 years old.

Wildlife: Lichens are an important winter food for caribou and reindeer in more northerly latitudes. Various invertebrates (including spiders and grasshoppers) mimic color patterns of lichens, making it difficult for predators such as birds to find them.

Uses: Lichens are indicators of air quality as they are particularly sensitive to air pollutants such as sulfur dioxide.

Claytonia caroliniana Michx.
CAROLINA SPRING BEAUTY
Portulacaceae (Purslane family)

Description: A short succulent perennial arising from a corm in early spring. A single pair of opposite leaves with distinct petioles occurs below a loose terminal raceme of showy white or pinkish flowers with 5 pink-veined petals. Fruit an ovoid capsule with shiny black seeds. Flowers Mar.–May.

Habitat/range: Moist forests at moderate to high elevations. Northern hardwood forests and rich cove forests. Common. A northern species extending south in the Appalachian Mountains to Georgia.

Taxonomy: A genus of 30 species of perennial herbs of North America and eastern Asia, including 2 in the Southeast. Spring beauty (*C. virginica*) has similar flowers but much narrower leaves lacking a distinct petiole. The 2 species occur in similar habitats, but spring beauty is less common at higher elevations. Where the 2 species occur together, hybrid individuals can occur.

Ecology: As early spring sun warms the leaf litter, overwintering corms initiate growth. Each corm produces several, or even many, flowering stems, each of which can produce up to a dozen flowers. Although the individual flowers are small, their massed display can be spectacular. The flowers open only in sunny conditions, closing at night and under cloudy skies. On warm, sunny days, the flowers open for about 4–5 hours from midmorning to early afternoon. The flowers depend on pollinators (mainly small bees and flies) for successful fruit production. Low temperatures limit pollinator availability and subsequent seed set early in the growing season, whereas resource availability limits seed set later in the growing season as increased shade decreases photosynthesis. As a result, flowers that open early or late in the growing season tend to produce fewer seeds than flowers that open midseason.

Wildlife: Ants disperse the seeds and mammals ranging from mice to black bears dig up and consume the corms.

Uses: The starchy corms (up to 1 in. in diameter) were a favorite food of Native Americans. Spring beauty's dainty flowers add spring color to woodland wildflower gardens.

Claytonia virginica L.
SPRING BEAUTY
Portulacaceae (Purslane family)

Description: Low-growing herbaceous perennial from a bulb-like corm with a single pair of opposite, narrow grass-like leaves midway up a wiry stem. Showy, one-half in. wide white or pink flowers lined with dark pink veins. Fruit a small capsule. Flowers Feb.–early Apr.; fruits Mar.–Apr.

Habitat/range: Rich, moist woods and clearings. Cove forests, floodplain forests, and basic-mesic forests. Common. Widespread in eastern North America.

Taxonomy: Carolina spring beauty (*C. caroliniana*) occurs in similar habitats but has broader leaves and is more common at higher elevations than *C. virginica*.

Ecology: Spring beauty, like other spring ephemerals, emerges in early spring while the canopy is still leafless. Amazingly, it manufactures its entire year's food supply (through photosynthesis), produces flowers, and matures seeds all within a few short weeks. By the time the forest floor is shaded by canopy foliage, the aboveground parts have withered and died. During the remaining 45–48 weeks of the year, only the underground food-storage organ persists. The initiation of growth and flowering in spring ephemerals depends on temperature, as does the emergence of their insect pollinators. Spring beauty's flowers open from mid-morning until late afternoon on warm, sunny days, often producing a spectacular massed display. The conspicuous pink veins guide small bees and flies to the nectaries at the base of each petal, increasing the likelihood of successful pollination. Unpollinated flowers can persist up to 6 days before withering, an adaptive trait in an environment where low spring temperatures frequently limit pollinator activity. Fruits ripen quickly, explosively dispersing the shiny black seeds. Ants attracted to the lipid-rich food body (the elaiosome) on the outer seed coat further disperse the seeds.

Wildlife: The marble-sized corms are dug up and eaten by chipmunks, mice, wild hogs, and black bears. Night-foraging slugs feed on the leaves.

Uses: Native Americans ate spring beauty's starchy corms. The plant is attractive in gardens.

Clematis viorna L.
LEATHER FLOWER
Ranunculaceae (Buttercup family)

Description: Climbing perennial vine with soft reddish brown stems that die back in winter. Opposite, pinnately compound leaves with 3–7 leaflets. Urn-shaped red-to-purple flowers with fused, fleshy, petal-like sepals up to 1 in. long, with recurved tips. Fruit a round cluster of achenes with long, plumose, curved tails. Flowers May–Sept.; fruits Aug.–Nov.

Habitat/range: Mesic forests, woodlands, and thickets, often on basic or limestone soil. Common in mountains and piedmont. Widespread in eastern and central United States.

Taxonomy: The genus *Clematis* is widely distributed in Eurasia, North and South America, and Africa. There are about 300 species of shrubs, vines, and herbaceous plants in the genus, including 18 species in the mountains and piedmont.

Ecology: Clematis vines climb with tendrils. Tendrils are slender, wiry, and sensitive to touch, coiling tightly around any slender support they contact. In *Clematis*, the stalks of leaves and leaflets have been modified to function as tendrils. Tendrils react to the slightest touch; even contact with a spider web will trigger a coiling growth response. While the mechanism isn't fully understood, it is clear that tendril cells on the inside of the tendril contract in response to direct contact, while those on the outer side of the tendril expand, causing a coiling response. The coiled tendril and its support are normally flexible enough to allow movement during windy conditions without breaking the connection. Tendril climbers require slimmer supports than twining vines (such as pipevine, wisteria, and kudzu) as twiners can wrap around larger objects such as tree trunks. Tendril climbers such as *Clematis*, greenbriers (*Smilax*), and wild grape (*Vitis*) often occur in forest openings or on woodland borders where slender supports are more readily available.

Uses: Leather flower is easily grown from seed and can be used as a groundcover or climbing vine in the garden. All species and parts of *Clematis* are poisonous if eaten.

Clintonia borealis (Aiton) Raf.
BLUEBEAD LILY
Liliaceae (Lily family)

Description: Perennial herb with 2–5 (usually 3) dark green basal leaves, 4–16 in. long, oblong to elliptic with a strongly depressed midvein. Nodding greenish yellow flowers in a terminal raceme of 3–8 flowers on a leafless stalk. Fruit a bright blue ovoid berry. Flowers May–June; fruits Aug.–Sept.

Habitat/range: Rich, moist woods. Mainly spruce-fir forests and northern hardwood forests, less common in red oak forests. Common. Widespread species in northeastern North America, extending south in Appalachian Mountains to Georgia.

Taxonomy: The genus *Clintonia* comprises 5 species (2 in eastern North America, 2 in western North America, and 1 in eastern Asia).

Ecology: A winter deciduous herb, the vegetative rosettes of bluebead lily die back in autumn and are replaced by new rosettes the following spring. By utilizing stored carbohydrates in overwintering rhizomes, newly emerged rosettes expand quickly, reaching full size in early spring. The early emergence and rapid development of rosettes allow the plant to take advantage of the high light levels present prior to the canopy leafing out. Individuals spread vegetatively by underground runners in such a way that a single plant comprises multiple vegetative rosettes that form a clone. If a rosette is damaged (e.g., by grazers) or is situated in an unfavorable microsite, nutrients can be shunted to it from sister rosettes, thereby enhancing survivorship among rosettes. Seedlings grow slowly and don't flower or spread vegetatively until they are at least 10 years old.

Wildlife: Overbrowsing by deer markedly decreases bluebead lily's populations.

Uses: A compound produced by the roots of bluebead lily with estrogenic and anti-inflammatory properties is being investigated for potential medicinal use. The bright blue berries are mildly poisonous to humans.

Clintonia umbellulata (Michx.) Morong
SPECKLED WOOD LILY
Liliaceae (Lily family)

Description: Perennial herb with 2–5 (usually 3) basal leaves from 6 to 12 in. long, elliptic to ovate with long hairs on leaf margins. Flowers with similar petals and sepals (3 each), white with purple and green speckles, in a terminal umbel of erect flowers at the end of a leafless stalk 8–15 in. tall. Fruits round, dark blue-black berries. Flowers May–June; fruits Aug.–Oct.

Habitat/range: Mesic to dry ridges and slopes, red oak forests, northern hardwood forests, and cove forests. Common in mountains. Appalachian Mountains from New York south to Georgia.

Taxonomy: The 2 species of *Clintonia* in our region can be distinguished by the color of their flowers and fruits: speckled wood lily has white flowers and dark blue-black berries while bluebead lily (*C. borealis*) has yellow flowers and bright blue berries. When not in flower or fruit, look for long hairs on the leaf margins: only speckled wood lily has such hairs. Bluebead lily generally occurs at higher elevations, but the 2 species occasionally occur together.

Ecology: The genus *Clintonia* is thought to have originated in eastern Asia and later migrated to North America across the Bering land bridge that joined present-day Alaska and eastern Siberia. Roughly 1,000 miles across, the land bridge became available several times over the last 70,000 years due to the rise and fall of global sea levels during the Pleistocene ice ages. The Bering land bridge is of immense biological significance, not only because humans from Asia migrated across this bridge to colonize the Americas, but also because many plant and animal species that evolved in Asia migrated across it to reach North America.

Wildlife: Various birds and small mammals seek out speckled wood lily's fruits and disperse the seeds.

Uses: Hunters rubbed the roots of speckled wood lily on their traps as the odor was thought to attract bears.

Commelina erecta L.
ERECT DAYFLOWER
Commelinaceae (Spiderwort family)

Description: Perennial herb with slender, branching stems from 6 to 24 in. tall with alternate, linear to lanceolate leaves with parallel veins and basal sheaths; the stems frequently weaken and recline with age. Showy flowers on slender stalks from a folded bract (spathe) consist of 2 pale blue (rarely pink) upper petals up to 1 in. long, and a much smaller, white lower petal. Fruit a capsule. Flowers June–Oct.

Habitat/range: Forest openings and woodlands, especially on deeper soils of granite outcrops. Common in piedmont, uncommon in mountains. Eastern and central United States.

Taxonomy: A genus of 170 species with a nearly worldwide distribution. The 4 species in the mountains and piedmont include 2 native species (*C. erecta* and *C. virginica*) and 2 introduced species (*C. communis* and *C. diffusa*).

Ecology: Although the flowering season is long, lasting from June through October, individual flowers are short-lived, opening at sunrise and closing by midday, never to open again, hence the name "dayflower." At first glance, the flowers appear to have just 2 petals; however, a much smaller petal is barely visible below the main part of the flower. Each flower has in its center several "feeding anthers" whose pollen functions as the primary pollinator attractant (the flowers lack nectar), and 2 "pollinating anthers" whose pollen is more likely to be inadvertently deposited on stigmas by pollen-foraging bees. Appropriately, the "feeding anthers" are a conspicuous bright yellow color, whereas the 2 blue "pollinating anthers" are relatively inconspicuous and less likely to be visited. If insect pollination fails to occur, the stigma curls, contacting 1 or more of the anthers as the flower closes, resulting in self-pollination.

Wildlife: Meloid beetles (also called blister beetles, because they produce a secretion that blisters the skin) feed on pollen and other parts of the flower. Because they mate within the inflorescence, their larvae can heavily infest the flowers by midsummer.

Uses: Dayflowers are used to make a tea to treat sore throats, colds, and urinary infections.

Conopholis americana (L.) Wallr.
SQUAWROOT, CANCER ROOT
Orobanchaceae (Broomrape family)

Description: Yellowish brown parasite on oak roots with short unbranched stems that resemble small ears of corn popping up through the leaf litter. Stems usually clumped and covered with numerous brown, overlapping scale-like leaves lacking chlorophyll. Small, white to yellowish tubular flowers in a dense terminal spike with leaf-like bracts make up half (or more) of the stem. Fruit an ovoid capsule. Flowers Mar.–June.

Habitat/range: Occurs under or near oaks in various forests, including oak-hickory forests, river bluff forests, and alluvial forests. Common in mountains, occasional in piedmont. Eastern North America.

Taxonomy: A genus of 2 species of parasitic herbs, 1 of eastern North America, the other of southwestern North America, south to Central America. Squawroot is easily identified by its distinctive growth form and yellowish brown color.

Ecology: The life cycle of this highly specialized holoparasite lacking roots and bearing non-photosynthetic, scale-like leaves is unusual. Seeds that germinate near a small oak root form a parasitic connection to the root, resulting in the formation of a gall-like mass called a tubercle (which consists of a combination of host and parasitic tissue). It takes about 5 years for the underground tubercle to mature, after which it produces multiple aboveground flowering stems each spring for a number of years. Larger tubercles (nearly a foot in diameter) produce as many as 8–12 flowering stalks per year, which are visited and pollinated by bumblebees. A single fleshy capsule (about the size of a large grape) contains about 5,000 tiny seeds; larger squawroot plants with multiple stems can produce more than 100,000 seeds in a single year. The seeds are dispersed by wind, by rainwater flowing over the ground surface, and by mammals.

Wildlife: Black bears, white-tailed deer, chipmunks, mice, and squirrels ingest the fleshy fruit stalks and disperse the seeds in their droppings.

Coreopsis major Walter
WHORLED COREOPSIS
Asteraceae (Sunflower family)

Description: Upright perennial herb 20–40 in. tall with opposite, sessile compound leaves, each consisting of 3 narrow leaflets, giving the appearance of 6 leaves in a whorl. Flowers in flat-topped heads with 7 or more, bright yellow ray flowers surrounding yellow (purplish with age) disk flowers. Fruit a flat-curved achene. Flowers June–Aug.

Habitat/range: Dry oak-hickory forests, woodlands, forest edges, fields, and roadsides. Common. Eastern and central United States.

Taxonomy: A genus of about 35 species of herbs distributed primarily in North America, including 12 species in the mountains and piedmont. Sometimes referred to as woodtickseed, not because ticks inhabit the plant but because of the tick-like shape of its achenes.

Ecology: Whorled coreopsis occurs as scattered plants or in loose groupings in relatively open areas. The ray and disk flowers collectively form a flower head that functions as a landing platform for butterflies, bees, and other insects that sip nectar or harvest pollen from the many tiny flowers within each head. The single seeded fruits (achenes) ripen in late summer with many persisting in tight, upright clumps well into winter. The entire plant turns black after the first frost; new upright stems emerge the following spring from dormant buds on long, slender rhizomes.

Wildlife: White-tailed deer browse the foliage, and finches, sparrows, and other songbirds feed on the seeds.

Uses: Whorled coreopsis is a desirable plant in gardens due to its showy flowers, long blooming season, and drought tolerance.

Cuscuta rostrata Shuttlw
APPALACHIAN DODDER
Convolvulaceae (Morning Glory family)

Description: Slender, leafless, bright orange or yellow twining parasitic vine with small, tubular, white flowers. Fruit a small capsule with 4 tiny seeds. Flowers Aug.–Sept.; fruits Aug.–Oct.

Habitat/range: High-elevation hardwood forests, grassy balds, and heath balds. Common. Appalachian Mountains from Maryland south to Georgia.

Taxonomy: Ten of the more than 150 species in the genus occur in the mountains and piedmont. Flowers are needed to distinguish between species as the stems are very similar.

Ecology: An obligate parasite, dodder seedlings must locate and become attached to a suitable host plant within a few days; if they do not, the seedling will die once the nutrients stored in the seed are consumed. Dodder seedlings use volatile cues (odors) to locate a suitable host plant. Recent research has demonstrated that once an appropriate scent cue has been detected, the seedling grows toward the preferred host. Dodder species differ in their host preferences; some occur on just a few host plants, while others parasitize numerous species. Appalachian dodder often parasitizes blackberries (*Rubus* spp.), but is also found on common hydrangea (*Hydrangea arborescens*), orange jewelweed (*Impatiens capensis*), and a few other species. When contact is made with a suitable host, the stem coils around it, and specialized root-like structures called haustoria penetrate the host plant along the stem. A vascular connection develops and the dodder plant obtains all the nutrients and water it requires from the host plant. While the host plant is rarely killed, it often loses vigor and appears unhealthy. A robust dodder plant can spread from one host plant to another, forming a dense, tangled mat of intertwined stems that looks like orange (or yellow) cooked spaghetti noodles.

Wildlife: Flies visit and apparently pollinate the small but fragrant flowers.

Uses: Dodder is sometimes referred to

as "strangleweed" or "witches shoelaces" as it can be a serious pest to both wild and cultivated plants.

Cymophyllus fraserianus (Ker-Gawl.) Kartesz & Gandhi
FRASER'S SEDGE
Cyperaceae (Sedge family)

Description: Evergreen herbaceous perennial forms dense clumps of strap-shaped leathery leaves 8–20 in. long and 1–2 in. wide with wavy margins and prominent, parallel veins that arise from a short, thick rhizome. Flower stalks 4–16 in. tall with a terminal spike up to 1 in. long, white and showy, with male flowers at tip, female flowers below. Fruit a single dry seed (achene) enclosed within an inflated sac (perigynium), about 20–30 fruit sacs per spike. Flowers Apr.–June; fruits May–July.

Habitat/range: On cool, moist slopes and streambanks at moderate elevations, usually with a dense heath shrub understory of rosebay (*Rhododendron maximum*) or mountain laurel (*Kalmia latifolia*). Cove forests. A rare species restricted to the Appalachian Mountains from Pennsylvania to Georgia.

Taxonomy: Fraser's sedge is the only species in what is considered to be a very primitive genus. *Cymophyllus* and its close relative *Carex* are the only grass-like plants that produce fruits in sacs (perigynia). Vegetative plants of Fraser's sedge are sometimes mistaken for lilies because of their wide, strap-shaped leaves.

Ecology: Fraser's sedge is a rare species and of concern to conservationists in most of the 9 states it occupies. Interestingly, it's much more common in mature or old-growth forests than in second-growth (previously disturbed) forests. Its absence from second-growth forest may be due to limited seed dispersal, lack of suitable habitat, or the presence of competing species. Small bees and flies pollinate the showy white flowers. Almost all other members of the Cyperaceae (sedge family) have nondescript wind-pollinated flowers.

Wildlife: White-tailed deer graze the foliage, flowers, and fruits.

Uses: This unusual sedge with its broad evergreen leaves and showy white flower clusters is sometimes grown in woodland gardens.

Cypripedium acaule Aiton
PINK LADY'S SLIPPER
Orchidaceae (Orchid family)

Description: Long-lived herbaceous perennial with 2 large, strongly ribbed, basal leaves. A solitary flower with a distinctive, large pink pouch (the "slipper") terminates a leafless stalk. Fruit an elliptic capsule. Flowers Apr.–June; fruits May–July.

Habitat/range: Dry to moist acidic forests, often under conifers and rosebay thickets. Pine-oak-heath, chestnut oak forests, and occasionally in mountain bogs. Common. Eastern North America.

Taxonomy: A genus of 45 species with distinctive pouch-like lip petals known as "slippers." Of the 4 mountain and piedmont species, this is the only 1 that has a leafless flowering stalk.

Ecology: Lady's slipper orchids are among the most unusual and prized plants in the Southeast. Conspicuous vein-like lines and a sweet odor direct large bees (mainly bumblebees) to a small opening in the large pink pouch. Once inside, bees first brush against the stigma (which is built like a comb to remove pollen) and then an anther (which contains a sticky mass of pollen), after which they exit through a small opening at the base of the flower. If a bee visits another lady's slipper, the stigma rakes off the previously deposited pollen, resulting in pollination, and the anther pastes a fresh load of pollen onto the bee's thorax. However, because no actual reward is provided, pollinator visitation rates are very infrequent and fewer than 5 percent of the flowers typically mature fruit. If a flower is pollinated, the resulting fruit contains thousands of tiny wind-dispersed seeds. Very few seeds find the right combination of microclimate, soil, and symbiotic fungus to germinate and establish a new plant. The very shallow root system doesn't typically penetrate the mineral soil but rather resides in the organic matter immediately above it. Periodic fires and other disturbance factors generally benefit this species as it grows best under a fairly open canopy.

Uses: It's best to simply enjoy this plant in its natural setting as wild orchids are nearly impossible to transplant successfully.

Cypripedium parviflorum Salisb.
YELLOW LADY'S SLIPPER
Orchidaceae (Orchid family)

Description: Showy perennial herb 8–32 in. tall with a hairy stem and 3–5 alternate, mostly sheathing stem leaves from 2 to 8 in. long and half as wide with parallel, raised veins. One or 2 terminal flowers each with 2 long, twisted, purplish brown lateral petals, 3 wavy-edged sepals (the lower 2 fused into 1), and a lower petal that forms a yellow pouch streaked or spotted with purple (known as the lady's slipper). Fruit an elliptic capsule. Flowers Apr.–June; fruits May–July.

Habitat/range: Rich mesic forests,

including rich cove forests and basic mesic forests. Uncommon. Eastern North America.

Taxonomy: A large, colorful pouch (the "slipper") enclosing the male and female parts of the flower distinguishes lady slipper orchids. Yellow lady's slipper differs from the pink lady's slipper (*C. acaule*) by its flower color and leafy stem.

Ecology: The large yellow flowers depend on pollinators for successful pollination yet offer no food reward. Instead, a form of deception is employed whereby the large colorful flowers and sweet fragrance falsely advertise the presence of food. Occasional visits by bees seeking nectar or pollen result in sporadic pollination. While few flowers set fruit, those that do produce thousands of tiny wind-dispersed seeds. Lady slipper orchids are unusual in exhibiting intermittent emergence; in some years adult plants remain dormant, without forming an aboveground plant. These dormant plants may persist underground for 1 or more years (in some cases, up to a decade) apparently using stored reserves and obtaining nutrients from a mycorrhizal (root) fungus. As a result, the size of a given population may be greater than that which meets the eye.

Wildlife: Crab spiders and other predatory insects sometimes occupy the pouch sacs, devouring pollinators as they enter the flower. Large bumblebees trapped in the pouch sometimes bite their way out, leaving behind a mutilated flower.

Uses: Unfortunately, this beautiful orchid, so exhilarating to see in the wild, is becoming increasingly uncommon due to unscrupulous individuals digging it up.

Synonym: Cypripedium calceolus L. var. *pubescens* (Wild.) Correll

Danthonia compressa Austin
MOUNTAIN OAT GRASS
Poaceae (Grass family)

Description: A perennial bunchgrass with mostly basal leaves. Culms (flowering stems) slender, compressed, sometimes lying on the ground with the tip curved upward. Inflorescence with slender branches bearing 2–3 spikelets. Flowers June–Aug.

Habitat/range: Grassy balds, rock outcrops, red oak forests, and chestnut oak forests. Common in mountains, less so in upper piedmont. Southeastern Canada and New England, south in the Appalachian Mountains to Georgia.

Taxonomy: Danthonia is a genus of about 20 species of Europe and the Americas, with 4 species in the mountains and the piedmont.

Ecology: A moderately shade-tolerant species, mountain oat grass grows in full sun and open woods but doesn't persist under a closed canopy. It forms dense clumps that restrict or hinder tree growth, thereby helping to maintain grassy balds. Mountain oat grass also occurs on thin soils associated with rock outcrops and colonizes disturbed areas such as recent clearcuts and burned areas. Individual plants produce both open (chasmogamous) and closed (cleistogamous) flowers. Because closed flowers occur lower on the plant than open flowers, the closed flowers and their developing seeds are less likely to be removed by grazers. Mountain oat grass is also susceptible to a systemic parasitic fungus that "sterilizes" open flowers in such a way that only closed flowers produce seeds in infected plants. This same fungus produces an alkaloid that benefits its host plant by making it less palatable to herbivores.

Dennstaedtia punctilobula (Michx.) T. Moore
HAYSCENTED FERN
Dennstaedtiaceae (Bracken family)

Description: Deciduous fern with pale green lacy fronds, often in large colonies. Leaf blades about 3 times as long as broad, widest near bottom, pointed at apex, thin-textured and easily broken. Spore clusters (sori) roundish, in cup-like indusia. Spores released June–Sept.

Habitat/range: Woodlands and forests, along streams and roadbanks, rock outcrops, and pastures. Common in mountains, uncommon in piedmont. Eastern North America.

Taxonomy: Hayscented fern is our only representative in the mostly tropical genus *Dennstaedtia*. It can be confused with New York fern (*Thelypteris noveboracensis*), but hayscented fern's fronds are triangular, rather than tapered at both ends. Crushed or bruised fronds release a fragrance similar to freshly mown hay, hence the common name.

Ecology: Hayscented fern grows in a variety of habitats, including moist to dry soils and full sunlight to fairly deep shade. It tends to be sparsely distributed in shaded areas but forms large colonies or thickets in forest openings where increased light reaches the forest floor. Established plants spread rapidly into open areas as buds at the base of leaves develop into long, creeping, underground stems. Once a dense carpet of fronds has formed, it can dominate the understory so thoroughly that there is little regeneration of trees. Apparently, a dense organic mat of roots, rhizomes, and dead fronds, coupled with a dense canopy of living fronds, inhibits seed germination and seedling establishment of other plants. Chemicals such as coumarin that leach from the fronds or rhizomes of hayscented fern also have an inhibitory effect on seeds and seedlings.

Wildlife: Hayscented fern has a variety of phenolic compounds that makes it unpalatable to most herbivores, including white-tailed deer. Heavy grazing associated with high deer densities tends to favor unpalatable species such as hayscented fern.

Uses: Hayscented fern is sometimes used in gardens because it tolerates a wide range of conditions and forms large colonies.

Desmodium nudiflorum (L.) DC.
BEGGAR'S TICKS
Fabaceae (Legume family)

Description: Smooth, upright perennial with a slender, arching, flowering stem up to 3 ft. tall and separate foliage bearing stems usually 1–2 ft. tall with trifoliate leaves clustered at the tip; the leaflets broadly ovate, about 3 in. long. Rose-purple, pea-like flowers in a loose raceme. Fruit a flattened pod covered with small, hooked hairs that break into several 1-seeded segments when mature. Flowers July–Aug.; fruits Aug.–Oct.

Habitat/range: Moist to dry forests, including river bluff forests and oak-hickory forests. Common. Widespread in eastern North America.

Taxonomy: The genus consists of 300 species of herbs and shrubs of temperate and tropical areas throughout much of the world. The more than 20 species in the mountains and piedmont are characterized by sticky seedpods. Species of *Desmodium* differ from *Lespedeza* in that the seedpods are flattened and have a small appendage (stipel) at the base of each leaflet.

Ecology: Don't worry about getting ticks from this plant, as the common name describes the seedpods that attach and cling like ticks. Covered with small, hooked hairs, the seedpods can be dispersed long distances by adhering to the fur of animals (or the clothing of humans). Like the roots of many legumes, the roots of beggar's ticks form nodules in a mutualistic association with nitrogen-fixing *Rhizobium* bacteria. The plant uses nitrogen fixed by the bacterium, and the bacterium is provided food and shelter. Bumblebees visit the flowers for nectar, pollen, or both and function as pollinators.

Wildlife: White-tailed deer actively browse most species of *Desmodium* and northern bobwhite, ruffed grouse, wild turkey, and various songbirds consume large quantities of the seeds.

Uses: Native Americans chewed on the roots as a remedy for inflamed gums.

Diamorpha smallii Britton ex Small
ELF ORPINE
Crassulaceae (Stonecrop family)

Description: A diminutive annual 1–3 in. tall with reddish semisucculent stems and leaves and small white flowers in flat-topped clusters. Fruit a cluster of 4 erect follicles. Flowers Apr.–May; fruits May–June.

Habitat/range: Grows in very thin soils on seasonally wet rock outcrop depressions. Common on piedmont outcrops, uncommon in mountains. From Virginia south to Georgia.

Taxonomy: This is the only species in the genus. Puck's orpine (*Sedum pusillum*) is similar but typically has green (rather than red) stems and leaves, the pistils are separate to the base, and it usually occurs under red cedar (*Juniperus virginiana*).

Ecology: Elf orpine is abundant in the shallowest soils in and around depressions of granite outcrops. A winter annual, the seeds germinate in late fall or winter, seedlings overwinter as small rosetteS, and plants flower and mature seed from April through June. The vegetative rosettes of winter are highly resistant to frost and can survive weeks submerged under water. Elf-orpine escapes the high temperatures and severe droughts of summer by completing its life cycle in late spring. However, even in spring, plants on thin soils experience extreme variability in moisture availability. Individuals resist drought by using water stored in their semisucculent stems and leaves, by reviving after periods of desiccation, and by adjusting plant height and flowering to moisture availability. Drought-stressed plants may be only one-half in. tall with fewer than 5 flowers at maturity, whereas plants growing on more favorable sites can be up to 3 in. tall with more than 50 flowers. On deeper soils where drought stress is reduced, larger, more competitive species invade, thereby limiting elf orpine to the periphery of depressions where the soil is thinner and competition is reduced. Elf orpine is a stress-tolerant species that occupies a highly specialized habitat that few other plants can tolerate.

Wildlife: Elf orpine is one of a relatively small number of plants whose primary pollinator is ants. Small bees and flies also visit and occasionally pollinate the flowers.

Dicentra cucullaria (L.) Bernh.
DUTCHMAN'S BRITCHES
Fumariaceae (Fumitory family)

Description: Perennial herb from 4 to 12 in. tall, arising from a short rhizome with long-stalked basal leaves and deeply divided, narrow leaf segments. The inflorescence is a raceme of hanging white flowers, each with 2 conspicuous, upward-pointing nectar spurs. Fruit a capsule with shiny black seeds. Flowers Mar.–Apr.; fruits May–June.

Habitat/range: Rich, moist forests, especially rich cove forests and basic mesic forests. Common in mountains, less so in piedmont. Primarily a northern species of eastern and central United States, south to Georgia and Arkansas.

Taxonomy: A genus of 12 species of eastern and western North America and eastern Asia. Similar to squirrel corn (*D. canadensis*) but its flowers have pointed (rather than rounded) nectar spurs and lack fragrance. The flowers look like a pair of old-fashioned knickers hanging out to dry, hence the common name.

Ecology: A spring ephemeral, plants emerge and flower in early spring before the canopy leafs out. The fruits mature in late spring and early summer, after which the plant dies back. The underground plant remains dormant until fall, at which time flower buds and leaf primordia (tiny leaves) are produced belowground, which remain dormant until the following spring. Long-tongued insects, mainly bumblebees, pollinate the upside-down flowers. Some bees and wasps with mouthparts too short to reach the nectar have learned to chew holes at the tips of the spurs to access the nectar. These insects are considered "nectar robbers" as they rarely pollinate the flowers. By scraping away the leaf litter, the nutrient-rich bulblets that cover the roots are easily seen. Squirrels reportedly harvest and store the bulblets in food caches and may inadvertently help distribute the plant.

Wildlife: Alkaloids in the leaves deter most animals from feeding on this plant (ranchers call it "staggerweed" because of its effect on cattle). Lipid-rich food bodies on the seed coat attract ants that disperse the seeds.

Uses: Alkaloids in the bulblets have been used to treat syphilis. The entire plant is poisonous if ingested.

Dioscorea villosa L.
WILD YAM
Dioscoreaceae (Yam family)

Description: Perennial climbing vine with smooth, twining stems up to 15 ft. long. Leaves whorled on lower stem, alternate on upper stem, heart-shaped with conspicuous veins. Tiny greenish yellow flowers in loose, hanging clusters from leaf axils. Fruit a 3-winged capsule, initially green, eventually turning light brown. Flowers Apr.–June; fruits Sept.–Oct.

Habitat/range: Moist forests and woodlands. Widespread in eastern United States.

Taxonomy: Dioscorea is a large genus of about 600 species of vines widely distributed in the tropical and warm temperate regions of the world. Of the 3 species of *Dioscorea* in the mountains and piedmont, cinnamon vine (*D. polystachya*) is most similar to wild yam. Both are climbing vines with heart-shaped leaves, but unlike wild yam, cinnamon vine has opposite leaves and small, potato-like aerial tubers in the leaf axils. The term yam is also commonly used for the cultivated sweet potato (*Ipomoea batatas*), an unrelated plant whose edible tubers are called sweet potatoes or yams.

Ecology: Like most plants, vines grow upward and outward toward the sun. Unable to support themselves, vines have devised various ways to hitch a ride on other structures, including neighboring plants, to reach heights where light is more readily available. Wild yam climbs other plants by attaching itself to the host plant with tendrils, thin wiry strands sensitive to touch that coil tightly around any slender support they come in contact with. The aerial stems of wild yam climb upward from right to left in a counter-clockwise direction, whereas the stems of cinnamon vine (native to China) twine in a clockwise direction. Wild yam's small, inconspicuous male and female flowers occur on separate plants. The female flowers develop into 3-winged fruits that hang like ornaments from twining stems from late summer through fall.

Uses: Most steroid hormones used in modern medicine, including progesterone and estrogens, and those used in oral contraceptives, were developed from chemical extracts of wild yam.

Diphasiastrum digitatum Dill. ex A. Braun
RUNNING CEDAR
Lycopodiaceae (Lycopodium family)

Description: A creeping evergreen nonflowering plant with horizontal stems on or just below the soil surface and multi-branched vertical stems with scale-like leaves that form fan-shaped branches in a horizontal plane. Cylindrical cones in upright, candelabra-like clusters above the foliage mature spores from July–Sept.

Habitat/range: Variety of dry to moist coniferous and hardwood forests and openings, including early successional pine-oak forests. Common. Widespread in eastern North America.

Taxonomy: A genus of about 15 species, mostly north-temperate and subarctic, including 2 species in the mountains and piedmont. Running cedar differs from blue running cedar (*D. tristachyum*) in that its foliage is dark green, rather than blue-green. Its scale-like leaves and growth form resemble dense clusters of tiny cedar trees, hence the common name.

Ecology: Clubmosses such as running cedar differ from true mosses in that they have a simple vascular system of food- and water-conducting tissues. Fossils indicate that ancient ancestors of clubmosses, as well as ferns and giant horsetails (*Equisetum*), once grew as huge trees that dominated the earth's vegetation. From about 360 to 290 million years ago, thick beds of this vegetation were buried, compressed, and carbonized into coal. Known as the Carboniferous period (or the coal age), enormous deposits of coal were created in various parts of Europe, Asia, and North America, including in the Appalachian Mountains, where coal mines are common. Today, clubmosses exist as prostrate, nonwoody plants that sometimes form a dense ground cover on acidic soils. Individuals reproduce by spores (rather than seeds) and spread vegetatively from creeping stems that root on the underside of the main stem.

Wildlife: Little is known about interactions between running cedar and animals, although birds such as the Nashville warbler build ground nests in the dense foliage.

Uses: The spores were used as a flash powder for early photography and for producing stage effects in theatrical performances as the oil-rich spores give off a flash when ignited.

Synonym: Lycopodium flabelliforme (Fernald) Blanch.

Diphylleia cymosa Michx.
UMBRELLA LEAF
Berberidaceae (Barberry family)

Description: Perennial herb 1–3 ft. tall from a thick rhizome. One or 2 large (up to 15 in. wide) leaves, each with a stout leaf stalk attached to the middle. Small clusters of white flowers at the tip of a long stalk above the broad, coarsely toothed leaves. Conspicuous dark blue berries on bright red stalks. Flowers Apr.–June; fruits July–Aug.

Habitat/range: Seepage areas and brooks, moist slopes, northern hardwood forests, and cove forests. Uncommon in mountains. Appalachian Mountains from Virginia south to Georgia.

Taxonomy: The genus *Diphylleia* has just 3 species, 1 in eastern North America, 2 in eastern Asia.

Ecology: Umbrella leaf is a loosely scattered, conspicuous herb that occurs along seepage areas and brooks at mid- to high elevations. Where surface water is lacking, it's usually associated with subterranean seepage flow. Like mayapple (*Podophyllum*), vegetative plants have a single leaf, flowering plants have 2. The large round leaves of both species look like open umbrellas standing in the woods. Their large surface area and horizontal orientation make them particularly efficient at capturing the limited amount of light that reaches the forest floor. The tradeoff is that large leaves lose tremendous amounts of water through transpiration, potentially subjecting the plant to severe water stress. Umbrella leaf avoids this problem by growing in wet areas where the water lost by transpiration is readily replaced by water taken up by roots.

Wildlife: The conspicuous dark blue berries on red stalks attract various birds and mammals that eat the pulp and disperse the seeds.

Uses: Umbrella leaf and mayapple are members of 2 closely related genera, both of which contain podophyllotoxin lignans. This relatively rare alkaloid is currently used in the treatment of various kinds of cancer.

Drosera rotundifolia L.
ROUNDLEAF SUNDEW
Droseraceae (Sundew family)

Description: Insectivorous perennial herb with a basal rosette of round leaves, the upper surface covered with reddish, glandular hairs tipped with a glistening sticky secretion that traps insects. Small white flowers often tinged with pink on one-sided racemes. Fruit a capsule with numerous tiny seeds. Flowers July–Sept; fruits Aug.–Oct.

Habitat/range: Mountain bogs and seepage slopes, often on rock or clay substrates, rarely on peat. Uncommon. A circumboreal species that in North America ranges from Canada south to Georgia, west to California.

Taxonomy: Four of the more than 100 species of small insectivorous plants that comprise the genus *Drosera* occur in the mountains and piedmont. "Sundew" refers to the glistening sticky droplets on the round leaves.

Ecology: Insectivorous plants capture prey such as insects, spiders, crustaceans, and protozoans. Most insectivorous plants grow in sunny, nutrient-poor bogs and other waterlogged habitats. Roundleaf sundew leaves capture insects on sticky leaf hairs, which then fold around the prey. Glands on the hairs secrete enzymes that digest the insect, allowing nutrients to be absorbed through the leaves. Experiments on sundews by Charles

Darwin and his son Francis were the first to show that insectivory benefits plants by increasing their growth and reproduction. Mosquitoes, midges, and gnats pollinate the flowers, which are elevated well above the sticky leaves. Roundleaf sundew spreads locally by seeds and by vegetative reproduction; occasional long-distance dispersal occurs when floods sweep away the buoyant seeds. The slow growth rate and prostrate growth form of many insectivorous plants makes them vulnerable to competitive displacement by taller, more vigorous vegetation, particularly in the absence of fires and other kinds of disturbance that keep the habitat open. Other major threats include overcollecting and habitat destruction.

Wildlife: Bog-dwelling ants rob up to two-thirds of the insects trapped in sundew leaves.

Uses: In Sweden, sundew leaves have been used to curdle the milk used in making cheese.

Dryopteris campyloptera Clarkson
MOUNTAIN WOOD FERN
Dryopteridaceae (Wood fern family)

Description: Deciduous fronds 2–3 ft. long, ovate to triangular, light green and glabrous. The leaf stalk makes up about one-third the length of the leaf and has brown scales, at least at the base. Sori (spore-producing clusters) covered by a thin flap of kidney-shaped tissue occur midway between the midvein and margin of the leaf segments. Spores dispersed July–Sept.

Habitat/range: Cool, moist woods, often on rocky summits of mountains. Spruce-fir forests and northern hardwood forests. Locally common. Occurs in northeastern United States and Canada, south in mountains to North Carolina and Tennessee.

Taxonomy: Seven of the 250 species in the genus occur in the mountains and piedmont.

Ecology: Whenever 2 or more *Dryopteris* species occur in close proximity, there is a good chance that hybrids are present. Hybrid individuals typically have characteristics intermediate between the 2 parental species, making field identification difficult. While hybrids are often sterile, hybridization followed by polyploidy (an increase in chromosome number) enhances fertility and promotes the formation of new species. This phenomenon is common in plants in general, and in the genus *Dryopteris* in particular. For example, *D. campyloptera* is a tetraploid (it has 4 sets of chromosomes) and is apparently derived from hybridization between 2 diploids, *D. expansa* and *D. intermedia*.

Wildlife: White-tailed deer eat the foliage, and a small pyralid moth caterpillar webs and rolls the tips of fronds.

Uses: The wide-spreading roots and rhizomes of wood ferns stabilize soil, thereby reducing erosion.

Echinacea laevigata (Boynt. & Beadle) Blake
SMOOTH CONEFLOWER
Asteraceae (Sunflower family)
Federally Endangered

Description: Perennial herb with smooth, generally unbranched stems 2–4 ft. tall, often in clumps. Basal leaves to 6 in. long and 3 in. wide, stem leaves similar but smaller with shorter leaf stalks. Solitary flower heads at shoot tips, the ray flowers (petal-like structures) light pink to purplish, drooping, disk flowers purple. Fruit an achene. Flowers May–July; fruits July–Oct.

Habitat/range: Dry, open woodlands, forest edges, power line corridors, roadsides, fields, generally on calcium-rich soil over mafic or calcareous rocks. Rare. Historic range extended from Pennsylvania south to Georgia, currently known only from Virginia, North Carolina, South Carolina, and Georgia.

Taxonomy: A genus of 9 species of herbaceous perennials of eastern and central North America, including 4 species in the mountains and piedmont.

Ecology: Only 23 of the 50 historically recorded populations of this federally endangered species survive. Most of the remaining populations are small, containing fewer than 100 plants. A poor competitor, it's restricted to relatively open sites, usually on calcium or magnesium-rich soils. Historically, the species probably occurred most frequently in prairie-like habitats and oak savannas maintained by fires (caused by lightning or intentionally set by Native Americans). Loss of relatively open habitats due to decades of fire suppression undoubtedly contributed to the decline of this species. Today, most populations occur in open woods and human-maintained clearings such as roadsides and utility rights-of-way. In addition to fire suppression, current threats include the collecting of wild plants, road widening, roadside utility maintenance, and exotic invasives.

Wildlife: The flowers depend on pollinators (mainly large bees) for cross-pollination and subsequent seed development.

Uses: Smooth coneflower's close relative, eastern purple coneflower (*E. purpurea*) is widely propagated and grown in gardens. Various species of *Echinacea* are used as an herbal remedy for treating colds.

Epifagus virginiana (L.) Barton
BEECHDROPS
Orobanchaceae (Broomrape family)

Description: Root parasite with thin, ascending pale brown stems 4–18 in. tall with brownish purple streaks and tiny scale-like leaves that lack chlorophyll. Flowers inconspicuous, cream with brown-purple stripes, born singly in leaf axils. Fruit a tiny brown capsule. Flowers Sept.–Nov.; fruits Oct.–Dec.

Habitat/range: Moist to rather dry forests beneath or within the vicinity of American beech (*Fagus grandifolia*), including northern hardwood forests, rich cove forests, river bluff forests, basic mesic forests. Common. Widespread in eastern North America.

Taxonomy: Beechdrops is the only species in the genus. The genus name is derived from the Greek words "epi" (upon) and "fagus" (beech). The more than 2,000 species in the broomrape family are either parasitic plants that lack chlorophyll (holoparasites) or plants that have green photosynthetic tissues (leaves and sometimes stems) that obtain additional nutrients from a host plant (hemiparasites).

Ecology: This inconspicuous but common plant is easily missed as its brownish purple stems blend in with the forest floor. Occurring singly or in small colonies, it generally occurs wherever American beech trees are found. Lacking chlorophyll (and therefore unable to photosynthesize), all its nutrients come from the roots of a single host species—American beech. Without this plant, beechdrops can't survive. Beechdrops produces 2 types of flowers. The upper flowers on the stem are larger (about one-half in. long), tubular, and usually sterile; the lower flowers are much smaller, never open, and produce abundant self-fertilized seeds. The tiny capsules form a splash cup, with raindrops dispersing the dust-like seeds. Carried down through soil by water, the seeds only germinate when in close proximity to beech roots, stimulated by an exudate produced by beech roots. Seedling roots that make contact with a beech root form a haustorium that transfers nutrients from the host tree to the parasite.

Wildlife: Ways in which animals might interact with this plant have yet to be discovered.

Uses: Beechdrops has been used as a folk medicine to treat various ailments, including dysentery and gonorrhea.

Epigaea repens L.
TRAILING ARBUTUS
Ericaceae (Heath family)

Description: A ground-level, slightly woody evergreen plant with creeping reddish brown stems with ovate to oblong leathery leaves, 2–3 in. long. White to pink, fragrant flowers form small clusters, often concealed under leaves. Fruit a berry-like capsule. Flowers Feb.–May; fruits Apr.–June.

Habitat/range: Found in variety of dry to somewhat moist habitats with acidic soils, including pine-oak-heath, heath balds, and forest edges. Common. Widespread in eastern North America.

Taxonomy: A genus of 3 species, 2 of which occur in Eurasia. Also known as mayflower, it purportedly was the first plant the Pilgrims saw in flower after enduring their first very difficult winter.

Ecology: One of the smallest members of the heath family (Ericaceae), this prostrate, mat-forming species occurs on acidic soils in woods and clearings, including road banks and trailside edges. Among the first plants to bloom in spring, bumblebees pollinate the spicy-scented flowers that are often partially or completely hidden from view under leathery leaves. Developing fruits, initially green, become red and then purple as they ripen. The 5-chambered, pea-sized capsule splits open at maturity, revealing hundreds of tiny brown seeds embedded on the surface of sticky, white placental tissue. Ants quickly and efficiently remove the sugary placental tissue, thereby dispersing the seeds.

Wildlife: Small mammals and birds, as well as ants, eat the pulp and disperse the seeds.

Uses: Trailing arbutus was used by Native Americans and in folk medicines to treat urinary disorders and kidney stones. Overcollecting in the early twentieth century by individuals in the florist trade nearly eliminated this plant from some areas.

Erigeron pulchellus Michx.
ROBIN'S PLANTAIN
Asteraceae (Aster family)

Description: Hairy perennial herb 8–24 in. tall with a basal rosette of spoon-shaped leaves 1–5 in. long, stem leaves, alternate, lance-shaped, progressively reduced upward. Usually 2–5 daisy-like flower heads with 50–100 white to lilac-colored ray flowers and yellow disk flowers. Fruit a shiny ribbed achene with a tuft of tan bristles. Flowers Apr.–early June; fruits May–June.

Habitat/range: Open, moist woods, including coves, oak-hickory forests, forest edges, and trailsides. Common. Widespread in eastern and central United States.

Taxonomy: The genus *Erigeron* has a nearly worldwide distribution, with 8 of the 150 species in the mountains and piedmont. Members of this genus usually have 50 or more very slender rays in each flower head, whereas "asters" typically have fewer but wider rays.

Ecology: Robin's plantain flowers in early spring, rather than in summer or fall, when most plants in the sunflower family bloom. Each flower head consists of hundreds of tiny flowers, with showy ray flowers on the outer rim and yellow disk flowers in the center. Within a head, the flowers open sequentially from the outer region toward the center. In a single visit, a pollinator can pollinate a number of flowers, each of which has a single ovule (a potential seed). Newly opened flowers are functionally male (pollen presenting), whereas older flowers have receptive stigmas and are functionally female. Individuals spread by wind-dispersed seeds as well as by stolons (aboveground runners), often forming colonies. One of the most common places to encounter Robin's plantain is on the margins of trails.

Wildlife: Lynx flower moth caterpillars feed on the flowers and seeds.

Uses: Species of *Erigeron* are sometimes called fleabane because they are said to keep flies, gnats, and other pesky insects away. Dried plants were formerly used as stuffing in mattresses to reduce bites from fleas.

Eryngium yuccifolium Michx.
RATTLESNAKE MASTER
Apiaceae (Carrot family)

Description: Coarse, erect perennial with a stout, glabrous stem up to 4 ft. tall with numerous long, strap-shaped, bluish green lower leaves with parallel veins and prickly margins; the upper leaves similar but fewer and smaller. Greenish white ball-like flower clusters almost 1 in. across contain numerous tiny white flowers surrounded by prickly bractlets. Fruit a schizocarp. Flowers June–Aug.

Habitat/range: Dry soils, open woods, edges of pine woodlands, fields, and roadsides. Uncommon. Widespread in Southeast and Midwest where it's often associated with prairie remnants.

Taxonomy: A genus of about 250 herbaceous species of tropical and temperate areas, including 3 species in the mountains and piedmont. From a distance, the foliage resembles a yucca, hence the species name.

Ecology: The tiny flowers in dense, ball-like clusters attract numerous visitors, including bees, wasps, butterflies, moths, flies, and beetles. Newly opened flowers within each inflorescence (or "ball") are in the male (pollen-shedding) phase; 2–3 days after the stamens have released their pollen, the female phase begins (the 2 stigmas per flower spread and become sticky when receptive). This temporal separation of male and female stages, a common trait in members of the carrot family, promotes cross-pollination, rather than self-pollination. The benefit of this strategy is that cross-fertilized seeds generally produce more vigorous offspring than self-fertilized seeds. Individual plants typically produce numerous seeds, some of which persist in the soil, forming a seed bank. Following disturbance, when conditions are often most favorable for successful seedling establishment and growth, seeds in the soil provide a source of new plants.

Wildlife: Mammalian herbivores generally avoid the coarse foliage and prickly flower heads.

Uses: Native Americans and early settlers used the roots as a poultice for snakebites, from which the common name is derived.

Erythronium umbilicatum
Parks & Hardin
DIMPLED TROUT LILY
Liliaceae (Lily family)

Description: A nodding, solitary yellow flower with strongly recurved sepals and petals rises above a pair of elongated, mottled leaves. Fruit a many-seeded capsule. Flowers Feb.–May; fruits Apr.–June.

Habitat/range: Rich, moist woods to somewhat dry habitats, including alluvial forests, basic mesic forests, and acidic cove forests. Common. Southeast.

Taxonomy: A genus of 25 species of North America and Eurasia. Dimpled trout lily is similar to yellow trout lily (*E. americanum*), but its petals have an auricle (or "ear") at the base, and mature seed capsules are indented at the top and lie flat on the ground. Markings on the leaf surface resemble splotches on a brook trout, hence the common name.

Ecology: Trout lilies are spring ephemerals with a very short growing season. Plants emerge in late winter–early spring as soil temperatures rise. A few weeks later, when the canopy trees leaf out and the forest floor is shaded, it goes dormant, persisting as an underground food-storage organ (bulb) for about 48 weeks each year. One of the earliest woodland herbs to bloom, its flowers track the sun and close at night (the sepals and petals curve backward as the flower opens each morning). While some early spring-flowering plants have difficulty with pollination, the pollination success rate of trout lily is high because large amounts of nectar and pollen attract a variety of bees. Only 2–3 bee visits per flower are needed to ensure successful fruit set, and because individual flowers can persist for 10 days or more, the likelihood of successful pollination is increased. Seeds germinate in spring, forming tiny bulbs that get larger and bury themselves deeper into the soil with age. Smaller bulbs produce single-leaved plants; larger bulbs produce 2 leaves and a single flower. Some populations form dense patches of plants, with few plants flowering in any one year.

Wildlife: Black bears and wild hogs dig up and eat the bulbs, white-tailed deer occasionally nip off the fruits, and ants disperse the seeds.

Uses: Nursery-propagated plants can be purchased and grown in moist woodland gardens.

Eurybia chlorolepis (Burgess) Nesom
MOUNTAIN WOOD ASTER
Asteraceae (Sunflower family)

Description: Perennial herb 1–3 ft. tall with a zigzag stem. Leaves alternate, toothed, lower leaves heart-shaped and conspicuously pointed at tip, upper leaves progressively smaller and less heart-shaped. Daisy-like flower heads with 10 or more ray flowers and yellow or red disk flowers. Fruit an achene with fine, pale cinnamon-colored bristles. Flowers Aug.–Oct.; fruits Sept.–Oct.

Habitat/range: Woodlands, thickets, and roadsides at high elevations. Spruce-fir forests and northern hardwood forests. Common. Southern Appalachian endemic from Virginia south to Georgia.

Taxonomy: Mountain wood aster is a tetraploid (has 4 sets of chromosomes) derived from a diploid ancestor, the white wood aster (*E. divaricatus*). Plants of the mountain wood aster are larger and essentially replace white wood aster at higher elevations.

Ecology: Newly opened flower heads have yellow disk flowers that turn red or purplish as the flowers age (usually within a week). This change in flower color is an adaptive trait that benefits both the plant and its insect pollinators. The yellow flowers offer more nectar and pollen than the red-purplish flowers. Pollinators cue in on this difference by visiting yellow disk flowers at a higher rate than red-purplish disk flowers. By preferentially visiting the more rewarding flowers, pollinators forage more efficiently for nectar and pollen. From a plant perspective, the advantage of maintaining its post-change (red-purplish) flowers is an increased floral display (as larger floral displays attract more pollinators). Reproduction occurs sexually by seed and vegetatively by rhizomes, resulting in dense patches of this plant.

Uses: A fall-blooming species, mountain wood aster makes an attractive garden plant.

Synonym: Aster divaricatus var. *chlorolepis* (Burgess) Ahles

Eurybia macrophylla (L.) Cassini
BIGLEAF ASTER
Asteraceae (Sunflower family)

Description: Herbaceous perennial up to 4 ft. tall with very large, rough, heart-shaped basal leaves with saw-toothed margins, upper leaves oval to lance-shaped, reduced in size upward on stem. Pale purple ray flowers surround yellow disk flowers that become reddish with age. Fruit a brown nutlet. Flowers July–Sept.; fruits Aug.–Oct.

Habitat/range: Moist to somewhat dry forests and woodlands, including red oak forests. Common in mountains. Eastern United States.

Taxonomy: Of the 250–300 species of asters worldwide, more than half are native to the United States and Canada. Formerly placed in a single genus (*Aster*), researchers over the past decade have split asters into several genera. Most of the North American asters are now in the genera *Eurybia* and *Symphyotrichum*.

Ecology: In asters and other members of the sunflower family, what appears to be a single large flower is actually a head of many tiny flowers crowded together. A head typically consists of a whorl of female flowers (rays) on the margin and a dense cluster of bisexual (disk) flowers in the center. The outer female flowers bear a large, conspicuous petal that helps attract pollinators. Because most North American asters are genetically self-incompatible, cross-pollination is necessary for successful seed-set. Asters generally bloom in late summer and fall and are pollinated by various insects, including bees, flies, butterflies, and moths. A ring-shaped nectary at the base secretes nectar that accumulates and rises to the upper part of each flower. The aggregation of tiny flowers into heads allows pollinators to rapidly visit many flowers for nectar or pollen. Many asters exhibit "sleep" movements, with the ray petals closing around the disk flowers at night. This helps insulate the reproductive parts from low nighttime temperatures and provides some protection from nocturnal herbivores.

Wildlife: Bumblebees are an important pollinator of bigleaf aster flowers.

Synonym: Aster macrophyllus L.

Eutrochium fistulosum (Barratt) Lamont
JOE PYE WEED
Asteraceae (Sunflower family)

Description: Multistemmed perennial 3–10 ft. tall, smooth, purplish, mostly hollow stems with vanilla odor. Leaves in whorls of 3–7, lanceolate, 4–12 in. long. Flowers in large, round-topped, showy pink to purplish clumps. Fruit a black achene topped with bristles. Flowers July–Oct.; fruits Sept.–Oct.

Habitat/range: Moist to wet areas, including rocky streamsides, mountain bogs, forest edges, and roadsides. Common. Widespread in eastern and central United States.

Taxonomy: The genus *Eutrochium* consists of 5 herbaceous perennials of eastern North America, all of which occur in the mountains and piedmont. Spotted Joe Pye weed (*E. maculatum*) is very similar to *E. fistulosum* but has solid stems and flat-topped inflorescences.

Ecology: Joe Pye weed grows best in open, sunny places where its leaves receive full sunlight. Take a close look down a stem; you'll notice that each whorl of leaves is slightly rotated from the whorl above and below. By reducing self-shading, this leaf arrangement maximizes the amount of light each leaf receives, thereby increasing photosynthesis and plant growth. Dense clusters of flowers provide abundant, easily accessible nectar for a wide range of flower visitors. It's not unusual to see hordes of bees, flies, wasps, and butterflies simultaneously visiting the flowers on a single plant. The growing (and flowering) seasons usually end with the first hard frost of autumn, but the tall dead stems remain standing overwinter, replaced by new stems that emerge in late spring from dormant buds on the persistent root crown.

Wildlife: Tiger swallowtails, great spangled fritillary, red admiral, painted lady, viceroy, monarchs, and sulphurs are among the many butterflies that visit the flowers. Goldfinches commonly glean seeds from fruiting heads in autumn.

Uses: One of our showiest fall-blooming species, Joe Pye weed is commonly planted in wildflower gardens.

Synonym: Eupatorium fistulosum Barratt

Fragaria virginiana Mill.
WILD STRAWBERRY
Rosaceae (Rose family)

Description: A low-growing perennial that spreads by runners. Leaves on long, slender stalks with 3 coarsely toothed leaflets. White flowers with 5 petals occur in flat clusters on stalks separate from the leaves. Achenes embedded in a fleshy receptacle (the strawberry). Flowers Mar.–June; fruits May–June.

Habitat/range: Fields, roadsides, and forest edges. Common. Eastern North America.

Taxonomy: Two of the 10 species of *Fragaria* occur in the mountains and piedmont. Wood strawberry (*F. vesca*) has smaller (one-half in. wide) flowers and its achenes occur on the surface of the fleshy fruit, rather than in depressions, as do the seeds of wild strawberry. The cultivated strawberry sold in markets is a hybrid that was formed by crossing *F. virginiana* and *F. chiloensis*.

Ecology: Wild strawberry grows in full to partial sun, often forming dense patches. Each flower cluster includes about 10 flowers, but usually only 1 flower is open at a time. Individual flowers typically open for a single day. Male, female, and hermaphrodite plants can all occur in the same population. The flowers attract a variety of insects, including bees, flies, small butterflies, skippers, and ants, but bees are the primary pollinators. Hermaphrodite flowers are larger, produce about 50 percent more nectar, and receive about 50 percent more bee visits than do female flowers. Plants spread by seeds as well as by runners that root at the nodes. The runners begin to decay by late summer and because the connections between nodes are usually lost by spring, single large plants separate into a number of smaller plants. Small, prostrate plants occur at higher elevations, including roadside areas along the Blue Ridge Parkway.

Wildlife: Numerous songbirds and small mammals consume the fleshy fruits and disperse the tiny seeds. White-tailed deer, eastern cottontail, and other small mammals eat the foliage.

Uses: The fleshy red fruits are smaller but sweeter than the cultivated strawberry. The leaves can be brewed into a tea rich in vitamin C.

Galax urceolata (Poir.) Brummitt
GALAX, SKUNKWEED
Diapensiaceae (Diapensia family)

Description: Low-growing evergreen perennial spreads vegetatively from rhizomes, forming dense colonies of round, shiny leaves on long stalks. Small white flowers in dense racemes on tall, slender stalks form small capsules. Flowers May–July; fruits Aug.–Oct.

Habitat/range: Moist to dry woods on acidic soils, often with mountain laurel (*Kalmia latifolia*) or rosebay (*Rhododendron maximum*). Nearly ubiquitous in mountains, less common in piedmont. From Maryland south to Georgia.

Taxonomy: The genus *Galax* has just 1 species. The plant sometimes smells like dog feces or skunk spray, hence the name skunkweed.

Ecology: Galax thrives in environments ranging from low-elevation coastal sites to high mountain spruce-fir forests, but grows best on cool, moist, acidic sites in partial shade. Once established, plants spread vegetatively from rhizomes, often forming continuous ground cover. The leaves typically change from dark green in summer to a red, bronze, or purple color in late fall. This color change is due to the production of anthocyanin pigments that absorb light and provide a kind of light screen for leaves exposed to potentially damaging light levels in winter. With the onset of warmer temperatures in spring (and shade as the deciduous overstory leafs out), the anthocyanins dissipate and the leaves become green again. In contrast, plants in continuous shade typically stay green year-round as the protective pigment isn't produced (or needed).

Wildlife: White-tailed deer browse the leaves in winter (particularly in years when acorns are in short supply) and the tiny white flowers (with their garlic-like odor) attract flies and other insect pollinators.

Uses: Its shiny, reddish brown autumn leaves (which can be stored for months) have been in high demand as background foliage in floral arrangements since the early 1900s. Overcollecting is a threat in some areas, as experienced workers can harvest 5,000 leaves in a single day.

Synonym: Galax aphylla L.

Galearis spectabilis (L.) Raf.
SHOWY ORCHIS
Orchidaceae (Orchid family)

Description: A low-growing orchid with 2 large, rather fleshy basal leaves and a single stout flower stalk with 2–12 colorful flowers in a loose raceme. Pink to lavender flowers with 2 lateral petals and 3 sepals, converging to form a hood with a third (lower) petal forming a white lip with a prominent nectar spur. Fruit an erect capsule with thousands of dust-like seeds. Flowers Apr.–May, fruits May–June.

Habitat/range: Rich mesic or calcareous woodlands, often at base of slopes and near streams. Cove forests, river bluff forests, floodplain forests, and basic mesic forests. Uncommon. Eastern North America.

Taxonomy: The genus *Galearis* has just 2 species, 1 in eastern North America, the other in eastern Asia.

Ecology: Showy orchis is a good example of a facultative calciphile: a plant that often occurs on calcium-rich soils, but not exclusively. Individuals emerge and flower in early spring, thereby taking advantage of the high light levels reaching the forest floor prior to canopy leaf out. Unlike spring ephemerals, showy orchis remains green throughout the summer and fall, prolonging its growing season before overwintering as a fleshy rootstalk. The showy flowers depend on insect pollinators (mainly early spring-emerging bumblebee queens) for successful pollination. The hood and nectar spur reflect ultraviolet light, which helps attract bees to the flowers. Bees use the white lower lip petal as a landing platform as they push their way into the hood. The lower lip petal also has a long, backward-pointing nectar spur that provides a rich nectar source for long-tongued insects. At the base of each flower is a conspicuous leaf-like bract that is green and photosynthetically active, an important nutrient source for developing fruits.

Wildlife: Skunks are known to feed on the fleshy roots.

Uses: Showy orchis, like almost all our native orchids, is best enjoyed in the wild, as it's very difficult to cultivate in gardens without its specific soil fungal associates.

Synonym: Orchis spectabilis L.

Galium aparine L.
CATCHWEED BEDSTRAW
Rubiaceae (Madder family)

Description: Numerous weak, scraggly stems, some erect, others adhering to or leaning against other plants, with narrow, sessile leaves in whorls of 4–8. Tiny white flowers, each with 4-petal lobes, in small clusters. Mature fruits consist of paired, seed-like structures covered with hooked bristles. Flowers Apr.–May.

Habitat/range: Shady, moist woodlands, meadows, lawns, roadsides, other disturbed areas. Common. Temperate regions throughout the world and at higher elevations in tropics.

Taxonomy: A large genus of about 300 species of herbs from around the world, including 17 species in the mountains and piedmont.

Ecology: The foliage is more likely to get your attention than the flowers, as its tiny flowers are easily overlooked, but if you brush against the foliage, it sticks, hence the name "catchweed." In most bedstraws it's the seeds, covered with tiny hook-shaped bristles that cling, like Velcro, to clothing and fur. In catchweed bedstraw, however, it's the stems (covered with recurved bristles) that adhere to you (and other animals). Because the stems typically have seeds attached, the stickiness of the plant provides a mechanism for seed dispersal. A winter annual, bedstraw seeds germinate in the fall, plants overwinter in a vegetative state and then flower, fruit, and die in spring. Ripe seeds germinate readily, but only if covered with soil, as light inhibits germination (this may help seedlings survive drought). Both native and introduced populations from Eurasia occur in the eastern United States.

Wildlife: More than 3 dozen insect species feed on this plant, including gall makers, leaf miners, sap-suckers, and leaf browsers. The small, hard-coated seeds readily pass through the guts of cattle, horses, goats, and birds without losing their viability.

Uses: Dried bedstraw was once used as mattress stuffing, hence the common name "bedstraw." Bedstraw can be a problem weed in both agricultural fields and gardens.

Gaultheria procumbens L.
WINTERGREEN
Ericaceae (Heath family)

Description: A low-growing (3–4 in tall), slightly woody plant with a few shiny evergreen leaves (mostly crowded toward stem tip) from a creeping rhizome. Solitary, white to pinkish urn-shaped flowers hang from stalks. Fruit a bright red berry with numerous seeds. Flowers June–Aug.; fruits Sept.–Nov., persisting through winter.

Habitat/range: Dry to moist, acidic woodlands and openings, including heath balds, pine-oak-heath, and mountain bogs. Common in mountains, occasional in piedmont. Widespread in northeastern United States and Canada, extending south in Appalachian Mountains to Georgia.

Taxonomy: A widespread genus of 130 species of shrubs and subshrubs, it's the only species in the mountains and piedmont.

Ecology: This prostrate plant is technically a subshrub, rather than a herbaceous plant, because of its slightly woody stems. Like almost all members of the heath family (Ericaceae), it's a good indicator of acidic soils. Bees, particularly bumblebees, pollinate the small, dangling, urn-shaped flowers, which develop into fragrant, bright red berries that typically persist on the plant over winter. The glossy green leaves turn a bronze to red color in winter and have a strong wintergreen odor if bruised.

Wildlife: Birds and mammals, such as chipmunks, white-tailed deer, and ruffed grouse consume the red aromatic fruits and disperse the tiny hard-coated seeds, which typically pass intact through their guts.

Uses: The leaves and red berries of *Gaultheria* and the twigs and bark of sweet and yellow birch (*Betula lenta* and *B. alleghaniensis*) are natural sources of oil of wintergreen (methyl salicylate), a chemical compound that was once used to flavor gum, candy, and toothpaste. Today, it's produced synthetically.

Gentiana saponaria L.
SOAPWORT GENTIAN
Gentianaceae (Gentian family)

Description: Erect herbaceous perennial with smooth stems up to 2 ft. tall, often in clumps. Leaves linear to elliptic, widest near middle, dark green. Large bluish purple, tubular flowers, usually closed at tip, in terminal clusters and in upper leaf axils. Fruit an elongate, tan capsule with numerous wind-dispersed seeds. Flowers late Sept.–Nov.

Habitat/range: Bogs, wet meadows, wet hardwood forests, roadside ditches, and other moist to wet habitats. Uncommon. Eastern United States.

Taxonomy: Gentians occur in Asia, the Americas, Europe, Africa, and Australia. The 8 species in the mountains and piedmont generally occur in moist to wet habitats and flower in late summer–fall. The closed gentian (*G. clausa*) is similar to soapwort gentian but lacks bicolored flowers. Soapwort gentian derives its name from its resemblance to the foliage of *Saponaria*, or soapwort, but its foliage doesn't produce a lather.

Ecology: The large tubular flowers are unusual in that they're virtually closed, restricting access to bumblebees, which are strong enough to push their way through the stiff, pleated corollas to access nectar and pollen. The exclusive nature of the flowers' pollination mechanism benefits the plant in that pollen and nectar aren't wasted on less efficient pollinators. As fruits mature, the flower stalk elongates and the capsule splits lengthwise, exposing tiny, winged seeds to the wind.

Wildlife: Gentians are an important nectar source for bumblebees from late summer–fall. Deer sometimes browse the tops of soapwort gentian, but bitter-tasting alkaloids deter most herbivores.

Uses: Gentian flowers are widely admired for their beauty and are sometimes incorporated into gardens.

Geranium maculatum L.
WILD GERANIUM
Geraniaceae (Geranium family)

Description: Herbaceous perennial from 1 to 2 ft. tall with deeply palmately-lobed basal leaves. Showy, bright pink to rose-purple flowers in loose terminal clusters above the leaves. Fruit a beaked capsule with 5 chambers, each containing a single seed. Flowers Apr.–June; fruits May–July.

Habitat/range: Moist, open woods, bluffs, and streambanks, including cove forests, river bluff forests, alluvial forests, and other calcium-rich forests. Common. Widely distributed in eastern North America.

Taxonomy: A genus of more than 300 species of herbaceous plants mostly of temperate areas, including 11 species in the mountains and piedmont. The "geranium" of home gardens and window boxes is in the same family, but a different genus (*Pelargonium*).

Ecology: This common spring wildflower has large, showy flowers. When flowers first open, the stamens release bright blue pollen and the flower is functionally male. On the second or third day, the anthers fall off and the stigmas open, resulting in a functionally female flower. This temporal separation of gender within a flower promotes cross-pollination, rather than self-pollination. Various butterflies visit the flowers for nectar, but bees are the primary pollinators. After pollination, the petals fall off and the pistil develops into a 5-parted capsule with beak-like projections. When ripe, each section of the capsule splits off from the others, the stalk curls up, twists as humidity changes, and finally catapults the seed up to 30 ft. away. On the ground, the long tail attached to the seed (called an awn) continues to curl when dry and straighten when wet, pushing the seed over the surface of the ground until it becomes stuck in a small hole or crack (the twisting motion may also help push the seed into the soil). This adaptive behavior helps ensure the seed is in a good place to germinate and establish as a seedling.

Wildlife: Dense clusters of wild geranium aphids (yellowish green with black markings) suck sap from the leaves and stems. Birds and small mammals eat the seeds.

Uses: Wild geranium is a robust and attractive garden plant.

Geum radiatum Michx.
SPREADING AVENS
Rosaceae (Rose family)
Federally Endangered

Description: Perennial herb 8–20 in. tall, densely hairy stems, leaves mostly basal, 3–6 in. across, with a large, rounded, deeply toothed terminal leaf, the stem leaves much smaller. One to several large bright-yellow flowers with numerous stamens and pistils at tips of erect stems. Fruit an aggregate of achenes. Flowers June–Aug.; fruits July–Sept.

Habitat/range: High-elevation rock outcrops and grassy balds. Rare. A southern Appalachian endemic known from only a small number of mountaintops in North Carolina and Tennessee.

Taxonomy: The famous French botanist André Michaux first described *G. radiatum* in 1803. It's easily distinguished from the other 9 species of *Geum* in the mountains and piedmont by its showy yellow flowers and mostly basal leaves with large rounded terminal leaves. *G. radiatum* is most closely related to *G. peckii*, whose southernmost occurrence is in the White Mountains of New Hampshire.

Ecology: Spreading avens most often occurs on exposed cliffs and ledges where small pockets of soil accumulate in the cracks and crevices of underlying rocks. These high mountaintops are often immersed in dense fog, and the condensation that forms on plants and other surfaces is an important source of soil moisture. The main threat to this federally endangered species is human-caused disturbance. The popularity of mountain summits for their scenic vistas, coupled with their thin soils, makes outcrop plants such as spreading avens particularly vulnerable to trampling by hikers, climbers, and sightseers. Seven of the 11 known populations of spreading avens have fewer than 50 plants (5 additional populations have been extirpated). Very small populations are particularly vulnerable to extinction and low levels of genetic variability limit their ability to adapt to environmental change (such as global climate change), further increasing their extinction risk.

Wildlife: Flies and bees pollinate the flowers as they seek nectar, pollen, or both.

Goodyera pubescens (Willd.) R. Br.
RATTLESNAKE ORCHID
Orchidaceae (Orchid family)

Description: Herbaceous perennial with 4–8 evergreen leaves in a basal rosette. Ovate leaves bluish green with a distinctive network of white veins and a broad white stripe down the midrib. Stout, hairy, flowering stalk up to 15 in. tall, the upper part densely packed with small, hairy white flowers with a sac-like lower lip. Fruit a small, erect capsule. Flowers June–Aug.

Habitat/range: Wide variety of moist to dry coniferous and hardwood forests on acidic soils. Common. Eastern North America.

Taxonomy: Orchids comprise the largest and most diverse family of flowering plants with over 800 genera and 25,000 species. Only 2 of the 100 species of *Goodyera* occur in the mountains and piedmont. The similar but less common lesser rattlesnake orchid (*G. repens*) has a basal rosette of dark green variegated leaves that lack a broad white stripe down the midrib. The infructescence (cluster of fruits) looks very much like the "rattle" at the tail end of a rattlesnake, and the unusual markings on the leaves resemble the skin of a rattlesnake, hence the common name.

Ecology: Rattlesnake orchid is one of our most common and easily recognized orchids. Individuals spread vegetatively by underground stems (rhizomes), so a single plant can have multiple rosettes, few of which bloom in any given year. After flowering, individual rosettes wither and die, but one or more new rosettes arise from a rhizome, ensuring survival. Enormous numbers of extremely tiny seeds are produced in each fruit. The seeds consist of a minute embryo surrounded by a single layer of protective cells. Because orchid seeds lack stored food (or endosperm), they depend upon a symbiotic relationship with a specialized soil fungus for seed germination and seedling growth. The chance of a seed encountering an appropriate fungus is very small. For this and other limiting factors, only a tiny fraction of the seeds produced develop into seedlings. Orchid seedlings develop so slowly that it may take 5–10 years or more before a plant is large enough to flower.

Wildlife: Bees pollinate the flowers.

Uses: The Cherokee made a tea from the leaves to treat colds and kidney problems.

Gratiola amphiantha Estes and Small
POOL SPRITE
Plantaginaceae (Plantain family)
Federally Threatened

Description: Diminutive aquatic annual consists of submerged and floating leaves, the latter in single pairs at the tips of long, threadlike stems. Tiny white to violet flowers in axils of both leaf types. Fruit a tiny capsule. Flowers Mar.–Apr.; fruits Apr.–May.

Habitat/range: Restricted to shallow pools on granite outcrops that retain rainwater for prolonged periods during cool months of late fall through early spring. Rare. The piedmont of South Carolina, Georgia, and Alabama.

Taxonomy: This unusual, easily identified plant is the only species in the genus.

Ecology: Pool sprite occupies an extremely specialized habitat—shallow depressions on rock outcrops that have a thin layer of mineral soil and an intact rim restricting water drainage. The seeds of this winter annual typically germinate from late fall through winter after pools form in depressions. Tiny rosettes of leaves are submerged through late winter when each rosette forms 1 to several threadlike stems, each bearing a single pair of tiny floating leaves. Inconspicuous self-pollinating flowers are produced until the pools dry up in spring, killing the plants. The population persists as dormant seeds in mostly dry pools until germination occurs in late fall or winter. Seeds are dormant when shed, a condition that is maintained throughout summer and early autumn by high temperatures. Because light is required for germination, buried seeds remain dormant, providing a buffer (in the form of a seed bank) against local extinction in years when early drought or other factors result in high mortality and low seed production. The seeds are dispersed by runoff during heavy rains as well as by adhering to mud on the feet of birds or mammals that visit the pools. Restricted to small, scattered pools on about 65 outcrops in the piedmont, the species is currently threatened by habitat degradation due to rock quarrying, off-road vehicles, and recreational impacts such as excess foot traffic, people and pets playing in pools, and the building of campfires in dry pools.

Synonym: Amphianthus pusillus Torr.

Grimmia laevigata (Brid.) Brid.
DRY ROCK MOSS
Grimmiaceae (Woolly Moss family)

Description: Grows in dense, prostrate cushions or mats, dark olive green to black or brown. Stem leaves minute, oblong-ovate to lanceolate with long, decurrent awns. Spore-producing capsules occasionally present.

Habitat/range: Rock outcrops in piedmont and lower mountains. Common. Across North America and on every continent except Antarctica.

Taxonomy: A cosmopolitan genus of 94 species, nearly all of which grow on acidic bedrock.

Ecology: Like many mosses, dry rock moss can grow directly on bare rock. While lichens also do this, other plants depend on the presence of soil for successful establishment and growth. Because moss mats gradually accumulate soil, they provide substrates that enable other plants to colonize rock outcrops. Mosses (and lichens) are the true pioneers of rock outcrops since their presence facilitates succession. Another remarkable feature of some mosses, including dry rock moss, is an ability to tolerate very high temperatures and prolonged desiccation, and then rehydrate and become metabolically active when moisture returns. Other than lichens, mosses, and a few ferns and flowering plants, very few plants can do this. With a nearly worldwide distribution on bare rock substrates, dry rock moss can tolerate a remarkably broad set of environmental conditions, including temperature extremes, low nutrients, and prolonged desiccation. In one study, individuals stored in dry cabinets for 10 years restored metabolic activity upon rehydration. On rock outcrops, individuals become black when dormant during droughts, turning bright green and becoming metabolically active after rain. Dry rock moss's wide distribution pattern is also a result of its tiny dust-sized spores traveling great distances in air currents. Once established, individuals spread laterally, sometimes coalescing with other mats to form large patches.

Wildlife: Few herbivores feed on the tiny leaves of this prostrate plant.

Uses: Adds interest to rock gardens.

Helianthus schweinitzii
Torr. & A. Gray
SCHWEINITZ'S SUNFLOWER
Asteraceae (Sunflower family)
Federally Endangered

Description: Upright perennial herb usually 3–6 ft. tall but can reach heights of 10 ft. Lance-shaped leaves opposite on lower stem, changing to alternate above, gradually reduced upwards, rough like sandpaper on upper surface, velvety smooth on lower surface. Flower heads less than 2 in. across with yellow ray and disk flowers. Fruit a dark brown nutlet. Flowers late Aug.–Sept.

Habitat/range: Glades in xeric hardpan forests, mowed power line corridors, roadsides, and field margins. Rare. Restricted to piedmont of North Carolina and South Carolina, mostly within 60 miles of Charlotte, North Carolina.

Taxonomy: A genus of 52 species of North America, including about 26 species in the mountains and piedmont.

Ecology: Like most sunflowers, Schweinitz's sunflower requires full to partial sunlight to grow, reproduce, and persist. Historically, it probably occurred in piedmont woodlands (open-canopy forests) and prairies that were kept open by periodic fires caused by lightning and Native Americans. By the early twentieth century, widespread fire suppression dramatically reduced the frequency of wildland fires and the amount of open forest, a habitat Schweinitz's sunflower and other sun-loving plants require. Today's remaining populations persist in marginal sites, including power line right-of-ways and roadsides where periodic bush hogging maintains a suitable habitat. Schweinitz's sunflower was designated a federally endangered species in 1991; fewer than 20 populations are now known, most of which are small and vulnerable to extirpation. In addition to fire suppression, current threats are development, mining, encroachment by invasive plants, highway construction, and roadside and utility right-of-way maintenance, including the use of herbicides.

Wildlife: Grazing by native herbivores, including buffalo and elk, and periodic fires historically played an important role in maintaining the open habitat required by this species.

Helianthus strumosus L.
ROUGHLEAF SUNFLOWER
Asteraceae (Sunflower family)

Description: Herbaceous perennial 3–9 ft. tall with smooth, bluish green stems, leaves mostly opposite, lanceolate to ovate, 3–6 in. long with a rough upper surface, hence the common name. Flower heads with yellow disk and ray flowers, the latter 1–2 in. long. Fruit an achene. Flowers late July–Sept.

Habitat/range: Woods, forest edges, fields, and roadsides. Common. Widespread in eastern United States.

Taxonomy: The genus name *Helianthus* comes from 2 Greek words, "helios" (sun) and "anthos" (flower). The yellow, maroon, or brown radial disks of sunflowers have been used artistically as symbols for the sun throughout the ages.

Ecology: The yellow flower heads of various sunflowers (including *Solidago*, *Packera*, and *Helianthus*) are a conspicuous component of roadsides, fields, and forest margins in late summer and early fall. The flowers of roughleaf sunflower (and various other plants) track the sun across the sky, facing east in the morning, and west as the sun sets at the end of the day. By tracking the sun, the surface temperature of the flower head is slightly elevated, which helps lure pollinating insects. The large, showy ray flowers help attract pollinators visually as well; experiments have shown that removing the ray flowers decreases insect visitation rates and seed set.

Wildlife: White-tailed deer commonly forage the flower heads and fresh foliage, various insects visit the flowers for nectar, pollen, or both, and songbirds consume the seeds. Silvery crescentspot butterflies use *Helianthus* species as a larval host plant.

Uses: Native Americans used the seeds of various sunflowers to make flour for bread and oil for cooking. Tolerant of both heat and dry conditions, sunflowers provide a splash of color in woodland gardens from summer through fall.

Helonias bullata L.
SWAMP PINK
Melanthiaceae (Bunchflower family)
Federally Threatened

Description: Herbaceous perennial with a basal rosette of evergreen spatulate leaves, 4–8 in. long. Dense clusters of pink flowers with blue anthers at tip of long stalk with many small, scale-like leaves (bracts). Fruit a capsule. Flowers Apr.–May; fruits June–July.

Habitat/range: Usually under dense shrubs in wet, peaty soils. Mountain bogs and swamps. Rare. Loosely scattered in Blue Ridge Mountains from Virginia south to Georgia, and in coastal plain from New Jersey south to Virginia.

Taxonomy: Swamp pink is the only species in the genus *Helonias*; its closest relatives are in the eastern Asian genus *Heloniopsis*.

Ecology: Flies, beetles, and other insects visit the showy pink flowers in search of nectar, pollen, or both. The slender seeds are initially dispersed by gravity and wind from fruiting stalks that reach heights of 3 ft. or more. The seeds may subsequently be dispersed by ants or by water as the seeds can float for days. Vegetative reproduction enables plants to spread locally as new rosettes develop from underground stems. Swamp pink is a habitat specialist in that it's restricted to fairly uncommon, often isolated wetland habitats. Although it typically occurs under dense shrubs, swamp pink flowers and grows best in openings created by windthrown trees. A federally listed species, swamp pink is at risk due to loss of wetlands as well as habitat degradation resulting from siltation, changes in the water table, and the introduction of excess nutrients and toxic chemicals from runoff. Other threats include trampling, illegal collection by gardeners (and commercial nurseries), dam building by beavers, and encroachment by woody plants, especially Chinese privet. Low levels of genetic variation increase swamp pink's vulnerability to disease and reduce its ability to adapt to changing conditions.

Wildlife: The foliage, flowers, and developing fruits are subject to heavy browsing by deer.

Hepatica acutiloba DC.
ACUTE-LOBED HEPATICA
Ranunculaceae (Buttercup family)

Description: A stemless herbaceous perennial up to 6 in. tall, with clusters of basal, 3-lobed evergreen leaves with sharply pointed tips, hence the common name. Solitary flowers on elongate, hairy stalks, the petal-like sepals vary in color, white, pink, lavender, purple or blue. Fruit a single-seeded achene. Flowers Feb.–Apr.; fruits Mar.–May.

Habitat/range: Moist forests, including cove forests, river bluff forests, and basic mesic forests. Common. Widespread in eastern North America.

Taxonomy: Hepatica is a small genus of herbaceous perennials of eastern North America, Europe, and eastern Asia. Round-lobed hepatica (*H. americana*) is similar but has rounded, rather than acute, leaf tips. These two species are sometimes placed in the genus *Anemone*.

Ecology: Acute-lobed hepatica is one of our earliest-blooming spring wildflowers. Because stigmas of open flowers are receptive to pollen for several days before the anthers dehisce, cross-pollination is promoted. If that fails, self-pollination can still occur, a beneficial trait given the precarious nature of pollinator availability in late winter and early spring. As seeds begin to ripen, the flower stalk lengthens and droops near the ground, increasing access to ants, which collect and disperse the seeds. After flowering, the reddish brown overwintering leaves senesce, and a new set of green leaves is produced that persist until the following spring. Hepatica leaves, unlike those of spring ephemerals, are relatively shade-tolerant and function efficiently under the leafy canopy of summer and fall.

Wildlife: Flies and bees pollinate the flowers and ants disperse the seeds.

Uses: Early herbalists developed the "Doctrine of Signatures," the belief that if a plant part has the shape of a human body part, the plant part would be useful in treating a disease of that body part (a similar belief was held in Native American and Asian cultures). Because the leaves of hepatica have lobes that resemble a human liver, it was traditionally used in the treatment of liver ailments.

Heuchera parviflora Bartlett
CAVE ALUMROOT
Saxifragaceae (Saxifrage family)

Description: Herbaceous perennial 4–20 in. tall with large, nearly circular basal leaves with broadly rounded lobes and teeth; the leaves, petioles, and stems soft and hairy. Tiny white flowers in multiple, branched racemes. Fruit a small capsule. Flowers July–Sept.; fruits Aug.–Oct.

Habitat/range: Shaded cliff bases and ledges, usually under overhangs, and spray cliffs. Uncommon and sporadic in mountains and piedmont. Eastern United States.

Taxonomy: *Heuchera* is a genus of about 55 species of perennial herbs, 8 of which occur in the mountains and piedmont. Rock alumroot (*H. villosa*) grows in similar habitats and blooms at the same time as cave alumroot but differs in having triangular, rather than rounded, leaf lobes.

Ecology: Cave alumroot is a rare species largely because it's restricted to a highly specialized habitat: shaded cliffs and ledges, often associated with waterfalls. A slow-growing species, it's able to occupy deeply shaded habitats where few other seed plants grow. The large (up to 6 in. wide) horizontally oriented leaves enhance the capture of light and therefore photosynthesis and growth in a dimly lit environment. Seeds are dispersed by a combination of gravity, wind, and water. Germination occurs in late winter or early spring when soil temperatures are increasing and conditions favor seedling growth.

Wildlife: The seeds are too small to be of much interest to birds or small mammals.

Uses: Cave alumroot makes a nice addition to woodland gardens.

Heuchera villosa Michx.
ROCK ALUMROOT, CRAG JANGLE
Saxifragaceae (Saxifrage family)

Description: Perennial herb 8–36 in. tall, the maple-like basal leaves 2–6 in. long and wide, palmately lobed with 5–7 sharp lobes. Tiny pink to white flowers occur in dense clusters that terminate a leafless, hairy stalk that extends well above the basal leaves. Fruit a capsule with tiny dark red seeds. Flowers June–Oct.; fruits Aug.–Oct.

Habitat/range: High-elevation rock outcrops. Common in mountains, rare in upper piedmont. Virginia south to Georgia, primarily in Blue Ridge Mountains.

Taxonomy: Rock alumroot is similar to common alumroot (*H. americana*) and cave alumroot (*H. parviflora*) but has sharp, rather than blunt or rounded, leaf lobes. Common alumroot differs from the other 2 species in that it blooms in spring, rather than summer.

Ecology: Rock alumroot occurs mostly on high-elevation cliffs and ledges where it grows in rock crevices and on thin soils over boulders. Loosely scattered plants occur on moist, shaded sites and on drier, more open exposures on a variety of rock substrates, including granites, quartzites, schists, and felsic and mafic gneisses. Successful seed set depends on flowers being cross-pollinated, rather than self-pollinated, as rock alumroot is genetically self-incompatible. Although the specific pollinators are unknown, small bees and flies are likely candidates. Most eastern North American species of *Heuchera* are interfertile, resulting in hybrid individuals often growing in areas where 2 or more species co-occur.

Uses: Native Americans used a powder from the dried roots as a topical remedy for sores, wounds, and ulcers. Species of *Heuchera* make attractive plants in rock gardens and containers.

Hexastylis arifolia (Michx.) Small
LITTLE BROWN JUGS
Aristolochiaceae (Birthwort family)

Description: Small, stemless perennial herb with smooth, shiny, arrowhead-shaped evergreen leaves arising from a short rhizome. Flower a jug-shaped fleshy calyx about 1 in. long, constricted at top, with 3 small, erect lobes, often hidden under leaf litter. Fruit a fleshy capsule. Flowers Mar.–May.

Habitat/range: Dry to moist deciduous forests, including acidic cove forests, chestnut oak forests, river bluff forests, and oak-hickory forests. Common in piedmont and lower mountains. Southeast.

Taxonomy: A genus of 10 species of evergreen herbaceous plants of the Southeast, including 9 species in the mountains and piedmont. The shape and size of the flower are the main criteria used to distinguish species in this genus.

Ecology: Like many woodland wildflowers, the leaves are oriented horizontally (at right angles to incident light), enabling the plant to more efficiently capture limited light energy, particularly in summer under a shaded canopy. Long petioles position the leaves well above the ground surface (reducing the likelihood of being overtopped by neighboring herbaceous plants). In winter, the leaf petioles collapse, positioning the leaf blade close to the ground surface where temperatures are warmer, thereby facilitating winter photosynthesis. The underground rhizome and overwintering leaves act as storage organs for carbohydrates (soluble sugars). The emergence of new leaves and flowers in spring correlates with a rapid decrease in stored sugars, which are gradually replaced during the spring and summer growing seasons. The unusual flowers hidden at the base of the plant typically depend on pollinators for successful seed set. Certain flies and thrips apparently function as pollinators while using the flowers as a source of nutritious pollen, as shelter, and as a breeding site. Seedlings develop and grow slowly, often taking more than 7 years before the first flowers are produced.

Wildlife: Like most ant-dispersed plants, the fruits are located close to the ground and the seeds ripen in spring when ants are most likely to disperse them (later in summer, ants are less interested in seeds as other more attractive foods are available).

Hexastylis shuttleworthii (Britten & Baker) Small
LARGE FLOWER HEARTLEAF, WILD GINGER
Aristolochiaceae (Birthwort family)

Description: Low-growing, stemless herbaceous perennial with heart-shaped to round evergreen leaves 2–4 in. long, often with light green or white along veins. Flower a brown urn-shaped calyx up to 1 ½ in. long, wide at bottom, constricted at top with 3 large, spreading lobes mottled with purple. Fruit a fleshy capsule. Flowers May–July.

Habitat/range: Often under rosebay (*Rhododendron maximum*) along creeks in acidic cove forests. Common in mountains, uncommon in piedmont. Restricted to southern Appalachians, from Virginia south to Georgia.

Taxonomy: Hexastylis and *Asarum* are closely related genera that share a number of characteristics, including the common name "wild ginger." *Hexastylis* differs from *Asarum* in having evergreen, rather than winter deciduous, leaves.

Ecology: Many herbaceous plants of eastern deciduous forests, including wild ginger, violets, trilliums, trout lily, hepatica, spring beauty, bloodroot and some sedges, have ant-dispersed seeds. Seeds of ant-dispersed species almost always have a small, lipid-rich food body called an elaiosome attached to the seed coat. Ants carry seeds back to the nest where the elaiosome is removed and fed to ant larvae in the nest. Seeds are frequently discarded on the soil surface near the nest where they may germinate and establish new plants. This interaction is mutualistic as both the ant and plant benefit.

Wildlife: Wild ginger contains aristolochic acid, a bitter-tasting plant-defense compound that deters most herbivores.

Uses: Ingesting plants that contain aristolochic acid may cause cancer and kidney failure in humans. Wild ginger is sometimes grown in woodland gardens.

Houstonia serpyllifolia Michx.
APPALACHIAN BLUET
Rubiaceae (Madder family)

Description: Low-growing herbaceous perennial, 4–8 in. tall, with a combination of diffusely branched, prostrate stems and numerous erect stems. Leaves opposite, ovate to roundish, less than one-third in. long, on short petioles. Tiny blue-violet solitary flowers on long stalks, each with 4 petal lobes, a light yellow center, the narrow tube hairy within. Fruit a flattened, 2-chambered capsule. Flowers Apr.–June.

Habitat/range: Occurs in cool, moist areas, including rocky streamsides, spray cliffs, seepage slopes, and grassy balds. Common in mountains. Restricted to Appalachian Mountains from Pennsylvania south to Georgia.

Taxonomy: The genus *Houstonia* comprises about 20 species of perennial herbs of North America, 11 of which occur in the mountains and piedmont. Quaker ladies (*H. caerulea*) is very similar to Appalachian bluet, but it lacks prostrate runners, the stem leaves lack a distinct petiole, and the petals are typically a lighter blue color.

Ecology: Appalachian bluet has delicate, prostrate stems that root at the nodes, forming dense carpets of small blue flowers in spring. Below the disk-shaped petal lobes, each flower has a narrow floral tube that encloses the pistil and stamens. A yellow nectar guide in the center of the flower helps insects locate the narrow opening that leads to the nectar. The flowers of Appalachian bluet have either a long style with 4 short stamens or a short style with 4 long stamens. This flower dimorphism, known as heterostyly ("different styles") occurs in at least 24 families of flowering plants. Heterostyly is particularly common in the madder (Rubiaceae) family, including members of the bluet genus. Heterostyly promotes cross-pollination because long-styled flowers can be pollinated only with pollen from short-styled flowers (and vice versa). Cross-pollination helps maintain genetic variability, enhancing the ability of species to adapt to changing environments.

Wildlife: Bees, hover flies, and butterflies visit the flowers for nectar, pollen, or both.

Uses: Appalachian bluet can be used as a low-growing groundcover in cool, shady places.

Hydrastis canadensis L.
GOLDENSEAL
Hydrastidaceae (Goldenseal family)

Description: Perennial herb 6–20 in. tall with a single basal leaf and 2 smaller leaves near top of stem. Up to 4 in. wide during flowering, the upper leaves expand to as large as 12 in. wide at maturity, with 3–5 (rarely 7) pointed lobes with a toothed margin and a hairy, wrinkled surface. Small, solitary flowers with 3 greenish white deciduous sepals, leaving the numerous white anther filaments as the primary visual cue attracting pollinators. Fruit a cluster of small, fleshy red berries. Flowers Apr.–May; fruits May–June.

Habitat/range: Moist, nutrient-rich forests on soils high in calcium or magnesium. Rich cove forests. Rare in mountains. Eastern North America.

Taxonomy: Goldenseal is the only species in the genus. The deeply lobed leaves and flowers of Tasselrue (*Trautvetteria caroliniensis*) are similar to goldenseal, but it has smooth (rather than hairy) stems and its leaves and flowers form branched clusters.

Ecology: Populations usually consist of flowering shoots with 3 leaves

(2 stem leaves and 1 basal leaf) as well as single-leafed nonreproductive shoots. While new individuals infrequently establish from seed, vegetative spread by an extensive network of rhizomes can result in dense patches of hundreds of leafy stems. Local patch proliferation is often greatest on forest edges or beneath small gaps in the forest canopy. Rare throughout its range, the species has declined in both distribution and abundance due to overcollecting (for medicinal purposes) and loss of habitat.

Wildlife: White-tailed deer browse the foliage and small bees pollinate the flowers. The fleshy red berries would seem to be attractive to birds and mammals but they often simply fall to the ground.

Uses: Goldenseal rhizomes contain various alkaloids that are used in herbal remedies to treat digestive ailments, bronchial infections, and to "boost" the immune system. A popular medicinal herb, several million wild-collected rhizomes are harvested annually from publicly managed forests in the eastern United States.

Hypericum gentianoides (L.) Britton, Sterns & Poggenb.
PINEWEED
Hypericaceae (St. John's wort family)

Description: Small, upright annual 4–16 in. tall with numerous thread-like branches and scale-like leaves. Tiny, star-shaped yellow flowers open in morning and close by afternoon. Fruit a slender cone-shaped capsule with numerous tiny seeds. Flowers July–Oct.

Habitat/range: Rock outcrops, woodland borders, fields, and roadsides. Common. Widespread in eastern United States.

Taxonomy: Stems resemble pine needles, hence the common name. Also called orange-grass as stems emit an orange-like odor when crushed.

Ecology: Pineweed flowers and produces fruit from midsummer through early fall, when most other piedmont outcrop plants are dormant. Unlike annuals such as elf orpine (*Diamorpha smallii*) and Appalachian sandwort (*Minuartia glabra*), which avoid the severe conditions of summer by completing their life cycle in spring, pineweed is a stress-tolerant annual that copes with the hot, dry conditions of summer. Its green (photosynthetic) thread-like stems and tiny scale-like leaves minimize transpirational water loss, thereby enhancing its ability to cope with very limited moisture availability. A poor competitor, it typically grows on relatively dry, shallow soils where most competing species can't survive. A prolific seed producer, pineweed rapidly invades disturbed soils, including forest plantations, roadsides, and power line corridors. Its seeds remain viable in the soil for several years or more, thereby providing a hedge against local extinction as well as a seed source following disturbance.

Wildlife: Plant defense chemicals deter most animals from feeding on pineweed.

Uses: Various species in the genus are used medicinally, including as a remedy for mild depression.

***Hypericum perforatum** L.*
COMMON ST. JOHN'S WORT
Hypericaceae (St. John's wort family)

Description: Leafy, much-branched herbaceous perennial commonly 1–3 ft. tall. Leaves opposite, sessile, linear-oblong with translucent dots. Showy yellow flowers with numerous stamens and black-dotted petal margins occur in open, flat-topped clusters. Fruit a sticky, cone-shaped capsule. Flowers June–Sept.

Habitat/range: Fields, pastures, grassy balds, roadsides, and forest edges. Common. Introduced from Europe, it occurs throughout the United States and southern Canada. Widely cultivated as a medicinal and garden plant, it has become naturalized in many temperate regions.

Taxonomy: It's the only nonnative species among our 26 species of *Hypericum*.

Ecology: First reported in Pennsylvania in the late eighteenth century, it now occurs in 44 states, 7 of which label it a "noxious" weed. A number of traits enhance its ability to readily colonize disturbed sites, including agricultural fields, overgrazed pastures, roadsides, and forest openings. It tolerates a wide range of soil types and produces an abundance of widely dispersed seeds. A large single plant, for example, can produce more than 15,000 seeds. The seeds mature within sticky capsules that adhere to the feet and bodies of mammals and birds, as well as to vehicles and farm equipment. A persistent soil seed bank makes it difficult to eradicate the plant once it has become established; it also spreads vegetatively by underground stems (rhizomes). Individuals generally experience relatively low levels of damage by grazing animals. Studies have shown that plants of this species introduced into North America experience less herbivore damage than do plants in their native habitats, perhaps because they have left behind their natural herbivores and pathogens.

Wildlife: Except in spring when growth is young and succulent, or at times when more palatable forage is scarce, most insects and mammals avoid this plant.

Uses: Common St. John's wort is a widely used herbal medicine to treat mild forms of depression. It can, however, cause serious interactions with prescription drugs and other herbal products, as well as mild photosensitization.

***Impatiens capensis** Meerb.*
**ORANGE JEWELWEED,
ORANGE TOUCH-ME-NOT**
Balsaminaceae (Touch-me-not family)

Description: Fleshy annual 2–5 ft. tall with smooth, hollow stems and alternate ovate to elliptic leaves 1–4 in. long. Orange-yellow, trumpet-shaped flowers about 1 in. long, on thread-like stalks. Fruit a translucent green capsule. Flowers May–Oct.; fruits June–Oct.

Habitat/range: Moist forests, including northern hardwood forests, cove forests, spray cliffs, rocky streamsides, mountain bogs, forest edges, and floodplain forests. Common. Widespread in eastern and central North America.

Taxonomy: The genus *Impatiens* comprises about 850 species, including 2 in the mountains and piedmont. Yellow jewelweed (*I. pallida*) is similar and grows in many of the same habitats as orange jewelweed but has bright yellow flowers, rather than orange-yellow flowers. Droplets of water bead on the leaves and sparkle in the sun, hence the common name "jewelweed."

Ecology: Most of our woodland wildflowers are perennials, but jewelweeds are annuals that reestablish from seed each year. In sunny, persistently moist habitats, individuals grow from small seedlings in early spring to mature plants up to 5 ft. tall by late summer, often forming dense colonies that suppress or shade out perennial herbs. A cold-sensitive species, jewelweed quickly wilts and dies in autumn when temperatures drop below about 40°F. An annual with relatively short-lived seeds, jewelweed depends on yearly seed production to reestablish populations each spring. In poor habitats, plants produce mostly cleistogamous flowers that self-pollinate in buds and mature seeds early in the growing season, thereby helping to ensure that some seeds are produced each year.

Wildlife: Hummingbirds and bumblebees pollinate jewelweed's nectar-rich flowers.

Uses: Crushed leaves applied to skin sooth the irritation caused by poison ivy and wood nettle. Makes an attractive garden plant in moist, sunny areas.

Impatiens pallida Nutt.
YELLOW JEWELWEED,
YELLOW TOUCH-ME-NOT
Balsaminaceae (Touch-me-not family)

Description: Annual with smooth, almost succulent stems 2–6 ft. tall, widely branching above. Ovate to elliptic toothed leaves on stalks 1–4 in. long. Yellow flowers lightly spotted with reddish brown on slender, drooping stalks from leaf axils, sac-shaped sepal with a narrow nectar spur curved downward at a sharp angle. Fruit an elongate, narrow green capsule. Flowers July–Sept.; fruits Aug.–Oct.

Habitat/range: Moist areas, including rocky streamsides, cove forests, northern hardwood forests, mountain bogs, and forest edges, usually on high pH soils. Common in mountains, rare in piedmont. Eastern and Central North America.

Taxonomy: The 2 species of *Impatiens* in the mountains and piedmont (*I. pallida* and *I. capensis*) are similar in appearance and overlap in habitat types. The easiest way to distinguish them is by flower color, as is reflected in their common names ("yellow" versus "orange jewelweed").

Ecology: Jewelweed produces 2 types of flowers: relatively large, showy, pollinator-dependent chasmogamous (CH) flowers and tiny, inconspicuous cleistogamous (CL) flowers that self-pollinate in the bud. The relative proportion of the 2 flower types is influenced by environmental factors. In less favorable sites (e.g., those with less light, drier soils), a higher proportion of CL flowers is produced. This may reflect the reduced energetic cost of CL flowers (nectaries are absent and the petals, sepals, and anthers are much reduced in size) as well as their higher probability of maturing fruit. Seeds of both flower types mature inside capsules held under tension that "explode" when touched by a passing animal, flinging seeds up to 9 ft. away.

Wildlife: Wild hogs devour the foliage, bees and hummingbirds pollinate the flowers, and birds, rodents, and insects (especially stink bug nymphs) feed on the seeds. Bumblebees and yellow jackets sometimes cut holes in the nectar spurs and steal nectar without pollinating the flowers.

Uses: Native Americans and pioneers applied crushed leaves of jewelweed to rashes caused by poison ivy and wood nettle to reduce inflammation and to relieve itching, a practice that continues today.

Ipomoea pandurata (L.) G. Mey.
BIGROOT MORNING GLORY
Convolvulaceae (Morning glory family)

Description: Trailing or twining perennial vine from a large, deep, tuber-like root with alternate, usually heart-shaped leaves with pointed tips. Large, white funnel-shaped flowers with a purplish center. Fruit an ovoid capsule. Flowers May–Sept.; fruits July–Sept.

Habitat/range: Open woods, thickets, fields, roadsides, other open areas. Common. Widespread in eastern North America.

Taxonomy: The large white flowers with a purplish center, heart-shaped leaves, and hairy seeds distinguish this species from the other 5 species of *Ipomoea* in the mountains and piedmont.

Ecology: Bigroot morning glory grows mostly in disturbed habitats where it sprawls across the open ground or climbs over (and sometimes smothers) low-growing vegetation. Multiple shoots emerge from tubers that lie several feet beneath the ground and weigh up to 30 lbs. Flowers are produced along continuously elongating shoots from May through September. The large, showy flowers produce abundant nectar, much of which is consumed by long-tongued bees within 30 minutes of flower opening. The 1-day flowers continue to produce small amounts of nectar throughout the morning, then wilt and collapse by early afternoon. Primary pollinators are bumblebees and 2 specialist bees that often become conspicuously covered with white pollen as they fly from flower to flower seeking nectar, pollen, or both. Cross-pollination is necessary for successful seed set.

Wildlife: Ants and wasps harvest nectar from extrafloral nectaries (located near the top of each flower stalk) and aggressively attack caterpillars and other insects that attempt to feed on the plant. The relationship is mutually beneficial as the ants and wasps receive food in the form of sugar-rich nectar and the flowers and developing fruits are protected from herbivorous insects.

Uses: The large, edible tuber-like root is somewhat similar to the cultivated sweet potato (*I. batatas*). Native Americans apparently spread this plant from cuttings.

Iris verna L.
DWARF IRIS
Iridaceae (**I**ris family)

Description: Erect perennial herb up to 6 in. tall from thick, spreading rhizomes that form dense patches of mostly straight leaves up to 4 in. long and one-half in. wide at flowering. Showy lavender flowers with 3 erect spatulate petals and 3 spreading or drooping sepals with a yellowish orange stripe bordered with white. Fruit a 3-lobed capsule. Flowers Apr.–May; fruits June–early Aug.

Habitat/range: Dry, rocky areas, including chestnut oak forests and oak-hickory forests. Common. Eastern United States.

Taxonomy: The genus *Iris* includes about 225 species of North America, Eurasia, and Africa, 12 of which occur in the mountains and piedmont. *I. cristata* (dwarf crested iris) is similar to *I. verna* but has crested sepals and wider leaves.

Ecology: Iris flowers are unusual. The outer whorl of 3 petal-like sepals is spreading or droopy, while the inner whorl of 3 petals is smaller and erect. Alternating with the petals and located directly above each sepal is a petaloid style whose pollen-receptive surface (the stigma) is a small flap of tissue that is pressed against the adjacent sepal. Between each sepal and petaloid stigma is a stamen. The long, tongue-like sepals serve as landing platforms for pollinators, and their brightly colored stripes function as nectar guides, directing pollinators towards the mouth of the flower, where the nectar is located. When a pollinator (primarily bees) enters an iris flower, it pushes its way between the petaloid style and sepal. During this process, it may inadvertently brush pollen from its body onto the stigmatic surface, thereby pollinating the flower. As the pollinator probes deeper into the flower for nectar, it becomes dusted with new pollen from the anthers. In backing out of the flower, the pollinator contacts only the nonreceptive lower face of the stigma, thereby reducing the likelihood of self-pollination.

Wildlife: Though the flowers are toxic to humans, white-tailed deer readily eat the flowers, leaves, and rhizomes.

Uses: Dwarf iris is an attractive plant in woodland gardens, due to its showy, fragrant flowers and dense clusters of leaves.

Justicia americana (L.) Vahl
AMERICAN WATER WILLOW
Acanthaceae (Acanthus family)

Description: Perennial herb with smooth, stout stems up to 3 ft. tall, forming dense colonies from rhizomes. Opposite, linear to lanceolate leaves 3–6 in. long. Flowers bluish white with 2-lipped corollas, the upper lip 2-lobed, the lower lip 3-lobed with purple markings. Flowers in dense, head-like clusters at tip of 2–6 in. long stalks arising from upper leaf axils. Fruit a brown capsule. Flowers June–Sept.

Habitat/range: Shallow streams and rivers, rocky shoals, margins of reservoirs and other impoundments. Common. Eastern North America.

Taxonomy: The genus consists of close to 600 species of herbs and shrubs of the tropics and warm, temperate North America, but only 1 species occurs in the mountains and piedmont. Its leaf shape and habitat are similar to willows (*Salix*), hence the common name.

Ecology: Water willow grows in wet areas with ample sunlight. Flexible stems enable it to withstand being scoured by flooding in river systems as well as the strong wave action along the margins of reservoirs. Once established, individuals form dense patches by spreading laterally from rhizomes. Stems knocked down by wave action can root at nodes, sending up new upright shoots. Fragmentation of stem and root segments enables populations to spread rapidly along shorelines. Large root and rhizome systems help stabilize streambed habitats by reducing stream velocity and facilitating the deposition and retention of sediments. While tolerant of moderate water-level fluctuations, extended periods of flooding can result in mortality.

Wildlife: Water willow benefits fish and various other aquatic organisms by providing refugia from predators. The bacteria and algae that grow on stems and leaves are also an important food source for many invertebrates, which in turn are consumed by fish and amphibians.

Uses: Water willow is sometimes planted along reservoirs because of its ability to form dense stands that reduce shoreline erosion and thereby improve water clarity.

*Lamium amplexicaule L.

HENBIT

Lamiaceae (Mint family)

Description: Winter annual 4–16 in. tall with a square stem and shallow taproot. The rounded upper leaves sessile, clasping, the lower leaves with long petioles. Pinkish purple, tubular, 2-lipped flowers in whorls from leaf axils. Fruits consist of 1–4 nutlets. Flowers Feb.–May; fruits Mar.–June.

Habitat/range: Lawns, fields, and gardens. Native to Europe, now widely distributed in temperate regions, including the United States.

Taxonomy: Of our 4 species of *Lamium* (all introduced), the 2 most common are henbit and purple deadnettle (*L. purpureum*). Crowded, overlapping, petioled upper leaves characterize purple deadnettle.

Ecology: Henbit is a common weed of open, sunny areas that is well known to farmers and gardeners as one of the first weeds to emerge in winter and spring. A winter annual, seeds germinate in fall and plants grow vegetatively, flowering in winter and early spring when competition is reduced. A cool-weather plant, this species spends the summer as dormant seeds in the soil. Two types of flowers are produced—larger showy flowers that produce nectar and are occasionally visited and cross-pollinated by long-tongued bees, and tiny, inconspicuous flowers that never open and self-pollinate in the bud. Depending on size, a single plant can produce anywhere from 200 to more than 2,000 seeds, some of which remain dormant in the soil for decades. Once established, it's difficult to eradicate as seedlings continue to emerge in future years.

Wildlife: Voles and box turtles consume the foliage and various birds eat the seeds.

Uses: Foliage of young plants can be added to salads and boiled as potherbs.

Laportea canadensis (L.) Weddell
WOOD NETTLE
Urticaceae (Nettle family)

Description: Herbaceous perennial up to 3 ft. tall with stinging hairs and alternate, broadly ovate leaves 3–6 in. long with coarsely toothed margins. Female flowers in dense clusters at base of upper leaves and at shoot tip, male flowers in clusters at base of leaves lower on stem. Fruit an achene. Flowers June–Aug.; fruits late July–Oct.

Habitat/range: Rich, moist woods and near streambanks, including cove forests, northern hardwood forests, and alluvial forests. Common. Widespread in eastern North America.

Taxonomy: Only 1 species of *Laportea* occurs in the mountains and piedmont. False nettle (*Boehmeria cylindrica*) is closely related and similar to wood nettle but lacks stinging hairs and has opposite, rather than alternate, leaves.

Ecology: Wood nettle is a shade-tolerant species that initiates growth about the same time the canopy trees leaf out. The spirally arranged leaves reduce the amount of self-shading, which likely increases photosynthesis and growth rate. A strong competitor, it often forms the dominant herbaceous layer in rich, moist cove forests, overtopping the diverse spring flora by midsummer. Wood nettle spreads vegetatively from an underground stem (rhizome) that sends up multiple upright shoots, forming dense patches. As crowding limits additional vegetative spread, plants reproduce mostly by seed, allowing them to colonize new sites. In alluvial forests and along streams, rhizomes uprooted during floods can wash up and establish new plants downstream.

Wildlife: Wood nettle's stinging hairs deter some but not all herbivores. For example, white-tailed deer and wild hogs feed on the foliage, as do certain butterfly larvae (caterpillars), beetles, and snails.

Uses: Stinging hairs cover all of the aboveground parts of the plant except for flowers and fruits. The stinging hairs penetrate bare skin (and thin pants) on contact, injecting formic acid, which causes a stinging sensation that normally lasts several minutes. Applying juice from dock plants (*Rumex*) or jewelweed (*Impatiens*) relieves the nettle's sting.

Liatris helleri Porter
HELLER'S BLAZING STAR
Asteraceae (Sunflower family)
Federally Threatened

Description: Perennial herb with 1 or more upright stems up to 16 in. tall, arising from a basal rosette of narrow leaves, the stem leaves gradually reduced in size before culminating in a dense spike of showy lavender flowers. Heads consist of 7–10 disk flowers subtended by several series of overlapping bracts. Fruit an achene. Flowers July–Sept.; fruits Aug.–Oct.

Habitat/range: Shallow soils on high-elevation rock outcrops, ledges, cliffs, and in rocky openings of heath balds. A rare species limited to small, scattered populations in mountains of West Virginia, Virginia, and North Carolina.

Taxonomy: The genus *Liatris* includes 40 species of herbaceous plants, 12 of which occur in the mountains and piedmont. Heller's blazing star can be distinguished from other species of *Liatris* in the mountains and piedmont by its shorter pappus, ciliate petioles, and short stature.

Ecology: With fewer than 10 known populations, most of which are small, Heller's blazing star is extremely vulnerable to extinction. Climatic fluctuations such as severe droughts, ice, and erosion caused by heavy rains could easily reduce the number and size of populations. Heller's blazing star is also vulnerable to invasion by woody plants as it requires open, sunny areas to persist. Other threats include trampling by hikers, climbers, and sightseers (attracted to mountain vistas), as well as commercial and residential development of rock outcrops. In spite of its rarity (or perhaps because of it) surprisingly little is known about its biology. While studying rare species in small, loosely scattered populations is difficult, such studies are needed for developing effective management plans.

Wildlife: Bees, moths, and butterflies pollinate the flowers as they forage for nectar, pollen, or both.

Uses: Species of *Liatris* contain medicinal compounds called liatrines that are effective in treating certain forms of cancer, including leukemia.

Lilium grayi S. Watson
GRAY'S LILY
Liliaceae (Lily family)

Description: Herbaceous perennial with a single smooth stem, 2–4 ft. tall, with multiple whorls of 3–8 leaves up to 4 in. long and 1 in. wide, narrowly elliptic, tapering to an acute or blunt tip, with a minutely serrulate margin. The bell-shaped flowers, on long stalks near the stem tip, consist of 6 petal-like structures, dark red on outside, lighter red on inside, yellowish in throat with many dark spots, the tips flared, rather than recurved or widely spreading. Fruit a capsule about 2 in. long. Flowers June–July; fruits Aug.–Sept.

Habitat/range: Mid- to high-elevation grassy balds, mountain bogs, wet meadows, seeps, cove forests, and openings in spruce-fir forests. Rare. A southern Appalachian endemic of Virginia, North Carolina, and Tennessee.

Taxonomy: Both the common and scientific names of this species honor Asa Gray, one of America's foremost botanists of the nineteenth century.

Ecology: Like most lilies, Gray's lily grows best in open areas that receive full sunlight. Populations consisting of several thousand individuals occur on the Roan Mountain massif, which borders North Carolina and Tennessee, and in Long Hope Valley, North Carolina. Elsewhere, populations tend to be very small and isolated. Woody plant invasion, overgrazing by cattle, habitat destruction, and illegal plant-collecting threaten this rare species. Gray's lily is also susceptible to at least 3 types of fungal infection, including an anthracnose fungus that causes flowers to senesce without maturing fruits and seeds.

Wildlife: Ruby-throated hummingbirds pollinate the flowers. Fritillary (*Speyeria* spp.) butterflies also visit the flowers but aren't effective pollinators. Herbivores such as white-tailed deer, European wild boar, and rabbits feed on the foliage.

Uses: Native Americans used the bulbs of many lily species for food and medicine. For example, bulbs were used to make flour for bread in times of famine, and mashed bulbs were used in the treatment of fever, stomachaches, and spider bites.

Lilium michauxii Poir.
CAROLINA LILY
Liliaceae (Lily family)

Description: Glabrous perennial 2–4 ft. tall with a stout, erect stem from a scaly bulb. Leaves widest at or above middle, becoming progressively smaller up stem, mostly in whorls of 3–7. Large, nodding flowers at top of stem, the flower segments strongly recurved, orange-red, becoming yellow in the throat with numerous purple spots. Upright green capsules turn brown and split into 3 segments when ripe. Flowers June–Aug.; fruits Sept.–Oct.

Habitat/range: Dry upland forests, ridges, and upper slopes. Pine-oak-heath, rock outcrops, and forest edges. Common. Southeast.

Taxonomy: Centers of diversity for *Lilium* are in North America and eastern Asia, where about 80 of the 110 species occur, including 8 species in the mountains and piedmont. It is one of about 6 plant species named after famous eighteenth-century French botanist André Michaux. Carolina lily is similar to Turk's cap lily (*Lilium superbum*) but is a much shorter plant with fewer leaves and flowers. It's the state wildflower of North Carolina and is described in *Flora of North America* as the only fragrant native lily east of the Rocky Mountains.

Ecology: Swallowtail butterflies, including the eastern tiger, pollinate the flowers. While the caterpillar larvae of butterflies and moths feed on plant tissues, including leaves, stems, and buds, adults feed on liquids only, primarily the nectar of flowers. Their long tongues, which are coiled into tight spirals when not in use, are able to reach nectar that accumulates at the bases of deep flowers such as Carolina lily. Because this species is self-incompatible, successful seed production depends on pollinators (primarily butterflies) carrying pollen from plant to plant.

Wildlife: White-tailed deer and voles feed on the foliage.

Uses: Lilies have been cultivated, eaten, and used medicinally for at least 2,000 years. Today, lilies are widely used in the horticultural bulb trade, including thousands of hybrids. Carolina lily is an attractive drought-tolerant plant that could be used more widely in wildflower gardens, but plants shouldn't be dug up in the wild.

Lilium superbum L.
TURK'S CAP LILY
Liliaceae (Lily family)

Description: Perennial herb 4–8 ft. tall with lance-shaped, whorled leaves, widest at or below middle, tapering at both ends, becoming alternate on upper stem. Large, showy, orange to red flowers, densely spotted with purple, with a distinguishing green "star" inside the flower tube, the sepals and petals strongly recurved. Fruit an angular capsule up to 2 in. long. Flowers July–Aug.; fruits Sept.–Oct.

Habitat/range: Moist forests, woods, and meadows, including northern hardwood forests, cove forests, forest edges, and grassy balds. Common in mountains, rare in piedmont. Eastern North America.

Taxonomy: A genus of 110 species of the northern hemisphere, including 8 species in the mountains and piedmont.

Ecology: This spectacular native lily is one of our showiest wildflowers. On rich, moist soils in full or partial sun, individual plants can reach heights of 8 ft. and bear a dozen or more large, showy, nodding flowers. The green "star" in the center of the flower functions as a nectar guide, helping to lure various swallowtail butterflies, including spicebush, pipevine, and eastern tiger to sip nectar and function as pollinators. Without these butterflies and other insect pollinators, there would be no Turk's cap lily, as cross-pollination is necessary for the production of viable seeds.

Wildlife: Herbaceous plants such as Turk's cap lily are particularly vulnerable to browsing by deer because they can't grow beyond their reach, as many woody shrubs and trees can. In one study, white-tailed deer consumed the shoot tips of more than 25 percent of Turk's cap lily plants, thereby halting growth and preventing flower, fruit, and seed production for that year. Rodents excavate and consume the bulbs, killing the plant.

Uses: The graceful foliage and striking flowers make a nice addition to woodland gardens, but only use nursery-grown plants, rather than plants dug up from the wild.

Lobelia cardinalis L.
CARDINAL FLOWER
Campanulaceae (Bellflower family)

Description: Upright, usually unbranched perennial with 1 to several stems from basal rosettes, 2–4 ft. tall. Leaves simple, alternate, lanceolate, 2–6 in. long with toothed margins. Intensely red or scarlet tubular flowers crowded in a terminal raceme. Fruit an ovoid or spherical capsule. Flowers July–Oct.; fruits Nov.–Feb.

Habitat/range: Wet soil, including rocky streamsides, mountain bogs, swamp forests, meadows, and wet roadsides. Common. Widely distributed in eastern North America.

Taxonomy: Brilliant red or scarlet flowers distinguish cardinal flower from the 10 other species of *Lobelia* in the mountains and piedmont. The common name alludes to the similarity in the color of the flower to the color of the robes worn by Roman Catholic cardinals.

Ecology: Cardinal flower is a hummingbird favorite. Having thread-like tongues that extend well past their bills, hummingbirds easily access nectar at the base of long flower tubes. The flowers lack scent, as do most flowers adapted to hummingbird pollinators. The inflorescence develops from the base upward so the oldest flowers are at the bottom, the youngest at the tip. By late summer, inflorescences often have upwards of 100 developing fruits, open flowers, and flower buds. The minuscule seeds (about 500 per fruit) are dispersed by wind and water. In addition to establishment from seed, vegetative offshoots can form new basal rosettes. Rosettes remain green year-round, allowing for photosynthesis in all seasons. Cardinal flower is a relatively poor competitor that requires open areas for establishment and persistence.

Wildlife: Mammals usually don't browse the foliage because of its toxic white latex, which contains the alkaloid lobeline. In addition to hummingbirds, the flowers attract long-tongued nectar-feeding butterflies such as black swallowtail, spicebush swallowtail, eastern tiger swallowtail, and cloudless sulphur.

Uses: One of the richest reds in nature, cardinal flower provides a welcome splash of color in wildflower gardens.

Lysimachia quadrifolia L.
WHORLED LOOSESTRIFE
Myrsinaceae (Myrsine family)

Description: Erect perennial herb with a smooth to sparsely hairy, rarely branched stem with lanceolate leaves in whorls of 4–6. Solitary yellow flowers in leaf axils of upper 2–6 whorls. Fruit a small, round capsule. Flowers May–Aug.; fruits July–Oct.

Habitat/range: Wide variety of moist to dry forests and openings. Common. Eastern United States.

Taxonomy: Lysimachia is a cosmopolitan genus of about 150 species, including 14 species in the mountains and piedmont. The name *Lysimachia* literally means "to release from strife," referring to the ancient tradition of attaching dried loosestrife plants to harnessed animals for its calming effect (the plant repels flies and other biting insects that might otherwise torment them).

Ecology: Plants generally attract potential pollinators with showy flowers, enticing scents, and by offering nectar and pollen as floral rewards. In lieu of nectar, whorled loosestrife produces floral oils that attract specialized pollinators. Over 2,300 plant species are known to secrete floral oils, most of which occur in the tropics. In whorled loosestrife, the basal part of the anther filaments have specialized gland-tipped hairs that secrete glistening droplets of oil. Female bees in the genus *Macropsis* function as pollinators as they collect oil and pollen from *Lysimachia* flowers. The female bee mixes the oil and pollen together to form a moistened ball and places it in a shallow, single-celled nest in the ground. A single egg is laid on the pollen mass, which becomes the sole food source for the bee larva that emerges. Female *Macropsis* bees also line their nests with *Lysimachia* oils to help regulate humidity within the nest.

Uses: Dried loosestrife plants were burned in houses to produce smoke that repelled biting insects and snakes.

Maianthemum canadense Desf.
CANADA MAYFLOWER
Ruscaceae (Ruscus family)

Description: Low-growing perennial herb with unbranched stems bearing 1–3 smooth, broadly ovate leaves with heart-shaped bases. Small white flowers in 1–2 in. long terminal racemes; fruits form clusters of red translucent berries. Flowers May–July; fruits Aug.–Sept.

Habitat/range: Moist forests and woods, especially at high elevations. Spruce fir forests, red oak forests, northern hardwood forests, and cove forests. Common in mountains. Across Canada and the northern United States, south in mountains to Georgia.

Taxonomy: The genus *Maianthemum* occurs in North and Central America, Europe, and eastern Asia. It contains 28 species of herbs, including 3 in the mountains and piedmont. False Solomon's seal (*M. racemosum*) can be distinguished from Canada mayflower by its larger size, many leaves, and bright red fruits.

Ecology: Canada mayflower is a woodland herb that tolerates a wide range of light conditions, from the shaded understory to relatively open, sunny sites. New shoots emerge in spring before the canopy leafs out. Flowering shoots have 2–3 leaves;

vegetative shoots have a single leaf. Canada mayflower spreads vegetatively from rhizomes, forming large, long-lived clones. Because individuals are genetically self-incompatible, cross-pollination, rather than self-pollination, is necessary for successful fruit set. Bumblebees visit the flowers for nectar and pollen and are the primary pollinator. Fruit production is variable and often limited by the amount of compatible pollen reaching stigmas, which is influenced by clone size and the distance between compatible clones. Large clones can have lower fertility than smaller clones because of more frequent pollen transfers within clones, whereas more distant, isolated clones often have reduced fruit set due to fewer visits by pollinators carrying pollen from other clones. Lack of sufficient resources can also limit the number of flowers that successfully mature fruit.

Wildlife: Mayflower is a preferred food plant of white-tailed deer in spring. Birds and mammals eat the berries and disperse the seeds.

Uses: Canada mayflower forms an attractive groundcover in woodland gardens.

Maianthemum racemosum (L.) Link
FALSE SOLOMON'S SEAL
Ruscaceae (Ruscus family)

Description: Herbaceous perennial 1–3 ft. tall with erect, arching, unbranched stems. Leaves alternate, in 2 rows, sessile, elliptic, 4–6 in. long with conspicuous parallel veins. Numerous tiny white flowers in lacy terminal clusters. Ripe berries a deep translucent red. Flowers Apr.–June; fruits June–Sept.

Habitat/range: Variety of moist, deciduous woods, including cove forests, northern hardwood forests, chestnut oak forests, oak-hickory forests, and forest edges. Common. Widespread in North America.

Taxonomy: False Solomon's seal resembles true Solomon's seal (*Polygonatum biflorum*) in the shape and arrangement of its leaves but differs in that its flowers and fruits are at the tip of the stem, rather than scattered beneath the stem.

Ecology: The small, densely clustered flowers depend on insects moving pollen from one plant to another for successful cross-pollination and subsequent seed set. The seeds have "double dormancy," sometimes called 2-year seeds, as it takes 2 years to complete germination. The seeds ripen in summer and require an overwintering period before the radicle (embryo root) emerges in spring. The following (second) spring, a single leaf emerges from the seed, completing germination. This unusual germination behavior is restricted to a small number of plants, mostly monocots. False Solomon's seal spreads by seeds and by a fleshy rhizome (underground stem) that gives rise to multiple shoots that form small colonies. Both diploid and tetraploid races are found ($2n = 36$ and 72); the tetraploids are usually larger than the diploids.

Wildlife: White-tailed deer graze the foliage, and birds and small mammals eat the fruits and disperse the seeds.

Uses: The berries are edible, but mildly cathartic. False Solomon's seal's arching, leafy stems, lacy white flowers, and colorful fruits add interest to woodland gardens.

Synonym: Smilacina racemosa (L.) Desf.

Marchantia species
LIVERWORT
Marchantiaceae (Liverwort family)

Description: Flat, leaf-like structures form dense prostrate mats on surface of bare soil or rocks. Liverworts are unisexual with male and female sex organs forming on different plants. Spores released in summer.

Habitat/range: *Marchantia* grows in cool, moist, shaded sites such as along shaded streambanks and in the spray zone of waterfalls.

Taxonomy: Mosses, liverworts, and hornworts are collectively known as bryophytes. There are approximately 6,000 species of liverworts, widely distributed from the tropics to the arctic.

Ecology: Liverworts, thought to be the first land plants, evolved from green algae about 400 million years ago. To put this in perspective, the oldest known flowering plants are about 130 million years old. Liverworts are considered to be the simplest land plants because they lack stomates for controlling gas exchange and specialized cells (in the form of vascular tissue) for conducting water and nutrients. Instead of roots, liverworts have numerous single-celled appendages called rhizoids that anchor the plant to its substrate. Like mosses and ferns, liverworts reproduce sexually by spores. *Marchantia* also reproduces asexually from gemmae, tiny, disk-shaped clusters of green cells produced in cup-shaped structures. The splash of raindrops propels gemmae up to 3 ft. away. If they land in a favorable site, they "germinate" and form a new liverwort genetically identical to the parent plant. Liverworts also spread when pieces of the parent plant break off and grow, a process known as fragmentation.

Uses: The name "liverwort" dates back to medieval times when the "Doctrine of Signatures" reflected the belief that plant shape was a sign of medicinal value. The liverwort, with its flattened body and lobes shaped somewhat like those of a human liver, were thought to be useful for treating liver ailments.

Medeola virginiana L.
INDIAN CUCUMBER ROOT
Liliaceae (Lily family)

Description: Erect herbaceous perennial 12–30 in. tall, with woolly tufts of hairs on stem. Vegetative plants have a single whorl of 5–11 leaves; flowering plants have a second upper whorl of 3 smaller leaves. Several yellowish green flowers hang beneath the upper whorl of leaves with 6 recurved, petal-like structures and 3 long, brown stigmas conspicuously curved outward. Fruit a round, dark purple-black berry. Flowers Apr.–June; fruits Sept.–Oct.

Habitat/range: Moist forests, including acid cove forests and oak-hickory forests. Common. Widespread in eastern North America.

Taxonomy: Indian cucumber root is the only species in the genus *Medeola*.

Ecology: Indian cucumber root has rather inconspicuous greenish yellow flowers for a species that must attract insect pollinators for successful fruit and seed set. Flower visitation rates are frequently low and a lack of pollen reaching stigmas often limits fruit set. The drooping stalks (pedicels) that position the flowers below the upper whorl of leaves straighten as the fruits develop, positioning the fruits above the leaves. As this occurs, the basal part of the upper whorl of leaves turns scarlet. The contrasting colors of the scarlet leaves, and the dark purple to black fruits in autumn help attract fruit-eating birds and mammals, which disperse the seeds.

Wildlife: Little is known about the pollinators, fruit-eaters, and herbivores that interact with this plant.

Uses: Native Americans and early settlers ate the crispy, white underground rhizomes, which taste like cucumber.

Micranthes petiolaris (Raf.) Bush
CLIFF SAXIFRAGE
Saxifragaceae (Saxifrage family)

Description: Perennial herb with a basal rosette of green to red, coarsely serrate leaves from 2 to 6 in. long, with an open inflorescence of white flowers with orange anthers. The upper 3 petals each with 2 yellow spots and the lower 2 unspotted petals readily distinguish this species when in bloom. Flowers Apr.–Aug.; fruits June–Sept.

Habitat/range: On moist to rather dry rock outcrops. Common in mountains, uncommon in piedmont. A southern Appalachian endemic from Virginia south to Georgia.

Taxonomy: A genus of about 65 species of perennial herbs of North America, South America, and Eurasia. Four of the 7 species in the mountains and piedmont are southern Appalachian endemics.

Ecology: Cliff saxifrage commonly occurs on high-elevation rock outcrops in the southern Appalachians, where it's an early colonizer of landslide scars and bare rock surfaces exposed when highways are cut through mountains (such as along the Blue Ridge Parkway). It grows in moist areas where seepage water flows over rock surfaces and on rather dry rock surfaces where plants are exposed to direct sunlight and desiccating winds. The prostrate leaves provide protection from drying winds and the semisucculent leaves, with waxy surfaces, help retain moisture. Surprisingly little is known about the ecology of this interesting plant.

Wildlife: Flies and small bees visit and pollinate the small but distinctive flowers.

Uses: Cliff saxifrage can be incorporated into rock gardens.

Synonym: Saxifraga michauxii Britton

*Microstegium vimineum (Trin.) A. Camus
JAPANESE STILTGRASS
Poaceae (Grass family)

Description: A sprawling annual grass 6–36 in. tall that forms dense colonies from lateral branches rooting at nodes. Leaves alternate with short, flat, lance-shaped blades 1–3 in. long with a pale silvery strip of hairs along the midrib. Flowers in narrow terminal, spike-like racemes; fruit a tiny grain. Flowers Aug.–Oct.; fruits Sept.–Nov.

Habitat/range: Disturbed areas, including streambanks, moist woodlands, alluvial forests, forest edges, fields, and roadside ditches. Common. Native to Asia, it has become naturalized throughout the eastern United States.

Taxonomy: It's the only species of *Microstegium* in the mountains and piedmont.

Ecology: Japanese stiltgrass grows in habitats ranging from open to closed forests, from floodplains to uplands, and from disturbed roadsides to intact forest. Inadvertently introduced to Knoxville, Tennessee, in packing material for porcelain in the early twentieth century, it currently occurs in 25 eastern states. A harmful pest, Japanese stiltgrass ranks as one of the most destructive invasive plants in the Southeast, forming thick mats up to 3 ft. tall that can smother other herbaceous plants. Inconspicuous at first, it can replace native plant cover within 3–5 years, particularly in moist, fertile sites such as floodplains, north-facing slopes, and cove forests. It frequently invades roadsides, trails, and other disturbed areas, which then serve as satellite populations for colonizing areas in the forest interior. Even minor disturbances such as a single tree-fall provide an opportunity for colonization, after which the plant spreads rapidly by seed and by rooting at stem nodes that touch the ground. As a result, this nonnative grass can dominate large areas of the forest floor. Once established, it's difficult to eradicate as large numbers of seeds persist in the soil for years, germinating readily following soil disturbance.

Wildlife: White-tailed deer and other grazers tend to avoid Japanese stiltgrass, which gives it a competitive advantage in heavily grazed areas.

Minuartia glabra (Michx.) Mattf.
APPALACHIAN SANDWORT
Caryophyllaceae (Pink family)

Description: Small, erect annual with green, wiry stems that develop from a basal rosette of leaves that wither prior to flowering; the stem leaves small, narrow, opposite. Small white flowers with 5 separate petals in open groups. Fruit a capsule. Flowers Apr.–May; fruits May–June.

Habitat/range: Rock outcrops in piedmont and at low to medium elevations in mountains. Uncommon. Maine south to Georgia.

Taxonomy: A genus of nearly 175 species of herbs, primarily in the northern hemisphere, including 7 species in the mountains and piedmont. Mountain sandwort (*M. groenlandica*) is similar but is a mat-forming perennial; piedmont sandwort (*M. uniflora*) is an annual distinguished by its short (less than one-quarter in.) stem leaves.

Ecology: Appalachian sandwort occurs in vegetation mats, in shallow depressions, and along the margins of granite outcrops. It can't survive in the extremely shallow soils occupied by elf orpine (*Diamorpha smallii*), but is more tolerant of competition. Like elf orpine, it's a winter annual whose seeds germinate in fall; plants overwinter as rosettes, and flowering and fruiting occur in spring. The vegetative rosettes are highly resistant to frost during winter, and because plants die after fruiting in spring, it escapes the severe heat and prolonged droughts of summer. Nonetheless, moisture stress resulting from shallow soil and sporadic spring rains results in reduced growth or "stunting" of individuals, as well as high mortality. Individuals growing in shallower soils are generally smaller, less branched, and produce fewer flowers and fruits than those in deeper soils. As a result, high densities of very small plants commonly occur on shallow soils, particularly in dry years. Syrphid flies and small bees visit the flowers for nectar, pollen, or both and function as pollinators. The opportunity for cross-pollination is increased by the anthers opening and releasing pollen before the stigmas are receptive. The seeds are dispersed by wind and by rainwater flowing across the rock surface.

Synonym: Arenaria glabra Michx.

Minuartia groenlandica (Retz.) Ostenf.
MOUNTAIN SANDWORT
Caryophyllaceae (Pink family)

Description: Mat-forming herbaceous perennial with small white flowers at tips of slender stalks rising above dense tufts of linear basal leaves. Flowers with 5 separate petals, each slightly notched at tip, developing into many-seeded capsules. Flowers May–Oct.; fruits July–Oct.

Habitat/range: On rocky or gravelly slopes and ledges of rock outcrops in mountains and upper piedmont. Regionally rare. Greenland, Canada, and higher mountains of New England, with disjunct populations in the southern Appalachians of Virginia, North Carolina, and Tennessee.

Taxonomy: Similar to *M. glabra* (Appalachian sandwort) but has slightly larger flowers, forms denser tufts of basal leaves, and occurs at higher elevations.

Ecology: Mountain sandwort occurs on dry, open, wind-swept substrates where small amounts of soil collect in crevices between rocks. The prostrate growth form and smooth, rounded surface of cushion plants such as mountain sandwort help buffer the plant from the chilling, drying, or the physical damage of high winds. The air within the cushion creates an almost closed system such that, on sunny days, the cushion temperature can be significantly warmer than the surrounding air. As the lateral branches spread outward, additional roots anchor the plant and increase its water-absorbing capacity. The dead leaves below the cushion persist, allowing some nutrient recycling by the parent plant. A slow-growing, stress-tolerant species, mountain sandwort is absent from deeper soils where larger, more competitive species grow.

Wildlife: Flies and bees pollinate the flowers. Both are important pollinators at high elevations because of their ability to remain active during inclement weather.

Uses: Sandworts are sometimes grown in rock gardens.

Synonym: Arenaria groenlandica (Retz) Spreng.

Mitchella repens L.
PARTRIDGE BERRY
Rubiaceae (Madder family)

Description: Prostrate evergreen perennial herb with small, shiny, opposite leaves on short stalks. Fragrant, white trumpet-shaped flowers in pairs fuse to form a single, round red berry that persists through winter. Flowers May–June; fruits June–July, persisting into winter.

Habitat/range: Deciduous and coniferous forests and streamsides, usually on acidic soils, including acidic cove forests, river bluff forests, and oak-hickory forests. Common. Widely distributed in eastern North America.

Taxonomy: The genus *Mitchella* has just 2 species, 1 in eastern North America and 1 in eastern Asia.

Ecology: Partridge berry has creeping stems that root at the nodes, forming dense patches in shady habitats. Plants have either short-styled flowers (thrums) with long, exserted stamens or long-styled flowers (pins) with exserted stigmas and short stamens. The flowers depend on insect pollinators (primarily bumblebees) to move pollen between plants, as compatible pollinations only occur between the 2 different flower types (from thrum to pin and vice versa). Since only one flower type typically occurs within a single patch, bumblebees must move pollen from patch to patch to pollinate flowers with compatible pollen. Most flowers contain small amounts of nectar, encouraging bumblebees to forage widely and to visit large numbers of flowers in multiple patches to meet their energy demands. Bumblebees apparently do a good job of moving pollen between patches (and flower types), as most flowers mature fruit.

Wildlife: Ruffed grouse, wild turkeys, gray squirrels, raccoons, and mice eat the berries and disperse the small hard-coated seeds.

Uses: Partridge berry makes an excellent groundcover in woodland gardens and is increasingly available in specialty nurseries. The berries are edible but bland.

Monarda didyma L.
CRIMSON BEE BALM
Lamiaceae (Mint family)

Description: Herbaceous perennial from 2 to 5 ft. tall, with a square stem and pungent opposite leaves with serrate margins. Terminal whorl of 2-lipped, bright red flowers subtended by showy, reddish leaf-like bracts. Fruits consist of 1–4 small nutlets. Flowers July–Oct.; fruits Sept.–Oct.

Habitat/range: Seepage slopes, streambanks, and roadside ditches, including northern hardwood forests, alluvial forests, and boulder fields. Common in mountains, rare in piedmont. A mostly northeastern species, south in mountains to North Carolina, Tennessee, and Georgia.

Taxonomy: Monarda is a North American genus of 20 species. Crimson bee balm is readily distinguished from the other 4 species in the mountains and piedmont by its bright red flowers.

Ecology: The odorless, red, tubular, nectar-rich flowers fit the classic profile of a hummingbird-pollinated plant. Hummingbirds use the lower lip of the flower to orient their beaks into the narrow opening of the corolla tube, within which the nectar is located. In the process, pollen is deposited on top of their heads between the eyes, producing a yellow spot that is easily seen. As hummingbirds fly from flower to flower of crimson bee balm, they deposit large amounts of pollen onto the exserted stigmas. Because anthers shed their pollen at a time when the stigmas aren't yet receptive, successful reproduction depends on pollinators transferring pollen from anthers to receptive stigmas on separate flowers. Individual flowers typically remain open for several days, increasing the chances of successful pollination.

Wildlife: White-tailed deer browse the plants and hummingbirds, bumblebees, and butterflies visit the flowers for nectar, pollen, or both.

Uses: Monarda leaves were widely used as a source of tea after the Boston Tea Party resulted in a tea shortage. These days, crimson bee balm is commonly grown in wildflower gardens.

Monotropa hypopithys L.
PINESAP
Ericaceae (Heath family)

Description: Small, 4–10 in. tall parasitic plant with clusters of yellow, pink, or red stems. The tiny, clasping, scale-like leaves lack chlorophyll. Nodding yellowish red urn-shaped flowers arranged mostly on one side of stem. Fruit an upright capsule. Flowers May–Oct.; fruits July–Nov.

Habitat/range: Moist to dry woods, usually on acidic soils. Chestnut oak forests, oak-hickory forests, and acidic cove forests. Uncommon. Widespread in North America, Asia, and Europe.

Taxonomy: Indian pipe (*M. uniflora*) has white, rather than yellowish red stems and a single flower at the stem tip, rather than multiple flowers at the stem tip. Some authors place pinesap in the genus *Hypopitys*.

Ecology: This widely distributed but generally scarce plant has 2 color morphs; late spring- and summer-flowering individuals tend to be yellow, whereas fall-flowering individuals are usually reddish. Since plants of this species obtain all of their nutrients from fungi associated with roots (usually of pines and oaks), they don't need green leaves for photosynthesis. The interaction between pinesap and tree roots was demonstrated nearly 50 years ago when labeled glucose injected into the phloem of spruce trees was subsequently found in nearby individuals of pinesap. Subsequent studies demonstrated that specialized mycorrhizal fungi function as a "bridge" moving glucose from spruce roots to pinesap. Since the movement of nutrients is unidirectional, pinesap is a parasite. Because it obtains nutrients indirectly from a neighboring photosynthetic plant through a shared root fungus, pinesap is technically known as an epiparasite. Nearly 400 species of flowering plants are epiparasites, most of which go unnoticed because the plant fungus–host plant interaction occurs underground.

Wildlife: Interactions between animals and this plant have yet to be discovered.

Uses: This edible but uncommon plant is best left alone.

Monotropa uniflora L.
INDIAN PIPE, GHOST FLOWER
Ericaceae (Heath family)

Description: Waxy-white (rarely pink), fleshy, perennial herb with 2–8 in. tall clusters of stems that turn black with age. Tiny, scale-like leaves the same color as stem. Solitary flowers at end of stem narrowly bell-shaped, nodding. Fruit an erect capsule. Flowers June–Oct.; fruits Aug.–Nov.

Habitat/range: Occurs in wide variety of forests, always in shade, never in open areas receiving direct sunlight. Common. Americas and eastern Asia.

Taxonomy: A genus of 2 species, both lack chlorophyll and depend on other organisms for nutrients. The common name "ghost flower" alludes to its white translucent color.

Ecology: This once-seen, never-forgotten plant looks more like a fungus than a flowering plant yet is loosely related to rhododendrons, mountain laurel, and blueberries. The albino shoots pop up suddenly, often after a heavy summer rain. A solitary nodding flower quickly forms; following fertilization, the developing fruit, a capsule, turns upright and numerous dust-like seeds are dispersed by wind, after which the stems turn black and wither away. Early botanists thought Indian pipe was a parasite, taking up nutrients directly from the roots of other plants; later, it was considered to be a saprophyte, living off decaying plants in the soil. Now, botanists consider it to be an epiparasite—a parasite that obtains nutrients from another parasite. As an epiparasite, Indian pipe obtains nutrients through its roots from mycorrhizal fungi that are connected to the roots of a nearby green (photosynthetic) plant. Indian pipe indirectly obtains nutrients from other plants via a "mycorrhizal bridge." Since it obtains all its organic nutrients from other plants, its green (photosynthetic) leaves were lost during evolution.

Wildlife. Bumblebees visit the flowers for nectar and pollen and function as pollinators. Plant defense compounds (glycosides) deter most herbivores.

Uses: Indian pipe isn't a plant for bouquets, as cut (or even bruised) stems quickly turn black and ooze a clear, gelatinous substance.

Oclemena acuminata (Michx.) Greene
WHORLED ASTER
Asteraceae (Sunflower family)

Description: Perennial herb 8–15 in. tall with large, closely crowded leaves on upper part of stem. About 15 white to pinkish ray flowers surround central yellow or red disk flowers within a head. Flowers July–Sept.; fruits Aug.–Sept.

Habitat/range: Cool, moist woods, mountain seeps, and streambanks at mid- to high elevations. Spruce-fir forests, northern hardwood forests, and red oak forests. Common. Northeastern United States and Canada, south to North Carolina, Tennessee, and Georgia.

Taxonomy: This is the only species of *Oclemena* in our region.

Ecology: Whorled aster is a good example of a forest herb whose persistence depends on periodic disturbance. Tree falls, logging roads, trails, animal burrows, and other kinds of disturbance create openings in the forest with higher light levels and reduced leaf litter. On such sites, seedlings of whorled aster can become established and a relatively large patch of plants can develop over a period of several years. The high light levels associated with forest openings enhance photosynthesis and increase the availability of resources for reproduction. This in turn can result in the production of large numbers of flowers, fruits, and seeds in the first years following disturbance. Underground runners also give rise to new plants, thereby increasing patch size. As the canopy fills in and light levels decrease, whorled aster plants gradually decrease in size and fewer individuals have sufficient resources to flower and produce seeds. After 2–3 decades under a shaded canopy, patches of whorled aster often die out, but new patches form as seedlings colonize other disturbed sites.

Uses: Ancient Greeks used asters as an antidote for snakebites.

Synonym: Aster acuminatus Michx.

Oenothera biennis L.
COMMON EVENING PRIMROSE
Onagraceae (Evening primrose family)

Description: Biennial or short-lived perennial up to 6 ft. tall, usually branching only near top, the alternate leaves reduced in size up the stalk. Flowers showy, with 4 yellow petals, 4 reflexed sepals, 8 stamens, and an X-shaped stigma. Fruit a cylindrical capsule. Flowers June–Oct.; fruits July–Nov.

Habitat/range: Fields, roadsides, other disturbed areas. Common. Coast to coast, from southern Canada south. Native to the United States, it has become a widespread weed in Europe and Japan.

Taxonomy: The most common species among the 16 species of *Oenothera* in the mountains and piedmont.

Ecology: Like many weedy species, common evening primrose grows best in disturbed areas where it can escape from competing vegetation. Its showy yellow flowers at the tips of tall, upright shoots brighten roadsides and fields in summer and fall. Plants usually form a basal rosette of leaves their first year, then send up an upright shoot, flowering, fruiting, and dying in their second year. In unfavorable conditions, such as low water availability or partial shade, plants remain in the rosette stage for a second year and flower in their third year. Conversely, plants growing in especially favorable conditions can accumulate sufficient resources to flower in their first year. In all cases, plants die after setting seed. The flowers open in the evening and close the next morning. The fragrant yellow flowers attract evening- and night-flying moths, some of which hover like hummingbirds as they suck up nectar. In the morning, bees visit the flowers and function as backup pollinators.

Wildlife: More than 100 insect species are known to use common evening primrose, including aphids, beetles, spittlebugs, and leaf miners. The caterpillars of several moths (including the white-lined sphinx moth) feed on the foliage, and the adults pollinate the flowers.

Uses: Common evening primrose is an excellent garden plant as it tolerates drought, grows in a variety of soils, and produces showy flowers over a long flowering season.

Oenothera fruticosa L.
SUNDROPS
Onagraceae (Evening primrose family)

Description: Perennial herb up to 3 ft. tall with narrow alternate leaves. Flowers mostly in dense terminal clusters with 4 bright yellow petals up to 1 in. long. Fruit a 4-chambered capsule with tiny brown seeds. Flowers Apr.–Aug.; fruits May–Sept.

Habitat/range: Moist to dry woodlands, forest edges, rock outcrops, fields, and roadsides. Common. Widespread in eastern North America.

Taxonomy: The genus *Oenothera* includes about 125 species of herbs of North and South America, with 16 species in the mountains and piedmont. The genus includes evening primroses (mostly evening-blooming species) and sundrops (day-blooming species).

Ecology: The flowers of most species of *Oenothera* open in the evening and are pollinated primarily by hawkmoths.

410

Other species, including sundrops, bloom during the day and are pollinated mainly by bees. Sundrops are self-incompatible, so fruit set depends on pollinators moving pollen from plant to plant. About three-quarters of all flowering plant species, including most food crops, depend on pollinators to bear fruit. Studies of many pollinators, including wild bees, as well as some butterflies, hummingbirds, and bats, show signs of declining populations. The causes of pollinator decline vary and are often difficult to identify but are often associated with habitat degradation or loss.

Wildlife: Songbirds such as mourning doves, American goldfinches, and dark-eyed juncos eat the seeds.

Uses: This hardy perennial, with its bright yellow flowers and long blooming season, makes a nice addition to wildflower gardens.

Onoclea sensibilis L.
SENSITIVE FERN
Onocleaceae (Sensitive fern family)

Description: Perennial fern from shallow, creeping rhizomes. Leaves dimorphic, the sterile fronds green, broad, almost triangular with 8–12 pairs of nearly opposite leaflets with wavy margins; fertile fronds at first dark green, soon turn brown, usually shorter than sterile leaves, the sori (spore clusters) grouped in bead-like clusters rolled in small leaf segments (pinnules) at upper end of fertile stalk. Spores released May–June.

Habitat/range: Mountain bogs, moist woodlands, and wet disturbed areas. Common. Widespread in eastern North America and Asia.

Taxonomy: Sensitive fern is the only member of the genus *Onoclea*. It resembles and sometimes occurs with netted chain fern (*Woodwardia areolata*) but has nearly opposite (rather than alternate) leaflets with entire (rather than serrate) margins, as well as distinctive fertile leaves.

Ecology: Sensitive fern is an ancient species; fossilized fragments 65 million years old have been found in Greenland, Japan, Russia, the United Kingdom, and the western United States. While its geographic distribution has shifted over time, the fern itself has remained virtually unchanged. Sensitive fern thrives in wet areas and full sun, but will grow almost anywhere that isn't too dry. Like most ferns, it spreads sexually by spores and vegetatively by rhizomes. In favorable conditions, the shallow, creeping rhizomes spread widely, forming dense stands of upright fronds. The fronds are neither fragile nor sensitive to touch; the common name alludes to the vulnerability of the fronds to cold, as they quickly die back with the first touch of autumn frost. A frost in late spring also kills newly emerged leaves, forcing plants to expend limited energy reserves on replacement leaves.

Wildlife: Horses that graze on sensitive fern are susceptible to poisoning and death.

Uses: Sensitive fern is occasionally grown in gardens, but it spreads.

Opuntia humifusa (Raf.) Raf.
EASTERN PRICKLY PEAR
Cactaceae (Cactus family)

Description: Low-growing succulent with round, flattened stem segments, usually with spines and small deciduous leaves. Showy, bright yellow flowers, about 3–4 in. across, with numerous stamens. Fruit a large, fleshy purplish berry. Flowers May–July; fruits Aug.–Oct.

Habitat/range: Dry, open places, including thin soils on rock outcrops. Common in piedmont, uncommon in mountains. Widespread in eastern United States.

Taxonomy: Opuntia is a genus of about 200 species of North America, south to Patagonia, with only 1 species in the mountains and piedmont. Most prickly pear cacti (*Opuntia* spp.) occur in the deserts of the southwestern United States and Mexico.

Ecology: This slow-growing, drought-tolerant species occurs in full sun and dry conditions but won't tolerate dense shade. Its shallow, fibrous, spreading roots efficiently absorb water near the soil surface. The water stored in its fleshy stems enables the plant to cope with extended periods of drought. The green, succulent stems also function as the primary photosynthetic organ of the plant as the leaves are small and short-lived. While the flowering season is relatively long, individual flowers last just a single day. Various bees, including large bumblebees and carpenter bees, actively visit and pollinate the showy yellow flowers. Individuals resprout from the base following low-intensity fires, but its shallow root system makes it vulnerable to hotter fires.

Wildlife: Birds and small mammals disperse the plant in 2 ways—by eating the fleshy fruits and disseminating the seeds and by fragmentation, whereby an upper pad segment breaks off and becomes attached to an animal (by the spines) and subsequently roots elsewhere. Birds such as northern bobwhites nest in the stems, using the sharp spines as protection. Caterpillars of an introduced moth (*Cactoblastis cactorum*) currently threaten prickly pears throughout the Southeast.

Uses: Ripe fruits can be eaten fresh, dried, or made into jelly, but handle this plant with care as the long spines and clusters of tiny bristles can penetrate the skin. Cochineal insects (a source of red food coloring) often infest prickly pear cacti.

Synonym: Opuntia compressa J. F. Macbr.

Osmunda cinnamomea L.
CINNAMON FERN
Osmundaceae (Royal fern family)

Description: A deciduous fern with erect dimorphic fronds (leaves), sterile fronds light green, ovate to lanceolate, 2–5 ft. tall, forming a clump. Fertile fronds lack expanded leaflets, bright green becoming cinnamon brown, shorter and narrower than sterile fronds, withering after spores dispersed. Sporangia in large globose clusters. Spores released Mar.–May.

Habitat/range: Moist areas with acidic soils and high organic content, including rocky streamsides, mountain bogs, and alluvial forests. Common. Widely distributed in Asia and the Americas.

Taxonomy: The genus *Osmunda* consists of 10 species of tropical and temperate ferns with dimorphic fronds, including 3 species in the mountains and piedmont. The common and scientific names allude to the woolly, cinnamon-colored spore clusters on the fertile fronds.

Ecology: The genus *Osmunda* is one of the most ancient fern genera, with fossils dating back more than 200 million years. Because cinnamon fern has undergone little or no anatomical change during this time, it's sometimes called a "living fossil." The tightly curled young fronds, called fiddleheads, are large and showy with silver-white hairs, which turn rusty as the fronds uncurl. It takes about a month for a fiddlehead to mature into a fully expanded leaf. The fertile fronds begin to wither in early summer after the spores are released, whereas the sterile (photosynthetically active) green fronds die back in late summer. Like many ferns, cinnamon fern reproduces both by spores and vegetatively by rhizomes. Individuals can be quite old, as the stout woody rhizomes with fibrous roots persist for many years. Although fires kill the fronds, dormant buds on the rhizome, insulated from the heat of the fire, give rise to new fronds. In many habitats, vigorous regrowth following a fire increases the area covered by cinnamon fern.

Wildlife: Deer sometimes browse the fronds, but the fronds' palatability decreases with age. Brown thrashers and veeries sometimes nest in the central "vases" of cinnamon fern clumps.

Uses: Cinnamon fern is widely cultivated as an ornamental and its fiddleheads are considered to be a delicacy.

Osmunda claytoniana L.
INTERRUPTED FERN
Osmundaceae (Royal fern family)

Description: Erect deciduous fern 1–3 ft. tall, the outer series of smaller leaves sterile, the inner series of leaves either all sterile, or with fertile leaflets midway between the lower and upper sterile leaflets. Short clusters of green sporangia resemble tiny grapes, which turn dark brown as spores mature. Spores released Mar.–June.

Habitat/range: Moist to somewhat dry upland forests, woodlands, and balds. Common in mountains, rare in piedmont. Eastern North America.

Taxonomy: Three species of *Osmunda* occur in the mountains and piedmont: interrupted fern, cinnamon fern (*O. cinnamomea*), and royal fern (*O. regalis*). Interrupted fern is distinctive in that its fertile and sterile leaflets are interspersed on the same frond. The spores ripen and the highly reduced fertile leaflets wither away, leaving a distinct gap in the otherwise "leafy" frond, hence the name "interrupted fern."

Ecology: Research based on the fossil record indicates that interrupted fern is the world's oldest known living fern. It was present in the early Mesozoic, more than 200 million years ago, when the dinosaurs first roamed the earth! Of the 10,000 species of ferns worldwide, about 450 occur in North America. With few exceptions, ferns of temperate regions have horizontal stems (rhizomes) that grow at or just below the ground surface, with all but the fronds hidden from view. In contrast, some tropical ferns have upright woody stems and are called tree ferns. A chemical released from the fronds of interrupted fern slows or inhibits the growth of woody plants, which helps to maintain the open habitat required by this fern.

Uses: Interrupted fern is occasionally grown in gardens.

Oxalis montana Raf.
MOUNTAIN WOOD SORREL
Oxalidaceae (Wood sorrel family)

Description: A low-growing perennial herb that forms small mats of basal leaves with 3 heart-shaped leaflets resembling clover. White flowers with pink veins borne singly on short stalks that barely surpass the leaves. Fruit a round capsule that contains up to 10 small seeds. Flowers June–July; fruits June–Sept.

Habitat/range: Cool, moist forests on acidic soils at high elevations. Spruce-fir forests, northern hardwood forests, and spray cliffs. Locally common. Southeastern Canada, south in mountains to northern Georgia.

Taxonomy: Plants in this genus aren't related to true sorrels (*Rumex*), although both genera have sour-tasting leaves.

Ecology: Mountain wood sorrel reproduces sexually by seeds and vegetatively by slender, creeping rhizomes that form dense patches. Two different kinds of flowers are produced. Chasmogamous flowers emerge just above the leaves and have deep pink veins that guide insect pollinators (bees and flies) to nectaries at the base of each petal. Seed set is often limited by the availability of pollinators. In contrast, cleistogamous flowers look like buds, are greatly reduced in size, and never open. Often hidden in moss or leaf litter at the base of the plant, these flowers self-pollinate within the bud, thereby insuring seed production in the absence of pollinators. Mature fruits have a ballistic dispersal mechanism whereby seeds are "flung" 3–6 ft away from the parent plant.

Wildlife: Oxalic acid in the leaves imparts a sour taste that deters snails and most other herbivores from feeding on the plant.

Uses: Native Americans used mountain wood sorrel as a food and a dye, although all parts of the plant are mildly toxic in sufficient quantity.

Synonym: Oxalis acetosella L.

Oxalis violacea L.
VIOLET WOOD SORREL
Oxalidaceae (Wood sorrel family)

Description: Low-growing perennial with basal leaves on long stalks and 3 broadly heart-shaped leaflets, notched at tip with purple markings on lower surface. Several purple to pink or white flowers at end of a leafless stalk that extends well above the leaves. Fruit a round capsule. Flowers Apr.–May (and sporadically in fall); fruits May–June.

Habitat/range: Moist to dry woodlands, including river bluff forests, alluvial forests, and oak-hickory forests. Common. Eastern and central United States.

Taxonomy: A genus of more than 500 species of herbs, shrubs, and vines, including 9 species in the mountains and piedmont.

Ecology: Populations of violet wood sorrel typically flower, produce seeds, and persist in relatively open forests but gradually disappear under a dense forest canopy. Both the leaves and the flowers exhibit "sleep" movements—the leaflets fold down at night and return to a horizontal position during the day, and the flowers close up at night (and in cloudy weather). These behaviors help protect the flowers and leaves from frost damage (and heavy rain). Two flower morphs are produced—1 has long styles and short stamens, the other morph has short styles and longer stamens. Both morphs depend on cross-pollination by insects (mainly small bees) because plants of this species are genetically self-incompatible. Plants spread by seeds and by runners.

Wildlife: Most herbivores avoid this plant because oxalic acid in its tissues gives it a bitter taste. Various birds consume the seeds.

Uses: Violet wood sorrel is an attractive plant in woodland gardens due to its showy flowers and interesting foliage.

Packera millefolium (Torr. & A. Gray) Weber & A. Love
BLUE RIDGE RAGWORT
Asteraceae (Sunflower family)

Description: Upright perennial herb 1–3 ft. tall with ribbed stems and patches of woolly hairs in leaf axils. Basal leaves up to 1 ft. long, deeply divided into many segments, each segment subdivided into many narrow segments giving the leaf a lacy texture; stem leaves similar but progressively reduced up stem. Small, compact flower heads with yellow ray and disk flowers at tips of numerous branches arching upward near top of stem. Fruit a brown achene topped with white bristles. Flowers late Apr.–early June.

Habitat/range: Restricted to shallow soils that form on and around granite or limestone outcrops. Rare. Restricted to Virginia, the Carolinas, and Georgia.

Taxonomy: Golden ragwort (*P. anonyma*) is similar but has coarsely toothed, rather than finely divided, leaf segments.

Ecology: Blue ridge ragwort occurs on rock outcrops in the upper piedmont and mountains at elevations up to 4,000 ft. within portions of just 4 states. The biggest threat to the species appears to be "genetic swamping" due to hybridization with golden ragwort (*P. anonyma*), a widespread "weedy" species that tolerates a wide range of environmental conditions. Where golden ragweed and blue ridge ragwort co-occur, hybrids readily form as the 2 species have overlapping flowering times, share a variety of pollinators, and are interfertile (pollen from 1 species can sire seeds of the other species). A recent study reported hybrids in about 40 percent of the populations of blue ridge ragwort in North and South Carolina. Small populations of blue ridge ragwort that occur in close proximity to large populations of golden ragwort are particularly vulnerable to loss of genetic integrity due to hybridization. Other risks include habitat loss due to the development of rocky areas with views and trampling by hikers.

Wildlife: Bees and other insects visit and pollinate the flowers.

Synonym: Senecio millefolium Torr. and A. Gray

Packera tomentosa (Michx.) C. Jeffrey
WOOLLY RAGWORT
Asteraceae (Sunflower family)

Description: Perennial herb 1–2 ft. tall with mostly basal leaves, the margins scalloped to nearly entire, the underside of leaves and lower part of stems covered in white woolly hairs, hence the common name. Heads of yellow ray and disk flowers in open, flat-topped clusters at stem tips. Fruit an achene. Flowers Apr.–June.

Habitat/range: Rock outcrops and roadside areas, usually in moist areas in full sun. Common in piedmont, occasional in mountains. Eastern United States.

Taxonomy: A genus of 64 species of annual and perennial herbs, mostly of North America, including 11 species in the mountains and piedmont.

Ecology: Plants on rock outcrops, particularly at lower elevations are exposed to high temperatures, intense sunlight, and potentially severe moisture stress. By reflecting light, the dense hairs of woolly ragwort help keep the leaf surface cool, thereby reducing transpirational water loss. The vertical orientation of the leaves has a similar effect because the leaves don't receive direct sunlight during the hottest parts of the day. Like the flowers of most members of the sunflower family, the flowers of woolly ragwort are clustered into more or less flattened heads that serve as landing platforms for potential pollinators seeking nectar, pollen, or both. Ragwort flowers typically attract a wide range of potential pollinators, including bees, wasps, butterflies, flies, and beetles. Although the nectar reward per flower is small, potential pollinators can quickly probe the many flowers within a head, and thereby obtain large amounts of nectar. Individuals spread by seeds and by basal offshoots and stolons, often forming large colonies.

Wildlife: Most herbivores avoid ragworts because they contain highly poisonous alkaloids. The seed bug *Neacoryphus bicrucis* is an exception, as it has circumvented the plant's chemical defenses. The seed bug sequesters alkaloids present in woolly ragwort seeds into its own tissues, thereby gaining protection from potential predators such as anole lizards.

Synonym: Senecio tomentosus Michx.

Panax quinquefolius L.
AMERICAN GINSENG, SANG
Araliaceae (Ginseng family)

Description: Perennial herb 8–24 in. tall with a solitary stem bearing 1–4 palmately compound leaves, each with 3–5 leaflets. Small greenish white flowers in a single terminal umbel. Red berry-like drupes form a compact round cluster. Flowers May–June; fruits Aug.–Oct.

Habitat/range: Rich, mesic deciduous forests, including cove forests, northern hardwood forests, and basic mesic forests. Once common throughout much of eastern North America, now increasingly rare.

Taxonomy: The genus *Panax* includes 14 species, 2 in the mountains and piedmont, the others in eastern Asia. Dwarf ginseng (*P. trifolius*) is similar to American ginseng, but smaller in size (4–8 in. tall).

Ecology: American ginseng occurs in relatively stable habitats, such as mid- to late-successional deciduous forests. Like many woodland herbs, ginseng is slow-growing but long-lived, with a potential life expectancy of about 60 years. Plants emerge each spring from an underground taproot after the forest canopy has partially or completely developed. Once widespread and abundant, ginseng populations have become fewer and smaller due to overharvesting by humans, grazing pressure by deer, and habitat destruction.

Wildlife: Flies and bees pollinate the flowers, birds and small mammals disperse the seeds, and deer graze on the foliage.

Uses: There is a long tradition of using ginseng roots for therapeutic and aphrodisiac purposes in China. Native Americans' use of ginseng for medicinal purposes and the plant's wide collection for export in colonial times are less well-known aspects of ginseng's history. Today, the dried roots continue to be in great demand both for export to Asia and for domestic consumption. Although ginseng can be cultivated, wild roots are considered more potent and therefore more valuable. Studies indicate the rate at which wild populations are harvested isn't sustainable.

Parnassia asarifolia Vent.
KIDNEYLEAF GRASS OF PARNASSUS
Parnassiaceae (Grass of Parnassus family)

Description: Herbaceous perennial from 8 to 16 in. tall with kidney-shaped basal leaves, 1–2 in. wide, on long stalks. Flowering stems with terminal white flower with prominent green veins and a single sessile leaf, similar to but smaller than the basal leaves. Fruit a 4-parted capsule with numerous seeds. Flowers Aug.–Oct.; fruits Sept.–Nov.

Habitat/range: Mountain bogs, seepage slopes, and streambanks. Uncommon in mountains, rare in piedmont. Virginia south to Georgia and Texas, primarily in southern Appalachians and Ozarks.

Taxonomy: The genus *Parnassia* includes about 70 herbaceous species, primarily in arctic and north-temperate areas, with 2 species in the mountains and piedmont. Bigleaf grass of parnassus (*P. grandifolia*) has ovate, rather than kidney-shaped, leaves and occurs mainly on circumneutral, rather than acidic, soils. Members of this genus aren't grasses, nor do they resemble grasses, despite the common name.

Ecology: The delicate green lines on the white petals, like spokes on a wheel, radiate toward the center of the flower, guiding insect pollinators to the nectar. The 5 stamens with pollen-bearing anthers alternate with 5 shorter, sterile stamens. The latter structures, called staminodes, are sham nectaries: they glisten like nectar droplets but are completely dry. The deceptive droplets are analogous to an advertisement that lures customers inside the store to look at other items. In *Parnassia*, the "real goods" are the nectar droplets at the base of the petals where the functional nectaries are located. Experimentally removing the staminodes from flowers results in a decrease in pollination success and a reduction in the number of fruits produced, indicating that advertising "hooks" used by flowers can pay off.

Wildlife: Small bees, flies, and butterflies visit the flowers for nectar, pollen, or both.

Uses: Grass of parnassus can be grown from seed and transplanted to open, wet areas of gardens.

Passiflora incarnata L.
MAYPOPS, PASSION VINE
Passifloraceae (Passion flower family)

Description: Climbing or trailing herbaceous vine with deeply 3-lobed leaves pointed at tip. Large, showy, white to purple flowers with a conspicuous circular fringe, the 5 prominent anthers form a circle below 3 arching styles with knobby stigmas. Large, oval-shaped, fleshy fruits, initially green, turning yellow when ripe, with numerous gelatinous covered seeds. Flowers May–Sept.; fruits July–Oct.

Habitat/range: Fields, roadsides, thickets, forest edges, and open places. Common in piedmont, occasional in mountains. Most of eastern United States.

Taxonomy: A genus of more than 400 mostly tropical species. The only other species in our region, yellow passionflower (*P. lutea*), is similar, but its leaves are much broader than they are long, and the greenish yellow flowers form relatively small, dark purple fruits.

Ecology: This fast-growing vine spreads over the ground or clambers over low-growing vegetation with tendrils that curl around twigs and other supports. It also spreads underground by roots and rhizomes that send up new shoots. Plants consist of 1–5 vines, each about 10 ft. long. The sweet-smelling flowers open about noon and last just 1 day. Within minutes of opening, large bees (mainly bumblebees and carpenter bees) land on the flowers and begin sucking up nectar. Bees continue to visit the flowers throughout the afternoon, accumulating large amounts of pollen on their dorsal surfaces, some of which is inadvertently transferred onto stigmas. Because the flowers require cross-pollination for successful seed set, bees play a critical role in the production of fruits. Without bees, no fruits or seeds are produced.

Wildlife: Caterpillars of the variegated and gulf fritillary can devour the foliage by late summer, reducing vegetative growth and fruit production. Fruits are rapidly harvested by mammals, which disperse the hard-coated seeds in their droppings.

Uses: A hardy vine with striking flowers, maypops makes an interesting addition to gardens, but it gets around.

Pedicularis canadensis L.
LOUSEWORT, WOOD BETONY
Orobanchaceae (Broomrape family)

Description: Upright, hairy, herbaceous perennial 6–16 in. tall. Forms dense colonies from short rhizomes. Lower leaves in basal cluster, stem leaves alternate, reduced in size upward, blades deeply divided into toothed segments, fern-like. Flowers sessile in dense terminal heads with small, leaf-like bracts and a 2-lipped corolla, the hood-like upper lip arches over a 3-lobed lower lip, forming a tube-like corolla, yellow to reddish brown. Fruit a flattened capsule. Flowers Apr.–May; fruits May–July.

Habitat/range: Moist to dry forests, woodlands, and meadows. Common. Widespread in eastern North America.

Taxonomy: The genus *Pedicularis* includes 350 species of hemiparasitic herbs in temperate regions of North America, South America, Europe, and Asia, including 2 species in the mountains and piedmont.

Ecology: Like many members of the broomrape family, the roots of *Pedicularis* tap into the roots of neighboring plants and divert water, mineral elements, and possibly carbohydrates. Because *Pedicularis* is green and photosynthetically active, it's called a hemiparasite. Holoparasites, in contrast, lack chlorophyll and can't manufacture their own food. Considered to be an obligate hemiparasite, its roots form thin rootlets that attach to almost any neighboring plant root by specialized organs called haustoria. Such parasitism can be detrimental to the host plant, causing reduced growth, reproduction, and survivorship. By reducing the growth of its neighbors, hemiparasites can gain a competitive advantage in obtaining light and other resources.

Wildlife: The nectar-rich flowers are actively visited and pollinated by bumblebees.

Uses: American Indians used lousewort to treat heart conditions, diarrhea, and anemia.

Phacelia fimbriata Michx.
FRINGED PHACELIA
Hydrophyllaceae (Waterleaf family)

Description: Annual from 4 to 16 in. tall, with weak, hairy stems. Lower leaves with petioles, upper leaves sessile, pinnately lobed, up to 1½ in. long. Flowers white, cup-shaped, about one-half in. wide with 5 deeply fringed petal lobes. Fruit a capsule with 2–4 seeds. Flowers Apr.–June; fruits May–July.

Habitat/range: Moist forests on slopes and floodplains, including northern hardwood forests and cove forests. Uncommon (but with locally dense populations) in mountains. Restricted to the southern Appalachians, from Virginia south to Georgia.

Taxonomy: The genus *Phacelia* includes 150 species in North and South America, including 9 species in the mountains and piedmont. Fringed phacelia is similar to Miami mist (*P. purshii*), but has more deeply fringed white (rather than lavender-blue) petals.

Ecology: Numerous annuals occur in open, well-lit areas such as fields, lawns, and roadsides. In contrast, very few annuals occur on the forest floor of deciduous forests. One of the interesting exceptions is fringed phacelia, an annual that germinates in the fall, produces a rosette of overwintering leaves, and then flowers, fruits, and dies the following spring or summer. Given that annuals must start each year from seed, they are likely to be handicapped by small size when competing with older and larger perennials for resources such as light, soil moisture, and nutrients. More so than perennials, annuals depend on frequent establishment of new individuals from seed. A thick layer of leaves, freezing temperatures, and seasonal droughts are just a few of the obstacles that limit seedling establishment on the forest floor. An additional constraint is that annuals have just one growing season to reproduce, thereby increasing the risk of reproductive failure. The ecological characteristics that enable annuals such as fringed phacelia to occupy a habitat dominated by perennials have yet to be determined.

Uses: In woodland gardens (and in the wild) dense patches of flowering fringed phacelia resemble light coverings of newly fallen snow.

Phemeranthus teretifolius (Pursh) Raf.
APPALACHIAN ROCK PINK
Portulacaceae (Purslane family)

Description: Small herbaceous perennial with a cluster of fleshy, linear basal leaves round in cross-section and 1–2 in. long. Flowering stems long and wiry with a few deep pink flowers in an open terminal cluster. Flowers one-half in. across with 2 green sepals, 5 small, rounded petals, and less than 20 stamens. Fruit a small roundish capsule. Flowers June–Sept.; fruits July–Oct.

Habitat/range: Thin, rocky, or sandy soils, usually on or near edges of rock outcrops. Common. From Pennsylvania south to Georgia.

Taxonomy: A genus of about 25 species of herbs and dwarf shrubs of the Americas, including 4 species in the mountains and piedmont. The similar but less common large-flowered rock pink (*P. mengesii*) has larger flowers that open earlier in the day.

Ecology: Appalachian rock pink occurs on shallow soils on a variety of rock substrates, including granite, sandstone, and serpentine. Unlike most other flowering plants on rock outcrops, it actively grows, flowers, and sets seeds in the summer months when temperatures are most severe and prolonged droughts are common. Appalachian rock pink survives drought by closing its stomates (thereby minimizing evaporative water loss) and by utilizing stored water in its succulent leaves. The pink flowers are open for only a few hours, opening by 3 p.m. and closing by about 7 p.m. On cloudy days, the flowers remain closed. The flowers are visited and pollinated by various species of bees. If cross-pollination fails, the flowers can self-pollinate as the stigma brushes against the stamens when the flowers close in the evening. This species is thought to have arisen as a result of hybridization between large-flowered rock pink (*P. mengesii*) and small-flowered rock pink (*P. parviflorus*). The 2 parental species are diploids, whereas *P. teretifolius* is tetraploid (has 4 sets of chromosomes). All 3 species are summer-flowering, drought-tolerant perennials with succulent leaves that grow in shallow soils on rock outcrops.

Synonym: Talinum teretifolium Pursh

*Phleum pratense L.
TIMOTHY GRASS
Poaceae (Grass family)

Description: A short-lived perennial bunchgrass from 1 to 4 ft. tall. Flowering stems (culms) smooth, erect or ascending, form large clumps. Leaf blades elongate, flat, 4–12 in. long, tapering to a thin point. Seed heads cylindrical, bristly, and very dense. Flowers June–Oct.

Habitat/range: Meadows, pastures, roadsides, and disturbed areas. Common. Native to Eurasia, now widely distributed throughout the temperate world, including all 50 states.

Taxonomy: Phleum is a genus of 15 species of annual and perennial grasses. Timothy grass is the only species in the mountains and piedmont; its common name honors Timothy Hanson, a farmer who promoted cultivation of it as hay beginning about 1720.

Ecology: As an important range plant, Timothy grass has been introduced over much of temperate North America, where it has often escaped cultivation and become established in fields, roadsides, and other open habitats. A prolific seed producer, it rapidly colonizes disturbed areas. Once established, Timothy grass stores carbohydrates and other products of photosynthesis in the base of swollen stems and in corms. These nutrient reserves are important to winter survival, to the initiation of early spring growth, and in the production of replacement tillers (shoots) following defoliation by grazers. Grasses, like other wind-pollinated plants, produce enormous amounts of pollen as a mechanism to facilitate successful pollination. A meadow dominated by Timothy grass, for example, can disperse over 1 billion pollen grains in just 2 weeks. Unfortunately, pollen produced by this grass is a common cause of hay fever. No matter how long a naturalized plant such as Timothy grass persists in an area, or how far it spreads, it doesn't become native to the area if its history there is traceable to human introduction.

Wildlife: Timothy grass is a palatable and nutritious forage plant for domestic livestock (horses, cattle, and sheep) as well as deer, elk, and small mammals.

Uses: One of the most important hay species in the United States, but it's weedy.

***Phlox carolina* L.**
CAROLINA PHLOX
Polemoniaceae (Phlox family)

Description: An erect perennial up to 3 ft. tall with opposite, ovate-lanceolate to elliptical leaves 2–5 in. long. Lavender to pink tubular flowers up to 1 in. long with 5 spreading lobes, the stamens project beyond the glabrous corolla tube. Fruit a capsule. Flowers May–July.

Habitat/range: Moist to dry forests, woodlands, and forest edges. Common. Widely distributed in eastern North America.

Taxonomy: The genus includes 70 species of herbs (and small shrubs) of temperate North America with 1 species in Asia and about 20 species in the mountains and piedmont.

Ecology: The wide diversity of flowers in the phlox family represents adaptations to a wide range of pollinators, including hummingbirds, bats, butterflies, moths, bees, flies, and beetles. Nectar-feeding butterflies, skippers, and moths pollinate the long, narrow, tubular flowers of Carolina phlox. The amount of nectar present at the base of the corolla tube varies depending on factors such as time of day, flower age, pollination status, and nectar removal rates. One potential advantage of a long corolla tube is that it can exclude some non-pollinating insects from reaching the nectar. Butterflies and moths with their long tongues (coiled into tight spirals when not in use) can readily access the nectar in tubular flowers such as those found on Carolina phlox.

Wildlife: Rabbits, groundhogs, and white-tailed deer feed on the foliage.

Uses: This showy perennial adds color to summer wildflower gardens. Numerous cultivars are available.

***Phytolacca americana* L.**
POKEWEED
Phytolaccaceae (Pokeweed family)

Description: Robust perennial herb 3–10 ft. tall with smooth, green to purplish red stems with large lanceolate to elliptic leaves. Small white flowers borne in 2–8 in. long racemes form purple-black berries when ripe. Flowers May–frost; fruits Aug.–Dec.

Habitat/range: Fields, fencerows, other disturbed areas. Common. Widespread in eastern North America.

Taxonomy: Of the 25 species in the genus *Phytolacca*, only 1 occurs in the mountains and piedmont.

Ecology: One of our largest non-woody plants, individuals emerge from a large, deep taproot or from newly germinated seeds in late spring. Plants consist of a single unbranched stem or multiple stems if browsed. Abundant in open, disturbed habitats, it also occurs along forest edges and in forest gaps. Because flowers are produced at the tips of racemes until autumn frost kills the meristems, small white flowers, green fruits, and purplish black berries (with red juice) can often be seen on the same plant from late summer–fall. About the time that fruits begin to ripen, the stems typically turn from green to red. The contrasting colors of the purplish black berries and red stems enhance the attractiveness of the plant to fruit-eating birds, which benefit the plant by dispersing its seeds. Abundant fruit production, high seed germinability, a persistent soil seed bank, and widespread seed dispersal contribute to the success of this common native weed.

Wildlife: Insect and mammalian herbivores generally won't consume the foliage because of its toxic properties, but birds and mammals consume the fleshy fruits and disperse the seeds.

Uses: Early colonists made ink from the juicy fruits. The younger leaves and shoots are sometimes cooked and eaten as greens (or "poke salad") but older parts of the plant are highly poisonous if ingested.

Pityopsis graminifolia (Michx.) Nutt.
GRASSLEAF GOLDEN ASTER
Asteraceae (Sunflower family)

Description: The leaves and stem of this grass-like herbaceous perennial appear silvery due to a dense cover of silky, appressed hairs. Alternate, mostly basal, parallel-veined leaves up to 12 in. long, reduced upward on stem. One to several erect flower stalks with small heads of bright yellow ray and disk flowers. Fruit a reddish brown achene topped with bristles. Flowers June–Oct.; fruits Nov.–Feb.

Habitat/range: Dry woodlands and open forests, including pine-oak-heath, oak-hickory forests, chestnut oak forests, and forest edges. Common. Eastern United States, south to Mexico and Central America.

Taxonomy: Three of the 8 species in the genus occur in the mountains and piedmont.

Ecology: The long, dense hairs that give this plant its silvery sheen reflect light, which moderates the surface temperature of the plant and reduces evaporative (transpirational) water loss, an important feature given the dry habitats it occupies. The bright yellow flower heads attract various bees and butterflies that function as pollinators. Plants spread vegetatively by underground stems (rhizomes), forming small to large colonies. Because seedling mortality is high, the persistence and vegetative spread of established individuals play a key role in maintaining populations. Following a fire, vegetative growth and flowering typically increase as a more open canopy increases the amount of light reaching the ground.

Wildlife: White-tailed deer browse the foliage.

Uses: This low-maintenance, drought-tolerant plant with silvery gray foliage and bright yellow flower heads does well in wildflower gardens.

Synonym: Heterotheca nervosa (Willd.) Shinners

Platanthera ciliaris (L.) Lindl.
YELLOW-FRINGED ORCHID
Orchidaceae (Orchid family)

Description: An upright perennial herb 1–3 ft. tall with alternate, lanceolate lower leaves 2–8 in. long, reduced to bracts above. Flowers bright yellow to deep orange with a deeply fringed lip petal and a long nectar spur. Fruit an elongate capsule with numerous dust-like seeds. Flowers July–Sept.

Habitat/range: Occurs mainly in open to lightly wooded, moist sites, including bogs, seepage slopes, meadows, roadbanks, and forest edges. Fairly common in mountains, rare in piedmont. Widespread in eastern North America.

Taxonomy: The genus includes about 200 species primarily in temperate regions of the northern hemisphere, including 12 species in the mountains and piedmont.

Ecology: The flowers open sequentially from the bottom of the inflorescence to the top. The markedly fringed lower petal serves as both a visual attractant and landing platform for potential pollinators as they sip nectar from the long, downturned spur. The primary pollinators are large butterflies, especially spicebush swallowtails and palamedes swallowtails. The pollen of orchids is produced in discrete bundles called pollinia. As butterflies probe the nectar spur with their long tongues, the sticky end of the pollinium adheres to the eye of the butterfly. When the butterfly visits another flower, the pollinium may brush against the stigma, resulting in pollination. Without pollinators, no seeds are produced.

Wildlife: White-tailed deer and rabbits browse the foliage, and rodents consume the fleshy tubers.

Uses: Native Americans used the flowers (which superficially resemble insects) as lures to catch fish. Enjoy this plant in the wild, as individuals dug up and transplanted simply die.

Synonym: Habenaria ciliaris (L.) R. Br.

Platanthera integrilabia (Correll) Luer
MONKEY FACE ORCHID
Orchidaceae (Orchid family)

Description: Perennial herb with an erect stem up to 4 ft. tall with 2–3 large, lanceolate leaves on lower stem, reduced to several small, bract-like leaves near stem tip. Pure white flowers with a slight hood on top, a spoon-shaped lower lip with a slightly toothed margin, and a long, strongly curved nectar spur occur in a loosely flowered terminal cluster. Fruit an elliptic capsule. Flowers July–Sept.; fruits Sept.–Oct.

Habitat/range: Sphagnum bogs, red maple–black gum swamps, damp stream margins, and rocky, thinly vegetated seepage slopes, primarily in mountains. Rare. Known from a small number of sites in the Southeast.

Taxonomy: The pure white color of the flowers, the long nectar spur, and the nearly entire margin of the lower lip distinguish this species from other members of the genus in our region.

Ecology: Vegetative plants with a single strap-shaped basal leaf far outnumber flowering plants in most populations. The showy flowers are adapted to evening-flying hawk moths as suggested by their white color, strong fragrance (especially at dusk), and long (1–2 in.) nectar spur. Day-flying butterflies, especially swallowtails, also function as pollinators. Some hawk moths hover in midair while feeding on nectar and are sometimes mistaken for hummingbirds. Other visitors use the lower lip of the flower as a landing platform before extending their (necessarily) long mouthparts into the spur to access nectar. Longer nectar spurs as seen in this species can benefit a plant by excluding less efficient pollinators from getting nectar, thereby promoting pollinator specialization. While relatively few flowers mature fruit, those that do contain more than 3,000 tiny seeds. Habitat loss, poaching by unscrupulous collectors, logging, and cattle grazing threaten this rare species.

Synonym: *Habenaria blephariglottis* (Willd.) Hook var. *integrilabia* Correll

Pleopeltis polypodioides (L.) Andrews & Windham
RESURRECTION FERN
Polypodiaceae (Polypody family)

Description: Evergreen epiphytic fern with long, creeping, much-branched stolons. Leaves (fronds) 2–7 in. long, borne singly along the rhizome, dark green and smooth above, densely scaly and silvery brown below. Spore clusters (sori) lack a cover (indusium) and occur near margins of leaflets (pinnae), June–Oct.

Habitat/range: On tree limbs and crotches of large trees with a deeply grooved bark and on rocks (usually limestone or sandstone). Common. Eastern United States, south to Mexico and Guatemala.

Taxonomy: Of the 50 species in the genus, resurrection fern is the only species in the mountains and piedmont. Common rockcap fern (*Polypodium virginianum*) occurs on rocks (rarely trees) and has similar leaves but lacks scales on the lower leaf surface.

Ecology: On a typical hot summer day, this fern completely dries up—its leaves curl up, turn brown, and it looks dead. During a soaking rain, the leaves absorb water, uncurl, and the plant is as alive and green as ever. By curling its leaves during dry periods, the plant exposes hundreds of tiny whitish scales that cover the underside of each leaf. When the leaf is wet, these scales absorb and funnel water into the leaf cells, rehydrating the plant. Remarkably, resurrection fern can survive without irreversible harm after losing more than 97 percent of its water content. In contrast, most plants die after losing less than 15 percent of their water content. On favorable sites, resurrection fern spreads vegetatively, forming dense patches. It spreads to other trees by wind-dispersed spores.

Uses: Resurrection fern adds interest to moist, shaded sites in woodland gardens.

Synonym: Polypodium polypodioides (L.) Watt.

Podophyllum peltatum L.
MAYAPPLE
Berberidaceae (Barberry family)

Description: Perennial herb from a creeping rhizome forms a dense carpet of large umbrella-like leaves on forest floor. Large, solitary, nodding flowers with waxy white petals and numerous stamens, usually partially hidden under leaves. Fruit a large, yellow, egg-shaped, many-seeded berry with a pleasant fragrance. Flowers Mar.–Apr.; fruits May–June.

Habitat/range: Rich, moist woods and meadows, including cove forests, alluvial forests, river bluff forests, and basic mesic forests. Common. Widespread in eastern North America.

Taxonomy: The genus *Podophyllum* consists of just 2 species, 1 in eastern North America, the other in eastern Asia.

Ecology: Like many woodland herbs, mayapple is both long-lived and clonal (a dense patch may consist of a single plant with multiple shoots interconnected by a branched rhizome). Leaves are produced on 2 types of stems: "singles" have a solitary stem terminating in a single umbrella-like leaf while "forks" have a branched stem with 2 smaller umbrella-like leaves and a single flower at the junction of the leafstalks. Bumblebees (the primary pollinator) infrequently visit the nectarless flowers, most of which fail to mature fruit due to lack of pollination. Mayapple plants near nectar-rich species, such as lousewort (*Pedicularis*), are more frequently visited by bumblebees and have higher fruit set. Other bottlenecks that limit reproduction include low seed-germination rates and a host-specific fungus (*Puccinia podophylli*) that kills young plants.

Wildlife: Small mammals, as well as the eastern box turtle, eat the fragrant, fleshy fruits and disperse the seeds. While ripe fruits are edible, all other parts of mayapple are highly poisonous to humans and most other organisms.

Uses: Mayapple has long been known to be a medicinal plant. Chemicals derived from mayapple are currently used to treat certain types of cancer.

Podostemum ceratophyllum Michx.
RIVERWEED
Podostemaceae (Riverweed family)

Description: This highly unusual, alga-like, aquatic vascular plant consists of a multibranched thallus with very narrow, highly dissected leaves, and tiny flowers and fruits (capsules) in leaf axils. Small, disk-like holdfasts anchor the plant to rocks and ledges of fast-flowing streams and waterfalls. Flowers May–July; fruits June–Oct.

Habitat/range: Submersed in rapids, rocky streambeds, and spray cliffs. Occasional. Mainly in eastern North America.

Taxonomy: Podostemum is a genus of 18 aquatic herbs of temperate and tropical regions, all of which grow in river rapids and waterfalls. This is the only North American species.

Ecology: Riverweeds are unique among flowering plants in that they grow submerged in fast-flowing currents, anchored by holdfasts firmly attached to rocks. Their rubbery texture is an apparent adaptation to the mechanical stress imposed by swift currents and rocky substrates. The inconspicuous flowers, which occur above, below, or at the water's surface, mostly self-pollinate within buds. The seeds of riverweed are dispersed downstream by the current or by the sticky mucilaginous seed coat adhering to the feet of wading birds. The seeds germinate underwater, first producing a green (photosynthetically active) seedling root that compensates for the lack of stored nutrients (endosperm) in the tiny seeds. Lest the seedling be washed away, adhesive hairs (rhizoids) on the underside of the root attach the seedling to the rocky substrate. Once established, riverweed spreads vegetatively from thread-like "roots" that spread across the substratum, sending up new shoots and laying down additional holdfasts that anchor the plant to the substrate. Heavy sedimentation in streams has markedly reduced the distribution and abundance of this species.

Wildlife: Dense beds of riverweed provide an important substrate for algae, including enormous numbers of diatoms, which are food for invertebrates, which in turn are prey for fish.

Uses: Riverweed is a useful indicator of water quality because it's intolerant of siltation and requires high concentrations of oxygen.

Polygala paucifolia Willd.
FRINGED POLYGALA,
BIRD-ON-THE-WING
Polygalaceae (Milkwort family)

Description: Herbaceous perennial from 3 to 6 in. tall with alternate, elliptic to ovate-shaped leaves crowded near stem tip. Pink to purple (rarely white) flowers in a terminal raceme, each consisting of 2 flaring lateral sepals (the "wings") and a fringe-tipped corolla tube borne in small clusters of 1–4 flowers. Fruit a small capsule. Flowers Apr.–June; fruits June–Sept.

Habitat/range: Moist forests at mid- to high elevations, including red oak forests, pine-oak-heath, and chestnut oak forests. Common in mountains. Primarily a northeastern species extending south in Appalachians to Georgia.

Taxonomy: This nearly cosmopolitan genus includes about 500 species of trees, shrubs, and herbs, including 7 species in the mountain and piedmont region.

Ecology: Like jewelweed, violets, and numerous other plants, fringed polygala produces 2 types of flowers—larger, showier (chasmogamous) flowers that attract potential pollinators and tiny (cleistogamous) flowers that never open and self-pollinate in the bud. The chasmogamous flowers attract bees that use the fringed central tube as a landing platform. The weight of the insect depresses the pouch and forces the anthers and stigmas through a slit at the top and into direct contact with the insect's lower abdomen, which accumulates pollen, some of which may subsequently contact a stigma, thereby promoting cross-pollination. The tiny self-pollinating flowers produce viable, if not genetically diverse, seeds. Look for cleistogamous flowers at the base of the plant under the leaf litter.

Wildlife: Ants quickly remove ripe seeds from capsules and carry them back to their nests where they remove the food body (elaiosome) that's attached to the seed coat and feed it to their larvae. They subsequently drop the otherwise intact seed near the nest, where it can germinate and potentially establish a new plant.

Uses: This low-growing colonial plant with its highly unusual flowers adds interest to shade gardens but shouldn't be removed from the wild.

Polygonatum biflorum (Walter) Elliott
SOLOMON'S SEAL
Ruscaceae (Ruscus Family)

Description: Perennial herb with 1–6 ft. long arching stems with alternate, smooth leaves, narrowly oval with prominent parallel veins. Greenish white, bell-shaped flowers and blue-black berries hang below leaves. Flowers May–June; fruits Sept.–Oct.

Habitat/range: Variety of dry-moist forests, including cove forests, oak-hickory forests, and chestnut oak forests. Common. Widespread in eastern and central North America, west to New Mexico.

Taxonomy: The genus *Polygonatum* consists of about 60 species of Europe, Asia, and North America, 2 of which occur in the mountains and piedmont. Solomon's seal and false Solomon seal (*Maianthemum racemosum*) are similar vegetatively but differ in that the flowers and fruits of Solomon's seal hang beneath the stem, whereas those of false Solomon's seal are clustered at the stem tips.

Ecology: Solomon's seal tolerates a wide range of conditions but grows best in rich, moist woodlands. Plants have either 2 or 4 sets of chromosomes, thus both diploid and tetraploid plants occur. Tetraploids are typically larger than diploids and produce more flowers and fruits. Rhizomes with knobby swellings run horizontally beneath the soil surface from which the arching stems arise. In winter, the deciduous stems leave a circular scar atop the rootstalk that is thought to resemble the seal of King Solomon, hence the common name. The location of the flowers beneath the leafy stem provides shelter from the potentially damaging effects of wind and rain.

Wildlife: Bumblebees pollinate the flowers in spring, birds disperse the seeds in autumn, and white-tailed deer graze the foliage throughout the growing season.

Uses: Its arching stems and graceful habit add interest to gardens.

Polystichum acrostichoides (Michx.) Schott
CHRISTMAS FERN
Dryopteridaceae (Wood fern Family)

Description: Evergreen fern with pinnate fronds from a stout, creeping rhizome, often forming circular arching clumps, 12–24 in. tall, leaflets (pinnules) resemble a Christmas stocking or sleigh. Spore clusters (sori) often cover underside of fertile leaflets near tips of fronds. Spores dispersed June–Sept.

Habitat/range: Moist to dry forests and woodlands, including cove forests, river bluff forests, and floodplain forests. Common. Widely distributed in eastern North America.

Taxonomy: The genus *Polystichum* comprises about 180 species, but Christmas fern is the only species in our region.

Ecology: Christmas fern is a widespread and abundant evergreen fern in eastern deciduous forests. Its fronds remain green through the winter and then die back as new fronds expand in spring. The new fronds are held in an upright position through the spring, summer, and fall, thereby reducing the likelihood of their being overtopped by nearby herbaceous plants. In late fall, the fronds become horizontal, where they remain green until new fronds are produced the following spring. Reorientation of fronds to a prostrate position in winter is advantageous because the fronds are less exposed to cold, drying winds, and because warmer ground temperatures increase leaf temperature, promoting photosynthetic activity, particularly on relatively mild winter days when Christmas fern is metabolically active. A cost of being wintergreen is increased vulnerability to herbivores, as other green plants are scarce and Christmas fern is highly visible on the forest floor.

Wildlife: Deer, rabbits, chipmunks, ruffed grouse, and box turtles graze the fronds to varying degrees, and Carolina chickadees line their nests with them.

Uses: The evergreen fronds were once cut and used as holiday greenery during the Christmas season. This hardy fern is relatively easy to grow in woodland gardens.

Portulaca smallii P. Wilson
SMALL'S PORTULACA
Portulacaceae (Purslane family)

Description: A small, prostrate to more or less erect summer annual with narrow, alternate, semisucculent leaves. Small, pink to almost white flowers in terminal inflorescences partially hidden by surrounding clusters of small leaves. Fruit a small capsule. Flowers June–Oct.; fruits June–Nov.

Habitat/range: Thin soils on rock outcrops in piedmont, sometimes spreading locally to adjacent fields and other disturbed areas. Rare. Virginia, the Carolinas, and Georgia.

Taxonomy: Portulaca is a nearly worldwide genus of annual and perennial herbs, including 7 species in the mountains and piedmont. Kiss-me-quick (*P. pilosa*) resembles Small's portulaca but has dark pink to purple petals.

Ecology: Small's portulaca grows on shallow soils in full sunlight where there is enough moisture for successful seedling establishment and growth. A narrow band on the edge of the outcrop is often ideal, since it receives and retains water from runoff and the vegetation is often sparse. Where conditions are more favorable (e.g., on deeper soils), it's outcompeted by larger plants. The seeds germinate in late spring or early summer and the first flowers are typically produced within 4 weeks of seedling emergence. Like other summer-growing rock outcrop plants, it has a remarkable ability to tolerate high temperatures. In one study, plants survived temperatures up to 130°F. Moisture availability has a strong influence on survivorship, growth, and reproductive output. Severely drought-stressed plants may survive but exhibit pronounced stunting and produce very few fruits. In prolonged droughts, individuals orient their leaves vertically, thereby reducing heat gain and evaporative water loss from the leaf surface. The inconspicuous flowers open for a short period around noon, but remain closed under cloudy skies. Small bees visit the flowers but if cross-pollination fails, the flowers can self-pollinate. Seeds buried beneath the soil surface remain dormant, providing a buffer (a seed bank) against local extinction in extremely dry years when few plants survive to produce seeds.

Primula meadia (L.) Mast and Reveal
SHOOTING STAR
Primulaceae (Primrose family)

Description: Smooth perennial herb with a basal rosette of mostly oblanceolate leaves 4–10 in. long. Flower stalk to 18 in. tall with a cluster of nodding, white flowers at tip. The unusual flowers consist of 5 petals swept backward with 5 fused stamens protruding forward, forming a pointed beak. Fruit an elliptic capsule that splits open at tip when ripe. Flowers late Mar.–early June; fruits late May–June.

Habitat/range: Rich, moist wooded slopes often associated with high-calcium soils, including basic mesic forests, rich cove forests, and rock outcrops. Uncommon. Eastern United States.

Taxonomy: The genus *Primula* includes 400 species of low-growing herbs in Europe, Asia, North America, South America, and East Africa. The common name alludes to the flower resembling a celestial shooting star.

Ecology: Shooting star is one of a number of bee-pollinated species whose flowers hang downward with the petals bent backward, away from the tightly united cone-shaped anthers. Other plants with this unusual flower-form include cranberry (*Vaccinium macrocarpon*) and horse nettle (*Solanum carolinense*). Pollen-collecting female bees cling to the anther cones and by rapidly vibrating their flight muscles cause a "shower" of fine, powdery pollen to be released from the anthers. The pollen typically accumulates on the ventral part of the bee's abdomen, some of which may subsequently contact a stigma, resulting in pollination. Because bees make a clearly audible buzzing sound while foraging for pollen in this way, it is called buzz pollination. Shooting star depends on buzz pollination by bees, especially bumblebee queens, for successful fruit set.

Wildlife: Rodents relish all parts of the plant.

Uses: The striking flowers and basal rosette of leaves make shooting star an attractive garden plant, but it takes 3–4 years for plants grown from seed to produce their first flowers.

Synonym: Dodecatheon meadia L.

Prunella vulgaris L.
HEAL ALL
Lamiaceae (Mint family)

Description: An erect or creeping perennial herb from 4 to 20 in. tall, with square stems and opposite, lanceolate or elliptical leaves 1–3 in. long. Blue-violet 2-lipped flowers occur in terminal spikes among fringed bracts; upper lip covers the 4 stamens, lower lip shorter, with 3 lobes. Up to 4 dark brown nutlets at base of calyx. Flowers Apr.–Oct.

Habitat/range: Fields, meadows, pastures, roadsides, alluvial forests, and forest edges. Common. Widespread in temperate North America.

Taxonomy: A genus of 4 species of herbs of north-temperate areas. Two varieties of this species occur in our area: var. *lanceolata* is native to North America, whereas var. *vulgaris* is introduced (from Eurasia).

Ecology: The growth form of this plant is highly variable, depending on its particular environment. Commonly low-growing and somewhat sprawling, plants exhibit a more upright growth form in more open sites where competition is reduced and resources are more readily available. While inferior competitors for light, plants with the creeping growth form produce long, horizontal, aboveground stems (stolons) that enable individuals to (at least partially) escape unfavorable conditions. In contrast, more upright plants have relatively short stolons enabling them to better exploit locally favorable conditions. Bees function as pollinators while visiting the flowers for nectar, pollen, or both. Raindrops hitting the calyx tube cause it to bend and reflex, flinging ripe seeds from the plant.

Wildlife: Most wildlife species avoid this plant because of its bitter taste.

Uses: Heal all has been used as a folk medicine to treat a wide variety of ailments. Recent research indicates it has antibiotic properties.

Pteridium aquilinum (L.) Kuhn
BRACKEN FERN
Dennstaedtiaceae (Bracken family)

Description: Large triangular-shaped fronds emerge from a creeping underground stem, often forming dense colonies. Spore clusters (sporangia) occur as a continuous band along leaf margins, partly covered by rolled leaf edges, July–Sept.

Habitat/range: Woodlands, forests, and fields, particularly on dry, acidic soils, including grassy and heath balds, chestnut oak forests, pine-oak-heath, oak-hickory forests, and forest edges. Common. Nearly worldwide distribution.

Taxonomy: The genus consists of a single species with multiple varieties.

Ecology: One of the 5 most common plants in the world, bracken fern occurs on all continents except Antarctica. Its widespread distribution reflects long-distance dispersal via airborne spores, coupled with an ability to tolerate a wide range of environmental conditions, including sites too dry for most other ferns. Once established, individuals spread rapidly from a creeping rhizome, often forming numerous fronds that cover a large area. The rhizomes, which can be more than half an inch thick, are the primary carbohydrate storage organ and also store water. A strong competitor, bracken fern develops a dense canopy and leaf litter layer. Subsequent shading, smothering, and the release of inhibitory chemicals reduces the growth of other species, thereby decreasing the diversity of the herbaceous layer. Under favorable conditions, a colony can persist for hundreds of years and fossils of this ancient fern go back at least 55 million years.

Wildlife: Most vertebrates avoid or feed sparingly on bracken fern because of its toxic chemicals. However, nearly 100 species of insects feed exclusively on this fern, having evolved specialized mechanisms to cope with the plant's defense compounds.

Uses: Has been used as a food source, as thatch for roofing, and in medicines. Eating bracken fern is now discouraged as it's thought to be carcinogenic.

Rudbeckia hirta L.
BLACK-EYED SUSAN
Asteraceae (Sunflower family)

Description: Coarsely hairy herbaceous plant from 1 to 3 ft. tall with alternate grayish green, entire or toothed (but not lobed) leaves, the lower leaves stalked, the upper mostly sessile. Flower heads about 2–3 in. across with a prominent central cone of dark brown disk flowers with showy yellow to orange-yellow ray flowers. Fruit a 4-angled, black achene. Flowers May–Oct.; fruits Aug.–Dec.

Habitat/range: Open habitats such as roadsides, fields, pastures, open woods, and forest edges. Common. Widely distributed in North America, naturalized in Europe and other parts of the world.

Taxonomy: Six of the 23 species in the genus occur in the mountains and piedmont. Asteraceae is one of the largest plant families with more than 1,500 genera and 23,000 species.

Ecology: Black-eyed Susan grows mostly in dry, open areas, including on poor soils, where there is less competition for space and other resources than on more favorable sites. A highly variable species, several different varieties have been recognized. Some individuals are annuals, completing their life cycles in 1 year or less, others are short-lived perennials. Bees are the primary pollinators, but flies, wasps, moths, and beetles also visit the flowers for nectar, pollen, or both.

Wildlife: Look for spittlebugs in the leaf axils. They imbibe sap from the plant and mix it with chemicals in their guts to produce conspicuous spittle that provides protection from both predators and desiccation. In one study, spittlebugs reduced the growth of black-eyed Susan by 25 percent and seed production by 35 percent.

Uses: Black-eyed Susans are widely planted in gardens and often included in wildflower meadow mixes and highway beautification projects.

Rudbeckia laciniata L.
CUTLEAF CONEFLOWER
Asteraceae (Sunflower family)

Description: Highly branched perennial herb 3–8 ft. tall with alternate, deeply cut, 3–5 lobed lower leaves up to 8 in. long, the upper leaves reduced in size and less dissected. Flowers in long-stalked, showy heads, the central disk flowers greenish yellow with drooping yellow ray flowers. Fruit a 4-angled, brown achene. Flowers July–Oct.

Habitat/range: Moist woodlands and forest edges, alluvial forests, and rocky streamsides. Common. Widely distributed in North America.

Taxonomy: This highly variable species, with 3 recognized varieties, is sometimes called green-headed coneflower because of its distinctive greenish yellow disk flowers.

Ecology: This large plant with showy flowers is a conspicuous component of forest margins from late summer–fall. Like many members of the sunflower family, its flowers are visited by a wide variety of insects, including bees, wasps, flies, butterflies, and moths. Plants often form dense colonies as slender rhizomes spread laterally, sending up new shoots. More than

90 species of plants show visible signs of damage due to the high ozone concentrations that characterize the southern Appalachians. Exposure symptoms in cutleaf coneflower, one of the species most sensitive to ozone damage, begin as patches of dull red, mottled areas between the veins on the upper surface of leaves at the base of the plant. By late summer or fall, the symptoms often spread up the plant to the youngest leaves.

Wildlife: Caterpillars of crescentspot butterflies feed on the leaves and goldfinches glean seeds from fruiting heads from late summer–fall.

Uses: Various cultivars are grown in gardens, including some that have traveled to Europe and returned as new and "improved" varieties with foreign names such as "herbstsonne" (German for autumn sun).

Sagittaria latifolia Willd.
ARROWHEAD, DUCK POTATO
Alismataceae (Water plantain family)

Description: A robust, aquatic perennial herb 1–3 ft. tall that spreads laterally, forming dense colonies. Basal, arrowhead-shaped leaves, 6–16 in. long and about half as wide, with petiole length varying depending on water depth. Showy white flowers with 3 petals and numerous pistils or stamens, lower flowers usually female, upper flowers male. Fruit a beaked achene clustered in heads. Flowers July–Sept.

Habitat/range: Bogs, marshes, wet ditches, and stream margins. Common. Widely distributed in the Americas.

Taxonomy: Sagittaria is a genus of about 25 species of herbs, including 9 species in the mountains and piedmont. Southern arrowhead (*S. australis*) is similar, but the bracts subtending flowers are longer than the pedicel and the beaks on the fruits turn upward, rather than to the side.

Ecology: Arrowhead spreads vegetatively, with single large individuals having more than 100 shoots. Separate male and female flowers typically occur on the same plant but some plants produce flowers of only 1 gender. Flower buds open from the base to the apex of an inflorescence over a period of days, with individual flowers usually opening for a single day. Bees, flies, wasps, and butterflies visit and pollinate the flowers. Individuals are self-compatible such that the pollen produced by a particular plant can fertilize the ovules (potential seeds) of that same plant. However, offspring derived from self-fertilized seeds are less vigorous than offspring resulting from cross-fertilized seeds. Separate male and female plants have the advantage of being able to produce only outcrossed seeds because self-fertilization isn't possible.

Wildlife: Various waterfowl eat the potato-like, tuberous roots, hence the common name "duck potato."

Uses: An important staple food for Native Americans, the starch-filled tubers can be eaten raw or cooked.

Sanguinaria canadensis L.
BLOODROOT
Papaveraceae (Poppy family)

Description: Low-growing perennial herb with a thick rhizome that oozes an orange-red juice when cut, hence the common name. Solitary, distinctively shaped, blue-green basal leaf with a deeply lobed margin. Solitary white flower up to 2 in. across on a leafless stalk with 8–24 petals and numerous golden stamens. Fruit an elongate green capsule, pointed at both ends. Flowers Mar.–Apr.; fruits Apr.–May.

Habitat/range: Variety of moist, rich forests, including cove forests, river bluff forests, and floodplain forests. Common. Patchily distributed in eastern and central North America.

Taxonomy: Bloodroot is the only species in the genus *Sanguinaria*.

Ecology: Bloodroot in bloom is one of the cherished signs of early spring. The large white flowers, partially encircled by an unfolding leaf, emerge well before the trees leaf out. The initially vertical leaves become horizontal as they expand, eventually reaching a diameter of 4–8 in. Unlike spring ephemerals, shade-tolerant herbs such as bloodroot retain their leaves and actively grow during the summer months. Bees and flies visit the showy but nectarless flowers for pollen. If cross-pollination doesn't occur within 3–4 days, the anthers bend toward the stigmas, covering them with self-pollen, a useful backup since cold or wet early spring weather hinders pollinator activity. A single plant with a highly branched rhizome may produce as many as 10 flowers (and leaves).

Wildlife: Bloodroot's brown seeds contain a white, lipid-rich appendage (an elaiosome) that attracts ants. The ants consume the elaiosome and leave the seed to germinate, usually near their nest.

Uses: Native Americans frequently used the bright orange-red juice (sanguinarine) from bloodroot's rhizomes as a dye for clothing and for body paint. Sanguinarine is currently used as an anti-plaque agent and as a supplement in cattle feed due to its antibacterial properties. With increasing demand, the overharvesting of bloodroot is a concern.

Sarracenia purpurea L.
PURPLE PITCHER PLANT
Sarraceniaceae (Pitcher plant family)

Description: Insectivorous herb with evergreen purple-streaked leaves, modified into keeled, pitcher-shaped containers arranged in a basal rosette with erect hoods. Solitary, purple, nodding flowers on leafless stalks, 8–16 in tall. Fruit a round, warty capsule with winged seeds. Flowers Apr.–May; fruits June–July.

Habitat/range: Mountain bogs, seepage bogs, and wet savannas. Uncommon. Eastern North America.

Taxonomy: Four of the 11 species of this eastern North American genus occur in the mountains and piedmont.

Ecology: The pitchers are highly modified leaves that function as pitfall traps. At the top of the pitcher is a flared out "lip," with nectar glands and conspicuous red veins that attract insects. On the inside of the lip are stiff, downward-pointing hairs that cause insects to lose their footing and fall into the trap. A smooth, waxy region occurs immediately below the slippery hairs that prevents insects from crawling out of the trap. Below is the water-filled area of the pitcher—it contains rainwater as well as bacterial and plant digestive enzymes that help decompose trapped insects, releasing nitrogen and other nutrients that are absorbed by specialized cells at the bottom of the pitcher. The lowest zone is a narrow stalk in which undigested insect parts accumulate. Draining and conversion of wetlands, plant poaching, and a lack of fire threaten this species.

Wildlife: Insects and other organisms interact with pitcher plants in various ways. The flowers depend on bumblebees for successful pollination, while insects captured in the leaves provide an important source of nutrients for the plant. Other insects function as herbivores on the leaves, sometimes cutting a hole in the pitcher and causing the "digestive fluid" and its contents to run out.

Uses: Nursery-propagated pitcher plants are well suited to bog gardens.

Schizachyrium scoparium (Michx.) Nash
LITTLE BLUESTEM
Poaceae (Grass family)

Description: A clump-forming grass with few to many long, slender, greenish blue to purplish stems, 2–5 ft. tall, arising from a common root system. Leaf blades linear, 3–14 in. long at maturity, rough on upper surface and margins, initially light green, changing to purplish from late summer–fall. Stems with numerous branches, each terminated by a spike-like raceme 1–2 in. long. Seeds tipped by hairlike awns that collectively give plants a fluffy appearance in fall and winter. Flowers Aug.–Oct.

Habitat/range: Wide range of moist to dry habitats. Common. Widespread in North America.

Taxonomy: Only 1 of the 60 species in this genus occurs in the mountains and piedmont.

Ecology: This widespread and abundant warm-season grass is extremely variable, which in part reflects the diversity of habitats it occupies. It typically grows upright in distinct clumps about 4–10 in. across, with flowering stems ranging from 2 to 5 ft. tall, depending on soil fertility and moisture availability. On wet sites, it sometimes spreads vegetatively, forming an open sod with short rhizomes connecting small tufts. A deep (up to 5 ft.) root system takes up water, stores carbohydrates, and holds the plant in place. Fall, winter, and spring fires typically stimulate growth, flowering, and seed production, due to increased light, soil temperature, and available nutrients. Conversely, summer fires (during the growing season) can be detrimental, as dry conditions result in hotter fires that can kill plants. Good seed crops are produced most years, except during drought years when inflorescences don't develop.

Wildlife: Little bluestem is an important source of forage for both wild and domestic animals.

Uses: Widely used in prairie restoration projects.

Synonym: Andropogon scoparius Michx.

Selaginella tortipila A. Braun
TWISTED HAIR SPIKEMOSS
Selaginellaceae (Spikemoss family)

Description: Grayish green moss-like evergreen forming thick, prostrate mounds. Aboveground stems with small, tightly overlapping, linear leaves with apical, twisted bristles. Spores produced in tiny cone-like structures, July–Sept.

Habitat/range: Rock outcrops. Common in mountains, rare in upper piedmont. Restricted to North Carolina, Tennessee, South Carolina, and Georgia.

Taxonomy: Selaginella is a genus of more than 700 species, including 5 species in the mountains and piedmont. A characteristic feature of *S. tortipila* is the twisted bristle that terminates each tiny leaf, from which the common name is derived.

Ecology: Twisted hair spikemoss is a common mat-forming species on outcrops. By trapping soil particles carried by wind and water, it accumulates soil, thereby facilitating the development of vegetation mats on rocky substrates. Superficially resembling a large moss, *Selaginella* species are actually primitive vascular plants related to ferns. Like ferns, they have specialized tissues for transporting water (xylem) and nutrients (phloem), and reproduce by spores, rather than by seeds. Along with bryophytes (mosses, liverworts, and hornworts), seedless vascular plants were the first terrestrial plants. Ancient lycophyte relatives of *Selaginella* included tree-like forms that grew up to 115 ft. tall. During most of the Carboniferous period, which extended from 360 to 286 million years ago, these lycophyte trees were the dominant plant group. As the climate became cooler and drier towards the end of the Carboniferous, these lycophytes died off, leaving behind huge amounts of dead organic matter that was buried, compressed, and chemically transformed, eventually forming a major part of the world's extensive coal deposits. Modern-day lycophytes, including *Selaginella*, are small herbaceous plants, most of which grow as epiphytes on the branches of tropical trees.

Shortia galacifolia Torr. & A. Gray
OCONEE BELLS

Diapensiaceae (Diapensia family)

Description: Low evergreen herb spreading by short shallow runners, forming dense clumps of shiny circular leaves, often purple-tinged, with prominent pale veins and long petioles. Solitary, white flowers with 5 separate petals toothed at apex, resembling a nodding bell. Fruit a small capsule with numerous tiny seeds. Flowers Mar.–Apr.; fruits July–Aug.

Habitat/range: Moist, humid slopes and creek banks usually in deep shade beneath rosebay (*Rhododendron maximum*) or mountain laurel (*Kalmia latifolia*). A rare species restricted to gorges of the Blue Ridge Escarpment in North Carolina, South Carolina, and Georgia.

Taxonomy: The genus *Shortia* includes 1 North American species and 5 eastern Asian species. Oconee Bells was first collected in 1787 in Oconee County, South Carolina, by the famous French botanist André Michaux. Harvard botanist Asa Gray discovered Michaux's collection in Paris nearly 50 years later and, recognizing it as a new species, described and named it. *Shortia* soon became a kind of Holy Grail for plant collectors, as numerous plant hunters (including Asa Gray) searched for it unsuccessfully in the "high mountains of the Carolinas" (the locality given by Michaux on his specimen label). Almost 90 years after Michaux first collected the plant, and nearly 40 years after Gray named it, *Shortia* was rediscovered by 17-year-old George Hyams in North Carolina, bringing additional fame to a plant that Gray once characterized as "perhaps the most interesting plant in North America." Vegetative plants closely resemble *Galax urceolata* but are readily distinguished in bloom, as *Shortia* has relatively large, solitary flowers, while *Galax* has small, numerous flowers in dense racemes.

Ecology: About 60 percent of the populations of Oconee Bells were lost due to the construction of 2 large reservoirs in South Carolina, the Jocassee and the Keowee, in the 1960s. In spite of its limited natural distribution, some fairly large populations persist in the wild.

Wildlife: Pollen-collecting bees sporadically visit the nectarless flowers.

Sibbaldiopsis tridentata (Aiton) Rydb.
THREE-TOOTH CINQUEFOIL

Rosaceae (Rose family)

Description: Low-growing perennial with slightly woody stems and mostly basal, evergreen leaves with 3 leaflets, each with 3 shallow teeth at apex. White flowers with 5 petals and numerous stamens in flat-topped terminal clusters. Fruit an aggregate of brown achenes covered with long, fine hairs. Flowers June–Aug.; fruits July–Sept.

Habitat/range: Rocky substrates in full sun. Grassy balds, rock outcrops, and glades at high elevations. This wide-ranging plant of Canada and the northern United States is uncommon in the southern Appalachians.

Taxonomy: Sibbaldiopsis is a small genus of herbs and subshrubs of North America and Asia with only 1 species in the mountains and piedmont. The word *tridentata* in the species name refers to the 3 teeth at the tip of each leaflet, a trait that characterizes this species.

Ecology: Three-tooth cinquefoil occurs on rocky substrates where the vegetation is typically sparse. It colonizes crevices in rocks as well as disturbed sites, including trailside areas. Successful seedling establishment occurs infrequently, but established plants can persist for many years and spread vegetatively from underground rhizomes. Although it looks herbaceous, three-tooth cinquefoil is technically a subshrub because it has slightly woody stems and is low growing. The bumblebee-pollinated, showy white flowers bloom over a long period (June–Aug.) and the evergreen leaves usually turn a rich burgundy red from late summer on.

Synonym: Potentilla tridentata Aiton

Silene virginica L.
FIRE PINK
Caryophyllaceae (Pink family)

Description: Upright perennial herb 1–3 ft. tall with a tuft of basal leaves 3–5 in. long and 2–4 pairs of narrow, sessile stem leaves. Deeply notched scarlet-red flowers with a tubular, sticky green calyx are unmistakable. Fruit an elliptic capsule that tilts downward at maturity to release the seeds. Flowers Apr.–June.

Habitat/range: Moist to dry, open habitats, including woodlands, forest edges, rock outcrops, and roadbanks. Common. Widely distributed in eastern North America.

Taxonomy: A genus of about 700 species of Eurasia and North America, with 14 species in the mountains and piedmont.

Ecology: A poor competitor, fire pink typically occurs as single plants or small clumps in areas where the vegetation is sparse. The spectacular scarlet-red blooms are classic hummingbird-pollinated flowers in that they are tubular red flowers with abundant nectar, no landing platforms, no nectar guides, and no detectable floral odor. The long corolla tube generally limits flower visitors to those with long tongues, and the sticky hairs on the surface of the tubular calyx deter nonpollinating crawling insects from stealing nectar. However, bees sometimes chew holes at the bases of flowers and rob nectar. Newly opened flowers function as "males," releasing pollen from anthers over a period of about 2 days; the "female phase" begins by day 4, when the stigmas become receptive. Because pollen is released before the stigmas become receptive, the flowers depend on pollinators for successful pollination and fruit set.

Wildlife: Caterpillars of the noctuid moth (*Hadena ectypa*) feed on the flowers and developing seeds.

Uses: The brilliant scarlet-red flowers of this hardy plant add color to wildflower gardens.

Silphium terebinthinaceum Jacq.
PRAIRIE DOCK
Asteraceae (Sunflower family)

Description: Herbaceous perennial with 1 or more upright stems from 3 to 10 ft. tall with large (up to 1 ft. wide), mostly basal leaves with heart-shaped bases on long stalks. Flowering stems with few, very small leaves and numerous large heads (2–4 in. wide) with yellow ray and disk flowers. Fruit a winged achene. Flowers July–Sept.

Habitat/range: Glades in xeric hardpan forests, barrens, woodlands, and roadsides. Rare. Southern Canada south to Georgia and Mississippi.

Taxonomy: A genus of 20 species of herbaceous plants of eastern North America, including 8 species in the mountains and piedmont. Lesser prairie dock (*S. compositum*) is similar, but the flower heads are smaller, with only 5–10 ray flowers.

Ecology: The large, nearly vertical leaves face east in the morning and west in the evening. Fewer than 10 plant species worldwide are considered to be compass plants, although a number of species have solar-tracking leaves that maintain their perpendicular angle to the sun throughout the day. The leaves of prairie dock receive the most light and photosynthesize at the highest rate in the morning and evening hours, when their nearly vertical leaves face the sun. Because temperatures are relatively low at these times of day, the leaves heat up less and transpirational water loss is reduced. From midday through early afternoon, when solar radiation and temperatures are typically highest, the nearly vertical leaves remain fairly cool, as they are oriented parallel (rather than perpendicular) to the sun's rays. These leaf-orientation characteristics are particularly beneficial to prairie dock because it grows during the summer months, when plants are exposed to high temperatures, intense sunlight, and periodic droughts, and also because it has unusually large, unlobed leaves that would otherwise be vulnerable to excessive heat gain and transpirational water loss.

Wildlife: Large mammalian herbivores readily eat the foliage, and goldfinches and other birds consume the seeds.

Uses: Early settlers aware of the compass-like orientation of the leaves used the plant as a navigational tool.

Smilax herbacea L.
CARRION FLOWER
Smilacaceae (Greenbrier family)

Description: Herbaceous perennial vine 3–9 ft. long that climbs with thread-like tendrils. Leaves ovate to round, 2–5 in. long, with smooth margins.

Numerous yellow-green clusters (umbels) of malodorous male and female flowers on separate plants. Dark blue-black berries in dense round clusters on long stalks. Flowers May–June; fruits Aug.–Oct.

Habitat/range: Moist deciduous forests, thickets, meadows, and roadsides. Common in mountains and piedmont. Southeastern Canada south to Georgia.

Taxonomy: The genus *Smilax* includes about 300 species of woody and herbaceous vines in tropical and temperate regions, including 15 species in the mountains and piedmont.

Ecology: Unlike most species of *Smilax*, carrion flower is an herbaceous, rather than woody, vine with smooth, rather than prickly, stems. Both male and female flowers are strongly odiferous, producing a carrion-like odor (hence the common name) that attracts flies, bees, and beetles. Bees and carrion flies are the primary pollinators. Beetles are less effective because they rarely move among flowers or plants, and their smooth bodies carry less pollen. The flowers lack nectar, so pollen (present only in male flowers) is the sole reward. The large stigma lobes of female flowers mimic the pollen-laden anthers of male flowers; thus, female flowers use a form of deception to attract potential pollinators. This deception is reinforced by the nearly identical appearance and odor of the male and female inflorescences. Most populations have more males than females because the higher energy costs of producing fruit results in higher mortality rates for female plants.

Wildlife: Songbirds, black bears, and small mammals feed on the fruits and disperse the seeds. Various wildlife species browse the shoots and dig up and eat the rhizomes.

Uses: Native Americans used carrion flower's roots and leaves for medicine, the woody rhizomes for smoking pipes, and the seeds as beads.

Solanum carolinense L.
HORSE NETTLE
Solanaceae (Nightshade family)

Description: Erect to sprawling perennial herb covered with sharp prickles. Coarsely lobed alternate leaves up to 6 in. long and 3 in. across. Small clusters of light purple to white, star-shaped flowers with a central cone of 5 conspicuously yellow anthers. Fruits resemble small yellow tomatoes. Flowers May–Sept.; fruits July–Oct.

Habitat/range: Roadsides, fields, pastures, croplands, lawns, and waste areas. Common. This weedy native has spread over much of the United States and has become naturalized in parts of Europe and Asia.

Taxonomy: Five of the 7 species of *Solanum* in our region are introduced. Other members of the nightshade family include tomatoes, potatoes, and peppers, as well as various medicinal, hallucinogenic, and poisonous plants.

Ecology: Horse nettle is considered to be a noxious weed in more than 35 states because it readily colonizes disturbed areas and reduces the yield and quality of pastures and forage crops. It grows rapidly during the hot days of summer, and dies back with the first frost of autumn. A single plant can spread about 20 ft. from a lateral root system that produces upright shoots. A deep, fleshy taproot (often reaching ground water) enables it to tolerate drought. Bumblebees and carpenter bees buzz pollinate the showy, nectarless flowers. Using rapid contractions of their flight muscles, these large-bodied bees produce vibrations that propel pollen grains out of tiny pores at the tips of the anthers, which then accumulate on the bees' body surfaces. While much of this pollen is used as food for bee larvae, some grains are incidentally deposited on the stigmas of other flowers. Successful seed set depends on cross-pollination by bees.

Wildlife: Most vertebrates avoid horse nettle due to its toxic alkaloids and sharp spines, but various insects have circumvented the plant's defense mechanism and feed on its tissues without harm.

Uses: The leaves and berries have medicinal properties, but the berries can be fatal if ingested by humans, cattle, sheep, and possibly deer.

Solidago altissima L.
TALL GOLDENROD
Asteraceae (Aster family)

Description: A tall perennial with multiple annual shoots arising from persistent underground rhizomes. Leaves narrowly oblanceolate, sessile, upper surface rough to the touch. Small yellow flowers in dense terminal clusters with long, arching branches. Fruit an achene. Flowers Aug.–Oct.

Habitat/range: Fields, roadsides, forest edges, and disturbed areas. Common. Native to eastern and central North America, it has become naturalized in western North America and Europe.

Taxonomy: Species identification can be difficult as hybridization within the genus is common, and variation within a species can be considerable.

Ecology: It's not unusual to find multiple species of goldenrod within the same field or roadside area. Blooming in late summer or fall, goldenrods often turn drab openings into fields of gold. Like many goldenrods, tall goldenrod spreads vegetatively from underground stems (rhizomes), with some clones consisting of more than 20 connected shoots. The tall stems (up to 6 ft.) emerge from winter-dormant rhizomes in late spring and die back in late fall. A long growing season means that individuals must tolerate a wide range of climatic conditions, including heat, drought, and cold. People sometimes associate goldenrods with runny noses, itchy eyes, and sneezing, but goldenrods are not the culprit. Goldenrods are insect-pollinated, and their pollen grains are too large and sticky to be carried by wind. Instead, the primary cause of late summer or fall hay fever is ragweed (*Ambrosia*), with its abundant, small, nonsticky, wind-borne pollen.

Wildlife: Look for cryptically colored yellow ambush bugs and goldenrod spiders sitting motionless within flower heads, waiting to prey on nectar-feeding bees, flies, and butterflies. More than 100 kinds of insects feed on tall goldenrod, including gall-forming midge and fly larvae that cause stem swellings of various shapes and sizes.

Uses: Goldenrods provide fall color in perennial borders and are used in the floral trade as cut flowers.

Solidago curtisii Torr. & A. Gray
CURTIS'S GOLDENROD
Asteraceae (Sunflower family)

Description: Herbaceous perennial 2–3 ft. tall with angled, finely grooved green stems. Leaves numerous, usually 3–10 times longer than broad, sharply toothed, tapered to a fine tip, the lower stem and basal leaves smaller than the upper leaves, early deciduous. Five to 10 yellow flowers per head, heads in clusters of 3–15 from axils of upper leaves, each cluster subtended by a long, narrow leaf. Fruit a hairy achene. Flowers Aug.–Oct.

Habitat/range: Moist, forested slopes, including northern hardwood forests, cove forests, and oak-hickory forests. Common in mountains, rare in piedmont. Appalachian Mountains from Pennsylvania south to Georgia.

Taxonomy: Solidago is a large genus of about 100 species of perennial herbs, most of which occur in North America. The grooved stems, numerous large stem leaves, and short clusters of heads in the axils of the upper leaves distinguish Curtis's goldenrod from other species in our region.

Ecology: Goldenrods commonly occur in open, sunny habitats such as early successional fields and roadside areas; in contrast, Curtis's goldenrod occurs in the forest understory. Goldenrods typically have vibrant golden yellow flowers that open from late summer–fall. In each head are several ray (female) flowers, each bearing a single petal that surrounds a dense cluster of small disk (bisexual) flowers. The female flowers attract pollinators with their conspicuous ray petals. Because goldenrods are typically self-incompatible (their pollen unable to fertilize their own ovules), the flowers depend on pollinators (mainly bumblebees) to transfer pollen from plant to plant.

Uses: Goldenrods are used as landscape plants, as well as a source of cut flowers.

Solidago glomerata Michx.
SKUNK GOLDENROD
Asteraceae (Sunflower family)

Description: Herbaceous perennial with smooth, angled stems 1–4 ft. tall, the basal and stem leaves 4–10 in. long, 1–3 in. wide with serrate margins. Clusters of yellow flowers (heads) form dense spike-like inflorescences at top of stems (in contrast, most goldenrods have flower clusters on nodding, arched branches). Flower heads with multiple achenes (one-seeded fruits), each with a small, feathery, parachute-like pappus for wind dispersal. Flowers July–frost.

Habitat/range: Spruce-fir forests, northern hardwood forests, grassy and heath balds, and rock outcrops at high elevations. Common. A southern Appalachian endemic restricted to North Carolina and Tennessee.

Taxonomy: The genus name means "to make whole," referring to the plant's purported herbal properties.

Ecology: If you smell skunk at high elevations, look around for skunk goldenrod, as it has a distinctly skunky odor. Goldenrods produce a variety of compounds that play a role in plant defense against herbivores. The skunky odor probably functions as a warning signal to potential herbivores that the plant is unpalatable (the odor forms a "cloud" around plants, making them easy to smell without contacting them). The evergreen basal rosettes stand out in winter on the mostly drab forest floor.

Wildlife: The skunky odor doesn't seem to bother bumblebees as they actively visit and pollinate the flowers.

Uses: Native Americans used goldenrods to make tea and as a medicine for urinary and kidney disorders.

Sorghastrum nutans (L.) Nash
INDIANGRASS
Poaceae (Grass family)

Description: Erect, perennial, clump-forming grass 3–8 ft. tall with long, upright leaves. Flower clusters (panicles) 4–12 in. long, yellow to golden brown with hairy grayish branches, often nodding at tips. Fruit a flat, reddish grain tipped with a hair-like, twisted awn. Flowers Sept.–Oct.

Habitat/range: Fields, roadsides, and open woods. Common. Widespread in North America.

Taxonomy: A genus of 18–20 species primarily of tropical and subtropical America and Africa, including 2 species in the piedmont and mountains. The genus name reflects its resemblance to sorghum.

Ecology: A warm-season grass, Indiangrass dies back in fall and sends up new shoots in mid-spring (after the soil has warmed up) from underground stems (rhizomes). The numerous short, scaly rhizomes form a dense sod with relatively deep roots that enhance the plant's ability to tolerate drought. It commonly occurs in a variety of open habitats, including woodlands, forest margins, abandoned farmlands, and rights-of-way. Indiangrass is also one of the dominant grasses in midwestern tallgrass prairies. It grows on a variety of soils, and while it tolerates partial shade, it grows best in full sun. Indiangrass responds favorably to non-growing season burns, as the underground rhizomes quickly send up new shoots. Fires help keep the habitat open and increase vegetative vigor, flowering, and seed production.

Wildlife: The foliage of Indiangrass is highly palatable to large grazers in summer when the leaves are green, but forage value decreases in fall and winter due to a reduction in digestibility and protein content. Numerous birds and small mammals consume the seeds.

Uses: This drought-tolerant native grass, with striking golden flowering plumes above dense clumps of foliage, makes a good substitute for exotic ornamental grasses such as Chinese silvergrass (*Miscanthus*) and pampas grass (*Cortaderia*).

Sphagnum species
SPHAGNUM
Sphagnaceae (Sphagnum family)

Description: Individual plants typically consist of a main stem with tightly arranged clusters of branches spreading in various directions. The tiny leaves vary in shape depending on species. Spores produced in specialized capsules at tips of thin stalks.

Habitat/range: Species of sphagnum occur primarily in nutrient-poor, acidic wetlands, including bogs, swamps, seepage slopes, and spray cliffs. Sphagnum moss occurs on all continents except for Antarctica.

Taxonomy: The genus consists of about 280 species, including 88 species in North America. The color of the plants, the shape of the branches and leaves, and the shape of the green cells are characteristics that delineate species of sphagnum.

Ecology: Sphagnum moss consists of low-growing plants densely packed together to form ground-hugging mats. Within a single mat, several sphagnum species may co-occur. Sphagnum leaves consist of large, dead cells surrounded by narrow, green or occasionally red-pigmented, living cells. The dead cells readily fill with water, so that the water-holding capacity of sphagnum moss may exceed 20 times its dry weight (in comparison, cotton absorbs only 4–6 times its dry weight). By holding great amounts of water and releasing it slowly, sphagnum plays a key role in maintaining the hydrology of bogs. The slow release of water by sphagnum mats is especially important in keeping upper layers of soil moist during extended dry periods. Moreover, many rare plant species live in sphagnum mats; salamanders and rare bog turtles also lay their eggs in this moss. Sphagnum is particularly susceptible to siltation, trampling, and excess nutrient input. With a reduction in sphagnum, bogs become drier and more susceptible to woody plant succession.

Wildlife: Surprisingly, almost nothing eats sphagnum.

Uses: Sphagnum has been used for centuries as a dressing for wounds as it's both absorptive and highly acidic and thereby inhibits the growth of most bacteria and fungi. Currently, decomposing *Sphagnum* (peat) is used by gardeners to enhance the water-holding capacity of potting mixtures.

Spigelia marilandica (L.) L.
INDIAN PINK
Loganiaceae (Logania family)

Description: Erect leafy perennial from 1 to 2 ft. tall with opposite, mostly sessile, lance-shaped leaves. Showy tubular flowers, scarlet on outside, greenish yellow on inside, with 5 conspicuous, spreading, pointed lobes. Fruit a 2-lobed green capsule, broader than tall. Flowers May–June; fruits late June–July.

Habitat/range: Forests and woodlands, usually on calcium-rich soils with a soil pH close to neutral. Common. Southeastern United States west to Indiana, Oklahoma, and Texas.

Taxonomy: A genus of about 50 species of herbaceous plants of North and South America, including 2 species in the mountains and piedmont. Indian pink is easily identified by its upright, tubular, bright scarlet flowers with a yellow interior.

Ecology: Like many woodland herbs, Indian pink dies back to the ground in winter then reemerges from an underground rhizome in spring. In so doing, it's less vulnerable to damage by herbivores and freezing temperatures in winter. The plant, however, has to reestablish its position on the forest floor each year, which reduces its competitive ability relative to woody plants whose aboveground stems persist from year to year. From late spring through early summer, the reddish tubular flowers are sporadically visited and pollinated by ruby-throated hummingbirds. About a month after the flowers fade, the ripe fruits (capsules) catapult the seeds away from the parent plant. The underground stems (rhizomes) spread horizontally, forming small colonies in favorable habitats.

Wildlife: A poisonous alkaloid (spigeline) deters most herbivores, although white-tailed deer occasionally feed on the leafy stems.

Uses: Indian pink can be grown in shady woodland gardens, but plants should be purchased from specialty nurseries, rather than dug up from the wild. The plant is highly toxic if eaten.

Spiranthes cernua (L.) Rich.
NODDING LADIES' TRESSES
Orchidaceae (Orchid family)

Description: Perennial herb often in large colonies, with basal leaves 2–10 in. long, less than 1 in. wide, reduced in size up stem. Small, white, slightly nodding, generally fragrant flowers packed into a dense spiral spike. Fruit an elliptical capsule with numerous tiny, wind-dispersed seeds. Flowers July–frost; fruits Aug.–frost.

Habitat/range: Moist, open habitats, including mountain bogs, marshes, meadows, lawns, and ditches. Common in mountains, uncommon in piedmont. Widespread in eastern North America.

Taxonomy: *Spiranthes* is a nearly cosmopolitan genus of 40 species, including 9 species in the mountains and piedmont. The genus name is derived from the Greek "speira," meaning "spiral," and "anthos," meaning "flower," alluding to the way in which the flowers appear to wrap around the stem, much like a spiral staircase.

Ecology: Orchids bring to mind large, showy, colorful flowers with elaborate shapes. The flowers of nodding ladies' tresses are small but just as interesting.

Bees visit the small, tubular flowers by starting at the bottom of an inflorescence (a spike) and moving progressively upward. In a maturing spike, the lower, older flowers are in the female phase (having receptive stigmas) while the upper, younger flowers are in the male phase (releasing pollen). Bees visiting upper flowers pick up pollen before moving to lower flowers on the next plant, where they deposit pollen on receptive stigmas of female-stage flowers. The bottom-to-top foraging behavior of bees, coupled with the sequential male-to-female gender expression of the flowers within an inflorescence, promotes cross-pollination. Should cross-pollination fail to occur, seeds are produced asexually (without fusion of egg and sperm), resulting in genetic replicates of the parent plant. Plants of this species often produce a mix of sexually and asexually derived seeds, something most plant species can't do.

Wildlife: Rabbits, voles, groundhogs, and white-tailed deer browse the foliage.

Uses: Native Americans made a tea from the leaves of nodding ladies' tresses to treat urinary infections and venereal disease.

Stellaria pubera Michx.
GIANT CHICKWEED
Caryophyllaceae (Pink family)

Description: An erect, weak-stemmed perennial 4–16 in. tall with opposite, mostly lanceolate leaves. Numerous white star-like flowers with 5 petals so deeply cleft as to appear to be 10. Fruit an ovoid capsule containing many small seeds. Flowers Apr.–June.

Habitat/range: Moist forests, including river bluff forests, alluvial forests, cove forests, and basic mesic forests. Common. Eastern United States.

Taxonomy: A genus of about 120 species centered in Asia but nearly worldwide in distribution, with 7 species in the mountains and piedmont. Common chickweed (*S. media*), an introduced, weedy species commonly found in lawns and gardens, is similar but has smaller leaves and flowers and weaker stems.

Ecology: Giant chickweed has an unusual growth pattern, with short, relatively small-leaved, flowering shoots produced in spring replaced by taller shoots with larger, thicker leaves in summer. The taller shoots persist until the aboveground plant dies back in autumn. New shoots arise the following spring from dormant underground buds. A poor competitor, giant chickweed tends to be restricted to more open areas on the forest floor. The conspicuous flowers produce both nectar and pollen and are pollinated by small bees and flies. For the first 1–3 days, upright anthers release pollen and the flowers are functionally male. The stigma then enlarges and becomes receptive (resulting in a functionally female flower), while the stamens reflex outward, resting on the petals. The spatial and temporal separation of anthers and stigmas prevents automatic self-pollination, but self-fertilized seeds can result if an insect pollinator transfers pollen between flowers on the same plant. Because pollinators typically visit flowers on multiple plants, a mix of self- and cross-fertilized seeds is produced.

Wildlife: Songbirds actively feed on the seeds, hence the common name "chickweed."

Uses: Makes a nice addition to woodland wildflower gardens due to its abundant flowers and attractive foliage.

Symplocarpus foetidus (L.) Salisb. ex Nutt.
SKUNK CABBAGE
Araceae (Arum family)

Description: Herbaceous perennial 1–2 ft. tall with basal, cabbage-like leaves 10–20 in. long and almost as wide, emerging in late spring, well after the flowers. Fleshy, hood-like spathe, brownish purple, usually striped or spotted, encloses a ball-like spadix with numerous tiny flowers. Numerous seeds embedded just below surface of enlarged spongy spadix. Flowers Jan.–Mar.; fruits July–Sept.

Habitat/range: Mountain bogs. Common in Virginia, rare in North Carolina and Tennessee. Widely distributed throughout northeastern North America, south in mountains to North Carolina and Tennessee.

Taxonomy: The genus *Symplocarpus* has just 2 species, the other is in eastern Asia.

Ecology: Skunk cabbage gives off a skunk-like odor when any part of the plant is bruised or damaged. The odor is beneficial because herbivores learn to associate the plant's odor with the sharply pointed crystals of calcium oxalate that irritate their mouths if the plant is chewed on. A strong odor also helps lure potential pollinators to the tiny flowers. One of the first plants to flower in winter, skunk cabbage develops spathes that can emerge through snow. The plant has the rare characteristic of being able to regulate flower temperature by producing its own heat. On cold winter days, when air temperatures hover around 40°F, skunk cabbage can generate enough heat to maintain a flower temperature of nearly 70°F. The elevated temperature of the flowers within the hood-like spathe provides a warm environment that attracts potential pollinators such as flies, beetles, and bees that feed on pollen (the flowers lack nectar). Carrion beetles that normally feed on the thawing corpses of dead animals are sometimes tricked into visiting the fetid flowers and may transfer a few pollen grains onto the stigma of the next flower that fools them. Strong odor, elevated temperatures, and the contrasting colors of the spathe function synergistically to attract insects at a time of year when potential pollinators are scarce.

Wildlife: The large leaves provide shelter for birds, frogs, and other animals, spiders spin their webs across the spathe to catch flower-visiting insects, and squirrels sometimes cache the seeds.

Uses: Skunk cabbage is a prized plant in European bog gardens.

*Taraxacum officinale F. H. Wigg.
COMMON DANDELION
Asteraceae (Sunflower family)

Description: Basal rosette of pinnately compound leaves, cut into triangular, backward-pointing lobes. Bright yellow strap-shaped ray flowers in heads on leafless stalks. Fruit a brown to tan achene topped by a parachute-like cluster of white hair-like bristles that aid dispersal. Flowers Jan.–Dec.

Habitat/range: Common weed of disturbed areas, including lawns, roadsides, and fields. Common. Native of Eurasia, now widely distributed throughout temperate regions of world.

Taxonomy: Red-seeded dandelion (*T. erythrospermum*) is similar, but has more deeply incised leaves and red-purple achenes.

Ecology: Tolerant of a wide range of climates, common dandelion grows from sea level to the high mountains, mostly in disturbed sites, as it's a poor competitor. Having a rosette of leaves at ground level has 2 advantages—it's more difficult for grazing animals to eat, and the leaves are below the blades of most lawnmowers. Peak flowering typically occurs in spring and fall, but plants can flower any month of the year. Dandelions produce seeds asexually (without fusion of egg and sperm), so the parent plant effectively clones itself from seeds, a strategy employed by less than 1 percent of flowering plants. As the seeds within a flowering head ripen, the flower stalk elongates 12–18 in. above the ground, positioning seeds to catch the wind with their parachute-like hairs. This highly effective dispersal mechanism, coupled with an ability to rapidly build up populations following disturbance, have enabled dandelions to become one of world's most widely distributed and common weeds.

Wildlife: Lawn weeds such as dandelions provide an important source of food (nectar and pollen) for bees and other insects, particularly in winter, when few other plants are in bloom.

Uses: Young leaves can be used in salads and cooked as a vegetable.

Tephrosia virginiana (L.) Pers.
GOAT'S RUE
Fabaceae (Legume family)

Description: Densely hairy perennial herb 1–2 ft. tall with 1 to several stems with alternate, pinnately compound leaves, the 15–25 narrow leaflets about 1 in. long. Short terminal racemes of bicolored pea-like flowers consisting of a large creamy yellow upper petal (the standard), pink to rose lateral petals (the wings), and 2 fused lower petals (the keel). Fruit a 1–2 in. long, soft, hairy pod. Flowers May–June; fruits July–Oct.

Habitat/range: Dry, open woods, including pine-oak-heath, oak-hickory forests, xeric hardpan forests, and forest edges. Common. Widespread in eastern United States.

Taxonomy: The genus comprises about 400 species of perennial herbs of tropical and warm temperate regions of the world, including 2 species in the mountains and piedmont. Our other species, southern goat's rue (*T. spicata*), has leaves with 9–17 leaflets with nearly white flowers that become reddish purple with age.

Ecology: A sun-loving plant, goat's rue grows more vigorously and produces many more flowers and fruits in the sun than in the shade. Its deep roots increase its ability to take up water, particularly in times of drought when the upper layers of the soil dry out. Like most legumes, its roots contain nodules that harbor nitrogen-fixing bacteria. The flowers depend on bees for successful pollination and fruit set. Various seed predators, including larvae of a weevil that feeds only on goat's rue, consume a high proportion of the developing seeds in some years. Growing-season fires kill aboveground plants, but encourage dormant underground buds to produce new shoots. Fires also stimulate flower and fruit production, and because seed predator populations are knocked back by fires, many more seeds typically mature in years that plants are burned.

Wildlife: White-tailed deer occasionally browse the foliage and various birds, including wild turkeys, eat the seeds.

Uses: Native Americans placed the roots (which contain rotenone) into pools to stupefy fish; after floating to the surface, the fish were easily gathered into baskets. Rotenone is still used as a fish poison and as an insecticide.

Thalictrum clavatum DC.
MOUNTAIN MEADOWRUE
Ranunculaceae (Buttercup family)

Description: Smooth herbaceous perennial 5–24 in. tall with biternately compound leaves and rounded leaf lobes. Flowers with white petal-like sepals, broad white stamens, and slender, elongate flower stalks in few-flowered inflorescences. Fruit an aggregate of achenes, 3–8 per flower. Flowers May–July.

Habitat/range: Rich, moist forests and along streams, including cove forests, northern hardwood forests, and spray cliffs. Common in mountains, rare in piedmont. Southern Appalachians from Virginia south to Georgia.

Taxonomy: Eight of the 330 species of *Thalictrum* occur in the mountains and piedmont.

Ecology: Mountain meadowrue differs from many early emerging woodland herbs in that it has a long flowering period that extends from spring well into summer. Unlike the flowers of many members of the genus, the flowers of meadowrue contain both male and female parts and are pollinated by insects, rather than wind. The flowers lack petals and nectar but have showy sepals and conspicuous white stamens that attract syrphid flies foraging for pollen. Due to their ability to hover in one spot, syrphid flies, also known as hover flies, are often mistaken for wasps or bees because of their black and yellow-striped abdomens, but they don't sting and they are beneficial to plants as pollinators. If syrphids and other insects fail to pollinate the flowers, self-pollination readily occurs. The tiny seeds are dispersed by gravity and by water, either "sheets" of rainwater flowing over the soil surface or downstream currents along river corridors.

Wildlife: Many different types of alkaloids have been identified in meadowrue, some of which deter herbivores.

Uses: Some of the alkaloids known from *Thalictrum* have pharmacologic potential, due to their ability to lower blood pressure and inhibit the growth of tumors.

vidual flowers persist up to 2 weeks, increasing the opportunity for successful pollination at a time of year when inclement weather limits pollinator activity. The seeds lack a specialized mechanism for dispersal: once ripe, they simply fall to the ground close to the parent plant. Seeds that germinate give rise to tiny seedlings that take 3 or more years to flower.

Wildlife: Pollen-foraging bees and flies pollinate the nectarless flowers.

Uses: Native Americans used infusions derived from meadowrue's roots to treat diarrhea and vomiting.

Thalictrum thalictroides (L.) Eames & B. Boivin
MEADOWRUE, WINDFLOWER
Ranunculaceae (Buttercup family)

Description: Smooth, slender perennial herb 3–8 in. tall. Stem leaves opposite, with wiry stalks and 3 leaflets each with 3 shallow, rounded lobes. Flowers in a single terminal umbel with 1 central and 1–4 lateral flowers; 5–10 white sepals surrounding a cluster of pistils and stamens. Fruit an achene, usually 8–12 per flower. Flowers Mar.–May.

Habitat/range: Moist, rich woods, including cove forests, river bluff forests, and floodplain forests. Common. Widespread in eastern North America.

Taxonomy: This species differs from the other 7 species of *Thalictrum* in our region by having flowers in umbels. The flowers "quiver" in a light breeze, hence the common name "windflower." Some authors place this species in the genus *Anemonella*.

Ecology: This small, delicate-looking plant is actually quite tough, as the leaves and blossoms tolerate hard frosts in early spring and the plant pops up readily after being stepped on by people and animals. Nutrients stored in underground rhizomes enable tiny leaf and flower buds formed the previous autumn to develop quickly in late winter or early spring. Indi-

Thelypteris noveboracensis (L.) Nieuwl.
NEW YORK FERN
Thelypteridaceae (Marsh fern family)

Description: Fronds about 1–2 ft. tall, about 6 in. wide, tapered almost equally at tip and base from a slender, creeping rootstalk. Spore clusters (sori) small, circular, near margins of lobes on underside of leaves. Spores released May–Aug.

Habitat/range: In moist or wet thickets and woodlands, often near streams, including acidic cove forests, red oak forests, mountain bogs, floodplain forests, and oak-hickory forests. Common. Widely distributed in eastern North America.

Taxonomy: The genus *Thelypteris* comprises almost 900 species, 5 of which occur in the mountains and piedmont. Both New York fern and hayscented fern (*Dennstaedtia punctilobula*) have fronds that appear delicate and often grow in large colonies that carpet the forest floor. Hayscented fern has a triangle-shaped frond that is broadest at the base, whereas New York fern has fronds that taper at both ends.

Ecology: New York fern is an opportunistic species that forms large colonies in forest openings. It reproduces sexually by wind-dispersed spores and asexually by long, creeping rhizomes, the fronds solitary or in closely packed tufts of 3–4. In slightly disturbed areas, it can form a dense groundcover that reduces the diversity of woodland herbs and inhibits establishment of woody plants, thereby slowing successional change.

Wildlife: The fronds are unpalatable to deer and most other grazers.

Uses: The pointed fronds of New York fern add interest to moist gardens.

Tiarella cordifolia L.
FOAMFLOWER
Saxifragaceae (Saxifrage family)

Description: Perennial herb from 4 to 20 in. tall with semi-evergreen, heart-shaped basal leaves resembling a maple leaf. Numerous white flowers in a terminal raceme extend well above the basal leaves. Fruit a 2-parted capsule. Flowers Apr.–June; fruits May–July.

Habitat/range: Moist forests, streambanks, and margins of rock outcrops, including cove forests, river bluff forests, and basic mesic forests. Common. Widely distributed in eastern North America.

Taxonomy: The genus *Tiarella* includes 5 species of perennial herbs of North America and eastern Asia. There are 2 varieties of *T. cordifolia*, 1 with stolons (aboveground horizontal stems), the other without.

Ecology: This spring-blooming wildflower is easily recognized by its airy raceme of white flowers on a hairy, leafless stalk. The long stamens extending beyond the petals add to the "foamy" appearance of the inflorescence, and the abundant pollen is a conspicuous orange color. The flowers bloom sequentially from the bottom to the top of the inflorescence and are pollinated by flies. The small seedpods split at maturity, dropping numerous tiny black seeds beneath the parent plant. Horizontal stems root at nodes, often forming dense colonies. The leaves have a relatively high photosynthetic rate in the spring before the canopy leafs out and in the fall after the canopy leaves drop. Because rates of photosynthesis and growth are very low under the shaded canopy of summer, nearly 75 percent of the plant's annual growth occurs during the spring and fall seasons. Removal of the forest canopy by logging or natural processes adversely affects foamflower, as its shallow root system makes it susceptible to soil drying caused by direct sunlight reaching the ground surface.

Wildlife: The tannin-rich leaves and stems deter most animals from feeding on foamflower.

Uses: The showy white flowers and

semi-evergreen leaves make foamflower a popular choice for moist woodland gardens.

Tipularia discolor (Pursh) Nutt.
CRANEFLY ORCHID
Orchidaceae (Orchid family)

Description: A perennial with a single annual leaf arising from a small corm, dull green above, purple below, emerging in fall, withering and disappearing in mid- to late spring before flowering. Purplish green to brown flowers in loose racemes. Fruit a capsule. Flowers July–Sept.; fruits Aug.–Sept.

Habitat/range: Variety of moist to dry forests, usually on acidic soils. Common. Eastern United States.

Taxonomy: A genus of 3 species—1 in the eastern United States, the Himalayas, and Japan. The common and genus names allude to the flowers resembling a crane fly (*Tipula* spp.).

Ecology: This relatively common orchid is easily missed because it's leafless in summer when the plant flowers and the slender flowering stalk and flowers blend in with leaf litter on the forest floor. In contrast, the dark green, 2–4 in. leaf (with a purple underside) stands out in winter against the mostly grayish brown forest floor. The only other wintergreen, summer-deciduous orchid in our eastern deciduous forests is putty root (*Aplectrum hyemale*). The flowers of cranefly orchid are pollinated by night-flying moths. As a moth inserts its head into the flower to obtain nectar, a pollinium (a tiny ball of pollen) is attached to the moth's eye and may inadvertently be deposited on the stigma of another flower. Amazingly, the deposition of pollinia on insect eyes is a common mode of pollen transfer in temperate orchids. Carbohydrates stored in the shallow-rooted corm are used to produce a new leaf in fall, and flowers, fruits, and seeds in summer. A lack of sufficient nutrients and pollen transfer typically results in fewer than 25 percent of the flowers maturing fruit. The tiny seeds (with very small nutrient reserves) require specific fungi for both seed germination and seedling growth.

Wildlife: White-tailed deer commonly eat the entire leaf, leaving the plant leafless until the following autumn; because such plants accumulate fewer carbohydrates, they are much less likely to flower and produce fruits that year.

Tradescantia hirsuticaulis Small
HAIRY SPIDERWORT
Commelinaceae (Spiderwort family)

Description: Densely hairy perennial herb up to 15 in. tall with linear leaves and parallel veins. Radially symmetrical flowers with 3 petals and 6 stamens varying in color from blue to rose. Fruit a capsule. Flowers Apr.–June (often flowering again in fall).

Habitat/range: Rock outcrops and dry, rocky woods. Occasional in piedmont, rare in mountains. Southeastern United States, west to Arkansas and Oklahoma.

Taxonomy: A genus of 70 herbaceous species of the Americas, including 6 species in the mountains and piedmont. Hairy spiderwort is the only species in the region that has both glandular and nonglandular hairs on its sepals. Spiderworts (*Tradescantia*) and dayflowers (*Commelina*) are similar but the flowers of spiderworts aren't enclosed in a spathe and their 3 petals are uniform in size and color.

Ecology: Hairy spiderwort copes with the extremely hot, dry summer environment of rock outcrops by actively growing primarily during the cooler months of late fall and spring. Also, by reflecting sunlight, the densely hairy leaves remain relatively cool, which in turn reduces evaporative water loss from the leaf surface. The large, showy flowers depend on large bees (mainly bumblebees) for successful pollination. Pollen is the sole food reward, as the flowers lack nectar. The small seeds are dispersed by gravity and by the flow of surface water following rain. Because *Tradescantia* species are interfertile, when 2 or more species are in close proximity, hybrids can occur.

Uses: Spiderworts have been used to detect air pollutants, including radioactive particles, as significant exposure to such chemicals causes the anther filaments to change from blue to pink. Spiderworts are occasionally grown in gardens for their showy flowers and attractive foliage.

*Trifolium repens L.
WHITE CLOVER
Fabaceae (Legume family)

Description: Creeping herbaceous perennial, often rooting at nodes, with trifoliate leaves (usually with a whitish "V" toward base) and round heads with white or pink-tinged flowers. Fruit a legume. Flowers and fruits Apr.–Oct.

Habitat/range: Disturbed areas, including lawns, roadsides, and fields. Common. Widespread in temperate regions.

Taxonomy: Fourteen of the 18 species of clover in the mountains and piedmont (including this species) were introduced from Eurasia as a forage crop. Well-established nonnatives such as white clover are sometimes said to be naturalized, but that doesn't make them native, even if they have been here for a long time.

Ecology: White clover is the common clover in lawns and pastures. It can grow in a wide range of climatic conditions, ranging from sea level to the high mountains. It flourishes in full sunlight and declines as plant cover increases. A shallow, fibrous root system makes it vulnerable to hot, dry conditions. Bees actively visit the flowers, and within 2 weeks of pollination, the seeds ripen. Most seeds lack dormancy and germinate right away, but they require disturbance of the existing vegetation for successful seedling establishment. The movement of livestock and wildlife species spreads the seeds (passing intact through animals' digestive tracts or becoming entangled in their body hairs) as does lawn and farm equipment and other human activities. Vegetative reproduction (from stolons rooting at the nodes) plays a primary role in local spread, whereas reproduction by seed is essential for colonizing new habitats.

Wildlife: White clover flowers provide an important source of nectar and pollen for bees and other insects, and the seeds are eaten by a variety of birds.

Uses: White clover is an excellent forage plant for livestock and is often sown as a companion plant in pasture mixtures because of its nitrogen-fixing root nodules.

Trillium catesbaei Elliott
CATESBY'S TRILLIUM
Trilliaceae (Trillium family)

Description: Herbaceous perennial 8–20 in. tall, with a whorl of 3 uniformly green leaves, ovate to widely elliptical, 3–6 in. long, on short stalks. Flower stalk bent downward, usually below leaves; petals white, pink, or rose, recurved, usually with a wavy margin. Pollen egg-yolk yellow, ovary white. Fruit a berry-like capsule, greenish or whitish. Flowers late Mar.–early June; fruits July–Aug.

Habitat/range: Moist to dry forests with acidic soils, including oak-hickory forests, pine-oak-heath, acidic cove forests, and alluvial forests. Common in piedmont and lower mountains. From North Carolina south to Georgia.

Taxonomy: A genus of about 50 species of eastern and western North America and eastern Asia, including about 22 species in the mountains and piedmont. The name honors Mark Catesby, a British naturalist who explored the plants and animals of the Southeast in the early 1700s.

Ecology: The most common trillium in the piedmont, it occurs on drier, more acidic soils than most trilliums. Because the stigmas extend beyond the anthers, the showy but nectarless flowers depend on pollinators to transfer pollen from the anthers to the stigmas. The primary pollinators are thought to be queen bumblebees, which visit the flowers for pollen. Individual flowers remain open for up to 2–3 weeks, thereby increasing the opportunity for successful pollination. Following pollination, or perhaps simply with age, the flowers change color from white to pale pink or deep rose.

Wildlife: White-tailed deer relish trilliums; a single bite can defoliate an entire plant, which prevents additional photosynthesis and the accumulation of carbohydrates during the current year. As a result, plants are shorter and less likely to flower the following year. In areas with overabundant deer populations, trillium populations decline dramatically while less palatable species such as hayscented fern (*Dennstaedtia punctilobula*) increase in abundance.

Trillium cuneatum Raf.
SWEET BETSY, PURPLE TOADSHADE
Trilliaceae (Trillium family)

Description: Erect perennial herb with 3 whorled, sessile, broadly ovate, mottled leaves from 3 to 6 in. long. A single sessile flower with 3 more or less erect purple, green, or yellow petals more than twice as long as stamens, the anthers blunt at tip. Fruit ovoid, mealy or pulpy, not juicy. Flowers early Mar.–Apr.; fruits late May–June.

Habitat/range: Moist woods, usually on calcium-rich soils derived from limestone. Rich cove forests, basic mesic forests, alluvial forests, and oak-hickory forests. Uncommon but locally abundant. From North Carolina and Kentucky south to Georgia and Alabama.

Taxonomy: The yellowish flower form of sweet Betsy is very similar to yellow trillium (*T. luteum*), but sweet Betsy has a purple (rather than green) ovary.

Ecology: The largest of the eastern sessile-flowered trilliums, its leaves are weakly to strongly mottled. On particularly favorable sites, thousands of plants can carpet the forest floor. One of the earliest trilliums to flower in spring, its flowers persist for a relatively long time. The majority of plants have maroon-purple flowers, but scattered plants with yellow or greenish flowers also occur. Flowers in most populations have a faint spice-like odor, but some populations (particularly in the North Carolina piedmont) have a strongly scented flower similar to that of sweetshrub (*Calycanthus*). While many plants flower, relatively few set fruit. Plants that successfully mature a fruit typically persist until late June or early July; in contrast, vegetative plants, as well as those that fail to mature a fruit, die back within a week of flowering in spring and remain dormant as underground rhizomes until early the following spring. Trilliums often reproduce vegetatively from small rhizome offshoots that remain attached to the parent rhizome for several years before the connection decays. Initially, the offshoots have just a single leaf, but as nutrients accumulate, the offshoots develop into 3-leafed reproductive plants.

Wildlife: Ants and yellow jackets are attracted to the lipid-rich food body (elaiosome) attached to the outer seed coat. While ants generally disperse the seeds short distances, yellow jackets disperse seeds longer distances.

Trillium discolor Wray ex Hook.
PALE YELLOW TRILLIUM
Trilliaceae (Trillium family)

Description: Herbaceous perennial 4–12 in. tall with a single whorl of 3 sessile leaves mottled with 2–3 shades of green, the mottling fading with time. Flowers sessile with 3 upright, pale yellow spoon-shaped petals with a greenish or purplish stalk-like base. Fruit roundish, pulpy, or mealy, greenish white at maturity, falling to ground when ripe. Flowers late Mar.–early May; fruits June–July.

Habitat/range: Basic mesic forests in piedmont and rich cove forests in mountains. Rare. Restricted to the Savannah River drainage of northwest South Carolina, northeast Georgia, and southwest North Carolina.

Taxonomy: Pale yellow trillium is similar to the yellow-flowered form of sweet Betsy (*T. cuneatum*) but has spoon-shaped petals with a greenish or purplish base. Yellow trillium (*T. luteum*) has similar flowers but has a green, rather than purple, ovary.

Ecology: Only 4 species of *Trillium* occur in the Northeast, each of which occurs over the entire region. In contrast, nearly 30 species of *Trillium* are found in the Southeast, many of which have small ranges. Trilliums occur in every southeastern state, but no one species occurs in every state. Pale yellow trillium is an example of a species with a limited distribution, restricted to a single river drainage. Yet, within this range, it can be locally abundant, particularly on calcium-rich soils. No one knows for sure why this species is restricted to a single river valley, but since it can be grown over a much wider geographic area, limited seed dispersal, rather than something unique about the soil or environment of the Savannah River drainage, probably limits its distribution.

Wildlife: White-tailed deer relish trilliums; in areas where deer are abundant, the number and size of trillium plants decrease markedly over time.

Trillium erectum L.
WAKE ROBIN, STINKING WILLIE
Trilliaceae (Trillium family)

Description: Herbaceous perennial from 4 to 18 in. tall, each stem with a whorl of 3 leaves and a single terminal flower. Leaves uniformly green, sessile, about as long as wide. Flowers maroon or white, less frequently yellow or green, on upright stalks with 3 widely spreading, lance-shaped petals surrounding a purple-black ovary. Fruit a dark maroon, somewhat juicy berry. Flowers Apr.–early June; fruits July–Aug.

Habitat/range: Wooded slopes at mid- to high elevations, northern hardwood forests, red oak forests, and acidic cove forests. Common in mountains. Mainly a northeastern species, from Canada south in mountains to Tennessee and Georgia.

Taxonomy: In habitats where multiple trillium species occur, hybrids with unusual flower colors sometimes appear.

The specific epithet *erectum* refers to the erect flower stalk, while the common name "stinking Willie" refers to the odor of the flowers, which has been described as "smelling like a wet dog."

Ecology: The fetid flower odor attracts various kinds of flies and beetles, which function as pollinators. In some populations and in some years, the flowers are visited infrequently and fruit set is low. When fruit set fails, the aerial stem (and leaves) quickly senesce. In contrast, stems with a developing fruit persist until the seeds mature in mid- to late summer. In early spring, when high light levels promote high rates of photosynthesis, the sugars produced are stored in aerial stems. This temporary reservoir of sugars serves as the main source of nutrients as fruits develop in summer. As such, the sugars produced by leaves in spring (rather than in summer) play a key role in fruit maturation.

Wildlife: White-tailed deer browse the foliage and ants disperse the seeds.

Uses: Early herbalists followed the "Doctrine of Signatures," whereby plants were used to treat body parts or symptoms they resembled. In this case, wake robin's foul-smelling flowers were used to treat gangrene.

Trillium grandiflorum (Michx.) Salisb.
LARGE-FLOWERED TRILLIUM
Trilliaceae (Trillium family)

Description: Erect perennial from 6 to 20 in. tall with a single whorl of 3 uniformly green, mostly ovate leaves at the top of a single stem. Large (2–4 in. across) solitary, funnel-shaped flower on an upright or gently arching stalk above the leaves; the white petals with wavy margins turn pink with age. Fruit a pale green fleshy capsule. Flowers Apr.–May; fruits July–Aug.

Habitat/range: Rich, moist forests, including cove forests, northern hardwood forests, and basic mesic forests. Common in mountains, rare in upper piedmont. Widespread in eastern North America.

Taxonomy: Trilliums are easily recognized by their single whorl of 3 leaves with a solitary terminal flower.

Ecology: One of our showiest and most common trilliums, often forming large colonies that emerge from underground rhizomes in early spring and die back in late summer. The scentless flowers attract and reward pollinators with both nectar and pollen (the flowers of some *Trillium* species lack nectar). Flower visitation rates are sometimes low, resulting in pollen-limited fruit and seed set. Ripe fruits drop to the ground below the parent plant and split open, thereby exposing the seeds to ants, which disperse the seeds. Seeds exhibit "double dormancy," meaning it takes almost 2 years to complete germination. The summer-dispersed seeds break dormancy the following spring when the embryo root (radicle) emerges from the seed coat, but the long, narrow cotyledon (seed leaf) doesn't appear aboveground until the next (second) spring. Young plants produce just a single leaf for several years before accumulating enough resources to transition to the more familiar 3-leaf stage.

Wildlife: Bees and flies pollinate the flowers, ants disperse the seeds, and deer feed voraciously on the foliage. White crab spiders hang out in the flowers and prey on flower-visiting insects.

Uses: Nursery-propagated trilliums are becoming more available and make a welcome addition to woodland gardens.

Trillium luteum (Muhl.) Harbison
YELLOW TRILLIUM
Trilliaceae (Trillium family)

Description: Herbaceous perennial 6–15 in. tall with a single whorl of 3 sessile, variably shaped leaves mottled with 2–3 shades of green, the mottling fading with time. Flowers solitary, sessile, with 3 yellow petals, widest near base, tapering to a long acuminate tip with a strong lemony fragrance. Roundish berry-like fruit, green to greenish white at maturity. Flowers mid-Mar.–early May; fruits late May–June.

Habitat/range: Most abundant in rich cove forests but also occurs in thin, open woods, rocky streambanks and flats, and roadside areas. Uncommon (but locally abundant) in southern Appalachians from North Carolina and Kentucky south to Georgia and Alabama.

Taxonomy: The name "Trillium" alludes to plants in this genus having parts in 3's — 3 leaves, 3 petals, 3 sepals, and 3-chambered ovaries. Yellow trillium is similar to pale yellow trillium (*T. discolor*) and the yellow-flowered form of sweet Betsy (*T. cuneatum*), but has a pale green, rather than dark purple, ovary.

Ecology: Nearly 30 species of *Trillium* occur in the Southeast, but only 4 species of trillium occur in the Northeast. This pattern reflects a general trend —

plant diversity decreases from the South to the North. Why should there be more species in the South than the North? In part, this reflects past glaciation. As recently as 18,000 years ago, the Northeast was covered by a thick layer of ice. Species there have colonized relatively recently. Because the Southeast wasn't glaciated, the flora is much older, allowing for a larger pool of species to accumulate over time.

Trillium reliquum J. D. Freeman
RELICT TRILLIUM
Trilliaceae (Trillium family)
Federally Endangered

Description: Perennial herb with a short, curved, hairless stem and a single sessile flower in the center of a whorl of 3 strongly mottled leaves with a silvery streak down the middle of each leaf, the leaves positioned on or near the ground surface. Flowers emit a foul carrion odor; the 3 upright petals range in color from dark purple to yellow. Fruit a fleshy capsule. Flowers Mar.–Apr.; fruits May–early June.

Habitat/range: Deep, loamy soils on river bluffs, ravine slopes, and adjacent bottomlands. Rare in piedmont. Widely scattered populations in Georgia, Alabama, and South Carolina near the fall-line.

Taxonomy: The following combination of traits distinguish this species from our other trilliums: a curved, hairless stem, a silver streak down the middle of each leaf, beaked anther tips, and flowers smelling like putrid meat.

Ecology: Though discovered near Augusta, Georgia, in 1901, it wasn't described as a new species until 1975. Fewer than 50 populations are known for this federally endangered species, most of which occur in Georgia. Current populations vary in size from 20 to several thousand individuals, with half of the known populations having fewer than 200 plants. Censusing populations can be tricky, as not all individuals produce an aboveground shoot in a given year, remaining underground in a dormant state during the summer growing season, as some wild orchids do. Nearly all of the existing populations occur on privately owned land, making conservation efforts more complicated. Current threats include habitat loss due to residential development, timber harvesting, and exotic invasive species, particularly kudzu (*Pueraria montana*), Japanese honeysuckle (*Lonicera japonica*), and Chinese privet (*Ligustrum sinense*).

Wildlife: White-tailed deer browse the foliage, flies and beetles pollinate the foul-smelling flowers, and ants disperse the seeds.

Trillium undulatum Willd.
PAINTED TRILLIUM
Trilliaceae (Trillium family)

Description: An erect herbaceous perennial 8–20 in. tall, topped by a whorl of 3 ovate leaves, each with a distinct petiole. Single upright flowers with 3 showy white petals, each with a red, inverted V-shaped mark near base, readily distinguishing this species. Red berry-like fruits fall from plant shortly after ripening. Flowers late Apr.–June; fruits July–Aug.

Habitat/range: Cool, moist environments and acidic soils, mostly at high elevations. Spruce-fir forests, balds, rhododendron thickets, hemlock forests, and margins of mountain bogs. Common. Northeastern United States and Canada, south in mountains to Georgia.

Taxonomy: The genus name from the Latin "trille" alludes to the flowers having parts in 3's, whereas the name "undulatum" refers to the petals' wavy margins.

Ecology: Of all our trilliums, painted trillium is best adapted to acidic soils. It generally occurs in shaded habitats, except at high elevations, where it grows in full sun. If exposed to a warm-spell in early spring, newly emerged shoots expand so quickly that plants not evident one day may be in flower the next. Individuals occur as single stems or in small, scattered clumps. The flowers are mostly self-pollinated, rather than cross-pollinated, and fruit set is often high. The fleshy red fruits contain numerous seeds, each of which contains an oily food body attached to the seed coat, which is called an elaiosome. Ants collect the seeds, feed on the elaiosomes, and discard the otherwise intact seeds in or near their nest. The seeds have a double dormancy mechanism causing seeds to germinate in spring but not to emerge as aboveground seedlings until the following spring.

Uses: Best enjoyed in the wild, as painted trillium is difficult to cultivate in the garden.

Trillium vaseyi Harbison
VASEY'S TRILLIUM
Trilliaceae (Trillium family)

Description: Perennial herb up to 2 ft. tall from a short, thick rhizome. Three large, whorled leaves, uniformly green, broadly elliptic, tapering at base. Solitary, maroon flower, 2–4 in. across, on long, nodding stalk, usually with strongly recurved petals. Fruit an obtusely angled dark maroon capsule. Flowers Apr.–early June; fruits June–early July.

Habitat/range: Rich woods, often on steep slopes, ravines, stream banks, mainly in cove forests. Uncommon. A southern Appalachian endemic restricted to Tennessee, North Carolina, South Carolina, Georgia, and Alabama.

Taxonomy: Vasey's trillium can be distinguished from wake robin (*T. erectum*) by its much larger nodding flower, sweet fragrance, and later flowering period.

Ecology: Vasey's trillium typically occurs as scattered, single-stemmed plants, rather than in large clumps or dense stands like some trilliums. With flowers up to 4 in. across, it has the largest flower of our native trilliums and is the latest to bloom, flowering from April to early June, depending on elevation and latitude. The maroon (rarely white) flowers with their unusual but pleasant fragrance occur on long, nodding stalks, often partially hidden beneath the whorled leaves. Slow-growing but long-lived, trilliums typically take upwards of 10 years to flower.

Wildlife: Trilliums are a preferred food of white-tailed deer, a common and increasingly abundant herbivore in some areas. When deer browse trilliums, they typically remove virtually all of the above-ground foliage, including any flowers or developing fruit. Since an individual plant produces only a single flush of 3 leaves each season, defoliation terminates growth (and reproduction) for that year. With fewer carbohydrates stored over winter, plants that emerge from rhizomes the following spring are smaller and less likely to reproduce. Defoliation in successive years, as often occurs in areas with high deer populations, results in smaller plants with fewer flowers.

Uses: Vasey's trillium is one of a number of trilliums available from specialist nurseries.

Umbilicaria mammulata (Ach.) Tuck.
SMOOTH ROCK TRIPE
Umbilicariaceae (Umbilicaria family)

Description: Large leathery lichen with a smooth (but not shiny) upper surface typically 2–6 in. across, reddish brown to grayish brown, the underside pitch black. Like other members of genus, it's attached to substrate by a thin central holdfast. The cup-shaped fruiting bodies (within which the spores are produced) rarely present.

Habitat/range: On boulders and steep rock walls in forests and open areas at higher elevations. Occasional. From southern Canada west to North Dakota, south in mountains to Georgia.

Taxonomy: The 30 North American species in the genus are commonly called rock tripe. Smooth rock tripe is by far the most common species in eastern North America. Plated rock tripe (*U. muehlenbergii*) has a similar growth form but has a somewhat shiny dark brown to grayish brown upper surface that is pitted with shallow depressions.

Ecology: Lichens are fungi that have a close relationship with a green alga or cyanobacterium. The interaction is generally mutually beneficial as the fungus provides protection, accumulates mineral nutrients, and helps retain moisture; in turn, the alga or cyanobacterium contributes carbohydrates through photosynthesis. The more than 14,000 species of lichens are divided into 3 types: species that form flat, circular, often brightly colored patches (crustose), freely branched species that look like miniature shrubs (fruticose), and flat leaf-like forms (foliose). Smooth rock tripe, a foliose lichen, curls up and appears brittle when dry, but has a slimy, rubbery appearance when wet. Individuals as large as 2 ft. across have been found in the Great Smoky Mountains of Tennessee, making it one of the largest lichens in the world.

Wildlife: Rock tripe is an important winter food of elk in Canada's boreal forests.

Uses: Lichens can be used as biomonitors of air pollution. For example, rock tripe lichens were used to monitor radionuclide levels after the Chernobyl nuclear disaster because its tissues absorb radioactive particles. Used as human food in times of emergency.

Uvularia grandiflora J. E. Smith
LARGE-FLOWERED BELLWORT
Colchicaceae (Meadow saffron family)

Description: Herbaceous perennial with branched stems, 8–30 in. tall. Leaves alternate, perfoliate, margins smooth, apex acute. Large, solitary butter yellow flowers hang from upper leaf axils. Long, narrow, twisted look-alike sepals and petals (3 each) appear limp, even when fresh. Fruit a 3-lobed capsule. Flowers Apr.–May; fruits July–Aug.

Habitat/range: Rich, moist woods, often on limestone or calcareous soils. Northern hardwood and cove forests. Common in mountains. Widespread in eastern and central North America.

Taxonomy: Four of the 5 species of *Uvularia* occur in the mountain and piedmont regions, all with nodding, bell-shaped, yellow flowers. Perfoliate bellwort (*U. perfoliata*) most closely resembles large-flowered bellwort but its petals and sepals aren't twisted. *Uvularia* was once a member of the lily (Liliaceae) family, a family now divided into about 17 smaller families, including the meadow saffron family (Colchicaceae).

Ecology: In early spring, 1 to several stems with narrow leaves curled around the stem tip (like an unfurled umbrella) emerge from a short rhizome. After flowering, the stems continue to elongate, eventually reaching up to 3 ft. tall. The slightly fragrant flowers are pollinated by queen bumblebees, which grasp the large hanging flowers at the bottom and crawl up the flower where they gather large amounts of pollen for raising their broods, and suck up sugar-rich nectar as an energy source.

Wildlife: White-tailed deer browse the foliage and both ants and rodents collect ripened seeds. Ants benefit large-flowered bellwort by dispersing its seeds, consuming only the lipid-rich food body (the elaiosome) attached to the outer seed coat. Rodents are seed predators, although cached (stored) seeds sometimes escape predation, germinate, and give rise to new plants.

Uses: Native Americans made an infusion from the rhizomes to treat backaches and sore muscles.

Uvularia perfoliata L.
PERFOLIATE BELLWORT
Colchicaceae (Meadow saffron family)

Description: Erect perennial herb 8–16 in. tall with smooth blue-green alternate leaves whose base appears to be pierced by the stem. Pale yellow to cream bell-shaped flowers nod singly from upper leaf axils. Fruit a 3-chambered green capsule. Flowers Apr.–May; fruits June–Aug.

Habitat/range: Moist to fairly dry hardwood forests, including river bluff forests, cove forests, and oak-hickory forests. Common. Widespread in eastern United States.

Taxonomy: The common name "perfoliate bellwort" refers to the piercing of the leaf base by the stem. Similar to large-flowered bellwort (*U. grandiflora*) but smaller, with pale (rather than lemon yellow) flowers and a granular (rather than smooth) petal surface.

Ecology: New shoots emerge through the leaf litter from late winter to early spring, flowering occurs in spring before the canopy completely fills in, and fruits mature in summer. Aboveground plants die back in autumn, and individuals overwinter as dormant belowground structures. Bumblebees grasp the petals and crawl up the nodding flowers to obtain nectar and pollen. The seeds germinate in the spring, following late summer dispersal, but only an embryo root emerges. The following (second) spring, the embryo shoot emerges from the seed, forming a small, leafy shoot. Thus, individuals exist entirely underground their first year. Perfoliate bellwort is shade tolerant, growing under a closed canopy as well as in forest openings (gaps) where light levels are considerably higher. In gaps, individuals are typically larger, produce more flowers and fruits, and exhibit greater vegetative reproduction than under a closed canopy.

Wildlife: Ripe seeds fall to the ground immediately beneath the plant, most of which are quickly removed by ants or rodents. Deer browse the foliage.

Uses: Perfoliate bellwort is a hardy plant whose nodding pale yellow flowers make an interesting addition to wildflower gardens.

Veratrum viride Aiton
FALSE HELLEBORE
Melanthiaceae (Bunchflower family)

Description: Poisonous perennial herb 2–6 ft. tall with a stout, leafy stem. Leaves mostly sessile, somewhat clasping, heavily ribbed, 6–12 in. long. Dense clusters of yellow-green flowers on a branching inflorescence. Fruit an elliptical capsule with numerous winged seeds. Flowers June–Aug.; fruits July–Sept.

Habitat/range: Mountain bogs, meadows, seeps, streambanks, and boulder fields. Common in mountains.

Taxonomy: Five of the 55 species of *Veratrum* occur in the mountains and piedmont. Small false hellebore (*V. parviflorum*) resembles false hellebore but is a less robust plant with narrower petiolate leaves mostly near the base of the plant.

Ecology: New shoots emerge early each spring from long-lived underground rhizomes. The thick leafy shoots grow rapidly, providing the plant a competitive advantage over its neighbors. False hellebore plants don't flower until they are about 7–10 years old. Thereafter, individuals typically flower every several years. The winged seeds are dispersed by wind in late summer. Initially dormant, cold stratification during winter facilitates germination the following spring. More than 25 different alkaloids have been identified in false hellebore. The type and concentration of alkaloids varies in different parts of the plant, as well as seasonally, but the entire plant is poisonous to all but a few herbivores.

Wildlife: False hellebore sometimes occurs in fields and pastures, where it can poison (and kill) cattle and sheep that consume large amounts of the plant. Certain caterpillar-like sawfly larvae are specialists on *Veratrum*. They sequester toxins from the plant in their tissues and use them as a defense against predators, much the way monarch butterfly caterpillars do with milkweeds.

Uses: All parts of the plant are highly toxic to humans, especially the roots. False hellebore is used in pharmaceutical drugs to slow heart rate and lower blood pressure.

*_Verbascum thapsus_ L.
WOOLLY MULLEIN
Scrophulariaceae (Snapdragon family)

Description: Densely woolly biennial to short-lived perennial with single stems 2–6 ft. tall. Basal rosette of large, thick, velvety leaves; stem leaves gradually reduced upwards. Yellow saucer-shaped flowers in dense terminal spike. Fruit a round woolly capsule. Flowers June–Sept.; fruits July–Oct.

Habitat/range: Fields, roadsides, other disturbed areas. Common. Introduced from Eurasia, now widespread in North America.

Taxonomy: Our 2 most common species of *Verbascum* are woolly mullein and moth mullein (*V. blattaria*); the latter species is recognizable by its mostly smooth leaves and open inflorescences with either white or yellow flowers.

Ecology: Normally a biennial, woolly mullein forms a large vegetative rosette, overwinters, and then flowers, fruits and dies the second year. Various insects visit the flowers, but bees are the only effective pollinators. If insect-mediated cross-pollination fails to occur, self-pollination occurs as the flowers close at midday. Delayed selfing provides an important backup mechanism because woolly mullein often occurs in small, isolated populations that may be overlooked by pollinators An early colonizer of disturbed habitats, woolly mullein requires bare soil and high light levels to establish and grow. Its populations are often short lived—as the vegetation fills in, new plants are unable to become established. When a new disturbance occurs, mullein seeds present in the soil can quickly germinate and, if the area remains open long enough, survive to reproduce. Its success as an early colonizing species is enhanced by the production of abundant seeds that persist in the soil for decades, waiting for a gap in the vegetation.

Wildlife: The densely hairy leaves are unpalatable to most herbivores.

Uses: Pioneers lined their shoes with the velvety leaves (today, hummingbirds use the leaves to line their tiny nests).

Vernonia noveboracensis (L.) Michx.
NEW YORK IRONWEED
Asteraceae (Sunflower family)

Description: Perennial herb 3–7 ft. tall. Stems with numerous alternate, lance-olate leaves, 4–8 in. long. A half dozen or more flower heads in flat-topped clusters, each head with 30–50 deep purple-violet disk flowers, ray flowers absent, green leafy bracts with long, slender tips enclose base of each head. Fruit a ribbed achene with dark brown to purple hair-like bristles. Flowers July–Sept.; fruits Aug.–Oct.

Habitat/range: Low woods and moist openings, including rocky streamsides, roadsides, and fields. Common in mountains, less so in piedmont. Widespread in eastern United States.

Taxonomy: The genus *Vernonia* consists of about 500 species of trees, shrubs, and herbs of tropical, subtropical, and warm temperate regions, including 5 species in the mountains and piedmont.

Ecology: Butterflies and long-tongued bees actively visit and pollinate the tubular flowers. While adult bees typically harvest food from flowers for their own consumption as well as their brood, all food collecting by adult butterflies is for their own use. Both butterflies and bees have a well-developed visual sense and are attracted to vividly colored flowers. The aggregation of brightly colored flowers into dense clusters (heads) compounds the visual effect and signals minimal travel costs, thereby increasing foraging efficiency of insect pollinators. Where 2 or more species of *Vernonia* occur together, interspecies pollinations often result in hybrid plants intermediate between those of the parents, making identification difficult.

Wildlife: Little is known about other wildlife interactions in this species of *Vernonia*; however, a particularly interesting interaction occurs between *V. amygdalina*, an African species, and chimpanzees experiencing gastrointestinal problems. Sick chimps apparently seek out this plant, thereby benefiting from its powerful antibiotic and antiparasitic properties. Relatively little is known about this intriguing interaction whereby animals (other than humans) use plants for medicinal purposes.

Uses: The vibrant purple-violet flower heads make a striking addition to mixed perennial borders.

Viola canadensis L.
CANADA VIOLET
Violaceae (Violet family)

Description: Perennial herb with leafy stems 8–16 in. tall from a short thick rhizome. Heart-shaped leaves with a sharp tip, 2–4 in. long, on elongate stalks. Flowers white with a yellow center, purple-veined near base, fading to pink-purple with age. Fruit a capsule. Flowers Apr.–July (less often Aug.–Sept.); fruits May–Aug. (occasionally Oct.).

Habitat/range: Mainly in rich cove forests. Common in mountains and upper piedmont. Widespread in eastern and central North America.

Taxonomy: The genus *Viola* comprises about 600 species of mostly perennial herbs found in both the Old and New Worlds, including about 30 species in the mountains and piedmont.

Ecology: Canada violet is one of the most characteristic species of cove forests, often forming dense patches that persist through summer. Like most violets, Canada violet produces both open (chasmogamous) flowers and small, bud-like (cleistogamous) flowers that never open. The chasmogamous flowers have a white corolla with a yellow center, purple veins (nectar guides), and a slightly sweet odor. Bumblebees, solitary bees, hoverflies, and skipper butterflies visit the flowers sporadically. If cross-pollination fails to occur, delayed selfing can occur by the stigmas curving down and contacting pollen grains that have fallen from the anthers onto the anterior petals. The tiny cleistogamous flowers self-pollinate in bud-like flowers that remain closed. The seeds from both types of flowers are ballistically dispersed up to 12 ft. from the parent plant. Secondary dispersal occurs with the cleistogamous seeds, as they (unlike the chasmogamous seeds) have lipid-rich food bodies (elaiosomes) that attract ants.

Wildlife: Various birds and small mammals eat the seeds, including wild turkeys, mourning doves, and white-footed mice.

Uses: Violets were widely grown for perfume in the nineteenth century until the chemical compound responsible for the scent was identified and synthesized in the laboratory.

Viola hastata Michx.
HALBERDLEAF YELLOW VIOLET
Violaceae (Violet family)

Description: Low-growing herbaceous perennial from a white fleshy rhizome. Arrowhead-shaped leaves (2–4) clustered near tip, the upper surfaces usually mottled with silvery blotches. Bright yellow flowers borne on slender stalks just above leaves. Fruit an elliptic capsule. Flowers Mar.–May; fruits Apr.–July.

Habitat/range: Moist deciduous forests, including acidic cove forests, oak-hickory forests, and river bluff forests. Common. Eastern United States.

Taxonomy: More than 80 species of *Viola* occur in North America, most of which are natives. Interbreeding between species has resulted in many intermediate forms, making species identification difficult.

Ecology: There are 3 different seed dispersal syndromes in violets. Some species have ballistic dispersal, some have ant dispersal, whereas other species combine both ballistic and ant dispersal. The flower stalks of ballistically dispersed species are typically long and erect, keeping dehiscing fruits well above the leaves. In contrast, species using only ant dispersal have short stalks close to the ground surface, providing easy access to ants. In addition, the capsules are drooping or nodding in ant-dispersed species, but are upright in ballistically dispersed species. Seeds in ballistic fruits can be "flung" 3–15 ft. from the parent plant, whereas ant-dispersed seeds are larger in size and fall directly beneath the parent plant. Because most violet seeds have an elaiosome, ballistically dispersed seeds often have secondary dispersal by ants.

Wildlife: Violets, like many plants, are subject to predispersal seed predators, including slugs, caterpillars of the butterfly genus *Argynnis*, and rodents such as mice and voles.

Uses: Some yellow-flowered violets are mildly cathartic and can be used as a gentle laxative. In Shakespeare's writings, the violet represents humility and loyalty paired with love.

Viola sororia Willd.
COMMON BLUE VIOLET
Violaceae (Violet family)

Description: The leaves and flowers of this low-growing (4–6 in. tall) herbaceous perennial arise directly from the rhizome, forming a basal rosette of ovate to broadly heart-shaped leaves on long stalks. Blue to violet flowers with a whitish center about 1 in. across, with tufts of hairs on lateral petals. Fruit an ovate capsule. Flowers Feb.–May.

Habitat/range: Woodlands, thickets, moist meadows, fields, other disturbed areas. Common. Widespread in eastern United States.

Taxonomy: Violets have either aboveground stems with leaves and flowers on the same stalk or belowground stems (rhizomes), with leaves and flowers on separate stalks (as in common blue violet). Flowers of most violets have 5 petals, the lowest petal conspicuously veined and extending back to form a nectar spur. Many violets also produce small, inconspicuous, fertile flowers that never open as they self-pollinate in the bud.

Ecology: Considered to be the most common and widespread violet in the eastern United States, common blue violet forms large clumps or colonies in forests, fields, and disturbed areas. A spring- and summer-growing species, individuals overwinter as underground stems (rhizomes). The timing of emergence of leaves and flowers varies from year to year, depending on soil temperature, although emergence always occurs before trees leaf out. In forest habitats, light levels are much higher during the first few weeks of growth than later in the growing season when the canopy closes. The leaves and aerial parts of the plant turn yellow and die in fall due to low temperatures, water stress, or both. In times of drought, the aboveground parts die back earlier and more rapidly. Fungal pathogens, as well as grazing by herbivores, can also cause premature die back.

Wildlife: White-tailed deer, rabbits, and livestock sometimes feed on the foliage. Dark spiny caterpillars (larvae) of the fritillary butterfly feed on violet leaves, leaving irregular holes. By feeding at night, the caterpillars reduce their risk of being discovered and eaten by birds.

Uses: Common blue violet is an attractive, low-maintenance groundcover in woodland gardens, but it can be weedy.

Xerophyllum asphodeloides (L.) Nutt.
TURKEYBEARD, BEARGRASS
Melanthiaceae (Bunchflower Family)

Description: Dense clusters of long, slender, grass-like leaves form a basal rosette that remains green through winter. Flowering stems 2–5 ft. tall with small, needle-like leaves end in a showy white inflorescence, at first compact, later elongating up to 12 in. Fruit a 3-lobed capsule. Flowers May–June; fruits July–Sept.

Habitat/range: On dry, acidic ridges and slopes that burn periodically, including heath balds, pine-oak-heath, xeric oak-hickory forests. Uncommon. Occurs mainly in 3 disjunct regions—at mid-elevations in the southern Appalachians, on monadnocks in the upper piedmont, and in the pine barrens of New Jersey.

Taxonomy: The genus includes 1 species in eastern and 1 in western North America. Vegetative plants resemble a bunchgrass, but the leaf bases are white and flattened, unlike those of grasses.

Ecology: Turkeybeard grows mainly in open woodlands dominated by various species of pine and oak, with scattered shrubs and herbaceous plants that can tolerate dry, acidic, nutrient-poor soils. Fires benefit this species because they open up the forest canopy, increasing the amount of light reaching the forest floor, reducing competition from other plants, and increasing the availability of soil nutrients. The grass-like clumps of basal leaves protect the growing tip (apical meristem) from the heat of fire, much like the "grass stage" of longleaf pine; large underground rhizomes also help plants survive fires and function as a storage organ for carbohydrates and water. In a typical year, relatively few individuals flower, but huge flower displays can occur following a fire. Dense clusters of showy, nectar-producing flowers attract bees and cerambycid beetles that function as pollinators. Cross-pollinated flowers are much more likely to produce fruits than are self-pollinated flowers. The flowering stalk, along with its surrounding leaves, dies after fruiting, but the plant typically persists through offshoots. Fire suppression over much of the past century has contributed to the rarity of this species.

Wildlife: White-tailed deer sometimes browse the flowering stalks.

Uses: Turkeybeard is cultivated for its showy white inflorescences.

Yucca filamentosa L.
BEARGRASS
Agavaceae (Agave family)

Description: Basal rosette of long, leathery leaves tapering to a sharp point with curly, thread-like fibers on margins. Large, nodding, creamy white flowers with 6 petal-like parts form a large, branched inflorescence on a 3–9 ft. tall stalk. Fruit an erect capsule with flattened black seeds stacked like coins. Flowers late Apr.–June; fruits Sept.–Oct.

Habitat/range: Dry, open woodlands, rock outcrops, and roadsides. Common. From New Jersey south to Georgia, west to Mississippi. Has escaped from cultivation over a larger area of the eastern United States.

Taxonomy: Most of the 40 species of *Yucca* occur in deserts of the southwestern United States and northern Mexico, with only 1 species in the mountains and piedmont.

Ecology: The tiny yucca moth pollinates the large, showy flowers. Female moths visit flowers for pollen, which they temporarily store in a specialized "pollen basket." They subsequently push a clump of pollen onto a stigma, the part of the pistil receptive to pollen. After pollinating the flower, the female moth lays eggs in the ovary, which hatch and feed on developing seeds (the larvae typically consume about 20–30 percent of the developing seeds). This highly specialized interaction is a classic example of a mutually beneficial relationship in which 2 different species are completely interdependent—the yucca moth is essentially the sole pollinator of yucca flowers and the developing seeds are the sole larval food source of yucca moths. This plant-pollinator interaction is unusual in several respects—most plants are pollinated by multiple (rather than a single) pollinator species, the yucca moths intentionally (rather than inadvertently) pollinate the flower, and developing seeds (rather than nectar or pollen) function as the food reward.

Wildlife: Herbivores tend to avoid the tough, leathery leaves.

Uses: Native Americans and early settlers used the plant as a source of food, fiber, and soap. Its showy flowers, evergreen foliage, and ability to tolerate drought make it an attractive landscape plant.

Zephyranthes atamasca (L.) Herbert
ATAMASCO LILY
Amaryllidaceae (Amaryllis family)

Description: A low perennial with a subterranean bulb and grass-like basal leaves up to 16 in. long with a single, erect, white to pinkish funnel-shaped flower at the tip of a leafless stalk. Fruit a thin-walled capsule that splits at maturity, releasing shiny black seeds. Flowers late Mar.–Apr.; fruits May–June.

Habitat/range: Alluvial forests, wet meadows, and adjacent road shoulders. Common in piedmont, rare in mountains. Southeast.

Taxonomy: A genus of about 50 species of the Americas and the West Indies, with just 1 species in the mountains and piedmont. Members of the Amaryllis family are similar to true lilies (Liliaceae family) except that their ovaries are located below, rather than above, the base of the flower tube. Daffodils (*Narcissus* spp.), spider lilies (*Lycoris radiata*), and amaryllis lilies (*Hippeastrum* hybrids) are other well-known members of the Amaryllis family.

Ecology: Atamasco lily grows well in partial to full sun and in damp soils, but doesn't tolerate continuously waterlogged soils. The large funnel-shaped flowers depend on pollinators (primarily bees) for successful pollination, since the receptive stigmas extend well beyond the dehiscing anthers. Because bees tend to contact stigmas prior to anthers when visiting flowers, cross-pollination is promoted. If self-pollen is deposited on the stigma, the flower can produce viable seed, as the plant is self-compatible. Following pollination, the flowers rapidly change color from pure white to pink. Plants spread sexually by seeds and vegetatively when bulblets (small bulbs) produced by the "mother" bulb develop into new plants.

Wildlife: Most herbivores avoid this plant due to toxic alkaloids present in both the leaves and bulbs.

Uses: The large, showy flowers provide a splash of color in early spring wildflower gardens.

Glossary of Botanical Terms

Terms marked with an asterisk (*) are illustrated at the back of the book, after the indexes.

Achene: A small, dry, single-seeded fruit.
Acidic soil: A soil with a pH less than 7.0.
Aerial rootlet: Small roots produced on stems, as in English ivy.
Alluvial soil: A fertile soil deposited by water flowing over floodplains.
*Alternate leaves: Leaves arranged singly along the stem.
Annual: A plant that germinates, flowers, sets seed, and dies in one year or less.
*Anther: The pollen-bearing part of a stamen.
Aril: An appendage or outer covering of certain seeds, as seen on the seeds of strawberry bush and maypops.
Awn: A slender terminal bristle.

Basic soil: A soil with a pH greater than 7.0; an alkaline soil.
Berry: A fleshy or pulpy fruit with several to many seeds within, such as the tomato.
Biennial: A plant that lives two years, generally producing a basal rosette of leaves the first year, and flowers and fruits the second.
Bottomland: Low-lying land along streams and rivers, in contrast to upland.
Bract: A leaf-like structure usually near the base of a flower or an inflorescence.
Browse: Leaves, twigs, and young shoots of woody plants used as food by deer and other animals.
Bulb: An underground food-storage organ composed of overlapping fleshy scales, such as an onion.
Bunchgrass: A grass that grows in tufts or clumps rather than forming a sod or mat.

Cache: Seeds and other food items stored by certain animals for later consumption.
Calcareous: Refers to soils that contain large amounts of calcium carbonate, usually from limestone.
*Calyx: The outermost whorl of a flower consisting of sepals; usually green.
Canopy: The uppermost layer of a forest, consisting of the branches and leaves of the taller trees.
Capsule: A dry fruit that splits open at maturity into two or more sections, as in azaleas.
Cathartic: A natural laxative, as found in some fruits.
Catkin: An inflorescence consisting of a dense spike of apetalous unisexual flowers, as in willows and birches.
Circumboreal: Refers to species that occur throughout the boreal (northern) regions of North America and Eurasia.
Circumneutral: Refers to soil that is neither strongly acidic nor basic, as the soil pH is near 7.0; such soils are usually relatively high in calcium, magnesium, or both.
Cleistogamous species: Refers to plants that produce two types of flowers—small self-pollinating flowers that don't open (cleistogamous flowers) and larger flowers that open and are potentially cross-pollinated (chasmogamous flowers).
Clone: A group of genetically identical individuals resulting from vegetative reproduction.
Closed cone: A long-lived cone that remains closed until the heat of a fire causes it to open and release its seeds, as in table mountain pine.

471

Community: An assemblage of species that occur together.
Compound leaf: A leaf divided into two or more leaflets.
Conifer: A cone-bearing (rather than flowering) tree or shrub such as pine, spruce, and fir.
*Cordate: Heart-shaped.
*Corolla: Collective name for the petals of a flower.
Cross-pollination: Transfer of pollen from the anthers of one plant to a stigma on another plant.
Crown: The top part of a tree.
Crown fire: A fire that burns the treetops, jumping from one tree to another.
Cuticle: The waxy layer on the surface of a leaf or stem.

Deciduous: Refers to plants that shed their leaves at the end of the growing season.
Defoliation: The shedding or loss of leaves due to herbivory, drought, or other factors.
*Dentate: Refers to coarse, sharp teeth along the leaf margin that point outward.
Dioecious: Refers to species that have male and female flowers on separate plants.
Diploid: Refers to plants that have two sets of chromosomes.
*Disk flower: A tubular flower in sunflower heads.
Disjunct: Refers to populations of the same species occurring in widely separated geographic areas.
Drupe: A fleshy fruit, such as a cherry, with a hard stone or pit that contains a single seed.

Elaiosome: A fleshy, lipid-rich structure attached to the seeds of some plants that entice ants to disperse the seeds.
*Elliptic: Broadest near the middle, tapering at both ends.
Endemic: Restricted to a relatively small geographic area.
Ephemeral: Lasting a short time.
Epiparasite: A parasite that obtains nutrients from a second parasite that in turn parasitizes a third species. In plants, the intermediate species is often a mycorrhizal fungus that functions as a bridge carrying nutrients from a photosynthetic plant to a parasitic plant.
Epiphyte: A plant that grows upon another plant but doesn't derive water or nutrients from it, such as a moss growing on a tree trunk.
Evergreen: Having green leaves throughout the year, not deciduous.
Exotic: A nonnative species introduced from elsewhere.
Extrafloral nectary: A nectar-producing gland that isn't associated with a flower.

Floodplain: Low-lying land along streams and rivers that is periodically flooded.
Flora: The plant species that occur in a particular place.
Follicle: A dry fruit that splits down one side when ripe, such as a milkweed pod.
Frond: A fern leaf.
Frugivore: An animal that eats fruits.

Gall: An abnormal growth caused by an insect, as often occurs on oak leaves.
Gap: A small to large opening in the vegetation.
Genus: A group of related species.
Glabrous: Smooth, without hairs.
Glade: A relatively open, grassy area within a woodland or forest.
Graze: Animal feeding on grass and other low-growing plants.

Habitat: The environment where an organism lives.
Hardwood: A general term that refers to broad-leaved flowering trees.
Haustorium: A specialized structure by which a parasite penetrates and draws nutrients from a host plant.
*Head: A dense cluster of sessile or nearly sessile flowers, as in sunflowers.
Heartwood: The innermost, usually darker wood of a woody trunk.
Hemiparasite: A parasitic plant that produces sugars via photosynthesis

and which obtains water and nutrients from a host plant.

Herb: A plant that lacks a persistent, aboveground woody stem.

Herbaceous: Refers to nonwoody plants.

Herbivore: An animal that consumes plants.

Hermaphrodite: Having both male and female parts (stamens and pistils) in the same flower or within separate flowers on the same plant.

Holoparasite: A nonphotosynthetic, parasitic plant that completely depends on a host plant for nourishment.

Host: A plant that provides nourishment to a parasite.

Hybrid: The offspring from a cross between parent plants of different species.

Indusium: A thin, scale-like covering of a sorus (cluster of sporangia) on a fern leaf.

Inflorescence: A cluster of flowers.

Insectivorous: Refers to a plant that captures and digests insects.

Introduced: Refers to a species that occurs in a geographic area outside its native range; also known as a non-indigenous, alien, or exotic species.

*Lanceolate: Lance-shaped, several times longer than wide, broadest at base, tapering to apex.

Layering: Occurs when low-growing branches on or partially buried in the soil form roots and new upright shoots.

Leaf axil: The upper angle between a leaf and a stem.

Leaf blade: The wide, flat portion of a leaf.

Leaf sinus: The depression or recess between two adjoining lobes.

Leaflet: A single segment of a compound leaf.

Legume: A dry fruit that splits along two sutures, characteristic of plants in the legume or bean family (Fabaceae).

Lemma: The lower of two chaff-like bracts enclosing a grass flower.

Lenticel: A slightly raised area of spongy tissue on the surface of stems (and other plant parts) that allows gas exchange with the atmosphere.

Masting: Refers to trees such as oaks and hickories that produce large seed crops in some years interspersed with years in which relatively few seeds are produced.

Mesic: Refers to habitats of moderate moisture, as opposed to xeric (dry) or hydric (wet).

Mesophyte: A plant that lives in moderately moist soils.

Microclimate: The climate of a small, defined area, which may be different from that of the general area.

Midrib: The main rib or vein of a leaf or other organ.

Monadnock: An isolated hill, ridge, or small mountain that rises abruptly from a sloping or level area.

Monoecious: Refers to species that have separate male and female flowers on the same plant.

Mycorrhiza: A mutualistic relationship between certain fungi and the roots of a plant.

Nectar: The sugary liquid produced in flowers that attracts insects and other potential pollinators.

Nectary: A nectar-secreting gland.

Nectar guide: Lines, spots, or odors that help direct potential pollinators to where the nectar is located within a flower.

Nectar spur: A slender, tubular or sac-like extension of the flower that bears nectar.

Nitrogen fixation: The conversion of atmospheric nitrogen into a compound that can be used by plants, usually either ammonium or nitrate.

Node: The point on the stem where leaves and branches emerge.

Nutlet: A small nut or nut-like fruit.

Oblanceolate: Lance- or spear-shaped with the broadest part above the middle.

Old-growth forest: Forests that have reached sufficient age to resemble the composition and structure of native forests prior to European settlement. They vary by forest type but generally include more large trees, canopy layers, standing snags, and native species than do young or intensively managed forests.

*Opposite leaves: A pair of leaves that grow directly across from each other on the stem.

Outcrop: Bedrock that is exposed and protruding through the soil.

*Ovary: The expanded basal portion of the pistil that contains the ovules (potential seeds).

*Ovate: Egg-shaped in outline with the widest point at the base.

*Palmately compound: A compound leaf in which the leaflets radiate out from a single point.

Pappus: The bristles, scales, or hairs at the apex of achenes in the sunflower family.

Parasitic plant: A plant that obtains part or all of its nutrients from another living organism to which it's attached.

Pendant: Hanging or drooping downward.

Perennial: A plant that lives three or more years.

*Petal: An individual segment of a corolla.

Petiole: The stalk of a leaf.

*Pinnately compound: Refers to a compound leaf in which the leaflets are arranged along a common axis.

Pioneer species: Plants that often colonize newly disturbed areas.

*Pistil: The female part of a flower consisting of a stigma, style, and ovary.

Pollination: The transfer of pollen from the anther to the stigma of a flower.

Prescribed burn: The controlled use of fire by land managers to maintain the health of forests and other naturally occurring vegetation types that benefit from periodic fires.

Pubescent: Covered with hairs.

*Raceme: An unbranched, elongate inflorescence with flowers on stalks.

Rachis: The central axis of an inflorescence or compound leaf.

*Ray flower: A strap-shaped flower in sunflower heads.

Rhizome: A horizontal underground stem from which shoots and roots emerge.

Rosette: A circular cluster of leaves usually at or near ground level.

Samara: A small, dry fruit with an attached wing that facilitates wind dispersal, as occurs in ash (single samara) and maple (double samara).

Sap: The "juice" of a plant, from either vascular tissue (xylem or phloem) or from damaged cells.

Sapling: A small tree.

Saprophyte: A non-photosynthetic plant that gets its nutrients from dead organic matter.

Seed bank: The reservoir of viable seeds in the soil.

Self-incompatible: Refers to species that require cross-pollination because an individual plant's pollen is genetically unable to fertilize its own ovules.

Self-pollination: The transfer of pollen from the anthers to a stigma on the same plant.

*Sepal: A segment of the calyx, usually green.

*Serrate: A saw-like margin, with the teeth directed forward.

Shade-intolerant: Refers to a species that grows well in the open or as a member of the forest canopy, but which dies out in densely shaded habitats.

Shade-tolerant: Refers to a species that can survive and reproduce in shaded habitats such as in the forest understory.

Shrub: A woody plant, usually with multiple stems, that is shorter than a typical tree.

*Simple leaf: A single leaf not divided into leaflets.

Sorus: A cluster of sporangia usually located on the underside of a fern leaf.

Spadix: A spike with small flowers on a fleshy axis.

Spathe: A large bract subtending or partially enclosing an inflorescence, as in Jack-in-the-pulpit.

Species richness: Refers to the number of species in a given area or community.

*Spike: An unbranched, elongate inflorescence with sessile flowers.

*Stamen: The pollen-bearing organ of a flower, consisting of an anther and filament.

*Stigma: The pollen-receptive tip of the pistil.

Stipule: A leaf-like appendage at the base of a petiole.

Stolon: A horizontal aboveground stem that roots at the nodes.

Stratification: Seeds that require exposure to an overwintering period (cold stratification) or summer period (warm stratification) prior to germinating.

Subshrub: A small shrub, slightly woody at the base.

Succulent: A plant with thick water-storing stems or leaves.

Sucker: A shoot originating from below ground roots.

Surface fire: A fire that burns the surface layer, including leaves, dead branches, and low vegetation.

Symbiosis: An intimate living-together of two different kinds of organisms, such as a fungus and green algae (or cyanobacteria) that together form a lichen; the relationship may or may not be mutually beneficial.

Taproot: A main root from which smaller root branches arise.

Tendril: A slender, twining structure used for climbing or support, such as those used by greenbriers.

Tetraploid: Refers to plants with four sets of chromosomes.

Thallus: A plant that is not differentiated into stems, leaves, and roots, such as a moss.

Thorax: The body region between the head and the abdomen of insects and other arthropods.

Topkill: When the aboveground parts of a plant die back due to fire, wind, logging, or other factors.

Trailing: Refers to a plant that runs along the soil or leaf litter surface, such as certain vines.

Transpiration: The loss of water (in vapor form) from plants, usually through stomatal pores on the leaves.

Tree: A large woody plant, usually with a single main stem or trunk.

Trifoliate: A compound leaf with three leaflets.

Tuber: A thickened underground stem modified for food storage, such as a potato.

*Umbel: A flat-topped or rounded inflorescence in which the flower stalks arise from a common point, as they do in members of the carrot family.

Understory: Refers to the plants growing under the forest canopy, including smaller trees, shrubs, and herbs.

Unisexual: Refers to a flower (or plant) that has either male or female reproductive parts but not both.

Vine: A weak-stemmed climbing or trailing plant that uses other plants (or structures) for support.

*Whorled: Refers to three or more structures (e.g., leaves, flowers, or fruits) that arise from a common point.

Windthrow: Refers to trees knocked down by high winds.

Xeric: Refers to dry environments.

SELECTED NATURAL AREAS

Selected Natural Areas

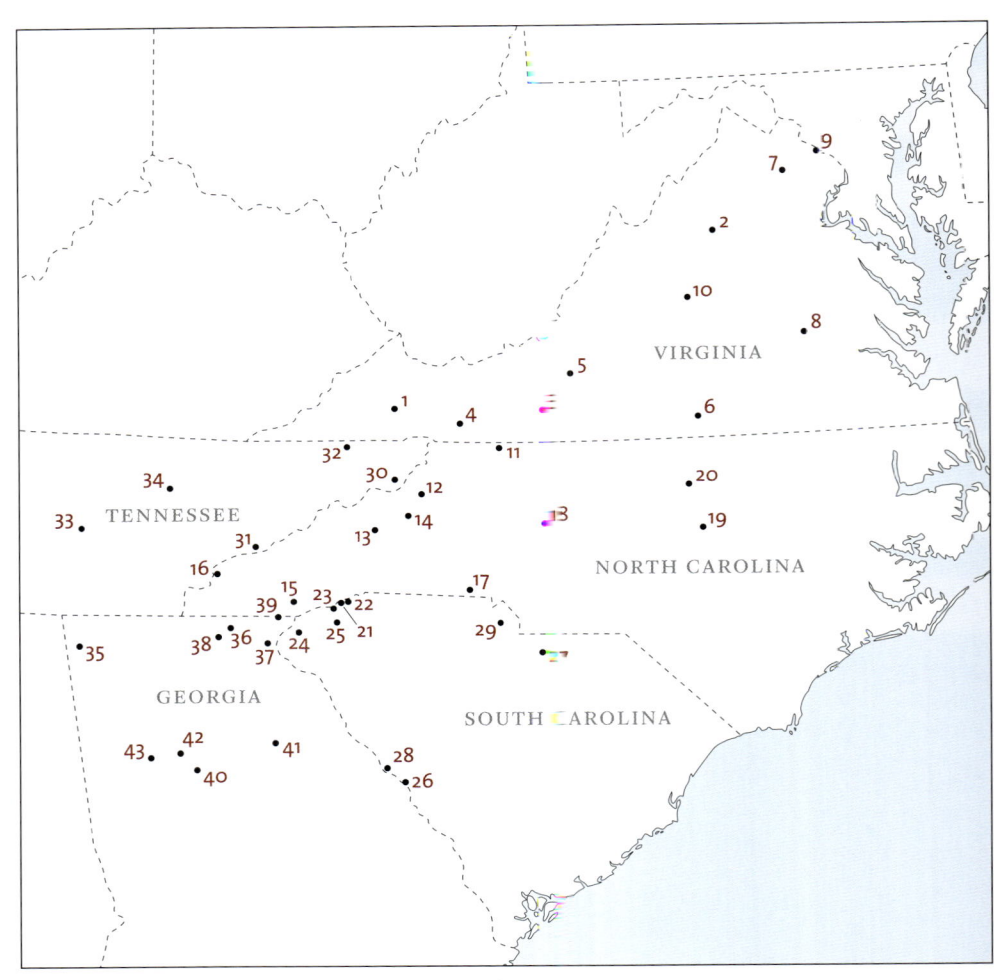

Map 2. Selected natural areas of the southeastern United States

476

SELECTED NATURAL AREAS

VIRGINIA MOUNTAINS
1. Pinnacle Natural Area Preserve
2. Shenandoah National Park
3. Buffalo Mountain Natural Area Preserve
4. Mount Rogers National Recreation Area
5. Poor Mountain Natural Area Preserve

VIRGINIA PIEDMONT
6. Difficult Creek Natural Area Preserve
7. Bull Run Mountains Natural Area Preserve
8. Pocahontas State Park
9. Fraser Preserve
10. Fortune's Cove Preserve

NORTH CAROLINA MOUNTAINS
11. Blue Ridge Parkway
12. Grandfather Mountain State Park
13. Mount Mitchell State Park
14. Linville Gorge Wilderness Area
15. Whiteside Mountain
16. Joyce Kilmer Memorial Forest

NORTH CAROLINA PIEDMONT
17. Crowders Mountain State Park
18. Boone's Cave Park
19. Swift Creek Bluffs Nature Preserve
20. Penny's Bend

SOUTH CAROLINA MOUNTAINS
21. Caesars Head State Park
22. Jones Gap State Park
23. Table Rock State Park
24. Station Cove Falls

SOUTH CAROLINA PIEDMONT
25. Glassy Mountain Heritage Preserve
26. Savannah River Bluffs Heritage Preserve
27. Flat Creek Heritage Reserve (Forty Acre Rock)
28. Stevens Creek Heritage Preserve
29. Rock Hill Blackjacks Heritage Preserve

TENNESSEE MOUNTAINS
30. Roan Mountain Massif
31. Great Smoky Mountains National Park
32. Bays Mountain Park and Natural Area
33. Fall Creek State Park and Natural Area
34. Frozen Head State Park and Natural Area

GEORGIA MOUNTAINS
35. Crockford-Pigeon Mountain Wildlife Management Area
36. Brasstown Bald and Brasstown Bald Wilderness Area
37. Tallulah Gorge State Park
38. Sosebee Cove
39. Rabun Bald

GEORGIA PIEDMONT
40. Panola Mountain State Conservation Park
41. Rock and Shoals Outcrop Natural Area
42. Fernbank Forest
43. Sweetwater Creek State Conservation Park

Virginia Mountains

PINNACLE NATURAL AREA PRESERVE

Features: Dramatic cliffs and ledges, scenic rivers, impressive waterfalls, numerous caves, and spectacular wildflower displays characterize this natural area. Towering above Big Cedar Creek, a nearly 400 ft. tall spire of dolomite known as the Pinnacle, gives the site its name. From the parking area, follow the footbridge across Big Cedar Creek to access the trail to the Clinch River. Communities include rich cove forest, spray cliff, rocky streamside, and dry, calcareous woodlands. Weathering of the calcium-rich limestone and dolomite cliffs and ledges has resulted in a nutrient-rich, nearly neutral (basic) soil with colorful wildflower displays, particularly in spring before the canopy trees leaf out. A dozen rare plants are known from the preserve, including Canby's mountain lover (*Paxistima canbyi*), Carolina saxifrage (*Micranthes caroliniana*), and glade spurge (*Euphorbia purpurea*).
Web: www.dcr.virginia.gov/dnh
Management: Virginia Department of Conservation and Recreation's Division of Natural Heritage Program (276) 676-5673
Nearest town: Lebanon, Russell County, Virginia

SHENANDOAH NATIONAL PARK

Features: A prominent feature of Shenandoah National Park is Skyline Drive, a 105-mile road that runs the entire length of the park along the crest of the northern Blue Ridge Mountains. Variation in elevation, slope, aspect, bedrock, precipitation, and other factors creates numerous habitats that support a diversity of natural communities and species. More than 95 percent forested, the park harbors more than 1,300 species of vascular plants, including 100 species of trees. On dry upper slopes, chestnut oak and high-elevation red oak forest are common, whereas on more mesic slopes with deeper, more nutrient-rich soils, rich cove forest and northern hardwood forest can be found. Spruce-fir forest is limited to small patches at the highest elevations (as on Hawksbill Mountain, one of two peaks in the park that exceed 4,000 ft.). The only large open area in the park is directly across from Big Meadows Visitor Center. Here, mountain bogs (technically mafic fens) and other wetland and upland habitats can be found, including a number of rare plants. Along the numerous small streams in the park, one can find acidic cove forest, rocky streamside, and spray cliff communities. Wildflowers are conspicuous in spring at lower elevations along streams such as the South River, Rose River, and Mill Prong. In summer and fall, Big Meadows, Hawksbill Mountain, Stony Man, and the banks along Skyline Drive are good places to view wildflowers. Fall colors typically reach their peak during the middle two weeks in October.
Web: www.nps.gov/shen
Management: National Park Service (540) 999-3500
Nearest town: The Park runs from the town of Front Royal (Warren County) south to the city of Waynesboro (Augusta County), Virginia.

BUFFALO MOUNTAIN NATURAL AREA PRESERVE

Features: At nearly 4,000 ft., the rounded summit of Buffalo Mountain stands well above the surrounding landscape. Considered one of Virginia's most significant natural areas, the preserve is distinctive in having subalpine forests with stunted trees, areas of magnesium-rich soils, and high-elevation prairie-like glades. A steep 1-mile trail to the top of the mountain provides stunning views of the surrounding

landscape, as well as numerous plant species. The south face of the mountain contains prairie-like openings with various wildflowers and native grasses generally associated with the Midwest, including big bluestem (*Andropogon gerardii*) and Indian grass (*Sorghastrum nutans*). More than a dozen rare plants occur on the mountain, including Gray's lily (*Lilium grayi*), mountain sandwort (*Minuartia groenlandica*), and mountain rattlesnake root (*Prenanthes roanensis*). Magnesium-rich seeps at the base of the mountain support additional rare plants, including large-leaved grass of Parnassus (*Parnassia grandifolia*). One of the best times to visit is late summer, when the prairie-like glades are in full bloom.
Web: www.dcr.virginia.gov/dnh
Management: Virginia Department of Conservation and Recreation's Division of Natural Heritage Program (276) 676-5673
Nearest town: Willis, Floyd County, Virginia

MOUNT ROGERS NATIONAL RECREATION AREA

Features: Mount Rogers, Virginia's highest peak at 5,729 ft., is surrounded by the 150,000-acre Mount Rogers National Recreation Area. One can reach the summit of Mount Rogers via an 8-mile round-trip trail that begins in Grayson Highlands State Park. Highlights include stunning views from open, wind-swept, grassy plateaus, lichen-covered boulders, herds of wild ponies, and numerous plants within grassy balds, high-elevation rock outcrops, and dense spruce-fir forests. Hikers should be prepared for quickly developing summer thunderstorms and frequent whiteouts from fog. Once heavily forested, the balds were created by heavy logging and subsequent wildfires in the early 1900s. The balds are currently kept open by a combination of controlled burns and grazing by cattle and feral ponies. While much of the trail traverses open plateaus, the summit is densely covered by spruce-fir forest. For unknown reasons, balsam woolly adelgids have had less of an impact on Fraser fir (*Abies fraseri*) on Mount Rogers than elsewhere in the southern Appalachians. Peak flowering occurs in summer.
Web: www.southernregion.fs.fed.us/gwj
Management: Mount Rogers National Recreation Area and the Jefferson National Forest (276) 783-5196
Nearest town: Troutdale, Grayson County, Virginia

POOR MOUNTAIN NATURAL AREA PRESERVE

Features: Located in the Blue Ridge Mountains, this nearly 1,000-acre preserve consists of steep slopes and ridges ranging from 1,500 to 2,700 ft. in elevation. The name of the mountain reflects its nutrient-poor acidic soils. The slopes and ridges are mostly covered with pine-oak-heath including chestnut oak (*Quercus montana*), scarlet oak (*Q. coccinea*), bear oak (*Q. ilicifolia*), Table mountain pine (*Pinus pungens*) and pitch pine (*P. rigida*). Heath shrubs dominate the understory, including huckleberry (*Gaylussacia* spp.), mountain laurel (*Kalmia latifolia*), and fetterbush (*Pieris floribunda*). The most distinctive feature of the site is a large population of piratebush (*Buckleya distichophylla*), a globally rare shrub restricted to the mountains of Virginia, North Carolina, and Tennessee. A root parasite, piratebush is most conspicuous in autumn when its brilliant yellow foliage brightens slopes and ridges.
Web: www.dcr.virginia.gov/dnh
Management: Virginia Department of Conservation and Recreation's Division of Natural Heritage (540) 265-5234
Nearest town: Roanoke, Roanoke County, Virginia

Virginia Piedmont

DIFFICULT CREEK NATURAL AREA PRESERVE

Features: Prior to European colonization, prairie-like grasslands with scattered pines and hardwoods covered the unusual soils that characterize this preserve. Fire suppression, coupled with the planting of loblolly pine (*Pinus taeda*) during the twentieth century, altered the vegetation in such a way that many of the sun-loving grasses and other herbaceous plants were displaced to remnant patches beneath power line clearings and roadside areas. Currently, prescribed fires are being used as a management tool to restore the open, grassy areas that once characterized this area. Rare species include Midwestern Indian physic (*Gillenia stipulata*), Carolina thistle (*Cirsium carolinianum*), winged loosestrife (*Lythrum alatum*), and rattlesnake master (*Eryngium yuccifolium*). More than 2 miles of hiking trails along fire lanes provide access to the preserve.
Web: www.dcr.virginia.gov/dnh
Management: Virginia Department of Conservation and Recreation's Division of Natural Heritage (540) 265-5234
Nearest town: South Boston, Halifax County, Virginia

BULL RUN MOUNTAINS NATURAL AREA PRESERVE

Features: Varied topography, soils, and hydrology result in a great diversity of habitats and species within this 2,486-acre preserve located within 50 miles of Washington, D.C. Communities include chestnut oak forest, pine-oak-heath, oak-hickory forest, and river bluff. A trail leads to a ridgetop with great views of the nearby Blue Ridge Mountains and surrounding piedmont.
Web: www.brmconservancy.org
Management: Bull Run Mountain Conservancy (703) 753-2631
Nearest town: Broad Run, Fauquier County, Virginia

POCAHONTAS STATE PARK

Features: This heavily forested 8,000-acre state park, just 20 minutes from downtown Richmond, includes wetland and upland habitats. Low areas along Swift Creek and the long, narrow Swift Creek Lake support bottomland forest with broad-leaved trees such as sweetgum (*Liquidambar styraciflua*), willow oak (*Quercus phellos*), and swamp chestnut oak (*Q. michauxii*). Marshy habitats with 10 ft. tall bulrush (*Scirpus* sp.) and both orange and yellow jewelweeds (*Impatiens capensis* and *I. pallida*) occur along the shores of Beaver Lake. With a slight increase in elevation, bottomland forest transitions to mesic forest with American beech (*Fagus grandifolia*), red mulberry (*Morus rubra*), pawpaw (*Asimina triloba*), and numerous spring wildflowers, including Solomon's seal (*Polygonatum biflorum*), dutchman's britches (*Dicentra cucullaria*), and bloodroot (*Sanguinaria canadensis*). On upper slopes and ridgetops, where the soil is shallow and exposure to sunlight and wind is greatest, dry forests dominated by loblolly pine (*Pinus taeda*) occur. Goldenrods (*Solidago* spp.) and asters (*Symphyotrichum* spp.) bloom in late summer and fall. A number of trails wind through the forests and along Beaver Lake.
Web: www.dcr.virginia.gov/state_parks
Management: Pocahontas State Park (804) 796-4255
Nearest town: Richmond, Chesterfield County, Virginia

FRASER PRESERVE

Features: The Potomac River forms the northern boundary of this small (220-acre) preserve only 15 miles from Washington, D.C. Numerous habitats are represented, including streams, marsh, swamp, meadows, seeps, fields in various stages of succession, alluvial forest, and river bluff forest. More than 300 species of wildflowers and over 100 species of birds (including bald eagles) have been identified in the preserve. Alder thickets (*Alnus* sp.) thrive in the floodplain, and box elder (*Acer negundo*) and sycamore (*Platanus occidentalis*) lean out over the river, seeking additional sunlight. An infestation of the invasive waxy-leaved basket grass (*Oplismenus hirtellus* ssp. *undulatifolius*) was discovered in the preserve several years ago. Similar to Japanese stiltgrass (*Microstegium vimineum*) in its ability to eliminate native wildflowers, efforts are currently underway to eradicate it. Several miles of trails provide access to the preserve.
Web: www.nature.org
Management: The Nature Conservancy (434) 295-6106
Nearest town: Great Falls, Fairfax County, Virginia

FORTUNE'S COVE PRESERVE

Features: Stretching across the crest of Woods Mountain, this 755-acre preserve provides spectacular views of the Blue Ridge Mountains. Because it straddles Virginia's piedmont and Blue Ridge provinces, the preserve contains an interesting mix of mountain and piedmont species. A challenging 5.5-mile loop trail gains about 1,500 ft. in elevation before reaching its highest point. Chestnut oak forest covers the dry ridgetops. Rocky glades on the west side of the mountain have an unusual assortment of species. The open, grassy areas are dominated by little bluestem (*Schizachyrium scoparium*). Fringetree (*Chionanthus virginicus*) is also abundant—you may notice the sweet fragrance of its white wispy inflorescences in early spring before actually seeing the plant. Numerous wildflowers occur along the stream at the base of the trail in summer.
Web: www.nature.org
Management: The Nature Conservancy (434) 295-6106
Nearest town: Lovingston, Nelson County, Virginia

North Carolina Mountains

BLUE RIDGE PARKWAY

Features: This linear national park follows the crest of the Blue Ridge Mountains for 469 miles, from Shenandoah National Park in Virginia to Great Smoky Mountains National Park in North Carolina. Ranging in elevation from 650 ft. to over 6,000 ft., it passes through numerous communities and has more than 1,400 species of vascular plants. In a single day's drive, one can observe summer-blooming species at lower elevations and spring-blooming species on the higher peaks. The moderately strenuous one-mile Craggy Gardens trail (milepost 364.6) winds through wind-stunted northern hardwood forest and heath and grassy balds. The area is particularly striking in mid- to late June when Catawba rhododendron (*Rhododendron catawbiense*) is in bloom. The Mount Pisgah area (milepost 408.6) is especially rich in wildflowers. The Buck Springs trail from the Pisgah Inn parking area to the Buck Springs overlook (a distance of 1.1 miles) has numerous wildflowers from spring through summer. The Mount Pisgah summit trail (3.2 miles round trip) traverses a high-elevation red oak

forest with scenic views and heath balds on top. A short (0.5 mile) but steep, mostly paved trail to the top of Devil's Courthouse (milepost 422.4) provides magnificent views of the surrounding mountains. Rock outcrops on the summit harbor rare plants and provide nesting sites for peregrine falcons. The spruce-fir forest looks healthier here than on higher peaks because the dominant species is red spruce, which, unlike Fraser fir, isn't susceptible to the balsam woolly adelgid. The Richland Balsam Overlook, at an elevation of 6,053 ft., is the highest point on the parkway. The standing dead trees are mostly Fraser firs killed by the balsam woolly adelgid in the late 1970s. For a closer look, take the 1.5-mile loop trail to the summit of Richland Balsam (elevation 6,420 ft.) which begins in the parking area at milepost 431, about 0.5 miles to the north of the Richland Balsam overlook.
Web: www.nps.gov
Management: National Park Service (828) 271-4779
Nearest town: The parkway begins near Waynesboro, Augusta County, Virginia and ends near Cherokee, Cherokee County, North Carolina.

GRANDFATHER MOUNTAIN STATE PARK

Features: Rising nearly 4,000 ft. above the adjoining piedmont, Grandfather Mountain, at an elevation of 5,964 ft., is the highest mountain in the Blue Ridge Escarpment. Its quartzite rocks are thought to be more than one billion years old, making it among the most ancient mountains in the world. The rugged terrain, shallow soils, and severe climate (including occasional 100 mph winds) along the high crests have resulted in a mixture of stunted red spruce (*Picea rubens*), Fraser fir (*Abies fraseri*), northern hardwoods, and heath shrubs. The short (2.2 mile) but steep Grandfather trail traverses this high-elevation vegetation. At lower elevations, chestnut oak forest commonly occurs on dry ridges and upper slopes, whereas cove forest covers moist, sheltered sites such as ravines, mountain valleys, and north-facing slopes. The Profile trail winds through rich cove and northern hardwood forests with abundant spring wildflowers. The scenic Rough Ridge Overlook trail, which can be accessed from the Blue Ridge Parkway, includes heath balds, rock outcrops, and northern hardwood forest, along with colorful wildflower displays.
Web: www.ncparks.gov and www.grandfather.com
Management: At the time of this writing, this site is managed jointly by Grandfather Mountain State Park (828) 297-7261 and Grandfather Mountain, Inc. (800) 468-7325
Nearest town: Linville, Avery County, North Carolina

MOUNT MITCHELL STATE PARK

Features: Mount Mitchell (at an elevation of 6,684 ft.) is the highest peak in the eastern United States. On clear days, an observation deck on the summit provides spectacular views of the surrounding mountains, almost all of which are covered in lush green vegetation. The climate is often cool to cold (even in summer), with frequent fog (or rain) and strong winds, but unlike the higher peaks in the northern Appalachians, Mount Mitchell (and other southern mountains) lacks alpine tundra. Up until several decades ago, mature stands of Fraser fir (*Abies fraseri*), with lesser amounts of red spruce (*Picea rubens*), densely covered the summit and upper slopes of Mount Mitchell. Today, the forest is much different, consisting of smaller living trees, many standing dead tree trunks, decomposing fallen logs, and dense shrubs. Almost all of the large old Fraser firs died in the 1960s and 1970s due to a tiny sucking insect known as the balsam woolly adelgid that was accidentally introduced from Europe. Younger fir and spruce trees, yellow birch (*Betula alleghaniensis*), mountain ash (*Sor-*

bus americana), blackberry bushes (*Rubus* spp.), and other species have colonized the forest openings created by dead firs. Other communities in the park include northern hardwood forest, high-elevation rock outcrop, heath bald, and spray cliff. About a half-dozen trails wind through the park, including the 0.75-mile Balsam trail, which begins near the observation deck.
Web: www.ncparks.gov
Management: Mount Mitchell State Park (828) 675-4611
Nearest town: Celo, Yancey County, North Carolina

LINVILLE GORGE WILDERNESS AREA

Features: This 11,000-acre wilderness area includes numerous natural communities, original-growth forests, and spectacular scenery, including a 600–2,000 ft. deep gorge that is one of the deepest cuts east of the Grand Canyon. Linville Gorge is characterized by rugged topography, quartzite cliffs, nutrient-poor soils, relatively low annual rainfall, and limited human disturbance (except for an introduced insect, the hemlock woolly adelgid, destroying eastern hemlock trees). Kistler Memorial Highway on the west and Forest Service road 210 on the east provide access to both sides of the gorge. The ridgelines and upper slopes are dominated by pine-oak-heath with pitch pine (*Pinus rigida*), table mountain pine (*P. pungens*), chestnut and scarlet oak (*Quercus montana* and *Q. coccinea*), and various heath shrubs. The rock outcrops that line both sides of the gorge include rare endemics such as mountain golden heather (*Hudsonia montana*) and Heller's blazing star (*Liatris helleri*), as well as scattered heath balds. Acidic cove forest is common on the sheltered, mid- and lower slopes, but rich cove forest is relatively rare because nutrient-rich soils are uncommon. Rocky streamside and spray cliff communities occur along the Linville River at the base of the gorge. It's easy to get lost without a good map of the numerous trails that wind through the rugged terrain.
Web: www.cs.unca.edu/nfsnc/recreation/Linville.pdf
Management: Pisgah National Forest (704) 652-2144
Nearest town: Linville Falls, Avery, Burke, and McDowell counties, North Carolina.

WHITESIDE MOUNTAIN

Features: This massive granitic dome, thought to be over 400 million years old, rises more than 2,000 ft. above the valley floor to reach an elevation of 4,930 ft. at its summit. A moderately difficult 2-mile loop trail to the summit begins at the parking area. Highlights include a rich diversity of plants and stunning views of the surrounding mountains. The trail follows an old roadbed through cool, moist north-facing slopes covered by northern hardwood forest. Common species include yellow birch (*Betula alleghaniensis*), wild hydrangea (*Hydrangea arborea*), mountain angelica (*Angelica triquinata*), and painted trillium (*Trillium undulatum*). The large area on top of the mountain includes old-growth high-elevation red oak forest, numerous rock outcrops, and scattered heath balds. Stunted northern red oaks (*Quercus rubra*), sculpted by wind and ice, dominate areas with deeper soils. The understory includes Catawba rhododendron (*Rhododendron catawbiense*), sprouts of American chestnut (*Castanea dentata*), and a fairly dense herbaceous layer. The rock outcrop community includes lichen-covered rocks with prostrate mats of twisted hair spikemoss (*Selaginella tortipila*), granite dome St. John's wort (*Hypericum buckleyi*) and rare species such as granite dome goldenrod (*Solidago simulans*). On the fringe of outcrops and forest are heath balds with sand myrtle (*Kalmia buxifolium*), mountain laurel (*K. latifolia*), and flame azalea (*R. calendulaceum*).

Web: www.cs.unca.edu/nfsnc/recreation/whiteside.pdf
Management: Nantahala National Forest, Nantahala Ranger District (828) 526-3765
Nearest town: Cashiers, Jackson County, North Carolina

JOYCE KILMER MEMORIAL FOREST

Features: Giant trees, old-growth forest, and spectacular wildflower displays highlight this living monument honoring Joyce Kilmer, an early twentieth century poet killed in World War I whose famous poem "Trees" begins, "I think I shall never see a poem lovely as a tree." Never having been logged, this preserve is one of the best examples of original-growth forest in the entire Appalachian Mountains. Particularly striking are huge tulip trees (*Liriodendron tulipifera*), white basswood (*Tilia americana*), and American beech (*Fagus grandifolia*), some of which are more than 100 ft. tall and 300–400 years old. Acidic cove forest occurs on moist, acidic soils, has a dense layer of heath shrubs (particularly rosebay, *Rhododendron maximum*), and a poorly developed herbaceous layer. Rich cove forest, in contrast, occurs on more nutrient-rich soils, has a species-rich and abundant herbaceous layer, and relatively few shrubs. Peak wildflower season occurs from mid-March through April, but anytime is a good time to visit. An easy 2-mile double loop trail provides insight into what mountain forests were like prior to logging.
Web: www.joycekilmerslickrock.com
Management: Nantahala National Forest (704) 479-6431
Nearest town: Robbinsville, Graham County, North Carolina

North Carolina Piedmont

CROWDERS MOUNTAIN STATE PARK

Features: This botanically rich 3,000-acre state park includes two prominent rock outcrops (monadnocks) with sheer vertical cliffs, impressive views, and mature forests. Erosion-resistant quartzite has enabled Crowders Mountain (at 1,625 ft.) and nearby Kings Pinnacle (at 1,725 ft.) to persist over time, while the surrounding landscape was gradually worn down by wind and water. Both peaks are readily visible off Interstate 85 (just north of the border with South Carolina). Chestnut oak forest at lower elevations gives way to stunted Virginia pine (*Pinus virginiana*) and other species on xeric cliffs and ridgetops. More than 15 miles of trails crisscross the park and its two peaks, including a short trail that showcases fern diversity. The visitor center has interpretive exhibits about the local geology, ecology, and plants.
Web: www.crowdersmountain.com
Management: Crowders Mountain State Park (704) 853-5375
Nearest town: Gastonia, Gaston County, North Carolina

BOONE'S CAVE PARK

Features: An overlook in the parking area provides views of the Yadkin River and relatively undisturbed floodplain and upland forests. A short trail leads to Boone's Cave where Daniel Boone reportedly once hid to avoid hostile Native Americans. A one-mile loop trail winds through various forest types. The alluvial (floodplain) forest has some exceptionally large trees, including a 154 ft. tall eastern cottonwood (*Populus deltoides*). On the lower slopes and ravines is a river bluff forest with mesic species such as American beech (*Fagus grandifolia*), white basswood (*Tilia americana*), and

tulip tree (*Liriodendron tulipifera*), and a rich herbaceous layer with species such as round-lobed hepatica (*Hepatica americana*), bloodroot (*Sanguinaria canadensis*), and meadowrue (*Thalictrum thalictroides*). Oak-hickory forest covers the relatively dry upper slopes and ridgetops.
Web: www.co.davidson.nc.us/leisure/BoonesCavePark.aspx
Management: Davidson County Recreation and Parks Department (336) 242-2285
Nearest town: Churchland, Davidson County, North Carolina

SWIFT CREEK BLUFFS NATURE PRESERVE

Features: This delightful preserve has a series of north-facing river bluffs, large old canopy trees, and a rich array of spring wildflowers. Numerous large American beech (*Fagus grandifolia*), some more than 200 years old, grow intermixed with massive northern red oak (*Quercus rubra*) and white ash (*Fraxinus americana*). The alluvial forest along Swift Creek includes swamp chestnut oak (*Quercus michauxii*), American elm (*Ulmus americana*), and sycamore (*Platanus occidentalis*) in the canopy, with species such as mayapple (*Podophyllum peltatum*), jack-in-the-pulpit (*Arisaema triphyllum*), and Atamasco lily (*Zephyranthes atamasca*) on the forest floor. The main trail from the parking area winds through the creek's floodplain to the base of the river bluff. Stairs lead up to the top of the bluff where impressive views and huge trees abound. The equally interesting Hemlock Bluff's Nature Preserve is located less than 2 miles downstream.
Web: www.triangleland.org/lands/places_to_visit.shtml
Management: Triangle Land Conservancy (919) 833-3662
Nearest town: Cary, Wake County, North Carolina

PENNY'S BEND

Features: Named after a sharp horseshoe bend in the Eno River, this small (84-acre) preserve includes alluvial forest, river bluff, and remnant piedmont prairie. More than 450 plant species have been identified in the preserve, including the federally listed smooth coneflower (*Echinacea laevigata*). The 1.5 mile river trail along the floodplain is rich in species, especially in early spring when numerous wildflowers bloom. Midwest prairie disjuncts such as prairie dock (*Silphium terebinthinaceum*), blue wild indigo (*Baptisia minor* var. *aberrans*), and blazing star (*Liatris squarrulosa*) occur in the remnant piedmont prairie adjacent to the parking area. The prairie has shallow soils with an underlying layer of magnesium-rich diabase rock that forms a nearly neutral (basic) soil. Thin soils, coupled with natural wildfires and intentional fires set by Native Americans, played a key role in maintaining open, prairie-like grasslands. Today, land managers at Penny's Bend and elsewhere use prescribed burns to maintain these habitats.
Web: www.ncbg.unc.edu/pages/42
Management: North Carolina Botanical Garden (919) 962-0522
Nearest town: Durham, Durham County, North Carolina

South Carolina Mountains

CAESARS HEAD STATE PARK

Features: An observation deck perched on a high elevation rock outcrop provides spectacular views of Table Rock, the Blue Ridge Escarpment, and the rolling hills of the piedmont. An ideal time to visit is late September or October when one can see fall-blooming wildflowers along with migrating raptors and monarch butterflies. This popular viewing area is also a fantastic spot to enjoy fall colors. The visitor center provides information on the regional landscape. The nearby Raven Cliff Falls trail leads to an observation platform with views of one of South Carolina's tallest (nearly 400 ft.) and most scenic waterfalls. Plant communities along the trail include oak-hickory forest, acidic cove forest, pine-oak heath, and chestnut oak forest.
Website: www.southcarolinaparks.com
Management: South Carolina State Park (864) 836-6115
Nearest town: Cleveland, Greenville County, South Carolina

JONES GAP STATE PARK

Features: The Jones Gap trail along the Middle Saluda River and several adjacent loop trails provide picturesque views of water cascading over boulders, impressive forests, and numerous wildflowers. Communities on moist to wet sites include alluvial forest, rocky streamside, spray cliff (waterfalls), and cove forest. Cataract bogs, which form alongside streams that slide down, rather than fall over, steeply sloped outcrops, also occur. Unusual plants such as the purple pitcher plant (*Sarracenia purpurea*) and kidneyleaf grass of parnassus (*Parnassia asarifolia*) occur in cataract bogs. Be careful when exploring cataract bogs as algae growing on wet rock surfaces makes them extremely slippery and dangerous! On upper slopes and ridges, where the soil is relatively shallow and dry, one encounters chestnut oak forest and pine-oak-heath woodlands.
Website: www.southcarolinaparks.com
Management: South Carolina State Park (864) 836-3647
Nearest town: Cleveland, Greenville County, South Carolina

TABLE ROCK STATE PARK

Features: This outstanding natural area includes Table Rock, an imposing granite dome with 1,000 ft. tall vertical cliffs, a scenic mountain lake, cascading streams, and a rich diversity of plants. The park includes several trails, all of which begin at Carrick Nature Center near Pinnacle Lake. The Carrick nature trail is a relatively easy 2-mile loop trail along Carrick Creek. The longer (about 7 miles round trip), more strenuous, but very interesting Table Rock trail traverses numerous communities, including acidic cove forest, oak-hickory forest, chestnut oak forest, pine-oak-heath, montane oak-hickory forest, and high-elevation granitic dome. The outcrop vegetation at the top is interesting and the views are spectacular.
Website: www.southcarolinaparks.com
Management: South Carolina State Park (864) 878-9813
Nearest town: Pickens, Pickens County, South Carolina

STATION COVE FALLS

Features: An easy half-mile trail leads from the parking area to Station Cove Falls, one of the premier wildflower sites in South Carolina. The scenic 60 ft. waterfall provides an attractive backdrop for an unusually species-rich and colorful herbaceous layer. The trail winds through a mixed pine-oak forest (heavily impacted by pine bark beetles), a mature oak-hickory forest, and a small wetland created by beavers damming the creek. As the trail approaches the falls, the slopes steepen, the vegetation gets lusher, and a rich cove forest begins. The cove is underlain with amphibolite, a mafic rock that releases magnesium into the soil, which elevates the soil pH and increases nutrient availability, thereby enabling a greater diversity of species to occupy the site. Early spring wildflowers include large populations of acute-lobed hepatica (*Hepatica acutiloba*), meadowrue (*Thalictrum thalictroides*), sweet Betsy (*Trillium cuneatum*), foamflower (*Tiarella cordifolia*), bloodroot (*Sanguinaria canadensis*), and mayapple (*Podophyllum peltatum*). A spray cliff community occurs behind and around the waterfall. Peak flowering is early spring (mid-March to mid-April), but anytime is a good time to visit.
Website: www.fs.fed.us/wildflowers/regions/southern
Management: Jointly managed by Sumter National Forest and South Carolina Park, Recreation, and Tourism (864) 638-9568
Nearest town: Walhalla, Oconee County, South Carolina

South Carolina Piedmont

GLASSY MOUNTAIN HERITAGE PRESERVE

Features: Glassy Mountain is a rounded granite dome (a monadnock) that rises 400 ft. above the surrounding piedmont landscape. From the small parking area at the top of the mountain (just past the fire tower), a nature trail descends a short distance to a viewing platform and then winds around the east side of the mountain. The vegetation consists of oak-hickory forest on deeper soils, scattered mats of low-growing plants on exposed rock outcrops, with transitional areas (glades) dominated by grasses with scattered trees and shrubs. Stunning views of the gently rolling piedmont below and the Blue Ridge Escarpment in the distance, along with a rich diversity of plants, make this an interesting destination any time of year.
Website: www.dnr.sc.gov/managed/heritage/glassymtn/description.html
Management: South Carolina Department of Natural Resources (803) 734-9100
Nearest town: Pickens, Pickens County, South Carolina.

SAVANNAH RIVER BLUFFS HERITAGE PRESERVE

Features: A short (1.5 mile) trail traverses a variety of communities, including oak-hickory forest, basic mesic forest, river bluff forest, and alluvial forest. The area is rich in species, including the rare rocky shoals spider lily (*Hymenocallis coronaria*), and the federally listed relict trillium (*Trillium reliquum*). The preserve also harbors South Carolina's only known population of bottlebrush buckeye (*Aesculus parviflora*). Look for coastal plain species such as bald cypress (*Taxodium distichum*), dwarf palmetto (*Sabal minor*), and Spanish moss (*Tillandsia usneoides*) in the narrow floodplain along the Savannah River. Peak flowering is mid-March to mid-April.
Website: www.dnr.sc.gov/managed/heritage/savrivbluffs/description.html
Management: South Carolina Department of Natural Resources (803) 734-9100
Nearest town: North Augusta, Aiken County, South Carolina

FLAT CREEK HERITAGE PRESERVE (FORTY ACRE ROCK)

Features: This 1,600-acre preserve is the most diverse protected area in the piedmont of South Carolina. The site is best known for Forty Acre Rock (actually 14 acres), one of the largest granite flatrocks in the eastern United States. This and other outcrops on the site harbor numerous rare and unusual species, including the tiny, floating aquatic known as pool sprite (*Gratiola amphiantha*). A double loop trail traverses a granite flatrock, chestnut oak forest, oak-hickory forest, alluvial forest, and winds around a large beaver pond. Because the preserve overlaps the fall-line sandhills and piedmont regions, characteristic plants of xeric sandhills also occur, including longleaf pine (*Pinus palustris*) and turkey oak (*Quercus laevis*). A basic mesic forest with an exceptionally rich herbaceous layer occurs in an area known as Flat Creek Dike (located just across the abandoned bridge over old Highway 601). The best time to visit the preserve is from late March to early April when the outcrop plants are in peak bloom. Water lilies (*Nymphaea odorata*) cover the beaver pond in summer, and various sunflowers and other plants provide a burst of color from late summer to fall.
Website: www.dnr.sc.gov/managed/heritage/fortyacrock/description.html
Management: South Carolina Department of Natural Resources (803) 734-9100
Nearest town: Kershaw, Lancaster County, South Carolina

STEVENS CREEK HERITAGE PRESERVE

Features: Spectacular wildflower displays makes this 434-acre preserve one of the most interesting botanical sites in the entire piedmont region. The rich diversity of wildflowers reflects the underlying bedrock, which weathers to produce a calcium-rich soil that is almost neutral (basic). Wildflowers such as spring beauty (*Claytonia virginica*), Dutchman's britches (*Dicentra cucullaria*), dimpled trout lily (*Erythronium umbilicatum*), round-lobed hepatica (*Hepatica americana*), and shooting star (*Primula meadia*) provide colorful displays on the north-facing river bluffs and adjacent basic mesic forest in early spring. Other communities include oak-hickory forest and a narrow strip of floodplain forest with some large trees and interesting herbaceous plants such as lanceleaf trillium (*Trillium lancifolium*) and wild ginger (*Asarum canadense*). The preserve harbors more than a dozen rare plants, including the federally threatened Miccosukee gooseberry (*Ribes echinellum*), known from only one other site near Lake Miccosukee, Florida. The best time to visit Stevens Creek is from late-March to mid-April. A relatively easy 2-mile loop trail traverses the site.
Website: www.dnr.sc.gov/managed/heritage/stevenscr/description.html
Management: Department of Natural Resources (803) 734-9100
Nearest town: Clark's Hill, McCormick County, South Carolina

ROCK HILL BLACKJACKS HERITAGE PRESERVE

Features: A flat 2-mile loop trail winds through several interesting communities in this 291-acre preserve. Prairie-like grasslands include a number of species more typically associated with midwestern prairies (including prairie dock, *Silphium terebinthinaceum*, which has huge basal leaves and tall flowering stems). Another unusual community is xeric hardpan forest, whose dominant tree, blackjack oak (*Quercus marilandica*), gives this site its name. Xeric hardpan forest occurs on shallow, nearly neutral (basic) soils that are typically wet and muddy in winter and dry and hard in summer. Small, scattered ephemeral springs with wetland species such as blackfoot quillwort (*Isoetes melanopoda*) occur in hardpan areas, as do open forests (glades)

with eastern red cedar (*Juniperus virginiana*) and other drought-tolerant species on especially rocky areas. The unusual flora of this preserve includes more than 20 rare plants, including the federally listed Schweinitz's sunflower (*Helianthus schweinitzii*). While many wildflowers bloom in spring, the most colorful displays occur from late summer to fall when the prairie-like habitats are in full bloom.
Website: www.dnr.sc.gov/managed/heritage/rockhlblkjacks/description.html
Management: South Carolina Department of Natural Resources (803) 734-9100
Nearest town: Rock Hill, York County, South Carolina

Tennessee Mountains

ROAN MOUNTAIN MASSIF

Features: Straddling the Tennessee and North Carolina border, the Roan Mountain Massif is undoubtedly one of the most scenic and interesting natural areas in the southern Appalachians. The word "massif" refers to Roan Mountain being a large mountain mass consisting of multiple peaks, the highest of which is 6,286 ft. tall. The area harbors an exceptional diversity of species as well as the largest expanse of grassy balds in the southern Appalachians. Unfortunately, various shrubs are invading the grassy balds, threatening to turn them into shrub balds. To prevent this, a combination of mowing and grazing (goats and cattle) are being used on various parts of the massif. The best-known heath bald is the 600-acre Rhododendron Gardens, where massive displays of the pink-purplish flowers of Catawba rhododendron (*Rhododendron catawbiense*) provide a spectacular sight in mid-June. Downslope from the balds and spruce-fir forest, stands of northern hardwood forest occur with yellow birch (*Betula alleghaniensis*), yellow buckeye (*Aesculus flava*), and American beech (*Fagus grandifolia*). Spreading avens (*Geum radiatum*), Gray's lily (*Lilium grayi*), and mountain sandwort (*Minuartia groenlandica*) are just a few of the more than 30 rare or endangered plants known from Roan Mountain.
Web: www.cs.unca.edu/nfsnc/recreation/roanmtn.pdf
Management: Cherokee National Forest, Unaka Ranger District
(423) 638-4109 in Tennessee and the Pisgah National Forest, Appalachian Ranger District (828) 682-6146 in North Carolina.
Nearest town: Roan Mountain, Carter County, Tennessee (and Bakersville, Mitchell County, North Carolina)

GREAT SMOKY MOUNTAINS NATIONAL PARK

Features: The broad crest of the Great Smoky Mountains extends into both Tennessee and North Carolina. This park is considered to have the most species-rich temperate forests in the eastern United States, the largest stands of original-growth forest in the southern Appalachians, and more species of vascular plants (more than 1,500) than any other U.S. National Park. The 130 species of trees in the Smokies is roughly equivalent to the number in all of Europe. A good place to begin is the interpretative center at the Sugarlands visitor center (near Gatlinburg). Exceptional wildflower sites (especially in early spring) on the Tennessee side of the park include the Cove Hardwood Nature Trail (an easy three-quarter mile loop trail through an old-growth rich cove forest), the first half-mile or so of the Chestnut Top trail, and the Porter's Creek trail. Clingman's Dome, the highest point in the park at an elevation of 6,643 ft., has an observation deck that overlooks a spruce-fir forest. The many dead gray trunks are Fraser firs that were killed by balsam woolly adelgids. The most accessible grassy

bald in the park is Andrews Bald, which can be reached by a 3.2 mile round-trip trail that begins near Clingman's Dome (peak bloom is mid-June). On the North Carolina side of the park, the Bradley Fork trail and the Kephart Prong trail are good sites for spring wildflowers.
Web: www.nps.gov/grsm
Management: National Park Service (865) 436-1200
Nearest town: Gatlinburg, Sevier County, Tennessee (and Cherokee, Cherokee County, North Carolina)

BAYS MOUNTAIN PARK AND NATURAL AREA

Features: Located in the ridge and valley physiographic province of eastern Tennessee, this 3,500-acre natural area occurs along the crest of two mountains that form a spectacular forested basin. Variation in underlying bedrock (made up of limestone, shale, and sandstone), slope, aspect, and moisture contribute to the diversity of plants and natural communities represented. Pine-oak-heath covers the relatively dry, nutrient-poor soils on upper slopes and ridges, whereas rich cove forests occur on moist, nutrient-rich soils over limestone. Moist areas with more acidic, less nutrient-rich soils typically have acidic cove forests with abundant heath shrubs and a low density and diversity of herbaceous plants. The park includes a nature center, 25 miles of hiking trails, and a large lake.
Web: www.baysmountain.com
Management: City of Kingsport (423) 229-9447
Nearest town: Kingsport, Sullivan County, Tennessee

FALL CREEK STATE PARK AND NATURAL AREA

Features: More than half of this 25,000-acre state park in the Cumberland Plateau has been designated a natural area. Among the highlights are species-rich forests, cascading streams, deep gorges, waterfalls, caves, and a large lake. Fall Creek Falls, which drops 256 ft., is one of the tallest waterfalls east of the Rocky Mountains. Several other waterfalls in the park are equally impressive. Oak-hickory forest covers much of the tabletop plateaus above the falls, whereas rich cove forest commonly occurs in the moist, sheltered gorges below. Among the many trees in the cove forest are tulip poplar (*Liriodendron tulipifera*), basswood (*Tilia* sp.), yellow buckeye (*Aesculus flava*), northern red oak (*Quercus rubra*), white oak (*Q. alba*), eastern hemlock (*Tsuga canadensis*), and American beech (*Fagus grandifolia*). The nature center includes interpretive exhibits on local ecology. About 25 miles of trails wind through the park.
Web: www.tnstateparks.com
Management: Fall Creek State Park (423) 881-5298
Nearest town: Spencer, Van Buren County, Tennessee

FROZEN HEAD STATE PARK AND NATURAL AREA

Features: This 13,000-acre state park and natural area in the Cumberland Mountains of Tennessee includes diverse vegetation, streams, waterfalls, and 14 peaks over 3,000 ft. It is also considered to be one of the best wildflower sites in Tennessee. The higher peaks are composed of hard, erosion-resistant rock that has remained in place while adjacent areas of softer rock have gradually been worn down by wind, water, and other factors, resulting in an undulating landscape of ridges and valleys. Frozen Head Mountain, whose 3,324 ft. summit is often covered with snow or ice in winter, is the tallest mountain in the park. From an observation deck on the summit,

one can see the Cumberland Plateau to the west, the Great Smoky Mountains to the east, and the Tennessee Ridge and Valley Region on a clear day. At upper elevations, and on dry slopes and ridges, chestnut oak forest is common. Dominant canopy trees include chestnut oak (*Quercus montana*), scarlet oak (*Q. coccinea*), and shortleaf pine (*Pinus echinata*). Oak-hickory forest occurs on mid-slopes with white oak (*Q. alba*) as the dominant species. The deep hollows and valleys support rich cove forest with many kinds of trees and abundant wildflowers. The 4.2-mile Panther Branch trail is especially good for spring wildflowers.
Web: www.tnstateparks.com
Management: Frozen Head State Park (423) 346-3318
Nearest town: Wartburg, Morgan County, Tennessee

Georgia Mountains

CROCKFORD-PIGEON MOUNTAIN WILDLIFE MANAGEMENT AREA

Features: In the Cumberland Plateau of western Georgia, Pigeon Mountain is well known for its many caves and limestone rock formations as well as its magnificent wildflowers. The Shirley Miller Wildflower trail is an 800 ft. wheelchair-accessible boardwalk that loops through a rich cove forest. Nestled within the northwest-facing side of Pigeon Mountain, the site is kept cool and moist while lime-rich colluvium washed down from the limestone cliffs above creates a nearly neutral (basic) soil, supporting a rich diversity of plants. At the far end of the boardwalk, a spur trail continues along a stream that provides more stunning wildflower displays as well as scenic views of a wet-season waterfall cascading down the steep cliffs. The abundance and diversity of wildflowers, along with the presence of many rare species, make this one of the premier spring wildflower sites in Georgia. Peak flowering is mid-March through mid-April.
Website: www.n-georgia.com/wildlife.htm
Management: Georgia Department of Natural Resources,
Wildlife Resources Division (706) 295-6041.
Nearest town: LaFayette, Walker County, Georgia.

BRASSTOWN BALD AND BRASSTOWN BALD WILDERNESS AREA

Features: The 13,000-acre Brasstown Bald Wilderness area includes steep slopes, remote coves, and narrow valleys that contain an exceptional diversity of plant species. The wilderness area encircles Brasstown Bald, Georgia's highest mountain at 4,784 ft. As one ascends the steep but short (0.5-mile paved trail) from the parking area to the summit of Brasstown Bald, the trees get progressively shorter and a dwarf forest of old, twisted red and white oaks (*Quercus rubra* and *Q. alba*) appears. At the top of the mountain is a shrub bald that contains plants such as Catawba rhododendron (*Rhododendron catawbiense*) and mountain ash (*Sorbus americana*) as well as a visitor center with interpretative displays, and an observation deck with panoramic views of the surrounding mountains and piedmont. Just below the visitor center, on the north side of Brasstown Bald, is a northern hardwood forest with huge yellow birches (*Betula alleghaniensis*) covered with lichens, often dripping with condensation from the frequent cloud cover.
Website: www.fs.fed.us/conf/rec/btb_overview.shtml
Management: Brasstown Bald Visitor Information Center (706) 896-2556
Chattahoochee-Oconee National Forests (706) 745-6928
Nearest town: Hiawassee, Towns County, Georgia

TALLULAH GORGE STATE PARK

Features: Over millions of years, the Tallulah River has eroded hard quartzite rock into a chasm more than two miles long and nearly 1,000 ft. deep, forming one of the deepest and most spectacular gorges in the Southeast. The thin, rocky, acidic soils of the rim and upper slopes are covered with pine-oak-heath. Here, one can find table mountain pine (*Pinus pungens*) and Carolina hemlock (*Tsuga caroliniana*). Chestnut oak forests occur on slightly less xeric (dry) sites, whereas rich cove forests occur on cooler north-facing slopes with deeper soils. Mesic species such as sycamore (*Platanus occidentalis*), tag alder (*Alnus serrulata*), and Virginia willow (*Itea virginica*) occur along the river channel, while numerous ferns, mosses and herbaceous plants grow on rocks kept moist by the 5 major waterfalls in the gorge. Rare and unusual plants include persistent trillium (*Trillium persistens*), monkey face orchid (*Platanthera integrilabia*), and kidneyleaf grass of parnassus (*Parnassia asarifolia*). The interpretative center displays information on the natural and cultural history of the area. Visitors can hike rim trails to scenic overlooks and (with a permit) hike down to the floor of the gorge.
Website: www.gastateparks.org
Management: Jointly managed by the Georgia Department of Natural Resources and the Georgia Power Company. Contact the State Park Office at (706) 754-7970.
Nearest town: Tallulah Falls, Habersham and Rabun Counties, Georgia

SOSEBEE COVE

Features: This 175-acre rich cove forest features large trees and abundant wildflowers. The cove has the feel of an old-growth forest as some trees are over 100 years old (it was clearcut about 1900). Canopy trees include tulip tree (*Liriodendron tulipifera*) and yellow buckeye (*Aesculus flava*), as well as white basswood (*Tilia americana*), sweet and yellow birch (*Betula lenta* and *B. alleghaniensis*), and the fairly rare yellowwood (*Cladrastis kentukea*). The north-facing orientation of the cove helps keep the soil moist, thereby contributing to the rich diversity of wildflowers in spring (late March through April) with a second peak in late summer and fall when goldenrods, sunflowers, and woodland asters (*Solidago*, *Helianthus*, and *Symphyotrichum* spp.) bloom. A short (0.6 mile) loop trail crisscrosses Wolf Creek as it winds through the cove.
Website: www.fs.fed.us/wildflowers/regions/southern
Management: Chattahoochee-Oconee National Forests (706) 745-6928
Nearest town: Blairsville, Union County, Georgia

RABUN BALD

Features: Located in the northeast corner of Georgia, within a few miles of North Carolina to the north and South Carolina to the east, Rabun Bald is Georgia's second highest peak, at 4,696 ft. With no other large mountains nearby, the 360-degree view from the observation tower on the summit of Rabun Bald has been described as the best in Georgia. Rabun Bald's main ridgeline is the Eastern Continental Divide, separating waters draining east to the Atlantic Ocean from those draining west and southwest to the Mississippi River and the Gulf of Mexico. The Rabun Bald trail is a 2 mile (one-way) hike from the Beegum parking area to the summit. Communities include pine-oak heath, rich cove forest, and high-elevation rock outcrop. The spring wildflowers are exceptional.

Website: www.sherpaguides.com/georgia/mountains
Management: Chattahoochee National Forest (706) 782-3320
Nearest town: Sky Valley, Rabun County, Georgia

Georgia Piedmont

PANOLA MOUNTAIN STATE CONSERVATION PARK

Features: This unusual park near Atlanta was created to protect one of the least disturbed granite domes (or monadnocks) in the region. Panola Mountain is a smaller version of the well-known Stone Mountain. The peak is 940 ft. above sea level, rising 260 ft. above the South River, which flows on its northern border. The park includes an interpretive center and two short self-guided nature trails (the rock outcrop and micro-watershed trails), each of which provides information on plants, animals, geology, and the history of the area. To protect the ecology of Panola Mountain, the trail to the top of the mountain is available only on guided hikes by park naturalists (call ahead or check the website for scheduled hikes). The vegetation includes patches of lichens and mosses growing on bare rocks, while mats of low-growing plants occupy thin soils, including in vernal pools where floral displays range from white to pink to red, yellow, and blue. On slightly deeper soils, a mixture of herbaceous plants, shrubs, and small trees often occur, while forests of oaks, hickories, pines and other trees occupy the deepest soils.
Website: www.gastateparks.org
Management: Panola Mountain State Conservation Park (770) 389-7801
Nearest town: Stockbridge, Henry County, Georgia

ROCK AND SHOALS OUTCROP NATURAL AREA

Features: This granite outcrop is considered to be a flatrock, rather than a dome (monadnock), because the area of exposed rock is not elevated above the surrounding landscape. Too rocky to farm or build on, this small outcrop has apparently changed little over the last several hundred years. An easy one-half mile trail winds through a second growth mixed oak-pine forest, which in the 1930s was a cotton field (look for remnant terraces on the hillside above the trail). The trail follows a small stream, which it crosses at a small cascade, before entering an open woodland dominated by eastern red cedar (*Juniperus virginiana*) and little bluestem (*Schizachyrium scoparium*) and then reaching the outcrop. The outcrop can be wet in winter but is typically hot and dry in summer. Lichens and mosses form a mosaic on bare rock while flowering plants require at least some soil to survive. Among the showier wildflowers are the large yellow flowers of prickly pear cactus (*Opuntia humifusa*), the dark blue to purplish flowers of hairy spiderwort (*Tradescantia hirsuticaulis*), and the bright pink flowers of Appalachian rock pink (*Phemeranthus teretifolius*). Peak flowering is from late March to mid-April, with a second burst of color in late summer and fall.
Website: www.n-georgia.com/wildlife.htm#Region3
Management: Georgia's Wildlife Resources Division and Wildlife Management Areas (770) 918-6411
Nearest town: Athens, Clarke County, Georgia

FERNBANK FOREST

Features: This small (65-acre) remnant patch of original-growth forest represents a type of vegetation that once covered large areas of the piedmont, including metropolitan Atlanta. Most such forests have been lost over the last several centuries to farming, logging, and urban and suburban development. White oaks (*Quercus alba*) and tulip trees (*Liriodendron tulipifera*), some over 125 ft. tall, dominate the canopy. More loosely scattered but equally tall loblolly pines (*Pinus taeda*) also occur. Common understory species include flowering dogwood (*Cornus florida*) and eastern redbud (*Cercis canadensis*), along with numerous shrubs and herbaceous plants. The name of the forest reflects the many ferns indigenous to the site. Many plants along trails in the forest are labeled. Call ahead or check the website for visiting hours. You may also want to visit the natural history museum in the main facility.
Website: www.fernbank.edu
Management: Fernbank Science Center (678) 874-7102
Nearest town: Atlanta, DeKalb County, Georgia

SWEETWATER CREEK STATE CONSERVATION PARK

Features: Highlights of this 2,500-acre conservation park include a cascading stream, a small lake, steep river bluffs, a rich diversity of plants, ruins of a Civil War–era textile mill, and a LEED-certified interpretive center. The landscape and plants are reminiscent of the mountains, yet downtown Atlanta is only 30 minutes away. Various trails meander through the park, including a 4-mile loop combining the white and red trails. From the parking area, the white trail traverses a mixed oak-pine forest to Jack's Hill Lake, which drops into a small cove with numerous spring wildflowers, including bloodroot (*Sanguinaria canadensis*), meadowrue (*Thalictrum thalictroides*), and giant chickweed (*Stellaria pubera*), along with dense clumps of cinnamon fern (*Osmunda cinnamomea*). Follow the trail along Sweetwater Creek to the factory ruins where an observation deck provides views of the creek, a small waterfall, and the piedmont landscape. The views are most stunning from mid- to late fall when the fall colors are at their peak. Along the creek, look for the yellow flowers of dimpled trout lily (*Erythronium umbilicatum*) in early spring and the bluish purple flowers of soapwort gentian (*Gentiana saponaria*) from mid- to late fall.
Website: www.georgiastateparks.org
Management: Sweetwater Creek State Conservation Park (770) 732-5871
Nearest town: Lithia Springs, Douglas County, Georgia

Suggested Reading

WILDFLOWERS

Alderman, J. A. 1997. *Wildflowers of the Blue Ridge Parkway*. Chapel Hill: University of North Carolina Press.

Bell, C. R., and A. H. Lindsey. 2005. *Seasonal Wildflowers of Eastern Forests* (DVD). Chapel Hill, N.C.: Laurel Hill Press.

Bentley, S. L. 2000. *Native Orchids of the Southern Appalachian Mountains*. Chapel Hill: University of North Carolina Press.

Campbell, C. C., A. J. Sharp, W. F. Hutson, and R. W. Hutson. 1996. *Great Smoky Mountains Wildflowers: When and Where to Find Them*. Northbrook, Ill.: Windy Pines Publishing.

Carman, J. B. 2001. *Wildflowers of Tennessee*. Tullahoma, Tenn.: Highland Rim Press.

Case, F. W., and R. B. Case. 1997. *Trilliums*. Portland, Ore.: Timber Press.

Chafin, L. G. 2007. *Field Guide to the Rare Plants of Georgia*. Athens: State Botanical Garden of Georgia.

Duncan, W. H., and M. B. Duncan. 1999. *Wildflowers of the Eastern United States*. Athens: University of Georgia Press.

Gupton, O. W., and F. C. Swope. 1979. *Wildflowers of the Shenandoah Valley and Blue Ridge Mountains*. Charlottesville: University Press of Virginia.

Hemmerly, T. E. 2000. *Appalachian Wildflowers*. Athens: University of Georgia Press.

Justice, W. S., C. R. Bell, and A. H. Lindsey. 2005. *Wild Flowers of North Carolina*. 2nd ed. Chapel Hill: University of North Carolina Press.

Midgley, J. W. 1999. *Southeastern Wildflowers*. Birmingham, Ala.: Crane Hill.

Murdy, W. H., and E. B. Carter. 2000. *Guide to the Plants of Granite Outcrops*. Athens: University of Georgia Press.

Nourse, H., and C. Nourse. 2000. *Wildflowers of Georgia*. Athens: University of Georgia Press.

———. 2007. *Favorite Wildflower Walks in Georgia*. Athens: University of Georgia Press.

Porcher, R. D., and D. A. Rayner. 2001. *A Guide to the Wildflowers of South Carolina*. Columbia: University of South Carolina Press.

Radford, A. E., H. E. Ahles, and C. R. Bell. 1968. *Manual of the Vascular Flora of the Carolinas*. Chapel Hill: University of North Carolina Press.

Smith, R. M. 1998. *Wildflowers of the Southern Mountains*. Knoxville: University of Tennessee Press.

Snyder, L. H., Jr., and J. G. Bruce. 1986. *Field Guide to the Ferns and Other Pteridophytes of Georgia*. Athens: University of Georgia Press.

White, P., T. Condon, J. Rock, C. A. McCormick, P. Beaty, and K. Langdon. 1996. *Wildflowers of the Smokies*. Gatlinburg, Tenn.: Great Smoky Mountains Natural History Association.

Wofford, B. E. 1989. *Guide to the Vascular Plants of the Blue Ridge*. Athens: University of Georgia Press.

TREES, SHRUBS, WOODY VINES

Duncan, W. H. 1975. *Woody Vines of the Southeastern United States*. Athens: University of Georgia Press.

Duncan, W. H., and M. B. Duncan. 1988. *Trees of the Southeastern United States*. Athens: University of Georgia Press.

Foote, L. E., and S. B. Jones Jr. 1989. *Native Shrubs and Woody Vines of the Southeast*. Portland, Ore.: Timber Press.

Kirkman, L. K., C. L. Brown, and D. L. Leopold. 2007. *Native Trees of the Southeast*. Portland, Ore.: Timber Press.

Lance, R. 2004. *Woody Plants of the Southeastern United States: A Winter Guide*. Athens: University of Georgia Press.

Peattie, D. C. 1966. *A Natural History of Trees of Eastern and Central North America*. New York: Bonanza Books.

Petrides, G. A. 1998. *A Field Guide to Eastern Trees*. Peterson Field Guide Series. Boston: Houghton Mifflin.

Swanson, R. E. 1994. *A Field Guide to the Trees and Shrubs of the Southern Appalachians*. Baltimore: John Hopkins University Press.

Wofford, B. E., and E. W. Chester. 2002. *Guide to the Trees, Shrubs, and Woody Vines of Tennessee*. Knoxville: University of Tennessee Press.

NATURAL HISTORY

Abrahamson, W. G., ed. 1989. *Plant-Animal Interactions*. New York: McGraw Hill.

Adams, K. 2004. *North Carolina's Best Wildflower Hikes*. Englewood, Colo.: Westcliffe Publishers.

Bell, C. R., and A. H. Lindsey. 2007. *Fall Color and Woodland Harvests*. Chapel Hill: University of North Carolina Press.

Braun, E. L. 1950. *Deciduous Forests of Eastern North America*. New York: Hafner.

Brown, F., and N. Jones, eds. 1996. *The Georgia Conservancy's Guide to the North Georgia Mountains*. 3rd ed. Atlanta: Georgia Conservancy.

Conners, J. A. 1988. *Shenandoah National Park: An Interpretive Guide*. Blacksburg, Va.: McDonald and Woodward.

Eastman, J. 1992. *The Book of Forest and Thicket: Trees, Shrubs, and Wildflowers of Eastern North America*. Mechanicsburg, Pa.: Stackpole Books.

Ellison, G., and E. Ellison. 2006. *Blue Ridge Nature Journal: Reflections on the Appalachian Mountains in Essays and Art*. Charleston, S.C.: Natural History Press.

Frankenberg, D., ed. 2000. *Exploring North Carolina's Natural Areas*. Chapel Hill: University of North Carolina Press.

Frick-Ruppert, J. 2010. *Mountain Nature: A Seasonal Natural History of the Southern Appalachians*. Chapel Hill: University of North Carolina Press.

Gaddy, L. L. 2000. *A Naturalist's Guide to the Southern Blue Ridge Front*. Columbia: University of South Carolina Press.

Godfrey, M. A. 1997. *Field Guide to the Piedmont*. Chapel Hill: University of North Carolina Press.

Houck, R. 1993. *A Natural History Guide: Great Smoky Mountains National Park*. Boston: Houghton Mifflin.

Kricher, J. 1998. *Eastern Forests*. Peterson Field Guide Series. Boston: Houghton Mifflin.

Martin, W. H., S. G. Boyce, and A. C. Echternacht, eds. 1993. *Biodiversity of the Southeastern United States: Upland Terrestrial Communities*. New York: Wiley and Sons.

McDaniel, L. 1998. *Highroad Guide to the North Carolina Mountains*. Marietta, Ga.: Longstreet Press.

Miller, J. H., and K. V. Miller. 2005. *Forest Plants of the Southeast and Their Wildlife Uses*. Athens: University of Georgia Press.

Shafale, M. P., and A. S. Weakley. 1990. *Classification of the Natural Communities of North Carolina*. Third Approximation. Raleigh, N.C.: North Carolina Natural Heritage Program, Division of Parks and Recreation, Department of Environment, Health, and Natural Resources.

Skeate, S. 2005. *A Nature Guide to Northwest North Carolina*. Boone, N.C.: Parkway Publishers.

Walker, L. C. 1990. *Forests: A Naturalist's Guide to Trees and Forest Ecology*. New York: Wiley.

Weidensaul, S. 2000. *Mountains of the Heart: A Natural History of the Appalachians*. Golden, Colo.: Fulcrum Publishing.

Wells, B. W. 2002. *The Natural Gardens of North Carolina*. Rev. ed. Chapel Hill: University of North Carolina Press.

Wharton, C. H. 1978. *The Natural Environments of Georgia*. Bulletin 114. Atlanta: Geologic and Water Resources Division and Resource Planning Section, Office of Planning and Research, Georgia Department of Natural Resources.

Websites

STATE NATIVE PLANT SOCIETIES

Georgia Native Plant Society
    www.gnps.org
North Carolina Native Plant Society
    www.ncwildflower.org
South Carolina Native Plant Society
    www.scnps.org
Tennessee Native Plant Society
    www.tnps.org
Virginia Native Plant Society
    www.vnps.org

OTHER BOTANICAL LINKS

Dendrology at Virginia Tech: Tree Fact Sheets
    www.dendro.cnre.vt.edu/dendrology/factsheets.cfm
Flora of the Southern and Mid-Atlantic States. Weakley, Alan S.
    www.herbarium.unc.edu/flora.htm
Georgia Botanical Society
    www.gabotsoc.org
Georgia Wildflowers
    www.plantbio.uga.edu/herbarium/herbarium/gaflowers/gaflrindex.htm
Great Smoky Mountains Wildflower Pilgrimage
    www.springwildflowerpilgrimage.org
Invasive Plants of the Southeast
    www.gaeppc.org/weeds/gpca.html
Native and Naturalized Plants of the Carolinas and Georgia
    www.namethatplant.net
Southeastern Flora
    www.southeasternflora.com
Wildflowers of the Southeastern United States
    www.2bnthewild.com/index2.shtml

Index of Scientific Plant Names

Page numbers for species profiles are shown in bold; page numbers in italic refer to the photo key.

Abies
  balsamea, 219
  fraseri, 20, 25, *31, 34, 39*, 105–9, 114, 120, 123, 129, **219**, 248, 262, 310, 479, 482, 489
Acer
  floridanum, 77, *84*, 182, 190, 193, **219–20**, 223
  leucoderme, 190, 220, 223
  negundo, *80*, 184–86, 188, **220–21**, 481
  pensylvanicum, *31, 42, 46, 50*, 109, 126–27, 129–30, 133, 136, 139, **221**, 223
  rubrum, *42, 54, 62, 66, 69, 72, 77, 80, 84, 88*, 124, 127, 141, 145, 157, 160–61, 164–66, 169–71, 176, 180, 182, 185, 188, 191, 193, 196–98, **222**, 258, 265, 425
  saccharum, *46, 50*, 129–31, 133, 136, 139, 220, **222–23**, 224
  saccharum ssp. floridanum. See Acer floridanum
  spicatum, *31, 46*, 106, 109, 130, 133, 221, **223–24**
Achillea millefolium, *35, 74, 100*, 111, 114, 175, 177, 212, 215, **325**
Aconitum reclinatum, 134
Actaea
  pachypoda, *52, 86*, 137, 139, 191, 194, **325–26**, 327
  racemosa, *48, 52, 86*, 130–31, 133, 136–39, 194, **326–27**
Adiantum
  capillus-veneris, 327
  pedatum, *52, 58, 86*, 139, 150, 194, **327**
Aesculus
  flava, 12, 21, *46, 50*, 129–30, 133, 136–39, **224–25**, 269, 489–90, 492
  glabra, 224
  octandra. See Aesculus flava
  parviflora, 274, 487
  pavia, 269
  sylvatica, *81, 85, 96*, 185, 188, 191, 194, 206, 209, **269**
Agalinis
  fasciculata, 328
  purpurea, *93*, 201, 203, **328**

Ageratina
  altissima, *32, 44, 48, 74*, 109, 125, 128, 130–31, 133, 175, 177, **328–29**
  aromatica, 329
Albizia julibrissin, *99*, 212, 216, **225**
Alliaria petiolata, 140
Allium tricoccum, *52*, 137, 139, **329–30**
Alnus serrulata, *59, 63, 81*, 152, 154, 157–58, 160–61, 189, **269–70**, 492
Ambrosia
  artemisiifolia, *101*, 212–13, 215, **330–31**
  trifida, 185, 330
Amelanchier
  arborea, 225–26
  arborea var. laevis. See Amelanchier laevis
  laevis, *31, 34, 39, 46*, 109, 111, 114, 120, 123, 125, 130, 133, **225–26**
Amianthium muscitoxicum, *68*, 165, 167, **331**
Amphianthus pusillus. See Gratiola amphiantha
Amphicarpaea bracteata, *90*, 199, **331–32**
Andropogon
  gerardii, 479
  scoparius. See Schizachyrium scoparium
  virginicus, *93, 97, 101*, 201, 203, 206, 209, 212–13, 215, **332–33**
Anemone
  acutiloba. See Hepatica acutiloba
  quinquefolia, *52*, 139, **333**
Anemonella thalictroides. See Thalictrum thalictroides
Angelica
  triquinata, *35*, 111, 114, **333–34**, 483
  venenosa, 334
Anisostichus capreolata. See Bignonia capreolata
Aplectrum hyemale, 453
Aquilegia canadensis, *97*, 210, **334–35**
Aralia spinosa, *73*, 174–75, 177, **270–71**
Arenaria
  glabra. See Minuartia glabra
  groenlandica. See Minuartia groenlandica
Arethusa bulbosa, 160
Arisaema
  dracontium, 335

triphyllum, 48, 52, 56, 83, 133, 137, 139, 143, 146, 189, **335**, 475, 485
Aristolochia
  macrophylla, 47, 51, 73, 130–31, 133, 139, 174–75, 177, **271–72**, 276, 297, 352
  tomentosa, 271
Aronia
  arbutifolia, 157, 272
  melanocarpa, 36, 39, 63, 116, 118, 123, 157, 161, **272**
Aruncus dioicus, 48, 74, 133, 175, 177, **336**
Arundinaria
  appalachiana, 67, 73, 89, 165, 167, 177, 199, **272–73**
  gigantea, 59, 82, 154, 185, 188, **273–74**
Asarum canadense, 52, 86, 139, 191, 194, **336–37**, 387, 488
Asclepias
  syriaca, 75, 175, 177, **337–38**
  tuberosa, 94, 101, 201, 203, 213, 215, **338**
Asimina
  parviflora, 274
  triloba, 51, 82, 85, 136–37, 139, 185, 189, 191, 194, **274**, 480
Asplenium
  ebenoides, 340
  montanum, 40, 58, 123, 150, 181, **339**, 340
  pinnatifidum, 340
  platyneuron, 340
  rhizophyllum, 58, 86, 150, 194, **339–40**
  trichomanes, 150
Aster
  acuminata. See *Oclemena acuminata*
  divaricatus var. *chlorolepis*. See *Eurybia chlorolepis*
  macrophyllus. See *Eurybia macrophylla*
Astilbe biternata, 336
Athyrium
  asplenioides, 32, 44, 106, 109, 128, **340**
  filix-femina ssp. *asplenioides*. See *Athyrium asplenioides*
Aureolaria
  flava, 341
  laevigata, 68, 71, 90, 164, 167, 169, 172, 199, **341**
  virginica, 341
Avenella flexuosa, 35, 40, 110, 114, 123, **341–42**

Baptisia minor var. *aberrans*, 485
Betula
  alleghaniensis, 12, 31, 39, 42, 46, 54, 62, 106, 109, 120, 123, 127, 129, 130–31, 133, 141, 143–45, 161, 186, 197, **226–27**, 228, 377, 482–83, 489, 491–92
  cordifolia, 109
  lenta, 50, 54, 136, 139, 141, 143–45, 186, 227, 228, 377, 492
  lutea. See *Betula alleghaniensis*
  nigra, 17, 59, 80, 152, 154, 184–86, 188, 228
Bignonia capreolata, 82, 96, 174, 185, 189, 208–9, **275**
Boehmeria cylindrica, 395
Botrychium virginianum. See *Botrypus virginianus*
Botrypus virginianus, 78, 180, 182, 327, **342**
Boykinia aconitifolia, 150
Buckleya distichophylla, 479

Calopogon tuberosus, 158
Caltha palustris, 157, 162
Calycanthus floridus, 51, 59, 86, 136–37, 139, 154, 191, 194, **275–76**
Campanula americana. See *Campanulastrum americanum*
Campanulastrum americanum, 61, 153, 155, **343**
Campsis radicans, 99, 213, 215, 275, **276–77**
Carex
  brunnescens, 111
  pensylvanica, 32, 35, 44, 48, 109, 111, 114, 128, 130, 133, **343–44**
  torta, 61, 152, 154–55, **344–45**
Carpinus caroliniana, 50, 81, 84, 136, 139, 185, 188, 190, 193, **228–29**, 246, 351
Carya
  carolinae-septentrionalis, 200, 203
  glabra, 66, 88, 92, 166, 196–98, 200, 203, **229–30**
  ovata, 81, 88, 185–86, 188, 198, **230**
  tomentosa, 66, 88, 164, 166, 196–98, **231**
Castanea
  dentata, 11, 14, 16, 25, 42, 66, 69, 124–27, 144, 163–64, 166, 171, 181, 197, **231–32**, 233
  pumila, 171
Castilleja coccinea, 97, 210, **345**
Caulophyllum thalictroides, 48, 52, 130, 133, 136–37, 139, 191, **345–46**
Celastrus
  orbiculatus, 47, 73, 134, 177, **277**
  scandens, 277
Celtis laevigata, 81, 85, 188, 193, **232–33**

Cephalanthus occidentalis, 59, 154, **278**
Cercis canadensis, 85, 88, 92, 191, 193, 196, 198, 201, 203, 225, **233–34**, 494
Chamaelirium luteum, 78, 180, 182, **346–47**
Chasmanthium latifolium, 83, 185, 189, **347**
Cheilanthes lanosa, 207, 210
Chelone
    glabra, 61, 153, 155, **347–48**
    lyonii, 32, 107, 109, **348–49**
Chimaphila
    maculata, 68, 71, 78, 90, 165, 167, 169, 172, 183, 192, 199, **349**
    umbellata, 349
Chionanthus virginicus, 92, 95, 201, 203, 206, 208–9, **234**, 481
Cimicifuga racemosa. See *Actaea racemosa*
Cirsium carolinianum, 480
Cladina rangiferina, 97, 206, 210, **350**
Cladrastis kentukea, 50, 136, 139, **234–35**, 492
Claytonia
    caroliniana, 48, 52, 130, 133, 139, **350–51**
    virginica, 83, 86, 132, 186, 189, 191–92, 194, 350, **351–52**, 387, 488
Clematis
    ochroleuca, 201, 203
    viorna, 44, 94, 125, 128, **352**
Clethra
    acuminata, 36, 60, 67, 116, 118, 154, 165, 167, **278–79**
    alnifolia, 279
Clintonia
    borealis, 32, 106, 109, **352–53**
    umbellulata, 44, 52, 125–26, 128, 137, 139, **353–54**
Collinsonia verticillata, 140
Commelina
    communis, 354
    diffusa, 354
    erecta, 94, 97, 201, 204, 208, 210, **354**
    virginica, 354
Conium maculatum, 334
Conopholis americana, 44, 91, 128, 196, 199, **355**
Conyza canadensis, 212
Corallorhiza maculata, 134
Coreopsis major, 71, 75, 94, 101, 169, 172, 175, 177, 204, 215, **355–56**
Cornus
    alternifolia, 43, 47, 125–26, 128, 133, **279**
    amomum, 60, 82, 152, 154, 185–86, 189, **280**
    florida, 19, 50, 77, 85, 88, 136–37, 139, 180, 182, 190–91, 193, 196, 198, **235–36**, 279, 306, 494
Cortaderia, 444
Corylus
    americana, 125, 281
    cornuta, 43, 67, 125, 128, 167, **280–81**
Crataegus macrosperma, 34, 42, 111, 114, 125–27, **236**
Cuscuta rostrata, 38, 116, 118, **356–57**
Cymophyllus fraserianus, 56, 58, 142, 146, 150, **357**
Cypripedium
    acaule, 71, 91, 169, 172, 199, **357–58**, 359
    calceolus var. *pubescens*. See *Cypripedium parviflorum*
    parviflorum, 52, 87, 140, 191, 194, **358–59**

Danthonia
    compressa, 35, 40, 110, 114, 123, **359–60**
    spicata, 201, 203
Decumaria barbara, 55, 142–43, 146, 174, **281**
Dennstaedtia punctilobula, 35, 44, 48, 68, 114, 128, 130, 133, 142, 164, 167, **360**, 452, 455
Deschampsia
    cespitosa, 342
    flexuosa. See *Avenella flexuosa*
Desmodium nudiflorum, 79, 91, 182, 199, **361**
Diamorpha smallii, 97, 206–7, 209, **361–62**, 389, 404
Dicentra
    canadensis, 362
    cucullaria, 52, 87, 139, 191–92, 194, **362–63**, 480, 488
Diervilla
    lonicera, 282
    sessilifolia, 37, 40, 116, 118, 121, 123, **282**
Dioscorea
    polystachya, 363
    villosa, 44, 125, 128, **363–64**
Diospyros virginiana, 92, 95, 99, 201, 203, 209, 215, **237**, 321
Diphasiastrum
    digitatum, 91, 199, **364**
    tristachyum, 364
Diphylleia cymosa, 48, 130–31, 133, **364–65**
Dodecatheon meadia. See *Primula meadia*
Drosera rotundifolia, 64, 158, 162, **365–66**
Dryopteris
    campyloptera, 33, 44, 106, 109, 128, **366**

expansa, 366
intermedia, 366

Echinacea
laevigata, 91, 94, 196, 199, 202, 204, 214, **367**, 485
purpurea, 367
Elaeagnus
pungens, 283
umbellata, 93, 100, 138, 201, 204, 212, 216, **282–83**
Epifagus virginiana, 48, 79, 130, 133, 180, 183, 238, **367–68**
Epigaea repens, 38, 56, 68, 71, 116, 118, 146, 164, 167, 169, 172, **368–69**
Equisetum, 364
Erigeron
annuus, 212
pulchellus, 56, 75, 142–43, 146, 177, **369**
Eriophorum virginicum, 160
Eryngium yuccifolium, 94, 201–2, 204, 214, **370**, 480
Erythronium
americanum, 371
umbilicatum, 48, 79, 83, 87, 97, 133, 180, 182, 185, 189, 191–92, 194, 210, **370–71**, 488, 494
Euonymus
americanus, 55, 78, 82, 143, 146, 180–82, 185, 189, **283–84**, 471
atropurpureus, 183
Eupatorium fistulosum. See *Eutrochium fistulosum*
Eupatorium rugosum. See *Ageratina altissima*
Euphorbia purpurea, 478
Eurybia
chlorolepis, 33, 75, 107, 109, 177, **371–72**
macrophylla, 44, 125, 128, **372**
Eutrochium
fistulosum, 61, 64, 75, 152, 155, 162, 175, 177, **373**
maculatum, 373
purpureum, 128

Fagus grandifolia, 12, 17, 19, 21, 46, 50, 55, 77, 85, 129–30, 132–33, 136, 138–39, 141, 144–45, 179–82, 190, 193, 197, 226, **237–38**, 368, 480, 484–85, 489–90
Festuca arundinacea, 157

Fothergilla major, 158, 167
Fragaria
chiloensis, 374
vesca, 374
virginiana, 35, 75, 101, 111, 114, 177, 212, 215, **373–74**
Fraxinus
americana, 46, 50, 92, 129, 133, 136, 139, 141, 200, 203, **238–39**, 259, 485
pennsylvanica, 185, 188

Galax
aphylla. See *Galax urceolata*
urceolata, 38, 44, 56, 58, 68, 71, 116, 118, 128, 142, 146, 150, 165, 167, 169, 172, 181, **374–75**, 438
Galearis spectabilis, 53, 137, 139, **375**
Galium aparine, 83, 101, 189, 215, **376**
Gaultheria procumbens, 38, 41, 64, 68, 71, 116, 118, 123, 159, 162, 164, 167, 169, 172, **376–77**
Gaylussacia
baccata, 118, 284
ursina, 43, 67, 70, 128, 164–65, 167, 169, 171, **284**
Gelsemium sempervirens, 90, 96, 174, 196, 199, 206, 208–9, **285**
Gentiana
austromontana, 114
clausa, 377
saponaria, 64, 158, **377–78**, 494
Gentianella quinquefolia, 111, 114
Geranium maculatum, 53, 79, 140, 180, 183, **378**
Geum
peckii, 379
radiatum, 38, 41, 118, 121, 123, **379**, 489
Gillenia stipulata, 480
Gleditsia triacanthos, 225
Goodyera
pubescens, 68, 91, 165, 167, 199, **379–80**
repens, 380
Gratiola amphiantha, 97, 206–7, 210, **380–81**, 488
Grimmia laevigata, 41, 97, 120, 123, 206, 209, **381**

Habenaria
blephariglottis var. *integrilabia*. See *Platanthera integrilabia*
ciliaris. See *Platanthera ciliaris*

502

Halesia
   diptera, 239
   carolina. See *Halesia tetraptera*
   tetraptera, *51*, *55*, *77*, 136–39, 142–43, 146, 180, 182, **239**
Hamamelis virginiana, *43*, 125–26, 128, 142, **285–86**
Hedera helix, 174, 281, 471
Helianthus
   porteri, 208, 210
   schweinitzii, *94*, 201-2, 204, 214, **382**, 489
   strumosus, *75*, *94*, 175, 177, 201, 204, **382–83**
Helonias bullata, *64*, 156–58, 162, **383–84**
Heloniopsis, 383
Hepatica
   acutiloba, *53*, *79*, *87*, 136, 140, 180, 183, 191, 194, **384–85**, 487
   americana, 384, 458, 488
Heterotheca
   latifolia, 212
   nervosa. See *Pityopsis graminifolia*
Heuchera
   americana, 386
   parviflora, *58*, 148, 150, **385**, 386
   villosa, *41*, 121, 123, **385–86**
Hexastylis
   arifolia, *79*, *91*, 180, 182, 199, **386–87**
   shuttleworthii, *56*, 142, 146, 337, **387**
Hieracium venosum, 199
Holcus lanatus, 110–11, 114, 157
Houstonia
   caerulea, 152, 388
   serpyllifolia, *35*, *58*, *61*, 111, 114, 148, 150, 152, 155, **387–88**
Hudsonia montana, *40*, 120–23, **286–87**, 483
Huperzia porophila, 150
Hybanthus concolor, 140, 191
Hydrangea
   arborescens, *47*, *51*, *73*, *86*, 130, 133, 136, 139, 174–75, 177, 191, 194, **287**, 356, 483
   cinerea, 287
   radiata, 287
Hydrastis canadensis, *53*, 138, 140, **388–89**
Hymenocallis coronaria, 487
Hypericum
   buckleyi, *40*, 120–21, 123, **287–88**, 483
   gentianoides, *97*, 206–8, 210, **389**
   hypericoides, 201, 203
   perforatum, *101*, 111, 215, **390**
Hypopitys, 407

Ilex
   montana, *31*, *43*, 109, 125–26, 128, **288–89**
   opaca, *55*, *77*, *81*, 146, 180–82, 185, 188, **239–40**, 288
   verticillata, *63*, 157, 159, 161, **289**
Impatiens
   capensis, *53*, *58*, *61*, 140, 148, 150, 153, 356, **390–91**, 480
   pallida, *48*, *61*, 130–31, 133, 153, 155, **391–92**, 480
Ipomoea
   batatas, 363, 393
   pandurata, *101*, 212, 215, **392–93**
Iris
   cristata, 393
   verna, *69*, 164, 167, **393**
Isoetes, 201, 206
   melanopoda, 488
   piedmontana, 210
Isotrema macrophyllum. See *Aristolochia macrophylla*
Itea virginica, *60*, *82*, 152, 154, 189, **289–90**, 492

Juglans
   cinerea, 240–41
   nigra, *81*, *85*, 185, 188, 193, **240–41**
Juniperus
   communis var. *depressa*, 241
   virginiana, *92*, *95*, *99*, 201, 203, 206, 209, 212, 215, **241–42**, 362, 489, 493
Justicia americana, *61*, 155, **393–94**

Kalmia
   buxifolia, *37*, *40*, 116, 118, 120–21, 123, 286, **290–91**, 483
   carolina, 160
   latifolia, *34*, *37*, *40*, *43*, *55*, *57*, *60*, *63*, *67*, *70*, *73*, *78*, 111, 114, 116, 118, 120, 123, 125, 128, 142–43, 146, 148, 150, 154, 157, 161, 164–65, 167, 169–71, 177, 181–82, 263, 265, **291–92**, 296, 357, 374, 408, 438, 479, 483
Krigia montana, 121, 123, 152, 155

Lamium
   amplexicaule, *101*, 212, 215, **394**
   purpureum, 394
Laportea canadensis, *45*, *49*, *53*, 128, 131, 133, 136, 140, 391–92, **395**
Leiophyllum buxifolia. See *Kalmia buxifolia*

Lespedeza, 301
  bicolor, 204
Leucothoe
  axillaris, 292
  axillaris var. *editorum*. See *Leucothoe fontanesiana*
  fontanesiana, 56, 60, 63, 82, 142–43, 146, 152, 154, 161, 186, 189, **292**
Liatris
  helleri, 41, 121–23, **396**, 483
  microcephala, 208, 210
  pilosa, 204
  squarrulosa, 485
Ligustrum
  japonicum, 293
  sinense, 56, 74, 82, 96, 100, 138, 145–46, 174–75, 177, 188–89, 193, 209–10, 212, 216, **292–93**, 384, 459
Lilium
  grayi, 35, 64, 111, 114, 156, 158, 162, **396–97**, 479, 489
  michauxii, 72, 169, 172, **397–98**
  superbum, 75, 175, 177, 397, **398**
Lindera benzoin, 51, 82, 86, 136–37, 139, 142, 175, 185–86, 189, 191, 194, **293–94**, 306
Liquidambar styraciflua, 17, 22, 72, 81, 89, 92, 99, 174, 176, 181, 185–86, 188, 193, 198, 203, 212, 215, **242**, 252, 480
Liriodendron
  chinense, 142
  tulipifera, 17, 51, 55, 66, 72, 77, 81, 85, 89, 99, 127, 136, 138–39, 141–43, 145, 157, 165–66, 174–76, 180–82, 185, 188, 190–91, 193, 196–97, 199, 212, 215, **242–43**, 258–59, 484–85, 490, 492, 494
Listera smallii, 142, 146
Lobelia cardinalis, 61, 153, 155, **399**
Lonicera
  japonica, 14, 74, 82, 86, 90, 93, 100, 174, 177, 180, 185, 188–89, 193–94, 196, 199, 201, 204, 212–13, 216, **294–95**, 459
  sempervirens, 78, 180, 182, **295**
Lotus helleri, 202, 204
Lycopodium flabelliforme. See *Diphasiastrum digitatum*
Lysimachia
  fraseri, 146
  quadrifolia, 35, 45, 111, 114, 125, 128, **399–400**
Lythrum alatum, 480

Magnolia
  acuminata, 46, 51, 55, 85, 133, 136, 139, 146, 191, 193, **243–44**
  fraseri, 51, 55, 136, 139, 142–44, 146, **244–45**
  macrophylla, 183, 191, 194
  tripetala, 243
Maianthemum
  canadense, 33, 45, 109, 125, 128, **400–401**
  racemosum, 49, 53, 69, 75, 130–31, 133, 140, 167, 177, 400, **401**, 428
Marchantia sp., 58, 148, 150, **402**
Medeola virginiana, 56, 69, 146, 167, **402–3**
Menispermum canadense, 191
Menziesia pilosa, 32, 37, 40, 63, 109, 116, 118, 123, 161, **295–96**
Micranthes
  caroliniana, 478
  petiolaris, 41, 58, 120–21, 123, 150, **403**
Microstegium vimineum, 53, 61, 83, 94, 140, 145, 155, 188–89, 204, **403–4**, 481
Minuartia
  glabra, 97, 206–7, 210, 389, **404–5**
  groenlandica, 35, 41, 114, 121–23, 404, **405**, 479, 489
  uniflora, 404
Miscanthus, 444
Mitchella repens, 57, 142–43, 146, **405**
Monarda didyma, 49, 130–31, 133, **406–7**
Monotropa
  hypopithys, 69, 164, 167, **407–8**
  uniflora, 91, 199, 407, **408–9**
Monotropsis odorata, 199
Morus
  alba, 245
  rubra, 81, 186, 188, **245**, 261, 480

Nuttallanthus canadensis, 206
Nymphaea odorata, 488
Nyssa sylvatica, 62, 66, 69, 73, 89, 157, 161, 164–66, 169–71, 177, 196, 199, 237, **245–46**, 306, 425

Oclemena acuminata, 33, 41, 45, 107, 109, 123, 128, **409**
Oenothera
  biennis, 101, 213, 215, **409–10**
  fruticosa, 58, 75, 94, 97, 148, 150, 175, 177, 201, 204, 210, **410–11**
Onoclea sensibilis, 64, 142, 162, **411**
Oplismenus hirtellus ssp. *undulatifolius*, 481

Opuntia
   compressa. See *Opuntia humifusa*
   humifusa, *98*, 208, 210, **412**, 493
Orchis spectabilis. See *Galearis spectabilis*
Osmunda
   cinnamomea, *61*, *65*, *83*, 152, 155, 157, 162, 189, 327, **412–13**, 494
   claytoniana, *45*, *65*, 128, 162, 327, **413–14**
   regalis, 152, 155, 185, 413
Ostrya virginiana, *51*, *77*, *85*, 136, 139, 180, 182, 190, 194, 229, **246–47**
Oxalis
   acetosella. See *Oxalis montana*
   montana, *33*, *58*, 106, 109, 150, **414**
   violacea, *79*, 183, **414–15**
Oxydendrum arboreum, 66, *70*, *73*, *77*, *89*, 167, 169, 171, 175, 177, 180, 182, 196, 199, 225, **247**

Packera
   anonyma, 415–16
   millefolium, *41*, *98*, 123, 208, 210, **415–16**
   tomentosa, *98*, 206–8, 210, **416–17**
Panax
   quinquefolius, *53*, *79*, *87*, 138, 140, 180, 183, 194, **417**
   trifolius, 417
Parnassia
   asarifolia, 65, 157–58, 162, **417–18**, 486, 492
   grandifolia, 418, 479
Parthenocissus quinquefolia, *74*, *82*, *100*, 142, 174, 177, 185, 189, 215, 281, **296–97**
Passiflora
   incarnata, *101*, 213, 215, **418–19**, 471
   lutea, 418
Paxistima canbyi, 478
Pedicularis canadensis, *45*, *69*, 125, 128, 167, **419**, 426
Pelargonium, 378
Phacelia
   fimbriata, *49*, 130, 133, **419–20**
   purshii, 420
Phemeranthus
   mengesii, 420, 421
   parviflorus, 421
   teretifolius, *98*, 201, 207–8, 210, **420–21**, 493
Philadelphus inodorus, 191
Phleum pratense, *35*, *65*, 111, 114, 157, 162, **421–22**

Phlox
   carolina, *75*, 175, 177, **422**
   latifolia, 111
Phoradendron serotinum, *74*, *90*, 177, 196, 199, **297–98**
Physostegia virginiana, 152, 155, 202
Phytolacca americana, *101*, 212, 215, **422–23**
Picea rubens, *31*, *39*, *47*, *63*, 105–9, 120, 123–24, 129, 133, 157, 161, **248**, 482
Pieris floribunda, 118, 123, 479
Pinus
   echinata, 17, *89*, *92*, *96*, 169, 196, 199, 201, 203, 209, 212, **248–49**, 250, 252, 491
   elliottii, 252
   palustris, 468, 488
   pungens, *39*, *70*, 120, 123, 169–71, **249–50**, 471, 479, 483, 492
   rigida, *63*, *70*, 157, 161, 169–71, 249, **250**, 479, 483
   strobus, *55*, *63*, 66, *89*, 146, 157, 161, 164–65, 167, 181, 196–97, 199, **251**, 308
   taeda, 17, *73*, *96*, *99*, 176, 196, 209, 212, 215, **251–52**, 480, 494
   virginiana, *70*, *73*, *89*, *92*, *96*, *99*, 169, 171, 174, 176, 196, 199–200, 203, 209, 212, 215, **252–53**, 484
Pityopsis graminifolia, *72*, *91*, 169, 172, 199, **423–24**
Platanthera
   ciliaris, *65*, *75*, 162, 175, 177, **424**
   integrilabia, *65*, 156, 162, **425**, 492
Platanus occidentalis, 17, *59*, *81*, 152–54, 184–86, 188, **253**, 481, 485, 492
Pleopeltis polypodioides, *83*, 185, 189, **425–26**
Poa pratensis, 212
Podophyllum peltatum, *53*, *79*, *87*, 136–37, 140, 142, 180, 182, 194, 365, **426**, 485, 487
Podostemum ceratophyllum, *59*, *61*, 148, 150, 152, 155, **427**
Polygala paucifolia, *72*, 172, **427–28**
Polygonatum biflorum, *53*, *69*, *94*, 136–37, 140, 167, 204, 401, **428–29**, 480
Polygonum pensylvanicum, 152, 155
Polypodium
   polypodioides. See *Pleopeltis polypodioides*
   virginianum, 150, 426
Polystichum acrostichoides, *57*, *79*, *84*, *87*, 142, 146, 181–82, 185, 189, 192, 194, **429**

Polytrichum
   appalachianum, 120
   commune, 210
Populus
   deltoides, 484
   heterophylla, 185
Portulaca
   pilosa, 430
   smallii, 98, 210, **430**
Potentilla
   canadensis, 111, 114
   tridentata. See *Sibbaldiopsis tridentata*
Prenanthes
   roanensis, 128, 479
   serpentaria, 181, 183
Primula meadia, 87, 191, 194, **430–31**, 488
Prunella vulgaris, 76, 175, 177, **431–32**
Prunus
   pensylvanica, 22, 31, 34, 36, 106, 109, 111, 114, 116, 118, 131, **254**
   serotina, 51, 99, 137, 139, 212, 215, **254–55**, 259
Ptelea trifoliata, 86, 96, 191, 194, 209, **298**
Pteridium aquilinum, 36, 38, 72, 102, 114, 116, 118, 169, 172, 212, 215, 342, **432**
Pueraria montana, 14, 74, 90, 100, 174–75, 177, 199, 212–13, 216, 252, 277, **298–99**, 352, 459
Pyrularia pubera, 67, 164, 167, **299–300**

Quercus
   alba, 6, 66, 89, 93, 126, 164, 167, 195, 197, 199, 201, 203, 247, **255–56**, 259, 490–91, 494
   coccinea, 67, 70, 126, 163–66, 169–71, 196, 247, **256**, 258, 479, 483, 491
   falcata, 89, 196, 199, **257**
   ilicifolia, 479
   laevis, 488
   marilandica, 93, 200, 203, **257–58**, 488
   michauxii, 185, 188, 258, 480, 485
   montana, 42, 66, 67, 70, 124, 126, 128, 163–66, 169–71, 197, 247, **258–59**, 265, 479, 491
   phellos, 185, 201, 203, 480
   prinus. See *Quercus montana*
   rubra, 11, 39, 43, 55, 67, 78, 85, 123–24, 126–27, 129, 146, 164, 167, 179–82, 190, 194, 196–97, 258, **259–60**, 483, 485, 490–91

stellata, 89, 93, 126, 196, 199–200, 203, 253, **260**
velutina, 126, 164, 167, 196, 199

Rhododendron
   arborescens, 60, 152, 155, **300**, 305
   calendulaceum, 34, 37, 43, 67, 111, 114, 116, 118, 125, 128, 164, 167, **301**, 483
   canescens, 304
   catawbiense, 17, 32, 34, 37, 40, 43, 47, 56, 70, 107, 109, 111, 114, 116, 118, 120, 123, 125, 128, 133, 146, 169, 171, 181, **301–2**, 304, 481, 483, 489, 491
   maximum, 37, 43, 56–57, 60, 63, 67, 71, 115, 125, 128, 142–46, 148, 150, 152, 155, 157, 161, 164–65, 167, 169, 171, 186, 291, **302–3**, 304, 357–58, 374, 387, 438, 481
   minus, 68, 78, 96, 164, 167, 180, 182, 209, 291, **302**, **303**
   nudiflorum. See *Rhododendron periclymenoides*
   periclymenoides, 60, 78, 152, 155, 180, 182, 304
   vaseyi, 32, 37, 40, 108–9, 116, 118, 121, 133, **304–5**
   viscosum, 60, 63, 152, 155, 157–58, 161, **305**
Rhus
   aromatica, 201, 203
   copallinum, 96, 100, 209, 215, **306**, 307
   glabra, 100, 215, **306–7**
   radicans. See *Toxicodendron radicans*
Rhynchospora, 157
Ribes
   echinellum, 86, 191, 194, **307–8**, 483
   rotundifolium, 32, 47, 106, 109, 130, 133, 308
Robinia pseudoacacia, 22, 43, 73, 125, 127–28, 131, 138, 175, 177, **260–61**
Rosa
   carolina, 93, 201, 203, **308–9**
   multiflora, 100, 145, 212, 216, **309–10**
   palustris, 160–61
Rubus
   alleghaniensis, 32, 34, 37, 43, 47, 109, 111, 114, 116, 118, 128, 133, **310**
   canadensis, 109, 118, 310
   odoratus, 47, 74, 130, 133, 177, **311**
Rudbeckia
   hirta, 76, 94, 102, 175, 177, 204, 215, **432–33**
   laciniata, 36, 49, 62, 76, 111, 114, 133, 155, 175, 177, **433–34**

Rugelia nudicaulis, 108–9
Rumex, 395, 414
    acetosella, 111, 114

Sabal minor, 487
Sagittaria
    australis, 434
    latifolia, 65, 157–58, 162, **434**
Salix
    nigra, 60, 64, 82, 152, 154, 161, 186, 189, **311–12**
    sericea, 161
Sambucus
    canadensis, 60, 74, 83, 152, 154, 174–75, 177, 189, **312–13**
    racemosa, 32, 47, 106, 109, 133, 312, **313**
Sanguinaria canadensis, 53, 79, 87, 136–38, 140, 180, 183, 194, 387, **435**, 480, 485, 487, 494
Saponaria, 377
Sarracenia
    jonesii, 158, 162
    purpurea, 65, 158, 160, 162, **435–36**, 486
Sassafras albidum, 67, 70, 73, 89, 164–65, 167, 169–71, 175, 177, 196, 199, **261–62**
Saxifraga michauxii. See Micranthes petiolaris
Schizachyrium scoparium, 36, 41, 62, 95, 98, 114, 123, 152, 155, 203, 210, 214, 332, **436–37**, 481, 493
Scirpus, 480
Sedum pusillum, 206, 362
Selaginella
    rupestris, 210
    tortipila, 41, 120, 123, **437**, 483
Senecio millefolium. See Packera millefolium
Shortia galacifolia, 57, 142–43, 146, 149, **438**
Sibbaldiopsis tridentata, 36, 41, 111, 114, 122–23, **438–39**
Silene virginica, 76, 175, 177, **439**
Silphium
    compositum, 440
    terebinthinaceum, 95, 201–2, 204, 214, **440**, 485, 488
Smilacina racemosa. See Maianthemum racemosum
Smilax
    glauca, 71, 90, 169, 171, 199, **314**, 315
    herbacea, 45, 125–26, 128, **440–41**
    rotundifolia, 37, 68, 71, 74, 100, 118, 167, 169, 171, 174, 177, 215, **314–15**

Solanum carolinense, 102, 213, 215, 431, **441–42**
Solidago
    altissima, 102, 215, **442**
    curtisii, 45, 49, 128, 130–31, 133, **443**
    glomerata, 33, 36, 42, 109, 111, 114, 123, **443–44**
    simulans, 483
Sorbus
    americana, 31, 39, 106, 109, 123, **262–63**, 482, 491
    melanocarpa. See Aronia melanocarpa
Sorghastrum nutans, 62, 95, 152, 155, 202, 204, 214, **444**, 479
Sorghum halepense, 155
Sphagnum, 59, 65, 148, 150, 156–57, 162, 206, 318, **445**
Spigelia marilandica, 91, 196, 199, **445–46**
Spiraea tomentosa, 161
Spiranthes cernua, 65, 158, 162, **446–47**
Stellaria
    media, 212, 215, 447
    pubera, 49, 79, 84, 134, 180, 183, 189, **447**, 494
Stenanthium leimanthoides, 120
Symphyotrichum georgianum, 202, 204
Symplocarpus foetidus, 65, 157, 159, 162, **448**
Symplocos tinctoria, 70, 78, 143, 169, 171, 180, 182, **263**

Talinum teretifolium. See Phemeranthus teretifolius
Taraxacum
    officinale, 102, 212, 215, 226, **448–49**
    erythrospermum, 449
Taxodium distichum, 487
Tephrosia
    spicata, 449
    virginiana, 72, 95, 172, 201, 204, **449–50**
Thalictrum
    clavatum, 59, 148, 150, **450**
    thalictroides, 54, 136, 140, **451**, 485, 487, 494
Thelypteris noveboracensis, 45, 57, 128, 142, 146, 360, **451–52**
Thermopsis mollis, 167
Tiarella cordifolia, 54, 80, 87, 137, 140, 142, 180, 182, 194, **452–53**, 487
Tilia
    americana, 23, 47, 51, 129, 133, 136, 138–39, 141, **263–64**, 484, 492
    heterophylla. See Tilia americana

Tillandsia usneoides, 487
Tipularia discolor, 91, 192, 199, 330, **453**
Toxicodendron
   pubescens, 315
   radicans, 74, 83, 90, 100, 143, 174, 177, 185, 189, 199, 215, 220, 281, 296, **315–16**, 391–92
   vernix, 161
Tradescantia hirsuticaulis, 98, 206–8, 210, **453–54**, 493
Trautvetteria caroliniensis, 388
Trichophorum cespitosum, 122
Trifolium repens, 102, 111, 212, 215, **454–55**
Trillium
   catesbaei, 80, 91, 181, 183, 196, 199, **455**
   cuneatum, 87, 191, 194, **455–56**, 458, 487
   discolor, 87, 194, **456–57**, 458
   erectum, 45, 49, 126, 128, 130–31, 134, **457**, 460
   grandiflorum, 54, 137, 140, **457–58**
   lancifolium, 488
   luteum, 456, **458–59**
   reliquum, 80, 88, 183, 191, 194, **459**, 487
   undulatum, 33, 38, 106, 109, 116, 118, **459–60**, 483
   vaseyi, 54, 140, **460–61**
Tsuga canadensis, 14, 17, 21, 25, 55, 63, 78, 141, 143–45, 157, 161, 181–82, **264–65**, 483, 490
Tsuga caroliniana, 14, 25, 39, 70, 120, 123, 144, 171, 264, **265–66**, 492

Ulmus
   alata, 17, 81, 93, 96, 188, 201, 203, 209, **266**
   americana, 188, 485
   parviflora, 267
   rubra, 85, 190, 194, **266–67**
Umbilicaria
   mammulata, 42, 120, 123, **461–62**
   muehlenbergii, 461
Uniola
   latifolia. See *Chasmanthium latifolium*
   paniculata, 347
Utricularia, 206
   cornuta, 158
Uvularia
   grandiflora, 49, 130–31, 134, **462**, 463
   perfoliata, 80, 180, 183, **462–63**

Vaccinium
   arboreum, 90, 93, 96, 196, 199, 201, 203, 209, **316**

   corymbosum, 34, 37, 40, 64, 111, 114, 116, 118, 121, 123, 161, **317**
   erythrocarpum, 109, 118
   macrocarpon, 64, 157, 159–61, **317–18**, 431
   pallidum, 68, 71, 93, 164–65, 167, 169, 171, 196, 201, 203, **318**
   stamineum, 68, 71, 78, 90, 93, 164, 167, 169, 171, 180, 182, 196, 199, 201, 203, **319**
   vacillans. See *Vaccinium pallidum*
Veratrum
   viride, 33, 65, 107, 109, 157–58, 162, **463–64**
   parviflorum, 463
Verbascum
   blattaria, 464
   thapsus, 102, 213, 215, **464**
Vernonia
   amygdalina, 465
   noveboracensis, 62, 84, 153, 155, 185–86, 189, **465**
Viburnum
   acerifolium, 56, 83, 146, 189, **319–20**
   cassinoides, 37, 64, 116, 118, 157, 161, **320–21**
   lantanoides, 32, 44, 47, 106, 109, 128, 130, 133, **321**
   prunifolium, 201, 203
   rafinesquianum, 199, 203
Viola
   canadensis, 49, 54, 133, 137, 140, **465–66**
   hastata, 57, 80, 143, 146, 183, **466–67**
   sororia, 102, 212, 215, **467**
Vitis rotundifolia, 90, 100, 174, 196, 199, 215, **322**
Vittaria appalachiana, 148, 150

Woodwardia areolata, 160, 411

Xanthorhiza simplicissima, 57, 60, 64, 83, 150, 152, 154, 158, 161, 189, **322–23**
Xerophyllum asphodeloides, 42, 72, 120, 123, 169, 172, 331, **468**

Yucca filamentosa, 98, 208, 210, **468–69**

Zephyranthes atamasca, 84, 189, **469–70**, 435
Zingiber officinale, 337

Index of Common Plant Names

Page numbers for species profiles are shown in bold; page numbers in italic refer to the photo key.

Acute-lobed hepatica, *53, 79, 87,* 136, 140, 180, 183, 191, 194, **384–85**, 487
Allegheny blackberry, *32, 34, 37, 43, 47,* 109, 111, 114, 116, 118, 128, 133, **310**
Alternate leaf dogwood, *43, 47,* 125–26, 128, 133, **279**
Alumroot
    cave, *58,* 148, 150, **385**, 386
    common, 386
    rock, *41,* 121, 123, **385–86**
American beech, 12, 17, 19, 21, *46, 50, 55, 77, 85,* 129–30, 132–33, 136, 138–39, 141, 144–45, 179–82, 190, 193, 197, 226, **237–38**, 368, 480, 484–85, 489–90
American bittersweet, 277
American chestnut, 11, 14, 16, 25, *42, 66, 69,* 124–27, 144, 163–64, 166, 171, 181, 197, **231–32**, 483
American elm, 188, 485
American ginseng, *53, 79, 87,* 138, 140, 180, 183, 194, **417**
American hazelnut, 125, 281
American holly, *55, 77, 81,* 146, 180–82, 185, 188, **239–40**, 288
American mistletoe, *74, 90,* 177, 196, 199, **297–98**
American water willow, *61,* 155, **393–94**
Angelica
    filmy. *See* mountain angelica
    hairy, 334
    mountain, *35,* 111, 114, **333–34**, 483
Appalachian bluet, *35, 58, 61,* 111, 114, 148, 150, 152, 155, **387–88**
Appalachian dodder, *38,* 116, 118, **356–57**
Appalachian false goat's beard, 336
Appalachian golden banner, 167
Appalachian gooseberry, *32, 47,* 106, 109, 130, 133, **308**
Appalachian haircap moss, 120
Appalachian oak leach, *68, 71, 90,* 164, 167, 169, 172, 199, **341**
Appalachian rattlesnake root. *See* Mountain rattlesnake root
Appalachian rock pink, *98,* 201, 207–8, 210, **420–21**, 493

Appalachian sandwort, *97,* 206–7, 210, 389, **404–5**
Appalachian shoestring fern, 148, 150
Appalachian twayblade, 142, 146
Arrowhead, *65,* 157–58, 162, **434**
    southern, 434
Ash
    green, 185, 188
    white, *46, 50, 92,* 129, 133, 136, 139, 141, 200, 203, **238–39**, 259, 485
Ashy hydrangea, 287
Aster
    bigleaf, *44,* 125, 128, **372**
    Georgia, 202, 204
    mountain wood, *33, 75,* 107, 109, 177, **371–72**
    whorled, *33, 41, 45,* 107, 109, 123, 128, **409**
Atamasco lily, *84,* 189, **469–70**, 485
Autumn olive, *93, 100,* 138, 201, 204, 212, 216, **282–83**
Azalea
    clammy. *See* swamp azalea
    flame, *34, 37, 43, 67,* 111, 114, 116, 118, 125, 128, 164, 167, **301**, 483
    mountain, 304
    pinkshell, *32, 37, 40,* 108–9, 116, 118, 121, 123, **304–5**
    swamp, *60, 63,* 152, 155, 157–58, 161, **305**
    sweet, *60,* 152, 155, **300**, 305
    wild, *60, 78,* 152, 155, 180, 182, **304**

Bald cypress, 487
Balsam fir, 219
Beaked hazelnut, *43, 67,* 125, 128, 167, **280–81**
Beargrass, *98,* 208, 210, **468–69**. *See also* Turkeybeard
Bear huckleberry, *43, 67, 70,* 128, 164–65, 167, 169, 171, **284**
Bear oak, 479
Beechdrops, *48, 79,* 130, 133, 180, 183, 238, **367–68**
Beggar's ticks, *79, 91,* 182, 199, **361**

509

Bellwort
    large-flowered, *49*, 130–31, 134, **462**, 463
    perfoliate, *80*, 180, 183, **462–63**
Big bluestem, 479
Bigfruit hawthorn, *34*, *42*, 111, 114, 125–27, 236
Bigleaf aster, *44*, 125, 128, **372**
Bigleaf grass of parnassus, 418, 479
Bigleaf magnolia, 183, 191, 194
Bigroot morning glory, *101*, 212, 215, **392–93**
Birch
    cherry. *See* sweet birch
    mountain paper, 109
    river, 17, *59*, *80*, 152, 154, 184–86, 188, **228**
    sweet, *50*, *54*, 136, *139*, 141, 143–45, 186, **227**, 228, 377, 492
    yellow, 12, *31*, *39*, *42*, *46*, *54*, *62*, 106, 109, 120, 123, 127, 129, 130–31, 133, 141, 143–45, 161, 186, 197, **226–27**, 228, 377, 482–83, 489, 491–92
Bird-on-the-wing. *See* Fringed polygala
Bittersweet
    American, 277
    oriental, *47*, *73*, 134, 177, **277**
Blackberry
    Allegheny, *32*, *34*, *37*, *43*, *47*, 109, 111, 114, 116, 118, 128, 133, **310**
    smooth, 109, 118, 310
Black cherry, *51*, *99*, 137, 139, 212, 215, **254–55**, 259
Black chokeberry, *36*, *39*, *63*, 116, 118, 123, 157, 161, **272**
Black cohosh, *48*, *52*, *86*, 130–31, 133, 136–39, 194, **326–27**
Black-eyed Susan, *76*, *94*, *102*, 175, 177, 204, 215, **432–33**
Blackfoot quillwort, 488
Black gum, *62*, *66*, *69*, *73*, *89*, 157, 161, 164–66, 169–71, 177, 196, 199, 237, **245–46**, 306, 425
Blackhaw, 201, 203
Black huckleberry, 118, 284
Blackjack oak, *93*, 200, 203, **257–58**, 488
Black locust, 22, *43*, *73*, 125, 127–28, 131, 138, 175, 177, **260–61**
Black oak, 126, 164, 167, 196, 199
Black walnut, *81*, *85*, 185, 188, 193, **240–41**
Black willow, *60*, *64*, *82*, 152, 154, 161, 186, 189, **311–12**
Bladderwort, 206
    horned, 158

Blazing star, 208, 210, 485
    Heller's, *41*, 121–23, **396**, 483
    shaggy, 204
Bloodroot, *53*, *79*, *87*, 136–38, 140, 180, 183, 194, 387, **435**, 480, 485, 487, 494
Bluebead lily, *32*, 106, 109, **352–53**
Blueberry
    highbush, *34*, *37*, *40*, *64*, 111, 114, 116, 118, 121, 123, 161, **317**
    lowbush, *68*, *71*, *93*, 164–65, 167, 169, 171, 196, 201, 203, **318**
Blue cohosh, *48*, *52*, 130, 133, 136–37, 139, 191, **345–46**
Blue ridge gentian, 114
Blue ridge ragwort, *41*, *98*, 123, 208, 210, **415–16**
Blue running cedar, 364
Bluestem
    big, 479
    little, *36*, *41*, *62*, *95*, *98*, 114, 123, 152, 155, 203, 210, 214, 332, **436–37**, 481, 493
Blue wild indigo, 485
Bottlebrush buckeye, 274, 487
Box elder, *80*, 184–86, 188, **220–21**, 481
Bracken fern, *36*, *38*, *72*, *102*, 114, 116, 118, 169, 172, 212, 215, 342, **432**
Brook saxifrage, 150
Broom sedge, *93*, *97*, *101*, 201, 203, 206, 209, 212–13, 215, **332–33**
Broom straw. *See* Broomsedge
Brown sedge, 111
Buckeye
    bottlebrush, 274, 487
    Ohio, 224
    painted, *81*, *85*, *96*, 185, 188, 191, 194, 206, 209, **269**
    red, 269
    yellow, 12, 21, *46*, *50*, 129–30, 133, 136–39, 224–25, 269, 489–90, 492
Buffalo nut, *67*, 164, 167, **299–300**
Bugbane, *48*, *52*, *86*, 130–31, 133, 136–39, 194, **326–27**
Bulrush, 480
Burning bush, 183
Bush honeysuckle
    northern, 282
    southern, *37*, *40*, 116, 118, 121, 123, **282**
Butterfly weed, *94*, *101*, 201, 203, 213, 215, **418**
Butternut, 240–41
Buttonbush, *59*, 154, **278**

Camphorweed, 212
Canada hemlock, 14, 17, 21, 25, 55, 63, 78, 141, 143–45, 157, 161, 181–82, **264–65**, 483, 490
Canada mayflower, 33, 45, 109, 125, 128, **400–401**
Canada violet, 49, 54, 133, 137, 140, **465–66**
Canby's mountain lover, 478
Cancer root. *See* Squawroot
Cane
    giant, 59, 82, 154, 185, 188, **273–74**
    hill, 67, 73, 89, 165, 167, 177, 199, **272–73**
    river. *See* giant cane
Cardinal flower, 61, 153, 155, **399**
Carolina hemlock, 14, 25, 39, 70, 120, 123, 144, 171, 264, **265–66**, 492
Carolina jessamine, 90, 96, 174, 196, 199, 206, 208–9, **285**
Carolina lily, 72, 169, 172, **397–98**
Carolina phlox, 75, 175, 177, **422**
Carolina prairie-trefoil, 202, 204
Carolina rose, 93, 201, 203, **308–9**
Carolina saxifrage, 478
Carolina sheeplaurel, 160
Carolina silverbell, 51, 55, 77, 136–39, 142–43, 146, 180, 182, **239**
Carolina spring beauty, 48, 52, 130, 133, 139, **350–51**
Carolina thistle, 480
Carrion flower, 45, 125–26, 128, **440–41**
Catawba rhododendron, 17, 32, 34, 37, 40, 43, 47, 56, 70, 107, 109, 111, 114, 116, 118, 120, 123, 125, 128, 133, 146, 169, 171, 181, **301–2**, 304, 481, 483, 489, 491
Catchweed bedstraw, 83, 101, 189, 215, **376**
Catesby's trillium, 80, 91, 181, 183, 196, 199, **455**
Cave alumroot, 58, 148, 150, **385**, 386
Chalk maple, 190, 220, 223
Cherry
    black, 51, 99, 137, 139, 212, 215, **254–55**, 259
    fire, 22, 31, 34, 36, 106, 109, 111, 114, 116, 118, 131, **254**
    pin. *See* fire cherry
Cherry birch. *See* Sweet birch
Chestnut oak, 42, 66, 67, 70, 124, 126, 128, 163–66, 169–71, 197, 247, **258–59**, 265, 479, 491
Chickweed
    common, 212, 215, 447

giant, 49, 79, 84, 134, 180, 183, 189, **447**, 494
Chinese elm, 267
Chinese privet, 56, 74, 82, 96, 100, 138, 145–46, 174–75, 177, 188–89, 193, 209–10, 212, 216, **292–93**, 384, 459
Chinese silvergrass, 444
Chinquapin, 171
Chokeberry
    black, 36, 39, 63, 116, 118, 123, 157, 161, **272**
    red, 157, 272
Christmas fern, 57, 79, 84, 87, 142, 146, 181–82, 185, 189, 192, 194, **429**
Cinnamon fern, 61, 65, 83, 152, 155, 157, 162, 189, 327, **412–13**, 494
Cinnamon vine, 363
Clammy azalea. *See* Swamp azalea
Cliff saxifrage, 41, 58, 120–21, 123, 150, **403**
Climbing hydrangea, 55, 142–43, 146, 174, **281**
Closed gentian, 377
Coastal doghobble, 292
Cohosh
    black, 48, 52, 86, 130–31, 133, 136–39, 194, **326–27**
    blue, 48, 52, 130, 133, 136–37, 139, 191, **345–46**
Common alumroot, 386
Common blue violet, 102, 212, 215, **467**
Common chickweed, 212, 215, 447
Common dandelion, 102, 212, 215, 226, **448–49**
Common elderberry, 60, 74, 83, 152, 154, 174–75, 177, 189, **312–13**
Common evening primrose, 101, 213, 215, **409–10**
Common grass pink, 158
Common greenbrier, 37, 68, 71, 74, 100, 118, 167, 169, 171, 174, 177, 215, **314–15**
Common milkweed, 75, 175, 177, **337–38**
Common ragweed, 101, 212–13, 215, **330–31**
Common rockcap fern, 150, 426
Common St. John's wort, 101, 111, 215, **390**
Coneflower
    cutleaf, 36, 49, 62, 76, 111, 114, 133, 155, 175, 177, **433–34**
    eastern purple, 367
    smooth, 91, 94, 196, 199, 202, 204, 214, **367**, 485
Confederate daisy, 208, 210
Coral honeysuckle, 78, 180, 182, **295**

INDEX OF COMMON PLANT NAMES

511

Cotton, 16, 187, 445
Cotton grass, 160
Cottonwood
　eastern, 484
　swamp, 185
Crag jangle. See Rock alumroot
Cranberry, 64, 157, 159–61, **317–18**, 431
　highbush, 109, 118
Cranefly orchid, 91, 192, 199, 330, **453**
Crimson bee balm, 49, 130–31, 133, **406–7**
Crossvine, 82, 96, 174, 185, 189, 208–9, **275**
Cucumber tree, 46, 51, 55, 85, 133, 136, 139, 146, 191, 193, **243–44**
Curlyheads, 201, 203
Curtis's goldenrod, 45, 49, 128, 130–31, 133, **443**
Cutleaf coneflower, 36, 49, 62, 76, 111, 114, 133, 155, 175, 177, **433–34**

Daisy fleabane, 212
Dandelion
　common, 102, 212, 215, 226, **448–49**
　red-seeded, 449
Deerberry, 68, 71, 78, 90, 93, 164, 167, 169, 171, 180, 182, 196, 199, 201, 203, **319**
Deerhair bulrush, 122
Devil's bit. See Fairywand
Devil's walkingstick, 73, 174–75, 177, **270–71**
Dimpled trout lily, 48, 79, 83, 87, 97, 133, 180, 182, 185, 189, 191–92, 194, 210, **370–71**, 488, 494
Dock, 395, 414
Doghobble
　coastal, 292
　mountain, 56, 60, 63, 82, 142–43, 146, 152, 154, 161, 186, 189, **292**
Dogwood
　alternate leaf, 43, 47, 125–26, 128, 133, **279**
　flowering, 19, 50, 77, 85, 88, 136–37, 139, 180, 182, 190–91, 193, 196, 198, **235–36**, 279, 306, 494
　pagoda. See alternate leaf dogwood
　silky, 60, 82, 152, 154, 185–86, 189, **280**
Doll's eyes, 52, 86, 137, 139, 191, 194, **325–26**, 327
Downy arrowwood, 199, 203
Downy oak-leach, 341
Downy serviceberry, 225–26
Dragon's mouth, 160
Dry rock moss, 41, 97, 120, 123, 206, 209, **381**

Duck potato. See Arrowhead
Dutchman's britches, 52, 87, 139, 191–92, 194, **362–63**, 480, 488
Dutchman's pipe. See Pipevine
Dwarf cinquefoil, 111, 114
Dwarf crested iris, 393
Dwarf ginseng, 417
Dwarf iris, 69, 164, 167, **393**
Dwarf palmetto, 487

Eastern columbine, 97, 210, **334–35**
Eastern cottonwood, 484
Eastern prickly pear, 98, 208, 210, 412, 493
Eastern purple coneflower, 367
Eastern redbud, 85, 88, 92, 191, 193, 196, 198, 201, 203, 225, **233–34**, 494
Eastern red cedar, 92, 95, 99, 201, 203, 206, 209, 212, 215, **241–42**, 362, 489, 493
Eastern white pine, 55, 63, 66, 89, 146, 157, 161, 164–65, 167, 181, 196–97, 199, **251**, 308
Ebony spleenwort, 340
Elderberry
　Common, 60, 74, 83, 152, 154, 174–75, 177, 189, **312–13**
　red, 32, 47, 106, 109, 133, 312, **313**
Elf orpine, 97, 206–7, 209, **361–62**, 389, 404
Elm
　American, 188, 485
　Chinese, 267
　lacebark. See Chinese elm
　slippery, 85, 190, 194, **266–67**
　winged, 17, 81, 93, 96, 188, 201, 203, 209, **256**
English ivy, 174, 281, 471
Erect dayflower, 94, 97, 201, 204, 208, 210, **354**

Fairywand, 78, 180, 182, **346–47**
False hellebore, 33, 65, 107, 109, 157–58, 162, **463–64**
　small, 463
False nettle, 395
False Solomon's seal, 49, 53, 69, 75, 130–31, 133, 140, 167, 177, 400, **401**, 428
Fascicled purple gerardia, 328
Fern
　Appalachian shoestring, 148, 150
　bracken, 36, 38, 72, 102, 114, 116, 118, 169, 172, 212, 215, 342, **432**
　Christmas, 57, 79, 84, 87, 142, 146, 181–82, 185, 189, 192, 194, **429**

cinnamon, *61*, *65*, *83*, 152, 155, 157, 162, 189, 327, **412–13**, 494
common rockcap, 150, 426
hairy lip, 207, 210
hayscented, *35*, *44*, *48*, *68*, 114, 128, 130, 133, 142, 164, 167, **360**, 452, 455
interrupted, *45*, *65*, 128, 162, 327, **413–14**
maidenhair, *52*, *58*, *86*, 139, 150, 194, **327**
netted chain, 160, 411
New York, *45*, *57*, 128, 142, 146, 360, **451–52**
resurrection, *83*, 185, 189, **425–26**
royal, 152, 155, 185, 413
sensitive, *64*, 142, 162, **411**
Venus' hair, 327
Fescue, 157
Filmy angelica. *See* Mountain angelica
Fir
balsam, 219
Fraser, 20, 25, *31*, *34*, *39*, 105–9, 114, 120, 123, 129, **219**, 248, 262, 310, 479, 482, 489
Fire cherry, 22, *31*, *34*, *36*, 106, 109, 111, 114, 116, 118, 131, **254**
Fire pink, *76*, 175, 177, **439**
Flame azalea, *34*, *37*, *43*, *67*, 111, 114, 116, 118, 125, 128, 164, 167, **301**, 483
Flowering dogwood, 19, *50*, *77*, *85*, *88*, 136–37, 139, 180, 182, 190–91, 193, 196, 198, **235–36**, 279, 306, 494
Flowering raspberry, *47*, *74*, 130, 133, 177, **311**
Fly poison, *68*, 165, 167, **331**
Foamflower, *54*, *80*, *87*, 137, 140, 142, 180, 182, 194, **452–53**, 487
Fragrant sumac, 201, 203
Fraser fir, 20, 25, *31*, *34*, *39*, 105–9, 114, 120, 123, 129, **219**, 248, 262, 310, 479, 482, 489
Fraser magnolia, *51*, *55*, 136, 139, 142–44, 146, **244–45**
Fraser's loosestrife, 146
Fraser's sedge, *56*, *58*, 142, 146, 150, **357**
Fringed phacelia, *49*, 130, 133, **419–20**
Fringed polygala, *72*, 172, **427–28**
Fringetree, *92*, *95*, 201, 203, 206, 208–9, **234**, 481

Galax, *38*, *44*, *56*, *58*, *68*, *71*, 116, 118, 128, 142, 146, 150, 165, 167, 169, 172, *181*, **374–75**, 438
Garlic mustard, 140

Gentian
blue ridge, 114
closed, 377
soapwort, *64*, 158, **377–78**, 494
stiff, 111, 114
Georgia aster, 202, 204
Gerardia
fascicled purple, 328
purple, *93*, 201, 203, **328**
Ghost flower. *See* Indian pipe
Giant cane, *59*, *82*, 154, 185, 188, **273–74**
Giant chickweed, *49*, *79*, *84*, 134, 180, 183, 189, **447**, 494
Giant ragweed, 185, 330
Ginger, 337
wild ginger, *52*, *86*, 139, 146, 191, 194, **336–37**, 387, 488
Ginseng
American, *53*, *79*, *87*, 138, 140, 180, 183, 194, **417**
dwarf, 417
Glade spurge, 478
Goat's beard, *48*, *74*, 133, 175, 177, **336**
Goat's rue, *72*, *95*, 172, 201, 204, **449–50**
Golden mountain heather, *40*, 120–23, **286–87**, 483
Golden ragwort, 415–16
Goldenrod
Curtis's, *45*, *49*, 128, 130–31, 133, **443**
granite dome, 483
skunk, *33*, *36*, *42*, 109, 111, 114, 123, **443–44**
tall, *102*, 215, **442**
Goldenseal, *53*, 138, 140, **388–89**
Gooseberry
Appalachian, *32*, *47*, 106, 109, 130, 133, **308**
Miccosukee, *86*, 191, 194, **307–8**, 488
Gorge rhododendron, *68*, *78*, *96*, 164, 167, 180, 182, 209, 291, 302, **303**
Granite dome goldenrod, 483
Granite dome St. John's wort, 40, 120–21, 123, **287–88**, 483
Grassleaf golden aster, *72*, *91*, 169, 172, *199*, **423–24**
Grass of parnassus
bigleaf, 418, 479
kidneyleaf, *65*, 157–58, 162, **417–18**, 486, 492
Gray reindeer lichen, *97*, 206, 210, **350**
Gray's lily, *35*, *64*, 111, 114, 156, 158, 162, **396–97**, 479, 489

513

INDEX OF COMMON PLANT NAMES

Greenbrier
    common, *37, 68, 71, 74, 100,* 118, 167, 169, 171, 174, 177, 215, **314–15**
    whiteleaf, *71, 90,* 169, 171, 199, **314**, 315
Green dragon, 335
Green violet, 140, 191
Ground juniper, 241

Hackberry, *81, 85,* 188, 193, **232–33**
Haircap moss, 210
    Appalachian, 120
Hairy angelica, 334
Hairy lip fern, 207, 210
Hairy spiderwort, *98,* 206–8, 210, **453–54**, 493
Halberdleaf yellow violet, *57, 80,* 143, 146, 183, **466–67**
Hayscented fern, *35, 44, 48, 68,* 114, 128, 130, 133, 142, 164, 167, **360**, 452, 455
Hazelnut
    American, 125, 281
    beaked, *43, 67,* 125, 128, 167, **280–81**
Heal all, *76,* 175, 177, **431–32**
Heart's-a-bustin'. *See* Strawberry bush
Heller's blazing star, *41,* 121–23, **396**, 483
Hemlock
    Canada, 14, 17, 21, 25, *55, 63, 78,* 141, 143–45, 157, 161, 181–82, **264–65**, 483, 490
    Carolina, 14, 25, *39, 70,* 120, 123, 144, 171, 264, **265–66**, 492
    eastern. *See* Canada hemlock
Henbit, *101,* 212, 215, **394**
Hickory
    Carolina shagbark, 200, 203
    mockernut, *66, 88,* 164, 166, 196–98, **231**
    pignut, *66, 88, 92,* 166, 196–98, 200, 203, **229–30**
    shagbark, *81, 88,* 185–86, 188, 198, **230**
Highbush blueberry, *34, 37, 40, 64,* 111, 114, 116, 118, 121, 123, 161, **317**
Highbush cranberry, 109, 118
Hill cane, *67, 73, 89,* 165, 167, 177, 199, **272–73**
Hobblebush. *See* Witch hobble
Hog peanut, *90,* 199, **331–32**
Holly
    American, *55, 77, 81,* 146, 180–82, 185, 188, **239–40**, 288
    mountain, *31, 43,* 109, 125–26, 128, **288–89**
Honey locust, 225

Honeysuckle
    coral, *78,* 180, 182, **295**
    Japanese, 14, *74, 82, 86, 90, 93, 100,* 174, 177, 180, 185, 188–89, 193–94, 196, 199, 201, 204, 212–13, 216, **294–95**, 459
Hop hornbeam, *51, 77, 85,* 136, 139, 180, 182, 190, 194, 229, **246–47**
Hoptree, *86, 96,* 191, 194, 209, **298**
Horned bladderwort, 158
Horse nettle, *102,* 213, 215, 431, **441–42**
Horse sugar, *70, 78,* 143, 169, 171, 180, 182, **283**
Horseweed, 212
Huckleberry
    bear, *43, 67, 70,* 128, 164–65, 167, 169, 174, **284**
    black, 118, 284
Hydrangea
    ashy, 287
    climbing, *55,* 142–43, 146, 174, **281**
    silverleaf, 287
    wild, *47, 51, 73, 86,* 130, 133, 136, 139, 174–75, 177, 191, 194, **287**, 356, 483
Indian cucumber root, *56, 69,* 146, 167, **402–3**
Indiangrass, *62, 95,* 152, 155, 202, 204, 214, **446**, 479
Indian paintbrush, *97,* 210, **345**
Indian pink, *91,* 196, 199, **445–46**
Indian pipe, *91,* 199, 407, **408–9**
Interrupted fern, *45, 65,* 128, 162, 327, **413–14**
Iris
    dwarf, *59,* 164, 167, **393**
    dwarf crested, 393
Ironwood, *50, 81, 84,* 136, 139, 185, 188, 190, 193, **228–29**, 246, 351

Jack-in-the-pulpit, *48, 52, 56, 83,* 133, 137, 139, 143, 146, 189, **335**, 475, 485
Jack pine, 50
Japanese honeysuckle, 14, *74, 82, 86, 90, 93, 100,* 174, 177, 180, 185, 188–89, 193–94, 196, 199, 201, 204, 212–13, 216, **294–95**, 459
Japanese privet, 293
Japanese stiltgrass, *53, 61, 83, 94,* 140, 145, 155, 183–89, 204, **403–4**, 481
Jessamine
    Carolina, *90, 96,* 174, 196, 199, 206, 208–9, **285**
    yellow. *See* Carolina jessamine

514

Jewelweed
    orange, *53*, *58*, *61*, *140*, *148*, *150*, *153*, *356*, **390–91**, *480*
    yellow, *48*, *61*, *130–31*, *133*, *153*, *155*, **391–92**, *480*
Joe Pye weed, *61*, *64*, *75*, *152*, *155*, *162*, *175*, *177*, **373**
    purple node, *128*
    spotted, *373*
Johnsongrass, *155*

Kentucky blue grass, *212*
Kidneyleaf grass of parnassus, *65*, *157–58*, *162*, **417–18**, *486*, *492*
Kiss-me-quick, *430*
Kudzu, *14*, *74*, *90*, *100*, *174–75*, *177*, *199*, *212–13*, *216*, *252*, *277*, **298–99**, *352*, *459*

Lacebark elm. *See* Chinese elm
Lady's slipper
    pink, *71*, *91*, *169*, *172*, *199*, **357–58**, *359*
    yellow, *52*, *87*, *140*, *191*, *194*, **358–59**
Lanceleaf trillium, *488*
Large-flowered bellwort, *49*, *130–31*, *134*, **462**, *463*
Large-flowered rock pink, *420*, *421*
Large-flowered trillium, *54*, *137*, *140*, **457–58**
Large flower heartleaf, *56*, *142*, *146*, *337*, **387**
Leather flower, *44*, *94*, *125*, *128*, **352**
Lesser prairie dock, *440*
Lesser rattlesnake orchid, *380*
Lily
    Atamasco, *84*, *189*, **469–70**, *485*
    Carolina, *72*, *169*, *172*, **397–98**
    dimpled trout, *48*, *79*, *83*, *87*, *97*, *133*, *180*, *182*, *185*, *189*, *191–92*, *194*, *210*, **370–71**, *488*, *494*
    Gray's, *35*, *64*, *111*, *114*, *156*, *158*, *162*, **396–97**, *479*, *489*
    Turk's cap, *75*, *175*, *177*, *397*, **398**
    yellow trout, *371*
Lion's foot, *181*, *183*
Little bluestem, *36*, *41*, *62*, *95*, *98*, *114*, *123*, *152*, *155*, *203*, *210*, *214*, *332*, **436–37**, *481*, *493*
Little brown jugs, *79*, *91*, *180*, *182*, *199*, **386–87**
Liverwort, *58*, *148*, *150*, **402**
Lobed spleenwort, *340*
Loblolly pine, *17*, *73*, *96*, *99*, *176*, *196*, *209*, *212*, *215*, **251–52**, *480*, *494*

Longleaf pine, *468*, *488*
Loosestrife
    Fraser's, *146*
    whorled, *35*, *45*, *111*, *114*, *125*, *128*, **399–400**
    winged, *480*
Lousewort, *45*, *69*, *125*, *128*, *167*, **419**, *426*
Lowbush blueberry, *68*, *71*, *93*, *164–65*, *167*, *169*, *171*, *196*, *201*, *203*, **318**

Magnolia
    bigleaf, *183*, *191*, *194*
    Fraser, *51*, *55*, *136*, *139*, *142–44*, *146*, **244–45**
    umbrella, *243*
Maidenhair fern, *52*, *58*, *86*, *139*, *150*, *194*, **327**
Maidenhair spleenwort, *150*
Maple
    chalk, *190*, *220*, *223*
    mountain, *31*, *46*, *106*, *109*, *130*, *133*, *221*, **223–24**
    red, *42*, *54*, *62*, *66*, *69*, *72*, *77*, *80*, *84*, *88*, *124*, *127*, *141*, *145*, *157*, *160–61*, *164–66*, *169–71*, *176*, *180*, *182*, *185*, *188*, *191*, *193*, *196–98*, **222**, *258*, *265*, *425*
    southern sugar, *77*, *84*, *182*, *190*, *193*, **219–20**, *223*
    striped, *31*, *42*, *46*, *50*, *109*, *126–27*, *129–30*, *133*, *136*, *139*, **221**, *223*
    sugar, *46*, *50*, *129–31*, *133*, *136*, *139*, *220*, **222–23**, *224*
Mapleleaf viburnum, *56*, *83*, *146*, *189*, **319–20**
Marsh marigold, *157*, *162*
Mayapple, *53*, *79*, *87*, *136–37*, *140*, *142*, *180*, *182*, *194*, *365*, **426**, *485*, *487*
Mayflower. *See* Trailing arbutus
Maypops, *101*, *213*, *215*, **418–19**, *471*
Meadowrue, *54*, *136*, *140*, **451**, *485*, *487*, *494*
    mountain, *59*, *148*, *150*, **450**
Miami mist, *420*
Miccosukee gooseberry, *86*, *191*, *194*, **307–8**, *488*
Midwestern Indian physic, *480*
Mimosa, *99*, *212*, *216*, **225**
Minniebush, *32*, *37*, *40*, *63*, *109*, *116*, *118*, *123*, *161*, **295–96**
Mockernut hickory, *66*, *88*, *164*, *166*, *196–98*, **231**
Mock orange, *191*
Monkey face orchid, *65*, *156*, *162*, **425**, *492*

INDEX OF COMMON PLANT NAMES

515

Moonseed, 191
Moth mullein, 464
Mountain angelica, *35*, 111, 114, **333–34**, 483
Mountain ash, *31*, *39*, 106, 109, 123, **262–63**, 482, 491
Mountain azalea, 304
Mountain dandelion, 121, 123, 152, 155
Mountain doghobble, *56*, *60*, *63*, *82*, 142–43, 146, 152, 154, *161*, 186, 189, **292**
Mountain fetterbush, 118, 123, 479
Mountain holly, *31*, *43*, 109, 125–26, 128, **288–89**
Mountain laurel, *34*, *37*, *40*, *43*, *55*, *57*, *60*, *63*, *67*, *70*, *73*, *78*, 111, 114, 116, 118, 120, 123, 125, 128, 142–43, 146, 148, 150, 154, 157, 161, 164–65, 167, 169–71, 177, 181–82, 263, 265, **291–92**, 296, 357, 374, 408, 438, 479, 483
Mountain maple, *31*, *46*, 106, 109, 130, 133, 221, **223–24**
Mountain meadowrue, *59*, 148, 150, **450**
Mountain oat grass, *35*, *40*, 110, 114, 123, **359–60**
Mountain paper birch, 109
Mountain phlox, 111
Mountain rattlesnake root, 128, 479
Mountain sandwort, *35*, *41*, 114, 121–23, 404, **405**, 479, 489
Mountain spleenwort, *40*, *58*, 123, 150, 181, **339**, 340
Mountain sweet pepperbush, *36*, *60*, *67*, 116, 118, 154, 165, *167*, **278–79**
Mountain sweet pitcher plant, 158, 162
Mountain wood aster, *33*, *75*, 107, 109, 177, **371–72**
Mountain wood fern, *33*, *44*, 106, 109, 128, **366**
Mountain wood sorrel, *33*, *58*, 106, 109, 150, **414**
Mulberry
    red, *81*, 186, 188, **245**, 261, 480
    white, 245
Mullein
    moth, 464
    woolly, *102*, 213, 215, **464**
Multiflora rose, *100*, 145, 212, 216, **309–10**
Muscadine, *90*, *100*, 174, 196, 199, 215, **322**
Musclewood. *See* Ironwood

Netted chain fern, 160, 411
New York fern, *45*, *57*, 128, 142, 146, 360, **451–52**

New York ironweed, *62*, *84*, 153, 155, 185–86, 189, **465**
Nodding ladies' tresses, *65*, 158, 162, **146–47**
Northern bush honeysuckle, 282
Northern red oak, 11, *39*, *43*, *55*, *67*, *78*, *85*, 123–24, 126–27, 129, 146, 164, 167, 179–82, 190, 194, 196–97, 258, **259–60**, 483, 485, 490–91

Oak
    bear, 479
    black, 126, 164, 167, 196, 199
    blackjack, *93*, 200, 203, **257–58**, 488
    chestnut, *42*, 66, *67*, *70*, 124, 126, 128, 163–66, 169–71, 197, 247, **258–59**, 265, 479, 491
    northern red, 11, *39*, *43*, *55*, *67*, *78*, *85*, 123–24, 126–27, 129, 146, 164, 167, 179–82, 190, 194, 196–97, 258, **259–60**, 483, 485, 490–91
    post, *89*, *93*, 126, 196, 199–200, 203, 258, 260
    scarlet, *67*, *70*, 126, 163–66, 169–71, 196, 247, **256**, 258, 479, 483, 491
    southern red, *89*, 196, 199, **257**
    swamp chestnut, 185, 188, 258, 480, 485
    turkey, 488
    white, 6, *66*, *89*, *93*, 126, 164, 167, 195, 197, 199, 201, 203, 247, **255–56**, 259, 490–91, 494
    willow, 185, 201, 203, 480
Oak beach
    Appalachian, *68*, *71*, *90*, 164, 167, 169, 172, 199, **341**
    downy, 341
Obedient plant, 152, 155, 202
Oconee bells, *57*, 142–43, 146, 149, **438**
Ohio buckeye, 224
Old man's beard. *See* Fringetree
Orange-grass. *See* Pineweed
Orange jewelweed, *53*, *58*, *61*, 140, 148, 150, 153, 356, **390–91**, 480
Orange touch-me-not. *See* Orange jewelweed
Orchid
    crane-fly, *91*, 192, 199, 330, **453**
    lesser rattlesnake, 380
    monkey face, *65*, 156, 162, **425**, 492
    rattlesnake, *68*, *91*, 165, 167, 199, **379–80**
    yellow-fringed, *65*, *75*, 162, 175, 177, **424**
Oriental bittersweet, *47*, *73*, 134, 177, **277**

Orpine
  elf, *97*, *206–7*, *209*, **361–62**, *389*, *404*
  Puck's, *206*, *362*

Pagoda dogwood. *See* Alternate leaf dogwood
Painted buckeye, *81*, *85*, *96*, *185*, *188*, *191*, *194*, *206*, *209*, **269**
Painted trillium, *33*, *38*, *106*, *109*, *116*, *118*, **459–60**, *483*
Pale yellow trillium, *87*, *194*, **456–57**, *458*
Pampas grass, *444*
Partridge berry, *57*, *142–43*, *146*, **406**
Passion vine. *See* Maypops
Pawpaw, *51*, *82*, *85*, *136–37*, *139*, *185*, *189*, *191*, *194*, **274**, *480*
  small-flowered, *274*
Pennsylvania sedge, *32*, *35*, *44*, *48*, *109*, *111*, *114*, *128*, *130*, *133*, **343–44**
Perfoliate bellwort, *80*, *180*, *183*, **462–63**
Persimmon, *92*, *95*, *99*, *201*, *203*, *209*, *215*, **237**, *321*
Phlox
  Carolina, *75*, *175*, *177*, **422**
  mountain, *111*
Piedmont quillwort, *210*
Piedmont sandwort, *404*
Pignut hickory, *66*, *88*, *92*, *166*, *196–98*, *200*, *203*, **229–30**
Pin cherry. *See* Fire cherry
Pine
  eastern white, *55*, *63*, *66*, *89*, *146*, *157*, *161*, *164–65*, *167*, *181*, *196–97*, *199*, **251**, *308*
  jack, *10*
  loblolly, *17*, *73*, *96*, *99*, *176*, *196*, *209*, *212*, *215*, **251–52**, *480*, *494*
  longleaf, *468*, *488*
  pitch, *63*, *70*, *157*, *161*, *169–71*, *249*, **250**, *479*, *483*
  shortleaf, *17*, *89*, *92*, *96*, *169*, *196*, *199*, *201*, *203*, *209*, *212*, **248–49**, *250*, *252*, *491*
  slash, *252*
  table mountain, *39*, *70*, *120*, *123*, *169–71*, *183*, **249–50**, *471*, *479*, *483*, *492*
  Virginia, *70*, *73*, *89*, *92*, *96*, *99*, *169*, *171*, *174*, *176*, *196*, *199–200*, *203*, *209*, *212*, *215*, **252–53**, *484*
Pinebarrens death camas, *120*
Pinesap, *69*, *164*, *167*, **407–8**
  sweet, *199*
Pineweed, *97*, *206–8*, *210*, **389**

Pink lady's slipper, *71*, *91*, *169*, *172*, *199*, **357–58**, *359*
Pinkshell azalea, *32*, *37*, *40*, *108–9*, *116*, *118*, *121*, *123*, **304–5**
Pink smartweed, *152*, *155*
Pink turtlehead, *32*, *107*, *109*, **348–49**
Pinxterflower. *See* Wild azalea
Pipevine, *47*, *51*, *73*, *130–31*, *133*, *139*, *174–75*, *177*, **271–72**, *276*, *297*, *352*
  woolly, *271*
Pipsissewa, *68*, *71*, *78*, *90*, *165*, *167*, *169*, *172*, *183*, *192*, *199*, **349**
Piratebush, *479*
Pitcher plant
  mountain sweet, *158*, *162*
  purple, *65*, *158*, *160*, *162*, **435–36**, *486*
Pitch pine, *63*, *70*, *157*, *161*, *169–71*, *249*, **250**, *479*, *483*
Plated rock tripe, *461*
Poison hemlock, *334*
Poison ivy, *74*, *83*, *90*, *100*, *143*, *174*, *177*, *185*, *189*, *199*, *215*, *220*, *281*, *296*, **315–16**, *391–92*
Poison oak, *315*
Pokeweed, *101*, *212*, *215*, **422–23**
Pool sprite, *97*, *206–7*, *210*, **380–81**, *488*
Post oak, *89*, *93*, *126*, *196*, *199–200*, *203*, *258*, **260**
Poverty grass, *201*, *203*
Prairie dock, *95*, *201–2*, *204*, *214*, **440**, *485*, *488*
  lesser, *440*
Prince's pine, *349*
Privet
  Chinese, *56*, *74*, *82*, *96*, *100*, *138*, *145–46*, *174–75*, *177*, *188–89*, *193*, *209–10*, *212*, *216*, **292–93**, *384*, *459*
  Japanese, *293*
Puck's orpine, *206*, *362*
Punctatum. *See* Gorge rhododendron
Purple deadnettle, *394*
Purple gerardia, *93*, *201*, *203*, **328**
Purple node Joe Pye weed, *128*
Purple pitcher plant, *65*, *158*, *160*, *162*, **435–36**, *486*
Purple toadshade. *See* Sweet Betsy
Putty root, *453*

Quaker ladies, *152*, *388*
Quillwort, *201*, *206*
  blackfoot, *488*
  piedmont, *210*

INDEX OF COMMON PLANT NAMES

Ragweed
  common, *101*, 212–13, 215, **330–31**
  giant, 185, 330
Ragwort
  blue ridge, *41*, *98*, *123*, *208*, *210*, **415–16**
  golden, 415–16
  Rugel's, 108–9
  woolly, *98*, 206–8, *210*, **416–17**
Ramps, *52*, 137, 139, **329–30**
Rattlesnake fern, *78*, *180*, *182*, 327, **342**
Rattlesnake master, *94*, 201–2, 204, 214, **370**, 480
Rattlesnake orchid, *68*, *91*, 165, 167, 199, **379–80**
Rattlesnake weed, 199
Red buckeye, 269
Red chokeberry, 157, 272
Red elderberry, *32*, *47*, 106, 109, 133, 312, **313**
Red maple, *42*, *54*, *62*, *66*, *69*, *72*, *77*, *80*, *84*, *88*, 124, 127, 141, 145, 157, 160–61, 164–66, 169–71, 176, 180, 182, 185, 188, 191, 193, 196–98, **222**, 258, 265, 425
Red mulberry, *81*, 186, 188, **245**, 261, 480
Red-seeded dandelion, 449
Red spruce, *31*, *39*, *47*, *63*, 105–9, 120, 123–24, 129, 133, 157, 161, **248**, 482
Relict trillium, *80*, *88*, 183, 191, 194, **459**, 487
Resurrection fern, *83*, 185, 189, **425–26**
Rhododendron
  Catawba, 17, *32*, *34*, *37*, *40*, *43*, *47*, *56*, *70*, 107, 109, 111, 114, 116, 118, 120, 123, 125, 128, 133, 146, 169, 171, 181, **301–2**, 304, 481, 483, 489, 492
  gorge, *68*, *78*, *96*, 164, 167, 180, 182, 209, 291, 302, **303**
River birch, 17, *59*, *80*, 152, 154, 184–86, 188, **228**
River cane. *See* Giant cane
River oats, *83*, 185, 189, **347**
Riverweed, *59*, *61*, 148, 150, 152, 155, **427**
Robin's plantain, *56*, *75*, 142–43, 146, 177, **369**
Rock alumroot, *41*, 121, 123, **385–86**
Rock clubmoss, 150
Rock pink
  Appalachian, *98*, *201*, 207–8, *210*, **420–21**, 493
  large-flowered, 420, 421
  small-flowered, 421
Rock spikemoss, 210

Rock tripe
  plated, 461
  smooth, *42*, 120, 123, **461–62**
Rocky shoals spider lily, 487
Rose
  Carolina, *93*, 201, 203, **308–9**
  multiflora, *100*, 145, 212, 216, **309–10**
  swamp, 160–61
Rosebay, *37*, *43*, *56–57*, *60*, *63*, *67*, *71*, 118, 124, 128, 142–46, 148, 150, 152, 155, 157, 161, 164–65, 167, 169, 171, 186, 291, 302–3, 304, 357–58, 374, 387, 438, 481
Rough-leaf sunflower, *75*, *94*, 175, 177, 201, 204, **382–83**
Round-leaf sundew, *64*, 158, 162, **365–66**
Royal fern, 152, 155, 185, 413
Rugel's ragwort, 108–9
Running cedar, *91*, 199, **364**
  blue, 364

Saint Andrew's cross, 201, 203
Sand myrtle, *37*, *40*, 116, 118, 120–21, 123, 128, **290–91**, 483
Sandwort
  Appalachian, *97*, 206–7, 210, 389, **404–5**
  mountain, *35*, *41*, 114, 121–23, 404, **405**, 419, 489
  piedmont, 404
Sang. *See* American ginseng
Sassafras, *67*, *70*, *73*, *89*, 164–65, 167, 169–72, 175, 177, 196, 199, **261–62**
Saxifrage
  brook, 150
  Carolina, 478
  cliff, *41*, *58*, 120–21, 123, 150, **403**
Scarlet oak, *67*, *70*, 126, 163–66, 169–71, 196, 247, **256**, 258, 479, 483, 491
Schweinitz's sunflower, *94*, 201–2, 204, 214, **382**, 489
Scott's spleenwort, 340
Scuppernong. *See* Muscadine
Sea oats, 347
Sedge
  brown, 111
  Fraser's, *56*, *58*, 142, 146, 150, **357**
  Pennsylvania, *32*, *35*, *44*, *48*, 109, 111, 114, 128, 130, 133, **343–44**
  twisted, *61*, 152, 154–55, **344–45**
Sensitive fern, *64*, 142, 162, **411**
Serviceberry
  downy, 225–26

518

smooth, *31*, *34*, *39*, *46*, 109, 111, 114, 120, 123, 125, 130, 133, **225–26**
Shagbark hickory, *81*, *88*, 185–86, 188, 198, 230
Sheep sorrel, 111, 114
Shooting star, *87*, 191, 194, **430–31**, 488
Shortleaf pine, 17, *89*, *92*, *96*, 169, 196, 199, 201, 203, 209, 212, **248–49**, 250, 252, 491
Showy orchis, *53*, 137, 139, **375**
Shrubby lespedeza, 204
Silktree. *See* Mimosa
Silky dogwood, *60*, *82*, 152, 154, 185–86, 189, **280**
Silky willow, 161
Silverthorn, 283
Skunk cabbage, *65*, 157, 159, 162, **448**
Skunk goldenrod, *33*, *36*, *42*, 109, 111, 114, 123, **443–44**
Skunkweed. *See* Galax
Slash pine, 252
Slippery elm, *85*, 190, 194, **266–67**
Small false hellebore, 463
Small-flowered rock pink, 421
Small's portulaca, *98*, 210, **430**
Small white snakeroot, 329
Smooth blackberry, 109, 118, 310
Smooth coneflower, *91*, *94*, 196, 199, 202, 204, 214, **367**, 485
Smooth rock tripe, *42*, 120, 123, **461–62**
Smooth serviceberry, *31*, *34*, *39*, *46*, 109, 111, 114, 120, 123, 125, 130, 133, **225–26**
Smooth sumac, *100*, 215, **306–7**
Soapwort gentian, *64*, 158, **377–78**, 494
Solomon's seal, *53*, *69*, *94*, 136–37, 140, 167, 204, 401, **428–29**, 480
Sourwood, *66*, *70*, *73*, *77*, *89*, 167, 169, 171, 175, 177, 180, 182, 196, 199, 225, **247**
Southern arrowhead, 434
Southern bush honeysuckle, *37*, *40*, 116, 118, 121, 123, **282**
Southern goat's rue, 449
Southern lady fern, *32*, *44*, 106, 109, 128, **340**
Southern red oak, *89*, 196, 199, **257**
Southern sugar maple, *77*, *84*, 182, 190, 193, **219–20**, 223
Spanish moss, 487
Sparkleberry, *90*, *93*, *96*, 196, 199, 201, 203, 209, **316**
Speckled wood lily, *44*, *52*, 125–26, 128, 137, 139, **353–54**

Sphagnum, *59*, *65*, 148, 150, 156–57, 162, 206, 318, **445**
Spicebush, *51*, *82*, *86*, 136–37, 139, 142, 175, 185–86, 189, 191, 194, **293–94**, 306
Spikemoss
  rock, 210
  twisted hair, *41*, 120, 123, **437**, 483
Spleenwort
  ebony, 340
  lobed, 340
  maidenhair, 150
  mountain, *40*, *58*, 123, 150, 181, **339**, 340
  Scot's, 340
Spotted coralroot, 134
Spotted Joe Pye weed, 373
Spreading avens, *38*, *41*, 118, 121, 123, **379**, 489
Spring beauty, *83*, *86*, 132, 186, 189, 191–92, 194, 350, **351–52**, 387, 488
  Carolina, *48*, *52*, 130, 133, 139, **350–51**
Squawroot, *44*, *91*, 128, 196, 199, **355**
Squirrel corn, 362
Steeplebush, 161
Stiff gentian, 111, 114
Stinking Willie. *See* Wake robin
Strawberry
  wild, *35*, *75*, *101*, 111, 114, 177, 212, 215, **373–74**
  wood, 374
Strawberry bush, *55*, *78*, *82*, 143, 146, 180–82, 185, 189, **283–84**, 471
Striped maple, *31*, *42*, *46*, *50*, 109, 126–27, 129–30, 133, 136, 139, **221**, 223
Striped wintergreen. *See* Pipsissewa
Sugarberry. *See* Hackberry
Sugar maple, *46*, *50*, 129–31, 133, 136, 139, 220, **222–23**, 224
Sumac
  fragrant, 201, 203
  poison, 161
  smooth, *100*, 215, **306–7**
  winged, *96*, *100*, 209, 215, **306**, 307
Sundrops, *58*, *75*, *94*, *97*, 148, 150, 175, 177, 201, 204, 210, **410–11**
Sunflower
  roughleaf, *75*, *94*, 175, 177, 201, 204, **382–83**
  Schweinitz's, *94*, 201–2, 204, 214, **382**, 489
Swamp azalea, *60*, *63*, 152, 155, 157–58, 161, **305**
Swamp chestnut oak, 185, 188, 258, 480, 485

INDEX OF COMMON PLANT NAMES

519

Swamp cottonwood, 185
Swamp pink, *64*, 156–58, *162*, **383–84**
Swamp rose, 160–61
Sweet azalea, *60*, 152, 155, 30C, 305
Sweet Betsy, *87*, 191, 194, **455–56**, 458, 487
Sweet birch, *50*, *54*, 136, 139, 141, 143–45, 186, **227**, 228, 377, 492
Sweetgum, 17, 22, *72*, *81*, *89*, *92*, *99*, 174, 176, 181, 185–86, 188, 192, 198, 203, 212, 215, 242, 252, 480
Sweetleaf. *See* Horse sugar
Sweet pepperbush, 279
  mountain, *36*, *60*, *67*, 116, 118, 154, 165, 167, **278–79**
Sweet pinesap, 199
Sweet potato, 363, 393
Sweet shrub, *51*, *59*, *86*, 136–37, 139, 154, 191, 194, **275–76**
Sycamore, 17, *59*, *81*, 152–54, 184–86, 188, 253, 481, 485, 492

Table mountain pine, *39*, *70*, 120, 123, 169–71, **249–50**, 471, 479, 483, 492
Tag alder, *59*, *63*, *81*, 152, 154, 157–58, 160–61, 189, **269–70**, 492
Tall bellflower, *61*, 153, 155, **343**
Tall goldenrod, *102*, 215, **442**
Tasselrue, 388
Three-tooth cinquefoil, *36*, *41*, 111, 114, 122–23, **438–39**
Timothy grass, *35*, *65*, 111, 114, 157, 162, **421–22**
Toadflax, 206
Tobacco, 16, 262, 279
Trailing arbutus, *38*, *56*, *68*, *71*, 116, 118, 146, 164, 167, 169, 172, **368–69**
Trillium
  Catesby's, *80*, *91*, 181, 183, 196, 199, **455**
  lanceleaf, 488
  large-flowered, *54*, 137, 140, **457–58**
  painted, *33*, *38*, 106, 109, 116, 118, **459–60**, 483
  pale yellow, *87*, 194, **456–57**, 458
  relict, *80*, *88*, 183, 191, 194, **459**, 487
  Vasey's, *54*, 140, **460–61**
  yellow, 456, **458–59**
Trumpet creeper. *See* Trumpet vine
Trumpet vine, *99*, 213, 215, 275, **276–77**
Tufted hairgrass, 342
Tulip tree, 17, *51*, *55*, *66*, *72*, *77*, *81*, *85*, *89*, *99*, 127, 136, 138–39, 141–43, 145, 157, 165–66, 174–76, 180–82, 185, 188,

190–91, 193, 196–97, 199, 212, 215, 242–43, 258–59, 484–85, 490, 492, 493
Turkeybeard, *42*, *72*, 120, 123, 169, 172, 331, **463**
Turkey oak, 488
Turk's cap lily, *75*, 175, 177, 397, **398**
Turtlehead
  pink, *32*, 107, 109, **348–49**
  white, *51*, 153, 155, **347–48**
Twisted hair spikemoss, *41*, 120, 123, **437**, 483
Twisted sedge, *61*, 152, 154–55, **344–45**

Umbrella leaf, *48*, 130–31, 133, **364–65**
Umbrella magnolia, 243

Vasey's trillium, *54*, 140, **460–61**
Velvet grass, 110–11, 114, 157
Venus' hair fern, 327
Violet
  Canada, *49*, *54*, 133, 137, 140, **465–66**
  common blue, *102*, 212, 215, **467**
  green, 140, 191
  halberdleaf yellow, *57*, *80*, 143, 146, 183, **466–67**
Violet wood sorrel, *79*, 183, **414–15**
Virginia creeper, *74*, *82*, *100*, 142, 174, 177, 185, 189, 215, 281, **296–97**
Virginia pine, *70*, *73*, *89*, *92*, *96*, *99*, 169, 171, 174, 176, 196, 199–200, 203, 209, 212, 215, **252–53**, 484
Virginia willow, 60, *82*, 152, 154, 189, **289–90**, 492

Wafer ash. *See* Hoptree
Wake robin, *45*, *49*, 126, 128, 130–31, 134, **457**, 460
Walking fern, *58*, *86*, 150, 194, **339–40**
Water lily, 488
Wavy hairgrass, *35*, *40*, 110, 114, 123, **341–42**
Waxy-leaved basket grass, 481
White ash, *46*, *50*, *92*, 129, 133, 136, 139, 141, 200, 203, **238–39**, 259, 485
White baneberry. *See* Doll's eyes
White basswood, 23, *47*, *51*, 129, 133, 136, 138–39, 141, **263–64**, 484, 492
White clover, *102*, 111, 212, 215, **454–55**
Whiteleaf greenbrier, *71*, *90*, 169, 171, 199, **314**, 315
White monkshood, 134
White mulberry, 245

Other **Southern Gateways Guides** you might enjoy

Backpacking North Carolina The Definitive Guide to 43 Can't-Miss Trips from Mountains to Sea
JOE MILLER

From classic mountain trails to little-known gems of the Piedmont and coastal regions

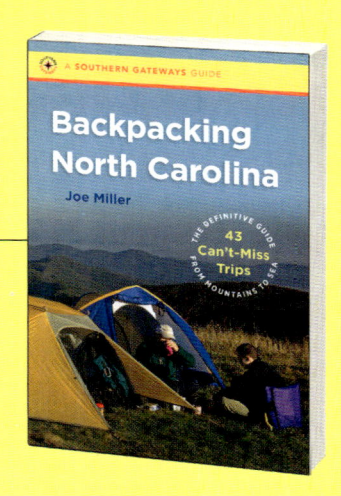

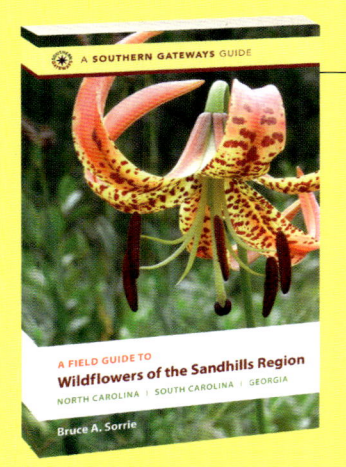

A Field Guide to Wildflowers of the Sandhills Region
North Carolina, South Carolina, and Georgia
BRUCE A. SORRIE

The first-ever field guide to the wildflowers of this vibrant, biodiverse region

Farm Fresh North Carolina The Go-To Guide to Great Farmers' Markets, Farm Stands, Farms, Apple Orchards, U-Picks, Kids' Activities, Lodging, Dining, Choose-and-Cut Christmas Trees, Vineyards and Wineries, and More **DIANE DANIEL**

The one and only guidebook to North Carolina's farms and fresh foods

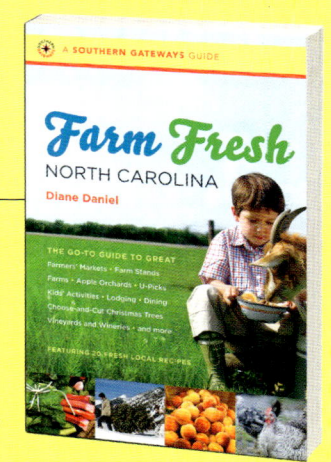

Available at bookstores, by phone at **1-800-848-6224**, or on the web at **www.uncpress.unc.e**

About the Author

Tim Spira's love for nature began in the mountains of California, where he studied alpine gentians as a graduate student and did rare plant surveys for the U.S. Forest Service. Since completing a Ph.D. in botany at the University of California, Berkeley, Tim has shared his passion for plants with students and colleagues for nearly 30 years, including 10 years as a faculty member at Georgia Southern University and 18 years at Clemson University, where he currently teaches plant ecology, field botany, and the natural history of wildflowers. Tim enjoys hiking, bicycling, gardening, and traveling to natural areas throughout the world, as well as exploring plants and habitats in the southern Appalachian mountains and adjoining piedmont. He has published more than 30 research papers in scientific journals, and his photographs have appeared in books, scientific journals, and magazines. Tim and his wife, Lisa Wagner, (along with their dog Mocha) divide their time between Clemson, South Carolina, and Asheville, North Carolina, where they've transformed their lawns into meadows, shrub borders, and woodlands featuring native plants.

LEAF TYPE:

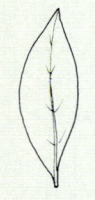

SIMPLE  PINNATELY COMPOUND  BIPINNATELY COMPOUND  PALMATELY COMPOUND

LEAF ARRANGEMENT:

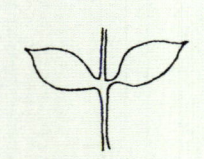

OPPOSITE  ALTERNATE  WHORLED  BASAL

LEAF SHAPE:

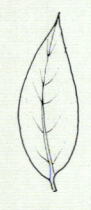

LANCEOLATE 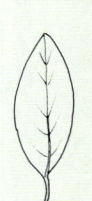 ELLIPTIC  OVATE 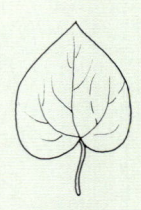 CORDATE

LEAF MARGIN:

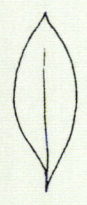

ENTIRE 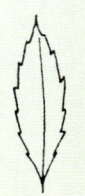 SERRATE 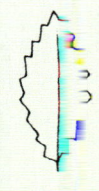 DENTATE  LOBED

Basic Plant Structures

INFLORESCENCE TYPE:

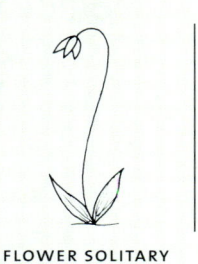

FLOWER SOLITARY | SPIKE | RACEME | UMBEL

THE PARTS OF A TYPICAL FLOWER:

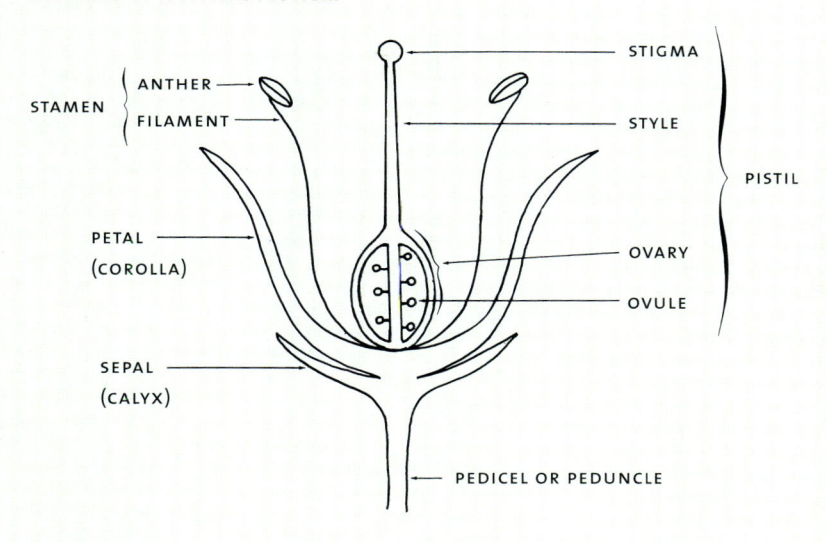

STAMEN { ANTHER, FILAMENT }

PETAL (COROLLA)

SEPAL (CALYX)

STIGMA

STYLE

OVARY

OVULE

PISTIL

PEDICEL OR PEDUNCLE

INFLORESCENCE OF A COMPOSITE (DAISY HEAD):

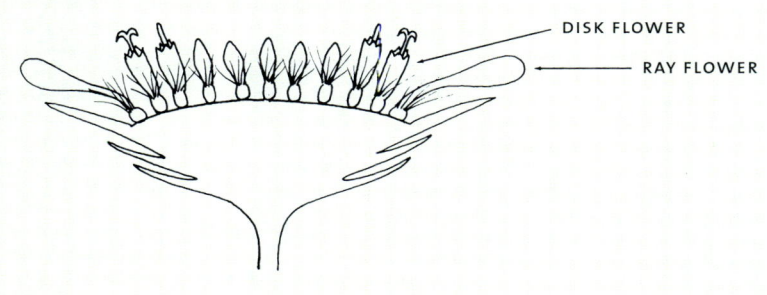

DISK FLOWER

RAY FLOWER

White oak, 6, 66, 89, 93, 126, 164, 167, 195, 197, 199, 201, 203, 247, 255–56, 259, 490–91, 494
White snakeroot, 32, 44, 48, 74, 109, 125, 128, 130–31, 133, 175, 177, 328–29
  small, 329
White turtlehead, 61, 153, 155, 347–48
Whorled aster, 33, 41, 45, 107, 109, 123, 128, 409
Whorled coreopsis, 71, 75, 94, 101, 169, 172, 175, 177, 204, 215, 355–56
Whorled horse balm, 140
Whorled loosestrife, 35, 45, 111, 114, 125, 128, 399–400
Wild azalea, 60, 78, 152, 155, 180, 182, 304
Wild geranium, 53, 79, 140, 180, 183, 378
Wild ginger, 52, 86, 139, 146, 191, 194, 336–37, 387, 488
Wild hydrangea, 47, 51, 73, 86, 130, 133, 136, 139, 174–75, 177, 191, 194, 287, 356, 483
Wild leek. *See* Ramps
Wild raisin, 37, 64, 116, 118, 157, 161, 320–21
Wild strawberry, 35, 75, 101, 111, 114, 177, 212, 215, 373–74
Wild yam, 44, 125, 128, 363–64
Willow
  black, 60, 64, 82, 152, 154, 161, 186, 189, 311–12
  silky, 161
Willow oak, 185, 201, 203, 480
Windflower. *See* Meadowrue
Winged elm, 17, 81, 93, 96, 188, 201, 203, 209, 266
Winged loosestrife, 480
Winged sumac, 96, 100, 209, 215, 306, 307
Winterberry, 63, 157, 159, 161, 239
Wintergreen, 38, 41, 64, 68, 71, 116, 118, 123, 159, 162, 164, 167, 169, 172, 376–77
Witch alder, 158, 167

Witch hazel, 43, 125–26, 128, 142, 285–86
Witch hobble, 32, 44, 47, 106, 109, 128, 130, 133, 321
Wood anemone, 52, 139, 333
Wood betony. *See* Lousewort
Wood nettle, 45, 49, 53, 128, 131, 133, 136, 140, 391–92, 395
Wood sorrel
  mountain, 33, 58, 106, 109, 150, 414
  violet, 79, 183, 414–15
Wood strawberry, 374
Wood tickseed. *See* Whorled coreopsis
Woolly mullein, 102, 213, 215, 464
Woolly pipevine, 271
Woolly ragwort, 98, 206–8, 210, 416–17

Yarrow, 35, 74, 100, 111, 114, 175, 177, 212, 215, 345
Yellow birch, 12, 31, 39, 42, 46, 54, 62, 106, 109, 120, 123, 127, 129, 130–31, 133, 141, 143–45, 161, 186, 197, 226–27, 228, 377, 482–83, 489, 491–92
Yellow buckeye, 12, 21, 46, 50, 129–30, 133, 136–37, 224–25, 269, 489–90, 492
Yellow false foxglove, 341
Yellow-fringed orchid, 65, 75, 162, 175, 177, 424
Yellow jewelweed, 48, 61, 130–31, 133, 153, 155, 391–92, 480
Yellow lady's slipper, 52, 87, 140, 191, 194, 358–59
Yellow passionflower, 418
Yellow poplar. *See* Tulip tree
Yellowroot, 57, 60, 64, 83, 150, 152, 154, 158, 161, 184, 322–23
Yellow touch-me-not. *See* Yellow jewelweed
Yellow trillium, 456, 458–59
Yellow trout lily, 371
Yellowwood, 50, 136, 139, 234–35, 492